THE MARKET

THE MACHINERY OF CAPITAL

JAG DESAINT

To the one who taught me that becoming who you are meant to be requires risk. You will make big mistakes. Let them deepen you, not shrink you. You will lose people and gain a few who respect you because you refused to fold. If you ever feel pressure to become smaller to make others comfortable, choose your spine. Choose your dignity. Choose your courage.

And to God—thank You for carrying me when I could not carry myself. Thank You for the doors You closed to protect me, the losses that taught me, and the strength You placed in me when I had none left. Thank You for the grace that kept finding me, and for the light that returned, again and again, when I thought it never would.

- Jag DeSaint

TABLE OF CONTENT

PART FOUR
THE PRIVATE ARCHITECTURE

PART FIVE
NATIONS THAT BUILD MARKETS & NATIONS THAT STAY DEPENDENT

PART SIX
THE POLITICAL STRUCTURE OF MARKETS

PART SEVEN

MARKET INSTRUMENTS MONEY THEORY

PART EIGHT

THE BLUEPRINT FOR THE NEXT MARKET

PART NINE

THE MAKING OF THE NEXT MARKET

APPENDICES

PREFACE

Markets are described as mirrors. They reflect information, aggregate beliefs, translate countless decisions into price. The metaphor is comforting because it suggests neutrality, as if the market merely reports what the world is. The truth is less polite. A market is also a factory. It manufactures liquidity, manufactures records that courts will honor, manufactures the time that allows institutions to carry risk without collapsing into panic. When it works, the factory disappears behind a screen. When it fails, the factory becomes the story, but even then the story is usually told in the vocabulary of emotion: greed, fear, mania, betrayal. Those words are not wrong. They are incomplete. The deeper question is mechanical and current: who is allowed to see first, who is allowed to settle first, who is allowed to borrow first, who is allowed to correct the record, and who is forced to accept delay as the price of being ordinary.

I wrote this book in a period when exchanges are treated as infrastructure and monetized like empires. The visible surface is busier than ever, faster than ever, more "transparent" than ever. Beneath it, the market has become more conditional, not less. Truth is segmented into tiers. Time is sold as a product. Settlement is treated as background until it becomes the crisis itself. The exchange is no longer only a public meeting place for price discovery. It is the central switchboard that decides which flows clear cheaply, which participants receive the best reality first, and which obligations become expensive to satisfy because the clock, not belief, is the real driver of behavior. The machine is not evil. It is incentive-driven. It builds hierarchies because hierarchies are profitable, and it defends them by calling them stability.

The present argument about markets is usually framed as a debate between "free markets" and "regulation," as if those were opposites. In practice the market is regulation. A market is a constitutional system for property rights, translated into minute-by-minute procedure. It assigns ownership. It assigns priority. It assigns finality. It decides when a transfer is finished and when it is still an argument. It sets the price of time, which is the price paid when obligations must be met on schedule. It builds hierarchies that feel like sophistication in calm and feel like extraction in stress: those who can buy speed, those who can buy proof, those who can buy discretion, and those who can only buy exposure. If you want to know where power sits, you look at who controls the record and who controls the clock.

This matters now because the exchange has become the invisible spine of national finance. A society that cannot settle cannot remain sovereign in a crisis. When funding tightens and confidence becomes fragile, the question is not only who will lose money. The question is who will accept external conditions to keep domestic obligations moving. Settlement and proof are not neutral plumbing. They determine whether long-duration finance is possible, whether project capital can be raised without punitive external clauses, whether a state is forced into improvisations that permanently raise the premium embedded in every future obligation. In the modern world, the architecture of the exchange and the post-trade stack is an element of national power. It decides whether a country finances ambition from within or rents ambition from outside.

That is why the future of markets will not be decided only by faster matching or by better analytics. It will be decided by what becomes public and what remains private: whether baseline truth stays thick or is thinned into subscription; whether finality is legally precise or kept elastic for those with influence; whether proof is admissible at speed or sold as a service; whether crisis time is allocated by criteria or by relationship; whether cross-border corridors expand sovereignty or become exit arbitrage for the fastest actors. Reform that touches these points will be fought, because no system built on extraction yields quietly. Resistance will arrive polished, moralized, and strategic. It will talk about liquidity because liquidity is the only word that can scare everyone at once. It will talk about protecting households because households are the moral shield behind which privilege hides. It will talk about competitiveness because competitiveness justifies fragmentation rents. It will demand more studies and more pilots and more alignment and more caution because delay is defeat without a vote.

The book treats the market as a machine whose outputs can be audited. It shows how obligations are manufactured, how schedules are monetized, how "passive" becomes forced flow, how the close becomes an institutional anchor, how clearing turns contracts into nettable exposures, how proof becomes a private product, how correction latency becomes a hidden haircut. It shows how a market can look chaotic on the surface and still produce stable winners underneath, because the winners are not always those who predict the world; they are those who own the rails that decide how the world's orders are processed. It shows how a market can be honest and still be unfair, because fairness is not only about intent; it is about access to the same reality at the same time under the same rules.

It also argues, from the same mechanical lens, that the exchange is approaching its next transformation: from a place where securities trade to a rail on which society settles. Market Instruments Money Theory is not a slogan that says securities should replace money in daily life. It is a constitutional claim that says a society can allow stocks, bonds, and listed products to extinguish obligations without turning daily commerce into speculation, but only if closure is money-grade: stable spend unit, legally defined finality, safe harbor for compliant recipients, funded restitution that repairs harm without retroactive clawback, admissible proof that prevents double-pledge, governed marks that prevent rumor-driven funding withdrawal, stress state machines that allocate time by rule, and corridors that operate as treaty-grade mutual recognition rather than as exit trap doors. If those conditions are not met, the future arrives as a private system for the powerful and a conditional system for everyone else. If those conditions are met, the future can arrive as democratized settlement capacity and longer domestic duration, which is another way of saying cheaper sovereignty.

I am not asking you to adopt a political ideology. I am asking you to accept practical chains. If a rule can be exploited by those who can see first, it will be. If a system depends on discretionary exceptions in crisis, it will allocate survival by proximity. If truth is degradable, it will be thinned into a product. If settlement is ambiguous, commerce will become credit. If cross-border corridors are misaligned, they will become exit arbitrage. If proofs are contestable, haircuts will rise. If haircuts rise, duration will shorten. If duration shortens, sovereignty becomes expensive. These are not philosophical claims. They are mechanical sequences that repeat until a society chooses to interrupt them.

The intended reader includes traders, regulators, exchange operators, bankers, allocators, lawmakers, and anyone who suspects that the most important things in markets happen before the public is told they happened. If you manage risk, this is about the rules that make risk financeable. If you write rules, this is about how rules become revenue and how revenue defends itself. If you allocate capital, this is about how allocation is already being guided by invisible calendars and eligibility lists. If you care about fairness, this is about how fairness is enforced or defeated at the level of timestamps, proofs, and closure. If you care about sovereignty, this is about how settlement and finality become national capacity rather than technical plumbing.

My commitment is simple. Every claim will be tied to a mechanism. Every mechanism will be traced to an incentive. Every incentive will be shown in motion, so what looks like chaos becomes a set of understandable, contestable rules. If you finish the book with only one conclusion, it should be this: the market is not only a place where value is discovered. It is an engineered system where reality is published, where time is priced, and where power sits inside the rails.

INTRODUCTION
THE MARKET - THE MACHINERY OF CAPITAL

On a Monday that begins like any other, a market learns, again, that price is not the event. A close print is disputed. A feed fracture widens the gap between what some participants see and what others can verify. A handful of marks diverge across venues just long enough to become a story. Funding desks do not wait for certainty; they price uncertainty as haircuts. Haircuts tighten. Tight haircuts pull repo lines and compress inventory. Inventory withdrawal widens spreads. Wider spreads increase mark volatility. Volatility triggers further margin add-ons. A few ordinary settlement delays become evidence in the wrong hands, and by Tuesday the narrative has hardened: the system is unstable, the public is being harmed, and the only responsible response is discretion. By Wednesday, "temporary" exemptions are proposed to keep liquidity alive, meaning private lanes are invited back as rescue. By Thursday, a corridor rumor turns into compliance de-risking and offshore spreads jump, because cross-border is where rule ambiguity becomes an exit route. By Friday, a ministry is forced to choose between rule-bound discomfort and improvised calm, and whichever choice it makes will be priced into the next refinancing. This is the machine: not a morality play, but a sequence in which truth, time, proof, and closure decide outcomes faster than sentiment ever could.

The first lie a modern market tells is that the trade is the event. The click, the fill, the confirmation, the sudden stillness that follows a decision and pretends it is complete. The truth is that the trade is a request. It asks a machine to produce closure: to decide whose reality counts, whose record is authoritative, whose proof is admissible, whose time is cheap, whose time is expensive, and whose mistake becomes a dispute that can be financed. The market's visible surface is price. The market's invisible surface is procedure. When procedure is coherent, the surface looks natural and inevitable. When procedure fractures, the surface looks like chaos, and the public is told the chaos is psychology. It is not. It is governance failing at speed.

This book is written for readers who know the slogans and want the rails. It does not treat markets as an argument about virtue. It treats markets as an engineered system that produces winners by allocating reality, time, proof, and closure. The promise is specific: when you are finished, you will be able to identify where the tolls are collected, how they are disguised as stability, how calendars and definitions create forced behavior, how marks become authority, how settlement becomes leverage, and how reforms fail when they trigger panic or allow "temporary" exceptions to harden into permanent privilege. You will be able to see how extraction hides in procedure, and you will be able to see what a redesign must include to survive sabotage and the politics of delay.

One can watch the machine work without believing in conspiracy or villainy. A large order arrives. It does not meet the public book the way the public imagines it should. It meets routing, internal discretion, inventory, latency, and prioritization. It meets fragmented venues that each claim to be the center. It meets a feed hierarchy that decides what is seen first. It meets an official mark that will later be treated as truth for performance, risk, and legal record. It meets clearing that compresses countless promises into net obligations. It meets funding that prices uncertainty as haircuts. It meets settlement that decides whether a confirmation becomes a final state or remains a conditional story. Then it meets the most underestimated force in finance: the clock. Obligations are most expensive when they must be met on schedule, because schedules convert judgment into compulsion, and compulsion is harvestable.

Markets do not merely discover prices; they manufacture consequences. Transparency is promised, then sold in tiers. Liquidity is praised, then monetized as a private lane. Fairness is invoked, then defined as equal access to a public surface that hides a private interior. Stability is demanded, then provided through exceptions that allocate survival by proximity. Innovation is celebrated, then used to justify new choke points that look like progress and behave like tolls. None of this requires bad intent to produce bad outcomes. It requires incentives that reward asymmetry and institutions that defend cash flow with the language of public virtue.

The market is not a neutral space between buyers and sellers. It is a constitutional system for property rights, translated into minute-by-minute procedure. It assigns ownership. It assigns priority. It assigns finality. It decides when a transfer is finished and when it is still an argument. It determines whether proof is cheap or expensive, whether correction is a public event or a private edit, whether a dispute is resolved quickly or becomes a slow haircut paid by those who cannot finance uncertainty. In calm, these mechanics look like sophistication. In stress, they look like extraction because stress reveals who can buy time and who must pay for it.

The stakes are present, not historical. Exchanges are treated as infrastructure and monetized like empires. The visible surface is faster than ever and louder than ever. Beneath it, truth is more segmented, settlement is more conditional, and time is more often sold as a product. The exchange is no longer only a public meeting place for price discovery. It is a switchboard that decides which flows clear cheaply, which participants receive the best reality first, and which obligations become expensive to satisfy because the clock, not belief, is the real driver of behavior. The market's modern hierarchy is built less by who is right about value and more by who can survive the gap between execution and finality.

The machine's evolution can be read as a long struggle over publication and authority. Before formal exchanges became institutions, markets lived in reputational credit, negotiable promises, and enforcement by courts and community. Early price sheets were not merely information; they were claims of authority. The right to publish became the right to define reality for others. Over time, mechanisms hardened: registries, brokers, quotation routines, standardized contracts, centralized venues. With legitimacy came concentration, and with concentration came the ability to sell access as a gradient rather than a binary. The market's history is the history of how an informational commons becomes a monetized hierarchy.

Modern structure added a second struggle: the struggle over completion. A trade is easy to announce and hard to finish. Completion requires netting and collateral, proof and priority, correction doctrine and dispute throughput, financing the gap between execution and finality, deciding which moments will be treated as canonical for marks and reporting, deciding who receives which reality first. The surface story speaks of discovery. The machine speaks of constraint resolution. When constraints align, markets move with a violence that looks irrational and is mechanically intelligible: margin rises, funding tightens, forced sales occur, spreads widen, and the cost of being late becomes larger than the cost of being wrong.

The surface story of modern capitalism says that "passive" investing reduced fees and democratized access. The machine story is that passive transformed definitions into obligations. Benchmarks became calendars of forced flow. Forced flow became predictable urgency.

Predictable urgency became monetizable. Definitions that looked neutral became private standards with public consequences, reallocating liquidity and cost of capital through methodology that few citizens can name and most institutions obey. In calm, these obligations produce stability. In stress, they amplify fragility because obligation does not pause when liquidity retreats.

Beneath public markets sits private architecture: leverage and access priced in systems the public rarely sees. Proof monopolies and delayed corrections, selective visibility and segmented data, discretionary exceptions and relationship time in crisis. This is where power becomes quiet. The public sees volatility. The machine sees who received the first warning, who was granted the first facility access, who was allowed to delay a margin call, whose marks were treated as authoritative, whose disputes were resolved quickly, whose claims lingered in backlog until their value was effectively discounted. The public debates morality. The machine allocates time.

Nations experience the machine differently depending on whether they have domestic market depth. Some countries finance ambition at home because they can settle, enforce, and publish truth credibly under stress. Others rent ambition from outside and pay for it twice: first in spread, then in clauses that shift enforcement and dispute authority outward. When market depth is thin, every shock becomes a legitimacy crisis because the state's only levers are improvisation and control. Improvisation raises future spreads. Control creates exit advantage for the most mobile. Exit advantage fractures politics. The machine does not merely trade securities; it decides whether development is domestically financeable or externally conditioned.

This is the fork that makes the present moment different. Markets already function as a hidden monetary layer through eligibility, haircuts, margins, and marks that convert instruments into time for institutions. The next step is not whether that layer will exist, but whether it remains aristocratic or becomes public infrastructure. Exchanges and post-trade stacks are being pulled, by their own mechanics, toward becoming settlement rails for society. The question is whether society will accept a future where closure is sold back as premium survival, or insist on rails where closure is a civic good.

Market Instruments Money Theory is the culmination of that fork, not a sudden detour. It is not a slogan that says securities should replace money in daily life. It is a constitutional claim that a society can allow stocks, bonds, and listed products to extinguish obligations without turning daily commerce into speculation, but only if closure is money-grade: stable spend unit for pricing, legally defined finality, safe harbor for compliant recipients, funded restitution that repairs harm without retroactive clawback, admissible proof that prevents double-pledge, governed marks that prevent rumor-driven funding withdrawal, stress state machines that allocate tightening by rule rather than by relationship, and corridors that operate as treaty-grade mutual recognition rather than as exit trap doors. If those conditions are not met, the future arrives as a private system for the powerful and a conditional system for everyone else. If those conditions are met, the future can arrive as democratized settlement capacity and longer domestic duration, which is another way of saying cheaper sovereignty.

The argument that follows holds to a discipline that is intentionally unfashionable. Every claim is tied to a mechanism. Every mechanism is tied to an incentive. Every incentive is shown in motion. The goal is not to make markets seem sinister. It is to make them legible, because legibility is the prerequisite to contesting the rules that quietly allocate advantage. If truth can be thinned into a product, it will be. If time can be sold in crisis, it will be. If proofs are contestable, haircuts will rise. If haircuts rise, duration will shorten. If duration shortens, sovereignty becomes expensive. The machine repeats those sequences until a society changes the rails.

PART ONE

THE INVENTION OF THE MACHINE

WHERE TRADE, DEBT, AND EMPIRE FUSED INTO A SYSTEM THAT COULD MOVE WEALTH AT SCALE AND RESHAPE POWER ITSELF.

A harbor at first light looks honest in the way paperwork never does. Salt hangs in the air. Rope fibers scratch palms. Wet timber creaks as hulls lean into the tide. On the pier, porters stack crates and roll barrels in plain view, but the harbor's real inventory lives inside rooms that smell of ink and damp wool, where promises sit in ledgers like cargo that never spoils.

A clerk arrives before the counting begins. He sets a satchel on a table and the wood gives a small complaint. Out come folded contracts, wax seals, a slim knife for opening letters without tearing the message, and a bound ledger whose spine has been handled by too many hands to stay pristine. He tops his inkwell, shakes sand across a test stroke, and does not look at the ships. He looks at names, because names are where obligation begins.

The first dispute of the day is not loud, but it is sharp. A merchant wants coin before his cargo sells. A lender wants certainty before money leaves a chest. A ship's agent wants speed because the tide does not negotiate. The clerk listens, then slides a finger along a clause and pins the room to a condition that sounds reasonable until it behaves like a lock. *"Payable on arrival, provided the cargo clears inspection and the captain's log matches the manifest."* The merchant hears delay. The lender hears protection. The agent hears friction. The clerk hears what he always hears: the price of trust when trust is forced to travel beyond the reach of a handshake.

That is the machine's first visible action: converting a private promise into a standardized claim that strangers will treat as real. Standard language makes the promise legible to outsiders, but it also trims away context and leaves seams where power can pry. Enforcement makes the promise collectible, but it also binds the machine to whoever controls courts, registries, and coercion. Recordkeeping makes the promise persistent, but it also turns the ledger into a weapon that can grant reality or deny it. Transferability makes the promise liquid, but it also creates a second market for speed, visibility, and privileged timing. A harbor can count crates by sight; a market can only count claims by rule.

The pipeline starts to look like routine the moment the paper begins to move. A merchant draws a bill of exchange on a distant buyer, seals it, and hands it to a broker who discounts it for coin today. The broker endorses the bill and passes it to a lender who wants a claim that can be sold again before the ship returns. The lender records the endorsement in a ledger, then carries the bill to a correspondent who presents it for acceptance when the buyer's agent arrives. If acceptance is delayed, a messenger runs with a protest note and a timestamp that marks who stalled and when. If payment fails, the holder brings the protested bill to a court, where a clerk reads a seal, compares signatures, checks the registry entry, and assigns priority against the buyer's assets. One document becomes a portable claim because multiple gates recognize it: seal, endorsement, ledger entry, protest, court order. The friction is the feature. Every gate slows someone down, and someone pays to move faster through it.

Once the paper can be endorsed and resold, money stops behaving like a private favor and starts behaving like an instrument. A merchant no longer needs a single wealthy patron who trusts him personally; he needs a document that other people will accept as collateral, and he needs a room where those people can compare notes. A lender no longer earns by waiting patiently for repayment; he earns by holding a claim that stays credible long enough to be transferred at a profit. The ship's agent no longer lives or dies on a single voyage; he learns to read credit conditions the way he reads weather, because the cost of money becomes another kind of tide.

The room where these papers change hands is not democratic. It is filtered by reputation, citizenship, guild standing, and proximity to enforcement. A person can be wealthy and still be refused a signature. Another person can arrive with less money and walk out with more leverage because his name carries weight that the ledger quietly honors. Access becomes a product before anyone calls it one. The clerk sees it in small gestures: whose letter is opened first, whose seal is trusted without argument, whose delay is excused as prudence and whose delay is labeled as default.

The market's earliest edge is not speed measured in microseconds. It is speed measured in minutes and hours: who hears a ship is late before the street hears, who knows an insurer is wobbling before premiums jump, who learns a court is tightening enforcement before credit widens. Information begins as gossip and becomes infrastructure. The moment the clerk writes a short note beside a name, the harbor's confidence shifts in a way that can be felt by evening. Credit extends to one merchant and retracts from another. Goods are purchased on promise or demanded in coin. A cargo is priced as real or priced as if it is already at the bottom of the sea.

This is where trade, debt, and state power fuse into a repeatable system. Trade creates the need for pooled funding. Pooled funding creates transferable instruments. Transferable instruments demand registries and enforcement. Enforcement demands a state that can compel payment and punish default. The state, in turn, discovers that a market that can mobilize private money can also fund wars, ports, and administration—so long as the market believes the rules will hold when stress arrives. That belief is legitimacy, and legitimacy is not a feeling. It is a routine maintained by visible records, predictable enforcement, and a shared understanding of who gets paid first when a promise breaks.

The machine does three jobs at once, and the tension between those jobs never goes away. It allocates capital toward enterprises that can use it. It manufactures liquidity so holders can exit before the underlying work finishes. It sustains legitimacy so enough participants keep showing up with money and faith in the ledger. When legitimacy weakens, liquidity thins and even good enterprises starve. When liquidity evaporates, enforcement becomes a scramble and the strongest claims turn sacred while weaker claims become optional. When allocation is captured, legitimacy and liquidity turn into props that keep the extraction quiet.

At dusk, the clerk ties the leather strap around the ledger and sets it in a locked cabinet. The key hangs on a ring that does not leave his belt. The cabinet is ordinary furniture in an ordinary room, and that is the point. The machinery of capital begins as mundane custody of paper, then becomes a method for moving power through rules that look like administration until they decide whose future is funded and whose is denied.

CHAPTER 1
BEFORE THE EXCHANGE
DEBT, TRUST, AND THE LONG ROAD TO TRADABLE PROMISES.

Before formal exchanges, there was still a market, but it did not behave like a room with a single rulebook. It behaved like a mesh of routes: routes for goods, routes for messages, routes for enforcement, routes for payment. Value moved, but it moved with friction that could not be wished away, and the central question was rarely what a cargo, a crop, or a claim was "worth" in the abstract. The central question was whether a promise could survive distance, delay, and denial long enough to be turned into spendable money again.

The most reliable way to misread early finance is to treat it as commerce with fewer institutions. The more accurate reading is harder: it was commerce with institutions that were personal, fragmented, uneven, and often slow, which made capital expensive because the machinery that makes promises portable was still being assembled. Scarcity of coin mattered, but scarcity of credible enforcement mattered more, because coin is not merely metal; coin is finality. When coin is scarce, credit expands. When enforcement is uneven, credit becomes selective, and selectivity is where hierarchy begins.

The pre-exchange economy is therefore not "pre-market." It is pre-standardization at scale. People already borrow, lend, insure, pledge, assign, and dispute. They already price risk. They already seek liquidity. They already build information advantages. They simply do it in a world where the gates are scattered, local, and inconsistent, which means each promise is evaluated not only on expected payment but on expected enforceability.

Picture an inland fair that appears like a temporary city, built from canvas, timber, and habit. Stalls arranged in rows; bundles of cloth; sacks of grain; barrels of oil; metal tools hung to catch the light; caged livestock; crates sealed with twine; small piles of coin on felt; larger sums kept out of sight. The air is thick with sweat, cooked fat, and wet wool. The obvious commerce is physical: goods changing hands. The decisive commerce is procedural: terms being negotiated behind the visible transaction, because terms decide whether the sale creates a liquid claim or a trapped one.

A buyer wants cloth now and will pay later after resale in a distant town. A seller wants payment now because wages and suppliers do not accept future optimism. A third actor appears, neither producer nor final buyer, and offers a bridge: money today in exchange for a claim tomorrow, priced at a discount. The discount is not merely interest. It is the price of time, verification, collection, and the right to be first in line if the claim fails.

The intermediary's constraint is not finding demand for cloth. The intermediary's constraint is finding a promise that can travel through gates that will recognize it in places the intermediary will never visit, against people the intermediary may never meet, under rules that may change across jurisdictions. When that travel is plausible, a promise can be discounted, sold, pledged, and used again. When that travel is not plausible, the promise is a local favor and cannot scale.

Early credit networks are built from social structures that double as enforcement. Guilds, religious communities, family alliances, municipal councils, and courts provide the muscle behind repayment. A borrower who defaults is not merely a debtor. He becomes difficult to trade with, difficult to hire, difficult to insure, difficult to defend in disputes. The penalty is exclusion, and exclusion is an economic sentence when commerce is access.

Yet exclusion loses power as distance grows. A borrower can default in one town and attempt to restart elsewhere. A buyer can stall in a district where courts are slow and harvest the benefit of time. A merchant can move assets across borders to evade seizure. The machine that will later make markets fluid begins here as an uneven terrain of enforcement speeds and information gaps.

The pre-exchange breakthrough is not a building or a central venue. It is a set of document technologies that convert reputation into a transferable instrument. Paper is not valuable because it is paper; paper is valuable because it triggers recognition routines across gatekeepers who have authority to certify, record, and enforce. Those routines are the earliest market infrastructure.

A bill of exchange is the cleanest example because it is simple, portable, and ruthless. One party draws an instruction on another party, directing payment at a specified time and place to a specified beneficiary, or to whoever legally holds the instrument under recognized transfer rules. The bill compresses a multi-party relationship into a portable claim. It also creates a chain, and chainability is how risk becomes distributable.

The pipeline can be traced as a sequence of gates rather than as a romantic tale. A seller delivers goods to a buyer in another town. The buyer cannot or will not pay immediately in coin. The seller draws a bill on the buyer and presents it for acceptance. Acceptance is the first decisive gate: once the buyer accepts, the buyer's obligation becomes legible to outsiders. The seller holds an accepted claim and can keep it until maturity or sell it at a discount to an intermediary who wants liquid paper. If the instrument permits transfer by endorsement, each holder signs it, creating a visible chain. The instrument travels via correspondents to the payment city. The correspondent presents it at maturity. If payment is refused or delayed, a protest is drawn by an authorized official, producing a formal record that the obligation was demanded and not honored. The protested instrument can then be enforced through courts that recognize the instrument's status and chain, allowing seizure, judgment, or negotiated settlement backed by coercion.

The instrument becomes tradable only because the gates recognize it: acceptance, endorsement, protest, court enforcement, and the practical willingness of the community to treat refusal as reputational damage. Each gate is friction. Each friction becomes a spread, a fee, a delay, or a bargaining advantage for whoever can pass the gate faster.

Merchant banking emerges as the professionalization of this gate navigation. The merchant banker is not merely a wealthy trader. The merchant banker is an operator of promises: verifying names, discounting bills, providing letters of credit, maintaining correspondents across cities, and using reputation as a balance sheet asset. The primary product is credibility, and credibility becomes a measurable input into pricing.

A bill bearing a widely respected name trades with a tighter discount because fewer buyers fear wasting time on enforcement. A bill bearing an obscure name trades with a wider discount because the buyer is purchasing delayed cash and delayed certainty. The discount rate is therefore not a pure judgment about productivity. It is a judgment about institutional travel time: how long it takes to verify, how long it takes to present, how long it takes to protest, how long it takes to collect, and how likely it is that collection will be blocked by politics.

Verification is expensive in a world without centralized data. A letter is a message traveling through uncertain channels, carried by couriers whose honesty is part of the system. A registry is a ledger kept by an institution whose legitimacy rests on the state's willingness to defend it. A signature is only meaningful if forgery is punishable and detection is plausible. That is why notaries and registrars become decisive. Certification converts a private agreement into a form courts will recognize without re-litigating the context. Registration converts a private fact into a public reference point that strangers can consult, if they can access it.

Uneven access is not incidental. It is early market power. Actors who can verify faster can price faster. Actors who can price faster can buy under uncertainty and sell after uncertainty resolves. The spread becomes compensation for information advantage and for the ability to traverse institutional gates without being delayed.

Early price sheets and posted quotations begin as attempts to reduce bargaining friction, but they do not eliminate asymmetry. A posted price reduces uncertainty for outsiders. It also creates a new fight over who sets the posted price, when it is updated, and who sees updates first. Public information is never fully public when timing is value. The earliest published rates often come from actors with interests: brokers, bankers, municipal offices, affiliated printers. Publication is framed as service, but it is also a claim to authority. Once a rate is printed, contracts can reference it, disputes can cite it, and the publisher becomes a quiet infrastructure node.

This is the first hint of a rule the machine repeats forever: reference signals are power. Whoever controls the signal can shape contracts, expectations, and enforcement outcomes. The fight is not only over truth; it is over whose version of truth becomes the default.

Letters of credit show the invention of trusted substitution. A buyer wants goods from a seller who does not trust the buyer's distant promise. A bank or merchant banker substitutes its own reputation and promises payment if conditions are met. This substitution is fee-based risk transformation. The seller accepts because the bank's promise is enforceable and easier to discount. The bank accepts because it can charge and because it can impose documentation requirements that act as gates.

Those documentation gates do double duty. They reduce fraud by forcing proof of shipment, proof of quality, proof of timing. They also concentrate power by making the bank the arbiter of what counts as compliant proof. The bank can decide which merchants qualify, which routes are acceptable, which jurisdictions are tolerable, which documents satisfy. Gatekeeping reduces loss but also concentrates advantage.

Once multiple banks and correspondents honor instruments across cities, an interbank layer appears. Correspondents present bills and collect payment. They also net obligations. Netting begins as a practical solution: if one correspondent owes another while being owed by that same correspondent, settle the difference rather than moving full coin both ways. Netting reduces the burden of settlement and increases the system's capacity. It also creates dependence. Dependence becomes a lever because the system now relies on a smaller set of nodes to compress obligations into manageable flows.

The same logic appears in merchant book credit. Merchant A sells on account to merchant B. Merchant B sells on account to merchant C. Merchant C sells on account to merchant A. The circle can persist until someone demands coin and forces settlement. The circle behaves like liquidity until stress forces finality. Stress is the most honest test because it reveals who relied on promises that cannot travel quickly through enforcement gates.

This is where the early system's crisis continuity becomes visible as a pipeline of pressure. A disruption reduces confidence in payment. Confidence reduction widens discounts on paper. Wider discounts reduce merchants' financing capacity. Reduced financing slows trade. Slower trade reduces tax receipts. Lower receipts increase the state's reliance on borrowing. Increased reliance makes the state more sensitive to credibility. Credibility depends on enforcement. Enforcement under stress becomes political. The pipe tightens at every seam.

The state enters this world not as a neutral referee but as a participant with solvency constraints and coercive capacity. Municipalities need funds for walls, roads, grain reserves, and administration. Raising money solely through direct taxation is politically costly and slow. Borrowing is faster, but borrowing requires credible repayment and enforceable routines. When a municipality issues obligations, it is making two claims at once: it will pay, and it will maintain the institutions that make its promise credible.

This dual role creates structural advantage. The state can shape the gatekeeping environment in which its own obligations are priced. It can define courts, protect registries, license notaries, and punish forgery. It can also shape priority in quiet ways: which claims are paid first under stress, which creditors have remedies, which revenues are pledged, which taxes can be increased, which assets can be seized.

Priority is the hidden lever of pre-exchange finance because priority decides whose loss becomes permanent when not all claims can be honored. Priority can be explicit in law or contract. It can be implicit in relationships with courts and registries. In practice it is often both: formal language on paper, and informal access to the officials who interpret the language when it matters.

Early public debt thus becomes a technology of statecraft, not merely a financial convenience. A polity that can mobilize credit can build infrastructure, fund conflict, and survive shocks. A polity that cannot is constrained by immediate revenue and immediate politics. The difference is not virtue; it is machinery.

Insurance markets develop as parallel machinery for converting uncertain loss into priced premium. Insurance makes ventures fundable by transforming uncertainty into a contract. But insurance depends on verification of loss and enforcement of claims, which turns insurers into information machines. They track routes, weather patterns, political risks, and reputations. They demand documentation. Documentation becomes a gate. The ability to satisfy the gate becomes an advantage.

Insurance also introduces layering: claims on claims. A bill might be insured. An insured bill might be discounted more cheaply. A discounted insured bill might be pledged again. Promises stack. Stacking increases capacity in calm times and increases fragility under stress because each layer assumes recognition routines will continue to function.

When stress hits, the machine reallocates survival through contractual switches rather than through public ceremony. Insurers raise premiums or withdraw coverage. Premium changes widen discounts on trade paper. Discount widening shrinks merchants' working capital. Working capital shrinkage reduces trade volume. Reduced volume tightens coin availability. Tightened coin availability increases demand for credit. Credit demand collides with tightened standards, and standards concentrate activity among the most credible names.

Concentration is not accidental. The machine prefers credibility because credibility is enforceability in disguise. Credibility is often inherited: family reputation, guild membership, political connections, institutional history. The pre-exchange system therefore builds a bias toward incumbency before modern language gives the bias a label.

Fraud is not a side plot in this world. Fraud is a structural pressure that appears wherever verification is slower than deception. Forged signatures, false bills, duplicate claims, fraudulent warehouse receipts appear wherever the gates are weak. Institutions respond by tightening gates: stronger seals, notarization, registry requirements, more witnesses, stricter acceptance routines. Each tightening increases cost and slows access, which benefits those already inside because they can navigate gates faster and can afford fees. The system's evolution is driven by two pressures that never fully align: expand participation and liquidity, protect credibility by restricting access.

Proto-brokers become human order books long before formal exchanges. They maintain lists of who wants what, who owes whom, who is reliable, whose paper should be discounted aggressively, whose paper should be refused. Their notebooks are live systems. Their advantage is information: who pays, who delays, which courts are slow, which registrars are strict, which notaries are trusted, which correspondents are competent.

Their advantage is also timing. A broker who hears a refusal early can widen discounts before others adjust. A broker who verifies acceptance quickly can buy paper before uncertainty resolves. The spread becomes a payment for being early and for having access to gates.

Early printed rate sheets intensify this dynamic. A printed rate sheet reduces bargaining friction and allows more participants to coordinate. It also creates authority contests. If contracts reference a printed rate, the printer's integrity becomes systemic. That integrity attracts both protection and capture attempts. Indexing contracts to a published rate turns publication into governance. Governance invites politics. Politics invites strategic ambiguity.

These are the seeds of the exchange. Not an abstract desire for transparency, but a practical bottleneck: too many bilateral bargains, too much duplicated verification, too much time spent finding counterparties, too many disputes clogging courts, too many private spreads being charged in rooms where outsiders cannot audit the terms. Once claims become tradable enough, the cost of finding the next buyer becomes a primary friction. A centralized venue can reduce that friction by concentrating buyers and sellers, standardizing rules, and publishing reference prices more consistently.

Centralization, however, introduces its own gate: access. Whoever controls the venue controls membership, rules, and the reference signal. Whoever controls the reference signal can charge for it. Whoever can charge for it can finance political protection. The exchange is not born as a neutral institution. It is born as a business model built on gatekeeping, justified as efficiency.

The pre-exchange world already contains the full pipeline, even if it is dispersed. There is origination: trade, venture, state need. There is instrument creation: bill, note, credit letter, insurance contract. There is verification: seals, acceptance routines, notarization, registry entries. There is transfer: endorsement, assignment, correspondent routes. There is enforcement: protest, judgment, seizure, reputational penalties. There is settlement: coin or book credit movement recognized as final. There is custody: the record that defines who owns the claim and can transfer it again.

Each stage contains a monetizable gate. Gate monetization becomes the seed of later market structure profits. Even before a formal exchange exists, there are already fees for discounting, fees for certification, fees for registry access, fees for correspondence, fees for collection, fees for dispute. The system is already charging for the right to make promises portable.

The most important historical takeaway is not romantic and not optional. Markets do not begin with price. Markets begin with enforceable claims. Price becomes meaningful at scale only after the machinery of portability exists: standardized instruments, recognized verification, reliable enforcement, transfer routines, and records that survive dispute. Once portability exists, liquidity becomes a sellable exit. Once liquidity becomes sellable, intermediaries become central. Once intermediaries become central, they defend the gates that preserve their profit. Once the gates are defended, the state becomes entwined because the state supplies coercion and also borrows through the same pipes. The loop is present before any formal exchange opens its doors.

A few phrases in this era function as switches, because legal language is the earliest code. The phrase *"to the order of"* creates transferability by endorsement. The phrase *"refused payment"* triggers a protest routine that makes denial costly. Those switches are not literary flourishes. They are operational commands embedded in paper.

By the time a formal exchange appears, the machine is already mature enough to industrialize. Claims are standardized enough to be compared. Verification routines exist. Enforcement is credible enough to support broader participation. Information is valuable enough to justify publication. Intermediaries are profitable enough to demand protection. The exchange consolidates these forces into a venue that scales matching, scales reference signals, and scales gatekeeping.

The chapter's irreversibility is structural: before exchanges, the market is already a machinery of gates, and the purpose of those gates is to convert local trust into portable claims. Exchanges do not create the claims. Exchanges concentrate the claims and monetize the concentration. If the reader holds onto one truth, it should be this: *the pre-exchange world is not pre-capital. It is capital assembling its operating system.*

CHAPTER 2
THE FIRST GREAT MARKET BREAKTHROUGH
HOW A MARITIME EMPIRE TURNED OWNERSHIP INTO A MACHINE OF SCALE.

A breakthrough in markets is rarely a new idea. It is usually a new routine that makes an old idea repeatable across distance and disagreement. Long before formal exchanges, people already pooled money for ventures, already lent against inventories, already insured cargo, already sold claims at discounts. The bottleneck was not imagination. The bottleneck was scalable ownership: a form of holding that strangers would recognize as real, transferable, enforceable, and legible enough to be priced without re-litigating the entire story each time a claim changed hands.

The maritime empire that solved this did not solve it by building a grand hall first. It solved it by building a disciplined chain of recognitions that made fractional ownership behave like a physical object. It fused registry discipline, contract standardization, enforcement certainty, and information publication into a machine that could mobilize private wealth at a scale large enough to change geopolitics. The ocean was the stage, but the breakthrough happened on land: in clerks' hands, in ledgers, in notarized routines, and in the courts' willingness to treat paper as reality.

The first pressure was scale. A long voyage consumes months, ties up capital, and faces risks that are not diversified by confidence: storms, spoilage, seizure, embargo, war, dishonest agents, and the ordinary fact that distance delays both news and remedies. A single wealthy backer can fund one voyage, perhaps several, but not indefinitely without exposing his entire fortune to correlated shock. A network of smaller backers can fund more ventures, but only if they can share upside and loss without dissolving into disputes at the first inconvenience.

That is the first requirement of scalable capital: converting shared exposure into shared ownership without requiring everyone to meet everyone else. If each voyage requires bespoke negotiation among dozens of backers, growth stalls. If each payout requires unanimous agreement about accounting, growth stalls. If each dispute requires personal leverage rather than institutional procedure, growth stalls. The breakthrough was to standardize ownership so it could be sliced, assigned, valued, and enforced with minimal reinvention.

The second pressure was sovereignty. Sea power is not merely ships. Sea power is finance that can pay for ships and provisions before ships generate revenue. A state that can mobilize private money quickly can project force, secure routes, and protect trade, which then returns revenues that justify mobilization. A state that cannot mobilize money quickly is trapped inside immediate tax receipts and immediate politics. Ownership machinery was state capacity disguised as commerce.

The third pressure was trust under distance. Distant trade creates permanent asymmetry: the seller's costs are local, the buyer's payment is remote, and enforcement in between is uneven. The breakthrough polity treated trust as a transport problem and solved transport with standardized routines. Not romance, not ethics, but protocols: known forms, known seals, known registries, known courts, known penalties, known priority.

The decisive move was to separate the venture from the individuals who financed it, then make the venture's ownership legible as standardized units. Pooled ventures existed earlier, but earlier pools often behaved like partnerships that dissolved into personal quarrels or demanded unanimous consent for change. The breakthrough venture persisted beyond individuals. It carried a charter or equivalent legal personality. It could hold assets, incur obligations, sue, and be sued. It could be governed by a layered structure that did not require every owner to negotiate every decision. It could issue units of ownership that were not merely moral claims but recognized property.

This legal architecture mattered because it created a fixed object for enforcement. If the venture can be sued as an entity, outsiders can lend to it and price risk without needing personal leverage over each backer. If the venture can hold inventory, inventory can be pledged. If the venture can maintain accounts, accounts can be examined. Auditability is the first cousin of liquidity because tradable claims require a plausible story about what is being traded, and plausibility in markets is always a function of whether the record can survive dispute.

The ownership unit did not need a modern label to be functionally identical to one. It needed definitional clarity: what fraction of profit or assets it represented. It needed transferability: assignment without renegotiating the venture's constitution. It needed enforceability: recognition by courts and registries that the holder had rights. It needed divisibility: a unit size small enough that many participants could buy and sell without rewriting terms.

The machine that made these units credible was built from mundane actions with severe consequences. A registrar wrote names into a register. A seal authenticated the register. A transfer was recorded as a dated entry. A receipt was issued. A court treated the entry as presumptive truth unless proven otherwise. A tax authority recognized the venture's status and demanded fees, which made the venture visible and therefore harder to deny. A set of standard contracts defined voting, distributions, dispute resolution, and the remedies available when someone tried to default through delay.

Infrastructure is not glamour, but infrastructure is how ownership scales.

Once ownership units exist, the next question becomes the question that defines every later market: how does a unit move from one holder to another in a way the system recognizes as final. Transfer must be fast enough to be useful and strict enough to prevent fraud. These goals collide. Strictness creates friction. Friction creates advantage for those who can pass gates quickly. The breakthrough system embraced this collision and monetized it while still expanding participation enough to increase total funding capacity.

A typical transfer event was not a shouted bargain. It was a chain of recognitions. A seller agreed to sell units. The seller delivered an instrument of transfer through a broker or directly. The buyer paid coin or book credit through a banker's account. A broker verified identities using known references. A registrar recorded the buyer as holder in the venture ledger. The registrar canceled the old certificate or marked it transferred. A confirmation was issued. A court recognized the ledger as authoritative in disputes.

Each step was a gate. Each gate could be priced. Verification cost money. Registrar speed cost money. Broker access cost money. Legal certainty cost money. Yet the existence of gates was also what allowed strangers to trade without personal leverage. Gates reduced the need for intimacy. Reducing intimacy is what makes scale possible.

The breakthrough included a cultural decision that looked minor and was not: acceptance that secondary sale of ownership units was normal rather than shameful. Many earlier societies treated transfer of participation as betrayal or destabilization. The breakthrough polity treated transfer as ordinary and designed rules around the fact that transfer would occur. When transfer is normalized, liquidity becomes a feature rather than a scandal. When liquidity becomes a feature, pricing becomes continuous rather than episodic. When pricing becomes continuous, capital becomes cheaper because backers can exit without waiting for the venture to liquidate.

The system also required information routines that did not yet resemble modern disclosure but served the same mechanical purpose: reducing uncertainty enough that strangers could price units without traveling to inspect warehouses and ships. The venture produced periodic accountings: cargo manifests, inventory ledgers, expense statements, distributions declared, losses recorded. These accountings were not pure transparency. They were negotiated. But negotiation still produced paper that could be referenced in disputes, and referenceable paper is the raw material of markets.

Once there is paper that can be referenced, there is an incentive to obtain it earlier than others. A broker with early access to the latest accounting can price units more accurately than a broker without it. That advantage creates a market for early visibility. Early visibility becomes a paid privilege. The machine develops its earliest information tolls: not only whether information exists, but who receives it first, in what form, and with what authority.

Authority is the missing variable in many naive histories. It is not enough for information to exist. A market needs a rule for which version counts when versions conflict. That rule is enforced by registries and courts.

Enforcement posture fused with commerce. Disputes over ownership entries were heard under specialized procedures. Disputes over venture losses were heard with attention to documents: manifests, logs, insurance policies, protest notes, witness statements. Documentation became the currency of legitimacy. In a documentation culture, the holder of the right document at the right time wins more often. That produces a predictable incentive: pay for better documents, pay for faster documents, pay for access to the clerks who certify documents.

The machine's winners emerge from a structural advantage: proximity to gates.

Now the breakthrough's deeper layer appears: ownership units alone do not create a machine of scale unless the payment system beneath them can absorb volume. A registry can record transfers all day, but transfers are not economically meaningful unless payment settles in a form recognized as final. The maritime system's financial infrastructure becomes less about voyages and more about settlement discipline, because settlement discipline is what allows secondary markets to thicken without snapping into fraud and dispute.

Settlement discipline begins with a simple institutional habit: separating agreement from extinguishment. Agreement can be spoken, written, witnessed. Extinguishment requires a medium and a rule: what counts as payment, when it counts, who can reverse it, and what evidence is sufficient to prove it happened. Early systems develop a hierarchy of acceptable settlement media: certain coins by weight and fineness, certain banker-ledger entries, certain correspondent balances treated as credible. The hierarchy is not merely convenience. It is a map of where enforceability is strongest.

Once banker-ledger settlement is broadly accepted, it becomes a throughput engine. Merchants and brokers hold accounts with banker-correspondents. Transfers become book entries rather than coin transport. Book settlement reduces theft risk and physical friction, but it concentrates dependence on the credibility and liquidity of the bankers whose ledgers now behave like quasi-money. That dependence brings new gates: who may hold an account, under what terms, with what collateral, and how quickly ledger balances can be converted into coin when stress rises.

Credibility becomes a balance sheet input. A banker with strong enforcement backing can settle claims quickly and at low friction. A banker whose jurisdiction is slow, or whose courts are easily pressured, becomes expensive to trust. The discount rates on paper drawn through that banker widen. The venture units held by investors who rely on that banker become less liquid. Liquidity differences become price differences.

The breakthrough polity's advantage was to knit these differences into a stable system rather than letting them remain purely local. It did this by building layered recognition routines: banker ledgers recognized by municipal courts, municipal courts protected by state authority, state authority financed by obligations that depended on the same credibility routines. The system stabilized circularity by making it predictable and by punishing behaviors that threatened predictability.

Predictability is the quiet definition of legitimacy in market machinery. Loss is survivable. Arbitrary enforcement is fatal.

Once book settlement is widespread, a second tension emerges: maturity mismatch. Venture capital is tied up in long voyages and long inventory cycles. Investors want liquidity. Brokers provide liquidity by holding units temporarily and quoting a spread between what they will pay and what they will sell. Bankers provide liquidity by lending against expected distributions and against pledged venture units. Credit expansion increases trade capacity. It also increases fragility if repayment depends on outcomes delayed by weather, conflict, or administrative bottlenecks.

The system's solution is not to eliminate mismatch. It is to formalize mismatch into instruments with known terms and known remedies. Short-term credit against trade paper. Longer-term credit against venture distributions. Secured credit against pledged inventories. Layered guarantees through letters of credit. The more formal these instruments become, the more they can be transferred, pledged again, and netted, increasing capacity while deepening dependence on gatekeeping accuracy.

Netting becomes the hidden throughput multiplier. If many parties owe each other, settling gross obligations requires moving large amounts of coin. Netting allows the system to settle only differences, compressing flows. A broker offsets what one merchant owes against what he is owed. A banker offsets correspondent obligations across cities. A municipal treasury offsets receipts and payments through designated accounts. Netting reduces immediate settlement burden and increases the machine's capacity. It also hides gross exposures, and hidden gross exposures are harmless in calm conditions only because the system assumes it can always roll or compress.

Under stress, netting can reverse from efficiency into fragility. A single broken link can force gross settlement at the worst time, revealing that apparent stability was a compression artifact.

Stress in early market systems is not only storm and war. It is information discontinuity. News arrives late, partially, or strategically. The market prices uncertainty as if uncertainty were a cost, because it is: uncertainty increases the probability that a claim will be delayed, disputed, or denied. Discounts widen. Brokers demand more compensation for holding paper. Bankers tighten credit. Sellers demand settlement in the most final medium available. Coin demand spikes. Coin transport becomes risky. The settlement engine tightens.

The breakthrough polity reduced the frequency with which uncertainty became existential by building routines for partial certainty: registrar confirmations, standardized protests, predictable enforcement pathways that turned refusal into a costly, bounded event rather than an open-ended negotiation. Predictability lowers the premium for fear and therefore lowers the cost of capital.

Municipal borrowing mechanics show how the breakthrough turned predictability into capacity. A municipality does not borrow cheaply by promising. It borrows cheaply by binding itself into routines outsiders can audit. Pledged revenues are specified: port fees, tolls, excise receipts, sometimes earmarked levies. Collection procedures are made visible. Payment dates are fixed. Priority is defined. Remedies are spelled out. Account publication is required. The goal is not moral display. The goal is to reduce the uncertainty that repayment will be renegotiated by delay or political discretion.

Creditor demands in this environment are covenant-like constraints: limits on additional senior obligations, pledges not to divert earmarked revenues, obligations to maintain specific taxes, requirements to publish accounts on schedule, requirements that disputes be heard under a particular jurisdiction, requirements that payments route through specified correspondents. These are gate designs. They shape what the municipality may do without triggering default. Default becomes a procedural definition rather than a mere failure to pay. Procedural default is powerful because it allows creditors to act before insolvency becomes complete.

The issuance also creates constituency. When public obligations are split across many holders, default becomes politically costly. Yet splitting across many holders can also create pressure for priority and for special treatment, because each holder fears being the one whose claim becomes optional under stress. Priority negotiations therefore harden. Priority becomes law-like.

The breakthrough polity's achievement was to make opportunism expensive enough that it was not the default strategy. Opportunism always exists because enforcement is a choice. The question is whether the system punishes opportunism reliably enough that participation remains rational. Punishment is not only jail. Punishment can be forced repayment, seizure, exclusion from future participation, and the widening of discounts that makes future borrowing expensive.

In the venture sphere, similar constraints emerge. Investors demand accounting routines, distribution schedules, and dispute procedures. Managers demand discretion. Brokers demand transferability. Registrars demand fees. Courts demand document compliance. The breakthrough aligns these demands into a repeatable pattern that can scale across many ventures without collapsing into bespoke chaos.

Repeatability produces secondary market episodes that begin to feel structurally modern. A rumor about delayed arrivals widens discounts on venture units. Confirmed arrivals tighten discounts. A sudden call for additional capital shifts prices. A disputed distribution freezes transfers because buyers fear unclear entitlement. Brokers widen spreads to compensate for uncertainty. Bankers tighten credit against units whose distributions are under dispute. Insurance premiums rise for routes perceived as riskier. The machine transmits stress through multiple pipes simultaneously: ownership pricing, credit terms, insurance cost, and municipal revenue expectations.

Secondary trading forces settlement conventions. A buyer wants assurance that his ownership will be recorded before a distribution record date. A seller wants assurance that payment is final before surrendering transfer documents. Brokers invent settlement sequences: payment first, then transfer; escrow through banker-correspondents; conditional delivery; notary-held documents until performance. These conventions reduce counterparty risk by inserting trusted nodes and by standardizing performance order. They also create fees and dependence, reinforcing the machine's loop: friction generates gates, gates generate profits, profits generate defenders.

Insurance layering intensifies both scale and disputes. Insurance reduces variance, allowing more ventures to be financed and more units to trade. But insurance claims are themselves obligations that must be verified and enforced. Policies specify documentation. Insurers impose conditions. Disputes arise over causality and exclusions. The system becomes, in effect, a market in documentation quality. Ventures with clean logs, certified inspections, and disciplined registrars trade at tighter discounts because insurers are less likely to refuse and investors are less likely to fear delayed payment. Ventures with sloppy records trade cheaper.

Friction becomes a priced variable. Once friction is priced, actors with resources can buy friction reduction and therefore buy advantage. Better notaries. Faster registrars. More credible correspondents. Stronger insurers. The system embeds a structural asymmetry: the cost of trust is lower for the already credible. Credibility compounds.

Information publication becomes the bridge that expands participation while preserving compounding. The polity tolerates or encourages periodic publication of rates and notices sufficient to keep broader participation engaged. Yet publication is never equalized. Early access remains purchasable. The first information toll is timing. The second is authority.

Authority is contested in price sheets and rate postings. A printed list reduces bargaining friction and provides a reference point for contracts. It also creates incentives to manipulate the reference. Brokers feed information to printers. Printers choose which sources to trust. Municipal offices may license printers or require certain postings. Courts may accept printed lists as evidence of customary value. Once a list has legal relevance, it becomes a strategic asset.

Strategic assets attract capture attempts. Capture can be blunt: bribery, intimidation. Capture can be procedural: influencing which transactions are counted, delaying publication until insiders have positioned, publishing in a place outsiders cannot access easily, embedding ambiguity in the terms that are "customary." The breakthrough polity survived these pressures by anchoring publication to recognized institutions and punishing obvious fraud enough to keep participation rational.

Participation at scale does not require purity. It requires a belief that cheating is risky and disputes have pathways. Pathways are the machine.

The transition toward a formal exchange is driven by arithmetic of volume. As secondary trading expands, bilateral matching costs grow. Duplicated verification grows. Bespoke settlement conventions multiply. Brokers become overwhelmed. Registrars become bottlenecks. Courts accumulate dispute load. The system searches for a new bottleneck to monetize: centralized matching and official price publication.

Centralized matching promises efficiency and produces rent. A venue can concentrate counterparties, standardize trade routines, define settlement cut-offs, and publish reference prices. It can also define membership. Membership can be sold. It can define priority. Priority can be sold. It can define officialness of prices. Officialness can be sold indirectly through controlled dissemination. The exchange is thus not a neutral endpoint but the formalization of the machine's next layer: centralized gatekeeping.

The breakthrough's historical importance is that it made centralized gatekeeping profitable by first making ownership units transferable and widely held enough to require industrialized matching. Without standardized units, an exchange has little to match. Without registries and enforcement routines, exchange trades are not credible. Without publication routines, exchange prices cannot become reference signals. Without insurance and financing layers, trading volume cannot sustain.

The first great market breakthrough, then, is the assembly of a complete ownership pipeline: legal personality for ventures, standardized units, registries treated as truth, courts enforcing ledger reality, brokers moving units, bankers settling payments, insurers reducing variance, printers and officials publishing reference signals, and a state whose strategic incentives align with defending credibility.

The system produces durable consequences. It lowers the cost of capital for favored ventures because investors can exit. Lower cost increases venture activity. Increased activity increases public revenue and strategic reach. Increased reach defends the enforcement perimeter that sustains credibility. Credibility attracts more capital. The loop tightens.

It also produces a permanent hierarchy. Those closest to registries, courts, and publication routines trade with tighter friction. Those far from those gates pay higher discounts, face slower transfers, and are more vulnerable to dispute. The machine expands participation enough to scale while preserving asymmetry enough to profit.

The irreversibility is structural: once a society treats standardized ledger-recognized ownership as transferable property, liquidity becomes normal, speculation becomes feasible, and the financial layer develops its own growth logic that can outrun underlying commerce. The exchange does not invent this logic. The exchange gives it a venue and sells access to it.

CHAPTER 3
THE FIRST STOCK
WHO CREATED IT, WHO BOUGHT IT, AND HOW THE FIRST SECONDARY MARKET CAME ALIVE.

Once a stock exists and transfer becomes routine, the market's next problem is not philosophical. It is operational: how to coordinate thousands of private judgments without forcing every trade to be renegotiated from first principles. Coordination requires reference, and reference requires a price signal stable enough to be used in other contracts, other debts, and other disputes. The first secondary market thus creates, almost immediately, a second system that becomes as important as ownership itself: the machinery of public valuation.

In early stock trading, price is not a number printed on a screen. Price is a claim of authority made by someone who expects to be believed. A broker's quote is a price, but it is also a statement about liquidity, risk, and how quickly the broker expects to be able to resell the unit if forced. A printed sheet is a price, but it is also a statement about what counts as representative. A municipal office's posted rate is a price, but it is also a declaration of what the polity wants to treat as normal. The system learns that price is a governance tool because people begin to index behavior to price.

The earliest reference prices therefore begin as a hybrid of reporting and persuasion. Brokers share lists of recent transfers and prevailing discounts. Printers publish summaries that claim to represent the market. Bankers reference those summaries when extending credit against stock units. Enterprises watch secondary prices when deciding whether to issue new units or call additional capital. Municipal treasuries watch secondary prices because prices signal the market's confidence in the venture and therefore the market's confidence in the enforcement perimeter the state is defending. The price signal becomes a lever long before it becomes a statistic.

A reference price must solve a credibility problem. It cannot simply exist. It must be recognized as something parties will accept in disputes. If two parties disagree about the value of units pledged as collateral, they need an external anchor. If an investor claims he was cheated because a broker sold him units at an unfair price, a court needs a concept of customary value. If a tax authority needs to assess duties or levies tied to transactions, it needs an assessable valuation framework. Price becomes institutional because institutions require it.

The first printed lists are therefore less like news and more like infrastructure. They gather bids, offers, recent transactions, and prevailing discounts, then present them as representative. Representation is contestable. Contestability is the beginning of manipulation. The most durable market struggle is not between truth and lies. It is between competing definitions of what counts as truth for purposes of enforcement.

Once a printed sheet becomes credible enough to be referenced, it becomes a profit surface. Brokers who can influence which trades are included can nudge the published signal in directions that benefit their inventory. Printers who control publication timing can favor those who see early. Bankers who are asked to extend credit can accept the sheet's authority when it supports conservative lending and reject it when it supports expansion. Enterprises can highlight favorable printed values to attract subscriptions and dismiss unfavorable values as rumor. The price signal becomes contested because it becomes useful, and usefulness creates incentive.

This is the moment the secondary market stops being merely a venue-less exchange of ownership and becomes a system that can coordinate capital allocation at scale. A credible price signal allows stock to be pledged as collateral, because collateral requires valuation. It allows contracts to include price-linked terms, because price-linked terms require reference. It allows structured finance in its earliest form: loans whose conditions change if stock prices fall, calls for additional collateral if prices move, and covenants that trigger when market value breaches thresholds. Even without modern math, the logic is mechanical: reference prices make conditional contracts enforceable.

Conditional enforceability is leverage. Leverage is capacity. Leverage is also fragility.

Once stock can be pledged for loans, a new loop appears. Higher stock prices increase borrowing capacity. Increased borrowing increases purchasing power. Increased purchasing power can drive stock prices higher. If prices then fall, borrowing capacity collapses, collateral calls arrive, forced selling begins, and the price signal becomes a conduit for panic. The first stock therefore brings the first recognizable reflexivity, not as a philosophical revelation but as a contractual feature of price-linked lending.

The machine learns to govern itself through thresholds. A banker sets a haircut: he will lend only a fraction of the stock's referenced value, because he expects volatility and enforcement delays. The haircut is a gate. A broker sets a spread: he will buy at one price and sell at another, because he expects inventory risk and registrar delay. The spread is a gate. A registrar sets processing fees and schedules, because capacity is finite and demand surges are monetizable. The schedule is a gate. A court recognizes certain references as customary, because courts need anchors. The anchor is a gate.

Gate multiplication is not an accident. It is how a system builds throughput while defending against fraud, and it is how a system creates revenue from the privilege of moving quickly through those defenses.

The registrar bottleneck becomes especially visible as trading volume increases. A transfer that is not recorded is an incomplete trade, and incomplete trades create disputes around distributions and voting. The system responds by formalizing record dates and eligibility windows. The enterprise declares a distribution and specifies that entitlement depends on being recorded as holder by a certain cut-off. That cut-off forces the market to care about registrar processing time. Processing time becomes a priced variable. Buyers pay less for units whose transfer might miss the record window. Sellers accept discounts to compensate buyers for that risk. Brokers charge higher spreads when registrar queues are long.

In this way, the registrar becomes a proto-clearing function. Not because it nets obligations, but because it determines finality of ownership. Finality is the condition for entitlement. Entitlement is why ownership is valuable. The market's velocity therefore depends on registry velocity, and registry velocity depends on administrative capacity and on who can buy priority.

Priority purchasing does not always appear as bribery. It often appears as "service": higher fees for faster processing, dedicated channels for frequent participants, relationship-based exceptions, informal understandings about whose paperwork is presumed clean. The machine is self-protective. It claims neutrality. Yet neutrality is often conditional on satisfying procedural preferences that are easier for insiders to satisfy because insiders built their operations around those preferences.

The first sustained speculative episodes emerge from this structure. A rumor about a delayed fleet widens discounts. Brokers become cautious. Bankers tighten lending against stock units. Sellers who need cash accept worse prices. Buyers with spare liquidity buy at discounts, expecting either arrival or a policy intervention that restores confidence. When the fleet arrives, discounts tighten and buyers profit. When the fleet does not arrive, discounts widen further and forced sellers are punished.

The speculation is not driven by a taste for gambling. It is driven by liquidity asymmetry. Those who can hold through uncertainty profit. Those who cannot are harvested by timing. Timing profit depends on earlier information and faster gate passage.

As these episodes repeat, the market begins to demand more formal rulemaking because ad hoc dispute resolution becomes too expensive. Brokers want standardized transfer instruments. Bankers want standardized collateral valuation routines. Enterprises want standardized distribution entitlement rules. Courts want standardized evidence of customary value. Printers want standardized inputs for their lists to protect themselves from accusations of manipulation. Standardization increases scale. It also increases the stakes of controlling the standard.

The first governance conflict in early stock markets is therefore a fight over standardization authority. Who defines the acceptable transfer form. Who defines the authoritative registry. Who defines which price list counts. Who defines how disputes are heard. Whoever wins defines which gates exist and who controls them.

This is where proto-exchanges begin to appear even before formal exchanges, as clubs or designated spaces where brokers coordinate, compare notes, and agree on conventions that later harden into rules.

The space does not become powerful because it is a space. It becomes powerful because it concentrates authority over reference signals and over recognized trading routines. Concentrated authority creates rents. Rents create defenders. Defenders influence enforcement. Enforcement stabilizes authority.

The secondary market thus evolves from scattered bilateral bargains into an institutionalized pattern: recognized intermediaries, recognized registries, recognized price publications, recognized dispute procedures. Each recognition step reduces friction for participants inside the recognition perimeter and increases friction for outsiders. Scale is achieved by partial openness: enough participation to deepen liquidity, enough gatekeeping to keep insiders profitable and fraud manageable.

A critical outcome of this evolution is that stock prices begin to influence the behavior of the enterprise itself. When the unit price rises, managers find it easier to issue more units or to call capital on favorable terms. When the unit price falls, managers face pressure to restrict payouts, to delay ventures, or to seek credit instead, which can increase leverage and therefore fragility. The stock becomes a feedback mechanism, and feedback mechanisms are governance even when nobody calls them governance.

A second critical outcome is that the state begins to treat stock prices as information about national capacity. A polity that relies on maritime ventures for revenue and strategic reach cannot ignore the market's valuation of those ventures. The state may not intervene directly, but it will shape enforcement and publication routines to stabilize credibility because credibility lowers borrowing costs and sustains trade volume. The state's self-interest therefore becomes part of market microstructure even in this early period.

This creates the first durable ambiguity that later markets inherit: when is enforcement neutrality, and when is enforcement policy. If courts accelerate certain disputes because the polity wants stability, is that fairness or favoritism. If registries prioritize frequent participants because capacity is limited, is that efficiency or capture. If printers publish with institutional backing, is that transparency or controlled narrative. The machine survives by turning these questions into procedure. Procedure does not answer moral questions; procedure allocates power.

The chapter's second movement therefore locks in a structural claim that will echo through every later chapter: a tradable unit without an authoritative price signal remains thin and local; a price signal without institutional backing remains rumor; institutional backing without credible enforcement remains theater; credible enforcement without gatekeeping becomes fraud-prone; gatekeeping without accountability becomes extraction. The first stock forced the system to assemble all of these simultaneously, and the first secondary market came alive in the tension between them.

The first sustained market break did not announce itself with collapse. It announced itself with timing friction that began to feel systemic. A convoy arrived late enough that rumors became the governing variable. The problem was not merely the delay. The problem was that the delay intersected with a distribution cycle, a record date, and a registry bottleneck at the exact moment secondary trading volume was thick enough that many holders were no longer "investors" in the old sense, but liquidity-seekers whose solvency depended on their ability to convert units into cash on schedule.

In calm conditions, uncertainty is priced as a spread. In stressed conditions, uncertainty becomes a gate. That is the difference between an ordinary fluctuation and a break. A break begins when gates stop behaving like friction and start behaving like denial, when liquidity becomes conditional on proximity to authority rather than on willingness to accept a slightly worse price.

The enterprise's managers had declared a distribution based on expected receipts. They had also declared, more consequentially, a record date: the ledger-recognized holders at a specified cut-off would be entitled. This is a technical decision disguised as administrative routine. It turns ownership into a timed property right. It also turns registry speed into a priced commodity because in a secondary market, ownership can change hands quickly relative to administrative processing.

In the days before the record date, transfer requests surge. Sellers who want cash before uncertainty worsens try to exit. Buyers who believe the convoy will arrive try to enter. Brokers quote wider spreads not because they suddenly forgot how to price risk, but because they are pricing registrar delay and the probability that a transfer will not be recorded in time to secure entitlement. A unit that may miss entitlement is not the same unit as one that is sure to qualify. The market now has two prices for the same instrument, separated not by fundamentals but by administrative throughput.

The registrar becomes a bottleneck and therefore a political actor. Clerks can process only so many entries per day. Documents must be verified. Signatures must be checked. Witness routines must be satisfied. Queues form. Once queues form, the question of priority becomes unavoidable. Priority can be formal, through fee schedules and service tiers, or informal, through relationships. Either way, priority becomes a shadow market in access.

The break begins when the registrar's queue stops being merely slow and becomes contested. A prominent broker submits a batch of transfers and expects them to be recorded before cut-off. Another broker submits earlier but through a less favored channel and is told the papers are incomplete. A third broker submits through a banker-correspondent whose seal is treated as presumptively clean and sees faster processing. The system can call this procedural variation. Participants experience it as hierarchy.

Dispute begins not with ideology but with arithmetic. If entitlements are large enough, missing record date is equivalent to losing cash.

Losing cash can trigger default on unrelated obligations. Default on unrelated obligations forces forced selling. Forced selling drives prices down. Price decline triggers collateral calls where units have been pledged. Collateral calls force more selling. The market break therefore begins as an entitlement bottleneck and becomes a leverage bottleneck, even in an early system, because once stock is used as collateral and once credit is extended against it, price becomes a contractual trigger.

The first wave of forced selling is not dramatic. It is scattered: merchants liquidating units to meet bills, bankers tightening credit against units whose entitlement is uncertain, brokers refusing to hold inventory because registry delay makes inventory dangerous. The secondary market thins. Spreads widen. Not because people have lost interest, but because the risk has shifted from economic outcome to procedural completion.

A rumor then crosses the market that turns thinning into panic: the convoy is not merely delayed; it has been diverted, or seized, or has suffered loss. Rumor is always present, but rumor becomes powerful when there is no authoritative mechanism for rapid verification. The polity's information routines are periodic, not continuous. Brokers with correspondents hear fragments early. Others hear later. Timing becomes survival.

In this period, the printed price sheet becomes a focal point because it is the closest thing to a public reference, and therefore the closest thing to legitimacy in disputes. The sheet's latest issue shows a downward move in unit prices and a widening of discount rates. Some participants accept the sheet's authority. Others claim it is manipulated. The argument is not over paper. The argument is over which reality will be enforced in contracts and in courts.

The price sheet becomes contested because credit contracts reference it. A loan secured by stock units may include a condition that if unit prices fall below a threshold, additional collateral is required.

That threshold is meaningless unless the market agrees which price counts. The sheet's authority therefore becomes a gate: if the sheet prints a lower value, debtors face collateral calls; if it prints a higher value, creditors feel underprotected. Each side has incentive to influence the printed number.

Influence is not necessarily fraud in the crude sense. It can be selection. Which trades are counted. Which brokers are treated as sources. Whether distressed trades are excluded as unrepresentative. Whether the sheet uses bid, offer, or last transfer. Whether publication timing favors morning insiders. The rules of publication become market structure.

Under stress, the system's missing component becomes obvious: a proto-clearing convention that can coordinate settlement and reduce the risk that one side performs while the other delays. The early secondary market relied on ad hoc escrow and trust nodes. During the break, trust nodes are overwhelmed. Too many transfers, too much cash movement, too many disputes about timing.

Brokers respond by tightening their own performance routines. They begin to require proof of funds before submitting transfer documents. They begin to require banker-confirmed settlement before delivering certificates. They begin to use standardized escrow arrangements through a small set of banker-correspondents whose ledgers are treated as credible. This is proto-clearing: an intermediary layer that aligns delivery and payment and reduces counterparty risk by centralizing performance sequencing.

Centralizing performance sequencing is not purely stabilizing. It also concentrates power. If a small set of correspondents become the clearing nodes, those correspondents can charge for speed and can ration access under stress. Rationing access becomes a political act even if described as prudence.

The break escalates when record date arrives and the registrar's ledger cannot keep up. Entries remain unprocessed at cut-off. Brokers argue about whether submission time or recording time determines entitlement. Buyers who paid believe they own. Sellers whose names remain on the ledger at cut-off are still recorded owners. The distribution is not yet paid, but entitlement has already become contested.

The registrar attempts to resolve by following the formal rule: entitlement belongs to recorded holders at cut-off. Formality protects the registry's authority, but it also creates injustice in the eyes of those who relied on submission timing. Submission timing feels like performance; recording timing feels like bureaucratic delay. Yet the machine must choose. Without a hard rule, every distribution becomes litigation. With a hard rule, legitimacy is preserved at the cost of individual pain.

Here the machine teaches its first brutal lesson: markets cannot scale without arbitrary-seeming cut-offs, and cut-offs become acceptable only when participants believe the rule is stable enough to price. Stability is not kindness. Stability is a predictable allocation of pain.

The immediate consequences are predictable and corrosive. Buyers who missed recording in time demand compensation or threaten suit. Brokers who promised entitlement face reputational damage. Bankers who extended credit against expected distributions tighten terms because entitlement is now uncertain. The enterprise faces pressure to delay the distribution until disputes are resolved, but delay punishes recorded holders who expected cash and triggers further stress in the credit web.

Managers attempt to preserve legitimacy by offering a compromise: maintain formal entitlement by ledger cut-off, but create a secondary compensation routine for those who can prove submission before cut-off. This creates a second ledger, an auxiliary claims list, which is itself a new gate. Who can prove submission. Which documents count as proof. Which witnesses are acceptable. Who certifies the proof.

The system is forced to invent a claims adjudication process, and the process becomes a new market. Intermediaries offer services to prepare proof packages. Brokers hire legal agents to argue for their clients. Notaries certify submission timestamps. The machine expands: when one gate fails to satisfy legitimacy, a new gate is built to absorb the overflow.

The price sheet's authority hardens during this moment because courts need a reference to settle disputes. If a claimant argues he suffered loss because he was denied entitlement, the value of the denied entitlement must be measured. A court that accepts a printed sheet as customary value effectively grants the sheet institutional power. That power then attracts capture attempts. The polity, recognizing that the sheet now influences legal outcomes, begins to regulate publication more directly: licensing printers, requiring source disclosure, imposing penalties for demonstrable misstatement.

The intention is stability. The effect is centralization of information authority. Centralization reduces some manipulations and creates new ones. If publication is licensed, access to licensing becomes a political lever. If sources are disclosed, sources become pressure points. If penalties exist, publishers become cautious and may exclude distressed trades, which can make the sheet lag reality, benefiting some parties and harming others.

The break also forces clearer rules around transfer finality. Participants learn that "I agreed" is not "I own." Ownership is "my name is recorded." This pushes markets toward faster and more standardized registry processes. The registrar's office expands capacity. Processing fees are standardized. Submission forms are standardized. Accepted identity proofs are standardized. Standardization improves throughput and reduces disputes, but it also increases the value of being able to comply cleanly. Clean compliance becomes a privilege of literacy, resources, and relationships.

The polity's role becomes more overt. Officials do not need to intervene in prices to intervene in machinery. They can strengthen registries, accelerate courts, punish forgery, and standardize publication. These actions lower the risk premium demanded by investors and lower borrowing costs for the state. They also entrench the state's influence over the market's core gates, which makes the market a tool of policy even when policy is not declared.

The break does not end with a single resolution. It ends when the convoy's fate becomes known. If the convoy arrives, prices rebound and disputes soften into grudging settlements. If the convoy is lost, prices fall further and disputes become sharper. Either way, the machine has changed. It has learned that secondary markets require more than tradable units. They require throughput, authoritative reference, and coordinated settlement routines that can withstand stress without collapsing into universal litigation.

From this break, three durable institutions emerge in clearer form. First, proto-clearing conventions become standardized: escrow routines, banker-correspondent settlement channels, and performance sequencing rules that reduce counterparty risk. Second, registry processing becomes formalized as a capacity problem with standardized fees and procedures, moving from personal discretion toward institutional schedule. Third, publication authority hardens: price sheets and notices become regulated reference signals rather than private rumors, because too many contracts and disputes depend on them.

None of these institutions eliminate asymmetry. They reorganize it. Those closest to the clearing nodes settle faster. Those closest to the registry pass gates with less friction. Those closest to publication see earlier. The market break therefore does not "fix" inequality. It reveals that inequality is produced by gate proximity, then encourages the building of gates sturdy enough that the system can scale without tearing apart.

The first sustained market break is thus a narrative about plumbing rather than emotion. It is the moment the system is forced to acknowledge that liquidity depends on processing capacity, that entitlement depends on recorded time, that recorded time depends on administrative throughput, and that administrative throughput depends on institutional design that is always political.

After the break, the market does what markets always do when survival requires it: it converts improvisation into routine. Improvisation is expensive because it forces every participant to renegotiate trust each time a transfer is attempted. Routine is cheaper because it allows strangers to assume a baseline of performance without knowing each other. The aftermath therefore is not a return to calm. It is a redesign of gates so the same failure cannot propagate as easily next time, and so the people who own the gates can charge more cleanly for passage.

The first redesign happens in settlement practice, not in price formation. Participants learned that bilateral escrow was insufficient under volume, because bilateral escrow scales linearly with counterparties and disputes scale faster than that. A handful of banker-correspondents had acted as ad hoc clearing nodes during the break, holding cash, holding transfer instruments, sequencing performance, and producing confirmations that courts would recognize. In the aftermath, the market formalizes this behavior.

Brokers begin routing more settlements through these nodes by default. Payment becomes book entry rather than coin movement whenever possible. Transfer instruments are held in standardized custody until the book entry is confirmed. Confirmation becomes a named object in itself: a recognized acknowledgment from a recognized ledger that settlement occurred. This is proto-clearing as a habit, and habits become infrastructure once enough participants rely on them.

Reliance produces dependence. Dependence produces pricing power. The clearing nodes can impose schedules, fees, and eligibility rules. Eligibility rules do not need to be announced as exclusion to function as exclusion. They can be written as prudence: account holders must be known, documentation must be complete, instruments must match accepted forms, transfers must be submitted through approved channels. Approved channels become the first quiet membership list in the market's bloodstream.

The second redesign happens in registry capacity. Before the break, registry throughput was treated as administration. After the break, registry throughput is treated as systemic stability. The registrar expands staffing, standardizes submission forms, standardizes identity proofs, standardizes fee schedules, and standardizes cut-off definitions. Standardization reduces ambiguity, but it also turns compliance into a barrier. Participants with literacy, clerical discipline, and money to pay expedited channels comply more easily. Participants without those resources become slower, more error-prone, and therefore more expensive to trust.

The registry also introduces what later markets would call batch processing logic. Instead of processing transfers purely in arrival order, registries adopt scheduled windows for recording, cancellation, and issuance, because windows make staffing predictable and reduce disputes about whether a transfer should have been recorded "immediately." Windows are stabilizing. Windows also create timing games. A broker who can submit early in the window can secure record-date eligibility for clients. A broker who submits late exposes clients to entitlement risk. Timing becomes a priced service.

The third redesign happens in publication authority. The break revealed that reference signals determine collateral calls, dispute valuations, and contract triggers. A printed list that courts accept as customary value becomes a quasi-regulator without admitting it. In the aftermath, publication becomes less plural and more hierarchical. Licenses, recognized sources, and standardized reporting practices emerge, justified as integrity and stabilized by the polity's enforcement interest.

This hardening does not purify the signal. It changes the battlefield. Instead of competing rumors, the market now competes to influence which transactions count as representative and how the published reference is computed. Computation is governance. If the reference uses last transfer, distressed prints can drag the signal down. If it uses a broker-averaged mid, insiders can keep the signal smoother than reality. If it excludes "unusual" trades, the signal can lag stress, benefiting debtors and harming creditors. Each methodology favors someone. Once methodology becomes stable, sophisticated actors design behavior around it.

These redesigns create a new structure: concentrated intermediation. More flows move through fewer trusted nodes. Fewer nodes means fewer points of catastrophic failure and fewer points of verification duplication. It also means more pricing power for those nodes and more capacity to shape rules.

That rule-shaping capacity becomes visible in broker behavior. During the break, brokers competed for clients and for information. After the break, brokers begin coordinating because coordination reduces their risk and increases their margins. Coordination does not always look like conspiracy. It can look like professional standards, common fee schedules, and shared rules for acceptable instruments. Yet the effect is cartel-like: a group of brokers defines what is tradable, under what documentation, through which settlement nodes, at what spreads during stress, and with what penalties for those who violate the norms.

This is a predictable result of a market that has learned that liquidity is fragile. Brokers who fear being trapped with inventory under stress prefer a world where they can collectively widen spreads without losing all clients to competitors who underprice risk. Collective widening stabilizes the brokers and transfers the cost to sellers who need cash. It also normalizes the idea that in stress, the "market" price includes a collective liquidity tax.

The cartel tendency is reinforced by registry and settlement gates. If brokers control the most efficient submission channels to registries and have the best relationships with clearing nodes, new entrants face a structural disadvantage. They can still trade, but they trade slower, with more errors, with more disputed entitlement risk, which forces them to charge wider spreads, which then looks like incompetence to outsiders even when the true cause is gate access.

The market's narrative now begins to diverge from its reality. The narrative says prices reflect value. The reality says prices reflect value plus gate friction plus timing privilege plus enforcement confidence. The narrative is useful because it encourages participation. The reality is profitable because it can be monetized.

The first durable membership logic emerges here, before a formal exchange is named. Membership is not a badge. Membership is access to the trusted settlement nodes, access to registry fast lanes, access to publication influence, and access to dispute pathways that resolve quickly. Those with membership can offer tighter prices because their cost of moving through gates is lower. Those without membership must charge for their higher friction.

The enforcement perimeter begins to codify this membership logic indirectly. Courts and officials, seeking stability, begin to prefer documents that follow standardized forms and originate from recognized intermediaries because those documents reduce dispute ambiguity. Preference becomes precedent. Precedent becomes advantage. Advantage attracts more volume. More volume increases the recognized intermediaries' centrality. Centrality becomes political. Political protection increases. The loop tightens.

The enterprise itself changes behavior in response. Managers learn that secondary prices and liquidity conditions affect their ability to raise new capital and to maintain public confidence. They therefore cultivate relationships with brokers and printers. They shape disclosures to stabilize the reference signal. They time distributions and capital calls in ways that reduce secondary market stress. They may seek to restrict transfers near record dates to reduce disputes, but restrictions reduce liquidity, and reduced liquidity raises the cost of capital. The enterprise becomes a manager not only of voyages and inventories, but of market microstructure.

This is the moment where stock becomes more than a financing instrument. It becomes a governance environment. The enterprise's policy decisions about record dates, eligibility, disclosure cadence, and transfer restrictions become market conditions that brokers and bankers price into spreads and haircuts. The market begins to discipline the enterprise through liquidity, and the enterprise begins to manage liquidity through policy.

The state's role becomes more explicit in the aftermath because the state has learned that market breaks are not only commercial disruptions; they are threats to fiscal capacity. If secondary markets seize, ventures cannot raise capital, trade slows, tax receipts fall, and state borrowing becomes more expensive. The state therefore strengthens registry integrity, improves court procedures for instrument disputes, and polices obvious fraud in publication. These interventions are framed as order and fairness. They are also fiscal self-defense.

With intervention comes a new class of disputes: disputes over who is inside the recognized perimeter and who is outside. If registry access is standardized, who qualifies for expedited processing. If clearing nodes are recognized, who can open accounts and under what collateral. If publications are licensed, whose quotes are accepted as sources. These questions are political because each answer distributes economic opportunity. The market learns to treat these questions as technical to avoid debating them in public moral language.

Technical language is a shield because it allows exclusion to masquerade as prudence. Documentation requirements can be framed as anti-fraud while functioning as barriers to entry. Fee schedules can be framed as cost recovery while functioning as rationing. Processing windows can be framed as capacity management while functioning as timing privilege.

In the aftermath, a new equilibrium forms. The system becomes more robust in one sense: fewer entitlement disputes, clearer transfer routines, more stable reference signals, and settlement sequences less dependent on personal trust. The system becomes more extractive in another sense: more concentrated intermediation, more monetized gates, more defensible insider advantage.

This is the permanent tradeoff introduced by the first stock's living secondary market. Scale requires routinization. Routinization requires gatekeeping. Gatekeeping creates rents. Rents attract power. Power shapes enforcement. Enforcement stabilizes the machine. The machine then claims its stability as legitimacy and its legitimacy as neutrality, even as neutrality remains conditional on passing gates that are easier for insiders to pass.

The first stock's aftermath therefore foreshadows the formal exchange without naming it. A formal exchange is simply the next institutional step: a declared venue that centralizes matching, centralizes publication, centralizes dispute routines, and sells access under the language of efficiency. The brokers' cartel behaviors, the registrars' fast lanes, the clearing nodes' eligibility rules, and the licensed price sheets are the exchange's organs before the exchange has a body.

The movement's irreversibility is procedural. Once settlement conventions harden, registry processing becomes scheduled, and publication authority becomes institutional, the market gains throughput and loses innocence. It becomes capable of scaling liquidity without constant renegotiation. It also becomes capable of selling gate passage as a durable business. That combination is the earliest complete outline of modern market structure: liquidity as product, access as privilege, and stability as a politically defended routine.

CHAPTER 4
PRICES IN THE COFFEEHOUSES
HOW RUMOR, PAPER, AND PUBLIC QUOTATIONS TURNED TRADING INTO A PUBLIC SYSTEM.

A trading culture does not begin with a building; it begins with a habit of believing that a number spoken aloud can coordinate strangers. Before formal exchanges, the place where that habit formed was not sacred finance space. It was a room that sold warmth, caffeine, news, and proximity, and then learned that proximity itself could be priced. The coffeehouse did not invent trade. It industrialized attention.

The most valuable commodity in early markets was not coin. It was credible information delivered before it became common knowledge. Credible meant it could survive dispute, which required either a document, a witness chain, or a source with enough reputation that denial would be punished by exclusion. Early trading culture is built on this enforcement-by-social-structure logic: the room remembers who lies, and memory becomes a cost.

Coffeehouses solved a logistical problem the pre-exchange world could not solve at scale: how to concentrate fragments of knowledge into a usable signal without requiring every merchant to maintain correspondents everywhere. A room where ships' agents, insurers, lenders, brokers, and printers regularly appeared could compress message travel time. It could turn letters into gossip, gossip into probability, probability into discount rates, and discount rates into prices.

The room's first infrastructure was not the table. It was the posting surface. A board, a wall, a ledger on a stand, a stack of circulars passed hand to hand. Notices arrived with couriers. People copied them. People summarized them. People argued about them. Then the argument produced a number that participants began to treat as a reference.

A reference price is an institutional claim. It tells the room: this is what a unit of ownership is worth today, not in metaphysical truth, but in the practical sense that this is what someone will pay and someone will accept. Once enough participants rely on the reference to settle disputes, pledge collateral, or negotiate loans, the reference becomes a governance tool. That is the moment rumor stops being entertainment and becomes infrastructure.

Coffeehouses created the early equivalent of a market data feed, but the feed was social and therefore unequal. Not everyone heard the same rumor at the same time. Not everyone could verify it. Not everyone could act on it. The room's hierarchy was enforced by proximity: proximity to the door when a courier arrived, proximity to the clerk who posted notices, proximity to the broker who kept a private notebook, proximity to the banker who knew which claims were being refused quietly.

The culture of quotation emerges because participants need to coordinate without constant renegotiation. A broker begins to say, consistently, what he will pay for a unit and what he will sell it for. Two numbers appear: a buy price and a sell price. The spread between them is not only profit. It is compensation for being a liquidity provider in a world where settlement takes time, registry recording takes time, and enforcement takes longer than either. The spread is the price of bridging those times.

Once spreads exist, the market has a structure. It can thin or thicken. It can widen or tighten. It can absorb selling or refuse it. It can punish desperation. It can reward patience. It can do all of this without needing a formal exchange, because the coffeehouse provides a repeated meeting place and therefore a repeated opportunity to make quotations behave like a public fact.

The mechanism is simple and brutal. A participant enters with paper: an ownership unit transfer instrument, a bill, an insurance claim, a municipal obligation. The participant wants liquidity. A broker quotes a price based on current rumor-weighted probability: probability of arrival, probability of enforcement, probability of registrar throughput before a record date, probability that an insurer will pay without dispute, probability that a municipality will meet its pledged revenue schedule. The broker's price includes an implicit map of gates. A buyer accepts or refuses. A transaction occurs. The transaction then must be made real: payment settled through an accepted medium, ownership transfer recorded in the registry, entitlement updated, and the room's collective belief adjusted.

The coffeehouse is where belief is manufactured. The registry is where belief becomes property. The court is where property becomes enforceable. The broker is the mobility layer that sells speed through those transitions.

Rumor enters this machine as raw input. A rumor is a message without official status. Yet a rumor can still govern prices if it is believed by those with the power to move liquidity. In early trading culture, belief is not democratic. Belief is weighted by reputation. If a rumor comes from a source with a history of accuracy, brokers will widen or tighten spreads quickly. If it comes from a source with a history of exaggeration, it will be discounted.

This creates the first credibility market inside the market. Sources compete not only to be heard, but to be believed. Belief yields influence. Influence yields profit, because influence moves prices before the wider public understands what has changed.

The room therefore develops verification routines that look informal and operate as gates. A broker will ask: who carried the letter. Whose seal is on the notice. Which correspondent signed. Whether the letter's phrasing matches known templates. Whether the news aligns with other fragments. Whether an insurer's clerk is quietly refusing to underwrite new policies on that route. Whether a banker has tightened credit terms on paper associated with that venture. Each verification question is a friction point. Each friction point favors insiders who can answer quickly.

The coffeehouse also solves a second bottleneck: coordination of settlement conventions. If trades are made in the room, the room must prevent the most dangerous outcome for liquidity: one side performing while the other delays. Early trading culture responds by relying on trusted nodes: banker-correspondents who can confirm payment posting, notaries who can hold transfer instruments, clerks who can witness handoff, and brokers whose reputation makes refusal costly.

These conventions are proto-clearing. They do not net obligations in a formal sense, but they sequence performance so that the probability of fraud is reduced enough that strangers will keep trading. The price of this safety is dependence on the trusted nodes. Dependence becomes a revenue model: the node charges for holding cash, for certifying documents, for expediting registry submissions, for providing confirmation letters that function as proof in disputes.

The room's culture thus begins to split into two layers. The visible layer is sociable: conversation, news, laughter, argument. The functional layer is procedural: who can access whose notebook, whose word is accepted as evidence, whose transfer documents are treated as presumptively clean, whose payment is treated as final. The second layer is where advantage is engineered.

Public quotations in this environment begin as a compromise between expansion and control. If quotations are too private, liquidity remains thin because newcomers cannot trust what they cannot see. If quotations are too public, spreads compress and insider advantages shrink. The coffeehouse resolves this tension by producing semi-public signals: numbers spoken in a room, written on a board, printed in a sheet that appears public but is distributed first to those who pay and participate.

Distribution timing becomes a toll road. A printed list is not simply information. It is a schedule advantage. Those who see it earlier can reposition. Those who see it later pay the price of being late. The printer becomes an infrastructure node. The sources who feed the printer become power brokers. The market learns, early, that controlling a reference signal is a way to control behavior without issuing commands.

Once a reference signal exists, contracts begin to point at it. Loans against ownership units include valuation thresholds. Insurance underwriting references prevailing rates. Municipal obligations negotiate spreads relative to "customary" discount rates. Courts ask what the market price was when evaluating damages or unfair dealing claims. The printed list becomes authority because institutions need anchors.

Authority invites manipulation pressure, which is not always dramatic. The simplest manipulation is selection: which transactions count as representative. If a distressed sale prints at a low price, should it be included. If it is included, collateral calls may trigger and forced selling may intensify. If it is excluded, creditors may feel underprotected. The choice is governance.

The coffeehouse becomes the venue where these governance choices are argued, then quietly implemented by those who control publication and recognition. The loudest voices do not always win. The most connected ones do, because connection determines access to the clerk, the printer, the banker, and the registrar.

Out of this emerges the first durable trading identity: the professional intermediary whose livelihood depends on maintaining a two-sided market. The intermediary learns to manage inventory, to manage rumor risk, to manage settlement timing, and to manage registry throughput. He widens spreads under stress to protect himself from being trapped. He tightens spreads in calm to attract flow. He cultivates relationships with registrars for faster recording. He cultivates relationships with printers for early visibility. He cultivates relationships with bankers for settlement confirmations.

This identity is the ancestor of the market maker. The coffeehouse is the ancestor of the exchange floor. The difference is not moral. It is degree of centralization.

The coffeehouse also creates a new species of conflict: conflicts over speech. Who may quote. Who may post. Who may challenge a posted number. Who may be treated as a source. These conflicts are not trivial. They determine who can shape expectations. Expectations determine prices. Prices determine who can borrow. Borrowing determines who can trade. Trading determines who can influence the next round of expectations.

The earliest enforcement tool inside the room is exclusion. A person who misreports can be pushed out. A person who fails to settle can be shunned. A person who refuses to honor a quoted bid can be treated as unreliable. The penalty is not a fine. It is loss of access to liquidity. Loss of access is a business death for intermediaries.

This social enforcement is powerful, but it is also selective. It applies most harshly to those who depend on the room. Those with alternative networks can escape and return. Those with political protection can survive reputational damage. That asymmetry is a preview of later market structure: enforcement is real, but it is uneven, and uneven enforcement is itself a priced variable.

Early quotation culture also forces the system to become more precise about time. When a quote is good for minutes rather than days, the market becomes a timing machine. When it becomes a timing machine, the ability to act quickly becomes profit. Profit attracts investment in speed. In early markets, speed is messenger networks, clerk access, and proximity to decision-makers. The coffeehouse intensifies this by concentrating decision-makers in one place, making it possible for some participants to become consistently earlier than others.

This is the seed of later speed races. The form changes. The logic does not.

A second seed is the discovery that rumor can be weaponized. A participant with inventory may benefit from driving prices up or down temporarily to sell or buy at advantageous levels. Rumor can be spread. Denial can be delayed. Confirmation can be withheld. The coffeehouse, being a human network, is vulnerable to these tactics.

The system responds with counter-tactics: demanding document-backed claims, privileging sources with reputations, punishing those caught fabricating, and anchoring disputes in printed or posted notices. Each counter-tactic strengthens the role of documents and therefore strengthens the gatekeeping power of those who control documents.

Over time, the coffeehouse becomes a place where paper evolves into protocol. Transfer forms become standardized because brokers and registrars want fewer disputes. Settlement confirmations become templated because bankers want fewer misunderstandings. Quotation lists become periodic because printers want predictable production. The entire culture becomes more machine-like because scale requires machine behavior.

This is where public quotations become more than speech. They become a thin rulebook. Not a formal rulebook, but an enforceable set of expectations: when quotes are binding, how long they are good, what constitutes a valid trade, what evidence is sufficient in dispute, how settlement must be confirmed, which registry entry counts for entitlement, and which publication is treated as customary value.

Each expectation reduces friction for insiders and raises barriers for outsiders. If you know the conventions, you can trade smoothly. If you do not, you will be forced into worse prices, slower settlement, and higher risk of dispute. Knowledge becomes a gate. The coffeehouse thus produces an early professional class whose advantage is not only capital but procedural fluency.

The chapter's irreversibility is that quotations, once public and repeated, begin to govern behavior. They shape collateral, credit, and enforcement decisions beyond the room. They transform local bargains into a proto-market that can coordinate strangers. They also introduce durable asymmetries: early visibility, faster verification, privileged access to registries and printers. The coffeehouse trading culture is therefore not a quaint prelude. It is the first scalable interface between rumor and law, between speech and property, between a number and an entitlement.

Movement Two. The quotation shock.

The shock began as a notice, because in early trading culture the notice is the closest thing to an official pulse. It arrived folded, carried by a courier who looked ordinary enough to pass without challenge, and it was read aloud near the posting board by a clerk whose voice had become a kind of metronome for the room. The content was not complex. Complexity was not required. All that mattered was that the notice sounded plausible, aligned with existing anxieties, and carried marks that suggested authority.

A single plausible notice can move prices because prices in this era are not computed. They are negotiated, and negotiation is a confidence machine. When a notice implies interruption—delayed receipts, disputed cargo, official seizure, unexpected levies—confidence translates into spreads in minutes. Brokers who quote both sides must protect themselves from being trapped, so they widen spreads and lower bids. Buyers interpret the change as signal. Sellers interpret it as punishment. The room begins to coordinate around the new number because coordination is safer than independent judgement when the penalty for being wrong is liquidity loss.

The shock becomes a break when the notice triggers three mechanical cascades at once: a quotation cascade, a collateral cascade, and a registry cascade.

The quotation cascade is immediate. Brokers reduce the prices at which they will buy venture units and raise the prices at which they will sell because uncertainty increases inventory risk and because inventory risk is paid for through spread. A thinner market forms inside the same room, visible not in empty chairs but in fewer willing bids at size. The printed list, which normally arrives on a predictable schedule, becomes a contested object because everyone knows the next print will be used as reference beyond the room: in loan valuations, in dispute arguments, in claims of customary value. Whoever can influence the next print can influence contracts, and influence contracts is power.

The collateral cascade follows because the secondary market is already entangled with credit. Units are pledged. Loans are extended against referenced values. A lower referenced value triggers collateral calls or margin-like demands for additional security. Collateral calls force holders who are short of coin to sell units into a widening spread market. Forced selling pushes prices lower. Lower prices trigger more collateral calls. This loop does not require modern leverage ratios to exist. It only requires that credit contracts use reference prices as thresholds, and that borrowers lack spare liquidity to satisfy demands without selling.

The registry cascade is slower in appearance and sharper in consequence. A price shock increases trading intent, and trading intent becomes transfer submissions. Transfer submissions require registry recording to become legal entitlement. If registries process slowly, ownership finality lags the market's trading behavior. Lag creates disputes near distribution windows and record dates. Disputes increase, and disputes make buyers more cautious, which widens spreads further. A registry that cannot keep up turns a price shock into a legitimacy shock.

During the first hours, the room acts as if the notice is true because acting is safer than waiting. Waiting is itself a position, and positions are punished under uncertainty. A broker tightens his acceptance rules, demanding cleaner documentation for transfers. A banker tightens credit, requiring higher haircuts against units. An insurer pauses underwriting on related routes because underwriting without credible information is a bet against the unknown. Each tightening is rational individually. Together they compress liquidity.

The merchant who wants to exit learns that the price is not just lower. The price is conditional. A broker offers a bid that is not truly a bid unless the broker can also be sure the registry will record the transfer promptly, and unless the broker can be sure the settlement intermediary will confirm payment finality before release. The trade becomes a chain of gates, and the shock is felt as longer, heavier gates.

The system's vulnerability becomes visible when a second notice arrives, contradicting the first. Contradiction is not merely confusion. Contradiction is a test of authority. If two notices exist and both claim legitimacy, the market must decide which one counts as reality. The coffeehouse does not have a sovereign truth mechanism. It has credibility hierarchies. A contradiction therefore forces the hierarchy onto the surface, and forced exposure is destabilizing because it reveals that what the market calls truth is often a function of whose documents are treated as real.

A small group of brokers move quickly to verify. Verification in this era is a network activity, not a calculation. They dispatch messengers to correspondents. They send runners to registry offices to ask whether any official entry aligns with the first notice. They contact insurer clerks to see whether policy terms are being interpreted differently. They visit banker desks to see whether ledger credit is tightening. They are not doing moral inquiry. They are tracing the pipe: what has actually changed in enforceable routines.

The verification finds what market shocks often find: the notice was not purely fabricated, but it was selectively framed. There was an administrative action, but it was narrower than implied. There was a delay, but it was not a seizure. There was a dispute, but it was not universal. The first notice magnified and generalized because magnification creates profitable mispricing when enough participants react.

This is where rumor becomes weapon rather than noise. The weapon is not the lie itself. The weapon is the timing. Those who spread a magnified notice can position before others update, then profit from the transition from fear to correction. Correction is slower than rumor because correction requires authority, and authority moves through institutions.

The printed list becomes central because it is the formalizable authority proxy. Printers, under pressure, must decide how to treat a day when prices are moving and when some trades are distressed. If they print the low distressed trades, they may trigger collateral cascades and intensify forced selling. If they exclude them, they may be accused of concealment and manipulation. If they delay publication to verify, they may be accused of favoring insiders who already know. If they publish quickly, they may publish error.

The printer's choice is therefore governance. The printer becomes a regulator in practice because the printed number will be used as a contractual anchor.

Under shock conditions, brokers attempt to influence publication through selection and framing rather than through crude falsification. They suggest which trades are "real." They argue that some trades reflect desperation and should not be treated as customary. They argue that certain counterparties are unreliable and their prints should be discounted. They argue that quotes should be used instead of transactions. Each suggestion, if accepted, protects the broker's position and shifts risk onto someone else.

The state's interest enters not through ideology but through fiscal arithmetic. If the price shock persists, venture units trade cheaper, credit tightens, trade slows, and tax receipts fall. The state also risks reputational damage: a market that appears manipulable becomes more expensive to fund, and state borrowing costs rise when credibility weakens. The state therefore has reason to stabilize the quotation system without appearing to fix prices. Stabilizing the system means stabilizing the gates.

The first stabilization step is stricter publication rules. The state or a municipal authority requires that published sheets disclose methodology: whether they use last transfers, broker quotes, or an average, and what time window is included. They require identifiable sources or at least a list of recognized contributors. They impose penalties for demonstrably false publication. Penalties do not need to eliminate manipulation to be effective. They need to make manipulation risky enough that participants treat publication as usable. Usable is what markets require.

The second stabilization step is faster registry routines. Registry offices extend hours during surge periods. They standardize submission forms more aggressively. They implement clearer cut-offs for record-date eligibility so disputes have fewer grey zones. They create expedited lanes with higher fees justified as capacity management. Capacity management is the neutral description. The operational truth is that access to speed becomes purchasable, and purchasable speed becomes a structural advantage.

The third stabilization step is broker coordination. Brokers, worried about being trapped and about losing legitimacy, agree on standardized settlement sequences. They formalize escrow norms with banker-correspondents. They formalize the order of performance: confirmation of payment finality before transfer release, confirmation of registry receipt before acceptance of trade as completed, standardized document packets required for submission. They may also agree on stress spreads, not as stated collusion but as "prudential norms" justified by volatility. The outcome is cartel-like stabilization: spreads widen together, preventing undercutting that could destroy broker inventories, transferring cost to liquidity seekers.

The quotation shock thus forces the market to become more institutional without yet becoming an exchange. It strengthens the role of recognized publication. It strengthens the role of registries as throughput engines. It strengthens the role of coordinated settlement conventions. It also strengthens the idea that legality is time-bound: ownership is not merely agreement, ownership is recorded status at the cut-off.

The shock's deepest consequence is that it teaches participants the difference between price and finality. Price can move on rumor. Finality cannot. Finality moves on registry and enforcement. In the shock, many participants discovered they could sell at a price but still fail to secure entitlement timing because the registry could not process fast enough. Others discovered they could borrow against a value but still face collateral calls because publication changed what the value "counted as" for contractual purposes. The machine's power lies in those definitions: what counts as a price, what counts as a holder, what counts as a completed transfer, what counts as proof.

When the corrected notice circulates widely enough, prices rebound partially, but the rebound does not erase what was learned. The market does not return to the old equilibrium. It returns to a tighter equilibrium: stricter documentation expectations, more formal publication authority, clearer but more expensive registry speed, and broker coordination that claims prudence while preserving rents.

That is why the quotation shock is a breakthrough episode in disguise. It is not merely a panic. It is the event that hardens a pre-exchange trading culture into a more rule-governed system by forcing everyone to admit that rumor must be turned into authoritative signal, that authority must be tied to enforceable routines, and that enforceable routines require gatekeepers whose incentives will never be neutral.

Movement Three. The blueprint hardens into membership, officialness, and surveillance.

After the quotation shock, the coffeehouse stops being merely a meeting place and becomes a governance layer that is not yet admitted as governance. Participants now understand, in their bones rather than in theory, that a quotation is not just a number; it is a contractual trigger, a collateral anchor, a litigation reference, and a reputational weapon. Once a number becomes those things, the system cannot tolerate unlimited authorship. Unlimited authorship is noise, and noise becomes instability when contracts point at the signal. The response is predictable: authority is narrowed, and narrowing authority produces membership.

Membership does not arrive as a proclamation. It arrives as an accumulation of "reasonable" requirements that function as gates. To contribute prices to the printed lists, you must be recognized. To be recognized, you must have a record of settling. To have a record of settling, you must have access to the clearing nodes and registry fast lanes. To have access to those nodes, you must meet collateral and documentation standards. Standards are framed as integrity, but they also define who is allowed to shape the reference signal that governs everyone else.

The first formal step is the creation of a recognized contributor set for quotation publication. Printers, now exposed to legal and political pressure, protect themselves by narrowing sources to those whose names carry settlement credibility and whose disputes can be routed through predictable remedies. This reduces the risk that the published list is attacked as reckless or manipulated. It also makes the published list a club product. If your quotes are included, you influence the signal. If your quotes are excluded, you must trade on someone else's definition of reality.

The second step is the tightening of what counts as a representative trade. Not every transaction is treated as informative. Distressed sales are labeled unrepresentative. Off-market transfers are excluded. Trades without clean documentation are treated as suspect. The criteria are justified as quality control. They also filter the data to favor those who can transact within the preferred pipes. Preferred pipes are accessible, faster, and more reliable for insiders. The published signal therefore becomes, quietly, a picture of the insider market rather than the whole market, and this is how the system can claim transparency while still monetizing opacity at the edges.

The third step is the formalization of officialness. In the pre-shock world, the printed list was persuasive. After the shock, the printed list becomes authoritative in disputes because courts and municipal offices need a stable anchor. Once authorities repeatedly reference a particular publication as customary value, the publication becomes the closest thing to an official price without being called that. Officialness changes behavior. People begin to design contracts around the list, lenders begin to write collateral thresholds using it, and brokers begin to defend spreads by pointing to it.

Officialness also creates vulnerability, because an official signal is an attack surface. If influencing the signal changes who gets margin calls, who faces collateral demands, and who wins damages claims, then influencing the signal becomes a high-return strategy. High-return strategies attract specialists. Specialists seek methods that do not look like crude fraud, because crude fraud is easier to punish. The system's next evolution is therefore the invention of early surveillance, not as a moral crusade, but as risk management for legitimacy.

Surveillance begins as pattern recognition. If a broker persistently prints trades at extreme values just before publication cut-offs, other brokers notice. If a set of transactions repeatedly occurs between the same counterparties in a way that seems designed to move the reference rather than to exchange risk, printers notice. If a rumor appears reliably before one broker's advantageous trades, rival brokers notice. Notice is the first layer. Documentation becomes the second.

Publication regimes respond by requiring transaction substantiation. Not full disclosure in the modern sense, but enough evidence that the listed trades were real transfers with real settlement and registry recording. The requirement creates a new gate: the ability to produce proof quickly. Proof is easier for those whose operations are already aligned with standard forms and recognized intermediaries. The requirement therefore improves integrity while increasing exclusion pressure.

Meanwhile, registries and courts respond by hardening time rules. Record dates and cut-offs become more explicit. Submission deadlines become more enforceable. Disputes about whether submission time or recording time matters are narrowed by standard language in venture instruments and by registry practice. This reduces ambiguity, but it increases the value of speed. When the rules are clearer, the advantage shifts from argument to timing. Timing is purchasable.

Broker coordination now becomes more than spreads under stress. It becomes a shared governance posture. Brokers begin to agree, informally at first and then with increasing formality, on acceptable documentation packets, settlement sequencing, and dispute escalation pathways. The reason is self-protection. When one broker's sloppy practice creates disputes, the entire room's legitimacy is threatened, and the printed signal's authority is threatened. Threatened authority raises financing costs. Higher financing costs reduce volume. Reduced volume reduces broker income. Brokers therefore have collective incentive to enforce standards that keep the machine credible.

Collective enforcement is never purely altruistic. It also functions as a barrier to entry. If the broker group can define what "proper" documentation looks like, then newcomers who do not have the same administrative capacity, correspondent relationships, and registry familiarity will fail more often, settle more slowly, and be treated as unreliable. Unreliable actors are excluded on the pretext of integrity. Integrity becomes the language of cartel behavior because integrity is difficult to argue against publicly.

The coffeehouse thus evolves into a proto-membership venue without declaring itself one. Access to the most profitable trading opportunities depends on being inside three overlapping perimeters: the settlement perimeter, the registry perimeter, and the publication perimeter. Settlement perimeter access means you can use recognized clearing nodes and can produce confirmation of final payment quickly. Registry perimeter access means you can record transfers quickly and reliably, securing entitlements and minimizing disputes. Publication perimeter access means your trades and quotes are treated as sources for the reference signal that governs contracts and litigation.

These perimeters create a distinct class of insiders whose cost of capital is lower because their transactions are treated as less risky by lenders and insurers. Lower cost of capital allows insiders to hold inventory through stress, which allows them to buy from forced sellers at discounts. The forced sellers are often not weak because they are foolish; they are weak because their liquidity is expensive. Expensive liquidity is the shadow cost of being outside the perimeters.

The state participates in this evolution by preferring stability to openness. Stability lowers borrowing costs. Stability preserves tax receipts. Stability reduces the probability of a legitimacy crisis that would force emergency measures. So the state tolerates, and sometimes quietly encourages, institutional narrowing: licensing of printers, recognition of certain registrars, preference for standardized instruments, and faster court routines for market disputes. Each measure can be defended as public order. Each measure also reinforces the power of the recognized intermediaries.

The market's internal surveillance grows in sophistication because manipulation becomes a threat to the entire financing architecture. If a reference signal is viewed as gameable, lenders widen haircuts, insurers raise premiums, and investors demand higher returns. Higher returns increase the cost of capital. Higher cost of capital reduces venture scale. Reduced venture scale reduces strategic capacity. The polity's incentives therefore align with discouraging obvious manipulation.

The discouragement does not require a modern regulator to exist. It can be achieved through a mix of penalties and exclusion. Printers refuse to list quotes from sources suspected of distortion. Brokers refuse to settle with parties suspected of gaming. Registries flag suspicious transfer patterns. Courts treat certain classes of transactions as suspect and demand heavier proof. Each action is procedural. The effect is surveillance by gatekeeping.

Surveillance by gatekeeping also produces a moral camouflage. The system can claim it is merely enforcing standards, not suppressing competition. Yet standards can be tuned. The tuning can favor incumbents. The same mechanism that stops fraud can also stop disruption. The machine does not distinguish cleanly between the two. It distinguishes based on what threatens stability and what threatens rents, and those threats overlap.

The next inevitable step is a dedicated space or committee that formalizes these norms into something closer to a rulebook. It may not call itself an exchange. It may call itself an association, a registry council, a committee of contributors, a licensing board. The name is less important than the function: defining who may quote, what counts as a trade, what documentation is required, what settlement conventions apply, and what evidence is admissible in dispute. Once these definitions are written and enforced repeatedly, the market has a rulebook whether or not it admits it.

The coffeehouse, in this sense, is the market's rehearsal space for institutional authority. It teaches participants to accept that prices are authoritative only when backed by recognized procedures. It teaches lenders to accept that collateral valuation depends on officialness. It teaches courts to accept that customary value must have a source. It teaches the state that credibility can be defended without setting prices, simply by defending the gates that make prices meaningful.

The irreversibility of this movement is that quotation becomes governance infrastructure, and governance infrastructure demands membership. Membership then becomes the first stable hierarchy in secondary trading: those who can shape the signal and pass the gates cheaply, and those who must accept the signal and pay for gates expensively. The exchange, when it finally appears as a named institution, will not be a sudden invention. It will be the public face of perimeters that were already operating quietly in rooms that sold caffeine and news while building the earliest version of market structure.

Movement Four. The proto-exchange charter: dues, disciplines, and the first formal boundary of "the market."

Once membership logic exists in practice, it eventually demands paperwork, because paperwork is how a system turns a social hierarchy into an enforceable one. The coffeehouse had already become a venue where quotations behaved like public facts, where settlement conventions behaved like proto-clearing, and where publication authority behaved like an official signal. That combination produced two conflicting needs: openness to deepen liquidity and narrowness to protect credibility and rents. A charter resolves the conflict by translating informal privilege into formal criteria that can be defended as integrity.

The charter does not arrive as a revolution. It arrives as a stabilization device after repeated shocks, disputes, and accusations that threaten the profitability of everyone who depends on the room. The brokers want spreads that remain defensible. The bankers want settlement sequences that reduce counterparty loss. The printers want sources that can survive legal challenge. The registrars want submission flows that do not drown capacity and then turn into entitlement litigation. The courts want fewer ambiguous disputes that require re-creating the market in testimony. The state wants fewer breakdowns that damage tax receipts and raise borrowing costs.

A proto-exchange charter is therefore a compact between gatekeepers. It defines who is allowed to produce the signal, how the signal is produced, and what evidence must exist when the signal is contested. It also defines the penalties for those who violate the compact, because a compact without punishments is merely etiquette.

The first artifact is a membership roll. The membership roll is not simply a list of names. It is a list of entities whose quotations and transactions will be treated as presumptively valid for publication and dispute purposes. Inclusion on the roll becomes a tradable advantage because inclusion reduces friction: members' documents are assumed cleaner, members' settlement confirmations are assumed more credible, members' transfer packets are processed with fewer questions. Exclusion becomes a cost because excluded actors must prove legitimacy repeatedly, and repeated proof is expensive.

Dues appear early because gatekeeping requires administration, and administration requires funding. Dues also serve another function: they price out casual participants. Pricing out casual participants is justified as quality control, but it is also how a group preserves market-making profit by limiting competition to those willing and able to pay. The dues become a filter that turns wealth and institutional backing into access.

The charter then defines quoting discipline. Quoting discipline is the set of rules that makes the published signal defensible as customary value. A member must quote in specified forms. Quotes must be firm within stated conditions. Quotes must be honored unless specific exceptions apply. Exceptions are critical because without exceptions, quoting becomes suicidal under stress. With too many exceptions, quoting becomes meaningless. The charter therefore balances two aims that never fully align: enforceability of the quote and survivability of the quoter.

The rules often hinge on time and size. A quote may be binding for a defined interval and for a defined quantity, beyond which it becomes indicative. Time and size boundaries transform obligation into something manageable. They also create a microstructure: small trades may clear easily at tighter spreads while larger trades face negotiation and wider spreads. The market becomes layered by size, and the layers create new opportunities for insiders who know how to break orders into smaller pieces, how to time submissions, and how to use relationships to avoid unfavorable terms.

Reporting discipline follows. If a printed list is authoritative, it cannot be built from rumors. It must be built from traceable inputs. The charter therefore defines what constitutes a reportable transaction and what constitutes a reportable quote. It defines which trades count, how they are verified, how they are timestamped, and how they are transmitted to the publisher. It may require that reportable trades be accompanied by proof of payment routing and proof of registry submission, not to reveal everything, but to make manipulation risky.

This introduces the earliest sustained surveillance mechanism: not a separate police force, but a compliance routine embedded in publication. If a member's reported trade cannot be substantiated with expected documentation, the trade is excluded, and repeated exclusions become grounds for discipline. Discipline can be a fine, but more often it is a loss of privilege: exclusion from publication sources, delayed processing in registry channels, refusal of settlement confirmation from key nodes, and ultimately expulsion from the membership roll. Expulsion is the harshest penalty because it removes the actor from the recognition perimeter that makes liquidity affordable.

The charter also defines dispute procedures because disputes are where legitimacy is tested. A dispute procedure specifies evidence standards: which documents are admissible, which confirmations count as proof of payment, which registry entries count as proof of ownership, which publication issues count as reference, and which time cut-offs apply. Evidence standards are a political allocation disguised as technical prudence. If evidence standards are too strict, outsiders cannot comply and are excluded. If evidence standards are too loose, manipulation thrives and credibility collapses. The charter sets standards that preserve insider advantage while keeping fraud manageable enough that the system can grow.

The settlement discipline portion of the charter is the clearest bridge between coffeehouse culture and exchange mechanics. Settlement discipline specifies performance sequencing: payment confirmation requirements before transfer release, escrow routines through recognized bankers, acceptable settlement media, and recognized acknowledgment forms that serve as proof. It also specifies what happens when settlement fails: penalties, time frames, and the circumstances under which forced replacement or compensation is triggered. This is proto-clearing as rulebook. It reduces counterparty fear and increases throughput. It also concentrates settlement into fewer trusted nodes, which strengthens those nodes' pricing power and strengthens the membership group's ability to exclude entrants who cannot access those nodes.

Registry discipline becomes integrated with charter membership because record dates and entitlement disputes had already proven that registry throughput is systemic. The charter therefore formalizes how transfers must be submitted, what identity proofs are acceptable, what fees apply, and how priority is assigned when capacity is strained. Priority is justified as capacity management and funded by expedited fees. The practical consequence is a tiered market in time: insiders buy speed, speed secures entitlements, secured entitlements preserve value, and preserved value lowers the cost of capital for those already inside.

Publication authority is the charter's most sensitive component because publication governs collateral and disputes. The charter therefore formalizes a calculation method or at least a methodology boundary: which time window is used, how distressed prints are treated, whether quotes or trades dominate, and how outliers are handled. Outlier handling is not merely statistical. It is distributive. Including distressed prints can intensify collateral cascades and forced selling. Excluding them can conceal stress and shift loss onto creditors. The charter's methodology chooses winners under pressure.

The publication authority also defines who may contribute inputs. Contribution is power. The charter often restricts contribution to members in good standing and to recognized correspondents whose credibility is itself gated. This creates an information perimeter. Information perimeters are the earliest form of market data monetization: members see earlier, members shape what counts, outsiders see later and pay wider spreads.

The charter's enforcement relies on two engines: social exclusion and institutional preference. Social exclusion is immediate: brokers refuse to trade with unreliable actors, bankers refuse escrow for those flagged, printers refuse to print their quotes, registrars slow their submissions. Institutional preference is slower and more decisive: courts begin to treat charter-compliant documentation as presumptively credible, and begin to treat non-compliant documentation as suspect. This preference shifts dispute outcomes. Once dispute outcomes shift, rational actors conform because nonconformity becomes expensive.

The state's role is subtle and decisive. The state does not need to write the charter to benefit from it. The state benefits when the charter stabilizes quotation authority, reduces disputes, and lowers the risk premium embedded in borrowing costs. Courts and municipal offices may reinforce the charter indirectly by accepting charter-published lists as customary value, by preferring charter-defined evidence standards, and by punishing overt manipulation when it threatens broader stability. The state thus becomes a silent partner in the consolidation of market authority, because consolidated authority is easier to monitor and easier to rely on for fiscal planning.

The proto-exchange charter therefore produces a boundary that did not exist earlier: the boundary between "the market" and "the public." Before, the market was dispersed and porous, though uneven. After, the market becomes a recognized perimeter of members whose transactions and quotations are treated as the official substrate for reference signals. Outsiders can still participate, but participation becomes mediated: they must trade through members, submit through member channels, and accept member-defined terms. Mediation is a revenue model.

This boundary also changes the meaning of transparency. The system can publish an official list and claim openness. Yet the process of producing the list is now more controlled. Control improves credibility and increases the value of being inside. The published list becomes a shop window for a machine whose levers remain behind the counter.

The charter solves a real problem and creates a durable one. It reduces fraud, reduces dispute ambiguity, and increases liquidity by standardizing gates. It also institutionalizes rent extraction by turning gate passage into a priced privilege defended by membership. The machine becomes more scalable and more political at the same time.

The coffeehouse trading culture has now produced the essential organs of a formal exchange without needing a grand building to declare itself. There is membership. There are quoting rules. There is publication methodology. There are settlement conventions. There are registry priorities. There are surveillance and discipline routines. There are dispute procedures. There is institutional preference that makes compliance profitable. Once these organs exist, the formal exchange is a naming event as much as an institutional one. The exchange, when named, will inherit these organs and enlarge them.

Movement Five. Compliance is born, precedent hardens, and manipulation becomes a case file.

Once a charter exists, the market's most dangerous vulnerability becomes obvious: the charter has created an official signal, and official signals are worth attacking. Before, manipulation could be dismissed as rumor and counter-rumor. Now, manipulation can be aimed at methodology, membership, and publication cadence, with the intent not merely to profit in the moment but to trigger contractual cascades: collateral calls, forced selling, damage claims, and renegotiated credit terms. The machinery of the market becomes, by design, sensitive to its own reference numbers, and sensitivity creates incentive.

The charter's authors understood this in practice even if they did not articulate it as theory. They had created a compact that relied on the public believing that published quotations were usable. Usable did not mean flawless. Usable meant that enough participants would accept the numbers as customary value when money, entitlement, and dispute demanded an anchor. The question then became how to defend usability without destroying liquidity by burdening every trade with investigation.

That defense begins with a new role: the compliance function, though it is not yet named that. A charter requires someone to check that members are honoring quoting disciplines, submitting proper documentation, and reporting trades according to the agreed rules. At first, these checks are performed by rotating clerks, by printers who refuse to publish suspect inputs, by registrars who flag irregular submissions, and by settlement nodes that deny services to those whose confirmations have become unreliable. Then the checks become continuous, because the market realizes that episodic policing is too slow to deter targeted manipulation.

Continuous policing does not arrive as moral concern. It arrives as risk management for legitimacy. If one manipulation episode produces a cascade large enough to cause broad losses, the credibility premium embedded in discounts and haircuts rises across the market. Higher discounts raise the cost of capital for ventures. Higher haircuts tighten credit. Tight credit reduces trade volume. Reduced volume reduces fee income for intermediaries and reduces fiscal receipts for the state. Everyone who depends on volume now has incentive to reduce the frequency of visible manipulation that threatens the signal's authority.

The compliance function therefore evolves into a three-part routine. First, documentation verification: ensuring that reported trades correspond to actual transfers with plausible settlement and registry submission. Second, pattern detection: identifying repeated behaviors that suggest trades exist primarily to influence the reference signal rather than to exchange risk. Third, discipline: applying penalties that are painful enough to deter without causing full market shutdown by making everyone fear participation.

Documentation verification is the easiest to formalize because it is gate-based. A reported trade that lacks the required packet is excluded from publication. Exclusion alone would be trivial if publication did not matter. Publication now governs contracts. Exclusion therefore becomes a penalty because it reduces a member's ability to shape the signal and reduces his ability to justify quotes by pointing to printed evidence. Repeated exclusions become reputational stains inside the membership perimeter, which then translate into practical costs: slower registry processing, tighter settlement terms, and reduced willingness of peers to trade.

Pattern detection is more subtle and more powerful. The market learns that manipulation does not require forged trades. It can be executed through real trades arranged for the purpose of printing a desired number at the right moment. The simplest pattern is self-reinforcing printing near cut-offs: a member repeatedly executes trades at extreme values just before publication windows, then benefits from the printed number through collateral triggers or through the ability to buy from forced sellers. Another pattern is circular trading between allied parties: A sells to B, B sells to C, C sells back to A, creating transaction volume that appears real but is structured to move the reference without changing net exposure meaningfully. A third pattern is selective reporting: only favorable trades are submitted as reportable, while unfavorable trades are concealed as private transfers, allowing the printed list to present a skewed market.

To detect such patterns, the charter's enforcement agents begin building what is effectively a case file culture. A file is not only paper; it is a memory system. The file collects trade reports, registry submission records, settlement confirmations, and publication timestamps. It collects complaints from counterparties. It collects the history of a member's quoting behavior relative to print cycles. It collects evidence of relationships between repeated counterparties. Over time, the file becomes the mechanism by which suspicion is converted into actionable discipline without requiring every incident to be argued from scratch.

That is the second breakthrough inside this chapter: the market begins to create an institutional memory of misconduct. Institutional memory is the difference between a scandal and a precedent. Precedent is how a system trains itself.

Discipline then becomes the question of proportional punishment. If punishment is too weak, manipulation becomes rational. If punishment is too strong, members fear accidental violation and reduce activity, thinning liquidity. The charter therefore tends to punish through exclusion and privilege withdrawal rather than through spectacular fines. Privilege withdrawal is economically surgical. It targets the member's ability to operate cheaply inside the gates. If a member is denied rapid registry channels, his settlement times worsen. If his settlement times worsen, his spreads widen. If his spreads widen, he loses flow. If he loses flow, his influence over publication declines. Influence decline is a loss of power disguised as administrative inconvenience.

Courts begin to reinforce this discipline indirectly. Once courts repeatedly accept charter-defined evidence standards and charter-published reference lists as customary value, courts also begin to treat charter violations as indicators of bad faith. Bad faith is an enforcement lever. It shifts burden of proof. It justifies harsher remedies. It increases the probability that a violator loses disputes. Losing disputes increases costs. Costs deter. The market's private discipline thus becomes public consequence without needing a modern regulator to declare it law.

The state's role strengthens further because the state has learned that the quotation system is now part of fiscal infrastructure. The state does not need to fix prices to shape outcomes. It can license publication. It can require recordkeeping standards. It can prioritize court handling of market disputes. It can criminalize certain forms of document tampering. Each action reduces the noise around the signal and therefore reduces the volatility premium demanded by lenders. Reduced premium improves the state's own borrowing costs. The state becomes an enforcer of signal integrity because signal integrity is revenue stability.

In this environment, the first long-running manipulation case becomes unavoidable. The case does not begin as a dramatic accusation. It begins as a pattern that too many people can see. A member repeatedly prints transactions at moments that align too neatly with publication cut-offs and collateral thresholds. His quotes consistently appear on the "right" side of the next day's printed list. His counterparties in these prints are unusually concentrated. His settlement confirmations arrive quickly, suggesting privileged access to clearing nodes. His registry submissions are rarely delayed, suggesting privileged access to recording lanes. His profits rise while others complain that the market feels "thin" at moments that matter.

The complaints, at first, are treated as rivalry. Rivalry is expected. But rivalry is not the same as an evidentiary file, and the file begins to fill. Printers notice that the same member's prints repeatedly dominate the tails of the distribution. Registrars notice unusual clusters of transfers that reverse quickly. Bankers notice collateral calls triggered in ways that seem to benefit a small circle. Brokers notice that forced sellers appear after specific publication outcomes. The pattern is not proof of fraud. It is proof of exploitation of the machine's rules. Exploitation can be punishable even when it is not illegal in the narrow sense, because punishability is how the charter defends legitimacy.

The compliance function then faces its own governing problem: what counts as manipulation when trades are real and documents are formally clean. If the trades are genuine transfers with genuine settlement, on what basis can the market punish behavior that merely uses the rules cleverly. The answer is precedent, because precedent is how a system defines its own moral boundary without admitting to moral language.

The case therefore becomes a test of intent, and intent is inferred from structure: repeated tail prints, repeated timing alignment, repeated counterparties, repeated reversal patterns, and the absence of plausible commercial rationale beyond signal influence. The enforcement group does not need to prove that a trade did not occur. It needs to prove that the trade was constructed to distort the reference signal and therefore to trigger contractual cascades. Contractual cascades are harm. Harm is the basis for remedy.

The hearing that follows is not a public trial. It is an internal procedure with external consequences, held in rooms where the charter's authority can be enforced without being embarrassed by the public's questions. Evidence is laid out: publication lists, trade tickets, settlement confirmations, registry entries, correspondent letters, complaint statements. Each artifact is a named object in action. Each object demonstrates how the machine can be steered. The steering is the offense.

The case produces the market's first durable set of anti-manipulation definitions. Not philosophical definitions, but operational ones. Trades executed within defined windows near publication cut-offs are subject to heightened scrutiny. Repeated reverse transfers between the same parties are treated as suspicious unless justified by documented commercial necessity. Reported trades must be accompanied by enhanced proof packages when they materially influence published references. A member whose trades repeatedly dominate publication tails may be required to disclose additional context to the enforcement group.

These rules do not eliminate manipulation. They change its cost. They also change who can afford compliance. Enhanced proof packages require administrative capacity. Administrative capacity is easier for large actors. The system therefore improves integrity while also increasing barriers to entry. Integrity and exclusion continue to travel together.

The punishment in the first precedent-setting case is carefully chosen to demonstrate authority without collapsing participation. The member is not necessarily expelled, because expulsion can create counterparty panic if too many positions depend on him. Instead, the member's privileges are curtailed: reduced access to expedited registry lanes, restricted ability to contribute quotes to published lists for a period, higher fees for settlement services, and mandatory additional documentation for reportable trades. The punishment is a throttling of gate access. It is a loss of speed. Speed loss reduces profit. Profit reduction deters.

Other members absorb the lesson quickly, because the lesson is not moral. It is economic. The system has demonstrated that it can change the cost of operating inside the gates.

The manipulation case also hardens a second precedent: the difference between public openness and internal accountability. The charter continues to present the printed list as a public service. Yet the governance of the list becomes increasingly private. The public sees the number, not the evidence trail that produced it. The public sees the method summary, not the enforcement deliberations. This is not accidental. The system prefers legitimacy without scrutiny because scrutiny can reveal how much of the signal is produced by negotiated gatekeeping rather than by neutral discovery.

The result is a more stable market and a more political one. Stability rises because obvious gaming becomes riskier and because registry and settlement routines become more standardized. Political content rises because the system now has an internal authority capable of deciding which behaviors are acceptable and which are punishable, and those decisions distribute profit.

The coffeehouse has become something else. It still sells warmth and news, but it now sits atop a layered enforcement stack: charter membership gates, settlement node eligibility, registry processing tiers, publication contributor lists, and compliance case files that create institutional memory. A participant can still trade outside the perimeter, but trading outside is slower, more expensive, and less protected. That is how the market's boundary becomes durable.

This movement's irreversibility is that the market learns to regulate itself through gate control, not through declared ideology. It learns to defend its reference signal because the signal is the machine's coordinating mechanism. It learns to create institutional memory of misconduct because memory allows precedent, and precedent allows a system to function without reinventing its legitimacy daily. It learns that manipulation is not merely lying; it is exploiting methodology, timing, and gate access in ways that convert the signal into a weapon.

The later exchange will inherit all of this. The exchange will formalize membership, formalize reporting, formalize surveillance, formalize discipline, and sell the resulting legitimacy as a product. The coffeehouse era is the prototype, not the prelude.

Movement Six. The bridge from talk to institution.

After the charter and the first manipulation case, the room's logic changes in a way that is easy to miss because the furniture does not. People still enter, still sit, still speak, still trade, still pass paper, still lean in when a notice is posted. Yet the center of gravity is no longer conversation. The center of gravity is recognition. Who is recognized as a valid quoter. Which prints are recognized as representative. Which confirmations are recognized as settlement proof. Which registry entry is recognized as final ownership. Which publication issue is recognized as customary value in court.

Recognition is a machine. It has inputs, outputs, and costs. It has bottlenecks. It can be gamed. It can be defended. When recognition becomes central, the market stops being a loose culture and becomes an institution in all but name, because an institution is simply a system that can enforce what counts.

The coffeehouse had always been a compression device: it compressed information travel time by concentrating messengers, correspondents, and decision-makers; it compressed search costs by concentrating brokers and buyers; it compressed enforcement ambiguity by concentrating witnesses and document practices that could later be referenced. The quotation shock revealed that compression can amplify as well as stabilize. The charter responded by narrowing authorship of the reference signal. The manipulation case responded by building institutional memory and discipline.

Now a final problem remains before a formal exchange becomes inevitable: the market still depends on a physical room whose rules are partly social. Social rules are powerful but fragile under scale. As volume grows, the room cannot hold all counterparties, cannot process all disputes, cannot verify all documents, cannot sustain all confirmation demands. A machine that scales must replace social enforcement with procedural enforcement that can run without the constant presence of the same people.

The first sign of that transition is the separation of functions that had been tangled together in the room. Quoting becomes one function. Reporting becomes another. Settlement confirmation becomes another. Registry processing becomes another. Dispute adjudication becomes another. Publication becomes another. In early phases, the same individuals touched multiple functions. In later phases, the functions begin to acquire their own personnel, their own schedules, and their own evidence requirements.

This is how bureaucracy enters markets without announcing itself. It enters as the price of volume.

The membership roll that once served primarily as a credibility filter begins to serve as an operational directory. Members are assigned identifiers. Their quotes are associated with those identifiers. Their reported trades are logged under those identifiers. Their settlement confirmations are routed through recognized nodes tied to those identifiers. Their registry submissions are tagged. The goal is not elegance. The goal is traceability. Traceability is the foundation of discipline because discipline requires evidence, and evidence requires a consistent way to say who did what, when, and through which gate.

Once traceability exists, a new artifact appears: the audit trail. The audit trail is not an abstract concept. It is a stack of documents and ledger entries that can be assembled to reconstruct a transaction's path from quote to report to settlement confirmation to registry update to publication inclusion. The audit trail becomes essential because the market has learned that its reference signal is an attack surface. An attack surface cannot be defended by vibes. It can be defended only by a trail that makes denial costly.

This shifts power toward those who can maintain trails. Trail maintenance requires clerical capacity. Clerical capacity is easier for larger actors. The market's integrity therefore improves at the same time that its hierarchy hardens.

Publication methodology tightens further because courts and lenders have become dependent on the printed list as a reference anchor. Dependency creates a need for continuity. Continuity creates rules about timing: publication windows become fixed, update cadence becomes predictable, cut-off times become formal. Predictable cadence reduces rumor-driven chaos but increases timing games. If everyone knows when the list prints, those who can trade just before printing can influence the signal, and those who can trade just after printing can exploit those influenced cascades.

The compliance response is predictable: publication introduces more explicit inclusion rules. Trades must meet minimal size thresholds to count. Trades must be accompanied by settlement proof to count. Trades must be submitted through approved channels to count. Outlier trades may be flagged and reviewed before inclusion. Review delays reduce the chance of printing distorted signals, but review delays create an inside lane for those who see preliminary prints or provisional decisions earlier. Every integrity improvement creates a new advantage surface.

The market's maturation is therefore not a march toward fairness. It is a march toward a stable distribution of advantages.

Registry routines accelerate and become more mechanical. The registrar expands processing windows, formalizes submission queues, and introduces standardized receipts that serve as proof of submission time. Proof of submission time matters because the market break taught everyone that entitlement disputes often hinge on timing, and timing disputes cannot be settled without receipts. Receipts become their own micro-asset because a receipt is evidence that can shift a distribution dispute. Evidence is leverage.

Receipts also create a new class of intermediaries who sell assistance in producing compliant submissions. Their service is administrative competence as a product. They help outsiders package documents, meet identity standards, and route submissions through channels that reduce rejection risk. Outsiders pay more, not because their trades are inherently riskier, but because they must purchase alignment with a machine designed around insider routines.

Settlement nodes become more formal in their role. Banker-correspondents who once served as trusted escrows now publish explicit schedules and accepted settlement media. They define what counts as final posting. They define reversal rules. They define fees for expedited confirmations. Confirmation becomes a priced service because confirmation is not merely reassurance; it is a document that can satisfy a gate at the registry, satisfy a lender in a collateral review, or satisfy a court in a dispute.

A confirmation, once priced, becomes an instrument of hierarchy. Those who can afford faster confirmation can settle trades more quickly, which allows them to recycle capital faster, which allows them to quote tighter spreads, which attracts more flow, which increases their dominance. The machine compounds.

Broker coordination shifts from informal norms to explicit committee behavior. A committee can exist without being called one. It exists whenever a small group has recurring meetings to define what counts as acceptable practice. They define acceptable documentation, acceptable reporting, acceptable settlement sequencing, acceptable dispute escalation, acceptable conduct in publication windows. They also define what counts as unacceptable manipulation.

The committee's most important product is not a moral code. It is boundary definition. Boundary definition is a market-making tool because it reduces uncertainty about whether a trade will be recognized. Reduced uncertainty tightens spreads. Tight spreads increase volume. Increased volume increases the committee's influence over the market's reality. Influence becomes self-legitimating because participation flows toward the most predictable pipes.

The system's enforcement begins to look less like scandal response and more like ordinary administration. Flags, lists, suspensions, reinstatements, documentation requirements, mandatory waiting periods, restricted quoting privileges. None of these punishments need to be dramatic. Their power lies in changing the cost of doing business.

When the market can change your cost of doing business, it can govern you.

This is the practical meaning of surveillance in early trading culture: not omniscience, but the ability to impose friction selectively. Selective friction is both integrity tool and rent defense. It is used to deter behavior that threatens the reference signal's usability. It is also used to manage competition by ensuring that the cheapest passage through gates remains concentrated among recognized actors.

Courts begin to adapt to this new reality. Judges and clerks develop a preference for charter-compliant evidence because charter compliance reduces ambiguity. Reduced ambiguity lowers court workload. Lower workload reduces delay. Reduced delay improves market predictability. The market then becomes more dependent on courts, and courts become more comfortable enforcing market-defined standards. This is how private rules become semi-public through repeated citation. The charter's evidence standards become customary. Customary becomes enforceable. Enforceable becomes law-like.

The state, observing that the market's stability is now tied to these routines, strengthens the enforcement perimeter selectively. It prosecutes forgery because forgery threatens registry integrity. It supports printer licensing because publication authority stabilizes collateral valuation and reduces dispute chaos. It supports standardized registry procedures because registry lag creates legitimacy crises that spill into fiscal stress.

These interventions are not purely technocratic. They are political choices about which institutions are trusted and which are allowed to fail. Trust is not evenly distributed. It is allocated. Allocation is power.

The result is a mature pre-exchange trading culture that no longer looks like casual conversation. It looks like a multi-layered machine with a visible interface and a hidden operating system. The visible interface is the coffeehouse: quotes, rumors, posted notices, printed lists. The operating system is the recognition stack: membership, documentation standards, settlement confirmations, registry processing tiers, publication methodology, and discipline routines that preserve signal usability.

At this point, the formal exchange is less an invention than an administrative consolidation. The market already has membership. It already has discipline. It already has a publication system. It already has settlement conventions. It already has surveillance. It already has dispute procedures that courts prefer. The formal exchange will simply bundle these into a declared institution, charge for access more openly, and present the resulting stability as public benefit.

The key transition is the conversion of a social venue into a governance venue. Once a governance venue exists, it can define what counts as a market price. Once a market price is definable, it can be used to value collateral, value damages, and value taxes. Once it is used for those purposes, the polity's fiscal system becomes entangled with the quotation system, and disentanglement becomes costly. Cost creates path dependence.

The bridge, then, is complete: a number spoken in a room becomes a number printed on a sheet, then becomes a number referenced in a contract, then becomes a number enforced in a dispute, then becomes a number that shapes who can borrow and at what terms. A trading culture becomes a capital allocation regime.

CHAPTER 5
THE STREET BEFORE THE TOWERS
DEBT, PANIC, AND THE STATE-MARKET BARGAIN THAT BUILT A FINANCIAL CENTER.

The street was narrow enough that two carts could not pass without negotiation. Its buildings were low, practical, and stained by rain and smoke. It sat close to the water and close to power, which is the combination that turns paper into money even when everyone swears it is only paper. In the mornings it smelled of damp timber, ink, and horse sweat. In the afternoons it smelled of tobacco and impatience. The street did not look like the future. It looked like commerce's back hallway, a place where men with obligations lingered because lingering was cheaper than default.

The city had grown faster than its settlement discipline. Trade expanded, credit chains lengthened, and public borrowing rose because wars and infrastructure both demand prepayment. Taxes arrived on schedule only in calm times, and calm times were never guaranteed. The state's obligations therefore began to circulate as instruments, not as one-to-one promises. A paper claim on the treasury became a medium for settling private debts, paying suppliers, and compensating soldiers, because coin was scarce and because the state's promise carried a kind of coercive shadow even when the treasury was empty.

These obligations were not uniform. Some were long-dated, some short-dated, some tied to particular revenues, some contingent on legislative approvals, some payable in designated coin, some payable in whatever the treasury could procure. Some had clear transfer rules. Some were transferred anyway, through custom and necessity. Custom hardened into practice. Practice hardened into expectation. Expectation turned into pricing.

In that street, debt acquired a second life. A promise issued for one purpose became tradable because someone else needed liquidity now and was willing to accept less than face value to get it. Discounting turned time into a market price. Discounting also turned the state's credibility into a private profit surface.

The first dealers were not born as an industry. They were born as adapters to mismatch. One person had a claim that would pay later. Another person needed coin today. A third person stood between them and offered to convert time into money for a fee. The fee looked like interest. It was also a payment for verification, for settlement sequencing, for rumor risk, and for the ability to survive a dispute.

The street's economy of paper was never merely about rates. It was about gates. Who could verify a claim quickly. Who could accept it as collateral. Who could resell it without waiting. Who could take it to a court if the issuer stalled. Who could petition an official for recognition of priority. Each gate created a spread. Each spread attracted capital and talent into the business of moving claims rather than producing goods.

The city's merchants tolerated these intermediaries because intermediaries made trade possible at scale. They also resented them because intermediaries profited from other people's urgency. That resentment mattered only when panic arrived, because in calm times the spread feels like a fee. Under panic, the spread feels like a verdict.

Panic arrived the way it often does in debt systems: first as a question about payment timing, then as a question about enforceability, then as a question about whose claims count as senior when money is insufficient. The immediate trigger was mundane and therefore lethal: a payment delay on a set of public obligations that many private contracts had begun to treat as near-cash. A delayed payment is not yet a default. A delayed payment is uncertainty, and uncertainty is what turns discounting from a trade into a stampede.

Dealers widened spreads within hours. They did it because they feared being trapped with paper that could not be converted back into coin, and because they feared that their own lenders would tighten credit if the paper's value became contested. The widening itself became a signal. Merchants who had been willing to accept public paper at a modest discount now demanded deeper cuts or demanded coin. Suppliers refused paper entirely unless it came through a trusted dealer's endorsement. Workers demanded payment in more final media because they could not eat a claim that might be disputed next week.

A run began, but it was not a run on a single bank. It was a run on settlement confidence. People tried to convert claims into coin. Coin demand rose. Coin supply did not. Prices for liquidity jumped.

This is the moment where a debt system shows its hidden architecture. The paper itself had not changed in legal text. What changed was the market's belief about how quickly the paper could be turned into final settlement. Liquidity is always a function of finality. Finality is always a function of enforceable routine.

The street's dealers had built their business on the assumption that the state would remain predictable enough that the paper would remain near-cash. Predictable did not mean generous. Predictable meant that delays would be bounded, that the courts would still treat the obligations as enforceable, that the legislature would not retroactively rewrite terms, and that the state would not privilege new claims at the expense of old ones without making the political cost unbearable.

Under stress, those assumptions became questionable, and the market began to reprice the entire hierarchy of claims. Some obligations traded at mild discounts because they were perceived as politically protected. Others traded at deep discounts because they were perceived as expendable. The hierarchy was not purely written. It was inferred from enforcement behavior, from political rumor, from which creditors had influence, and from which revenue streams were plausibly collectible.

Dealers responded by triaging what they would make markets in. Triaging is not ideology; it is survival. If a dealer quotes too tightly and is forced to inventory paper that becomes illiquid, he may be unable to meet his own obligations. If he quotes too wide, he loses clients and invites accusation. Under stress, accusation is also a risk because reputational damage can remove access to credit.

Credit access tightened first in the least visible way: haircuts rose. A lender who would previously lend a high percentage against a claim now demanded more collateral. This is the earliest form of margin logic: the borrower must post more value than the loan because the collateral's price is now uncertain. Higher haircuts forced borrowers to sell claims to raise coin, which pushed prices down further. A credit system under stress becomes a forced sale engine unless someone supplies liquidity willing to hold risk.

The street's dealers could have supplied that liquidity if they had had unlimited balance sheets. They did not. Their balance sheets were personal, fragile, and dependent on short-term lending from merchants and bankers who themselves were becoming cautious. The street therefore faced a choice: either accept a spiral of forced selling and widening discounts, or create a stabilization mechanism that could keep trading and settlement functioning long enough for political decisions to catch up.

Stabilization did not begin with speeches. It began with a bargain among intermediaries and power.

The intermediaries needed three things: enforceable recognition of the paper's legitimacy, a predictable schedule of payments or conversions, and a way to clear obligations among themselves without moving scarce coin for every transaction. The state needed two things: continued ability to finance itself and continued functioning of trade so tax receipts would not collapse further. The merchants needed one thing: a market where paper could be turned into usable settlement without being skinned alive by panic spreads.

These needs intersected on the narrow street because the street was where paper became price, and price became behavior.

The bargaining began in a room off the street, where the doors could close and the voices could drop. No one wanted the public to see that the market's stability depended on negotiated privilege, because public recognition of negotiated privilege invites anger. Anger invites political intervention. Political intervention can be clumsy and destructive. So the bargain was framed as order, prudence, and civic necessity.

The first term was recognition. Courts would treat the state's obligations as enforceable contracts with defined remedies, and officials would make that treatment visible through expedited hearings for instrument disputes. Expedited hearings are not charity. They are a liquidity tool because enforcement speed is a pricing variable. When enforcement is faster, discounts tighten. When discounts tighten, collateral haircuts fall. When haircuts fall, forced selling slows.

The second term was schedule. The state could not promise immediate payment in coin for all claims, but it could promise a predictable conversion routine: specific dates, specific windows, specific revenues prioritized. Predictable schedules convert panic into planning. Planning lowers the premium for fear. Fear is expensive; predictable fear is cheaper.

The third term was clearing. Dealers and their lenders needed a way to offset obligations so that only net differences required coin. The street's problem was not merely that coin was scarce. It was that coin movement was inefficient under volume. Without netting, a hundred trades could require a hundred settlements. With netting, a hundred trades could require a few. Netting is throughput. Throughput is survival.

The clearing arrangement emerged as a private ledger discipline operated by a small set of trusted nodes. Trades between dealers were logged. Obligations were offset. Settlement occurred in batches at defined times. Participants were required to maintain balances or collateral with the clearing node to reduce default risk. This is prefunding logic without the modern name. The key is not terminology. The key is that the system shifted from bilateral trust to centralized routine.

Centralized routine created a new gate: membership. Only those deemed reliable could participate. Reliability was defined by capital, by documentation discipline, by willingness to submit to the clearing node's rules, and by relationships that could be framed as reputational history. Membership lowered costs for members because it lowered uncertainty and accelerated settlement. Membership raised costs for outsiders because outsiders now had to transact through members or accept slower, riskier settlement.

This is how a financial center forms: not by building towers, but by building perimeters.

The perimeter then needed a reference signal. Under stress, private quotes vary wildly, and wild variation increases dispute probability. Disputes are throughput killers. So the bargain included publication discipline. A recognized publication would print reference prices and discount rates at scheduled times. The publication would use defined inputs, and those inputs would come from members in good standing whose trades could be substantiated through clearing records and registry submissions.

The publication was framed as transparency. It was also a control surface. A reference signal anchored collateral haircuts, anchored loan valuations, anchored damages claims, and anchored bargaining in private contracts. The market's stability therefore became sensitive to the publication's methodology, and methodology became governance.

Governance did not appear as a single rulebook. It appeared as a stack of routines.

A dealer quoting into the reference had to honor quotes within defined limits or face privilege withdrawal. A dealer reporting trades had to produce proof packets. A dealer settling through the clearing node had to meet collateral requirements. A registrar had to process member submissions quickly to prevent record-date disputes. A court had to treat the clearing confirmations and registry entries as authoritative evidence. A printer had to publish on schedule to prevent rumor-driven vacuums.

Each routine reduced one class of uncertainty while creating a new advantage surface. Faster settlement became purchasable. Faster registry processing became purchasable. Earlier access to publication became purchasable. The machine stabilized and stratified simultaneously.

The panic did not disappear immediately. It slowed, then changed character. Instead of a pure flight into coin, the market began to price claims according to membership-recognized credibility. Claims routed through the clearing node and verified by registry confirmation traded with tighter discounts. Claims outside the perimeter traded with wider discounts. The system had found a way to keep trading functioning by narrowing the definition of what counted as clean paper. Clean paper is always a social construction enforced by institutions.

The state's commitments, once routinized, began to pull the market toward a new equilibrium. Payment schedules reduced the uncertainty premium. Courts' expedited posture reduced enforcement risk. The clearing arrangement reduced settlement friction. The printed reference reduced bargaining chaos. Trade resumed, but it resumed through the perimeter.

This is the bargain that shaped the financial center: a private-public compact that traded stability for controlled access. The center's core advantage was not mystical genius. It was institutional throughput: the ability to turn claims into final settlement faster and more predictably than elsewhere.

Once that advantage existed, it attracted volume. Merchants preferred to discount paper where discounts were tighter. Governments preferred to issue obligations where there was continuous demand. Insurers preferred to underwrite where claims could be enforced predictably. Bankers preferred to lend where collateral could be valued against authoritative references. Volume attracted specialists. Specialists demanded more standardized routines. Standardized routines deepened the perimeter. Deepened perimeters increased the center's dominance.

The street then became more than geography. It became protocol. A claim "from the street" meant it had passed through recognized gates: verified trade, clearing record, registry entry, publication-anchored value. That meaning traveled to other cities and other jurisdictions. Other markets began referencing the street's printed lists because courts needed anchors and lenders needed standards. The center's reference signal became a remote governance tool, exporting its methodology and exporting its hierarchy.

Exported hierarchy appears as convenience to those who benefit. It appears as dependence to those who pay.

The dealers, now bound by clearing and publication disciplines, faced a new internal problem: default within the perimeter. If a member fails, losses can spread through netting. The perimeter therefore required loss allocation rules. Loss allocation is the most political aspect of clearing because it decides whether default is isolated or socialized. The chosen design tends to protect insiders: pre-funding requirements, collateral calls, and privilege withdrawal before default becomes catastrophic. When default still occurs, the loss is allocated through documented priority: who is paid first, whose claims are delayed, whose claims become impaired.

These rules created a moral camouflage that later markets would perfect. When a loss is allocated through procedure, no single person "chooses" who loses, yet someone designed the procedure, and the design reflects power.

The bargain also hardened the relationship between market stability and state capacity. The state learned that a functioning market in its obligations lowered borrowing costs and increased strategic flexibility. The market learned that state enforcement speed and registry integrity were liquidity inputs. The two became entwined. Entwinement made the center resilient. It also made it politically sensitive, because any challenge to the center's privilege could be framed as a threat to stability. Stability became the argument used to defend gatekeeping.

Over time, the street's routines became a template for formal exchange design. Membership rolls became exchange admission. Clearing ledgers became clearinghouses. Printed lists became official market data. Quoting disciplines became market-making obligations. Dispute procedures became rulebooks. Surveillance of manipulation became compliance offices.

The towers came later. The essential work happened earlier, when panic forced a bargain that converted a loose culture of trading into a disciplined stack of gates capable of clearing volume. The street shaped the center not by glamour but by constraints: scarcity of coin, fragility of trust, and the need to keep the state solvent without letting every shock become a collapse.

CHAPTER 6

WHY EXCHANGES HAD TO EXIST

THE SCALE PROBLEM: TRUST, MATCHING, AND ENFORCEABLE LIQUIDITY.

An exchange is not born from the love of price discovery; it is born from the hatred of unfinished trades. Before an exchange, bargains already happen, quotations already circulate, ownership units already transfer, and paper already moves. What does not scale is completion. Completion is the conversion of agreement into recognized finality across a chain that includes payment, registry recording, entitlement eligibility, and dispute survivability. A market can tolerate dispersed bargaining; it cannot tolerate dispersed finality once volume grows, because dispersed finality multiplies failure surfaces faster than it multiplies opportunity.

The pre-exchange world accumulates friction in five places that eventually become intolerable at scale: search, verification, settlement sequencing, registry throughput, and reference authority. Each friction begins as a cost and becomes a risk. Each risk becomes a spread. Each spread becomes a political problem once enough households, merchants, and public obligations depend on those spreads not widening into a freeze.

Search is the first. In dispersed trading, finding a counterparty is an expense that grows nonlinearly with participation because every actor must maintain networks or pay brokers to do it. Broker notebooks reduce the cost by centralizing knowledge privately, but private centralization is a fragility: liquidity becomes dependent on a handful of people and their willingness to show up, quote, and take inventory. When those people withdraw under stress, the market does not merely become expensive; it becomes intermittent, which is the beginning of paralysis. A persistent venue exists because search must be industrialized into a process that survives individual withdrawal: a standing pool of bids and offers, a known place where flow arrives, and a set of rules that keeps the pool from evaporating the moment rumor sharpens.

Verification is the second. In dispersed trading, every transaction re-verifies identity, ownership, and instrument validity. Re-verification is labor and vulnerability. It is labor because each counterparty repeats checks. It is vulnerability because each repeated check is a window for forged documents, disputed signatures, and procedural ambush. Re-verification also creates inequality because insiders verify faster through relationships while outsiders pay delay as a discount. The market tolerates that inequality until volume makes delay systemic, because systemic delay converts ordinary trading into a backlog of unresolved entitlements. A venue exists because verification must be standardized: listed instruments with known forms, known transfer rules, recognized participants, and predictable evidence standards that reduce the need to re-litigate legitimacy each time.

Settlement sequencing is the third. Dispersed markets rely on ad hoc escrow, personal trust nodes, and improvised performance order. Under volume, sequencing becomes the system's heart because the system's greatest fear is one-sided performance. A trade that completes only on one leg produces disputes, and disputes are liquidity poison because they force participants to hoard final media, widen spreads, and refuse to quote size. A venue exists because sequencing cannot remain improvisational once trades become numerous enough that even a small percentage of failures becomes a daily event. A centralized perimeter can impose sequencing conventions, require proof artifacts, and discipline repeat failures.

Registry throughput is the fourth. Registry lag turns trading into entitlement risk. Entitlement risk widens spreads near record dates. Wider spreads raise the cost of capital exactly when enterprises and the state need stable funding. Registry lag also creates disputes that courts must resolve, and court delay multiplies under load. A venue exists because it can integrate registry timing into trading conventions: standardized submission packets, recognized timestamps, accepted confirmations, and synchronized cut-offs that reduce ambiguity and therefore reduce litigation.

Reference authority is the fifth and most political. Once quotations become anchors for collateral, damages, taxes, and covenant triggers, the question of whose price counts becomes decisive. Pre-exchange price sheets are contested because they are simultaneously public-facing and privately influenced. Contested authority raises the risk premium embedded in credit. Higher premium raises borrowing costs for both enterprises and the state. A venue exists because it can claim officialness: publish an official price under rule-defined reporting, disciplined membership, and evidentiary preference in courts. Officialness is sold as stability. Stability lowers the premium for fear.

These five frictions entangle at scale into a single bottleneck: enforceable liquidity. Liquidity is not the ability to trade; it is the ability to trade and then finish the trade under stress without being forced into dispute. Enforceable liquidity therefore requires a chain: recognized participants, standardized instruments, verified ownership, coordinated settlement, registry integration, and authoritative reference. A dispersed market can supply pieces. A venue exists because it bundles the pieces into a repeatable system and sells access to that repeatability.

The necessity becomes obvious only when the system experiences a full failure cascade, because cascades are how a market learns what it is made of. The cascade begins in the least glamorous place: a timing mismatch between trading intent and administrative capacity. A rumor or notice widens spreads. Wider spreads trigger collateral calls in credit contracts that reference customary prices. Collateral calls force selling by borrowers who cannot meet demands with coin. Forced selling increases volume at precisely the moment brokers are least willing to hold inventory. Inventory aversion widens spreads further.

Volume floods registries with transfer submissions. Registry lag increases, turning immediate trades into delayed entitlements. Delayed entitlements increase the probability that buyers will not receive distributions or voting rights they believed they purchased. That probability is priced into discounts, widening spreads further. Wider spreads reduce the value of pledged units, triggering more collateral calls.

Courts congest because the system starts disputing not only prices but finality: whether a transfer is effective at submission, at recording, or at confirmation. Court delay becomes a pricing variable because delay increases the time capital is trapped. Capital trapped is the opposite of liquidity.

Bankers tighten credit because uncertain collateral is expensive collateral. Tightened credit reduces intraday liquidity for brokers and dealers. Reduced liquidity reduces their ability to make markets. Reduced market-making reduces depth. Reduced depth increases the price impact of forced selling.

This loop is not an abstraction. It is a practical chain reaction driven by three facts that pre-exchange systems cannot escape. First, price shocks turn into funding shocks because collateral is valued by reference. Second, funding shocks turn into forced behavior because most participants cannot absorb margin-like demands without liquidating. Third, forced behavior turns into administrative overload because transfer and proof systems have finite throughput.

A market can survive losses inside this loop. It cannot survive indefinite ambiguity. Ambiguity is the true poison because ambiguity turns every claim into a bespoke dispute, and bespoke dispute collapses throughput. The institutional answer is to concentrate gates so the system can say what counts quickly enough that trading remains possible.

Gate concentration is the core exchange function. The visible story is matching. The operational story is standardization of recognition: which instruments, which participants, which proofs, which timelines, which penalties. Under stress, participants do not need the perfect price. They need a recognized price that contracts can reference and courts can enforce. Under stress, participants do not need universal fairness. They need predictable procedure. Predictable procedure allows pricing. Pricing allows liquidity. Liquidity allows survival.

The exchange's first act is therefore not to create liquidity from nothing, but to compress liquidity's cost by reducing uncertainty about completion. It does this by building a perimeter with four pillars: membership, listing, reporting, and discipline.

Membership limits who can trade directly under the perimeter's rules. It is justified as integrity. It functions as gatekeeping. Membership provides the perimeter a way to impose obligations: settlement discipline, reporting requirements, and performance sequencing. It also provides a way to punish: removal of privileges, suspension, exclusion. The punishment is economic because exclusion removes access to the cheapest path to finality.

Listing limits what can be traded under standardized forms. A listed instrument has known transfer rules, known entitlement conventions, and known evidence standards. Listing reduces the need for bespoke verification. Listing also creates a revenue model: fees, control over disclosure cadence, and the ability to define which features of an instrument are treated as essential.

Reporting creates an authoritative record that can anchor reference prices. Reporting is the foundation of officialness. Without reporting discipline, published quotations remain rumor. With reporting discipline, published quotations become a contractual anchor. That anchor is valuable enough that it attracts manipulation attempts, which is why reporting discipline implies surveillance.

Discipline is the enforcement layer that makes membership and reporting meaningful. Discipline is how the perimeter defends its core product: officialness. Officialness is what allows collateral, damages, taxes, and covenants to reference a price and remain enforceable without turning every dispute into a new trial.

The perimeter's second act is to compress settlement friction through clearing routines. Clearing is not merely administrative; it is the throughput engine. A venue cannot scale on bilateral settlement. It must integrate a netting mechanism so gross movement compresses into net obligations. Netting reduces coin demand. Reduced coin demand increases volume capacity. Increased capacity deepens liquidity. Deep liquidity tightens spreads. Tight spreads increase participation.

Netting creates dependency. A netting node becomes systemic. Systemic nodes need rules about pre-funding and loss allocation because if a participant fails, losses propagate through netting links. The perimeter therefore builds or partners with a clearing structure that requires members to post balances or collateral, and that defines how shortfalls are handled.

These rules appear technical and are political. Pre-funding requirements protect insiders by reducing default risk. They also exclude entrants who cannot post. Loss allocation rules define whether losses are socialized among members or isolated to the failing member's counterparties. Socialization preserves system stability and concentrates control among members. Isolation preserves the appearance of individual responsibility and encourages tighter exclusion. Real systems blend both and defend the blend as prudence.

The perimeter's third act is time discipline. Pre-exchange markets already discovered that cut-offs govern entitlement and that publication cadence governs collateral triggers. A venue formalizes time as schedule: trading hours, settlement windows, reporting deadlines, publication times, and rule-defined record dates. Schedule reduces ambiguity and reduces dispute load. It also creates timing advantage, then monetizes the mitigation of that advantage by selling faster lanes and earlier visibility to those who can pay.

The perimeter's fourth act is to export its authority into courts and contracts. A venue becomes infrastructure when external systems treat its outputs as presumptively valid. Courts accept venue publication as customary value. Lenders write collateral contracts referencing venue prices. Tax authorities assess based on venue prints. Those references create dependence. Dependence creates power.

At this point the question shifts from why the perimeter exists to why it survives political challenge. The perimeter survives because it can claim that it reduces systemic risk, and it can demonstrate that claim by reducing the frequency and severity of cascades. It makes completion cheaper for those inside. It also makes completion more expensive for those outside, but it frames that expense as the cost of integrity rather than as the price of exclusion.

The decisive argument for existence is therefore not ideological. It is operational. In the pre-exchange world, price discovery could exist without a venue, but completion could not remain cheap without one. Once completion is expensive, capital formation becomes expensive. Once capital formation is expensive, strategic capacity falls. A polity that needs capital formation to fund trade and public borrowing will prefer the institution that lowers completion cost, even if that institution must be monitored and occasionally constrained.

The exchange's necessity can be shown by tracing the same shock under two regimes: dispersed completion and perimeter completion. Under dispersed completion, a rumor widens spreads, triggers collateral calls, floods registries, clogs courts, and tightens credit, producing a spiral. Under perimeter completion, the venue can slow the spiral by enforcing standardized settlement sequencing, imposing prefunding constraints that reduce default probability, widening haircuts in a coordinated way that preserves clearing stability, and publishing authoritative prices that reduce disputes about valuation.

Each intervention is a gate adjustment. Gate adjustment is the venue's control lever.

Gate adjustment is also the origin of the venue's power problem. If a venue can adjust gates, it can privilege some participants and punish others. It can do this openly through rules or quietly through exceptions. The market will tolerate that power if the venue delivers stability and cheap completion in the aggregate. The market will fight that power if it becomes too extractive or too obviously captured. This is the permanent tension built into exchange existence: stability requires gatekeeping; gatekeeping creates rents; rents attract capture; capture threatens legitimacy; legitimacy is required for stability.

Legitimacy is therefore not a moral ornament. It is an engineering requirement for throughput. If participants do not believe the system's outputs are acceptable, they withdraw. Withdrawal widens spreads. Wider spreads reduce capital formation. Reduced capital formation reduces state revenue. Reduced state revenue weakens enforcement. Weak enforcement raises risk premiums. Risk premiums widen spreads further. Legitimacy is a feedback loop controller.

The exchange's design is a response to this feedback problem. It creates a visible interface and a hidden operating system. The visible interface is trading: bids, offers, printed prices. The operating system is procedure: membership, listing, reporting, clearing, time discipline, evidence standards, and punishments that maintain order.

In a pre-exchange market, each of those procedures exists somewhere, but nowhere can claim authority over the bundle. The bundle is the breakthrough. The bundle reduces coordination cost. It also creates a single point of political contest.

The market chooses the bundle because the alternative is repeated fragmentation under stress. Fragmentation produces intermittent liquidity. Intermittent liquidity makes long-duration ventures harder to finance. Harder financing reduces trade expansion. Reduced trade expansion reduces public receipts. Reduced receipts increase the cost of war and infrastructure. That cost becomes strategic vulnerability. The exchange becomes a strategic asset because it reduces the cost of mobilizing capital without requiring every crisis to be settled by emergency political decisions.

That strategic asset status explains the oldest pattern: exchanges are tolerated, protected, and sometimes privileged, because they are part of a polity's capacity to convert private wealth into public power indirectly.

The necessity also explains the oldest hypocrisy: the market will speak about openness while defending exclusion. Openness deepens liquidity. Exclusion preserves credibility. The exchange resolves the contradiction by constructing a narrative where exclusion is framed as integrity, and integrity is framed as public good. The narrative is not always false; it is simply incomplete. Integrity is real. The rents that accompany integrity are also real.

The system then begins to use exchange outputs as inputs everywhere else, which further locks the exchange into necessity. Once a reference price is used to value collateral, the exchange becomes part of the credit system. Once it becomes part of the credit system, its outages and distortions are systemic. That creates demand for surveillance and discipline. Surveillance produces audit trails. Audit trails produce administrative burden. Administrative burden raises the minimum competence to participate cheaply. That, again, stratifies.

Stratification does not end exchange necessity. Stratification deepens it, because insiders become dependent on the perimeter's stability and outsiders become dependent on insider mediation. Mediation becomes a business model. A business model attracts defense. Defense becomes lobbying and legal preference. Legal preference makes the perimeter more authoritative. Authority deepens dependence.

The exchange is therefore not a neutral outcome. It is a stable point in a political economy where the cost of unfinished trades becomes too high to tolerate. The exchange exists because it is cheaper to accept one concentrated gatekeeper than to pay the cost of repeated systemic disputes.

CHAPTER 7
THE MARKET'S ORIGINAL DEAL
WHY INVESTORS ACCEPTED RISK, WHY STATES ACCEPTED SPECULATION, AND WHAT EACH SIDE WANTED.

The market's original deal was never a handshake between equals. It was a negotiated truce between three appetites that could not be satisfied at the same time without rules. The investor's appetite was upside without captivity. The state's appetite was money without revolt. The intermediary's appetite was profit without liability so large that a single shock could wipe him out. The deal held only when the enforcement perimeter made promises portable and when the gatekeepers could charge for portability without making the price of participation so insulting that the system lost legitimacy.

In early markets, risk is not a graph. Risk is what happens when a clerk is slow, when a registry is contested, when a court delays, when an issuer stalls, when a rumor widens a spread, when a lender demands more collateral than a borrower can produce, and when a transfer misses a record date by one administrative breath. Investors accept that risk only if it can be converted into something priceable. Priceability is not philosophy. Priceability is procedure: recognized instruments, recognized proofs, recognized timelines, and a credible exit path that does not require the underlying enterprise to end before the investor can regain cash.

The state's side begins in scarcity and time. War, fortification, administration, grain reserves, and roads require payment before returns arrive. Taxes arrive slowly and ignite political resentment precisely because they are visible. Borrowing pulls future receipts into present capacity, but borrowing is only cheap when creditors believe the state's promise will be honored more reliably than the state's temptation to improvise. That reliability is never moral purity. It is predictable self-restraint: honoring payment calendars, respecting priority, not rewriting terms retroactively, allowing enforcement to function even when it is inconvenient, maintaining registries so ownership is legible, maintaining courts so claims can be resolved without violence.

The intermediary's side is the conversion engine. He converts illiquid claims into liquidity by accepting risk and charging for it. He converts rumors into spreads, spreads into inventory decisions, inventory decisions into quoted markets, and quoted markets into a continuous exit path for others. His profit is the toll on movement through gates. His existence is tolerated because gates are necessary. His extraction is resented because tolls feel like punishment during stress.

The original deal forms where those three sides become mutually dependent. Investors will fund ventures and buy state paper if they can exit. Exits require secondary markets. Secondary markets require completion routines. Completion routines require registries, settlement sequencing, authoritative references, and courts that treat evidence as real. The state will tolerate secondary trading and speculative liquidity if it lowers the cost of capital, increases tax receipts indirectly through expanded trade, and provides a standing pool of buyers for public issuance. Intermediaries will provide liquidity if they can secure privileges that reduce their own risk: membership perimeters, access to clearing nodes, faster registry channels, and participation in publication authority that makes prices usable in contracts.

The system's dependency triangle is therefore structural. Investors need officialness: an ownership record and price signal treated as real outside the room. States need depth: a financing base that can absorb issuance without immediate taxation. Intermediaries need privilege: gate access that lets them sell liquidity at a spread without being exposed to open-ended disputes. Officialness lowers uncertainty. Lower uncertainty deepens participation. Deeper participation increases volume. Volume increases the value of privilege. Privilege finances the infrastructure that maintains officialness.

That triangle becomes the deal's operating system, but it only runs if three concrete mechanisms are aligned: public debt issuance discipline, venture equity exit mechanics, and bounded speculation supported by enforceable routines. Each mechanism is a machine with levers, attack surfaces, and political costs.

Public debt issuance discipline is the state's conversion of coercion into credibility. A sovereign instrument is fundable only when it contains a believable path from promise to payment that strangers can audit. The instrument must specify what is owed, when it is owed, and what constitutes default. Default cannot be left as a moral accusation. Default must be defined as a procedural trigger: a missed date, a delayed window, a diversion of pledged revenue, interference with registry integrity, obstruction of evidence, or refusal to honor defined priority. Procedural default definitions make slow-default expensive because they allow creditors to act before the state can use ambiguity as delay.

The discipline also requires legibility. Accounts must be published. Collections must be recorded. Pledged revenues must be visible enough that creditors can estimate whether repayment is plausible. Legibility is a constraint because it exposes weakness. The state accepts the constraint because legibility reduces the risk premium demanded by lenders. Lower premium lowers borrowing cost. Lower cost increases state capacity.

The discipline requires enforceability. Courts must treat the instruments as contracts with remedies that function in practice rather than in rhetoric. Remedies must be time-bound and credible enough that refusal is costly. If remedies are slow, discounts widen. If discounts widen, issuance becomes expensive. If issuance becomes expensive, the state's only alternative is taxation or debasement-like improvisation, both politically dangerous.

The state therefore trades discretion for access. It accepts that some revenues will be pledged. It accepts that some payments will occur even when the public grumbles. It accepts that priority rules will constrain later policy. It accepts that its own paper will be priced publicly, which creates a reputational signal it cannot fully control. It accepts these costs because the benefit is the ability to mobilize resources without immediate revolt.

Yet discipline creates its own secondary market because discipline makes the paper tradable. Tradable paper creates reference prices. Reference prices become contractual anchors in private credit. Once private credit references state paper valuations, state credibility becomes embedded in private liquidity, and the state becomes even more invested in preventing credibility collapses. The market is no longer merely a mirror. It becomes a transmission line.

Venture equity exit mechanics are the investor's conversion of duration into tradability. Debt is brittle under uncertain outcomes because it demands schedule obedience regardless of weather, war, or administrative delay. Equity-like claims absorb variance because they promise residual outcomes rather than fixed repayment. But equity-like claims are still unacceptable at scale without exit because residual outcomes can be delayed and uncertain for years.

Exit is created by secondary trading under enforceable transfer rules. Transfer rules require registries that can treat ownership as property. Registries require authority and evidence standards. Evidence standards require courts and enforcement. The private venture therefore depends on public coercion to scale, because tradability is a public-legal phenomenon even when the venture is privately motivated.

Exit reduces the risk premium demanded at issuance. Lower premium lowers the cost of capital. Lower cost increases venture scale. Increased venture scale increases trade and tax receipts. Increased receipts stabilize the state's own credit. Stabilized credit lowers borrowing costs. The cycle reinforces.

But exit also creates the appearance of gambling, because once an ownership unit can be sold tomorrow, people will buy and sell for reasons unrelated to long-term productivity: rumor, timing, credit conditions, and anticipated policy. The state tolerates the ugliness because the ugliness is the lubricant that keeps capital formation continuous rather than episodic. It tries to bound the ugliness because legitimacy is required for participation, and participation is required for depth.

Bounded speculation is the deal's most delicate component because it must be strict enough to protect officialness and loose enough to preserve liquidity. Bounded does not mean virtuous. It means procedural: membership perimeters, publication methodology, reporting discipline, evidence standards, settlement sequencing, registry timing rules, and punishments that can be applied without reinventing the system each time scandal erupts.

The state's bargain with intermediaries lives here. Intermediaries can profit from spreads and information if they maintain enough order that the system remains financeable. In return, the state protects the infrastructure that makes profits possible: registries, courts, notarial routines, forgery penalties, and institutional preference for charter-compliant evidence.

Institutional preference is the most powerful lever because it turns private rules into public consequence. If courts prefer charter-compliant documentation, then compliance becomes cheaper than noncompliance, and markets converge on the charter's standards. Convergence produces stability. It also produces exclusion because compliance requires administrative capacity and gate access.

This is the deal's permanent asymmetry. Insiders buy cheaper passage through gates. Outsiders pay more in spreads, delays, and proof burdens. The system expands participation enough to deepen liquidity while preserving hierarchy enough to monetize it. The system then defends hierarchy by calling it integrity, because integrity is difficult to oppose publicly.

The deal is stable only if each party can plausibly claim it benefits. Investors must believe the system offers real exit and real upside, not only extraction. States must believe the system lowers financing costs and supports trade, not only destabilization. Intermediaries must believe enforcement is predictable, not arbitrary. Predictability is the condition for pricing. Without pricing, liquidity collapses into hoarding.

The best way to see the deal is to watch it under stress, because stress reveals which promises are real. The first stress test is a sovereign funding shock, the kind that starts as a schedule question and becomes an enforcement question. A payment is delayed on instruments that private contracts have begun treating as near-cash. The delay widens discounts. Wider discounts tighten credit because lenders reprice collateral. Tight credit forces liquidation by borrowers who cannot meet demands. Liquidation pushes down the prices of venture units and other tradable claims. Lower prices trigger further collateral demands.

The shock moves from price to throughput when registries and settlement nodes are flooded. Transfers surge because investors attempt to reposition. Registry lag increases, and lag transforms trades into entitlement uncertainty. Entitlement uncertainty widens spreads because buyers demand compensation for the risk of missing eligibility windows. Wider spreads reduce liquidity. Reduced liquidity raises default probability in credit chains. Default probability makes bankers tighten credit further. The loop tightens.

In that moment, the state's discipline is tested. If the state responds by rewriting terms retroactively or by privileging new obligations over old in ways that appear opportunistic, the market's belief in predictability collapses. The collapse shows up as widened discounts that make future borrowing expensive and as hoarding that freezes trade. The state therefore learns that even when it cannot pay immediately, it must preserve procedural credibility: publish clear schedules, honor priority rules, allow courts to enforce remedies, and avoid using ambiguity as delay. Predictability becomes the cheaper form of pain compared to collapse.

The market's side is tested at the same time. If intermediaries hoard liquidity completely, spreads widen so far that exit becomes meaningless, and investors refuse to hold risk. If intermediaries continue quoting without protections, they risk insolvency. The compromise is procedural tightening: higher haircuts, stricter proof requirements, narrower quoting size, and increased reliance on clearing nodes to net obligations and reduce coin strain.

This is the moment bounded speculation proves its function. It is not to eliminate volatility. It is to prevent volatility from becoming paralysis by ensuring there are recognized procedures for completion and for evidence when disputes arise.

The second stress test is an equity exit panic, because equity panics expose whether the system's exit promise is real or theatrical. A rumor spreads that a record date is near and registry processing is slow. Buyers demand discounts. Sellers accept worse prices. Brokers widen spreads because they fear being trapped with units whose entitlement status will be disputed. If credit contracts reference published prices, falling prints trigger collateral calls. Collateral calls force selling. Forced selling worsens prints. The spiral accelerates.

The system can survive this only by adjusting gates. Registry offices must increase throughput or at least issue standardized receipts that define submission timing, reducing the ambiguity that fuels disputes. Publication methodology must avoid being steered by distressed prints designed to trigger cascades, which requires stricter reporting and proof packets. Clearing and settlement sequencing must reduce counterparty fear so that trading does not stop entirely. Brokers must continue quoting under discipline, even if at wider spreads, because zero bids is a legitimacy crisis.

Every intervention redistributes pain. Tight publication rules protect lenders by making the reference harder to game, but they burden smaller participants who struggle to produce proof packets quickly. Faster registry lanes reduce entitlement ambiguity, but they become purchasable privilege. Higher haircuts protect clearing stability, but they force selling by those without buffers. The deal holds only if the redistribution is perceived as procedural rather than arbitrary, because arbitrary redistribution destroys predictability, and predictability is the priceable base of the entire system.

The third stress test is legitimacy, because legitimacy is what keeps people willing to accept gatekeeping as integrity rather than as theft. When manipulation becomes visible, the public's tolerance collapses quickly. Yet the system cannot function without intermediaries and without gatekeepers, because fraud and disputes explode without them. The response is ritualized proof and ritualized punishment.

Proof rituals are not merely bureaucracy. They are legitimacy manufacturing. Audit trails, documentation packets, registry receipts, and substantiated publication inputs allow the system to claim that outcomes are produced by rules rather than by private whim. Punishment rituals are similarly instrumental. Visible discipline of a manipulator signals that the market is not purely extractive. The punishment is often privilege withdrawal rather than imprisonment because privilege withdrawal is faster and more controllable. It changes the cost of doing business and forces behavior change without destabilizing the entire node network.

This is why the market's original deal is enforced by gate control. Gate control is the system's core coercion. The state supplies coercion through courts and penalties. The market supplies coercion through exclusion, slower lanes, higher fees, and refusal to recognize certain claims as clean. Both are coercion. Both are defended as order.

The deal's most persistent outcome is that markets become part of state capacity. A polity with a functioning market can mobilize resources faster than a polity that relies only on taxes and bilateral loans. Market institutions become defended because they are strategic infrastructure. They also become instruments of leverage because controlling officialness means controlling credit triggers, collateral valuations, and the legitimacy of ownership claims.

This is where the deal's geopolitical edge appears. Nations that can maintain officialness at home can borrow in their own systems and sustain domestic capital formation. Nations that cannot must rent officialness elsewhere, borrowing confidence from foreign institutions and paying for it in dependence. The original deal therefore is not merely economic; it is the seed of capital sovereignty.

The deal's moral camouflage is procedural neutrality. The system distributes winners and losers through procedure, so responsibility appears to reside in rules rather than in people. Yet rules are designed and design reflects power. The market survives because procedure makes the distribution of pain predictable enough that participants can price it, and because predictability is cheaper than chaos.

PART TWO
INSIDE THE MARKET MACHINE

WHY A MARKET CAN LOOK CHAOTIC ON THE SURFACE AND STILL PRODUCE STABLE WINNERS UNDERNEATH.

The market most people think they know ends at the screen; the real system begins in routing, data, clearing, custody, and settlement.

The market's public face is a price. The machine's real face is a chain of permissions, timestamps, and obligations that decide whether the price can be turned into enforceable ownership without causing a cascade. In Part I, the system learned to make promises portable by building registries, publication authority, disciplined intermediaries, and early clearing routines. Here the machine is already mature. It does not merely move claims; it industrializes movement, monetizes movement, and embeds power inside procedure so that control can be exercised without describing itself as control.

The screen shows a number and a timestamp. The machine decides whether the number is usable. Usable means: it can be referenced in a contract, pledged as collateral, valued for a tax assessment, defended in a dispute, and converted into settlement without triggering failures that spread. The machine is therefore less an abstract market and more a protocol stack. The top layer is what the public sees. The lower layers are where the system's advantage surfaces live: routing economics, fee schedules, data entitlements, margin models, settlement cut-offs, and custody hierarchies that define what ownership means when someone challenges it.

The machine's defining property is that it can look transparent while remaining privately governed. A public quote looks like a fact. A public fact is a produced artifact: it is created by a matching logic, filtered by a rule about what counts as official, and disseminated through a data system that sells speed and completeness as products. A public print looks like a neutral outcome. It is the result of prioritization rules, queue design, and eligibility constraints that distribute advantage while claiming neutrality.

The machine's second defining property is that integrity becomes a revenue model. Every routine that reduces fraud and dispute also creates a gate. Every gate can be priced. The system is never only a public utility. It is also a toll road, and toll roads behave predictably: they expand capacity while charging for the right to move quickly, to move with certainty, and to be recognized without delay. The fees are not incidental. Fees are how the system funds the infrastructure that keeps it from collapsing, and also how the system concentrates profit among those who control the infrastructure.

The machine's third defining property is that completion is the scarce commodity. Trading is easy to imitate. Completion is hard to guarantee. Completion means: an order is routed, executed, confirmed, cleared, margined, settled, and recorded in custody systems in a way that survives dispute. Each stage has cut-offs. Each cut-off can become a choke point under stress. Each choke point can become a liquidity tax that only some can pay.

This is why modern market power is less about predicting prices and more about finishing cheaply. If you can finish cheaply, you can quote tighter. If you can quote tighter, you attract flow. If you attract flow, you see more, learn more, and can invest in faster infrastructure. Faster infrastructure lowers cost further. The machine compounds advantage through operational efficiency and institutional privilege. It does not require collusion to produce stable winners. It requires only that gate access is unequal and that unequal access can be priced.

The machine's fragility is not primarily volatility. Volatility is visible and often survivable. Fragility is timing mismatch. A system can endure large price moves if settlement and funding remain predictable. A system fails when settlement becomes uncertain, when margin models tighten simultaneously, when liquidity providers withdraw, and when queues become clogged with cancellations and re-pricings that turn execution into a lottery. The machine's role is to keep the visible surface trading while quietly reallocating pain through procedures: higher margin, wider haircuts, stricter eligibility, slower processing, and privilege withdrawal for those who break rules.

These procedures are defended as risk control. They are also distributive. When a margin model tightens, someone must post more collateral. Those with buffers survive; those without buffers liquidate. When a settlement cut-off is missed, someone pays fail penalties and someone gains optionality. When data is sold in tiers, someone sees earlier and someone trades later at worse prices. When routing rules privilege internalization, someone captures spread and someone else receives a price that looks fair while the informational edge is harvested.

What looks like one market is therefore a stack of markets stitched together by rules that are rarely read by the people whose savings and taxes depend on the outcome. One layer allocates capital to enterprises and states. Another layer allocates liquidity to intermediaries through spreads and fees. Another layer allocates visibility: who sees the signal first, in what shape, with what latency, and at what price. Another layer allocates risk: where volatility is absorbed, where it is warehoused, where it is netted, and where it explodes when a gate fails. Another layer allocates legal reality: who is recognized as owner, when, by which record, and under which evidence regime.

The machine survives because it produces enough stability to keep participation rational. It produces stability by narrowing what counts as official and by enforcing completion discipline. That narrowing is a form of governance. The exchange defines what counts as an official print. The broker-dealer complex defines where orders are allowed to go and on what terms. Data vendors define how the market is seen and who pays for clarity. Clearinghouses define how risk is netted and how quickly margin must be posted. Custodians define the hierarchy of title and the layers between beneficial holders and legal reality. Settlement systems define when a trade becomes final.

Each node is marketed as a service. Each node is also a power center because each can decide who gets access, who pays more, who is delayed, and who is forced to liquidate first under stress. The machine is therefore political without needing speeches. It distributes opportunity and pain through technical language. Technical language is the system's shield because technical language makes distribution feel inevitable.

Part II is a teardown of this stack as a system of gates. It treats market structure as engineering with political outputs. If you want to understand why liquidity can look endless for years and then freeze in hours, you do not start with sentiment. You start with routing incentives, data entitlements, margin rules, settlement cut-offs, and custody ambiguity. If you want to understand why a small set of firms can consistently win in environments that look competitive, you do not start with genius. You start with gate proximity: cheaper access to liquidity, earlier visibility into signals, faster completion pathways, lower clearing costs, and privileged influence over what counts as official.

The market most participants think they inhabit ends at execution. The real market begins at clearing. Clearing decides net exposure. Margin decides who can keep positions open. Settlement decides whether ownership is real. Custody decides whether ownership is recognized when challenged. Data decides whether you are acting on the same reality as everyone else or on a delayed imitation of it. Routing decides whether your order is exposed to competition or harvested as flow. These are the machine's organs. They do not merely support the market. They are the market.

Interlude II. The Queue You Never See

The invisible chain of signals that begins before the investor sees a confirmation.

Before an investor sees a fill, the machine has already made decisions about eligibility and priority. It has checked whether an order can be internalized, whether it can be routed to a venue that pays for the flow, whether it can be exposed to an auction that might improve the printed price, whether it can be sliced into smaller pieces that reduce visible impact, and whether it should be delayed to avoid showing intent. These decisions are defended as best execution and risk control. They are also revenue decisions because each route has fees, rebates, spreads, and information consequences.

A queue is where the market hides its politics. Queues decide whose order gets priority, whose quote sets the price, whose cancellation arrives first, whose fill happens at a better level, and whose trade becomes the official print. Queues are governed by rules that look neutral and behave distributively. Under stress, queues become choke points. Choke points become a liquidity tax. Those who can pay the tax through speed, priority, and infrastructure survive. Those who cannot pay are forced to accept worse outcomes or withdraw.

The interlude's purpose is not to romanticize hidden complexity. It is to establish that what feels like a single click is a sequence of gate checks and queue placements that determine who gets to be early, who gets to be certain, and who gets to be official. In the machine, early and official are assets. Assets are priced.

CHAPTER 8
WHERE CAPITAL IS BORN — AND WHERE IT GETS TRADED

THE SPLIT BETWEEN FINANCING BUSINESSES AND FEEDING THE MARKET ENGINE.

The market sells a story that feels clean because it flatters the citizen and calms the policymaker: savings become investment, investment becomes growth, growth becomes jobs, and price becomes a scoreboard for value. The machine sells that story because the story is the social license that allows the rest of the system to charge tolls. The operational reality is split. One side is capital formation, where new money is raised for enterprises and states. The other side is capital circulation, where existing claims are traded, financed, hedged, and optimized for spread, speed, and balance-sheet efficiency. The split is not an accident. It is how a system can appear to serve the public while building a private economy around completion, visibility, and gate access.

Capital formation is episodic by design. A firm or state cannot issue continuously without collapsing its own pricing, its own governance, and its own credibility. It must pick windows, build narratives, prepare disclosures, negotiate terms, and convince buyers that the claim is worth holding. The formation moment is where capital is born: cash moves to the issuer, and the issuer uses the cash to fund operations, investment, infrastructure, or public capacity. Formation has a moral aura because it is easy to point at the bridge, the factory, the payroll, the public project. Formation produces tangible outcomes, and tangible outcomes justify the system's legitimacy.

Capital circulation is continuous by design. A claim that exists can be traded endlessly without sending one additional dollar to the issuer. That continuity is defended as liquidity, and liquidity is real in its effects: it lowers the cost of issuance because buyers accept lower returns when they believe they can exit quickly. Yet continuity also becomes a revenue engine independent of formation. Circulation monetizes the spread between buyers and sellers, the financing of inventory, the sale of visibility, and the pricing of completion under stress. Circulation is not a moral defect. It is a second economy that grows out of the need to provide exits and out of the opportunity to sell the gates that make exits real.

The split begins at the first boundary: who gets paid when a trade happens. At issuance, the issuer gets paid. In secondary trading, the issuer does not. The proceeds go to the selling holder and to the intermediaries who sit between. This is not a nuance. It is the foundation of the machine's political signature: the public believes activity equals investment, while the system's most profitable activity can be the trading of already-issued claims.

The machine protects the legitimacy of circulation by making it look like a continuous referendum on value. It also protects circulation by making it essential to formation. That dependency is the key: formation requires liquidity to be cheap, and liquidity becomes cheap only when circulation is thick enough that exits are credible. The market therefore builds a circulation engine and then uses the engine's existence as evidence that formation is efficient.

The circulation engine has inputs, and those inputs are where power accumulates. Inventory capacity is the first input. An intermediary providing liquidity must be able to buy when others sell and sell when others buy. That requires balance sheet. Balance sheet is costly because it must be funded. Funding cost rises under stress. Stress is precisely when liquidity is most valuable. The system therefore rewards intermediaries who can fund inventories cheaply across cycles. Those intermediaries can quote tighter. Those who cannot must widen spreads or withdraw.

Completion capacity is the second input. A trade that cannot be cleared, settled, and recorded without fails is not liquidity, it is a future dispute with a price tag. Completion requires access to clearing and settlement infrastructure, predictable settlement windows, and operational discipline that prevents breaks. Completion is a gate. Gate access can be purchased through membership, infrastructure investment, and relationships with the nodes that define what counts as clean. Clean completion reduces cost. Reduced cost allows tighter quoting. Tighter quoting attracts flow. Flow compounds the advantage.

Visibility is the third input. The ability to see the market is not evenly distributed. There is the public signal, and then there are the higher-fidelity signals: faster timestamps, deeper order information, richer prints, and earlier access to changes in supply and demand. Visibility is not merely comfort. It changes expected outcomes. If you see earlier, you can avoid adverse selection. Avoiding adverse selection lowers your cost of providing liquidity. Lower cost allows tighter quoting. Tighter quoting attracts flow, and flow yields more information. The loop becomes self-reinforcing, and it is built from the sale of visibility as a product.

These inputs explain why the same market can appear competitive and still produce stable winners. The competition is real at the surface. The stability is produced underneath by compounding advantages in funding, completion, and visibility.

The formation engine has its own gates, and these gates are public-facing. Listing standards, disclosure obligations, governance structures, and legal liabilities. These gates are justified as investor protection and market integrity. They also serve a rationing function: they limit which issuers can access public capital and on what terms. Rationing is not always malicious. Rationing is necessary when credibility is scarce. Yet rationing also concentrates issuance among larger issuers and among those who can afford compliance costs.

The circulation engine's gates are less visible and often more profitable. Routing, execution priority, data entitlements, clearing membership, margin terms, settlement cut-offs, and custody arrangements. These gates determine who can trade cheaply at speed and who must trade expensively with friction. If you want to see why circulation grows faster than formation, follow the gates that can be monetized without requiring a new bridge to be built.

The machine's first distortion is therefore predictable. The participants who influence prices most are often not the participants supplying new capital. Long-term holders supply stability and absorb risk, but they trade infrequently. Intermediaries and arbitrageurs trade continuously and therefore influence the marginal price. The marginal price is what becomes the public signal. The public signal then feeds back into corporate cost of capital, into executive incentives, and into policy debates. The machine is not lying when it says prices matter. The machine is simply not admitting that the price is often driven by circulation constraints rather than by formation fundamentals.

A price in the circulation engine is a clearing point for constraints. It reflects risk limits, funding rates, inventory scarcity, hedging costs, benchmark flows, index inclusion rules, and settlement considerations. Under stress, it also reflects margin rules and the availability of balance sheet. These are not philosophical drivers. They are mechanical.

Consider the simplest formation-to-circulation chain. An issuer raises money once, and claims are created. Those claims then become collateral for financing. Financing allows leveraged holding. Leveraged holding increases demand for the claim. Demand pushes price. Price increases collateral value. Higher collateral value allows more financing. The cycle expands until funding tightens, margins rise, haircuts widen, and forced selling begins. Forced selling pushes price down. Lower price triggers more margin calls. The cycle contracts. The issuer receives no additional capital during this expansion or contraction, yet the issuer's perceived value swings and the issuer's financing conditions change. That is the circulation engine influencing formation conditions without funding formation directly.

This is why buybacks and index inclusion matter inside the machine. They are not merely corporate decisions or passive categorizations. They are liquidity and flow engineering. If an issuer supports its own price through buybacks, it supports the collateral value of its claim and reduces the probability of violent funding-driven selloffs. It also makes the claim more attractive to holders who care about liquidity and stability rather than about long-run productivity. If an issuer is included in an index, it receives predictable flows that thicken liquidity, and thicker liquidity lowers trading costs and lowers the issuer's cost of capital. The issuer then shapes behavior to remain eligible, and eligibility becomes a corporate governance influence that is not voted on by citizens.

The machine's second distortion is that formation begins to adapt to serve circulation. Issuers learn that being easy to trade is itself an asset. Easy to trade means stable disclosure cadence, predictable governance, sufficient free float, and a narrative that supports continuous attention. Enterprises that do not fit the machine's preferences are punished with illiquidity discounts. Illiquidity discounts raise the cost of capital. Higher cost forces issuers to avoid public markets or to accept worse terms. The machine therefore narrows which kinds of enterprises can raise public capital cheaply.

The machine's third distortion is the emergence of a shadow subsidy from formation to circulation. Because formation confers legitimacy, circulation can charge tolls without being seen as a separate industry extracting rents. Fees for execution, fees for data, fees for clearing, and spreads charged by liquidity providers can be defended as necessary costs of maintaining a liquid market. They are necessary in part. They are also revenue streams that scale with volume regardless of whether new capital is being formed.

The split matters for how we interpret "market growth." Market growth can mean more issuers, more capital raised, and more productive investment. Market growth can also mean more trading volume, more data products, more fee extraction, and more balance-sheet intermediation on existing claims. The machine blurs these meanings because blurring protects legitimacy.

The split also matters for how we interpret "market efficiency." Efficiency in circulation is often measured as tight spreads and fast execution. Those are real achievements. Yet tight spreads can be financed by data tolls and by privileged internalization that extracts value in places the spread metric does not capture. Efficiency can also be concentrated: the most traded claims become extremely efficient while less liquid claims become more expensive to trade, more expensive to finance, and therefore more expensive to issue. Efficiency becomes a tiered product rather than a universal condition.

The machine's outputs are therefore distributive even when they are defended as neutral. Investors with cheaper access to visibility and cheaper access to completion can trade with less adverse selection and lower cost. They can capture more of the spread and pay less of the toll. Investors without those advantages pay more through worse execution, delayed information, wider spreads in the instruments they can access, and higher financing costs when they borrow against holdings.

The state experiences the same split in a sharper form because state instruments become collateral. Sovereign issuance funds public capacity. Secondary trading in sovereign obligations becomes a global liquidity and collateral engine. The state wants low borrowing costs. The machine wants reliable collateral, stable reference prices, and predictable settlement. Under stress, the machine's needs can conflict with political constraints. If the machine tightens financing conditions quickly, the state is forced into choices it would prefer not to make. The state may then intervene to preserve stability, which can look like prudence and feel like coercion. The market's original deal is active here: the state tolerates speculation and secondary trading because they lower borrowing costs, but the state reserves the right to protect legitimacy and capacity when financing conditions become a threat.

The cleanest way to see the split is to compare two metrics: how much money flows to issuers, and how much money flows through intermediaries as fees and spreads. Formation is measured in net proceeds to issuers and public projects. Circulation is measured in volume, turnover, financing spreads, data revenue, and the profitability of those who sit between. A market can be "booming" on circulation metrics while formation is flat, and the public can confuse the boom with productive investment. The confusion is not accidental. It is functional.

The machine's governance consequence is that debates about markets often focus on the visible symbol rather than the invisible gates. People argue about whether prices are too high or too low. The machine argues about whether completion is cheap and whether visibility is controlled. People argue about whether markets allocate capital to the best enterprises. The machine allocates gate access: who gets the best execution, who gets the best data, who gets the lowest clearing costs, who gets the fastest settlement pathways, who gets priority at the choke points. Those allocations decide who profits from circulation, which then decides who has the resources to influence the rules of formation.

The split produces a predictable policy trap. If policymakers try to reduce circulation profits without understanding the gates, they risk thinning liquidity and raising the cost of capital, harming formation. If policymakers ignore circulation profits entirely, gate rents compound and legitimacy erodes, provoking backlash that can be politically destabilizing and can result in clumsy interventions that harm both formation and circulation. The machine survives by presenting itself as necessary infrastructure while negotiating which rents are tolerable and which abuses must be punished to preserve social license.

The investor's side of the deal is therefore acceptance of two forms of payment. The first is explicit: fees, spreads, and the fact that the best liquidity is not free. The second is implicit: acceptance that the game is tiered by gate proximity, and that returns for those without gate proximity will be lower than the market's headline stories suggest. Investors accept this because the alternative is illiquid ownership that cannot be exited cheaply, which raises required returns and shrinks formation.

The intermediary's side of the deal is acceptance of two constraints. The first is discipline: surveillance, reporting, and the risk of privilege withdrawal if behavior threatens officialness. The second is cyclicality: funding costs rise under stress and inventory becomes dangerous, so even privileged actors face moments when survival requires withdrawal or coordinated widening. Intermediaries accept this because the alternative is a system where disputes and fraud overwhelm trading, destroying volume and therefore profit.

The state's side of the deal is acceptance of two compromises. The first is tolerance of speculation as the price of cheaper financing and deeper liquidity. The second is defense of private gatekeeping under the language of integrity because gatekeeping prevents fraud and keeps completion possible under volume. The state accepts this because the alternative is a brittle financing system dependent on taxation and emergency measures.

The machine's signature move is to keep the formation story alive while building a circulation economy that can grow faster than formation. It does this by tying formation to liquidity, liquidity to completion, completion to gate access, and gate access to priced privileges that can be defended as necessary for integrity. The result is a system where capital is born episodically but traded continuously, where the public perceives continuous activity as continuous investment, and where the most consistent profits often accrue to those who control the gates rather than to those who fund the issuer.

CHAPTER 9
THE CAST INSIDE THE MACHINE
EXCHANGES, BROKERS, DEALERS, MARKET MAKERS, CUSTODIANS, AND THE HIDDEN LABOR OF MODERN MARKETS.

The market machine is often described as if it were a single institution. It is not. It is a cast of specialized actors stitched together by contracts, message standards, and enforcement routines. Each actor claims to provide efficiency. Each actor controls a gate. Gates are where power accumulates, because gates decide who can trade cheaply, who can finish reliably, who can see clearly, and who must accept delay as a hidden fee.

The cast begins with the exchange, but the exchange is not the market. The exchange is the venue that sells officialness: the right to produce prints and reference prices other systems will treat as real, the right to list claims under standardized rules, and the right to operate queues whose priority rules distribute advantage without describing who benefits. The exchange's public face is fairness and transparency. Its operational face is governance through microstructure: what counts as an order type, what counts as a valid trade, what counts as a valid cancellation, what timestamps are authoritative, what sequence of events becomes the official record.

Exchange power is exercised through queue design, eligibility, and the definition of the official print. The queue is a rulebook in motion:

it decides which orders can interact, which orders can hide, which orders can jump, which orders must wait, and which trades become prints that other contracts will reference. A queue rule that decides priority decides execution quality, and execution quality decides who can provide liquidity at lower cost. Lower cost liquidity provision becomes market share. Market share becomes information. Information becomes pricing advantage.

The exchange is also a revenue architecture disguised as public utility. Listing monetizes admission. Trading fees monetize churn. Data fees monetize visibility. Connectivity fees monetize speed. Surveillance products monetize the right to sit closer to matching logic and the reference signal. The exchange can defend the pricing as necessary for integrity and capacity. It is necessary in part. It is also a way to convert officialness into cash and cash into influence, acquisitions, and institutional power that further entrenches officialness.

Exchanges also define the vocabulary the machine uses to ration outcomes. Order types are not neutral options. They embed priorities. They define who can demand immediacy, who can supply it, who can hide, and who must expose. They define whether an order is allowed to rest or must chase. They define whether the system rewards patience with queue priority or rewards speed with cancellation agility. The list of allowed behaviors becomes a distributional map because certain strategies only exist if the rules admit them.

The next cast member is not a single firm but a class of venues that exists because one venue cannot satisfy all incentives at once. Alternative venues, off-book venues, and segmented pools appear when participants demand different mixes of impact, visibility, and certainty. The existence of multiple venues then forces a second industry: cross-venue navigation. Once navigation exists, fragmentation becomes a profit surface. Fragmentation is defended as competition. It also creates a condition where the best outcomes go to those who can see and route across fragments faster than others.

Brokers sit between end investors and the machine. The broker's public story is agency: route the investor's order for best execution. The broker's operational reality is that routing is an economic decision under constraints. Routes differ in fees, rebates, likelihood of fill, likelihood of price improvement, information leakage, and completion risk. Completion risk matters because a cheap fill that creates expensive downstream failure is not cheap. The broker must also produce proof: why the order went where it went, what alternatives existed, what conflicts were mitigated, what the outcome was relative to reasonably available options. Proof is not a legal ornament. Proof is a cost center that becomes a competitive advantage when it can be automated and industrialized.

Broker economics therefore splits into three tasks that collide under stress. First, satisfy execution obligations by producing outcomes that look good at the surface. Second, optimize the firm's routing economics by managing fees, rebates, and internalization arrangements. Third, minimize downstream completion cost by avoiding paths that create settlement fails, high margin consumption, or compliance exposure. A broker that can balance these tasks cheaply can scale. A broker that cannot will either subsidize client outcomes with firm profit or will charge higher commissions, losing flow and losing leverage.

Brokers also manage order intent. An investor's instruction is rarely a single binary decision. It is an intent: buy or sell, but with sensitivity to price impact, timing, and probability of completion. The broker's job is to translate intent into a sequence of messages to the machine: how much to reveal, how much to hide, how quickly to seek fill, how much to rest, how much to route away from public visibility. Translation is where hidden cost enters, because translation choices change how much information leaks to the market and how much the broker pays in spread, fees, and impact.

Dealers and market makers provide immediacy. Their spread is a price for inventory risk, funding risk, adverse selection, completion cost, and visibility disadvantage. Inventory risk is obvious: hold an asset, face movement. Funding risk is structural: inventory must be financed, and financing rates rise under stress precisely when inventory is hardest to unload. Adverse selection is the invisible tax: informed traders trade when you are wrong. Completion cost is the buried tax: clearing and settlement consume margin and operational capacity and create fail exposure. Visibility disadvantage is the latency tax: if you see the market later than others, you are the last to know you are being picked off.

The best liquidity providers win by engineering away each tax. They fund cheaply, hedge efficiently, avoid being last to information, and finish cheaply through privileged completion pathways. Privileged completion means: netting efficiency at clearing, favorable margin terms, stable settlement performance, and operational systems that avoid breaks. Those advantages make spreads tighter, and tighter spreads attract more flow. Flow yields better information about the order stream. Better information reduces adverse selection. Reduced adverse selection reduces cost further.

Internalizers and wholesalers are the middle of the middle. They receive a large share of smaller, predictable flows before they reach public venues. They execute against internal inventory or internal matching and then hedge externally. Their public defense is price improvement and reduced market impact. Their operational advantage is flow predictability. Predictability is an asset because it reduces adverse selection and allows hedging to be scheduled. The internalizer captures spread that would otherwise be competed away on public venues. It also captures early visibility into the order stream that is unavailable to those who only see public prints.

Internalization changes the economics of public quotes. If a large share of certain flow never hits the displayed market, displayed markets can become a thinner reflection of the true supply and demand balance. That makes the displayed signal more sensitive to professional flow and less anchored by broad participation. The system can still claim price improvement at the point of retail execution while shifting the composition of displayed liquidity toward those whose intent is most informational. The result is that some parts of the market can appear to have tight spreads while the underlying informational asymmetry grows.

Fragmented venues and dark pools exist because visibility is double-edged. Showing size invites predation. Hiding intent reduces impact but increases fragmentation. Fragmentation increases the value of those who can stitch markets together faster than others. Stitching markets is expensive: it requires infrastructure, analytics, and relationships across venues. Those who can afford stitching become the system's navigators. Those who cannot become price takers, trading in slower, thinner layers.

Routing intelligence becomes an industry. Its product is not simply speed. Its product is selective exposure: show enough to get filled without showing enough to be exploited. Selective exposure requires models of how different venues behave, how different participants react, and how quickly conditions shift. The firm that owns these models owns a form of structural foresight. Structural foresight is monetizable even when it never predicts direction, because it predicts where friction will be lowest and where adverse selection will be highest.

Data vendors and feed operators are visibility gates. Market reality is a stream of messages. Those messages can be packaged in tiers: slower consolidated feeds, faster direct feeds, deeper order detail, richer timestamps, and analytics overlays. When visibility is tiered, the market becomes layered perception. Those who see first avoid adverse selection and quote tighter. Those who see later pay the tax of delay. Delay is one of the most scalable hidden fees in the machine because it can be sold as technical product rather than as explicit financial price.

Visibility gates also define whose version of the market becomes authoritative. If two parties see different timestamps and different depth at the same moment, they are not trading in the same market. They are trading in layered realities. The machine tolerates this layering because it is profitable. It also manages the legitimacy risk by keeping the public feed good enough to maintain social license while selling higher-fidelity feeds to those who pay.

The data layer also creates a second kind of gate: interpretation. Raw messages are abundant, but actionable interpretation requires normalization, historical context, and models of how microstructure converts flow into price. Vendors sell not only speed but comprehension. Comprehension is a competitive advantage because it reduces the time between seeing and acting. Reduced time reduces adverse selection and reduces opportunity cost. It is another way the machine sells time.

Clearinghouses are the risk warehouse. They interpose themselves, net exposures, demand margin, and manage default. Their public story is stability. Their operational power is cost setting. They can make trading cheaper or more expensive by changing margin models, eligibility, and stress add-ons. Margin is a gate because it determines who can keep positions and who must liquidate. When margin tightens, the system forces selling. Forced selling increases volatility. Volatility justifies tighter margin. The loop becomes self-reinforcing even when nobody intends to create a spiral.

Clearinghouses also define what counts as acceptable risk. Netting rules decide which exposures offset. Margin rules decide how quickly collateral must be posted. Default management rules decide how losses are allocated. Each decision is defended as risk discipline, but each decision is also distributive. If netting is generous for certain portfolios, those portfolios become cheaper to hold. If margin is punitive for certain instruments, those instruments become expensive to trade. The clearinghouse therefore shapes market structure by shaping the price of balance sheet.

Funding providers and securities lenders are leverage gates. Many strategies require financing of inventory and short positions. Financing terms depend on collateral quality, volatility, counterparty credit, and stress conditions. When financing tightens, strategies unwind. Unwinds move prices. Price moves tighten financing further. Funding is therefore a hidden governor of market behavior, and it favors those who have diversified balance sheets and access to cheap liquidity during stress.

Funding gates also define who can be patient. Patience is not a personality trait in markets. It is a funding privilege. If your funding is stable, you can wait for spreads to normalize and for adverse moves to revert. If your funding is fragile, you must sell into stress and buy into calm, paying the system's hidden tax. The machine therefore transfers wealth through funding asymmetry even when everyone is trading the same instrument.

Custodians, depositories, and settlement systems are finality gates. A trade is not enforceable reality until it settles and is recorded in custody layers that define legal title and beneficial ownership. Custody is layered because scale requires intermediated recordkeeping: end investors see statements; behind those statements sit omnibus accounts, depository positions, and sub-ledgers. Layering allows throughput. Layering creates opacity. Opacity creates reconciliation work. Reconciliation work becomes cost, delay, and leverage for those who control exception pathways.

Settlement is not merely a back-office formality. Settlement is where the machine decides whether it will honor the visible trade as a legal fact. A settlement fail is not just an operational glitch. It is an event that can trigger penalties, credit tightening, and reputational damage that changes future access to clearing and funding. Settlement therefore feeds back into liquidity provision. Liquidity providers price the probability of fails into spreads.

Transfer agents and registrars sit at the boundary between issuer records and market records. They control corporate action eligibility, voting, distributions, and record dates. Their throughput and evidence standards define whether entitlement is clean or contested. Entitlement risk becomes a trading input around key dates, and entitlement risk is amplified by custody layering because beneficial ownership and legal title can diverge operationally even when the investor believes they own.

Corporate actions expose the machine's legal reality because they force the system to name a holder. A trade can be economically meaningful even if ownership is still in flight operationally. A dividend or a vote forces the system to decide whose name counts at a cut-off. That cut-off is a gate, and gate timing is a distributive event. Traders who can finish before cut-off receive entitlement. Those who cannot may be forced into claims and adjustments, which are slower and riskier.

Regulators and courts are the enforcement perimeter. They make records meaningful. They define evidence standards and time horizons. If enforcement is predictable, liquidity deepens because disputes can be resolved without endless delay. If enforcement is slow, spreads widen to price the time cost of trapped capital. If enforcement is inconsistent or captured, legitimacy collapses and the system charges a larger premium for fear.

The hidden labor of the market is the operational workforce that keeps completion possible: reconciliations, exception processing, margin calls, settlement instructions, corporate action processing, compliance logging, audit trail maintenance, and dispute handling. The market's public image is speed. Its private reality is constant repair. The machine does not collapse daily because this labor absorbs friction before friction becomes cascade.

The cast, however, is not merely a taxonomy. The cast is a wiring diagram for incentives, because each role has a different capacity to shift cost downstream. Some can charge explicit fees. Some can widen spreads without calling them fees. Some can sell delay as product. Some can tighten margin as model output. Some can define what counts as official and therefore what other contracts must accept as reality.

To make the cast operationally intelligible, the chapter must move from roles to interactions: how these actors pass risk, cost, and information across the chain, and how a small change at one gate becomes a large redistribution downstream.

The first interaction is between exchanges and market makers. Market makers need predictable queues and data. Exchanges need market makers to provide depth so official prints are usable and spreads are socially tolerable. This creates a reciprocity that looks like competition and behaves like co-dependence. The exchange designs order types and incentives that attract liquidity provision. Liquidity providers adapt with strategies that exploit those designs. Each side claims it is serving efficiency. Each side is also defending revenue.

A venue that cannot keep spreads tight loses flow. A market maker that cannot manage adverse selection loses money and withdraws. Withdrawal widens spreads. Wider spreads make the venue less attractive. Less attractive venues lose reference relevance. Loss of relevance reduces data revenue. The exchange therefore has incentive to structure queues and fee schedules to keep liquidity providers engaged, especially under stress when the legitimacy of officialness is tested.

The second interaction is between brokers and internalizers. Brokers are judged on execution outcomes and on economics. Internalizers offer brokers consistent fills, reduced visible impact, and often price improvement. Internalizers also offer economic terms that improve broker profitability. The broker's client sees a fill and a price. The broker sees a tradeoff: route to the public venue and risk higher impact, or route to the internalizer and accept that the internalizer captures spread and early-flow information.

The client's welfare depends not only on the fill but on the system's long-term structure. If too much flow is internalized, public quotes can become thinner and more sensitive to informed flow. Price discovery becomes more fragile and more dependent on private hedging behavior. Yet internalization can produce better short-run outcomes for individual retail trades. The machine's political tension lives here: short-run improvement can be purchased with long-run concentration of informational advantage.

The third interaction is between data vendors and everyone else. Visibility is sold at multiple layers. Venues sell direct feeds. Consolidators sell aggregated views. Vendors sell analytics. Brokers buy these products to route intelligently. Market makers buy them to avoid being picked off. Clearing and risk systems buy them to monitor exposures. The system becomes dependent on data products to operate, which means the data layer becomes a tax on participation.

This tax is regressive in a technical sense: large firms pay and amortize the cost across huge volume; small firms pay and cannot. The outcome is not merely cost difference; it is reality difference. A participant with slower, thinner data is acting in a different market than a participant with faster, richer data. The market looks like one field and behaves like layered terrain.

The fourth interaction is between clearinghouses and liquidity providers. Clearinghouses demand margin based on models that reflect volatility, concentration, and stress. Liquidity providers hold inventories and hedges that consume margin. When volatility rises, margin rises. Rising margin forces liquidity providers to either post more collateral or reduce positions. Reducing positions withdraws liquidity. Withdrawal widens spreads. Wider spreads increase price moves. Price moves increase volatility. Volatility increases margin again.

This loop is how a system amplifies stress without conspiracy. It is also how clearing becomes a political choke point: models allocate pain by forcing collateral demands on some portfolios earlier than others. Those with cheap funding post. Those without liquidate. The model allocates survivability.

The fifth interaction is between custodians, settlement systems, and the rest of the chain. Traders care about execution. The machine cares about finality. Finality is delivered by settlement and custody. Settlement has cut-offs. Cut-offs create fail risk. Fail risk creates penalties and reputational damage. Penalties and reputational damage create higher clearing costs and tighter credit terms.

When settlement friction rises, market makers widen spreads to compensate. Brokers route differently to avoid trades likely to fail. Internalizers prefer instruments with lower settlement risk. Liquidity concentrates where completion is cheaper, not necessarily where productive value is greatest.

The sixth interaction is between corporate actions and trading behavior. Corporate actions expose custody layers. Dividends, splits, votes, and tender offers require record dates. Record dates require clear ownership records. Clear records require settlement and custody alignment. Misalignment creates entitlement disputes. Entitlement disputes create risk. Risk widens spreads around key dates. Wider spreads increase trading cost and influence issuer behavior, because issuers see liquidity conditions and may change timing of actions to reduce disruption. Issuers begin making governance decisions with the circulation machine in mind.

The seventh interaction is between compliance and the whole stack. Markets are proof-based. Proof burden grows with fragmentation, internalization, and speed. Proof burden is not free. It requires systems, logs, surveillance, and reconciliation. Large firms can automate. Small firms cannot. Automation becomes competitive advantage. Competitive advantage attracts flow. Flow yields revenue to fund more automation. The machine compounds.

The cast's hidden logic is compounding through gate access. It is not only money. It is the ability to finish cheaply and defend decisions with evidence. If you can do that, you can operate with tighter tolerances, larger scale, and more strategies. If you cannot, you will be constrained to slower, more expensive participation, and your outcomes will look worse even when your intent is honest and your skill is strong.

The cast includes rule-writers whose influence is often invisible at the moment rules are written. Benchmark administrators decide what counts as included and what counts as excluded. Index inclusion directs passive flows. Passive flows stabilize liquidity for included names and reduce it for excluded names. The index becomes a gate. The gate is defended as rules-based. Rules-based is the market's preferred legitimacy language because it makes allocation feel neutral even when it is distributive.

Risk model vendors influence financing terms. Risk models decide haircuts, margin multipliers, and eligibility. Eligibility determines whether an instrument can be used as collateral. Collateral eligibility determines funding cost. Funding cost determines who can hold inventory. Inventory determines liquidity. Liquidity determines spreads. Spreads determine who can trade. The model becomes a lever. Those who influence the model influence the market without trading.

Technology providers and connectivity providers are also cast members because proximity to matching engines and low-latency networks reduce adverse selection and allow tighter quoting. This looks like an arms race. It is also the sale of certainty. Certainty is purchased by those who can pay for infrastructure. The public sees speed as progress. The machine experiences speed as gate premium.

The cast must also include the issuer-side professionals who make formation possible and who shape circulation indirectly: underwriters, syndicate managers, listing advisers, and counsel who design disclosure and governance to satisfy admission standards. Their role is to turn a real enterprise into a claim the machine will accept as tradable. Tradable does not mean good. Tradable means legible: predictable reporting, defined governance, and clear eligibility for corporate actions. Legibility is a gate.

The cast includes passive allocators whose flows operate like weather. When flows are steady, liquidity is deep and spreads tighten. When flows reverse, liquidity becomes scarce and spreads widen. The passive allocator is not "passive" in the machine's effect. It is automatic. Automatic flows create predictable demand or supply that intermediaries can anticipate and monetize. Anticipation reduces risk and increases profit.

The cast includes the firms that translate the legal into the operational: identifier standards bodies, corporate action processors, and message protocol maintainers. Their job is to keep the system from collapsing into mismatched records. When identifiers fail, settlement fails. When settlement fails, credit tightens. When credit tightens, liquidity withdraws. When liquidity withdraws, spreads widen. When spreads widen, legitimacy falls. Identifier discipline is therefore stability infrastructure even though it looks like clerical trivia.

The cast includes the exception handlers whose work is invisible until it is missing. Breaks occur daily: mismatched quantities, missing confirmations, failed deliveries, disputed ownership, corporate action misallocations. The exception handler's job is to repair without stopping the machine. Repair is not merely administrative. It is a source of advantage because those who repair faster recycle capital faster and avoid penalties. Speed of repair is another form of gate access.

The cast includes credit committees and risk committees that sit above trading desks and decide what strategies are allowed, which exposures are capped, and which instruments become expensive to hold because internal capital charges are raised. These committees are internal regulators. Their constraints can force liquidation just as surely as a clearinghouse margin call. Internal governance therefore becomes part of market behavior, and the firms with better internal capital efficiency can run larger books and quote tighter.

The cast includes the auditors of the market's own claims: those who test whether best execution is real, whether surveillance is effective, whether controls can withstand stress, whether proof trails exist and are coherent. Their presence is a response to political legitimacy demands. Their effect is to increase the cost of participation because compliance becomes heavier. That cost again advantages scale.

To understand why the cast produces stable winners, the chapter must treat the machine as a layered optimization problem. Each actor optimizes its own objective subject to gates imposed by others. The exchange optimizes revenue and officialness relevance. The broker optimizes routing economics, client outcomes, and proof burden. The market maker optimizes spread capture, adverse selection control, and funding efficiency. The internalizer optimizes flow capture and hedging cost. The data vendor optimizes tiered pricing and dependence. The clearinghouse optimizes stability and loss containment through margin models. The custodian optimizes throughput and exception handling with fee schedules. The regulator optimizes legitimacy and enforcement priorities.

Each optimization changes the environment. When the exchange sells more tiered visibility, the data layer becomes more unequal. When the broker routes more flow to internalizers, public venues thin. When public venues thin, market makers widen. When market makers widen, internalizers become more attractive. When internalizers become more central, price discovery becomes more dependent on their hedges. When hedges flow to venues, venues adjust microstructure to attract them. The loop becomes a self-organizing market structure.

This self-organization has a distributional signature: it pulls activity toward places where completion is cheapest and where visibility is richest. Places where completion is expensive are punished with illiquidity. Illiquidity raises cost of capital for issuers in those places. Higher cost of capital reduces formation. Reduced formation reduces political attention. Reduced attention reduces infrastructure investment. Infrastructure stagnation increases completion cost further. The cast therefore produces geographic and institutional concentration even when the surface story is global access.

The cast also produces a moral signature: outcomes can be defended as rule-following even when rules distribute advantage. This is the machine's central legitimacy trick. Not because it is deceitful, but because procedure is the only way to scale without constant conflict. Procedure distributes pain and profit. The cast is the set of entities that write procedure, enforce it, sell access to it, and profit from those who cannot pass it cheaply.

CHAPTER 10
THE JOURNEY OF AN ORDER
WHAT HAPPENS BETWEEN YOUR CLICK AND THE PRICE YOU ARE TOLD YOU GOT.

An order is not a request for a price. An order is a request for priority inside a machine that sells completion, visibility, and risk transfer. The click is a surface event. The machine treats the click as a packet of intent that must be translated, routed, exposed or withheld, executed or internalized, cleared, margined, settled, and proven. The investor sees a fill. The machine sees obligations: defend the outcome as compliant, avoid leaking intent into the wrong hands, minimize market impact, minimize completion risk, minimize margin consumption, and choose a route that optimizes economics without tripping enforcement or client backlash.

The journey begins before the click because the machine pre-sorts the investor. It learns account behavior, typical sizes, time-of-day patterns, instrument preferences, and the likelihood that the order is information-driven or noise-driven. This pre-sorting is cost control. If the order is likely uninformed and small, the machine treats it as flow that can be internalized cheaply. If the order is large, time-sensitive, or correlated with other signals that suggest information, the machine treats it as potentially toxic. Toxic does not mean illegal. Toxic means adverse selection: the counterparty who fills it is more likely to lose.

When adverse selection probability rises, spreads widen, price improvement vanishes, and routing logic becomes more conservative.

At the click, the order becomes a message with more than quantity. It carries limit or market, time-in-force, and optional constraints. The broker system adds metadata: client category, risk checks, compliance flags, and routing preferences shaped by the broker's economics and obligations. The first hidden gate is eligibility. Not every order is eligible for every route. Some routes require particular attributes. Some require minimum size. Some require that the broker can certify conditions the client never sees. Eligibility is a silent filter that changes reachable liquidity without announcing itself.

The machine then performs risk checks. These checks determine whether the broker accepts the order at all and under what conditions. An order can be rejected, delayed, throttled, or re-shaped by controls that exist to protect capital and compliance posture. Delay is not a trivial inconvenience. Delay is a price input because delay changes where the market is when execution occurs. Delay becomes a hidden fee paid in slippage while being defended as protection.

After acceptance, the order enters a routing decision that is not a single decision but a decision tree. The broker chooses whether to expose the order to displayed venues, route it to an internalizer, send it into auction logic, split it across venues, or rest it passively to seek a better price. Each path has a different footprint. Displayed exposure can create competition but leaks intent and worsens impact. Internalization can reduce impact and produce an outcome that looks like improvement while shifting value to the internalizer through spread capture and information advantage. Auctions can create genuine competition for the order while creating new timing surfaces. Splitting can reduce impact while increasing complexity and proof burden. Resting can improve price while increasing non-execution risk and exposing the order to being bypassed by faster actors.

Execution quality is not one metric. It is a bundle: price, speed, likelihood of fill, likelihood of partial fill, market impact, information leakage, and completion certainty. The broker's obligation is to produce a defensible outcome under this bundle. Defensible does not necessarily mean optimal in hindsight. Defensible means consistent with rules and with the documented process the broker can later prove.

The next gate is interaction style. The order can be posted to add liquidity or sent to remove liquidity. Adding liquidity means joining a queue. Joining a queue means accepting priority rules that decide whether the order will be filled quickly, whether it will be filled at all, and whether it will be filled ahead of other orders that arrived earlier in clock time but later in priority time. Priority time is produced by microstructure: timestamps, order type privileges, and cancellation behavior.

Removing liquidity means crossing the spread. Crossing the spread pays the immediacy toll instantly. That toll can be smaller than the cost of waiting if the market moves. It can be larger if the market is stable. The machine chooses removal when it fears time risk or information risk, and chooses posting when it wants improvement and believes it can wait without being picked off. Being picked off is the risk that the order rests and is executed only when it becomes unfavorable relative to new information.

If the broker routes to a displayed venue, the order enters a matching engine with defined rules. The engine applies priority rules and may run auctions for certain moments. In continuous matching, the first resting order at the best price trades first unless special instructions alter precedence. In auction logic, orders accumulate and then execute together to produce a clearing price. Auctions can reduce some speed advantage while creating other advantage surfaces: imbalance information, cut-off timing, and order classification.

The investor sees a fill and a timestamp. The timestamp is not singular. There is an internal broker timestamp, a venue timestamp, a feed timestamp, and a consolidated display timestamp. Each can differ. Each difference matters because disputes, audits, and performance comparisons depend on which timestamp is treated as authoritative. The system chooses authoritative timestamps through rules that appear technical and behave distributively.

If the broker routes to an internalizer, the order executes in a private node. The internalizer's promise is that the investor receives at least the displayed benchmark, often slightly better. That promise can be real in isolation while still shifting economic value. First, the internalizer captures spread that would otherwise be competed away. Second, the internalizer captures information about the flow and uses it to hedge efficiently, reducing its risk and increasing its profit.

Hedging is where private execution connects back to the public market. After filling internal flow, the internalizer manages net exposure by trading in displayed venues or other private venues. Those hedge trades become prints that influence the public price. The visible market is therefore partially a shadow of private execution decisions.

Fragmentation changes the journey because liquidity is split. The router evaluates multiple books at once, weighing fee schedules, fill probabilities, information leakage, and completion risk. This evaluation is not neutral because broker incentives are not neutral. Some venues pay rebates. Some charge fees. Some routes generate valuable data relationships. Some routes create higher fail risk. The router's objective is firm optimization under constraints, and the client's outcome is one constraint among several. That is why the proof burden exists: it forces the broker to justify that conflicts were managed.

Execution produces a record and downstream obligations. Confirmation to the client is immediate. Confirmation is not finality. Confirmation is a promise that finality will follow. Finality requires clearing and settlement.

Clearing turns bilateral trades into standardized exposures against a central counterparty or a netting system. Clearing nets exposures, reducing gross movement and reducing settlement burden. Netting increases throughput. Netting also concentrates systemic dependence on clearing rules and models.

The next gate is margin. Margin is the machine's fastest pain allocator. When the machine senses risk rising, it demands more collateral. The demand is computed by models that translate volatility and concentration into required resources. Those models can tighten rapidly. Rapid tightening forces participants to post collateral or liquidate. Liquidation is a mechanical response to a demand, not a mood.

The investor's order is part of a collateral metabolism. If many investors buy or sell at once, liquidity providers accumulate exposures and hedges. Those exposures consume margin. If volatility rises, margin rises. If margin rises, liquidity providers reduce activity. Reduced activity widens spreads. Wider spreads worsen execution outcomes for new orders. New orders pay the price of earlier stress through visible widening of costs.

Settlement delivers legal finality. Settlement means delivery of cash and delivery of the security, recorded in custody. Settlement is constrained by cut-offs, calendars, and custody capacity. Settlement fails trigger penalties. Penalties change future access to credit and clearing. Fail risk is priced into spreads because liquidity providers expect some probability of operational penalty.

Settlement reveals custody layering. The end investor's statement is not the legal registry. Ownership is recorded in centralized depositories and custodial ledgers. The investor holds beneficial ownership. Legal title sits higher in the stack. Layering allows scale and speed. It also creates ambiguity in edge cases: entitlement at record dates, voting rights, and correction of errors. The machine relies on reconciliation labor to keep layering from becoming visible conflict.

Reconciliation is the hidden labor that transforms a story into a stable system. Records across brokers, venues, clearinghouses, custodians, and internal systems must match. When they do not match, exceptions are processed. Exceptions require time. Time is cost. Firms with better infrastructure resolve exceptions faster, reducing capital trapped in fails. Faster resolution reduces funding costs. Lower funding costs allow tighter quoting. Advantage compounds through operational competence as surely as through speed.

The final gate is proof. A broker must defend routing. A venue must defend the trade record. A clearinghouse must defend margin computation. A custodian must defend ownership records. Proof burdens exist because legitimacy requires enforceable routines. Proof burdens create advantage surfaces because proof cost is not uniform. Large actors automate. Smaller actors struggle. Automation becomes competitive advantage.

The journey of an order is therefore a journey through priced invisibilities. The investor sees a fill. The machine prices the gates that make the fill real. The prices appear as fees, spreads, latency, margin, haircuts, and delayed finality.

A full journey can be mapped as a sequence of decisions and state changes. The order is classified. Risk checks accept or delay it. The router selects a path. The path can include internalization, auctions, or displayed venues. The order interacts with a queue. It is executed. The execution is confirmed. The trade is cleared and netted. Margin is computed and posted. Settlement instructions flow to custody. Settlement occurs or fails. If it fails, penalties apply and exceptions are processed. Records are reconciled. Proof packets are stored for audit and dispute.

Each stage has an associated failure mode, and each failure mode creates a business that sells mitigation. Routing failure risk creates routing intelligence. Information leakage risk creates hidden order types and off-book matching. Adverse selection risk creates premium data and internalization. Margin stress creates collateral optimization and financing products. Settlement fails create custodial services and reconciliation systems. Proof burdens create surveillance tooling and audit trail platforms.

The journey's political characteristic is that it can be described as best execution while being designed as revenue optimization. Best execution obligations exist. The machine responds by building audit trails and narratives that justify routing. Yet as long as multiple routes can be defended as reasonable, routing remains an optimization problem. Optimization finds revenue. Revenue reinforces infrastructure that controls routes. Route control concentrates. Concentration changes what is reasonable because alternatives shrink or become expensive.

The click is therefore a demand for completion. Completion is sold in layers. Layers are priced. The price of layers creates winners.

The doubled layer begins where the first telling often ends: at the moment the machine decides whether the investor's intent should be allowed to become visible competition or should be translated into private completion. Visibility is the market's raw ingredient for fairness and also the market's raw ingredient for exploitation. Show an order and others can compete to fill it, improving price. Show an order and others can infer intent, positioning against it, worsening price. The machine's job is to sell a controlled compromise.

Controlled compromise is implemented through slicing and staging. A large intent is rarely sent as a single message. It is broken into child orders, each with its own behavior. Some children rest passively to earn spread. Some children sweep aggressively to ensure completion. Some children probe multiple venues to discover hidden liquidity. Some children route to private nodes to reduce impact. Slicing reduces the visible footprint, but it increases the number of interactions and therefore increases the number of points where the market can extract tolls.

Each child order must be shaped to the venue's microstructure. Microstructure is not uniform. Some venues reward displayed liquidity; others reward immediate removal. Some run auctions at specified moments; others run continuous matching. Some allow midpoint-like executions that reduce spread cost; others impose rules that make midpoint execution conditional on hidden constraints. The router must choose not just where to send but what order behavior to use when sending. Behavior choice is a gate because behavior determines exposure to adverse selection and determines the probability of being filled only when it becomes unfavorable.

A simple example of behavior choice is the difference between a marketable limit and a pure market instruction. A market instruction accepts the best available price at that moment. A marketable limit accepts the best available price up to a defined boundary. The difference looks like safety. Operationally, it changes how the order interacts with fragmented books and how internalizers evaluate it. A pure market instruction can be seen as urgency and can be priced accordingly by liquidity providers. A marketable limit can be seen as willingness to wait and can invite different treatment. The same intent expressed differently can travel through different pipes and pay different tolls.

The machine also chooses whether to request liquidity from competition or to accept liquidity from privilege. Competition is displayed venues where many participants can respond. Privilege is internalization where a private node fills and then hedges. Competition can reduce price because more responders compete. Privilege can reduce impact because the trade does not hit the public book. The machine decides based on toxicity assessment and on economics. If the order is likely uninformed, privilege is cheap and profitable for the internalizer while still delivering outcomes that look fair. If the order is likely informed, the internalizer may refuse or may widen its implied spread, pushing the order toward public venues where competition can distribute the risk across more participants.

The order's journey therefore includes a negotiation the investor never sees: the market's willingness to be the other side. Willingness is not a moral state. It is a price. If willingness is high, spreads tighten and fills are easy. If willingness is low, spreads widen and fills become conditional. Conditional fills appear as partial execution, delayed execution, or execution at worse levels than expected.

The route decision is also shaped by fee schedules that can invert what looks like cheap. A venue can charge explicit fees or pay rebates. An internalizer can pay a broker for flow or offer improved economics through bilateral arrangements. The investor sees a fill price. The broker sees a combined objective: minimize total cost including fees, maximize predictable completion, and minimize proof burden. The broker can defend choices as compliant as long as there is a documented process and as long as outcomes fall within reasonable bounds. That defendability creates the space where economics can dominate.

Proof burden shapes route choice more than many narratives admit. A route that is hard to explain is expensive. A route that creates many partial fills across many venues is expensive. A route that increases the risk of settlement fails is expensive. The machine often prefers a slightly worse visible price if it reduces downstream cost and reduces the probability of dispute. This is one way the system prices the cost of being audited.

Auctions deserve a deeper view because they are marketed as fairness tools and used as strategic surfaces. An auction collects orders and executes them at a single price, reducing the advantage of being a tiny bit faster within the auction window. Yet auctions introduce new advantage: knowing imbalance, predicting the clearing price, and positioning just outside the auction to profit from the liquidity shock it creates. Auction information dissemination becomes a product. If some participants see imbalance earlier or with more fidelity, they can position. If they can position, they can trade just ahead of the clearing print. If they can trade ahead, they can extract value from those who are forced to execute inside the auction.

The journey also includes hidden cancellation logic. Many strategies depend on the ability to cancel quickly when the environment changes. Quick cancel protects from being picked off. The ability to cancel is itself a privilege because cancellation travels through queues and message systems. If your cancellation is late, you trade when you no longer want to. Late cancellation is adverse selection realized. Firms invest to make cancellation faster because faster cancellation reduces loss. That investment is a tax paid to avoid paying an even larger tax.

Cancellation speed changes how resting liquidity behaves. If liquidity can evaporate instantly, displayed depth becomes less reliable under stress. Less reliable depth increases uncertainty. Increased uncertainty widens spreads. Wider spreads increase execution costs for everyone. The machine then sells solutions: premium liquidity programs, private completion routes, and data products that help participants infer whether displayed depth is real or fleeting.

The order journey also includes the decision to hide or to display. Hidden orders reduce signaling but also reduce the market's ability to compete for the order. Reduced competition can worsen price. The machine chooses hiding when it fears predation more than it values competition. Predation here is not necessarily illegal front-running. Predation is microstructure exploitation: detecting intent and adjusting quotes to extract more value from the predictable path of the order.

Predictability is the order's enemy and the machine's business. If your path is predictable, others can position to profit from it. If others can profit from it, your execution cost rises. The machine sells unpredictability through smarter routing and through private venues. It also sells predictability to those who can exploit it through richer order flow signals and better data. The same system sells both sides, which is why it can claim neutrality while producing concentrated advantage.

Once execution occurs, the clearing layer introduces its own journey, and that journey can change the cost of the original trade after the fact. Clearing nets exposures, which can reduce margin if positions offset. But margin models can be procyclical, tightening when volatility rises. A participant can execute a trade cheaply and then find that holding it is expensive because margin has tightened or because the position increases concentration. The cost of holding feeds back into the willingness to quote. Willingness to quote feeds back into spreads. Spreads feed back into execution. The order journey is therefore not linear; it is a loop between execution and funding.

Margin is not merely collateral. Margin is a schedule. The schedule matters because when collateral must be posted quickly, those without immediate liquidity must liquidate. Liquidation is the machine's fastest enforcement. Liquidation is also a source of profit for those who can buy when others must sell. The order journey thus includes the market's asymmetric timing: some participants are forced to act by margin deadlines, others are free to wait. The free participants harvest the forced participants through spreads and through better entry prices.

Settlement adds calendar risk and fail risk. Fail risk is not only operational. Fail risk changes credit terms. If a firm has a pattern of failing, its counterparties tighten credit, its clearing costs rise, and its ability to quote tight spreads declines. Firms therefore invest heavily in settlement reliability. Settlement reliability is a hidden competitive advantage because it reduces the probability of penalties and reduces the probability of capital being trapped.

The custody layer adds legal reality risk. Beneficial ownership is not always the same as legal title, and record dates force the system to choose whose name counts. The machine handles this with standardized record date rules and with adjustment mechanisms for errors, but adjustment mechanisms are slower and create disputes. The possibility of dispute is priced into spreads around corporate actions. That pricing affects issuer cost of capital indirectly. Issuers then adapt behavior to reduce entitlement disputes, which is the circulation engine shaping corporate behavior.

The journey also includes a compliance mirror. Everything the machine does becomes evidence. Evidence must be stored. Evidence must be coherent. Evidence must explain why the outcome was acceptable. The market's speed therefore produces a second system that runs alongside it: logging, surveillance, and audit trail preservation. This second system is heavy. It raises the minimum efficient scale. It gives large firms a compounding advantage because they can spread the cost of proof across enormous volume.

Proof then shapes route choice again. The machine prefers paths that are easier to justify and easier to log. Paths that create messy exceptions are expensive. Paths that create clean confirmations are cheaper. The machine can therefore sacrifice a small amount of visible price improvement to reduce proof and completion risk. That sacrifice is rarely visible to the investor because the investor sees only the final print, not the alternative universe of paths not taken.

The journey ends not at settlement, but at the moment the system can defend the outcome as legitimate if challenged. Legitimate here means: the record exists, the timestamps align with accepted definitions, the routing decisions are documented, the fees are disclosed appropriately, the clearing and settlement completed or were managed through defined exception procedures, and custody records reflect entitlement. The investor thinks the market is the fill. The machine thinks the market is the defendable chain.

CHAPTER 11
THE PRICE FIGHT
AUCTIONS, SPREADS, LIQUIDITY, AND THE HIDDEN CONTEST THAT DECIDES VALUE IN REAL TIME.

A market price is not a consensus about value. It is a temporary ceasefire between competing constraints. The price fight is the process by which that ceasefire is negotiated continuously, and the negotiation is not a polite debate. It is a contest between those who demand immediacy and those who sell it, between those who reveal and those who hide, between those who see early and those who see late, and between those who can finish cheaply and those who pay extra to be finished.

The simplest story says buyers bid, sellers offer, and the midpoint is value. The machine's story is that spreads are the price of uncertainty and the price of protection. A spread compensates a liquidity provider for inventory risk, adverse selection, funding cost, completion cost, and the risk that the quote will be hit only when it is wrong. The spread is therefore not merely a cost paid by impatient traders. It is a tax that funds market stability by paying someone to stand ready.

The fight begins with liquidity as a scarce resource. Liquidity is not volume. Liquidity is the ability to transact at size without moving the price too much and without triggering downstream completion penalties. Liquidity is produced by market makers and by passive limit orders, but both forms are conditional. Market makers provide liquidity only when the expected cost of being wrong is smaller than the spread they can earn. Passive limit orders provide liquidity only when the poster believes the price is fair and believes they will not be picked off. The market's depth is therefore always contingent, and the price fight is the continuous adjustment of contingencies.

Adverse selection is the central asymmetry. If the counterparty to your quote knows more than you do, you lose. The liquidity provider's problem is not that markets move. The problem is that markets move in a way that correlates with the moments when the liquidity provider is forced to trade. That is why liquidity provision becomes an information business. The best liquidity providers are those who can infer whether incoming flow is informed, whether it is urgent, whether it is correlated with news, and whether it is likely to continue. They price differently based on these inferences. The public sees one quote. The machine sees a conditional quote adjusted by toxicity.

Toxicity is not a slur. It is a risk classification. A flow can be toxic because it arrives when volatility is rising, because it arrives just after a news release, because it arrives in patterns associated with larger informed sequences, or because it arrives from venues that tend to concentrate informed trades. A liquidity provider who fails to classify toxicity pays for it through inventory losses. A liquidity provider who classifies well can quote tighter when the flow is benign and widen when it is dangerous, preserving profit and preserving endurance.

Endurance is the quiet currency of the price fight. The side that can keep quoting under stress can extract wider spreads and can buy from forced sellers. The side that cannot must withdraw and accept worse prices later. Endurance is balance sheet plus funding plus risk limits plus completion capacity. Endurance is not only wealth. It is institutional permission to hold risk without being forced out by internal constraints, external margin demands, or settlement penalties.

This is why the price fight has two arenas. There is the visible arena where orders meet and prints occur. There is the funding arena where inventories must be financed, margins must be posted, and risk limits must be respected. The funding arena is the arena that decides who remains standing when uncertainty rises. When funding tightens, liquidity disappears and spreads widen. The public experiences this as the market becoming nervous. The machine experiences it as the cost of holding inventory becoming too high for too many participants at once.

Auctions are marketed as fairness mechanisms because they can reduce the advantage of being marginally faster. By collecting orders and executing them at a single clearing price, auctions can compress the fight into discrete moments where participation is broader and where the price is determined by aggregated supply and demand rather than by a thin sequence of trades. Yet auctions also introduce new advantage surfaces: imbalance information, cut-off timing, and order classification.

Imbalance information is the most direct advantage surface. If participants can see that demand is outweighing supply before the auction prints, they can position. If they can position, they can profit from the move the auction will create. If imbalance information is disseminated unevenly or can be inferred more precisely by those with richer data, the auction becomes a venue where fairness is performed while advantage is still purchased.

Cut-off timing is the second surface. Orders submitted before cut-off participate fully. Orders submitted after cut-off either wait or must chase in the next continuous period. Those who can time submission with precision can influence the auction's clearing point or can avoid being trapped in the wrong side of a sudden imbalance. Timing is a gate. The auction simply moves the gate from microseconds of continuous matching into the engineered rhythm of discrete windows.

Order classification is the third surface. Not all orders are treated equally within an auction. Some orders are conditional, some are hidden, some are pegged to reference points, and some are prioritized in particular ways. Classification can advantage certain strategies by granting them participation without full exposure. That is why auction fairness is not a moral state. It is a design problem with distributive outputs.

Continuous markets and auction markets distribute advantage differently. Continuous markets reward speed, cancellation agility, and queue strategy. Auction markets reward forecasting of the clearing price, control of order placement timing, and interpretation of imbalance signals. The machine often uses a hybrid because it wants the legitimacy of auctions and the throughput of continuous matching. Hybridization increases complexity, and complexity increases gate value.

Spread formation is where the price fight becomes visible. In calm conditions, spreads narrow because uncertainty is low, funding is cheap, and adverse selection is manageable. In stress, spreads widen because volatility rises, funding tightens, and adverse selection risk increases. Widening is not merely fear. Widening is self-defense. A liquidity provider who does not widen under stress may be forced to trade at the worst moments and may be unable to fund inventory.

The spread is also a negotiation between liquidity providers. They compete, but their competition is bounded by the floor set by toxicity. If one liquidity provider quotes too tight when toxicity is high, informed traders will hit that quote first, transferring losses to the naive quoter. The naive quoter then withdraws. Withdrawal reduces competition. Reduced competition widens spreads. The system therefore creates a paradox: competition is strongest when information is most evenly distributed and weakest when information is most asymmetric. That is why spreads widen sharply around uncertainty even in markets with many participants.

Fee schedules and rebates alter the visible fight without changing the underlying economics. If a venue pays for posted liquidity, displayed spreads can appear tight because posters are subsidized. If takers pay fees, takers experience a higher effective spread than the screen suggests. If certain participants receive better fee tiers, their effective spread is lower than others, letting them compete more aggressively and still profit. This is how the machine turns pricing into an eligibility gradient: two participants can trade at the same displayed price while paying different real prices to access that trade.

The price fight is also a contest over where the trade happens. Fragmentation means multiple venues can display similar prices. Routing decides which venue receives the order, which venue earns the fee, and which venue's print becomes part of the reference signal. Venues compete with microstructure features and with economic incentives. The visible competition is for volume. The hidden competition is for the right to define officialness and to sell the most valuable data products.

Officialness is the prize because official prints are used outside trading. If an official print triggers collateral rules, benchmark calculations, or valuation disputes, then controlling which prints count is controlling downstream reality. That control is monetizable through data products and through membership privileges. It is also defendable as integrity because officialness must be protected from manipulation.

Manipulation in the price fight is often procedural rather than theatrical. It can be executed through timing, through the selection of venues, through the use of small prints designed to influence a reference, or through strategies that exploit how quotes are formed from dispersed liquidity. When manipulation becomes visible, the machine responds by tightening reporting requirements and by raising the proof burden. Proof burden reduces manipulation. Proof burden also advantages scale, because producing clean proof packets and maintaining clean audit trails is expensive.

The fight includes the cost of cancellation. Cancellation is not neutral. Fast cancellation allows a liquidity provider to avoid being picked off when new information arrives. If cancellations are slow, resting liquidity becomes riskier, and liquidity providers demand compensation. Compensation appears as wider spreads. Fast cancellation therefore tightens spreads for those who can cancel fast and widens spreads for those who cannot. The machine sells cancellation advantage through better connectivity, better data, and better infrastructure.

This creates a visible paradox: displayed depth can be large and still evaporate under stress. Depth that can be cancelled instantly is not the same as depth that will remain when hit. The difference is survivability of liquidity. Survivability becomes a product. Some venues attempt to create more reliable liquidity through rules that penalize certain cancellations or that reward certain forms of commitment. Those rules create new gates: which participants can afford to commit and which cannot.

Another dimension of the price fight is hidden liquidity. Hidden liquidity exists because participants want to trade without being seen. Hidden liquidity can reduce market impact for the initiator. It can also reduce transparency for everyone else, shifting the fight toward those who can infer hidden supply and demand from indirect signals. When hidden liquidity grows, the visible quote becomes less representative. The visible quote remains the public signal anyway, which increases the value of privileged inference.

Privileged inference does not require illegal access. It can be achieved through better data tiers, better models, and better knowledge of routing patterns. If you know how routers behave and which venues they prefer, you can anticipate where flow will appear. Anticipation reduces adverse selection. Reduced adverse selection reduces spread. Reduced spread attracts more flow. The machine compounds.

The price fight therefore includes a contest over who gets to avoid trading when the price is wrong. Avoidance is not cowardice. Avoidance is survivability. Liquidity providers survive by withdrawing or widening when their risk rises. This withdrawal, collectively, is what the public experiences as the market becoming thin. The machine tolerates thinning because thinning protects the survival of key nodes. It manages legitimacy by keeping the thinning from becoming a complete freeze.

This is where clearing and margin enter the price fight even though they occur after execution. Liquidity providers quote with knowledge of what the trade will cost them in margin and settlement. If the clearinghouse tightens margin or adds stress charges, the cost of holding inventory rises, and liquidity providers must widen spreads to compensate. A change in margin policy therefore changes the price fight at the quote level. It does not need to be labeled as a pricing intervention to be one.

Funding conditions enter the fight through haircuts and financing rates. A liquidity provider who must fund inventory at a higher rate requires a wider spread. A liquidity provider whose inventory is eligible for cheap financing can quote tighter. Funding advantage becomes quote advantage. Quote advantage becomes flow advantage. Flow advantage becomes information advantage. The machine again compounds through a gate that looks like ordinary credit.

The fight is also shaped by benchmark and index flows because these flows create predictable demand and supply. Predictable flows create an opportunity for intermediaries to position. Positioning reduces risk and increases profitability. Profitability allows intermediaries to provide liquidity more consistently. Consistent liquidity tightens spreads. Tight spreads attract more flow. Flow makes the benchmark and index effects stronger because more participants reference them.

The result is that passive flows can become an engine of microstructure behavior even without intent.

The fight includes the contest over what counts as a meaningful price. A small trade can print at an extreme level and still influence perception. If officialness rules allow that print to be part of the reference, then micro prints can become leverage points. The machine responds by defining which trades are eligible for officialness or for benchmark use. Eligibility is a gate. Gate design distributes advantage.

This is why price discovery is never simply discovery. It is construction. Prices are constructed from eligible prints, eligible quotes, and eligible venues under rules that decide what counts. Those rules are defended as integrity and are also exploited as opportunity.

The price fight includes the economics of resting orders. A passive order provides liquidity but is exposed to being executed when it becomes unfavorable. This risk is selection risk. Passive liquidity is therefore not free. It is compensated either by earning spread or by receiving economic incentives. Incentives can be explicit, like rebates, or implicit, like queue priority. Those incentives are gates because they determine who can afford to provide passive liquidity and under what conditions.

Queue priority is itself a price. If you can obtain priority, you can be filled earlier, reducing your time exposed to adverse moves. If you can protect priority through cancellation strategies and order types, you can maintain a favorable position. Those protections cost money through infrastructure and through data. Money buys priority. Priority buys better fills. Better fills buy profit. Profit buys more infrastructure.

The fight also has a behavioral layer: how participants interpret the same signal. Some participants respond to prints; some respond to order book changes; some respond to volatility measures; some respond to funding rates; some respond to correlated instruments. These interpretations create cross-instrument linkages that can move price rapidly. Rapid movement increases toxicity. Increased toxicity widens spreads. Wider spreads increase the cost of trading for everyone.

Volatility is often treated as external. In the machine it is partly endogenous. Volatility rises when liquidity withdraws. Liquidity withdraws when volatility rises. That feedback loop is mediated by risk limits, margin models, and funding conditions. The price fight is where the loop is expressed as spread widening and thinning depth.

The market's legitimacy story says competition decides the price. The machine's reality is that competition is structured. It is structured by who can see, who can cancel, who can fund, who can clear, who can settle, who can internalize, and who can influence officialness. The price at any moment is a compromise across these constraints.

The nested structure of the fight can be stated as four contests happening at once. First, a contest over immediacy: takers pay spread to get done now, makers earn spread to wait and to absorb risk. Second, a contest over information: those who infer toxicity better trade with less loss. Third, a contest over infrastructure: those who cancel faster and see earlier avoid being harvested. Fourth, a contest over completion: those who can clear and fund cheaply can stay in the market longer under stress.

Each contest has a gate and each gate has a toll. Immediacy is priced as spread. Information is priced as data. Infrastructure is priced as connectivity and speed. Completion is priced as margin and funding. The public sees only the spread. The machine sees all four tolls and allocates advantage accordingly.

The reason the price fight matters is that it sets the terms of participation for everyone else. A firm raising capital pays indirectly through the liquidity conditions of its claim. A household investing pays directly through spreads and execution quality. A state borrowing pays through reference yields influenced by the same gates. A crisis is often not a change in fundamentals but a change in the price of these gates all at once.

CHAPTER 12
THE PRICE FEED ECONOMY
HOW MARKET DATA BECAME INFRASTRUCTURE, PRODUCT, AND TOLL ROAD.

Market data is treated as a mirror, but it is a manufactured mirror. A feed is not merely a stream of numbers. It is a governance artifact. It decides what counts as the market at a given moment, and once contracts, benchmarks, collateral rules, and enforcement regimes reference that artifact, the artifact becomes infrastructure. Infrastructure is never neutral because infrastructure decides who can move cheaply and who must pay friction as tax. The price feed economy is the story of how a public signal became a private industry, and how the private industry became a toll road with lanes that distribute advantage while claiming transparency.

The first economic insight behind the feed economy is that information is not valuable because it is mysterious. It is valuable because it is timely, authoritative, and actionable under completion constraints. A number that arrives after the quote has already moved is a narrative, not a tool. A number that arrives before the quote moves is a shield: it lets a liquidity provider cancel before being picked off, lets a router avoid sweeping into a vacuum, lets a risk desk tighten exposure before a margin model tightens, lets an internalizer hedge before the public sees the hedge pressure. Timeliness is survivability. Survivability is priced.

The second insight is that visibility is not binary. There is no single market view. There are layers of view produced by technical design and by business strategy. A public display might show a best bid and offer. A richer feed shows depth across multiple levels. An even richer feed shows order-level updates, auctions, imbalance messages, cancellations, modifications, and hidden state changes that do not appear in a simplified view. A view with better timestamps and richer event types is a higher-fidelity version of reality. High fidelity reduces adverse selection. Reduced adverse selection reduces the cost of liquidity provision. Reduced cost allows tighter quoting. Tighter quoting attracts flow. Flow increases profits. Profits fund more data. The loop is circular and self-reinforcing.

The third insight is authority. A price that is not treated as authoritative cannot be used safely in contracts. A price treated as authoritative becomes a legal and economic anchor. It becomes the reference for collateral valuations, for margin disputes, for benchmark calculations, for damages in litigation, for tax assessments, and for compliance reconstructions. The feed that carries authoritative prices becomes a privileged channel not because it is fast, but because it is recognized. Recognition is the rarest commodity in markets because recognition requires collective acceptance and enforcement preference.

Once timeliness, fidelity, and authority exist, the feed economy becomes inevitable. Someone must pay to produce the stream, normalize it, distribute it, time-stamp it, store it, and defend it in disputes. That payment can be collected as a fee. A fee can be structured as a public utility cost. A fee can also be structured as a revenue maximization program. Markets almost always choose the second structure once competition and shareholder incentives are introduced, because the feed is the cleanest monetization surface in the entire system: it can be sold repeatedly without consuming balance sheet the way liquidity provision does.

The feed economy begins with an apparent contradiction: markets claim transparency and then sell vision. The contradiction is resolved through layering. A minimal public feed is distributed widely enough that the system can claim openness. Premium feeds are sold to those who require survival-grade visibility. The system can defend this by saying the public feed is sufficient for ordinary participation, while professionals pay for professional needs. The distributional reality is that professionals pay for an advantage that compounds into tighter spreads, better routing, fewer losses, and therefore stable dominance. The public feed becomes a civic window. The premium feed becomes the machine's operating system.

The first lane of the toll road is latency. Lower latency is not just about being earlier in an absolute sense. It is about reducing the probability of trading on stale information. A liquidity provider exposed to stale information is exposed to being hit when wrong. A router exposed to stale information is exposed to chasing phantom liquidity and paying impact. A risk desk exposed to stale information is exposed to margin shocks arriving before internal adjustments can be made. Lower latency converts these risks into manageable costs.

Latency has multiple sources. There is the time between an event and the venue's dissemination. There is the time between dissemination and network transmission. There is the time between reception and processing. There is the time between processing and decision. Each layer can be optimized. Each optimization can be purchased. The feed economy therefore is not merely a price list. It is a market in microseconds and in the right to sit closer to the source. The participant who sits closer is not necessarily smarter. The participant who sits closer is less vulnerable to adverse selection. Less vulnerability is profit.

The second lane is depth and message richness. Depth reduces uncertainty about whether the displayed quote is supported by real size. In a fragmented market, the best quote on one venue may be small and fleeting while deeper liquidity sits elsewhere. A shallow view can cause a router to sweep a thin quote and then pay a worse price for the remainder. A deeper view allows smarter slicing and smarter venue choice. Smart slicing reduces impact. Reduced impact is a hidden performance advantage that can be converted into marketing, client retention, and regulatory defense.

Richness also matters because the market is not only trades and quotes. It is cancellations, modifications, auction updates, imbalance messages, and state changes. These messages signal intent and stress. A participant with access to them can infer whether liquidity is stable or fragile. Inferential advantage allows better quoting and better avoidance of toxic flow. This is why the market can sell depth as a product without having to call it a privilege. It can call it a professional tool.

The third lane is consolidation. The market is fragmented, and fragmentation creates a new product: a consolidated view that claims to show the market as a whole. Consolidation seems like a public good. It is also a point of contest because consolidation can be done in different ways. Which venues are included, how timestamps are aligned, how conflicts are resolved, which messages are treated as primary, and how errors are corrected. These are not purely technical decisions. They shape what the market appears to be.

If a consolidated feed is slow or incomplete, participants with direct feeds can exploit those relying on consolidated views. If a consolidated feed becomes authoritative for retail and for many compliance functions, direct feed users gain an advantage that is difficult for outsiders to perceive because outsiders believe they are seeing the market. They are seeing a delayed abstraction.

The fourth lane is redistribution rights. Data is valuable not only to the direct buyer but to any downstream client, and the right to redistribute becomes a gate. Venues monetize redistribution rights by charging vendors for licensing. Vendors then charge clients. Each layer adds a toll. The end user pays not because the data is scarce in an absolute sense, but because the right to distribute is controlled. Control is the business model.

The fifth lane is interpretation. Raw data is overwhelming. Actionable data requires normalization, mapping, and analytics. Interpretation is sold as a value add, but it also creates dependence. If your trading and risk systems rely on a vendor's normalization rules, you become locked into that vendor. Lock-in increases pricing power. Pricing power raises cost of participation. High costs of participation advantage scale.

Interpretation also changes behavior because analytics become signals that many participants follow. When many follow the same signal, flows become predictable. Predictable flows can be traded against. The data provider therefore sells signals that can be used to exploit those following signals. The system is self-referential: the feed does not merely report the market; it becomes part of what moves the market.

Authority is where the feed economy becomes a political economy. Official prices exist because legal and economic systems require anchors. Collateral agreements reference prices. Benchmarks compute returns. Courts assess damages. Regulators reconstruct events. All of these require a number that counts. The venue that can define which number counts can sell that definition. It can also shape behavior because participants adapt to what counts.

Officialness therefore becomes a product and a liability. It is a product because it can be monetized through data sales and through the prestige of being the reference. It is a liability because if officialness is perceived as manipulable, the legitimacy of the whole market is threatened. The feed economy must therefore invest in surveillance, audit trails, and reconstruction capability. These investments are costly. They also create additional products: compliance data services, forensic reconstructions, and historical datasets priced at levels small participants cannot afford.

The feed economy also creates an asymmetry between those who can pay for history and those who cannot. History matters because risk models and strategy development depend on historical data. If you can buy richer history with cleaner timestamps and deeper message coverage, you can build better models. Better models improve execution and risk control. Improved execution attracts flow. Flow funds more data. This is another compounding loop that concentrates advantage.

A feed is also a queue. Not only in the sense of message ordering, but in the sense that dissemination itself is prioritized. Some clients receive messages earlier through direct connections. Some receive later through consolidated distribution. Some receive only summaries. Summaries can be "good enough" for a human observer and harmful for an automated strategy. When decisions are automated, a small latency difference becomes a large profit difference because it repeats across thousands of events. That repetition turns tiny time differences into structural rents.

The feed economy's most visible legitimacy tactic is the minimum viable public feed. The public feed must exist because the market needs a public narrative of openness. Yet the public feed is often designed not to eliminate informational advantage but to define the boundary of acceptable inequality. Acceptable inequality is a political choice. Too much inequality invites outrage and regulatory intervention. Too little inequality reduces revenue and reduces the ability of venues and vendors to fund infrastructure. The system tends to settle at an equilibrium where inequality is large enough to be profitable and small enough to be deniable to most participants.

Denial is not necessarily deception. It is complexity. Most participants cannot see the difference between a public feed and a premium feed because they do not have a reason to compare them event by event. Professionals do compare. Professionals buy premium. Professionals benefit. The public sees price discovery. The machine sees perception engineering.

The feed economy also reshapes corporate behavior indirectly. If a company's stock is widely followed and heavily traded, data products and analytics proliferate. Proliferation increases attention. Attention increases liquidity. Liquidity lowers cost of capital. The company is rewarded for being in the feed economy's center. Companies outside the center face illiquidity discounts. Those discounts are not moral judgments. They are the price of being hard to trade and hard to monetize. The feed economy therefore pushes capital formation toward assets that are easy to signal and easy to package, reinforcing concentration.

The feed economy is deeply entangled with benchmarks. Benchmarks use data to compute inclusion, weights, and performance. Benchmark changes create flows. Flows create predictable trading patterns. Those patterns can be anticipated. Anticipation becomes profit. Profit attracts more capital to strategies that trade benchmark-driven flow. That increases demand for better benchmark data. Benchmark data becomes a premium product. The benchmark becomes a gate because inclusion directs flows. The benchmark administrator becomes a quasi-governor because rules decide who receives flows. The data provider becomes a toll collector because rules require data.

This is how a feed becomes a political instrument without speeches. If inclusion rules or price definitions change, flows move and financing conditions shift. Those shifts can affect corporate strategy, public borrowing costs, and household wealth. The feed economy is therefore not merely about traders. It is about who controls the definitions that allocate money automatically.

The feed economy's final function is forensic. When markets break, everyone demands a replay. Who traded when. Who canceled first. Which quote was visible. Which print counted. Which messages were delayed. Which systems failed. Forensic reconstruction requires full message capture, timestamp precision, and storage. Those capabilities are expensive. They are sold. The ability to reconstruct becomes a privilege. Privilege matters because in disputes, the party with better reconstruction can win. Winning disputes is a hidden profit surface because it reduces loss and deters claims.

Forensic capability also shapes regulation because regulators rely on evidence. If evidence is incomplete or inconsistent, enforcement becomes weaker. Weaker enforcement increases manipulation incentives. Manipulation threatens officialness. Officialness is the product. The system therefore sells evidence to preserve its own legitimacy while charging for it.

The feed economy's distributive output can be stated as a simple rule. Those who pay see earlier and see more. Seeing earlier and more reduces adverse selection, reduces impact, reduces completion cost, and improves model quality. Improved outcomes attract flow and profit. Profit funds further payment. Those who do not pay see later and see less. They trade on abstractions and pay the tax of delay through worse execution and higher uncertainty.

The machine can present this as natural segmentation. It is segmentation. It is also the core of how modern markets turn information into rent while keeping enough public visibility to preserve legitimacy.

CHAPTER 13
THE RISK WAREHOUSE
CLEARINGHOUSES, NETTING, MARGIN, AND THE MACHINERY THAT KEEPS PANIC FROM SPREADING.

The market's most important institution is rarely the one on the screen. It is the one that decides whether a failure stays local. A clearinghouse is a risk warehouse. It takes bilateral promises and turns them into a centralized obligation system that can be netted, margined, and, in crisis, liquidated without requiring every participant to sue every other participant. The clearinghouse exists because dispersed completion fails under scale. It is the machine's answer to the oldest problem: a chain of promises is only as strong as the first link that breaks, and without a warehouse, breaks propagate.

A clearinghouse performs three functions that look technical and behave political. It interposes itself as counterparty. It nets exposures to compress gross obligations into manageable net amounts. It demands margin to ensure that if a participant fails, the warehouse can absorb the shock long enough to manage an orderly unwind. Each function is a gate. Gates allocate pain, allocate time, and allocate survivability.

Interposition replaces counterparty uncertainty with institutional uncertainty. Instead of worrying about whether the other side will pay, participants worry about whether the warehouse's rules will tighten, how margin will be calculated under stress, and whether the warehouse will declare a participant noncompliant fast enough to prevent losses from becoming shared. This trade is accepted because institutional uncertainty is more predictable than bilateral uncertainty in a complex system. Predictability is the priceable base of liquidity.

Netting is the throughput engine. Without netting, every trade would require full settlement of cash and securities. Under volume, full settlement overwhelms operational capacity and consumes scarce final settlement media at the worst moments. Netting reduces movement. It also hides gross exposures. Hiding gross exposures is efficient in calm conditions and dangerous in stress, because stress forces gross exposures into visibility when a participant cannot meet net obligations and the system must determine who absorbs the gap.

Margin is the warehouse's primary lever. Margin is collateral demanded to cover potential losses between now and the time a position can be closed. Margin is not static. It is computed by models that incorporate volatility, concentration, liquidity, correlations, and jump risk. When volatility rises, margin rises. When margin rises, participants must post collateral or reduce positions. Reducing positions under stress often means selling into falling markets and buying into rising ones. Margin therefore can be procyclical: it tightens when the system is weakest, forcing behavior that can worsen price moves and justify further tightening.

Procyclicality is not a defect to be eliminated. It is a protective reflex. The warehouse is designed to survive its members. It would rather force liquidation than absorb exposures without collateral. Yet this reflex allocates pain. Those with cheap funding and high-quality collateral can post. Those without must liquidate. The warehouse redistributes survivability.

Default management is where the warehouse becomes an emergency government inside the market. When a member fails to meet margin or settlement obligations, the warehouse triggers a process: isolate the member's positions, hedge or auction them, use the member's posted margin first, then use the default fund, and only then consider assessments that call on surviving members. This sequence is a loss waterfall. The waterfall is not only accounting. It is a political economy because it defines who pays for failure and in what order.

The risk warehouse is therefore a machine that converts private risk into public-like stability through mutualization, and then sells that stability back to participants through cheaper netting, lower counterparty uncertainty, and deeper liquidity. The price is membership discipline and collateral discipline. The byproduct is concentration of power in the institution that sets the models.

The warehouse cannot be understood as a single entity. It is a layered architecture of accounts, obligations, and safeguards. At the surface, members trade with each other. The warehouse novates trades so each member faces the warehouse rather than each other. This novation creates two equal and opposite obligations: one for the buyer and one for the seller. Those obligations are then compressed through netting at defined intervals.

Netting itself is not a single technique. It is a family of compressions that reduce settlement movement and reduce risk, but each compression has a cost in hidden dependency.

Trade netting is the most intuitive. If a member buys and sells the same instrument, net position is smaller than gross. Netting reduces settlement volume and reduces exposure. It also reduces the need for cash and securities delivery.

Payment netting compresses cash flows from multiple trades into a single net payable or receivable. Without payment netting, a member would face many separate cash transfers, each with its own fail risk. Netting reduces operational risk.

Exposure netting is more subtle and more powerful. When the warehouse calculates risk, it can allow offsets across correlated positions. If a member holds a long position and a hedge, the net exposure may be smaller than the sum. Cross offsets reduce required margin. Reduced margin increases leverage capacity. Increased leverage can increase systemic fragility. The warehouse must balance the benefit of recognizing genuine hedges with the danger of over-recognizing correlations that break in crisis.

Portfolio netting is where advantage accumulates. A large, diversified member can present a portfolio whose internal offsets reduce required margin. A smaller, concentrated member cannot. This is not favoritism. It is arithmetic. Yet arithmetic is distributive: the warehouse's models reward scale and diversification by lowering collateral demands per unit of activity. Those who receive that benefit can trade more, provide more liquidity, and earn more. Their increased activity further entrenches their centrality.

Netting is the warehouse's promise of efficiency. Netting is also the warehouse's promise of entanglement. The more netting compresses the system, the more the system depends on the warehouse to be correct about offsets, to be correct about correlations, and to be willing to tighten fast enough that losses do not spill beyond the default waterfall.

The warehouse's second architecture layer is margining, which is not one number but a set of collateral demands with different purposes and time horizons.

Initial margin is the buffer for potential future exposure. It is sized to cover losses that could occur if a member defaults and the warehouse must liquidate positions over a defined liquidation horizon. The horizon matters. If a product is liquid, horizon can be short. If a product is illiquid or concentrated, horizon is longer. Longer horizon increases margin. Increasing margin reduces participation and can thin liquidity. Thinner liquidity increases liquidation cost. Increased liquidation cost justifies longer horizons. The loop is structural.

Variation margin is the daily or intraday transfer of gains and losses. Variation margin is intended to prevent losses from accumulating invisibly. It is a discipline mechanism. It forces the system to pay its mark-to-market costs now. Paying now reduces the chance that losses become unpayable later. It also creates funding stress because large variation margin demands require immediate liquidity. Under stress, immediate liquidity is scarce.

Additional margin, concentration add-ons, and stress add-ons are the warehouse's adaptive tools. They are used when a member holds positions that are too large relative to market depth or when volatility regimes shift. These add-ons are often where pain allocation becomes most controversial because they can change rapidly and can target specific members or specific positions. Targeting is not necessarily punitive. It is protective. Yet targeted demands can force liquidation and can be read as discretionary power.

The third architecture layer is collateral eligibility and haircut policy. Margin must be posted in acceptable collateral. Acceptability is a gate. A warehouse may accept cash, high-quality government securities, or other high-quality liquid assets under haircuts. Haircuts are the warehouse's way of pricing collateral risk. If the collateral itself can fall in value under stress, the warehouse must demand more of it. Higher haircuts reduce the usefulness of collateral for members and can tighten funding conditions.

Collateral policy is therefore a hidden governor of the entire machine. If the warehouse accepts a wide range of collateral, members can fund margin more easily and trade more. If the warehouse tightens eligibility, members scramble for accepted collateral, creating stress in collateral markets. That stress can spill back into broader markets. Collateral eligibility therefore has a macro dimension. It decides which assets become money-like in the clearing ecosystem.

The warehouse's fourth architecture layer is membership and client clearing. Not every participant clears directly. Direct clearing membership requires capital, operational competence, and compliance capacity. Those requirements create a perimeter. Participants outside the perimeter clear through members, paying fees and accepting indirect access. Indirect access is safer for the system and profitable for members. It also concentrates power and can concentrate risk if too much activity funnels through a few members.

Client clearing creates a second hierarchy inside the warehouse: the hierarchy of porting and protection. If a client's positions are held through a clearing member and that member fails, the warehouse must decide whether and how the client's positions can be transferred to another member. Porting is the mechanism that prevents a member's failure from destroying clients. Porting requires that client positions are segregated properly and that receiving members are willing to take them. Willingness depends on collateral and on operational readiness.

Segregation regimes are therefore not administrative details. They are survival design. If client collateral is commingled, clients become unsecured creditors in a failure. If collateral is segregated and legally protected, clients have a better chance of porting. Yet segregation has cost. It reduces netting efficiency for the member and can increase overall margin requirements. The warehouse and regulators choose a balance: more protection and less efficiency, or more efficiency and more contagion risk.

The fifth architecture layer is default resources beyond margin: the default fund and assessment powers.

The default fund is mutualized. Members contribute. The fund exists because margin is never perfect. There are always tail risks: gap moves, correlation breaks, liquidation cost spikes, and operational failures. The fund is a shared buffer. Shared buffers create collective discipline incentives: members want the warehouse to be strict because strictness protects the fund. They also want strictness to be predictable, because unpredictable strictness can force them into unnecessary liquidation.

Assessment powers allow the warehouse to call for additional contributions from surviving members in extreme cases. Assessments are a mutualization backstop. Their existence supports confidence that the warehouse can survive beyond the default fund. Their existence also creates a fear: being forced to pay for others. That fear shapes member politics and shapes lobbying around model governance.

These architecture layers interact to create a single operating outcome: the warehouse can keep trading possible by ensuring that credit risk and settlement risk are managed centrally and by ensuring that losses are absorbed in a controlled sequence rather than spreading indiscriminately.

The warehouse's control levers are model parameters and time. It decides liquidation horizons. It decides confidence levels. It decides stress scenarios. It decides add-on triggers. It decides margin call timing. It decides collateral eligibility. These are technical knobs that decide who must post collateral today and who can wait. Time is the most powerful distributional variable because time decides who is forced to act. Those who can wait harvest those who cannot.

A warehouse does not merely warehouse risk. It warehouses time. It imposes deadlines. It defines when losses must be paid. It defines when collateral must be delivered. It defines when default is declared. Those definitions allocate the ability to survive.

The warehouse's stabilizing function can be described as containment. Containment is achieved through four routines: novation, netting, margining, and default management. Each routine reduces one dimension of panic propagation.

Novation reduces bilateral credit risk propagation. If one participant fails, the warehouse absorbs the credit event, preventing the failure from creating a chain of direct counterparty losses across many participants.

Netting reduces settlement volume and reduces the number of transfers that can fail. It also reduces the amount of funding required to settle gross obligations.

Margining forces losses to be paid continuously rather than accumulating. This reduces the chance that a participant becomes insolvent without warning.

Default management provides a structured response to failure: positions are hedged, auctioned, or liquidated; losses are allocated through the waterfall; the system continues.

This containment is why the warehouse is tolerated and often protected. It is also why the warehouse is feared. The warehouse is the institution that can force liquidation at scale through margin calls. It is the institution whose model updates can transform a strategy from profitable to impossible overnight. It is the institution whose definitions of eligible collateral can create a scramble for certain assets. It is the institution whose declarations of default can trigger reputational and funding cascades.

The warehouse therefore lives inside a permanent tension: it must be strict enough to protect itself and the system, but not so strict that it causes the very destabilization it is meant to prevent.

That tension is managed through model governance, and model governance is the warehouse's hidden politics.

Model governance begins with the question of tail probability. How extreme a move should margin cover. Cover too little and the warehouse becomes vulnerable. Cover too much and margin becomes a tax that shrinks participation and makes liquidity brittle. Liquidity brittleness increases liquidation cost, which justifies higher margin. The warehouse must find an equilibrium. The equilibrium is not morally correct. It is operationally survivable given member economics and political tolerance.

Model governance also includes the choice of stress scenarios. Stress scenarios determine how large the default fund must be and how much margin add-ons can be demanded. Scenarios that assume severe correlation breaks increase margin and increase default fund contributions. Increased costs push marginal participants out or into client clearing, increasing concentration. Concentration increases systemic risk because fewer members carry more flow. The warehouse must therefore consider that increasing safety at the instrument level can create risk at the concentration level.

Procyclicality management is the warehouse's most contentious design problem. If margin rises sharply when volatility spikes, forced selling can amplify moves. If margin does not rise, the warehouse can be under-collateralized. Warehouses often attempt to smooth procyclicality by using anti-procyclical buffers in calm times. That means higher margin in calm times than would otherwise be required, building slack that can be used in stress. The political challenge is that participants resent paying more in calm times for a risk that feels hypothetical. Yet the cost of not paying is the forced liquidation spiral in stress.

The warehouse's ability to demand intraday margin is another critical lever. Intraday demands can prevent losses from accumulating, but they can also drain liquidity at the worst moments. A warehouse that calls too aggressively can cause a liquidity shock. A warehouse that calls too slowly can allow losses to grow. Timing is governance.

Default management is where model governance meets real economics. When a member fails, the warehouse must liquidate positions. The liquidation mechanism matters. It can hedge first and auction later. It can auction directly. It can attempt to transfer positions to surviving members. Each option has tradeoffs. Hedging can stabilize price risk but can move markets. Auctions can distribute risk but can be thin if participants are fearful. Transfers can preserve value but require willing recipients and clean porting structures.

Auction design is therefore part of the risk warehouse's core. Auction design includes who can bid, how quickly, with what collateral requirements, and under what confidentiality. If the auction is too open, bidders may fear adverse selection and bid conservatively. If the auction is too closed, competition is limited and liquidation costs rise. If collateral requirements for bidders are too tight, fewer bidders participate. If requirements are too loose, bidders may default, creating secondary failures. The warehouse must design auctions that create participation even when stress is high.

Auction participation depends on member incentives. Members will bid if they believe the terms are favorable relative to risk and if they have funding capacity. Funding capacity depends on margin and on external financing. In crisis, financing tightens. That reduces bidding. Reduced bidding increases liquidation costs. Increased liquidation costs increase the warehouse's losses. Losses threaten the default fund. Threats to the default fund trigger assessments. Assessments threaten surviving members. Threatened members become more conservative, reducing future participation. The warehouse must therefore protect confidence in its own process because confidence affects the willingness of members to absorb risk in auctions.

This is why the warehouse invests in transparency to members and secrecy to the public. Members need enough visibility into positions and risk to bid intelligently. Public disclosure of details can create panic and political intervention. The warehouse chooses a boundary: publish enough to preserve legitimacy, reveal enough internally to create orderly liquidation.

The risk warehouse's politics also include conflict between members. Large members often prefer robust netting and broad offsets because they hold diversified portfolios and can benefit from lower margin. Smaller members may prefer simpler models that do not disadvantage them through scale-based netting advantages. Clients may prefer strong segregation and porting protections even if those protections reduce netting efficiency and raise costs. The warehouse must balance these constituencies because losing any constituency can weaken the system: losing large members reduces liquidity and auction capacity; losing small members reduces competition and increases concentration; losing client confidence pushes risk into less transparent spaces.

The warehouse also interacts with regulators who care about systemic stability and with policymakers who care about legitimacy. Systemic stability prefers strong margin and strong default resources. Legitimacy prefers avoiding sudden, sharp demands that force visible liquidations. The warehouse's choices are therefore never purely internal. They are shaped by political tolerance for market stress outcomes.

A risk warehouse also shapes market structure through product eligibility. If a product is cleared, participants can trade it with lower counterparty risk and often with greater netting benefits. If a product is not cleared, it may remain bilateral, requiring more capital and more counterparty risk management, making it more expensive. Clearing therefore can push markets toward standardized products and away from bespoke contracts. Standardization increases volume and netting efficiency. It also can reduce customization that some users need. The warehouse thus becomes a force for homogenization, which can be stabilizing and can also concentrate risk in standard channels.

The warehouse's role in "keeping panic from spreading" can be understood through contagion pathways it blocks and contagion pathways it creates.

It blocks direct counterparty contagion by interposing itself. A member does not face hundreds of counterparties; it faces the warehouse. That reduces the network of direct exposures.

It blocks settlement contagion by netting, reducing the number and size of settlement transfers.

It blocks information contagion by providing a structured process for default rather than allowing rumor-driven lawsuits and bilateral refusal to settle.

It creates funding contagion through margin calls. When margin rises, the demand for high-quality collateral rises. This can stress collateral markets. Collateral stress can force selling of other assets to raise cash. Asset selling spreads stress.

It creates concentration contagion through membership structure. If client clearing funnels risk through a few members, the failure or stress of those members becomes systemic.

It creates model contagion because many participants respond to the same margin models and risk signals. When the model tightens, many sell. Selling moves prices. Price moves tighten the model further.

The warehouse must therefore be evaluated not only by whether it reduces bilateral failures, but by how its own mechanisms shape systemic behavior under stress.

The procyclicality loop deserves explicit mapping because it is the warehouse's most important macro effect. Volatility rises. Margin rises. Margin calls force liquidation. Liquidation increases volatility. Volatility rises further. This loop is amplified if participants have limited access to liquidity or if collateral is concentrated in a few assets.

Warehouses attempt to dampen this loop through buffers, through discretion on intraday calls, through staged margin increases, and through default resources that reduce the need to tighten as aggressively. Yet these dampeners create their own legitimacy issues. Discretion invites accusations of favoritism. Staged increases may be too slow. Buffers impose costs in calm times. Every dampener is a political choice about when pain is paid.

A warehouse also controls the definition of "stress enough" to tighten. If it tightens early, it may prevent default but may cause avoidable liquidation. If it tightens late, it may allow positions to grow too large and then require more violent tightening later. The system's preference depends on who holds positions and who can pay margin. Large actors tend to prefer early tightening if it disadvantages smaller, more leveraged actors, because early tightening can create forced sellers. Smaller actors tend to prefer gradual tightening because sudden tightening can wipe them out. The warehouse is in the middle.

Client clearing introduces another mechanism that can prevent panic from spreading: porting. Porting is the transfer of client positions and collateral from a failing clearing member to a surviving one. Porting is the warehouse's promise that a member failure does not automatically become a client failure. Yet porting only works if positions are properly segregated, if records are clean, if collateral is sufficient, and if receiving members are willing. Willingness depends on collateral quality and on the receiving member's risk appetite and funding capacity. Under stress, willingness can vanish. Porting then fails, and clients become exposed.

This is why segregation is not just protection; it is a participation constraint. Segregation can increase total collateral demand and reduce netting efficiency. Increased demand for collateral can itself increase stress. Again, stability and efficiency conflict.

The warehouse's mutualization mechanisms also deserve explicit detail because they are the core of the risk warehouse's social contract. The default waterfall typically follows a sequence: defaulter's variation margin and initial margin, defaulter's contributions to default funds, warehouse capital, mutualized default fund contributions, and assessment calls on members. The sequence matters because it shapes incentives. If members believe warehouse capital is at risk early, they trust that the warehouse will be disciplined. If members believe mutualized funds are used too quickly, they resent subsidizing risk. If defaulter resources are insufficient, everyone faces shared loss. That creates a collective incentive to demand higher margin and stricter membership standards.

Membership standards therefore tend to tighten over time because each crisis produces a memory of shared pain. Tightening reduces participation and increases concentration. Increased concentration increases systemic significance of the remaining members. This is another loop: crisis leads to tighter standards, tighter standards lead to concentration, concentration increases systemic risk, systemic risk leads to more regulatory scrutiny, scrutiny leads to higher costs, higher costs reinforce concentration.

The warehouse is also embedded in a hierarchy of legal regimes. It relies on enforceable rules across jurisdictions. If a member operates across borders, the warehouse must be able to seize collateral, liquidate positions, and enforce obligations across legal systems. Legal enforceability is a gate. It determines which participants can operate at scale. It also determines which jurisdictions can host major clearing nodes. Jurisdictions that provide strong enforceability become hubs. Hubs become geopolitical assets.

The warehouse therefore has a geopolitics even when it claims to be technical. If a clearinghouse is located within a particular jurisdiction, that jurisdiction has leverage over the rules and can influence the boundary conditions of global risk management. Leverage is rarely exercised overtly, but it exists through regulation, through sanctions regimes, through emergency authorities, and through the ability to define what counts as compliant participation. The warehouse becomes part of statecraft.

A modern risk warehouse also interacts with central bank liquidity indirectly. When margin demands rise sharply, the demand for cash rises. If the system cannot obtain cash, forced selling accelerates. Central bank interventions that supply liquidity can therefore stabilize markets by allowing participants to meet margin without liquidation. The public may interpret this as bailout. Operationally, it is an attempt to prevent the warehouse's procyclical loop from becoming an uncontrolled spiral. Yet supplying liquidity changes incentives because it reduces the perceived cost of leverage. The system then grows again and requires stronger future tightening. The warehouse lives inside this macro cycle.

The warehouse's internal controls include stress testing, backtesting, and governance committees that decide model adjustments. Stress testing is an attempt to imagine failure before it arrives. Backtesting is an attempt to measure whether margin would have covered past moves. Both are limited. Past moves are not future moves. Correlations shift. Liquidity disappears. Jump risk appears. The warehouse therefore must maintain conservative assumptions. Conservative assumptions increase costs. Higher costs reduce participation. Reduced participation concentrates. Concentration increases liquidation cost. Increased liquidation cost requires more conservative assumptions. The loop returns.

This is the warehouse's central engineering problem: it must model a system that changes in response to the model. If margin is low, participants leverage more. If participants leverage more, risk increases. If risk increases, margin must rise. If margin rises, participants deleverage. Deleveraging can crash prices. Crashed prices validate higher margin. The model is not external. It is part of behavior.

The warehouse's model is therefore not a measurement device. It is a policy device. It sets the price of risk. Pricing risk changes behavior.

Behavior changes risk. This is why the warehouse's decisions are political even when they are expressed as statistics.

The warehouse also manages the boundary between cleared and uncleared risk. Some risk remains bilateral. Bilateral risk requires bilateral collateral agreements. Those agreements can be messy. They can fail. They can create disputes. Clearing is often promoted as a solution. Yet forcing everything into clearing can create concentration and can push bespoke risks into standardized categories that do not fit well, increasing model error. The system therefore chooses a split: clear standardized products, keep bespoke risks bilateral, and require higher capital and collateral for bilateral exposures. This encourages standardization and shapes the evolution of markets.

The warehouse's relationship to exchanges is symbiotic. Exchanges produce trades. Warehouses finalize them. Exchanges sell officialness at the execution layer. Warehouses sell stability at the completion layer. Execution can be fast and visible. Completion must be enforceable and resilient. In crises, the warehouse often becomes more important than the exchange because the exchange can match trades that cannot be funded. The warehouse's margin demands can cause trading to slow or shift. The warehouse can effectively shut down leverage by making collateral too expensive.

This power is used rarely because using it openly can create legitimacy backlash. Yet it exists and is often the quiet reason markets stabilize: collateral requirements throttle risk. Throttling can look like prudence. It can also look like the warehouse deciding who gets to survive.

The warehouse's rulebook also embeds a philosophy of error. Errors happen daily: settlement fails, mismatched records, late deliveries, operational glitches. The warehouse's systems must be robust to these errors. Robustness is achieved through penalties and through exception processing. Penalties enforce discipline. Exception processing prevents penalties from causing cascades when errors are harmless.

The design of penalties is a gate. Strong penalties reduce fails but can increase liquidity costs. Weak penalties reduce cost but increase fail risk.

Fail risk matters because a settlement fail can propagate through funding. If a participant expects to receive securities and does not, it may be unable to deliver elsewhere. That creates chain fails. Chain fails create distrust. Distrust widens spreads. Wider spreads reduce liquidity. The warehouse's fail penalties and buy-in procedures are therefore systemic controls. They decide whether failures are contained or amplified.

The warehouse also controls the unit of finality. Finality is not instantaneous. It is defined by settlement cycles and by legal definitions of when a transfer is irrevocable. Irrevocability is critical because risk management depends on it. If a transfer can be reversed easily, counterparties will hoard. Hoarding reduces liquidity. The warehouse's role is to create a credible notion of finality by enforcing settlement discipline and by coordinating with settlement institutions and custody systems.

The warehouse is therefore a coordinator of time across the system. Trading occurs continuously, but clearing and settlement occur on schedules. Schedules create cut-offs. Cut-offs create timing games. Timing games create advantage for those who can predict and manage the cut-offs. The warehouse's schedules are therefore part of the market's competitive terrain.

The warehouse also has a business model. It charges fees. It sells clearing services. It sells risk management as a product. Fees appear small per trade and enormous in aggregate. Fee design can influence behavior: lower fees for certain participants, volume tiers, incentives for certain products, penalties for certain fails. These designs are policy levers.

The warehouse's governance includes membership committees, risk committees, and rule-change processes. These bodies decide model updates and eligibility. Decisions are influenced by member interests. Members are not identical. Some want more netting, some want less. Some want lower margin, some want higher. The warehouse must appear neutral while balancing these interests. Neutrality is maintained through procedure: documented decisions, published methodologies, and regulatory oversight. Procedure is legitimacy manufacturing.

The warehouse's legitimacy rests on a paradox. It must be trusted as a neutral guardian of stability, yet it must also be flexible enough to tighten rules rapidly under stress. Flexibility looks like discretion. Discretion invites accusations. Accusations threaten legitimacy. Threatened legitimacy can itself create stress.

This is why warehouses often prefer rule-based tightening even when discretion might be economically smoother. Rule-based tightening can be defended as automatic. Automatic tightening can still be procyclical, but it is easier to justify. The machine chooses what it can justify as much as what it can optimize, because justification preserves social license.

A risk warehouse must also plan for its own failure. Recovery and resolution planning is the admission that the warehouse is systemic. Systemic means its collapse is unacceptable. Unacceptable does not mean impossible. It means the political system will intervene. Recovery tools include margin increases, default fund replenishment, assessment calls, and in extreme cases partial tear-up or allocation of losses in ways that preserve continuity. These tools are last resorts. They are also the reason participants accept the warehouse: the warehouse can impose pain in a controlled way rather than allowing uncontrolled contagion.

Controlled pain is still pain. The warehouse's role is to decide whose pain comes first. The waterfall is the algorithm of pain. The model is the schedule of pain. Collateral eligibility is the currency of pain.

The warehouse keeps panic from spreading by turning panic into a funding problem with deadlines and by ensuring that the largest funding demands are backed by collateral. It also spreads panic through its own procyclical demands when many participants must meet deadlines at once. The warehouse is therefore not a cure. It is a containment system that can generate its own side effects.

The machine depends on the warehouse because without it, the market would revert to bilateral distrust, gross settlement overload, and litigation cascades. With it, the market can trade at scale and survive member failures. The price is that an institution with model power, membership power, and collateral power sits at the system's center.

CHAPTER 14

THE FINAL HANDSHAKE

SETTLEMENT, FINALITY, AND THE MOMENT A MARKET PROMISE BECOMES ENFORCEABLE.

A trade is not real when it is executed. A trade becomes real when it becomes irreversible enough that both sides stop treating it as a conditional claim and begin treating it as property. That conversion is the final handshake. Everything before it is negotiation and exposure. Everything after it is entitlement, accounting, and enforceable reality. The system can create obligations at the speed of signals; it can only create ownership at the speed of settlement discipline.

Settlement is the market's most underestimated engine because it does not create excitement. It creates certainty. Certainty is what makes leverage possible, what makes collateral usable, what makes corporate actions coherent, and what makes disputes resolvable without re-litigating every intermediate step. A system that can trade but cannot settle at scale is not a market. It is a promise factory whose products accumulate faster than the system can extinguish them, and accumulation is how panic becomes systemic.

Finality is layered and timed. At execution, a venue declares a match. At clearing, exposures are netted and margined. At settlement, cash and securities are delivered through cut-offs and calendars. At custody, ownership is recorded in the ledgers that corporate actions and courts recognize. At law, the transfer becomes binding such that reversal is either impossible or so costly and narrow that it functions as impossible for ordinary commerce. Each layer can fail. Each failure creates a mitigation business. Each mitigation becomes a gate. Gates are priced, and priced gates distribute advantage by controlling who can finish cheaply and who must pay in delay, funding cost, and exception risk.

The final handshake exists because the market has a permanent asymmetry: it can create obligations instantly and extinguish them only on schedule. Trading creates promises now. Settlement extinguishes promises later. The gap between now and later is exposure, and exposure is the distance between what has been agreed and what has been delivered. That distance is managed through netting, margin, and discipline, but it cannot be eliminated. It can only be contained and priced.

A settlement system performs four tasks that look administrative and behave systemic. It transfers cash in accepted final media. It transfers securities as control of a claim inside a custody hierarchy. It enforces cut-offs and calendars that decide what counts as on-time. It produces records that become evidence. The third and fourth tasks allocate penalties and decide disputes, which is why they are the most political parts of the handshake.

The cash leg is not merely paying money. It is paying in accepted final media under accepted timelines. Final media is the instrument the system treats as extinguishment rather than as another promise. When final media is strong, settlement becomes less about credit and more about timing and operational correctness. When final media is scarce, settlement becomes a liquidity contest and not a solvency contest. A participant can be economically sound and still fail because it cannot produce final media at the deadline. The system punishes deadline failure because deadline failure is a contagion generator.

The securities leg is not merely delivering a share. It is delivering control of a claim inside a custody stack designed for scale. A central depository holds the top record. Custodians hold sub-records. Brokers hold omnibus accounts. End investors hold beneficial claims. This layering exists because direct registration for every trade would not scale. The cost is that the handshake is a reconciliation event across multiple ledgers, and reconciliation is where settlement risk becomes visible.

Reconciliation is the stability labor that keeps layering from turning into conflict. If the broker ledger says a customer owns, the custodian ledger says the broker owns, and the depository ledger says the custodian owns, the system is stable only if these statements align precisely at cut-offs. When they do not align, exceptions occur. Exceptions create delays. Delays create fails. Fails create penalties and funding stress. Funding stress forces liquidation. The handshake is therefore not back-office detail. It is the machine's core stabilizer because it determines whether trades become property without producing disputes that freeze liquidity.

Settlement cut-offs are the machine's hidden time gates. Trades can execute continuously, but settlement must occur within cycles and within daily deadlines for instruction, collateral, and delivery. Instructions must be submitted by a cut-off. Securities must be delivered by a cut-off. Cash must be delivered by a cut-off. Missing a cut-off can turn a trade into a fail even if both sides still want completion. Once a trade is in fail status, it becomes chargeable: penalties, buy-ins, higher funding costs, tighter credit terms, and reputational damage that increases future margin demands.

Cut-offs shape behavior upstream. Market makers price settlement risk into spreads. Brokers route away from counterparties and venues associated with higher fail rates. Internalizers prefer paths that minimize downstream settlement complexity. Liquidity concentrates where completion is cheap, not necessarily where fundamentals are strongest. The surface narrative calls this efficiency. The operational reality is that the system rewards assets and pathways with low completion friction.

Finality is a legal definition enforced by irreversibility and evidence. If transfers can be reversed easily, participants hoard, spreads widen, and activity collapses because every completion becomes contestable. Irrevocability is therefore a stability requirement. Yet irreversibility is dangerous if errors cannot be corrected. Operational errors occur constantly: mismatched identifiers, misrouted instructions, incorrect quantities, late confirmations, corporate action misallocations, and custody breaks. The system must therefore define an error-correction regime that does not destroy finality. Error correction exists, but it is constrained: defined windows, defined procedures, and evidence thresholds that prevent correction from becoming a tool of opportunism.

Delivery-versus-payment discipline is the handshake's core method for preventing one-sided performance. If cash moves and securities do not, the buyer faces loss. If securities move and cash does not, the seller faces loss. One-sided performance is the oldest source of credit contagion in markets. The system therefore enforces synchronized exchange: both legs happen under controlled conditions, or neither happens, with rule-defined sequencing that minimizes temporary exposure.

Synchronization is not automatic. It requires systems aligned on time and instruction formats, and it requires liquidity in final media at the moment of settlement. When synchronization fails, temporary credit exposures appear through intraday credit, settlement guarantees, or liquidity facilities. These facilities are gates. Those who can access them settle reliably. Those who cannot face higher fail risk and must widen spreads or reduce activity. The market's fairness narrative rarely mentions intraday liquidity because mentioning it reveals that completion is subsidized by privileged access to funding.

Settlement is also a compression engine. The system cannot move gross obligations in real time for every trade without overwhelming capacity. It compresses through netting, through centralized clearing, and through batching. Batching is not merely operational convenience. Batching is how the system converts continuous trading into scheduled finality. Scheduled finality creates exposure windows. Exposure windows are funded by margin and by credit. Credit availability becomes a market condition, and market conditions become pricing inputs.

The handshake's structure can be understood by tracing the lifecycle of a trade through the completion stack without relying on slogans.

Trade capture produces an execution record and timestamps across multiple systems. The record is replicated in broker ledgers, venue logs, and downstream clearing files. If record replication is imperfect, mismatches occur later in instruction generation and in reconciliation. This is why messaging standards and identifier discipline are not clerical trivia. They are settlement stability inputs.

Allocation and affirmation translate a fill into ownership claims inside pooled accounts. A single execution can be split among subaccounts. Splitting must occur under deadlines. Splitting errors are settlement errors because settlement systems do not care about intent. They care about correct instructions. Automation reduces splitting errors. Automation is a scale advantage because it lowers exception costs per trade.

Clearing acceptance transforms a bilateral match into a centrally managed obligation. If clearing is delayed or if eligibility checks fail, the trade's completion path becomes uncertain. Uncertainty changes funding behavior because participants hold extra liquidity buffers. Buffers reduce risk-taking. Reduced risk-taking widens spreads.

Instruction generation converts the trade into deliverable formats: which account delivers, which account receives, which identifier is valid, which cash account pays, which settlement date applies, which corporate action eligibility is implied. This step is where small data errors become expensive market outcomes. A single wrong identifier can turn a clean trade into a fail and a penalty.

Matching at settlement utilities is where both sides must agree on the same instruction. Unmatched instructions create exceptions. Exceptions are time bombs under cut-offs. The system's stability depends on the speed of exception resolution, which is why operational labor is a hidden liquidity provision function.

Delivery is the actual movement. Finality is the legal condition attached to the movement. Post-settlement reporting is the preservation of evidence: who did what, when, and under which rule. Evidence is what allows the system to punish bad behavior without punishing ordinary participation.

Settlement fails are the most visible output of handshake fragility. A fail is not one thing. It is a category. It includes instruction fails, inventory fails, funding fails, system outage fails, and strategic withholding. Because fails have multiple causes, the system must punish fails in a way that deters opportunism without turning ordinary error into systemic liquidation. That balance is why fail policy becomes a continuous object of negotiation between stability and profitability.

The penalty regime is the first line of deterrence. Penalties can be daily fees, escalating fees, loss of privileges, higher clearing charges, and reputational consequences that tighten financing terms. Penalties do not need to be dramatic. Their power lies in changing the cost of using the market as an option rather than as a commitment. If failing is cheap, failing becomes a strategy. If failing is expensive, failing becomes rare, and liquidity providers can price completion risk lower.

Yet penalty regimes create their own feedback loops. If penalties are high, liquidity providers price penalty risk into spreads, and spreads widen for everyone. If penalties are low, fails increase, and spreads widen because completion becomes uncertain. The system searches for an equilibrium that keeps average completion reliable while keeping trading volume high.

Buy-ins are the system's forced correction tool. They exist because delivery must be enforceable if prices are to be trusted. A buy-in forces procurement of the undelivered security and charges the failing party. Buy-ins preserve finality and protect the receiving side. They also create forced demand that can amplify scarcity. Scarcity amplification can create squeezes in instruments with limited lendable supply. The system therefore designs buy-ins with timing and thresholds, and those design choices allocate pain between stability and market impact.

Securities lending is embedded inside settlement, not adjacent to it. A short sale is a promise to deliver on settlement date, and delivery often requires borrowing. Borrowing is funded, collateralized, and priced. Borrow cost rises under stress, and borrow availability can collapse in the instruments that matter most. When borrow collapses, fails rise. When fails rise, buy-ins increase. When buy-ins increase, scarcity worsens. Scarcity loops are settlement loops.

Funding is the other embedded dependency. Settlement requires cash at the deadline. Cash must be obtained through funding markets or through internal liquidity. In stress, funding markets tighten. Tightening is expressed as higher haircuts, reduced credit lines, and higher rates. These changes force participants to liquidate assets to raise cash. Liquidation changes prices. Price changes increase volatility. Volatility increases margin. Margin increases cash demand. The settlement layer therefore couples to the risk warehouse through funding loops.

This coupling is why the final handshake is the system's choke point during crises. Execution can continue even when funding is stressed, but settlement cannot. Settlement deadlines convert funding stress into forced behavior. Forced behavior creates price dislocations. Dislocations increase volatility. Volatility increases margin calls. The spiral becomes mechanical.

The system uses redundancy to protect settlement: netting and collateralization. Netting reduces movement and reduces the number of opportunities for failure. Collateralization ensures that if failure occurs, losses are covered. Yet redundancy creates dependence on central nodes and their rulebooks, and dependence concentrates power. Central nodes control haircuts, eligibility, and timing. Those controls decide who survives a stress episode without liquidation.

Custody layering is the handshake's quiet source of legal ambiguity and therefore of power. Investors experience ownership as a statement. Legal reality is a record in a depository and its sub-ledgers. Under normal conditions, the difference is invisible because the system reconciles continuously. Under stress, the difference becomes decisive because disputes require authoritative records and authoritative timestamps.

Corporate actions expose this layering with ruthless clarity. A dividend, a vote, a split, or a tender forces the system to name a holder at a cut-off. Naming depends on settlement status and custody status. If settlement lags, entitlement becomes contested. Contested entitlement creates risk premiums around key dates. Those premiums widen spreads. Wider spreads increase cost of capital. Issuers then adjust timing of actions and disclosure, not only for governance reasons but for completion reasons. The market machine shapes issuer governance through the settlement calendar.

Record dates also reveal the difference between recognized ownership and economic exposure. A participant can have economic exposure through derivatives or through unsettled trades and still lack recognized entitlement at record date. The difference matters because entitlements are cash and votes. The settlement and custody layers therefore allocate rights through timing. Timing becomes a distribution mechanism, and distribution mechanisms become political when large sums and control rights are involved.

Cross-border settlement multiplies handshake risk because time zones, legal regimes, and payment systems differ. One leg can settle in one system while the other leg is delayed elsewhere. Temporary exposures appear and must be funded. Funding is a gate. Institutions with global liquidity access and robust legal enforceability settle smoothly. Institutions without pay through delays, higher spreads, and higher fail risk. Cross-border settlement therefore reinforces concentration in institutions and jurisdictions with superior enforcement and funding infrastructure.

Legal enforceability is a settlement prerequisite. Settlement depends on enforceable netting, enforceable collateral seizure, enforceable finality rules, and predictable default treatment. Jurisdictions that provide these become hubs. Hubs become leverage points because they host critical completion infrastructure. This is why completion plumbing has geopolitical weight even when it is described as neutral infrastructure.

Settlement capacity is not just system throughput. It includes human exception handling and reconciliation staffing. A capacity shortage creates hidden illiquidity because capital becomes trapped in unsettled positions. Trapped capital increases funding demand. Funding demand tightens credit. Credit tightening reduces liquidity provision. Liquidity reduction widens spreads. The market looks volatile. The driver can be settlement capacity strain rather than new information about value.

Capacity strain becomes visible in backlogs and unmatched instructions. Unmatched instructions signal higher fail probability. Brokers route away from counterparties with high mismatch rates. Liquidity concentrates in counterparties with better settlement performance. Better performance attracts more flow. More flow funds better systems. Settlement becomes a selection mechanism favoring operational competence and funding access. The system defends this as integrity. The distributional effect is that scale compounds.

Good delivery standards define what counts as valid for settlement. Standards reduce disputes and prevent delivery of questionable instruments. Standards also create gates because only instruments that meet standards are easy to settle. Instruments with complex features or unclear eligibility become expensive to trade because settlement risk is higher. The machine nudges markets toward standardization, and standardization concentrates liquidity in standardized instruments and standardized pathways.

Clearing and settlement are coupled. If settlement fails rise, clearinghouses tighten margin and reduce tolerance for exposures that could become losses. If margin tightens, participants liquidate and scramble for collateral and cash. That scramble increases settlement stress. The handshake sits inside this feedback system. Preventing a spiral requires liquidity supply, operational resilience, and an error-correction regime that keeps finality credible while allowing repairs.

Central bank liquidity regimes shape the handshake because they shape the availability of final media. If final media is expensive or scarce under stress, margin calls and settlement deadlines force liquidation. If final media is available, participants can meet deadlines without selling into stress, damping the spiral. Crisis response often takes the form of liquidity provision because liquidity provision prevents the handshake's deadlines from turning into forced selling cascades.

Proof is the handshake's legitimacy layer. Markets must prove. Proof requires records. Records require timestamp integrity and preservation. Evidence standards determine which records count. Evidence standards allocate power: the party with authoritative records wins disputes. The party without must accept negotiated outcomes. This is another gate that advantages those with infrastructure and scale.

Timestamp authority is consequential because multiple timestamps exist: venue time, broker time, clearing time, settlement utility time, custody update time. Which timestamp is authoritative decides who is early, who is late, and who is penalized. Participants invest to align with authoritative clocks and logs. These are costs of participation that larger firms amortize easily.

The handshake's governing variables can be stated without metaphor: time, collateral, records, and penalties. Time decides who must act and who can wait. Collateral decides who can hold and who must liquidate. Records decide reality in disputes. Penalties decide whether failure is option or violation. These variables are expressed as technical rules. They allocate cost and survival.

Expansion begins at the edge cases where settlement stops being a routine and becomes a stress amplifier. Edge cases matter because they reveal what the machine protects and what it sacrifices.

Consider a clustered fail event. Many trades fail at once, not because many traders suddenly become dishonest, but because a shared funding shock drains final media and a shared operational shock reduces exception capacity. The system sees a surge in unmatched instructions. Settlement utilities issue warnings. Clearinghouses increase intraday margin calls because exposures are now riskier. Participants scramble for cash and eligible collateral. To raise cash, participants sell liquid assets. The selling pushes prices down. Prices down raise volatility. Volatility triggers higher margin. Higher margin drains more cash. The loop accelerates.

In this scenario, the settlement system is not a passive victim. It is a gate that turns uncertainty into deadlines. Deadlines force action. Forced action produces price movement. Price movement feeds back into funding. The system's stabilizing move is to create an orderly priority: who must pay now, who can defer, and what counts as acceptable collateral. That priority is implemented by clearing and settlement rules, and those rules distribute pain.

The system's second stabilizing move is to ration final media through collateral eligibility. In stress, only high-quality collateral is accepted widely. This creates a collateral squeeze. A collateral squeeze forces participants to sell less eligible assets to obtain eligible collateral. Asset selling spreads stress across markets, even markets unrelated to the initial shock. This is how settlement systems can propagate panic indirectly: the need to meet deadlines creates a demand for certain collateral and a supply of other assets.

The system's third stabilizing move is to tighten settlement discipline. This can include stricter matching requirements, stricter instruction formats, and stricter penalties. Stricter discipline reduces strategic failing and improves long-run reliability. In the short run, stricter discipline can increase fails if participants are already strained. This is why discipline is often staged rather than imposed instantly. Staging is discretion. Discretion invites accusations. Accusations threaten legitimacy. The system therefore prefers rule-based staging that can be defended as automatic.

The system's fourth stabilizing move is to expand exception processing. That means staffing, automation, and triage. Triage is where politics enters operationally: which exceptions are resolved first, which counterparties receive priority assistance, which instruments are treated as critical. Criticality is not moral. It is systemic: instruments used widely as collateral or benchmarks receive priority because their failure would ripple. Priority is power.

The handshake is also where the market's clock meets the legal clock. The market clock is fast and continuous. The legal clock is slower and cut-off driven. Record dates, settlement cycles, and evidence windows are legal-clock constructs. The market's ability to treat trades as real depends on these legal clocks not being overwhelmed.

When legal clocks are overwhelmed, disputes rise. When disputes rise, participants widen spreads to price the probability that completion will be contested.

This is why legal infrastructure is settlement infrastructure. Courts that can handle disputes quickly reduce the risk premium. Registries that can confirm ownership quickly reduce entitlement uncertainty. Evidence regimes that are predictable reduce the cost of proof. Predictable proof reduces the cost of participation. Lower cost deepens liquidity. The handshake is therefore a public-capacity dependent mechanism even though it is administered by private nodes.

The final handshake also defines the border between trading and money. A claim can be traded without being money. A claim becomes money-like only when it can be settled with near certainty and near speed. Settlement certainty is the condition for using a claim as collateral widely. Collateral use is what turns the claim into funding capacity. Funding capacity is money-like. The handshake is the conversion process.

This is why settlement modernization is often framed as efficiency while behaving as a power shift. Shorter settlement cycles reduce exposure windows, reducing margin needs and reducing funding stress. They also increase the value of automation and increase the penalty for those without operational capacity. Shorter cycles can reduce systemic risk while increasing exclusion pressure. The system often accepts this because exclusion can be defended as integrity.

The handshake's final observation is that markets do not fail first at execution. They fail first at completion. Completion is where promises become property. Property requires records, time gates, collateral, and enforcement. The institutions that control those levers control the market's real sovereignty.

CHAPTER 15
WHO OWNS THE SHARE — REALLY?
BENEFICIAL OWNERSHIP, LEGAL TITLE, AND THE LAYERS BETWEEN INVESTOR AND ASSET.

Ownership in modern markets is a layered claim, not a single fact. The investor experiences ownership as a statement line and a quantity of units. The issuer experiences ownership as a registry and a list of recognized holders. The legal system experiences ownership as title recorded in a depository-ledger hierarchy and as rights that attach to whoever is recognized at cut-offs. These experiences align often enough that daily commerce can treat ownership as simple. They diverge in the moments that decide money and control: corporate actions, votes, disputes, insolvencies, enforcement, collateral seizures, and record-date eligibility. The gap between lived ownership and recognized ownership is where power and risk accumulate, because the gap decides who receives entitlements, who can pledge collateral, who is protected in default, and who can enforce rights without negotiating through an intermediary.

The first distinction is beneficial ownership versus legal title. Beneficial ownership is the economic exposure and entitlement expectation held by the end investor. Legal title is the name in the ledger that the settlement system and issuer-side recordkeeping treat as the holder. In a layered custody stack, legal title often sits at a central depository or at its nominee, with custodians and brokers holding sub-positions. Beneficial ownership sits at the edge. The market scales by allowing beneficial owners to trade through intermediaries without updating issuer registries for every trade. The cost of scale is that the legal system must decide what beneficial ownership means when it is not identical to title, and must decide how far beneficial claims travel when the intermediary fails or when records conflict.

The second distinction is record ownership versus control rights. Many rights attach to record date: dividends, distributions, votes, tender eligibility, corporate action participation, and sometimes tax reporting obligations. Record date is a time gate. The system must name a holder at that gate. The named holder is typically the legal title holder at the top of the custody chain rather than the ultimate beneficial owner. The system then relies on intermediaries to pass through entitlements and instructions to beneficial owners. Pass-through works in calm conditions because incentives and operations align. Pass-through becomes fragile under stress because timing tightens, funding strains, and the legal system prioritizes the top-of-stack record when conflicts arise.

The third distinction is contract rights versus property rights. An investor's relationship with a broker is usually contractual. The broker owes the investor a claim on assets held in omnibus form, governed by account agreements, segregation rules, and insolvency regimes. A contractual claim can be strong, but it is still mediated. Property rights are rights against the world, enforceable through courts and registries without needing an intermediary's cooperation. In layered custody, the beneficial owner often holds a contractual right that behaves like property most of the time, and then discovers its boundaries when the machine is stressed. The system's legitimacy depends on those boundaries not being experienced as arbitrary.

The custody stack exists because direct registration for every trade would collapse throughput. If every transfer required issuer registry updates and individualized confirmation, settlement would slow, disputes would multiply, and liquidity would thin. The system therefore centralizes the master record and allows intermediaries to maintain sub-ledgers. That creates two systemic risks. First, reconciliation risk: ledgers must match. Second, recognition risk: the party who controls the authoritative ledger controls who is treated as owner at the moment rights are assigned. Recognition determines entitlement and enforcement, which is why the custody layer is not an administrative footnote but a governance layer.

A modern share can be thought of as three things at once: a claim on cash flows, a claim on governance rights, and a token used in funding chains. The first two are obvious. The third is the machine's hidden use. Shares are pledged as collateral, lent to enable shorting, rehypothecated to fund inventories, and used as balance-sheet lubricant. The beneficial owner can believe the asset sits quietly while the system uses it as a movable unit in multiple financing relationships, all of which depend on custody records and on legal title definitions.

The ownership machine therefore is a chain of recordkeeping and entitlement processing roles: issuer registrars and transfer agents, central depositories, custodians, brokers, securities lenders, and corporate action processors. Each maintains records under different formats, cut-offs, and evidence standards. The investor's "ownership" is the product of these records being consistent enough that the system can treat the investor as owner for practical purposes.

The simplest way to see why ownership is layered is to trace how a share is born and then how it is traded. At issuance, the issuer creates shares, and the initial ownership is recorded at the issuer registry. In practice, large issuance is mediated through depositories and intermediaries so that the issuer's registry does not need to track millions of small holders. The registry will show a small number of record holders that represent aggregated positions. That aggregation is the seed of the beneficial-title split. It is how the system scales and how the system creates the need for pass-through.

Once the share exists, secondary trading occurs at high speed. Each trade is recorded in broker systems and venue logs. Clearing and settlement then net and deliver positions at the depository and custodian level. The issuer's registry is often unchanged by this daily churn because the record holder remains the depository nominee while beneficial interests are updated within intermediary sub-ledgers. This is why the public can trade continuously while the issuer's list of record holders remains stable. The system is effectively operating two markets at once: a market of beneficial claims and a market of legal title records. The bridge between them is custody and corporate action processing.

Corporate actions are the moments when the bridge must hold weight. A dividend requires that cash be assigned to holders. The issuer pays to the record holder. The record holder passes funds to custodians. Custodians pass to brokers. Brokers pass to customers. Each step relies on accurate position records as of record date and on accurate mapping between accounts and beneficial owners. If mapping fails, money is misallocated. Misallocation creates disputes. Disputes require evidence. Evidence is drawn from custody records and time-stamped positions. The participant with stronger evidence and recognized authority tends to win.

Voting is similar but more politically sensitive because votes are control rights. The issuer solicits votes from record holders. Record holders distribute voting entitlements to beneficial owners via proxy mechanisms. Beneficial owners submit instructions. Those instructions are aggregated and passed back up. The process is necessarily indirect because the issuer does not know individual beneficial owners in a layered system. This indirection creates space for errors, delays, and mismatches between who believes they can vote and who is recognized as entitled to vote. The system's legitimacy depends on these mismatches being rare and repairable, because governance legitimacy is an ownership legitimacy.

Record date timing is therefore a fundamental gate. A share purchased after record date may carry economic exposure but not the right to receive the next dividend. A share sold before record date may remove ownership exposure but still leave the seller entitled if settlement timing is misaligned. The system manages these edge cases with due-bill regimes and entitlement adjustments. Due bills are the mechanism by which an entitlement is transferred economically even if legal record ownership at record date does not reflect the trade. Due bills are complex. Complexity creates disputes. Disputes create proof burdens. Proof burdens advantage scale.

The custody stack is also designed to allow securities lending and shorting. Lending depends on the ability to deliver a share to a borrower while maintaining a claim to get it back. That is a custody and contract problem. It requires records of loaned shares, collateral posted by the borrower, and mechanisms to recall shares when needed. When shares are loaned, the lender may lose voting rights or may need to recall to vote. This is another instance where beneficial ownership is economic exposure but not necessarily control. The market tolerates this because lending improves liquidity and tightens spreads. It also creates governance distortions because votes can be separated from economic exposure. The system manages this through disclosure rules and through institutional norms, but the separation remains a structural feature.

Rehypothecation and collateral chains deepen the separation. A share can be pledged as collateral by an intermediary, then re-pledged by the receiving party, creating multiple layers of claims on the same underlying asset. Each layer is governed by contract and by custody entries. In calm times, these chains increase liquidity and reduce funding costs. In stress, chains reveal their fragility because multiple parties believe they have a right to the same collateral.

Priority rules then decide who is protected. Priority rules are the hidden constitution of ownership in crisis.

Insolvency is the moment when ownership becomes real. When an intermediary fails, beneficial owners discover whether their claims are treated as segregated client assets, as protected interests, or as unsecured claims. The outcome depends on segregation practices, custody arrangements, and legal regimes. Segregation is not just a label. It is operational discipline: whether the intermediary actually maintained separation in its books, whether securities were properly held in protected accounts, whether loans and rehypothecation were within contractual limits, and whether records are clean enough to support rapid transfer.

Transfer in insolvency is often called porting. Porting is moving client positions from a failing intermediary to a surviving one without forcing liquidation. Porting is crucial because forced liquidation in insolvency can amplify market stress and can punish beneficial owners for an intermediary's failure. Porting requires clean records and willing recipients. Willing recipients require that positions are properly collateralized and that exposures are manageable. Under stress, willingness can vanish. If willingness vanishes, beneficial owners become trapped in the insolvency process. Trapped owners experience ownership as a claim, not as property. This is why the custody stack's stability depends on incentives and backstop arrangements that keep porting feasible even when fear rises.

The ownership stack also defines who bears operational error. If a broker misallocates a corporate action, the broker may correct through adjustments, but correction depends on rules and evidence windows. If a custodian mismatches positions, settlement fails can occur. Settlement fails can trigger penalties and buy-ins. Penalties and buy-ins can move prices. Price moves can create losses for participants uninvolved in the original error. The system therefore socializes some operational error costs through spreads, because liquidity providers price the probability of settlement disruption. The public experiences this as trading cost. The machine experiences it as the price of running layered ownership at scale.

Beneficial ownership is therefore a social fiction backed by enforcement: a claim that society agrees to treat as property because the system's routines make it reliable enough. The fiction must remain reliable enough in edge cases, because edge cases are where legitimacy is tested. A system that works in calm times and fails in stressed times is not stable; it is merely quiet until tested.

Ownership layers also create asymmetry in enforcement. If a beneficial owner wants to enforce rights against the issuer, the beneficial owner may have to act through the intermediary chain because the issuer recognizes record holders. If a beneficial owner wants to enforce in court, the evidence may sit at the depository and custodian levels. Access to evidence becomes a gate. Parties with better access to records can litigate more effectively. Parties without access must settle or accept disadvantage. Evidence access is therefore a power surface embedded inside custody.

The system defends this arrangement by claiming that intermediaries represent beneficial owners. Representation can be real and can also be conflicted. An intermediary may have incentives that differ from those of its customers, especially in situations involving corporate actions, voting, or settlement disputes. The law attempts to manage this through fiduciary duties and through client protection rules. Yet the operational reality is that representation is mediated by procedures, and procedures can fail. The beneficial owner's protection is therefore not only legal text. It is operational competence and enforcement willingness.

The ownership stack is also a timing stack. Beneficial ownership statements update quickly. Legal title updates on settlement cycles. Corporate actions assign rights at record dates. Disputes are resolved on legal clocks. These clocks can be misaligned. Misalignment creates opportunities for arbitrage and creates risks of misallocation. Those who understand timing can profit. Those who do not pay hidden taxes. Timing is therefore an ownership gate just as it is a trading gate.

The system's approach to timing misalignment often relies on standardized conventions: ex-date conventions, due-bill processes, settlement cycle definitions, and correction windows. These conventions are necessary. They also create complexity that can be exploited by sophisticated participants and can confuse ordinary participants. Complexity is not merely a byproduct. Complexity is also a moat because it makes full participation expensive.

Ownership also interacts with taxes. Tax authorities often require identification of holders and timing of realization. In a layered system, beneficial owners may have tax obligations while legal title holders appear on registry records. Reporting then relies on intermediaries. Intermediary reporting errors can create tax disputes. Tax disputes rely on evidence. Evidence relies on records. Again, ownership becomes a recordkeeping power contest under the surface of everyday statements.

The ownership machine therefore must be understood as a bundle of constraints the system manages to preserve scale. It preserves scale by aggregating record ownership, by netting settlement, by allowing intermediated pass-through, and by using standardized conventions for entitlements and voting. Each choice reduces friction. Each choice creates a gate. Gates are priced. The resulting structure allows billions of trades to be processed while keeping issuer registries stable. It also ensures that the people with the most direct control over authoritative records are not necessarily the ultimate owners. That separation is the machine's core feature and its core legitimacy risk.

The deepest consequence of the layered system is that the investor's ownership is a claim on a chain of institutions. The chain works because each node is regulated, capitalized, and operationally disciplined enough that society trusts the chain. Trust is not sentimental. Trust is the expectation that if a node fails, procedures will protect beneficial owners. Those procedures include segregation, porting, default waterfalls, and insurance-like protections. Each protection has limits. Limits are often discovered only in stress.

Stress episodes expose which protections are structural and which are rhetorical. Structural protections are those that operate automatically: segregation that is truly maintained, title records that can be reconstructed quickly, porting that is executable, and legal regimes that prioritize client assets. Rhetorical protections are those that sound comforting but depend on discretion, on slow litigation, or on incomplete records. The system's stability depends on structural protections dominating rhetorical ones.

Ownership is therefore less a noun and more a process. It is the process by which a claim becomes recognized at the right cut-offs and remains defensible in disputes. The process requires records, reconciliation, and enforcement. Each component is a business and a gate. Central depositories and custodians sell recordkeeping. Brokers sell access. Corporate action processors sell entitlement distribution. Securities lenders sell borrowing and liquidity. Each fee is justified as service. Each also is a toll for the privilege of having ownership behave like property at scale.

The ownership stack also affects market power. Institutions that sit closer to legal title and custody records can influence how quickly entitlements are processed and how disputes are resolved. They can also influence how collateral is treated, because collateral depends on clear title. Clear title depends on their ledgers. This gives them indirect power over funding conditions. Funding conditions influence who can hold positions and who must liquidate. Thus ownership records influence trading outcomes, not only legal outcomes.

The machine's final ownership paradox is that it must be both centralized and distributed. Centralized enough that records are authoritative and disputes can be resolved. Distributed enough that millions of owners can trade without direct registry interaction. The compromise is layered custody. Layered custody makes ownership scalable and makes ownership contestable. The system maintains legitimacy by keeping contest rare and by providing procedures when contest occurs. The procedures are the real definition of ownership.

CHAPTER 16
THE MYTHS THE MARKET TELLS ABOUT ITSELF
THE STORIES THAT PRESERVE LEGITIMACY, DISGUISE GATES, AND TURN TOLL ROADS INTO "FAIRNESS."

The market survives on a set of stories that are simple enough to repeat, moral enough to defend, and elastic enough to contain contradiction. These stories are not merely public relations. They are functional myths that stabilize participation, justify gatekeeping, and turn a machine built on tolls into a civic institution in the imagination. A myth in this context is not a lie in the childish sense. It is a framing that hides mechanisms in plain sight by replacing them with a narrative that feels like common sense. The machine needs myths because the machine's real operating logic is distributive. If the distribution were stated plainly, legitimacy would fracture.

The first myth is that the market is a place. The market is not a place. It is a protocol stack of permissions, queues, timestamps, and recognition rules. People picture a room where buyers meet sellers and agree on a price. That picture is comforting because it implies symmetry and immediacy. The machine is asymmetric and delayed. Orders do not merely "meet." They are routed through eligibility filters, exposed or internalized, sliced and staged, and executed under microstructure rules that allocate priority. Trades do not merely "happen." They become obligations, then exposures, then net positions, then margin demands, then settlement instructions, then custody entries, then entitlement assignments. The market is not a place because a place suggests one coherent view. The machine exists as layered reality with paid visibility tiers.

The second myth is that prices are discovered. Prices are produced. Discovery implies that value already exists and the market finds it through competition. Production is closer to the truth: price is the output of a contest among constraints. Liquidity providers quote under adverse selection risk. Funding conditions determine how long they can hold inventory. Margin models determine when they must liquidate. Data tiers determine who can cancel before being picked off. Routing determines which trades become visible prints and which are internalized. Officialness rules determine which prints count as reference. A produced price can be a useful signal. It is still produced, which means it is shaped by gates and by paid proximity to those gates.

The third myth is that the market rewards the best information. The market rewards the best completion. Information matters, but information without the ability to finish is only opinion. The machine rewards those who can execute without impact, clear without consuming expensive margin, settle without fails, and defend their decisions with proof packets. Completion is the scarce commodity because completion is what turns a probabilistic trade into enforceable property. Those who can complete cheaply can quote tighter. Those who quote tighter attract flow. Flow yields better information. Information then reinforces completion. The myth reverses causality to preserve the image of meritocracy.

The fourth myth is that liquidity is a public good. Liquidity is a product sold under conditions. Liquidity is offered by market makers and by passive resting orders when the expected cost of being wrong is lower than the expected compensation. Under stress, the compensation demanded rises, and the offered liquidity evaporates. Evaporation is not betrayal. It is the price of survival. The myth treats liquidity as an ambient property of a healthy market so that participants feel entitled to it. The machine treats liquidity as inventory capacity funded by balance sheets and protected by the ability to withdraw quickly. When liquidity disappears, the myth says panic. The mechanism says margin tightening, funding withdrawal, toxicity increases, and queue fragility.

The fifth myth is that the market is neutral. The machine is procedural, not neutral. Procedure is not neutrality. Procedure allocates advantage and pain. The queue decides who trades first. The feed decides who sees first. The clearing model decides who must post collateral now and who can wait. The settlement calendar decides who is entitled at cut-offs. The custody stack decides whose record counts in dispute. The routing logic decides who captures spread and who receives internalized fills. Each of these is defended as technical design. Technical design is a distribution mechanism. The market's neutrality myth exists to make distribution feel like gravity rather than governance.

The sixth myth is that regulation restrains the market. Regulation builds the market. Without enforceable evidence standards, registries, finality definitions, and penalty regimes, the machine would collapse into dispute and hoarding. Regulation does restrain some behavior. More fundamentally, it creates the conditions under which participants can treat a trade as property rather than as a fragile promise. The machine depends on regulation as the enforcement perimeter that makes records meaningful. The myth casts regulation as an external enemy so that the market can claim purity when it succeeds and blame when it fails. The truth is entanglement: enforcement and market design are braided.

The seventh myth is that the market allocates capital. The market allocates gate access, and capital allocation follows. Capital formation is episodic. Capital circulation is continuous. Most trading does not send money to issuers. It sends money between holders and intermediaries. The machine's activity can grow while formation is flat, and the public can confuse activity with investment. Capital allocation does occur through prices and through financing conditions, but those conditions are themselves shaped by completion costs, index rules, benchmark flows, and data-driven microstructure incentives. The market allocates capital partly by allocating liquidity. Liquidity is allocated by those who control completion and visibility. The myth compresses this into a moral statement: markets fund the best ideas. The mechanism is harsher: markets fund what is easiest to trade, easiest to collateralize, easiest to benchmark, and safest to clear under the warehouse's models.

The eighth myth is that volatility is irrational emotion. Volatility is often a funding and completion phenomenon. When margin rises, participants must post collateral or liquidate. Liquidation is forced. Forced liquidation moves price. Moving price increases volatility. Increased volatility increases margin again. This is not sentiment first. It is model-driven behavior expressed through spreads and depth. Emotion can amplify. The engine is mechanical: procyclical constraints, funding scarcity, and settlement deadlines. The myth is useful because it locates blame in psychology rather than in design.

The ninth myth is that the market is transparent because a price is visible. Visibility is tiered. The public feed is a civic window. Premium feeds are survivability tools. Depth, timestamp fidelity, imbalance messages, and venue-specific state changes are not experienced uniformly. A participant operating on slow abstraction pays the delay tax through adverse selection and worse routing. A participant operating on high-fidelity reality avoids being picked off and can quote tighter. The market can claim transparency because a number is visible. The machine profits because the useful reality is sold.

The tenth myth is that competition ensures fairness. Competition is bounded by gates. Markets can have many participants and still produce stable winners because gate access compounds. Those with cheaper funding can withstand stress and harvest forced sellers. Those with better data can cancel and avoid toxicity. Those with better routing intelligence can select favorable liquidity and avoid impact. Those with clearing advantages can hold inventory with less margin. Those with custody and settlement competence can recycle capital faster. Competition then plays out among those already inside the high-privilege perimeter. The myth exists because it makes the outcome feel like a tournament rather than like a layered toll road.

The eleventh myth is that best execution means best outcome. Best execution is a defensibility standard inside a range, not a guarantee of the optimal fill in hindsight. The machine uses that range. Routing choices can be justified as reasonable while also being optimized for broker economics, internalization arrangements, and proof burden. The investor sees the fill and believes it is the market. The machine sees the fill as one point in a set of defensible paths. The myth is necessary because admitting the range openly would raise the question of whose interests define the range, and the answer would point to gate power.

The twelfth myth is that market makers "provide" liquidity out of service. Market makers sell liquidity for a spread and for the right to withdraw. Their willingness is conditional on toxicity and funding. Their ability is conditional on margin and settlement. Their profit is conditional on seeing and canceling fast enough. The myth of service keeps the public from recognizing that liquidity provision is not charity and not purely competitive. It is a business that is structurally advantaged by data tiers, internalized flow, and the ability to hedge with lower friction than others.

The thirteenth myth is that the clearinghouse is a neutral safety net. The clearinghouse is a model-driven governor that sets the price of survival. Its margin rules determine who must liquidate. Its netting rules determine whose portfolios receive offsets. Its collateral rules determine which assets become money-like inside the machine. Its default procedures determine how pain is allocated. The clearinghouse is stability infrastructure. It is also a distribution mechanism. The myth of neutrality exists because the alternative is to admit that systemic safety is achieved by forcing certain participants to sell first and by charging certain participants more for the right to hold risk.

The fourteenth myth is that settlement is plumbing. Settlement is sovereignty. Settlement defines finality. Finality defines whether a trade is property. Property defines whether collateral is usable. Usable collateral defines whether leverage is possible. Leverage defines whether liquidity can be offered at tight spreads. Tight spreads define whether participation feels fair. The entire legitimacy chain runs through settlement and custody, and custody is layered. The myth of plumbing is convenient because it hides power in the back room.

The fifteenth myth is that ownership is simple. Ownership is layered and time-gated. Beneficial owners hold economic exposure. Legal title holders hold recognized record. Record dates assign rights. Pass-through relies on intermediaries. Securities lending and collateral chains create multiple claims. Insolvency reveals whose claim is protected. The myth exists because if ownership felt contingent, participation would demand a premium or withdraw. The system maintains the myth by making the layers work quietly most of the time.

The sixteenth myth is that markets are efficient in a way that implies justice. Efficiency is a measure of throughput and cost under the rules. A market can be efficient at extracting tolls, allocating visibility, and compressing settlement risk while still producing outcomes that feel unfair to those without gate access. The myth equates efficiency with virtue so that the machine's distributive outcomes can be defended as the result of natural laws rather than as a design.

The seventeenth myth is that fees are small and therefore irrelevant. Fees are often the least important toll. Delay is a toll. Spread is a toll. Margin is a toll. Haircuts are a toll. Financing rates are a toll. Data access is a toll. Proof burden is a toll. Custody and corporate action processing are tolls. These tolls do not appear on a single receipt. They appear as worse execution, as forced liquidation, as higher borrowing costs, as lost entitlements, and as the need to outsource complexity to intermediaries. The myth persists because visible fees are easy to debate. Hidden tolls are harder to see and therefore harder to contest.

The eighteenth myth is that crises are anomalies. Crises are stress tests of design. The machine is built to survive shocks by reallocating pain through margin, by throttling risk through funding, and by protecting officialness through tightening gates. Crises reveal who is allowed to fail and who is protected. They reveal which records count, which cut-offs are enforced, which exceptions are tolerated, and which behaviors are punished. The myth treats crises as rare storms. The mechanism treats crises as the moments when the machine shows its constitution.

The nineteenth myth is that innovation makes markets better by default. Innovation often means new gates and new tolls. Faster routing creates more fragmentation. More fragmentation increases the value of analytics and smart execution. Premium data becomes more valuable. Completion becomes more complex. Proof burden increases. Increased complexity advantages scale. Innovation can reduce certain costs and can also create new rents. The myth is progress. The mechanism is shifting advantage surfaces while preserving the need for legitimacy.

The twentieth myth is that participation is a choice made by individuals. Participation is shaped by institutions: retirement systems, benchmarks, passive flows, and the fact that household savings are routed into market products by default. When participation is structural, legitimacy becomes a public matter. The machine then must preserve a narrative of fairness while operating a tiered system. The myth of choice reduces pressure for redesign because it suggests that those harmed opted in. In reality, many are inside the system because wealth formation channels run through it.

These myths are not independent. They form a self-supporting architecture. Neutrality depends on the place myth. Fairness depends on the competition myth. Legitimacy depends on the transparency myth. Stability depends on the crisis-as-anomaly myth. Virtue depends on the efficiency myth. The machine's ability to charge tolls depends on the belief that it is a public utility rather than a private toll road.

The machine maintains myths through selective visibility and selective language. It highlights price discovery and hides completion. It highlights spreads and hides margin. It highlights execution and hides settlement. It highlights ownership statements and hides custody hierarchy. It highlights regulation as restraint and hides regulation as construction. It highlights volatility as emotion and hides volatility as model-driven funding behavior.

The purpose of Part II is not to sneer at these myths. The purpose is to treat them as operational necessities that can be redesigned. A society needs a capital allocation system that can scale. It also needs a legitimacy structure that allows households and enterprises to participate without feeling that the game is rigged beyond repair. If the myths collapse without replacement, participation shrinks, liquidity thins, and capital formation becomes expensive. The machine then becomes more extractive, because scarcity increases tolls.

The deeper danger is that myths can become brittle. When participants begin to experience too many visible contradictions at once, they stop believing. They hoard, withdraw, or demand higher returns. Higher returns raise the cost of capital. Higher cost reduces growth. Reduced growth increases political anger. Political anger triggers clumsy intervention. Clumsy intervention increases uncertainty. Uncertainty widens spreads. The spiral is not only financial. It is legitimacy-driven.

The exit from myth is not cynicism. It is mechanism literacy. Once the public understands that markets are designed systems with gates, tolls, and evidence regimes, debate can move from moral accusation to design choices: how to price visibility, how to constrain internalization, how to smooth margin procyclicality, how to strengthen beneficial ownership protections, how to reduce settlement fails, how to make officialness less steerable, and how to keep participation broad without making integrity impossible.

PART THREE

THE HOUSE BUILDS THE EDGE

WHY A MARKET CAN LOOK CHAOTIC ON THE SURFACE AND STILL PRODUCE STABLE WINNERS UNDERNEATH.

The surface looks like weather: a gust of orders, a sudden gap, a reversal that mocks the last story told about it, and a dozen explanations offered after the fact that fit only because they are vague enough to fit anything. Underneath, the system is not weather. It is a set of engineered constraints, and engineered constraints produce repeatable advantage for whoever owns the constraints, sells access to the constraints, or can endure the constraints when others cannot. The House is the ecosystem that profits from constraint. The House is not one villain in one room. It is the set of institutions that convert market functioning into tolls: officialness, visibility, completion, and the right to be early where being early matters.

Chaos is compatible with stable winners because stable winners do not need to forecast direction. They need to be paid for standing between forced buyers and forced sellers, between deadlines and inventory, between margin models and desperate funding, between benchmarks and the funds that must track them, between settlement cut-offs and the parties who will pay penalties if they miss them. The edge is built where behavior is not optional. Optional behavior is noisy. Forced behavior is harvestable. The machine produces forced behavior through schedules, models, and eligibility definitions, and then allows the House to price the cost of passing through those gates.

The edge begins with the price of immediacy. When a participant must trade now, that participant pays spread. Spread looks like a small tax until the market is stressed, and stress is when the House earns its most reliable rents because urgency spikes and willingness evaporates. A liquidity provider that can remain present when others withdraw can charge a higher price for immediacy. Remaining present is not courage. It is balance sheet, funding access, margin efficiency, hedging pathways, and the ability to see toxicity early enough to widen before being selected against. The market's surface sees widening spreads. The machine sees the price of survivability being repriced upward.

The edge continues with the price of visibility. A public quote is a civic artifact, good enough to preserve belief. The usable version of reality is higher fidelity: richer timestamps, deeper book information, more event types, faster delivery, and better inference about where liquidity actually is across fragmented venues. Higher fidelity reduces adverse selection, improves routing, and improves hedging. Those improvements can be turned into tighter quoting, which attracts flow. Flow yields more information. More information further reduces adverse selection. The loop compounds into dominance that looks like skill and is often gate proximity plus scale.

The House builds the edge by owning the path between intention and execution. Routing is a revenue decision disguised as an obligation. An order can be exposed to open competition or handled privately. Open competition can improve price while leaking intent. Private handling can reduce visible impact while shifting spread capture and informational advantage to the internalizer. The House profits when flow is predictable, because predictable flow can be warehoused and hedged cheaply. Flow becomes an asset class: not because it is mystical, but because it is statistically stable enough to optimize against. Stability of flow is purchased through broker relationships, payment arrangements, and the promise of consistent outcomes that can be defended as best execution within a plausible range.

Fragmentation is the House's amplifier. Fragmentation is defended as competition, but competition creates navigation costs, and navigation costs create dependence on those who can stitch the market together. The stitching requires data, connectivity, and strategy. Those require fixed costs. Fixed costs create scale advantages. Scale advantages allow operation across more venues, which makes fragmentation more tolerable for the largest participants and more punishing for smaller ones. The market becomes more complex, and complexity becomes a moat that does not need secrecy to work; it needs only that the cost of full participation is high.

The edge also lives in fee geometry. Fees are not merely charges; they are incentives that sculpt behavior. Rebates subsidize displayed liquidity and can make spreads look tight while moving the cost elsewhere. Connectivity fees sell priority access to the matching engine. Data licensing fees sell the right to see the market's usable reality. Clearing fees and netting rules sell balance-sheet efficiency. Custody fees sell the ability to have ownership behave like property without having to touch issuer registries directly. Each fee is a toll for passage through a gate, and the House's advantage is that it can pay wholesale and charge retail.

Wholesale versus retail is not only price. It is timing. The House buys earlier timestamps, faster cancels, and richer imbalance information. The House sells the appearance of fairness by keeping the public lane usable while monetizing the premium lanes. This design preserves legitimacy because most participants do not experience the premium lane directly; they experience it indirectly through consistent underperformance relative to headline prices that seem publicly visible but are not the same reality the House is trading in.

The edge is reinforced by the risk warehouse. Clearinghouses do not merely protect stability; they set the price of survival through margin. Margin rises when volatility rises. Rising margin forces collateral posting or liquidation. Those with cheap funding post. Those without liquidate. Liquidation creates price movement. Price movement increases volatility. Volatility increases margin again. The House profits when it is positioned to buy from forced sellers or to sell to forced buyers, and it is positioned because it can fund inventory longer and can absorb short-term mark-to-market pain without breaching constraints. This is endurance, and endurance is the compounder that converts small structural advantages into stable dominance.

The edge extends into collateral itself. Not all collateral is equal. Eligibility, haircuts, and reuse rights determine what can be turned into funding quickly. A participant with eligible collateral can meet deadlines without selling core positions. A participant without eligible collateral must sell to raise cash. The House accumulates eligible collateral and builds financing relationships that treat it as money-like. This turns collateral access into a quiet barrier to entry, because strategies that look simple at the surface become impossible when funding and haircuts are unfavorable.

Settlement is another edge surface that rarely looks like one. A participant that settles cleanly recycles capital quickly. Capital that is recycled quickly can be redeployed more times per period. A participant that suffers fails traps capital, pays penalties, and faces tighter credit terms. Operational competence becomes competitive advantage because it reduces the tax of delay. The House invests in operations not for virtue but for throughput: faster reconciliation, fewer mismatches, better corporate action processing, better evidence capture. Throughput reduces cost. Reduced cost allows tighter quoting. Tight quoting attracts flow. Flow yields information. The loop repeats.

Indexes and benchmarks create the House's favorite kind of constraint: scheduled forced behavior at scale. Rebalance windows, inclusion changes, and benchmark cut-offs force large funds to trade within defined windows. Windowed trading is predictable, and predictable trading is monetizable. The House positions ahead of these windows, sells liquidity into them, and buys liquidity from them, often without needing to predict anything beyond the fact that the trades must occur. The public sees volatility. The machine sees scheduled demand and supply. The House sees inventory opportunity and spread opportunity.

The edge also lives in the definition of officialness. The market needs a reference price that contracts and collateral systems can use. Whoever influences what counts as a valid print, which venues count for reference, and how anomalies are filtered influences downstream reality. This influence is exercised through microstructure, through data policy, through eligibility criteria, and through the methods that define consolidated reference signals. The House does not need to control officialness absolutely. It needs to know how officialness is computed and to trade around the computation with better visibility and better timing.

The edge becomes stable when the machine's enforcement and proof burdens are heavy. Proof burdens create fixed costs. Fixed costs advantage scale. Scale allows better compliance infrastructure, faster audit trail reconstruction, and more defensible routing choices. Better defensibility allows more aggressive optimization because the optimization can be wrapped in a documented process. Smaller participants face higher marginal proof cost per trade, which forces them into simpler strategies and worse execution, which reduces profitability, which reduces their ability to invest in infrastructure, which keeps them behind.

The House builds the edge by turning every mechanism that stabilizes the market into a product and every product into a tier. Tiers are not necessarily announced as tiers. They can be announced as professional tools, premium services, membership benefits, or technical connectivity. The distributional outcome is the same: the closer you are to the gate, the cheaper it is to trade and the easier it is to survive stress.

A market can therefore look chaotic and still produce stable winners because the chaos is expressed in price movement, while the winners are created by control over visibility, completion, funding, and scheduled forced behavior. The public reacts to the noise. The House prices the constraint. The machine keeps functioning because functioning is profitable, and profitable functioning attracts defense in the form of institutional privilege justified as integrity.

The system's most durable misdirection is that it frames the edge as talent. Talent exists. The deeper truth is that talent is paid most consistently when it is attached to gates. A brilliant forecast without funding is fragile. A mediocre forecast with privileged completion can still be profitable because the profit comes from being the conduit, not the oracle.

Part III maps how the edge is built without requiring conspiracy. It is built by owning or renting the points where the system must pass: data, routing, clearing, settlement, and the calendar-driven forced trades that make liquidity valuable.

The Bell Rings, the House Collects

The bell is theater. The collection is procedure. A new session begins with a collision of constraints: overnight inventory, scheduled orders, benchmark flows, risk limits resetting, and the need to convert yesterday's exposure into today's funded positions. The first visible prints look like a scramble because many intents arrive at once, and the public interprets simultaneity as unpredictability. Underneath, simultaneity is an opportunity because it concentrates urgency. Urgency is where spreads widen and where liquidity can be sold at a premium.

The House collects first by being the option seller in a world of deadlines. Some participants must buy now. Some must sell now. The House can stand between them if it has the balance sheet and the funding to warehouse inventory without immediate liquidation. The market maker who can quote when others step back collects spread. The internalizer who sees predictable flow collects spread. The broker who can steer flow collects economics. The exchange collects data and connectivity fees from everyone who must participate. The warehouse collects margin discipline, which is not a fee in name but is a cost that redistributes survivability.

The House collects second through time compression. Faster visibility allows faster cancellation. Faster cancellation reduces loss. Reduced loss allows tighter quoting. Tight quoting attracts flow. Flow yields more information about urgency and toxicity. More information reduces adverse selection. The loop is quiet and repeatable. The public sees a price and believes it is shared reality. The House sees a richer and earlier version of the same reality and trades against those who act on delayed abstraction.

The House collects third through scheduling. Many of the largest flows are not discretionary. They are required by index rules, benchmark reporting, and risk constraints. These flows arrive in patterns tied to calendars and cut-offs. Predictable patterns are monetizable. The House does not need to predict the world. It needs to predict when the world must transact.

The House collects fourth through completion advantage. Clean settlement, clean custody records, and fast exception repair recycle capital faster. Recycled capital can be redeployed more times. More redeployments mean more spread opportunities captured. The public lane experiences this as smooth functioning. The House experiences it as throughput that turns small per-trade edges into large aggregate rent.

The interlude's function is to set the tone: visible chaos can coexist with private stability because the machine's stability is not a moral state. It is the product of gates that allocate time, visibility, and completion, and of tolls that fund the gates. Whoever owns the toll road does not need to control the weather.

CHAPTER 17
WHAT THE EXCHANGE REALLY SELLS
LISTINGS, TRADING, DATA, AND THE REVENUE ARCHITECTURE BEHIND THE PUBLIC FACE OF THE MARKET.

An exchange is not primarily a place where buyers and sellers meet. It is a business that sells recognition, and recognition is the most valuable commodity in a system built on promises. Recognition is the ability to turn a private intention into a public fact other systems will accept: a listed instrument that mandates can hold, a printed trade that collateral agreements and benchmarks can reference, a timestamped sequence that survives dispute, and a venue status that regulators and courts treat as presumptively legitimate. The exchange sells recognition through products that look separate and behave as one machine: admission, execution, visibility, and enforceability.

Admission is listing, and listing is not ceremony. Listing is the conversion of an issuer into a tradable object with standardized obligations. The issuer pays to be admitted because admission purchases eligibility, and eligibility is demand. Many pools of capital do not choose freely among all claims; they choose among claims that satisfy rules. Admission gives a claim a passport: it becomes eligible for vehicles with strict mandates, for portfolios governed by rules-based constraints, and for fiduciaries who can defend holding decisions by pointing at the exchange's wrapper. Listing therefore is not only a business transaction between issuer and venue. It is a conversion of a claim into a reference-grade instrument.

A listing has three economic functions that are often discussed as one. It lowers perceived fraud risk by forcing disclosure and governance routines. It lowers liquidity risk by concentrating attention and flow, which attracts liquidity providers. It lowers evidence risk by embedding the claim inside a rulebook whose records are treated as clean. The issuer pays for these functions because they reduce the discount demanded by buyers. The exchange charges for these functions because they create dependence. Once a claim is wrapped in the exchange's recognition layer, it becomes costly to exit that layer without losing eligibility, liquidity, and reference status.

The listing bargain is frequently described as issuer quality control. It is also issuer monetization. The exchange's true listing product is not admission alone. It is the right to be a compulsory reference point for the issuer's public price formation. If the market's most widely used quotes, prints, and corporate action calendars flow through the exchange's infrastructure, then the exchange sits upstream of the issuer's cost of capital. That upstream position is a revenue architecture, because the exchange can monetize every layer that depends on reference status: listing fees, ongoing compliance fees, data fees, connectivity fees, and the prestige premium that attracts additional listings.

Listing also converts the issuer into a perpetual throughput generator for the venue's other products. A listed instrument produces quotes, trades, auctions, cancellations, and state changes that become a data stream. That stream is not a side effect. It is the most scalable product the exchange owns because it can be sold repeatedly without consuming balance sheet. Trading consumes risk and capital for liquidity providers. Data consumes bandwidth and storage. Bandwidth and storage are cheap relative to the value of being the canonical narrator of the market's facts.

To understand what the exchange sells, treat it as a firm that owns a definition. It defines what counts as an eligible instrument, what counts as a valid order, what counts as a valid trade, what counts as an official print, and what counts as an admissible record. Definitions are power in a system built on reference and proof. A price is only useful if it is recognized. Recognition is produced by definitions plus enforcement.

Execution is the exchange's second product, and execution is not merely matching. It is the sale of priority inside a rule-defined battlefield. The exchange sells a queue. The queue is not neutral plumbing. The queue decides who trades first at the best price, who can rest without being harvested, who can cancel before being selected against, whose size is visible, whose intent is hidden, and whose order type privileges allow the participant to harvest the queue itself. The exchange does not need to pick winners explicitly. It needs to offer a microstructure in which winners can be produced by those who can pay for speed, data, and operational capacity.

Queue design is where the exchange's public fairness narrative and its private revenue logic meet. Rules-based fairness means everyone is subject to the same priority rules. Outcome equality does not follow because capacity determines who can exploit the priority rules. Capacity means: faster perception, faster cancellation, better models of when the book is fragile, and the ability to hedge with lower friction. The exchange sells the tools that amplify capacity: richer feeds, lower-latency access paths, and in many cases order type menus that reward those whose systems can react fastest.

Every order type admitted is a distribution choice. An order type that hides size without losing priority changes who can provide liquidity without being exploited. An order type that can rest with special priority changes who gets filled first. An order type that can reprice automatically changes how quickly a participant can avoid being picked off. These are not conveniences. These are the exchange's policy instruments, and policy instruments in markets are profit instruments because they can shift rent from one strategy class to another.

The exchange's most delicate execution product is the official print. A market can trade in many venues, but contracts and disputes require a reference. Officialness is the right to define the reference. Officialness is an economic asset because it is used outside the exchange: in collateral triggers, in benchmarks, in index calculations, in litigation damages, in tax assessments, and in compliance reconstructions. The exchange sells officialness by operating the venue whose prints and time stamps are treated as canonical.

Canonical status is defended as integrity. Integrity requires surveillance, discipline, and evidentiary standards. Those requirements create fixed costs. Fixed costs justify fees. Fees then fund better infrastructure that makes canonical status harder to challenge. The exchange's business model becomes a self-reinforcing loop: officialness attracts flow, flow increases the value of data, data revenue funds infrastructure and surveillance, infrastructure and surveillance reinforce officialness.

Auctions are the exchange's legitimacy theater and its strategic surface at once. Auctions are presented as fairness mechanisms because they can reduce the advantage of being marginally faster in continuous matching. By collecting orders and printing a single clearing price, auctions can broaden participation and create a reference moment that looks democratic. Yet auctions introduce new advantage surfaces: imbalance information, cut-off timing, order classification, and the ability to position around the auction's predictable liquidity event.

If imbalance information is disseminated in tiers, earlier perception becomes a tradable asset. If cut-offs are known, participants can stage orders to influence or to avoid the clearing print. If certain order types receive special treatment inside auctions, order type access becomes a gate. The exchange can frame auction design as integrity and efficiency. Auction design is also a rent allocator because it determines who can harvest the predictable flows that auctions concentrate.

Fee schedules are the exchange's execution economics, and they are not merely prices. They are incentives that sculpt behavior. A fee schedule can subsidize posting and charge taking, making displayed liquidity appear deeper and spreads appear tighter. It can do the opposite. It can create volume tiers that lower marginal fees for large participants, which effectively grants those participants a cost advantage that can be converted into tighter quoting. It can create specialized programs that reward certain behaviors, such as providing liquidity in auctions or maintaining quotes within defined parameters.

The exchange's fee geometry therefore shapes the market's microstructure. If posting is subsidized, more liquidity rests. If taking is penalized, takers become more selective or route elsewhere. If certain participants receive better tiers, they can outcompete others while still profiting. The public sees the same displayed price. The machine sees different effective prices because the same trade can carry different fee burdens depending on who executes it and under which schedule.

The exchange also sells access to its fee geometry through membership and through connectivity. Membership is not just permission. It is a contract that defines obligations and privileges. Membership defines who can interact directly with the matching engine, who must access through intermediaries, and who bears which responsibilities for compliance and surveillance. Membership privileges can include lower fees, more direct data access, and operational pathways that reduce latency. These privileges are defended as necessary for quality participation. They are also commercial products.

Visibility is the exchange's third product and its cleanest toll road. The exchange produces a stream of messages: quotes, trades, cancels, auction updates, status changes, and timestamps. That stream is the market's raw material for perception. The exchange can distribute a public summary that preserves belief and then sell higher-fidelity versions that preserve profit. Higher fidelity is not a luxury. It is survivability.

A liquidity provider that sees the book update earlier can cancel before being selected against. A router that sees deeper can avoid chasing phantom size. A risk desk that sees shifts earlier can tighten exposure before external margin schedules tighten. These are not cosmetic improvements. They translate directly into lower adverse selection loss, lower market impact, and lower inventory risk. Lower risk allows tighter quoting. Tighter quoting attracts more flow. More flow yields better inference. Better inference reduces risk further. The feed becomes a compounding advantage engine.

The exchange's data products typically split into three categories that align with three kinds of dependence. First, real-time feeds that sell timeliness. Second, depth and message richness that sell completeness. Third, licensing and redistribution rights that sell control over who can narrate the market to whom. A participant paying for only the public view is operating on an abstraction. A participant paying for direct feeds is operating on a higher-fidelity market reality. When automation governs decisions, small differences in fidelity repeated thousands of times become large differences in outcome.

Data also becomes evidence. A market cannot claim integrity without the ability to reconstruct what happened. Reconstruction requires full message capture, timestamp integrity, and storage. That forensic capacity is not an afterthought. It is the legal product behind the commercial product. If a dispute arises, the party that can reconstruct the event chain can defend itself. Defense reduces liability. Reduced liability is profit. The exchange's ability to sell reconstruction capability, directly or via licensed vendors, is part of how it monetizes officialness.

The exchange's data economics are inseparable from fragmentation. In a fragmented market, many venues trade the same instrument. Yet one venue often remains the prestige reference for auctions, opening and closing prints, and widely used official signals. Even when volume is dispersed, reference can remain concentrated. Reference concentration increases the value of the exchange's feeds because participants must see and manage risk around the reference moments.

Connectivity is the exchange's fourth product and the one most easily defended as technical. Connectivity sells time compression. It sells lower delay in receiving and sending messages. Delay is an economic disadvantage because it increases adverse selection and reduces cancellation effectiveness. Participants pay not because they love speed for its own sake, but because speed is the difference between being the liquidity provider who earns spread and the liquidity provider who is harvested.

Connectivity products are not neutral to competition. If some participants can afford lower-latency paths, they can keep quotes tighter without being selected against as often. Their tighter quotes attract flow. Their flow yields more information. Their information yields more profitability. Profit funds better connectivity. The exchange can claim it does not choose winners because anyone can buy connectivity. In practice, the price of connectivity creates a threshold that favors scale.

The exchange's enforceability product is easy to ignore because it is not marketed as a product. It is surveillance, discipline, and integration into the enforcement perimeter. Officialness must be defended. If prints are manipulable, their reference value declines. If reference value declines, the exchange's data revenues decline. Surveillance and discipline therefore protect the exchange's commercial core.

Discipline includes sanctions that are economic rather than moral: fines, restrictions, suspensions, and expulsion. Expulsion is the strongest sanction because it removes access to recognition and liquidity. Recognition and liquidity are the exchange's products. Exclusion is therefore not merely punishment. It is the withdrawal of a commercial privilege that the participant needs to operate cheaply.

Enforceability also includes the exchange's role in producing acceptable evidence. The exchange's logs and timestamps become the raw material for compliance and for disputes. If the exchange's records are treated as presumptively accurate, the exchange's venue becomes the default narrative for what occurred. Narrative authority is power in a system where contracts reference prices and regulators reconstruct events.

The exchange is therefore a hybrid of utility and platform. It must preserve a public lane that is usable enough to sustain legitimacy. It must also preserve premium lanes that are meaningfully better to sustain profit. The public lane is the civic window: a price, a quote, and the promise that ordinary participation is possible. The premium lanes are survivability lanes: richer data, faster data, deeper market state, earlier auction imbalance insight, and connectivity that allows cancellation to be protective rather than ornamental.

This balance is the exchange's political economy: enough openness to avoid backlash, enough inequality to monetize. The public does not need to be blind. It only needs to be unable to measure the advantage precisely enough to politicize it continuously. Complexity performs that function.

The exchange's edge-building role is magnified by the way other systems reference it. Benchmarks use exchange prints. Collateral triggers reference exchange prices. Index providers use exchange reference data and sometimes exchange-derived methodologies. Corporate action calendars use exchange schedule conventions. When the exchange's outputs become inputs to other systems, dependence increases. Increased dependence increases the value of the exchange's products, especially data authority and connectivity.

The exchange's most durable rent is not per-trade fees. It is being the canonical clock. If the exchange's timestamps are treated as authoritative, then the exchange can define the sequence of events that matter. Sequence matters in disputes, in best-execution comparisons, in manipulation detection, and in the determination of what counts as the official close or open. Owning the canonical clock is owning a large portion of the market's legal reality.

Stable winners are produced when they can buy or influence the exchange's advantage surfaces. They do not need inside knowledge. They need earlier sightlines, faster reaction, and cheaper completion. The exchange sells sightlines and reaction capability. The exchange does not clear and settle by itself, but it sells the front end of the chain that produces the most important evidence. Those who are closest to that chain can avoid being selected against and can monetize the spread.

The exchange's role in producing stable winners also flows through its relationship with brokers and internalizers. If a large portion of flow never reaches the displayed venue, the displayed venue becomes more sensitive to professional, informational flow. That increases toxicity. Increased toxicity makes displayed liquidity provision harder. Liquidity providers widen spreads or withdraw. Wider spreads make internalization more attractive. Internalization then captures more flow and more informational advantage. The displayed exchange can still remain the reference venue for officialness while losing some volume. That can be a stable equilibrium for the exchange because reference status is more monetizable than raw volume when data is priced aggressively.

This reveals a counterintuitive point: an exchange can "win" as a business even if it does not dominate all executions, as long as it dominates officialness and sells the most valuable data and connectivity. Officialness is the exchange's crown. Volume is one way to defend the crown. Prestige and reference dependence are another.

The exchange's listing and market data products also shape issuer behavior. Issuers are pressured to maintain disclosure cadence, governance practices, and corporate action timing that sustain continuous liquidity and stable reference status. Liquidity and reference status lower cost of capital. Lower cost of capital rewards behavior that suits the machine's needs: predictable reporting, predictable corporate actions, and structures that reduce settlement and entitlement ambiguity. The exchange thus influences corporate behavior indirectly by making tradability and reference stability valuable.

The exchange's rulemaking therefore is not merely internal policy. It is a governance function with economic consequences. Microstructure changes redistribute rent among strategies. Fee changes redistribute rent among participants. Data policy changes redistribute visibility. Connectivity policy changes redistribute reaction advantage. Each change can be defended as modernization or integrity. Each change is also a redistribution of edge.

Because the exchange can claim neutrality and integrity, it can present edge redistribution as technical necessity rather than as political choice. That is why exchange governance is both powerful and hard to contest publicly: its outcomes are real, but its language is technical.

The exchange also faces a structural temptation: to expand the number of things it can monetize around the same core asset, which is being the canonical narrator. It can expand into indices, analytics, and derived data. It can expand into technology services for participants. It can expand into adjacent infrastructure that increases dependence: connectivity hubs, monitoring services, and compliance tooling. These expansions deepen the exchange's position as the place where the market is defined rather than merely traded.

This is how the exchange builds its own edge, and how it helps the House build edge. The House builds edge by paying wholesale for what the exchange sells and by charging retail to those who cannot or will not pay for premium access. Those paying retail experience the exchange as a public place. Those paying wholesale experience it as a controllable interface.

The exchange's edge is therefore not an accident. It is engineered into the business model. Recognition is sold through listing. Priority is sold through microstructure. Visibility is sold through data. Reaction advantage is sold through connectivity. Enforceability is sold through surveillance-backed officialness.

The exchange's most honest description is not that it sells liquidity. Liquidity is behavior. The exchange sells the conditions under which liquidity can be trusted and referenced. Trust and reference are recognition. Recognition is the asset.

CHAPTER 18

WHEN MEMBERS BECAME SHAREHOLDERS

WHY DEMUTUALIZATION CHANGED THE SOUL, INCENTIVES, AND FUTURE OF THE EXCHANGE.

An exchange begins as a club because a market begins as trust among insiders. The first requirement is not speed, innovation, or growth. The first requirement is an enforceable boundary: who is allowed to quote, whose trade counts, whose failure is punished, and whose records are believed. Membership is the original technology. It is a governance perimeter disguised as a venue. Inside the perimeter, the exchange can impose rules, impose discipline, and impose evidence standards that make completion plausible. Outside the perimeter, the venue is only a meeting place with no credible method for resolving disputes at scale.

In the member-owned form, the exchange's ownership logic is circular. Members provide liquidity, accept obligations, and police each other because the venue's reputation is their franchise, and the franchise is their wealth. The exchange is not merely where they earn spreads. It is the reason spreads exist at all. It protects the value of their intermediation by defending officialness, defending evidence, and defending a common clock. The club is not altruistic, but its incentives are anchored to a shared existential fear: if trust in quotes, execution, and completion collapses, every member loses.

Demutualization breaks this circle and rebuilds it around a different center of gravity. The exchange stops being a member-governed club and becomes a shareholder-owned enterprise. That change is not a cosmetic adjustment to corporate form. It is a rewiring of what the exchange is optimizing for, and optimization is destiny in a machine where small parameter shifts compound into stable outcomes. The exchange's incentives shift from preserving a durable ecology for member intermediation to maximizing scalable revenue and defensible margin under legitimacy constraints. The result is not a sudden moral collapse. The result is a predictable migration of strategy toward products that compound cleanly: data, indices, connectivity, licensing, and the right to define what counts.

The simplest way to see the difference is to ask who the exchange thinks it serves. In the club model, the exchange is owned by the same actors who must trade, quote, and shoulder obligations. When those actors pay fees, they are paying themselves in a roundabout way to fund the infrastructure that preserves their franchise. Complaints exist, but the argument is internal: fees must be high enough to preserve integrity and low enough not to strangle the members' own profitability. In the shareholder model, the owners are not the daily users. The daily users become customers. The owners become investors who demand growth. Growth demands either more volume or more extraction per unit of volume. Volume is competitive and cyclical. Extraction is more controllable if the exchange can make its products hard to avoid.

This is the soul change. A club exchange is built to be indispensable to its members' business, but it is constrained by co-ownership politics. A shareholder exchange is built to be indispensable to the system itself, and it is constrained primarily by regulation, competition, and the risk of public legitimacy fracture. When indispensability shifts from member franchise to system dependence, the exchange's product mix changes.

Demutualization also changes the exchange's view of its own risk. In a club form, the exchange's failure is a direct member failure because the exchange is the members' collective instrument. In a shareholder form, the exchange can diversify revenue away from pure execution volume and can design itself to profit in more market conditions. That diversification makes the exchange more resilient as a corporation, but it can also make it more willing to design market structure in ways that increase complexity and deepen dependence, because complexity increases the value of data, connectivity, and licensing.

The exchange's most valuable asset is recognition. Recognition is the ability to convert private intention into public fact: eligible listing status, canonical prints, authoritative timestamps, and evidence that courts and regulators will accept. Recognition is the root from which every scalable product grows. Demutualization intensifies the incentive to own and monetize recognition, because recognition creates pricing power that does not require the exchange to take directional risk.

In the club era, recognition is a shared public good for members. Members need officialness to be credible because their intermediation depends on it. In the shareholder era, recognition is a monetizable platform. The exchange sells the right to interact with recognition cheaply, the right to see recognition earlier, the right to redistribute recognition to others, and the right to reference recognition in derived products. These are tolls on perception, tolls on timing, and tolls on proof.

The mechanical consequence is that demutualization turns the exchange into a toll road owner. A toll road owner can raise revenue not only by increasing traffic but by pricing lanes. The public lane must remain usable enough to preserve legitimacy. The premium lanes must remain meaningfully better to preserve pricing power. Meaningfully better means earlier, deeper, faster, more reliable, and more defensible in dispute. The exchange is pushed to design and sell these differences continuously because shareholders demand recurring revenue growth.

This is why the shift changes incentives around market structure. In the club model, structure tends to be designed to preserve a stable member ecology and defend the venue's reputation. In the shareholder model, structure tends to be designed to expand monetization surfaces while maintaining enough integrity to keep officialness credible. The difference is not whether integrity matters. Integrity always matters. The difference is whether integrity is the primary objective or the enabling constraint for revenue expansion.

Fee geometry becomes more central under demutualization. A member-owned exchange can treat fee schedules as funding mechanisms and behavior nudges. A shareholder exchange treats fee schedules as product design. Fees can be engineered to subsidize displayed liquidity and to charge for taking liquidity, shaping the visible spread while moving economic cost into less visible components. Fees can be tiered to reward volume and therefore reward scale. Fees can be bundled with data and connectivity to create packages that are hard to avoid for serious participants. The exchange's objective becomes to extract more value from the same flow by distributing costs through a structure that participants cannot easily contest, because it can be framed as market quality engineering.

Market quality language becomes an instrument. Under demutualization, the exchange must justify profitability in public and to regulators. It cannot announce that it is raising rents. It must announce that it is improving resilience, improving transparency, improving fairness, improving liquidity, improving surveillance, improving technology, and improving investor protection. Those improvements can be real. They also create gates. Gates can be priced. Pricing gates is revenue.

Order type design is a prime example. Order types look like menu options, but they are distribution rules. They decide who can hide, who must display, who can gain queue priority, who can cancel without losing position, and who can interact with auctions in privileged ways. A club exchange tends to manage order types primarily as tools for orderly trading and member interests. A shareholder exchange treats order types as levers that can increase demand for premium data and premium connectivity, because more complex order interactions reward those who can see and react fastest. The exchange can describe this as innovation. The mechanical effect is a shift of profit toward participants with the infrastructure to exploit the complexity, and toward the exchange that sells the infrastructure inputs.

Demutualization also shifts how the exchange thinks about fragmentation. Fragmentation is often framed as competition between venues. In a club model, fragmentation can be viewed as a threat because it disperses liquidity and weakens the venue's centrality. In a shareholder model, fragmentation can be an opportunity if the exchange can remain the canonical reference while execution disperses. Reference is more monetizable than volume if data is priced aggressively. If the exchange remains the canonical open, canonical close, and canonical time-stamped record, it can profit from being referenced even if some trades occur elsewhere.

This is why shareholder exchanges often pursue a strategy of owning reference rather than owning all executions. Owning reference means: maintain prestige and officialness for opening and closing auctions, maintain authoritative timestamping and surveillance credibility, and maintain the most valuable data products and licensing relationships. Execution volume then becomes one input to reference credibility rather than the only objective.

The transformation can be seen most clearly in the rise of data and index businesses. Trading fees are competitive and cyclical. Data is scalable, repeatable, and sticky. Participants build systems around specific formats, timestamps, and historical archives. Once embedded, switching is expensive and risky. That stickiness becomes pricing power. Pricing power becomes predictable revenue, and predictable revenue is what shareholders reward. Demutualization therefore naturally pushes the exchange to become a data and analytics firm as much as an execution venue.

Data is not just a stream of numbers. It is a legal-economic record. Many external systems reference it: collateral triggers, benchmark calculations, damages assessment, and compliance reconstruction. When the exchange sells data, it sells authority. Authority is scarce because authority requires recognition by regulators and courts. This is why exchanges defend data pricing aggressively and why they pursue licensing controls: the product is not only the bytes, it is the right to treat those bytes as reality.

Demutualization also increases the incentive to expand vertically and horizontally through acquisitions. A club exchange is constrained in capital raising and in merger logic because its owners are members with complex local politics and divergent interests. A shareholder exchange can raise capital, issue equity, and pursue mergers as a growth mandate. The easiest acquisitions to justify are those that widen the stack of dependence: buy other venues, buy data vendors, buy index providers, buy analytics platforms, buy connectivity hubs, buy surveillance tooling, buy clearing-adjacent services. Each acquisition is defended as modernization and integration. The mechanical outcome is more toll points.

The exchange thus becomes less a single venue and more a platform that owns multiple interfaces. Each interface is a place where participants must pass: to execute, to see, to prove, to benchmark, to list, to distribute corporate action information, to reconstruct disputes. When one firm owns multiple interfaces, it can bundle products and price them in ways that make them harder to avoid. Bundling is a classic infrastructure strategy: reduce contestability by turning stand-alone products into a package that participants must buy to remain competitive.

The governance implications are significant. In a club model, governance is negotiated among those who bear the consequences directly as traders and market makers. In a shareholder model, governance becomes corporate product strategy. Rule changes are evaluated for market quality, but also for monetization surfaces: will the change increase demand for premium data, will it increase connectivity value, will it create new auction products, will it increase volume at reference moments, will it shift behavior toward chargeable interactions. The exchange can present changes as improvements, and they may be improvements, but the incentive to align improvements with revenue expansion becomes stronger.

Surveillance and enforcement become inseparable from the business model. Officialness is the exchange's asset. Officialness collapses if manipulation is perceived as easy. The exchange therefore invests in surveillance not only for civic duty but to protect its revenue base. This produces a particular pattern: aggressive policing of visible, confidence-destroying abuses, alongside structural design choices that allow legal stratification through speed, data tiering, and membership privileges. The exchange becomes both the policeman of obvious fraud and the architect of legal advantage.

The change also alters the exchange's relationship to participants. Under a club model, participants are owners, and price increases feel like self-taxation. Under a shareholder model, participants become cost centers whose expenditures become the exchange's revenue. The exchange seeks ways to increase participant spending without triggering participant exit. The easiest way is to raise the value of must-have products: data authority, connectivity, and reference events. If the exchange can make its open and close indispensable for benchmarks, index tracking, and valuation, then participants must pay to see and to participate.

That is why opening and closing auctions become strategic assets. These are the moments where officialness is most visible and most referenced. If the exchange controls these moments, it controls the canonical daily narrative. The canonical narrative is used by performance reporting, index calculation, and collateral valuation. The exchange can monetize participation in these moments through fees, through auction data products, and through connectivity demand to react to auction imbalances. Auctions are sold as fairness and price discovery. They are also monetizable reference events.

The exchange's incentives under demutualization therefore include protecting the value of the canonical daily moments. Protecting that value often means designing auction procedures that maintain confidence while also disseminating imbalance information in ways that support premium data sales. Imbalance information is a high-value product because it allows participants to position around predictable liquidity shocks. Predictable shocks are where spreads widen and where inventory can be moved at better terms for those who can see and react early. The exchange can sell this as market transparency. It is also a lane.

Demutualization also changes the relationship between the exchange and the broader market ecosystem by encouraging strategic tolerance of certain forms of off-venue trading. If internalization and off-venue execution draw away some flow, displayed liquidity can thin, and that can appear to threaten the exchange's relevance. Yet if the exchange retains reference status and can monetize data authority, it can remain dominant as a business even while volume disperses. This is a key structural reason stable winners can exist: the most profitable layers are not necessarily the visible trading layers; they are the definition layers.

Definition layers are the layers that decide what counts as a quote, what counts as a trade, what counts as the official open, what counts as the official close, what counts as an admissible record in dispute, and what counts as eligible reference data for indices. Demutualization pushes exchanges to expand control over definition layers because these layers create pricing power that is durable.

The exchange's transformation also reshapes the cost structure of market participation. When more functions become priced products, participation costs become more fixed and less variable. Data subscriptions, connectivity, and compliance tooling become recurring expenses. Recurring expenses increase the minimum efficient scale. When minimum efficient scale rises, smaller participants are disadvantaged. This is not necessarily intentional exclusion. It is the predictable result of infrastructure monetization. The market becomes more concentrated because the cost of being fully informed and fully connected is high.

Concentration then feeds back into exchange strategy. If fewer, larger participants dominate, the exchange can negotiate and price products differently, offering volume tiers and bundles that reinforce the dominance of large players. Large players benefit from lower per-unit costs and from better economics, allowing them to quote tighter and capture more flow. More flow yields more informational advantage. The exchange profits because the large players spend heavily on premium lanes.

This creates a subtle dynamic: the exchange can maintain the public narrative of broad access while relying economically on a smaller subset of heavy-spending participants who buy premium access. The public lane remains open. The premium lane becomes the primary profit engine. The exchange must keep the public lane good enough to preserve legitimacy and regulatory tolerance. It must keep the premium lane good enough to preserve revenue.

Demutualization also changes the exchange's incentives around technology cycles. A club exchange can be conservative, because its members might prefer stability and predictability over constant change. A shareholder exchange must justify growth, and growth can be framed as technology modernization. Modernization creates new product categories: new feeds, new analytics, new surveillance services, new connectivity offerings, new order types. Modernization also creates complexity, and complexity increases the value of premium products. The exchange can profit from the arms race by selling the inputs to the arms race.

This is the hidden compounding loop demutualization enables. The exchange invests in technology that increases message richness and market complexity. Market complexity increases the advantage of those who can buy richer feeds and faster connectivity. Those participants demand more premium products. Premium product revenue funds more technology investment and acquisitions. The exchange's dependence grows. The exchange's pricing power grows.

The exchange also gains more leverage over regulatory narratives. A club exchange can claim it is a quasi-public institution serving market integrity. A shareholder exchange must still claim integrity, but it can also claim modernization and resilience as reasons for fee structures and data pricing. Regulators are often concerned with stability and fairness. The exchange can frame premium products as necessary for sophisticated risk management and for maintaining stable markets. The exchange can frame data licensing as necessary to fund surveillance and reconstruction capabilities. These arguments can be partly true and still function as revenue justification.

A critical consequence is that rulemaking becomes more strategic. Under demutualization, the exchange has stronger incentive to design rules that increase the demand for products it sells. This does not require corrupt intent. It requires only that the exchange's profit depends on product demand. If the exchange can introduce features that make high-fidelity data more valuable, demand for high-fidelity data rises. If it can introduce features that make low latency more valuable, demand for low latency rises. If it can introduce features that increase the importance of auction imbalance information, demand rises. Each feature can be defended as improving execution quality or fairness. The revenue effect remains.

The exchange's evolution can be described as a shift from being a meeting place to being a platform for the market's evidence and clocks. Evidence and clocks are the core of enforceable markets. They are also the core of monetizable dependence. When a platform owns the evidence and the clock, it owns the narration of reality. That narration can be sold.

The exchange's clock matters because sequence matters. Sequence determines who is early and who is late, whose cancellation arrived in time, whose quote was displayed when the trade occurred, and whose fill is defensible. Sequence is central to surveillance and to disputes. If the exchange's timestamps are treated as authoritative, the exchange owns the canonical sequence. The canonical sequence is referenced in compliance, in litigation, in best-execution comparisons, and in manipulation investigations. Owning canonical sequence is governance power that can be monetized through data products and through premium access to the most precise timestamping.

Demutualization also encourages the exchange to deepen its involvement in benchmark and index ecosystems, because these ecosystems create forced flows and increase reference dependence. Benchmarks and indices require a reference price and reference methodology. If the exchange's data is used to compute indices, index-linked funds must reference the exchange's outputs. That creates demand for the exchange's feeds and for participation in reference moments. The exchange can monetize the chain: data licensing to index providers, fees and products around rebalance windows, and premium data products for participants positioning around those flows.

This produces a system where the exchange profits from the same mechanism that creates stability and volatility. Index flows can stabilize liquidity by creating consistent demand and supply. They can also create predictable, concentrated flows around cut-offs that can be harvested by those with visibility and inventory. The exchange profits because predictable concentrated flows increase demand for premium lanes. Demutualization strengthens the incentive to cultivate these flows as part of the market's structure, not necessarily by direct manipulation, but by integrating with the index and benchmark infrastructure that channels large quantities of capital through defined windows.

The exchange's incentives around listing also change. Listing is no longer simply admission to a club. It becomes an integrated product line: admission plus visibility plus analytics plus index pathways plus corporate action integration. Issuers seek lower cost of capital and higher liquidity. The exchange can offer those outcomes indirectly by making the issuer's instrument central to the data and index ecosystems. In return, the exchange extracts more ongoing revenue from the issuer and from the ecosystem that trades the issuer. The issuer becomes a durable revenue generator, not only through listing fees but through the data stream and reference events it produces.

The exchange's relationship with issuers becomes more platform-like. The issuer is not just a client. The issuer is content. Content in this context is not marketing fluff. Content is tradable signals and corporate action events that generate data products and forced flows. A shareholder exchange thinks in content economics: which listings generate the most attention, the most data demand, the most index inclusion, and the most derivative products. Derivatives and related products increase volume and data richness, which increase profitability.

Demutualization also changes the exchange's interaction with clearing and settlement indirectly. Exchanges do not typically clear and settle on their own, but their rules and products shape the composition of trading that reaches clearinghouses and settlement systems. If the exchange designs structures that increase high-frequency interaction and fragment order flow, the downstream completion chain must process more messages and more complex states. Complexity increases the value of sophisticated clearing members and sophisticated participants. Sophisticated participants buy more premium products. The exchange profits.

This is a second-order compounding loop: microstructure complexity drives completion complexity; completion complexity raises fixed costs; fixed costs raise scale advantages; scale advantages concentrate activity; concentrated activity increases premium lane spending; premium lane spending funds more microstructure complexity and acquisitions.

The political constraint on demutualization is legitimacy. The exchange cannot openly declare that it is selling a tiered market reality. It must preserve the appearance of fairness and equal access while monetizing tiered access. The system resolves this through two techniques. First, it provides a public lane that is adequate for ordinary human participation and preserves the civic narrative. Second, it sells premium lanes as professional tools required for advanced strategies, framing inequality as a consequence of sophistication rather than as a structural design.

The public lane is not fake. It allows participation. The premium lane is not merely convenience. It changes survivability. A participant with earlier visibility can cancel before being selected against and can quote tighter. Tighter quoting attracts flow. Flow yields information. Information yields profit. Profit buys more premium access. The loop is stable and self-reinforcing. The exchange benefits because it sells the premium access.

This is why demutualization changes the future of market inequality. In the club model, inequality exists but is constrained by member politics and by the need to preserve broad trust in the venue. In the shareholder model, inequality becomes a revenue strategy, constrained mainly by the risk of backlash. As long as the inequality is framed as technology and professional necessity, it can be sustained.

Demutualization also changes how exchanges respond to crises. In the club model, crises threaten the member franchise directly, and members may be willing to accept lower fees or temporary measures that prioritize stability over revenue. In the shareholder model, crises can increase demand for premium products: volatility increases demand for data, connectivity, and surveillance; stress increases demand for reliable reference prints; stress increases demand for auction information and for definitive officialness. The exchange can profit in crisis by selling the tools that participants believe they need to survive. This creates a potentially uncomfortable alignment: the exchange's revenue can be countercyclical in ways that deepen its incentive to sell more tiering under stress.

The exchange must manage this carefully because the public interprets crisis profits as extraction. The response is again procedural and rhetorical: frame premium products as necessary for stability, frame data pricing as funding surveillance and integrity, frame connectivity as technical modernization.

The deepest structural change demutualization produces is the conversion of the exchange from member governance institution into infrastructure rent extractor. Rent extraction here does not mean illegality. It means collecting recurring revenue from controlling interfaces others must use. The exchange controls interfaces of recognition: listing standards, officialness, canonical prints, canonical clocks, and admissible evidence. Once these interfaces are controlled, the exchange can price access.

The exchange's future under this model is expansion of interface control. That means more acquisitions, more integration into indices and benchmarks, more licensing control, more data product sophistication, more surveillance and forensic capability as a sellable asset, and more connectivity tiering. It also means more subtle microstructure design that increases the value of premium lanes while preserving the appearance of fairness.

The exchange becomes stable not because markets are calm but because the exchange's revenue does not require calm. It requires participation. Participation is maintained by legitimacy and by structural dependence. Legitimacy is maintained by visible integrity enforcement. Dependence is maintained by owning reference and evidence. Demutualization shifts the balance toward dependence as the primary defense because dependence is monetizable and is scalable.

This is why demutualization changed the soul. The exchange's soul is its objective function. A club objective function emphasizes member franchise durability and market integrity as a shared asset. A shareholder objective function emphasizes recurring revenue, margin expansion, and growth through controlling interfaces. Integrity remains, but it becomes the enabling constraint rather than the shared purpose.

CHAPTER 19
CONSOLIDATION AND THE NEW EXCHANGE EMPIRES
HOW MERGERS TURNED MARKET VENUES INTO GLOBAL INFRASTRUCTURE GROUPS.

Consolidation did not begin as romance. It began as math. A venue is expensive to run, politically difficult to govern, and increasingly hard to differentiate on matching alone once execution becomes fast, commoditized, and fragmented. If matching is a commodity, durable advantage migrates to what can be owned and resold: authoritative data, canonical reference moments, licensing rights, index methodologies, compliance-grade reconstruction, and the clocks that define sequence when disputes arise. These assets scale better than per-trade fees and, crucially, scale across borders. Consolidation is how venues stop competing trade by trade and start behaving as infrastructure landlords that price passage through interfaces the market cannot avoid.

The old exchange was a venue. The new exchange empire is a stack. It can sell admission to issuers, sell execution to participants, sell visibility to professionals, sell redistribution rights to vendors, sell index and benchmark plumbing to allocators, sell surveillance and forensic reconstruction to the enforcement perimeter, and sell connectivity that converts delay into an economic handicap. A stack is resilient because revenue does not depend on one layer surviving intact. If execution fees compress, data can expand. If listings slow, licensing can rise. If one region weakens, another can subsidize. Consolidation is the assembly of multiple toll points into one corporate perimeter, with one billing engine, one sales force, and one strategic objective: deepen dependence, then price it.

The mechanical driver is fixed cost and marginal revenue. Running a modern venue requires fixed-cost heavy systems: matching engines with redundancy, security, surveillance, compliance logging, time synchronization, and data distribution. The marginal cost of one additional message or one additional subscriber is low relative to what can be charged for authoritative visibility and reconstruction. The spread between low marginal cost and high willingness-to-pay produces an inevitable compounding incentive: build a larger client base, then increase the value of the must-have products by embedding them deeper into the market's workflows. Consolidation increases the base. Vertical integration deepens the workflow dependence. Workflow dependence creates pricing power.

Consolidation converts competition into category design. A venue that competes only on execution faces headwinds: routing can divert flow, internalization can siphon volume, fragmentation can thin displayed liquidity, and price discovery can migrate. An infrastructure group can tolerate those headwinds if it owns the reference layer and the evidence layer. Reference can remain concentrated even when execution disperses, as long as the market's most referenced moments remain anchored: opening and closing reference events, canonical prints treated as valuation anchors, and timestamp standards that become the baseline for reconstruction. Consolidation makes that defense easier because the group can bundle venues, standardize methodologies, and market itself as the stable center that other systems must orbit.

The first consolidation motive is survival of officialness under fragmentation. Fragmentation creates multiple execution points.

Multiple execution points create ambiguity: which prints count, which venue defines the canonical open and close, which message stream becomes admissible evidence. Ambiguity is toxic to collateral triggers, benchmarks, index tracking, and enforcement. The system therefore wants a small number of authoritative narrators even if execution is dispersed. An exchange empire becomes that narrator by owning critical venues, owning key licensing relationships, and securing regulatory and legal recognition such that its records become presumptive reality in disputes.

The second motive is rent stability through recurring revenue. Transactional trading fees are cyclical. Data licenses, indices, connectivity subscriptions, historical archives, and compliance tooling are recurring and sticky. Stickiness comes from integration costs. Institutions build systems around specific feed formats, time stamps, identifiers, and archives. Switching risks misalignment, mispricing, compliance gaps, and operational breaks. The more the exchange empire sells integrated products, the higher the switching cost and the stronger the pricing power. Consolidation is the fastest method to acquire sticky businesses and cross-sell them into an existing base.

The third motive is regulatory leverage through centrality. A small venue can be regulated with relatively blunt instruments because collateral damage is limited. A system-critical infrastructure group is harder to discipline aggressively because discipline can disrupt the market's evidence layer, reference layer, and liquidity routines simultaneously. This does not require overt capture. It is a structural bargaining advantage: the more central the infrastructure, the more carefully enforcement must be applied to avoid destabilizing spillovers. Consolidation increases centrality. Centrality increases the group's ability to frame pricing changes, bundling strategies, and rule adjustments as stability enhancements. Stability language becomes the shield for rent extraction because stability is politically hard to oppose.

The fourth motive is global expansion of definition control. Markets are local in law and global in capital. Global capital wants interoperable signals: comparable prints, comparable reference moments, comparable index levels, comparable evidence standards. An exchange empire sells interoperability by standardizing products across jurisdictions and offering large institutions one relationship for many markets. The product is uniformity: fewer interfaces, fewer legal reconciliation processes, fewer vendor contracts. Uniformity reduces compliance burden for large clients, which makes the empire more attractive. Once attractive, uniformity becomes a premium feature that can be priced, because the alternative is operational sprawl.

Consolidation changes the objective function beyond demutualization. Demutualization shifts the venue from member ecology to shareholder growth. Consolidation shifts it from growth to dependency engineering. A dependency model is defined by how many actors must use the group's interfaces and how costly it is to route around them. The empire's strategy becomes creation of unavoidable pathways.

The simplest unavoidable pathway is data authority. If a venue's prints and time stamps are treated as authoritative, they become inputs into external systems. External systems include indices, risk models, collateral valuation, regulatory reconstruction, litigation. Once records become inputs, participants must buy access to validate, hedge, and prove, even if they execute elsewhere. Consolidation expands the range of authoritative records owned. Ownership of records becomes ownership of the market's memory. Memory is monetizable because proof requires memory.

The second unavoidable pathway is benchmark and index integration. Indices are flow engines. A methodology change or inclusion event forces trading. Forced trading is predictable trading. Predictable trading is monetizable by those who can provide liquidity into that window, and by those who can position around it with better visibility. When an exchange empire owns both reference prints and index methodology, it can capture value across the loop: sell data licensing to index clients, sell participation tools around rebalance windows, sell premium visibility into imbalance dynamics, and sell connectivity needed to react. Consolidation aims to assemble this loop because it compounds: reference feeds indices, indices drive flow, flow increases the value of premium lanes, premium lanes fund further acquisitions.

The third unavoidable pathway is connectivity and time compression. Fragmentation makes being late more expensive. Being late means being selected against, chasing phantom size, failing to cancel in time. Participants respond by buying faster paths. The exchange empire sells those paths. Consolidation increases the number of venues, products, and reference moments bound to the same connectivity ecosystem, making a connectivity subscription more valuable and harder to replace. Price increases can be framed as investment in capacity and resilience rather than as extraction, because the buyer is paying for time compression and risk reduction rather than a visible fee.

The fourth unavoidable pathway is listing prestige and issuer dependence. Issuers seek liquidity, attention, and a stable reference signal that reduces cost of capital. The empire sells that by controlling the most referenced listing venues and integrating listings into data and index ecosystems. A listing becomes content: not entertainment, but tradable signal production and reference events. Attention increases liquidity, liquidity increases data value, data revenue funds products that sustain attention. Issuers become part of the loop. Once inside, leaving is costly because eligibility, liquidity, and perception are tied to the empire's prestige and the market's reliance on its reference moments.

Consolidation pushes exchanges away from execution as the main profit center and toward scalable products that do not require holding risk. Execution is contested. Data and licensing are controllable. This shift alters which market design choices are favored. Designs that increase message richness and increase demand for premium feeds become more attractive. Designs that simplify markets and reduce dependence become less attractive unless compelled by regulation. Complexity becomes profitable as long as it can be framed as innovation or resilience.

That framing matters because consolidation turns exchanges into quasi-utilities: publicly essential, privately owned, priced through tiering. The group's leadership learns to translate revenue expansion into resilience narratives because resilience is hard to oppose and often aligned with regulator priorities. The empire becomes adept at selling the same change twice: as integrity to the public and as growth to shareholders.

Consolidation changes bargaining power by reducing counterparties. A fragmented ecosystem produces many bilateral negotiations: venue fees, data licenses, redistribution rights, connectivity arrangements, surveillance data access. A consolidated empire reduces negotiation counterparties. Fewer counterparties increases negotiating power. Negotiating power enables bundle pricing, volume tiers, and long-term contracts that lock in clients. Lock-in reduces contestability. Reduced contestability increases pricing power.

Bundling also changes distribution. A small participant buys the minimum and operates on delayed abstraction. A large participant buys the bundle and receives wholesale economics: lower per-unit data costs, better connectivity, better licensing terms, integrated access across multiple venues. Wholesale economics can be converted into tighter quoting and better routing, capturing more flow. The empire profits because the large participant spends heavily on premium lanes, and the small participant remains a price taker.

Consolidation shifts innovation from product invention to interface capture. When an empire buys multiple venues, it can standardize identifiers, standardize protocols, centralize surveillance, centralize reconstruction, and then sell uniformity as an advantage. Standardization becomes the baseline the ecosystem must build around. Baseline control is monetizable because it makes licensing unavoidable: default formats become default costs.

Centralized surveillance and reconstruction is particularly valuable. Reconstruction capability is demanded by regulated institutions. It is also demanded by the enforcement perimeter. If the empire controls event streams across multiple venues, it can sell higher-fidelity reconstruction services, longer historical archives, and analytic layers that interpret event causality. These products are inelastic for many institutions because proof obligations do not vanish when budgets tighten. Inelastic demand is the best revenue category an infrastructure owner can have.

Consolidation also reshapes failure dynamics. When one group owns more of the stack, outages or policy changes have wider impact. Wider impact increases systemic importance. Increased systemic importance increases political caution. Political caution reduces aggressive interventions. Reduced intervention risk can embolden monetization strategies, as long as they remain inside technical language and integrity narratives. The equilibrium is predictable: central infrastructure is allowed to price itself because the alternative is destabilization.

This reshaping produces a new form of sovereignty: sovereignty of definition and evidence. The state remains the enforcement perimeter, but the exchange empire becomes the everyday governor of market reality because participants must use its clocks, its records, and its reference moments to function. Sovereignty of definition is not lawmaking, but it is reality-making inside the market's operational system.

Consolidation also changes the geopolitics of finance. When reference and evidence are centralized in a few hubs, global finance becomes dependent on those hubs. Dependence creates vulnerability and power simultaneously. Vulnerability because hub failure can ripple through collateral valuation, index calculations, and compliance systems. Power because hub owners can set terms for access and can influence standards that other jurisdictions must accommodate.

Exchange empires therefore pursue two parallel strategies: expand territorial reach and expand control over standards. Territorial reach means buying venues in multiple jurisdictions. Standards control means making the group's data formats, time synchronization, auction methodologies, and evidence requirements the default. Defaults are sticky. Sticky defaults are pricing power.

A consolidation wave also changes how the market's narrative is curated. A local venue narrates a local market. An empire narrates a category. Category narration is valuable because it shapes how institutional products are built: indices, benchmarks, risk models, and passive vehicles rely on category definitions. If the empire controls category definitions and category-level data products, it controls how capital is packaged. Packaging controls flow. Flow creates forced trading windows. Forced windows create monetizable demand for premium lanes.

The mechanics of forced windows deserve specific treatment because they are the most reliable engine of edge. A forced window exists whenever a large set of participants must trade inside a deadline: benchmark reporting cut-offs, index rebalance events, auction cut-offs, settlement cut-offs, margin call schedules. These deadlines create predictable urgency. Predictable urgency allows inventory to be priced higher. The empire profits indirectly by selling products that help participants navigate these windows: premium imbalance data, premium timestamps, premium connectivity, analytics that forecast flow pressure, and venue features that concentrate liquidity at reference moments. The empire also profits directly by charging for participation in those reference moments through fee design.

Consolidation helps concentrate reference moments. If an empire owns multiple venues, it can coordinate their reference events and can market certain events as canonical. Canonical status attracts liquidity. Liquidity increases data value. Data value increases premium lane pricing. Premium lane pricing funds more acquisitions. This is the compounding loop of empire building.

Consolidation also changes how internal conflicts are resolved. In a local venue, member politics can restrain fee increases and rule changes. In an empire, internal governance is corporate governance. The firm resolves conflicts by optimizing revenue and regulatory tolerance. Corporate governance has a stronger incentive to price aggressively because shareholders demand growth and because the firm can rely on dependence to prevent exit. The restraint becomes external: antitrust risk, regulatory intervention, and public legitimacy.

Antitrust risk shapes consolidation strategy but rarely eliminates it because infrastructure markets can be defended as natural monopolies. The defense is practical: duplication is expensive, fragmentation can increase instability, and standardization can improve resilience. Those arguments can be partly true and still serve as shields for rent extraction. The empire's task is to remain on the defensible side of concentration while still deepening pricing power.

Consolidation also alters market structure through the design of "best execution" landscapes. When venues are owned by multiple separate entities, routing can be a competition. When venues are inside one empire, routing becomes internal allocation. Internal allocation can reduce friction and can also increase the empire's ability to capture value across the path. The empire can set internal transfer prices, design bundled services, and shape which routes appear economically attractive to brokers. This can be defended as efficiency. It also deepens dependence because alternatives outside the empire must compete against an integrated stack.

The empire's ability to bundle across execution, data, and indices also changes how costs are hidden. A participant may see low per-trade fees but pay high data subscription fees. Another may see high per-trade fees but receive rebates that reduce effective cost if volume is large. Bundle design can make comparisons difficult, which reduces competitive pressure. Difficulty of comparison is a moat. Complexity becomes a strategy.

Consolidation also shifts the labor market inside finance. As infrastructures consolidate, the locus of high-paying technical work shifts toward firms that own the stack: data engineering, surveillance analytics, protocol design, and reconstruction. Those capabilities are both integrity and product. That dual role further reinforces the empire because integrity investments can be monetized, and monetized integrity funds more integrity investment.

The empire also leverages crisis as a sales moment. Volatility increases demand for faster visibility, deeper feeds, and more reliable reference prints. Stress increases demand for forensic reconstruction and compliance proof. Funding stress increases demand for clear officialness to value collateral. The empire can profit from stress without calling it a surcharge because demand naturally shifts toward premium products. The risk is legitimacy backlash if this looks like crisis profiteering. The empire responds by framing premium product demand as stability necessities.

Consolidation changes how innovation is justified. Innovation becomes easier to sell as resilience and modernization when the innovator is an infrastructure group. Resilience justifications can be used to introduce more complexity and more tiering. More tiering increases revenue. The empire must calibrate so that tiering remains politically tolerable while still meaningfully better for paying clients.

Consolidation's deepest effect is that it restructures the market's boundary between public and private. The public lane must exist: basic price visibility, basic access, basic integrity. The private lanes can be sold: faster clocks, deeper data, better analytics, better connectivity, better reconstruction. As consolidation increases the empire's control over more of the market's essential records, the private lanes can become more valuable because they are more directly connected to authoritative sources. This can produce stable winners even when surface prices look chaotic, because the winners are those who buy the reality that matters for survivability.

Consolidation also alters the geography of disputes. When an empire owns evidence and clocks, disputes are resolved within its definitions. Regulators and courts will still intervene, but the raw record is often the empire's record. The party that owns the record owns the starting point of the dispute. Owning the starting point is an advantage because it shapes what evidence is available and what sequence is treated as plausible.

The empire's creation is therefore not merely corporate. It is epistemic. It is ownership of how the market knows what happened. Once an entity owns that epistemic layer, it can sell access to knowledge in tiers and can sell proof as a product. Proof is not optional for regulated institutions. That is why exchange empires behave like infrastructure landlords: they own necessity.

The consolidation wave also changes how market participants are categorized. Under local venues, membership identities can be specific and negotiated. Under empires, categories become standardized: retail-facing brokers, professional liquidity providers, data vendors, index clients, institutional allocators. Standardization makes pricing easier. Pricing easier makes extraction easier. Extraction easier increases profit. Profit funds acquisitions. The loop continues.

The market's public narrative often treats consolidation as inevitability: globalization, technology, competition. The operational reality is that consolidation is an active strategy to own interfaces and to price dependence. It can produce efficiency gains and still concentrate power. It can reduce duplication and still increase inequality in who can see, who can cancel, who can prove, who can clear cheaply, and who can settle without penalties.

Consolidation is therefore not a neutral corporate trend. It is a restructuring of how the market defines reality and how the market sells access to that reality. In the club era, reality was defined locally with local politics and local enforcement. In the empire era, reality is defined by a global infrastructure group whose incentives are shareholder returns, whose products are tiered access to recognition, and whose legitimacy is maintained by keeping the public lane credible while selling professional lanes as survivability.

CHAPTER 20
THE FLOOR, THE SCREEN, AND THE VICTORY OF SPEED

WHICH TRADING MODELS SCALED, WHICH FADED, AND WHY THE MACHINE CHOSE ELECTRONS OVER VOICES.

The market did not "innovate" into speed the way a gadget gets upgraded. It migrated into speed because speed solved three institutional problems at once: it made the record easier to defend, it made the queue easier to scale, and it made intermediation easier to monetize without showing the toll as a toll. The floor, the screen, and the victory of speed is not a morality tale about progress. It is a selection story about which microstructures survived once volume, fragmentation, leverage, and proof burdens became too large for human choreography to contain.

The floor was never simply a place. It was a governance arrangement. It solved a hard problem that early markets could not solve with paper alone: how to create a shared clock, a shared witness, and a shared enforcement perimeter in a world where credit and reputation were the settlement system. A floor made trading public to the insiders who mattered. It made manipulation harder to deny and easier to punish. It produced a visible sequence of bids, offers, and consummated bargains that could be remembered, recorded, and appealed to when disputes erupted. The floor's greatest product was not liquidity. It was an agreed story about what happened.

The screen did not replace the floor because screens are faster. It replaced the floor because the floor's story became too expensive to maintain under modern scale. As participation expanded and instruments multiplied, the floor's governance advantages turned into capacity bottlenecks. The market needed a witness that could observe everything at once, time-stamp it precisely, store it indefinitely, and reproduce it on demand. Human witnesses could not. Human memory could not. Human paper trails could not. Speed was a side effect of the deeper requirement: mechanically reproducible evidence.

The victory of speed is therefore the victory of a certain kind of legitimacy: legitimacy that can be proven by log files rather than by reputations and shouted recollection. When the market's money moved into institutions that demanded proof, and when regulation demanded reconstructible order lifecycles, the market selected for systems that could generate proof automatically. The screen won because the screen could be audited.

The floor's other hidden function was discretion. Discretion is often romanticized as human judgment. On the floor, discretion was a practical shock absorber. If a quote looked absurd, people could refuse it. If a buyer seemed predatory, people could lean away. If a sequence smelled wrong, someone could slow it down. The floor's discretion created a form of informal volatility control. That discretion also created room for favoritism, opacity, and negotiated privilege, which became politically intolerable as the market claimed to be open and rules-based. The screen won partly because it could offer the appearance of neutrality: same rules, same timestamps, same queue. Appearance matters because markets run on belief.

The machine chose electrons over voices because electrons can produce a queue that is both scalable and justifiable. A voice-based market cannot guarantee that everyone heard the same thing at the same time. It cannot guarantee that the order of bids was recorded consistently. It cannot guarantee that someone was not leaned on or excluded by a crowd. It can claim fairness as culture. It cannot prove fairness as procedure. Once the market required provable fairness, the floor became a liability.

The shift also changed what a trade is. On the floor, a trade is a social contract made in public among those inside the perimeter. On the screen, a trade is a message accepted by a protocol, matched by an engine, recorded by a log, and defended by timestamps. The contractual moment moved from the human handshake to the system acknowledgment. That moved sovereignty from people to design. The market's constitution became software plus rulebook plus evidence policy.

Three pressures forced this selection: throughput pressure, fragmentation pressure, and the proof burden. Throughput pressure meant the floor could not handle the number of interactions without becoming slow, uneven, and vulnerable to disorder. Fragmentation pressure meant the market could not remain a single room; it became many rooms, many instruments, many overlapping venues, and many simultaneous events. Proof burden meant that whatever happened had to be reconstructible, defensible, and consistent across records in the presence of disputes and enforcement. The floor could manage one room well. It could not manage many rooms at once.

The floor survived longer than it should have, which reveals its real strengths. A floor produces liquidity under ambiguity by using human negotiation to bridge gaps in information. It can clear large blocks by allowing parties to communicate context and manage information leakage through tone and relationship. It can impose informal discipline on those who behave predatory because repeated interactions create reputational consequences. These strengths mattered in eras when credit was local and information moved slowly. Those strengths become weaker when participants are anonymous, capital is global, and repeated interactions are mediated by machines.

The screen's strengths are different. It produces continuous auditable priority. It produces instantaneous dissemination. It produces precise timestamps. It supports automation. It supports fragmentation by allowing routers to compare venues. It supports surveillance by generating complete message trails. The screen's strengths align with modern institutional needs.

This migration also changed who could win. On the floor, advantage often came from relationships, social positioning, and human interpretation of momentum in a crowd. On the screen, advantage comes from perception speed, cancellation speed, routing intelligence, fee geometry exploitation, and the ability to survive margin and settlement pressure. The winners changed because the game changed. The machine selected the kinds of advantage that can be purchased and scaled.

The victory of speed is therefore the victory of scale economics. Once markets became message factories, the marginal cost of processing one more message fell, and the advantage shifted to those who could invest in fixed-cost infrastructure: better connectivity, better data, better models, and better proof systems. Fixed costs create minimum efficient scale. Minimum efficient scale concentrates. Concentration creates stable winners.

The floor's decline is often explained as inevitability. The deeper truth is that the floor was incompatible with the market's claim to be rules-based, broadly accessible, and auditable. If the market wanted to be a public utility in narrative, it needed a public utility in evidence. The screen is evidence infrastructure. The floor is witness culture. Witness culture cannot scale to global capital without becoming scandal-prone.

The market did not remove humans from price formation. It removed humans from the core queue. Humans remained in the edges: block negotiation, crisis modes, auction stewardship, and rulemaking. That is the hybrid that refused to die. The core queue became electronic because the core queue needed to be provable. The edges remained human because the edges involve ambiguity and legitimacy management.

The transition also forced a choice among trading models. Several models coexisted before the screen's dominance: continuous open outcry, scheduled call markets, dealer-based quotation, specialist mediation, and negotiated bilateral trading. Each model has a different relationship to information, volatility, and fairness. The models that survived did not survive because they were morally superior. They survived because they fit the system's constraints: they could scale, they could be audited, and they could be monetized without provoking immediate political backlash.

Begin with the call market. A call market collects orders over a period and then clears them at one price. It reduces the advantage of being slightly faster inside the call window. It produces a clean reference print. It can absorb large imbalances by allowing many participants to respond before clearing. Call markets are powerful stability tools. They did not dominate the full day because they are slow for those who need immediacy and because modern markets demand continuous hedging and continuous risk transfer. The call market survives at the open and close and in special auctions because those are the moments where reference quality matters more than continuous immediacy.

The continuous market, whether floor-based or screen-based, provides immediacy. It allows risk to be transferred at any moment. It is the model that aligns with continuous hedging, continuous news flow, and global time zones. Continuous markets therefore won the day's main trading because modern finance requires continuous adjustment.

Dealer markets and specialists solved a different problem: they supplied immediacy when the crowd was thin by using balance sheet to make a price. They were the original liquidity guarantee. Their weakness is that their discretion is both stabilizer and conflict. Discretion can protect the market from disorderly prints; discretion can also hide preferential treatment and extract hidden rents. As markets became more regulated and more skeptical of discretionary privilege, the system moved toward rules-based market making rather than role-based specialists, and toward automated quoting that can be audited.

Negotiated bilateral trading never disappeared because it is the most efficient way to move large risk without advertising intent. It moved into private channels and block mechanisms. It became part of fragmentation and internalization. The market kept it because impact is a real cost and because displayed markets cannot absorb very large transfers without producing predation.

Each model therefore survives where it fits: continuous screens for ordinary flow and hedging, auctions for reference moments and imbalance handling, private negotiation for large risk transfer, and human discretionary governance for crisis containment and rule evolution. The victory of speed is not total replacement. It is reallocation of functions across layers.

The screen's victory also created a new definition of fairness: fairness by protocol. Protocol fairness says everyone can send messages under the same rules. Protocol fairness is compelling politically. Protocol fairness is also compatible with outcome inequality because capacity to exploit protocol differs. If you can see sooner, you can cancel sooner. If you can cancel sooner, you can quote tighter without being selected against. If you can quote tighter, you attract flow. Flow yields information. Information yields profit. Profit buys more capacity. Protocol fairness therefore produces a stable inequality engine under a formally equal rule set. The floor's inequality was social; the screen's inequality is infrastructural. Infrastructural inequality is easier to defend because it is priced as technology rather than as exclusion.

The market chose electrons over voices because electrons allowed the market to sell technology as necessity. Speed became a product. Data became a product. Connectivity became a product. Proof became a product. These products are scalable and recurring. A floor is expensive and local. A screen is global and subscription-friendly. Once exchanges demutualized and became shareholder enterprises, the pressure to prefer scalable subscription-like products intensified. The screen was not only a technological improvement; it was a business model transformation.

The transition from floor to screen therefore cannot be separated from the exchange's shift in revenue mix. When matching is on the screen, every event is a message that can be packaged and sold. The exchange becomes a narrator selling its narration. It sells public summaries to preserve legitimacy and premium feeds to preserve profit. It sells connectivity to reduce latency. It sells historical archives to build models. It sells licensing rights to control redistribution. These are the tollbooths of visibility, and the screen is the infrastructure that makes them possible.

The floor could not sell visibility in the same way because visibility on the floor is embodied. It is limited to presence. Presence is not scalable and not easily licensed. The screen turned presence into a purchasable stream. That stream became the exchange's most defensible rent because the market cannot function without a shared perception and a shared record.

The victory of speed also changed the role of time. On the floor, time is approximate; sequence is negotiated by social perception. On the screen, time is precise; sequence is an enforceable order of events. Precise time makes disputes resolvable. It also makes micro-advantage possible because micro-advantage is the profit of being slightly earlier within precise sequence. A world without precise sequence cannot monetize micro-advantage reliably. A world with precise sequence can. This is why time became a commodity. The market sells earlier time through lower latency feeds and connectivity.

The screen also made cancellation a core competitive weapon. On the floor, canceling a displayed intention carries social cost and is slower. On the screen, canceling is instant and nearly frictionless. Frictionless cancellation changes liquidity's nature. Displayed depth becomes less committal. It can vanish in response to information. Under stress, cancellation surges. Depth becomes a mirage. This mirage is one reason the hybrid survives: the market needs halts, auctions, and mode switches to prevent mirage-driven prints from becoming official reality.

The mirage also explains why speed won even though it increases fragility. Speed increases fragility because it allows feedback loops to accelerate. Yet speed also allows participants to protect themselves by canceling and repricing, which keeps them in the market in calm times. The system tolerates fragility because it can be managed by hybrid safety mechanisms and because speed produces profits that fund the infrastructure and the political defense of the system.

The victory of speed therefore is a negotiated equilibrium among three constituencies: participants who demand cheap continuous hedging, infrastructure owners who demand scalable recurring revenue, and regulators who demand auditable fairness. The screen satisfies all three better than the floor, even while creating new inequality and new fragility.

The decisive selection event was the growth of institutional obligations that require proof. When portfolios became large and mandates became formal, "trust us" became insufficient. Best execution had to be demonstrated. Manipulation had to be reconstructed. Errors had to be adjudicated with logs. The evidence burden became constant. A floor cannot produce complete evidence at scale. A screen can.

The evidence burden also reshaped the cost structure of trading firms. They had to store and analyze message trails. They had to maintain surveillance. They had to produce compliance reports. These are fixed costs. Fixed costs raised minimum efficient scale. Raised minimum efficient scale concentrated market making and routing into larger entities. Concentration made speed arms races more intense because the remaining competitors could afford to invest. The screen's victory is therefore linked to the concentration of participants as much as to the concentration of exchanges.

The story of the floor versus the screen is often told as romantic decline. The real story is that the floor's strengths became less valuable than the costs it imposed. The floor's discretion became politically dangerous. The floor's human latency became economically expensive. The floor's inability to generate machine-readable evidence became legally untenable. The screen offered a clean alternative: protocol fairness, auditable logs, and scalable dissemination.

The screen also enabled fragmentation. A floor-based market naturally concentrates because physical presence is a barrier. A screen-based market can be duplicated. Multiple venues can offer matching. That creates competition and fragmentation. Fragmentation then creates routing. Routing creates new rents. Those rents are sold as execution intelligence. The screen did not just replace the floor; it multiplied the number of markets and made the act of selecting among them profitable.

Fragmentation then pushed the system further toward speed because routing and cross-venue arbitrage require fast perception. If prices diverge across venues, those who see divergence earlier can capture it. If quotes are stale, those who see staleness earlier can avoid being selected against. The screen created many rooms; speed became the ability to navigate the rooms before the doors moved.

The victory of speed also redefined what a market participant is. On the floor, participants are human bodies with relationships. On the screen, participants are systems. Systems can be optimized. Systems can be scaled. Systems can be audited. Systems can also be weaponized. This is why surveillance expanded. The screen produced the evidence needed to police behavior, but it also produced the complexity that requires policing.

The market's speed turn also changed how value is extracted. On the floor, value is extracted through spread and through relationships. On the screen, value is extracted through microstructure: rebates, fee tiers, order type privileges, data access tiers, connectivity, and internalization. These are structural rents that do not require being right about direction. They require controlling or purchasing the interface. That aligns with Part III's theme: stable winners under visible chaos.

The screen's dominance also depended on a change in what society demanded from markets. As households became structurally invested through retirement systems and as markets became central to wealth formation, the market needed to look fairer and more open. The screen is visually democratic: anyone can access through a broker interface. The floor is visibly exclusive. The screen's narrative advantage is huge. It can claim openness even if practical inequality persists through paid lanes. The floor could not plausibly make that claim.

The market chose electrons over voices because electrons let it sell openness and monetize inequality simultaneously. The public lane can be maintained with public quotes and basic access. The premium lanes can be sold to professionals as survivability tools. This satisfies political demand for inclusion and shareholder demand for rent. It is the system's compromise.

The floor did not die entirely because some functions resist full electronization: block negotiation, illiquid risk transfer, and crisis discretion. Those functions moved to the edges and became part of the hybrid safety architecture and private completion ecosystem. The floor's spirit remains in auction stewardship and block negotiation, but the floor as the core queue lost because it could not meet modern proof and scale requirements.

The victory of speed also produced a new kind of vulnerability: the vulnerability of being governed by a clock. When everything is time-stamped, time becomes a weapon and a dependency. If clocks drift, evidence fractures. If feeds delay, perception diverges. If one participant is earlier, that participant can harvest those who are later. The market therefore invests heavily in time synchronization and in defining which clock counts. Defining which clock counts is governance. Governance is power. Power is monetizable when it is embedded in evidence and reference.

The victory of speed is therefore a victory of the clock as sovereign. The old sovereign was the crowd. The new sovereign is the time-stamp. The crowd was messy and discretionary. The timestamp is precise and monetizable. Precision is what allowed modern markets to scale into global infrastructure groups and to sell visibility as a subscription.

A final note on what "speed" actually won. Speed did not win because it produced better prices in a moral sense. Speed won because it produced a system that could be defended. Defended against disputes. Defended against enforcement. Defended against political backlash with a story of protocol fairness. Defended economically with recurring revenue streams tied to data and connectivity. The screen won the legitimacy war by offering proof. It won the business war by offering subscription. It won the competitive war by making micro-advantage purchasable and scalable.

"The crowd decided with its throat; the machine decides with its clock."

The crowd's decision was human and therefore contestable. The machine's decision is procedural and therefore defensible. Defensibility is the currency that allowed the market to become the modern machine.

CHAPTER 21

THE HYBRID THAT REFUSED TO DIE

WHY HUMAN JUDGMENT STILL SURVIVES WHEN MACHINE MARKETS STRUGGLE TO ABSORB SHOCK.

A machine market is built to be fast, consistent, and scalable. Those virtues are also its failure modes under stress, because speed amplifies feedback, consistency hardens procyclical behavior, and scale turns small errors into systemic events. The system never fully eliminated the human layer because the system cannot outsource legitimacy to literalness. It relocated humans into bounded roles, wrote procedures around them, and priced access to the moments when discretion matters. The hybrid survives because the market's real job is not to trade; it is to finish trading in a way that can be defended when the inputs become unreliable and the outputs become politically visible.

The public story says humans faded because electrons are better. The operating truth is humans remain because electrons are literal. A matching engine will do exactly what it is told, in the sequence it is told, on the timestamps it is told, with no understanding of whether the feed is corrupted, whether the book is momentarily one-sided, whether the best quote is a mirage built from cancelable liquidity, whether a price is stale relative to a cross-venue state, or whether the next millisecond reveals that the market is already somewhere else.

Literal obedience can be perfect and still be wrong because wrongness in markets is often contextual: a technically valid print can be socially illegitimate if it is produced from a transient vacuum and then used as a reference anchor for collateral, benchmarks, and disputes.

The hybrid is not nostalgia. It is the market's safety architecture. It exists because there are states of the world where automated matching produces outputs that cannot be defended without adding qualifiers that would collapse the belief that a price is a fact. A market needs moments where it can slow down, collect information, widen participation, and decide what counts as a valid record. Those moments are not daily for most participants. They are frequent enough that the system cannot remove the option without increasing the probability of a legitimacy fracture.

The hybrid endures because markets are not only computational systems. They are legal systems and evidence systems. Legal systems require definitions of finality, error, and authority. Evidence systems require stable records that can be reconstructed and defended. When inputs become unreliable, an automated system can still produce records, but the records may be impossible to defend without admitting the machine created a value from noise. The hybrid is the system's method for preventing noise from becoming officialness.

The survival of human judgment is easiest to understand by mapping the conditions under which purely automated markets become dangerous. The first condition is liquidity discontinuity. Liquidity discontinuity occurs when displayed depth evaporates faster than takers can adapt. In calm times, continuous posting and cancelling is treated as normal market maintenance. In stress, cancellation rates surge and displayed depth becomes a mirage: it exists in the feed and disappears at the moment it is targeted. A marketable order arrives and finds an empty book. The result is extreme slippage that is technically valid and politically explosive. The system responds with mechanisms that create time and simultaneity: pauses, limit bands, auction extensions, and discretionary intervention. These mechanisms are hybrid because they require human authority to invoke, to calibrate, and to explain afterward.

The second condition is cross-venue incoherence. Fragmentation means multiple venues are live simultaneously. Under normal conditions, arbitrage and routing keep prices aligned within tolerances. Under stress or outage, alignment breaks. One venue may show stale quotes. Another may be functioning normally. A third may be impaired by message delays. The consolidated public view may lag all of them. A purely automated system could continue matching locally and produce prints that are coherent inside that venue and incoherent globally. Global incoherence cannot be accepted because hedging, collateral valuation, and risk limits require a coherent reference. The hybrid exists to impose coherence: pause here, extend there, declare which prints are eligible for reference, and decide which feed is authoritative for reconstruction.

The third condition is price discontinuity driven by forced behavior. Forced behavior arrives in windows: open, close, rebalance events, benchmark cut-offs, margin call schedules, settlement cut-offs, and corporate-action record dates. These windows concentrate urgency. When urgency concentrates, spreads widen and depth thins. Continuous matching can produce extreme prints at those moments, and those extreme prints can become official reference prices if the system does not intervene. The hybrid exists because the system wants reference moments that can be defended as representative rather than as accidents of sequencing.

The fourth condition is operational error in a high-speed environment. Markets generate errors daily: broken symbol mapping, misapplied corporate action adjustments, duplicated messages, missing messages, crossed markets, mispriced orders, runaway algorithms, and data vendor glitches. The system survives not because errors are absent, but because errors are contained through controlled correction regimes. A fully automatic correction regime is exploitable because it can be gamed to manufacture free options. A fully irreversible regime is illegitimate because obvious glitches become binding reality. The hybrid survives as the compromise: correction is possible, but only through controlled processes, within windows, with evidence thresholds, and with discretion to deny opportunistic claims.

The hybrid is also a labor architecture. Human judgment is not simply one person stopping a market. It is distributed among roles, committees, and escalation pathways. These roles are designed to preserve two properties at once: operational throughput in normal times and defensible discretion in abnormal times. The hybrid is therefore not an exception to the system. It is a mode the system enters when the conditions that make automation socially acceptable are no longer present.

The first hybrid component is the volatility governor. This includes limit bands, halts, and mode shifts. A volatility governor is not meant to prevent price movement. It is meant to prevent the market from being forced to clear at prices formed under conditions of impaired liquidity and extreme adverse selection. When a book is thin and cancellations surge, the marginal trade can be a liquidation artifact rather than a price that represents broad agreement. A volatility governor creates time so that liquidity providers can re-enter and so that price formation can occur with broader participation. Time is the simplest stabilizer because time allows information to disseminate and allows more counterparties to respond.

The second component is the auction steward. Auctions are the hybrid's primary legitimacy tool because they replace microsecond sequencing with discrete simultaneity. Simultaneity reduces the advantage of being marginally faster inside the auction window. It does not remove advantage. It shifts advantage toward forecasting the clearing price, interpreting imbalance signals, and choosing submission timing. The auction steward's job is to manage these windows when imbalance is extreme or when the normal schedule would produce a reference print that is difficult to defend. Extending the auction, adjusting dissemination, and applying participation rules are human-governed actions even when executed through software, because they are discretionary choices about what the market will treat as a valid reference.

The third component is the error arbiter. This role evaluates contested trades, decides whether they stand, and manages corrections. The error arbiter preserves two competing requirements: finality must be strong enough that markets can function and flexible enough that obvious malfunctions do not become permanent facts. Error arbitration is the system's defense against free-option behavior. If a participant can always claim error when losing and accept trades when winning, markets collapse. The arbiter exists to demand evidence and to apply correction only when the event meets defined criteria. Defined criteria must still be interpreted, because criteria cannot anticipate every failure mode in a complex machine.

The fourth component is the kill-switch operator and containment team. Automated markets can transmit a malfunction across venues quickly. A runaway strategy can flood order books, cancel liquidity, and create false prints. Containment exists to throttle, disconnect, or suspend. This is not mercy. It is preventing a local malfunction from becoming a distributed liquidity vacuum. Containment must be fast, and it must be accountable, because the act of disconnecting a participant is both safety and redistribution: it changes who is allowed to participate and therefore changes price formation.

The fifth component is the continuity manager. When communications degrade or feeds disagree, the system must decide which view counts for officialness, for surveillance, and for reconstruction. The continuity manager enforces the single-story requirement: the market cannot have two competing realities that both claim to be official. Competing realities create disputes. Disputes create paralysis. The market cannot function if participants believe reference is negotiable on demand. Continuity management includes declaring a primary record, defining outage procedures, and coordinating with downstream systems that rely on the record.

These human roles persist because machine markets struggle with one specific property of stress: feedback loops that are fast enough to outrun discretion but slow enough to be exploited. In calm times, speed makes markets cheap. In stress, speed can make markets brittle. Brittleness emerges when the system responds to its own outputs. Volatility rises, which tightens risk limits, which triggers liquidation, which increases volatility. Depth evaporates, which increases slippage, which triggers more protective cancellations, which evaporates depth further. A pure machine will faithfully execute the loop. The hybrid exists to break the loop by inserting time and discretion.

The hybrid's methods are mostly temporal and procedural. Temporal means: pause, extend, delay, stage, batch, and auction. Procedural means: define which prints count, define what error correction is permitted, define which participants are throttled, define which data is authoritative, define which collateral valuations are used when reference prints are contested. These methods produce a market that can be defended as fair enough to keep participation broad.

The hybrid also survives because the market is not only about execution; it is about reference. Reference prices are used in collateral agreements, benchmark calculations, risk models, and performance evaluation. A reference price formed in a liquidity vacuum can trigger collateral calls, margin increases, and forced selling. A forced selling cascade can then create more vacuum prints. The hybrid exists to protect reference quality because reference quality is a stability prerequisite. A market can tolerate some noise in continuous prints. It cannot tolerate official reference prints being obviously wrong, because officialness is the foundation of trust.

The hybrid therefore is a subsystem that protects officialness. It does not protect participants from losses. It protects the system from producing official records that invite mass dispute. Mass dispute is existential because it turns trading into litigation and turns liquidity into hoarding. Hoarding is the death of a market because it eliminates the willingness to be the other side.

The hybrid's persistence is also explained by the incompleteness of any rulebook. Rulebooks encode past knowledge. Stress produces new combinations. New combinations create edge cases where the rulebook yields outcomes that are technically valid and socially unacceptable. The market cannot admit that it is socially unacceptable without undermining the neutrality narrative. The market therefore encodes discretion as rule-defined exceptions: volatility halts, error trade policies, auction extensions, and extraordinary session declarations. The exceptions are the hybrid's legal mechanism. Humans are the interpreters and executors of the exceptions.

The hybrid also performs a signaling function. When a market pauses or extends, it signals that the system is choosing stability over speed. This signal has a public audience and a professional audience. The public audience needs to believe the system is not rigged by machines for insiders. The professional audience needs to believe the system will not allow exploitation through obvious glitches. Both audiences require that someone is accountable for the decision. Accountability is a legitimacy product.

Accountability creates a second reason for the hybrid: politics. A market that breaks publicly requires a narrative with responsibility. A log file does not satisfy politics. Politics demands that someone can be questioned, blamed, and explained. That demand is not irrational. It is a stability mechanism because it forces institutions to maintain procedures and to plan for exceptional events. The hybrid persists because the market is embedded in social systems that require blame and remedy, not only computation.

The hybrid also survives because some trading problems remain negotiation problems. Illiquid instruments, large blocks, complex corporate events, and cross-border transfers often require discretion about timing, sizing, and information leakage. A pure electronic order book can be too costly in impact for a very large transfer. Private completion pathways require judgment about how to stage risk transfer without inviting predation. Humans persist in these channels because judgment is the cheapest way to manage certain forms of information risk and because negotiated completion can reduce downstream settlement breaks.

Negotiated completion is also a gate. If large transfers can be handled privately, then those with access to private pathways can avoid paying the full cost of public exposure. The system justifies private pathways as efficiency and stability. They can be both. They also create inequality in execution outcomes because private pathways often require scale, relationships, and compliance infrastructure. The hybrid therefore is not only safety. It is also a stratification mechanism.

The market's hybrid features are monetizable, which helps explain their persistence. Auctions create valuable imbalance information. Pauses create valuable restart dynamics. Exceptional handling creates privileged access pathways. A system that has hybrid modes can sell products that help participants survive those modes: premium auction data, premium timestamps, premium connectivity, and analytics that predict when the system is likely to enter a pause or extension state. The hybrid therefore is both a stabilizer and a revenue surface.

The most important hybrid moments are those that define the day's canonical record. The open and the close are not just times; they are reference anchors used for valuation, performance, and reporting. If a close is printed from a vacuum, it becomes a systemic hazard because it triggers benchmarking errors and collateral disputes. The system therefore invests heavily in closing auction procedures, extension rules, imbalance dissemination, and participation incentives. Each investment is framed as fairness. Each also increases the value of premium tools used to navigate the close. The hybrid persists because it protects the reference and because the reference is profitable.

The hybrid's interaction with the index engine is direct. Index tracking forces trades into windows, especially at the close. Forced trades increase imbalance risk. Imbalance risk increases the probability of dislocated prints. Dislocated prints threaten reference credibility. The hybrid responds by strengthening auction mechanisms, extension rules, and error-correction regimes. Those mechanisms reduce the probability that forced flows produce indefensible records. They also create predictable structural events that can be traded around by those with visibility and inventory capacity.

The hybrid's interaction with the risk warehouse is equally direct. If volatility rises, margin rises. Margin calls force liquidation. Liquidation concentrates at the most liquid instruments and at the most liquid times. Concentration can overwhelm depth. Overwhelmed depth increases slippage and increases print dislocations. Print dislocations can trigger more risk model tightening. The loop can accelerate. The hybrid exists to slow the loop: pauses, auctions, and extraordinary handling create time for funding to arrive and for liquidity to re-enter.

Funding is the invisible fuel of the hybrid. A pause is not just a pause. It is a funding window. It is a chance for participants to meet margin, to obtain collateral, to reduce exposure, and to decide whether to re-enter liquidity provision. A purely continuous market leaves no funding window. It forces immediate clearance and can therefore force liquidation at the worst moment. Hybrid tools create the slack needed for funding to catch up to price movement. Slack is stability.

The hybrid also exists because the market's evidence layer must remain coherent. In stress, feeds can disagree, timestamps can drift, and venues can diverge. If the evidence layer fractures, disputes become unresolvable because there is no shared record. A fractured evidence layer invites opportunism: participants can choose the record that favors them. The system must prevent record choice. It does so by defining authoritative sources and by enabling human decisions when authority is contested. The hybrid thus protects the single-story property of markets: one market reality for legal and contractual purposes.

The single-story property requires discipline in error policy. Error policy has two goals that are in tension. The first goal is deterrence of opportunism: participants must not be allowed to treat the market as a free option. The second goal is correction of genuine malfunction: the system must not allow obvious breakdowns to become binding. The hybrid reconciles the tension by requiring evidence thresholds and by granting decision authority to designated arbiters. This authority is limited by policy and documented procedures. Documentation is essential because documentation produces defensibility, and defensibility is legitimacy.

Defensibility is not abstract. Defensibility determines whether a correction will be accepted by courts, regulators, and counterparties. It determines whether the correction will trigger additional disputes. It determines whether the market can continue trading without participants fearing that trades will be reversed unpredictably. A market with unpredictable reversals is not liquid because liquidity providers will widen spreads or withdraw to protect against reversal risk. The hybrid therefore must be predictable enough to preserve liquidity while flexible enough to correct malfunctions. Predictability is engineered through explicit thresholds and time windows. Flexibility is preserved through discretion inside those thresholds.

Hybrid mechanisms also serve as a coordination device. In fragmentation, coordination is hard because multiple venues must remain coherent. A pause in one venue can create an arbitrage problem if another venue continues. The system therefore coordinates pauses, halts, and extraordinary procedures to preserve cross-venue coherence. Coordination is governance. Governance requires authority. Authority requires humans and procedures. This is another reason the hybrid persists: the market needs a coordination layer that sits above local matching engines.

Coordination is also where exchange groups and infrastructure owners gain leverage. A group that owns multiple venues can coordinate more easily and can standardize procedures. Standardization reduces confusion and reduces disputes. It also increases dependence on the group's procedures and data products. Thus the hybrid's coordination layer is both a stability tool and a consolidation tool.

The hybrid's durability is also explained by a simple behavioral reality: participants adapt. If the market is purely automated, participants will search for the edges of automation and exploit them. If the market includes discretionary correction, participants will search for ways to manufacture conditions that trigger discretionary correction in their favor. The system must therefore design hybrid mechanisms to be hard to game. Hard to game means: evidence thresholds, limited windows, and penalties for abuse. Designing for anti-gaming is itself a human judgment problem because gaming evolves. The hybrid persists because adversarial adaptation is permanent.

Adversarial adaptation creates a recurring design cycle. A new microstructure feature is introduced to improve stability or fairness. Participants learn how to exploit it. Exploitation produces distortions. The system responds by tightening rules, adding surveillance, and adding new hybrid triggers. Each change increases complexity. Complexity increases dependence on premium tools. Premium tools increase spending. Spending funds more surveillance and more product development. The hybrid becomes embedded as part of the market's evolution because evolution is adversarial and cannot be solved once.

The hybrid therefore is not a temporary compromise on the way to full automation. It is a permanent feature of a market that must be both fast and socially legitimate. Legitimacy is a constraint, and constraints create mechanisms. The hybrid is the mechanism that reconciles speed with legitimacy by allowing the market to change mode when the conditions for fair-by-rule matching are not present.

The hybrid's final property is that it is selective. Not all participants benefit equally from hybrid modes. Those who can buy premium imbalance data can position around auctions. Those who can buy premium connectivity can react faster when trading resumes. Those with cheaper funding can warehouse inventory through a pause and then sell into the restart. Those without are often forced to trade at worse levels because they must reduce risk quickly. Hybrid modes can therefore stabilize the system while still producing stable winners. Stability and inequality are compatible because stability is achieved through gate-based access to time, information, and funding.

That compatibility is why the hybrid refused to die. A fully automated market would be cheaper in calm times and more fragile in stress. A fully discretionary market would be harder to scale and easier to contest legally. The hybrid is the equilibrium: automation for throughput, discretion for legitimacy, and priced interfaces for those who want to survive the moments when the system changes mode.

CHAPTER 22

THE FRAGMENTED MARKET

ROUTING, VENUE COMPETITION, AND THE HIDDEN ECONOMICS OF WHERE ORDERS VANISH, SURFACE, AND GET PAID THROUGH.

A single market is a comforting idea: one price, one queue, one public truth. The modern system is not built that way. It is built as a network of venues, each with its own rulebook, fee geometry, data products, order type menus, and priority logic, stitched together by routers, internalizers, and a compliance narrative that insists the stitching produces one coherent best price. Fragmentation is defended as competition. It behaves as a tax paid in invisible tolls: latency, inference cost, slippage from partial visibility, higher proof burdens, and the compounding advantage of those who can treat the network as one integrated machine while others experience it as scattered rooms with doors they cannot find quickly enough.

Fragmentation exists because no single venue can satisfy every incentive at once. A venue that maximizes transparency exposes intent and increases predation risk for large traders. A venue that maximizes anonymity reduces signaling but weakens the public story of price discovery. A venue that subsidizes posting deepens displayed depth but shifts cost into fee channels and behavior incentives. A venue that sells premium data creates paid perception tiers that can be defended as infrastructure funding. A venue that optimizes for speed attracts cancellation-heavy liquidity that looks like depth in calm times and becomes fragile in stress. The system resolves these conflicts by allowing multiple venues to specialize and then selling navigation as a product, which means the system creates complexity and then sells the right to survive that complexity.

The first economic function of fragmentation is segmentation of intent. Different participants want different completion shapes. Some want immediacy at any cost. Some want minimal impact and accept slow completion. Some want hidden size to avoid being leaned on. Some want displayed priority to earn spread. Some want private completion to avoid broadcasting intent and to capture predictable spread. Fragmentation allows each preference to find a venue form, which looks like choice. The cost is that the market now requires a new governor: the router, the actor that decides where intent goes and which liquidity is reachable for a given order under a given definition of best execution.

Routing is the core governance act of fragmented markets because it decides which liquidity you are allowed to interact with, which fees you will pay, which signals you will reveal, which record becomes evidence for your execution, and which party captures the spread. Routing is presented as optimization. It is also allocation. Allocation is what determines who earns rents in a system where "best price" is an abstraction and "best execution" is a defensibility standard within a range rather than a provable optimum.

A fragmented market has two prices at every moment. There is the displayed price, the best visible quote across venues under defined rules and defined sizes. There is the achievable price, which depends on hidden liquidity, internalization willingness, queue position, partial fills, latency, and the probability that the liquidity still exists when you reach it. The achievable price determines real outcomes.

The displayed price preserves legitimacy. The gap between them is not an anomaly; it is the profit surface created by fragmentation and sold through data, connectivity, and routing services.

Fragmentation immediately creates a technical problem that becomes political economy: the same instrument can be quoted differently across venues at the same time. Without a unifying reference, disputes would explode and hedging would become unstable because "the price" would be contestable. The system constructs a unifying benchmark derived from venue quotes and defines it as the shared truth. The benchmark is necessary. It is also a convenience narrative because it compresses a layered reality into a single number that can be used for compliance and marketing. The machine then monetizes the difference between the benchmark and the real, reachable state of liquidity.

A composite quote is not the book. It is an abstraction. In a fragmented system the abstraction is incomplete by design. Even if every venue publishes its best quote, that quote can be stale by the time it is consumed. Even if it is timely, it can be fragile because it can be cancelled instantly by those with faster perception. Even if it is stable, it can be small because the deepest liquidity may be hidden or may sit behind order types that do not display. The result is that "best price" is often a best price for a specific fraction of a second, for a specific small size, under a specific definition of displayed. The market can still claim fairness because the definition is written. The system still produces inequality because the ability to exploit the definition depends on paid perception and paid reaction.

Fragmentation's second economic function is the creation of routing economics. In a single-venue world, a broker earns commissions and competes on service. In a fragmented world, the broker earns value by choosing destinations that generate rebates, reduce explicit fees, lower completion risk, or produce favorable bilateral arrangements with internalizers. The broker's obligation is to deliver best execution, but best execution is evaluated through metrics that must be defensible rather than perfect. If multiple routes can be defended as reasonable, routing becomes a space where broker economics and ecosystem relationships can dominate while still passing formal tests.

The most important routing conflict is the tension between public interaction and private completion. Public interaction exposes the order to open competition and can produce genuine improvement when many liquidity providers respond. Public interaction also leaks intent and can increase impact, particularly for orders large enough to move the book. Private completion reduces visible impact and can deliver a price at least as good as the public benchmark, often with a small improvement. Private completion also shifts value: the internalizer captures spread and captures early flow information that can be hedged efficiently. The public experiences a fill. The machine experiences a transfer of information and rent.

Private completion's advantage is predictability. Predictable flow is less toxic. Less toxic flow allows tighter pricing. Tighter pricing attracts more flow. More flow increases predictability. The loop compounds, and fragmentation makes it possible because fragmentation allows flow to be diverted away from the public book before it can influence the benchmark in a way that would reveal how much private completion has changed the composition of displayed liquidity.

Fragmentation therefore changes who the displayed market is for. The displayed market becomes the arena where professional, informational, and hedging flows interact, while a large share of smaller, predictable orders are handled privately and expressed indirectly through hedging prints. The public sees the displayed market and believes it is the whole market. The machine treats it as one layer among several, and it prices access to the layers.

The third economic function of fragmentation is the sale of venue differentiation. Venues compete by changing fee schedules, adding order types, running auctions, and selling premium data. A venue's goal is not merely to attract trades. It is to attract the kinds of trades that produce the most scalable revenue: message-rich activity that increases the value of data products, reference moments that increase licensing demand, and participant behavior that increases reliance on premium connectivity. A venue can make more money selling visibility and time than selling execution, as long as it retains enough relevance that its records remain valuable as evidence and reference.

Fee schedules are the venue's primary steering instrument. A venue can subsidize posting through rebates and charge takers, making displayed liquidity appear deeper while moving cost into the taker side. A venue can reverse the economics, changing where liquidity rests. A venue can offer volume tiers that lower effective costs for large participants, making scale a structural advantage that can be converted into tighter quoting and more flow capture. A venue can create programs that reward specific behaviors: consistent quoting, participation in auctions, or maintenance of certain order-to-trade ratios. Each schedule shapes where liquidity rests and how stable it is under stress.

Fee geometry also shapes routing. If a broker earns rebates by routing to specific venues, the broker has an incentive to choose those venues when the execution outcome is still defensible. This creates a conflict that must be managed through policies and reporting. Reporting itself is a cost. Cost advantages scale. Scale advantages allow better reporting, which allows more aggressive optimization inside defensible boundaries.

Fragmentation's fourth function is the creation of a navigation arms race. If liquidity is dispersed, the ability to discover it and access it quickly becomes valuable. Smart routing becomes an industry. A router must decide, quickly, whether to post or take, whether to split, whether to probe hidden liquidity, whether to interact with auctions, whether to avoid venues associated with high adverse selection, and whether to prioritize completion certainty over marginal price improvement. The router must also decide how much information to reveal and when, because revealing too much makes you a target.

Navigation is expensive because it requires data, models, and connectivity. Expensive navigation creates fixed costs. Fixed costs advantage scale. Scale funds better navigation. Better navigation produces better execution outcomes and lower adverse selection losses. Better outcomes attract more flow. More flow provides more information to improve navigation models. The loop compounds. Fragmentation therefore creates a structural advantage for the largest navigators and a structural disadvantage for participants who must navigate with delayed or simplified visibility.

The visible symptom of fragmentation is that the market can look deep and still behave thin. Depth is dispersed. The best visible quote can be small and cancelable. A participant attempts to execute size at the visible best and finds liquidity disappears, forcing the order to sweep worse prices across multiple venues. The participant pays slippage not because liquidity did not exist in aggregate, but because the participant could not see where it truly was or could not reach it fast enough. This is fragmentation tax paid as slippage.

The fifth function of fragmentation is the creation of latency value. When there are multiple venues and multiple feeds, there is no single moment when everyone sees the same state. Those who see earlier can cancel earlier, reprice earlier, and route earlier. Those who see later trade on stale abstraction and get selected against. Latency is not only time; it is survivability. Survivability is monetizable. Fragmentation increases survivability value because cross-venue divergence is more frequent and because the volume of micro-events is larger. Small perception advantages repeated thousands of times become large outcome differences.

This produces a stratified perception market. A public feed preserves legitimacy. Premium feeds preserve survivability. Participants who buy premium feeds can operate on higher fidelity and lower delay, making their liquidity more stable and their loss rates lower. Lower losses allow tighter quoting. Tighter quoting attracts flow. Flow improves inference. The loop compounds. Fragmentation amplifies the loop because it increases the number of micro-events where being slightly earlier changes whether you are harvested.

Fragmentation also changes the meaning of "best price." Best price becomes an obligation defined by rules rather than an objective truth. The system specifies what counts: which venues are included, which sizes are protected, how odd sizes are handled, how quote validity is defined, how stale quotes are treated, how timestamps are reconciled. These definitions are necessary. They also create edges. If the definition excludes certain liquidity, that liquidity can be interacted with privately without moving the benchmark. If the definition lags, those with faster perception can exploit the lag. If the definition treats some quotes as protected and others not, routing priorities change.

The market's unifying benchmark becomes both stabilizer and target. It stabilizes by creating a shared story. It becomes a target because contracts, valuations, and strategies reference it. If a participant can predict how the benchmark is computed and when it will move, the participant can position and capture value from those forced to trade relative to it. Fragmentation makes benchmark computation more complex. Complexity increases positioning opportunities.

Fragmentation's sixth function is the creation of hidden liquidity ecosystems. Hidden liquidity exists because visible intent is expensive. Participants who do not want to be leaned on seek mechanisms that allow execution without advertising size. Hidden liquidity reduces impact for the initiator. It also reduces transparency for everyone else. Reduced transparency shifts advantage toward those who can infer hidden supply and demand from indirect signals:

partial fills, timing patterns, venue-specific prints, and hedging behavior that leaks through public venues.

The system tolerates hidden liquidity because it is a release valve. Without it, large trades would crash through displayed books and create more visible volatility. Yet hidden liquidity weakens the public story that displayed markets reflect total supply and demand. Fragmentation allows the release valve to exist while keeping the public story anchored to a displayed benchmark that remains usable for most purposes.

The seventh function is completion selection. In a fragmented system, some paths settle more reliably than others. Some venues have fewer operational breaks. Some counterparties are more reliable. Some workflows are smoother. These differences matter because settlement failures and exception processing trap capital and impose penalties. Brokers and liquidity providers therefore route and quote not only based on execution price but based on completion risk. Completion risk becomes another hidden dimension of best execution.

Completion risk reinforces concentration. Participants with better operational infrastructure have fewer fails and recycle capital faster. Faster recycling allows more trading capacity. More capacity supports tighter quoting. Tighter quoting attracts flow. Flow yields revenue. Revenue funds better operations. The loop compounds. Fragmentation increases the value of this loop because more venues and more interactions create more opportunities for breaks.

Fragmentation also changes surveillance economics. Dispersed activity is harder to monitor. A manipulative sequence can be split across venues. A suspicious pattern may only become visible when consolidated across multiple data streams. Consolidation requires expensive tooling. Expensive tooling advantages scale, including infrastructure owners and the largest participants. The system responds by selling surveillance and reconstruction as products. Fragmentation increases demand for proof products, and proof products become revenue surfaces for those who own records and clocks.

The rules designed to unify fragmented markets often take the form of best-price obligations and order protection obligations. These rules are meant to prevent systematic execution at inferior prices when better displayed quotes exist elsewhere. They preserve a semblance of one market. They also create boundary conditions: latency allowances, quote validity windows, exceptions, and definitions of protected size. Those boundary conditions create edges because those who can exploit them can route around protection while remaining compliant.

Routing becomes the arena where boundary conditions are monetized. A router can comply with best-price obligations while selecting venues that optimize broker economics, minimize information leakage, and maximize completion certainty. Compliance can be proven by showing execution at or within the benchmark at the time. The public sees compliance. The machine sees optimization inside the compliance range.

Fragmentation also changes what competition means. Competition at the surface is among venues for volume. Competition underneath is among interfaces for reference and evidence. The venue group that controls the most valuable interface is the one whose records become default proof and whose reference moments become mandatory for valuation and tracking. That group can lose some executions and still win economically because it can monetize the need to see and to prove.

Fragmentation produces stable winners without requiring directional forecasting. Stable winners include the largest routers, the most efficient internalizers, the most capitalized liquidity providers, the data and evidence sellers, and the venue groups that own reference and clocks. Their advantage is being positioned where the system must pass. Fragmentation increases passes. Passes increase tolls.

The public's relationship with price changes under fragmentation. The public sees a quote and believes it is the market. The actual price experienced depends on route, size, timing, queue position, and whether the order is internalized or exposed. The difference is often small per trade. Across a lifetime of trading, the difference compounds. This compounding is a reliable extraction pathway because it looks like normal slippage rather than a visible fee.

The defense is that fragmentation lowers explicit costs through competition. Explicit fees can fall. Hidden costs can rise. Hidden costs include data subscriptions required for high-quality routing, connectivity required for protective cancellation, slippage caused by partial visibility, and proof burdens that raise minimum efficient scale. Fragmentation can therefore reduce visible tolls while increasing invisible tolls. The system persists because invisible tolls are harder to politicize.

To meet the full mechanism burden, the fragmented market must be described as a sequence of state changes rather than as a static map. Consider the order journey in a fragmented environment with three simultaneous decisions: where to seek execution, how much to reveal, and how to preserve completion certainty.

The first state is classification. The order is classified as likely benign or likely toxic. The classification depends on size, urgency, instrument characteristics, and current regime conditions. If classified benign, the router prefers private completion because private completion offers consistent fills and small improvements without forcing the order into the public book. If classified toxic, private completion may refuse or widen implied spreads, pushing the order toward public venues where competition distributes risk. This is not morality. This is adverse selection pricing.

The second state is venue evaluation. The router evaluates displayed quotes, depth, auction states, and known fee schedules. It also evaluates expected cancellation fragility: how likely displayed size is to disappear before interaction. It evaluates the probability of partial fill, and the cost of partial fill is not merely inconvenience. Partial fills increase exposure time and increase signaling. Exposure time increases predation probability. Predation probability increases impact.

The third state is slicing. The router breaks the parent order into child orders with different behaviors: a portion posted to earn spread, a portion routed to private completion, a portion staged to interact with auction windows, and a portion reserved to sweep if completion becomes urgent. Each child order reveals different information to the market and pays different tolls.

The fourth state is interaction and cancellation. Posted child orders rest in queues. Their success depends on priority and on whether they are bypassed by faster orders and special order types. Their safety depends on cancellation speed. Cancellation speed depends on connectivity and data. Those are paid inputs. The child orders that seek private completion are evaluated by internalizers who decide whether the flow is profitable and whether to provide price improvement.

The fifth state is hedging echo. If private completion fills the order, the internalizer may hedge externally. The hedge becomes a public print. The public print influences the benchmark and therefore influences the next set of best-price obligations and routing decisions. The private completion thus influences public price indirectly.

The sixth state is proof. The broker must produce a defensible explanation of why the order went where it went. The explanation relies on benchmark snapshots, timestamps, and execution outcomes relative to reasonably available alternatives. This is why evidence and clocks matter: the broker's defense depends on which record is treated as authoritative.

This journey illustrates why fragmentation is not just more venues. It is an entire second economy: the economy of selecting and defending the path. The House profits from that economy by selling the path tools and by capturing spread through private completion.

Fee geometry deserves a concrete mechanism chain because fee geometry is where fragmentation's surface competition becomes a hidden transfer system. Take the common pattern of subsidizing posted liquidity and charging takers. The venue that offers posting rebates attracts displayed orders because posters are paid to be visible. The displayed spread tightens. The public sees improved liquidity. The taker pays fees and therefore pays a wider effective spread than the screen implies. A broker routing retail-sized flow may route to a venue offering better internal economics for the broker while still delivering benchmark-compliant pricing for the client. The broker captures economics via rebates or arrangements. The venue captures revenue via data and connectivity. The client sees a fill and does not see the transfer.

The next step is that venues compete by altering fee schedules, and routers adapt by altering routing. This produces a dynamic equilibrium where displayed liquidity migrates in response to rebates rather than to fundamental value. Displayed depth becomes partly a purchased artifact. In stress, purchased depth is more fragile because it is maintained by economic incentives that can be suspended when adverse selection rises. This fragility produces the most visible symptom of fragmentation: sudden thinning and sudden slippage at precisely the moments when the public expects markets to be most reliable.

Completion risk deserves a concrete mechanism chain because completion risk is the hidden governor of routing under stress. In calm times, a router can chase marginal improvement across more venues because settlement fails are manageable and capital is not trapped. In stress, settlement fails and mismatches become more likely. A router then prioritizes paths known to settle cleanly, even if the displayed price elsewhere appears marginally better. The broker can defend this as best execution by including completion certainty in the analysis. Completion certainty becomes an allowable reason to accept slightly worse nominal prices. This is a legitimate consideration. It also moves flow toward participants and venues with better completion infrastructure, reinforcing concentration.

Fragmentation also amplifies the importance of the order types that control exposure. A hidden or partially hidden order can reduce signaling while still participating in the queue. A pegged instruction can follow reference prices without constant cancellation. A conditional instruction can interact only when certain criteria are met. Each of these reduces one cost and introduces another. Reducing signaling can reduce impact. Introducing conditionality can reduce fill probability and increase exposure time. Exposure time increases the probability of being selected only when wrong. Those who can manage these tradeoffs with better data and faster reaction have an advantage. Fragmentation multiplies the number of these tradeoffs because each venue has its own menus and its own rule quirks. Quirk mastery becomes edge.

The relationship between fragmentation and auctions must be treated as a distinct mechanism because auctions are where fragmentation tries to heal itself while creating new profit surfaces. The open and close are attempts to create a single, defensible print that can be used as a reference. In a fragmented system, reference is most fragile when it is most needed: at times used for valuation and reporting. Auctions concentrate liquidity to produce a reference that can be defended. The auction then produces imbalance information and timing games. The venue sells imbalance information in premium tiers. Participants pay to see it early. Early sight allows positioning. Positioning allows profit. Profit funds more premium access. The loop compounds. Fragmentation therefore both motivates auctions and monetizes auctions.

Fragmentation also alters how risk is transmitted. When markets are fragmented, a shock in one venue can propagate through routing systems into others as algorithms chase liquidity and hedge exposures. A small dislocation becomes a cross-venue event because routers seek completion and internalizers hedge. If one venue's feed is delayed, algorithms can misinterpret state and overreact. The system must then rely on hybrid mechanisms: halts, pauses, and error correction. Fragmentation increases the value of coordination, and coordination increases the value of the groups that can coordinate across many venues. Consolidation becomes the response to fragmentation, and the combined effect is that the system becomes both more complex and more centralized in ownership of evidence and clocks.

The fragmented market also deepens the value of the evidence layer. When execution occurs across many venues and via private completion, proving best execution becomes heavier. Proof requires snapshots of benchmarks, time-aligned records, and routing rationale. This increases fixed compliance costs and increases the minimum efficient scale. Larger firms amortize the cost and can build better proof systems. Better proof systems allow more aggressive optimization within defensible boundaries. Smaller firms face higher marginal proof cost and therefore less ability to optimize. Fragmentation thus increases inequality by increasing proof burdens.

A key feature of fragmentation is that it lets the system claim competition while preserving rent. Competition exists among venues. Rent exists in the interfaces that cannot be avoided: data authority, benchmark reference moments, connectivity, and the evidence layer. The system can reduce explicit execution fees and still increase total extraction by raising the price of seeing and proving. Participants experience lower headline fees and higher infrastructure bills. The public sees progress. The machine sees toll migration from explicit to invisible.

A fragmented market also produces a specific kind of moral hazard: the temptation to externalize costs downstream. A venue can introduce features that increase message traffic, increasing data product value while increasing burden on participants who must process more messages and maintain more complex risk controls. A broker can route in ways that improve broker economics while remaining within defensible best execution. An internalizer can capture flow and hedge externally, shifting market impact into public venues while keeping private profits. Each actor can claim compliance with rules. The system's distributive outcome emerges from compliant optimization.

Fragmentation persists because it solves real problems and creates profitable ones. It solves the problem of diverse intent by providing specialized venues and mechanisms. It solves the problem of excessive impact by providing hidden completion channels. It solves the problem of monopoly optics by enabling surface competition. At the same time, it creates navigation complexity, and navigation complexity is monetizable. It creates tiered perception demand, and tiered perception is monetizable. It creates proof complexity, and proof is monetizable. The system settles at an equilibrium where fragmentation is tolerated because it is profitable and politically defensible.

The Dark Pool Bargain

A dark pool exists because visibility is expensive. In a displayed market, an order is not just a request to trade. It is a broadcast of intent. Intent can be exploited through queue positioning, quote adjustment, and the gradual leaning of prices against a predictable buyer or seller. The dark pool bargain is the promise that intent can be hidden long enough to complete without paying the full cost of being seen. The system sells this bargain as protection for the large trader and as efficiency for the market. The bargain is real. The bargain is also a rent mechanism because the act of hiding intent creates a new gate: who can access private completion, on what terms, and with what information advantages for the operators of the private venue.

A dark pool is not one thing. It is a family of mechanisms that trade visibility for conditional liquidity. In a displayed venue, liquidity is visible and priority is governed by the public queue. In a dark pool, liquidity is conditional and priority is governed by matching rules that are not fully legible to outsiders. The dark pool's central promise is reduced market impact. The central cost is reduced certainty: you may not trade, you may trade partially, and the price you receive depends on reference points produced elsewhere. Dark pools therefore parasitize displayed markets for price discovery while claiming to protect displayed markets from the impact that would otherwise distort discovery. That paradox is not a defect; it is the operating equilibrium.

The dark pool bargain begins with the problem it claims to solve: information leakage. For a large order, the most expensive cost is rarely explicit fees. It is price drift caused by others adjusting against the order once they infer it exists. In a displayed market, inference does not require illegal access. It can be achieved by observing repeated small buys, by noticing consistent participation at the bid, by seeing depth disappear when the order arrives, and by watching correlated instruments move. The market does not need to know the full size of the order to profit from it. It needs only to know direction and persistence. Persistence is the signal.

A dark pool attempts to remove persistence from the public surface. Instead of slicing and exposing, the trader seeks hidden crossing. The ideal outcome is a block executed at a fair reference price without moving the displayed market. The trader avoids impact. The market avoids a visible shock. This is the civic justification.

The private justification is more precise. A dark pool allows an intermediary to internalize flow and to monetize the spread that would otherwise be competed away on a lit venue. It also allows the intermediary to capture information about latent demand and supply without broadcasting it. This information can be used to hedge efficiently. Efficient hedging reduces the intermediary's risk. Reduced risk allows tighter pricing. Tighter pricing attracts more flow. The loop compounds, and the dark pool becomes a liquidity magnet not because it is altruistic but because it is an engine that converts hidden intent into predictable profit.

The first mechanism of dark pools is reference pricing. Many dark executions are priced at or near a midpoint derived from displayed best quotes. This creates the appearance of price improvement: trading at the midpoint is better than paying the full spread. The improvement is real as arithmetic. The transfer is that the dark pool is using the displayed market's price discovery as a free input. The lit venue bears the cost of producing a reference price through visible competition. The dark venue captures volume and monetizes access. This is the core subsidy: displayed markets fund private completion by providing the benchmark.

Because the dark pool depends on reference, it also depends on the quality of the reference. When displayed liquidity is thin or stale, midpoint pricing can produce executions at prices that are not truly representative of available supply and demand. In those conditions, dark pools can either fail to match or can produce trades that feel unfair to one side. The operator then must design eligibility and interaction rules to manage adverse selection: who is allowed in, which order types can interact, and under what conditions trades occur.

Adverse selection is the dark pool's central threat. If informed traders can use the pool to trade against uninformed flow without revealing their information, the pool becomes toxic. Liquidity providers withdraw. The pool's fill rates collapse. The operator therefore performs a constant sorting function: encourage benign flow, deter toxic flow, and maintain enough volume that the pool remains attractive. This sorting is done through participant categories, minimum sizes, conditional order types, and sometimes subtle matching logic that is presented as fairness. The matching logic is also the rent allocator.

The dark pool bargain therefore includes a hidden trade: the trader gives up the right to open competition in exchange for privacy, and the operator gains the right to discriminate among flows to protect the pool's economics. Discrimination here means selection under rules. It is not necessarily illegal or unethical. It is the mechanism that keeps the pool from collapsing. Yet it creates a stratified market in which access and treatment can vary by participant type and by perceived toxicity.

The second mechanism is information shaping. A dark pool limits what others can see about your order. Yet the operator sees your order. The operator learns direction, size, urgency, and patterns across time. Even if the operator is constrained from misusing information directly, the operator's economic position improves because it can hedge and manage inventory with better knowledge than the public. This is why private completion is profitable: it transforms public uncertainty into private certainty, and the spread between them is rent.

The third mechanism is conditionality and partial fill control. Dark pools often allow conditional orders that interact only if certain criteria are met, such as minimum size or midpoint eligibility. These conditions reduce signaling because they reduce the chance that a large order is exposed through many small prints. They also reduce fill certainty because they limit interaction. The trader accepts uncertainty because the alternative is paying impact publicly. This is the bargain.

The fourth mechanism is the creation of a private queue. Even if liquidity is not displayed, priority still exists. Priority is determined by time, size, and participant privileges, often in ways that are not as transparent as in lit venues. The operator can design priority to attract desired flow types. Attracting desired flow types is an economic strategy: more benign flow increases fill rates and reduces adverse selection losses, making the pool more attractive. This is how the pool builds liquidity without displaying it: by shaping the ecology through rules.

The fifth mechanism is the internalization-to-lit feedback loop. Many dark fills are hedged in lit markets. The operator fills privately, then trades publicly to neutralize risk. The public prints reflect the hedge, not the original investor order. This creates a reversal of causality in public narratives. Observers may attribute the public print to investor demand when it is actually the intermediary's hedge response. The displayed market becomes the shadow of private execution decisions. The dark pool therefore does not remove impact; it often relocates impact and changes its timing. Relocated impact can be more manageable and less predatory for the initiating trader. It can also create new microstructure patterns that can be exploited by those who understand the hedging behavior.

The dark pool bargain also affects the economics of the lit venue. If too much benign flow is internalized privately, the displayed market becomes more dominated by toxic and informational flow. That increases adverse selection risk for displayed liquidity providers. They widen spreads or withdraw. Wider spreads make midpoint dark trading more attractive. More dark trading siphons more benign flow. The loop is self-reinforcing. This is why dark pools can be both stabilizing for large traders and destabilizing for displayed price discovery if they drain too much benign volume. The system tolerates this because the lit market's role shifts: it becomes the price discovery and hedging venue rather than the primary completion venue for all flows.

Dark pools therefore create a market with two publics. There is the formal public: displayed quotes and prints. There is the economic public: the set of participants with enough access to private completion and enough data to infer what private completion is doing. The wider population participates in the formal public and pays the slippage of delayed abstraction. The House participates in the economic public and pays for the tools that reveal and monetize private flow patterns.

CHAPTER 23
THE TOLLBOOTHS OF VISIBILITY

SUBTITLE: PREMIUM ACCESS, FASTER SIGHTLINES, AND THE PRICE OF SEEING THE MARKET SOONER.

PART FOUR

THE PRIVATE ARCHITECTURE

PUBLIC MARKETS FACE THE CROWD, BUT LEVERAGE, ACCESS, AND ASYMMETRY ARE PRICED IN PRIVATE SYSTEMS THE PUBLIC NEVER SEES.

Public markets are the stage where legitimacy is performed: a visible quote, a visible print, a visible close, and a civic story that a price is a fact anyone can observe. The real power sits behind the stage in systems where visibility is restricted, credit is negotiated, and risk is transformed into products that never need to show their faces on a tape. Those systems are not "outside" the market. They are the market's spine. They decide who can obtain balance sheet at the right moment, who can survive a margin cycle without selling, who can turn collateral into time, who can enter a deal before it becomes a symbol, and who can exit without broadcasting intent. Public prices are the broadcast. Private architecture is the transmission tower.

The private architecture begins with a simple observation that the public rarely has to articulate: a price is only meaningful if a participant can finance and hold the position that price implies. Financing is not a background utility. Financing is the constraint that converts ideas into trades and trades into sustained exposure. The public sees a rally and calls it confidence. The private layer sees haircuts tightening, repo terms shifting, dealer balance sheets rationing, and margin models rewriting the feasible set of positions. The crowd faces the screen. The real contest is the ability to borrow against a claim, roll the borrowing, and do it on terms that do not force liquidation at the first shock.

Private power is priced in admission, not in execution. Admission to public trading is not primarily the ability to click. It is the ability to be accepted by the machines that sit downstream: underwriting committees, allocation decisions, collateral eligibility lists, internal risk limits, and counterparty credit lines that determine whether a trade is even allowed. The public believes markets are open because access to the quote is open. The system is selective because access to cheap leverage and reliable completion is not open. Selectivity is enforced by documentation, by balance sheet, by relationships, and by the invisible veto of risk managers who can refuse a trade without ever touching a matching engine.

In the private layer, asymmetry is sold explicitly rather than denied implicitly. The public lane sells fairness by protocol. The private lane sells advantage by contract. Better terms, earlier information, preferential allocation, lower haircuts, longer maturities, tighter financing spreads, and conditional access to inventory are negotiated, priced, and renewed like any other supply relationship. A participant can be perfectly rational and still lose if it pays retail for leverage while competitors pay wholesale. Wholesale leverage is not a slogan. It is the right to endure volatility without being forced to trade at the worst moment.

The private architecture is also where risk is packaged before the public feels it. Volatility is not only a market state. It is a tradable product created by positioning, hedging, and forced behavior under constraints. A portfolio that looks stable on paper can be fragile because its financing is fragile. A basis position can look hedged and still be lethal if its legs are funded differently under stress. A carry strategy can look conservative until a haircut shift turns it into a fire sale. What the public experiences as "sudden" moves is often the visible result of private funding terms changing quietly and then expressing themselves through forced transactions at scale.

The private layer is built on collateral pathways. Collateral is not a static object. It is a claim whose acceptability changes with regime, counterparty, and time. Eligibility is negotiated. Haircuts are adjusted. Reuse rights are granted or withdrawn. The same asset can be money-like in one relationship and nearly useless in another. This is why power concentrates around the institutions that can declare acceptability and around the participants that can source the right collateral on demand. If public markets are about price, private markets are about what can be turned into financing at the deadline.

Private architecture is also where information becomes timing rather than content. The public imagines "information" as news and analysis. In private systems, the most valuable information is often a schedule and a constraint: who must roll financing this week, which inventories are crowded, where basis is funded thinly, what haircuts are being demanded, which counterparties are reducing exposure, which allocation decisions are being made, and which risk limits are tightening. This information does not need to be secret in a dramatic sense. It needs to be early, actionable, and tied to funding reality. That is why private meetings, counterparty calls, and term sheet negotiations can matter more than any headline.

Private power is also the power to choose the moment of visibility. The public lane forces transparency at execution. The private lane allows negotiation, staging, and delayed revelation. A position can be built quietly, financed quietly, and only later expressed through public hedges or through a controlled offering that looks orderly. The capacity to delay revelation is not cosmetic. It reduces the cost of being leaned on and reduces the probability of being forced into the crowd's price. The public sees a smooth move and assumes calm. The private layer did the work of controlling impact and controlling the clock.

The most dangerous feature of private architecture is that it can look stabilizing while it accumulates fragility. Private systems reduce visible volatility by absorbing flow internally, by financing inventories, and by smoothing execution through negotiated pathways. That smoothing can hide leverage concentration and hide maturity mismatch. When stress arrives, hidden leverage becomes visible as a liquidation wave. The market then looks like it "changed mood." It did not. The private layer simply ran out of room to warehouse the pressure.

"The public price is the headline; the private term is the verdict."

This section follows the verdict layer: the gatekeepers that decide who gets to be public at all, the plumbing that turns collateral into leverage, the intelligence businesses that trade on asymmetry as a model rather than a crime, the engineered control systems that operate away from the screen, and the quiet governors that allocate capital automatically without ever needing a speech.

CHAPTER 24
THE GATEKEEPERS OF GOING PUBLIC
UNDERWRITING POWER, PRICING CONTROL, AND THE REAL COST OF ADMISSION TO PUBLIC CAPITAL.

The public market pretends admission is a formality: file, disclose, list, ring a bell, become liquid. The private market knows admission is a purchase, and the price is paid in control. Going public is not an issuer "accessing capital" in the abstract. It is an issuer entering a governed perimeter where a small set of intermediaries decide what the issuer is allowed to be, how its story will be priced, how volatility will be distributed, who will receive early allocation, which investors will be courted, and which behaviors will be punished by exclusion from future offerings. The gatekeeper function is the conversion of a firm into a tradable object that the system can finance, hedge, index, lend against, litigate over, and repackage without requiring the firm's consent each time its equity becomes somebody else's inventory.

Underwriting begins as risk and ends as power because the risk is not symmetrical. The issuer risks mispricing and reputational damage. The underwriter risks being stuck with inventory, being blamed for a broken deal, and losing the right to allocate future deals. The system resolves this by giving the underwriter tools to control outcomes: price discovery rights, allocation discretion, stabilization mechanisms, syndicate coordination, and the ability to ration access as a reward or penalty. Underwriting is not merely matching capital to opportunity. It is manufacturing a marketable security and designing the first weeks of its social life so that it looks "successful" enough to become eligible for the next layer of demand.

The first gate is eligibility, and eligibility is not the exchange's listing checklist. Eligibility is institutional. It is the question of whether the claim can be held by the institutions that dominate flows: whether the disclosure package is defensible, whether the governance structure is tolerable, whether the float is sufficient, whether the story fits allocation preferences, whether the sector is in favor with allocators, whether the deal can be sold without creating embarrassment for the buyers who must justify it to committees. A public instrument is not only a share. It is a compliance artifact. Underwriters sell the compliance artifact and charge for the privilege.

The second gate is the book, and the book is not a list of orders. It is a map of relationships. The book is a negotiated construction of demand that reflects who matters to the syndicate, who will be rewarded for loyalty, who can provide supportive secondary behavior, and who will be excluded because they are viewed as flippers, troublemakers, or price-aggressive. "Demand" is curated, because curated demand reduces the probability of a first-day collapse. The underwriter's most valuable product is not the printed offer price. It is the ability to claim that the printed price reflects real appetite, and to produce a distribution that makes the claim self-fulfilling.

A book can be over-subscribed and still be weak. Oversubscription can be created by small orders, conditional interest, and strategic signaling designed to gain allocation. The underwriter knows this and applies a private taxonomy. Interest is categorized: long-only, hedge, momentum, tactical, strategic, supportive, indifferent. The public sees a single headline: oversubscribed. The machine sees a distribution problem: allocate enough to supportive holders to reduce immediate selling pressure, allocate enough to powerful accounts to maintain relationships, allocate enough to create trading volume without creating a cascade, and keep enough scarcity that price can lift and make the deal look like a win.

Scarcity is not a natural outcome. Scarcity is engineered. If the issuer sells too much, there is no scarcity and the price can sag. If the issuer sells too little, there is not enough float and the price can become unstable or too easily cornered. The underwriter negotiates the float with an objective that is not aligned perfectly with the issuer's desire to raise maximum proceeds. The underwriter's objective is an offering that trades well enough to preserve the underwriter's reputation and to protect the buyers that were allocated. Protecting buyers is not kindness. It is franchise protection.

The third gate is pricing, and pricing is not "what the market will pay." Pricing is what can be defended. A deal price must be defendable to the issuer, to the allocation clients, and to the public narrative that will be used as marketing for the next deal. The underwriter's pricing power comes from two asymmetries: information asymmetry and timing asymmetry. The underwriter sees the book, sees investor objections, sees where demand is real and where it is performative. The issuer does not see this cleanly. The public does not see it at all. Timing asymmetry matters because the underwriter controls the sequence: when the range is set, when it is revised, when allocations are communicated, and when final price is printed. Control over sequence is control over momentum, and momentum is a financing variable because momentum changes the cost at which secondary liquidity can be obtained.

The "real cost of admission" is paid in concessions embedded in structure. These concessions can include discounts to comparable valuations, conservative guidance expectations, governance compromises that reassure institutional buyers, lockup agreements that prevent insider selling, and greenshoe options that give underwriters inventory tools to manage post-offer trading. The issuer pays with money left on the table, with delayed liquidity for insiders, and with the acceptance that the security's early life will be managed by parties whose primary loyalty is to their own franchises and to the buyers they must keep happy for the next syndicate cycle.

The greenshoe is an instructive mechanism because it reveals how much of "market pricing" is actually controlled distribution plus controlled supply. A greenshoe gives the syndicate the ability to sell more than the base deal and then buy back in the aftermarket if needed. In one direction it supports price by creating buying pressure. In the other direction it supplies additional shares to meet demand without allowing the price to spike too violently. This tool is presented as stabilization. It is also a lever for shaping the first narrative: a stable price suggests a clean deal; a messy price suggests a failed admission. The underwriter's incentive is to avoid visible mess because visible mess invites scrutiny, reduces future fees, and destabilizes the syndicate's ability to demand concessions on the next issuer.

Stabilization is not an abstract term. It is a set of authorized behaviors executed under defined rules, often through syndicate desks that manage inventory and coordinate actions across participants. The fact that stabilization is allowed at all is the admission that "the market" is not a neutral discovery mechanism at the moment of birth. Birth is managed. Birth must be managed because the new instrument is fragile: limited float, uneven holder composition, incomplete information diffusion, and a public narrative that can be derailed by early volatility. The gatekeepers are paid to manage fragility so that the instrument can graduate into the machine's next stage: eligibility for passive inclusion, borrow availability, derivatives, and leverage against the shares.

Allocation is the underwriter's most durable power, because allocation is not only about this deal. It is about future access. If an investor wants to be allocated tomorrow, the investor behaves today. Behavior can include participating in secondary offerings, providing supportive bids during choppy periods, not publicly criticizing pricing, and not flipping aggressively. These behaviors are rarely written as explicit obligations. They are enforced through memory and exclusion. Exclusion is the private enforcement mechanism of primary markets. A public court is not needed; the underwriter can punish by not inviting. That is why primary markets remain private architecture even when the product becomes public.

The underwriter's pricing control is often misdescribed as "underpricing" versus "fair pricing." The deeper mechanism is risk distribution. If the deal is priced conservatively, early buyers receive an immediate cushion, which reduces the probability of rapid losses and reduces the probability of visible selling cascades. The cushion is a transfer from issuer to allocated buyers. It is justified as the cost of certainty and the cost of building a stable holder base. The issuer can accept this because the issuer values admission, ongoing access to capital markets, and the reputational effect of a successful debut. The underwriter values the ability to claim competence. Everyone values the avoidance of embarrassment.

The public sees a first-day jump and calls it excitement. The machine sees a controlled transfer that purchased cooperation from the buyers most likely to matter in the next cycles. A first-day jump can also be a sign that the issuer sold too cheaply. The underwriter does not mind that interpretation as much as the issuer does, because the underwriter's penalty for "leaving money on the table" is often lower than the penalty for a broken deal. A broken deal harms relationships and harms the narrative that the underwriter can place paper successfully.

Underwriting is a coordination business because primary markets require coordinated discipline across many actors. A syndicate exists because no single intermediary wants the full inventory risk and because broad distribution requires many client relationships. Coordination produces a cartel-like effect without requiring overt conspiracy: the syndicate shares information, aligns incentives, and manages allocation to prevent destructive competition among intermediaries. Destructive competition would look like fee cutting, more aggressive pricing, and less discipline in allocation. That would increase the probability of post-offer volatility and reputational damage. The system selects for discipline because discipline preserves the franchise value of underwriting itself.

The fee is rarely the main profit. The fee is the visible justification. The deeper profits include relationship reinforcement, secondary trading opportunities, access to flow, and the ability to position around the offering's known calendar. Primary events create predictable secondary behavior: lockup expirations, index eligibility windows, analyst initiation timelines, and the gradual opening of borrow and derivative markets. Predictable calendars are monetizable. The gatekeepers sit at the origin of the calendar and can trade the calendar with superior context.

The admission process also creates informational theater. A roadshow is not only marketing. It is demand shaping and narrative rehearsal. The issuer learns what the institutional audience will tolerate. The underwriter learns which objections are negotiable and which are fatal. The story is edited to fit committee heuristics and to avoid triggering red flags that can reduce demand. This is not mere persuasion; it is the transformation of messy corporate reality into a standardized claim that can be held by large institutions without requiring them to explain themselves constantly. Standardization is what makes a claim scalable.

The story is also used to define what the market will punish later. When an issuer goes public, it implicitly agrees to a monitoring regime: periodic disclosures, guidance expectations, and a style of communication that the market can digest. Deviations are punished through price. Price punishment is framed as discovery. It is also governance by crowd. The private gatekeepers help design the issuer's contract with that crowd, then charge for it, then later profit from the continued trading activity the contract generates.

The gatekeepers also price access by shaping who gets early shares. Early shares can be valuable not only because of immediate price moves but because early ownership can be used to build influence over corporate governance and to establish positions that can later be lent, hedged, or used as collateral. The underwriter's allocation decisions therefore shape the future microstructure of the security: who holds stable inventory, who provides lendable supply, who trades actively, and who will be the first forced sellers if risk limits tighten. This is how primary markets pre-load the secondary market's behavior.

If the allocation favors long-only institutions that hold, the public float becomes more scarce, and price can be more sensitive to marginal demand. If the allocation favors more active holders, volume increases and the security becomes easier to trade, but it can also become more volatile. The underwriter seeks an equilibrium that supports a tradable security that looks healthy: enough volume to appear liquid, enough stability to appear trustworthy, enough scarcity to allow price support, enough diversity to avoid one-sided selling. That equilibrium is engineered.

The admission gate also includes legal and procedural gates that look neutral and behave selective. Documentation requirements, audit standards, disclosure burdens, and governance structures create fixed costs. Fixed costs exclude smaller firms and concentrate public markets among firms that can afford the compliance machine. This exclusion is often defended as investor protection. It also concentrates the set of public claims and increases the value of private markets for firms that cannot afford admission. The gatekeepers profit on both sides: they sell admission for those that can pay and they sell private financing architecture for those that cannot.

The issuer's true admission cost is therefore a bundle: fee, discount, disclosure burden, governance burden, timing submission to external calendars, and acceptance of an enforcement regime based on public price reaction. Public markets face the crowd. Private gatekeepers face the issuer and price the issuer's entrance to the crowd. The crowd thinks it is judging the issuer. The underwriter has already shaped what the crowd will be allowed to judge and under what liquidity conditions the judgment will be expressed.

"Public capital is not raised; it is granted under terms."

Those terms are enforced through allocation memory, through future deal access, through stabilization tools, through narrative control, and through the underwriter's ability to coordinate the first weeks of trading so that the security becomes eligible for the deeper machine: passive demand, borrow markets, derivative references, collateral eligibility, and levered strategies that require a stable, liquid, reference-grade instrument.

The pricing gate is also a liability gate. A public admission creates a future dispute surface, and the system prices that surface into how it structures disclosure, how it chooses language, and how it sets the first set of expectations. The prospectus is not a brochure; it is a legal artifact designed to be survivable under stress, because what looks like optimism in calm conditions can become a cause of action when price falls and anger seeks a target. Underwriters are not paid only to sell; they are paid to structure defensibility. Defensibility includes what is said, what is omitted, what is emphasized, and how the issuer's risks are rendered legible enough that future disappointment can be framed as known risk rather than as concealed defect.

This is where underwriting power becomes institutional discipline. The issuer may want maximum narrative freedom. The underwriter demands a narrative that can be defended to committees and later to regulators and courts. That defense constraint pushes issuers toward standardized language and standardized metrics. Standardization reduces the issuer's ability to differentiate itself verbally. It also increases the system's ability to compare and to price quickly. Quick comparability is liquidity's friend. Quick comparability is also the enemy of nuance. Admission is the trade: nuance is sacrificed so that capital can scale into the claim without requiring constant interpretation.

Allocation is not only who gets shares. Allocation is also who gets information first, and information first is advantage in the aftermarket. The most obvious channel is access to management during the process, the ability to ask questions, and the ability to infer how aggressively the deal is being supported. The underwriter controls access and controls timing. Controlling timing is a form of soft power because it shapes who can position calmly and who must react publicly after the fact. A public investor sees the first prints. A privileged participant has already calibrated exposure and hedges around the offering calendar.

Syndicate behavior in the aftermarket is often misunderstood as spontaneous demand. It is frequently pre-planned risk management. A syndicate can coordinate to avoid a disorderly opening by managing how shares are released into the market, how stabilization is applied, and how inventory is handled when early selling pressure appears. Inventory control is not just the greenshoe. It includes penalty bids and allocation discipline: a buyer who flips quickly can be penalized by losing future access, and in some structures can indirectly cause the underwriter to claw back part of a selling concession from a distributing participant. The details vary by structure, but the mechanism is consistent: early selling is discouraged because early selling threatens the narrative of successful admission.

This discouragement is why allocation is rarely given purely to the highest bidder in a moralized sense. A bidder can be enthusiastic and still be a future seller. The underwriter prefers a buyer whose behavior supports a stable secondary market because stability is the currency of the underwriter's franchise. The underwriter's franchise is the right to be believed by issuers and by investors. If the underwriter repeatedly delivers unstable debuts, it loses belief. Loss of belief is loss of fees and loss of allocation authority.

Stabilization tools also shape who profits from early volatility. If a stock trades down immediately, a syndicate can provide support within allowed rules, reducing the downside and reducing the incentive for panic selling. That support can protect allocated buyers and preserve the appearance of orderly price formation. It can also create a predictable pattern: early weakness is cushioned until the stabilization window ends, at which point the price must stand on its own. Participants who understand the pattern can trade around it. The gatekeepers' attempt to smooth becomes a structural event. Structural events are monetizable by those with the right visibility and the right patience.

The quiet period around research initiation is another gate. Research coverage is not merely analysis; it is a legitimacy mechanism that widens the investor base and provides language committees can cite. Timing of initiation can influence secondary demand. The underwriter can manage this timing to avoid overwhelming the market with too much uncertainty and to create a staged narrative: first stability, then broader promotion. This staging is not marketing fluff. It is the sequencing of demand so that the float is absorbed without creating a visible collapse. The underwriter's sequencing power is a kind of time monopoly during admission.

Lockups are a further sequencing tool and one of the most direct examples of private power shaping public price. A lockup prevents insiders and early holders from selling for a period. This reduces immediate supply and supports price by engineering scarcity. Lockups also create a future forced window: expiration. Expiration is predictable. Predictable windows are tradable. The market knows supply may arrive. Buyers adjust. Lenders adjust. Borrow markets adjust. The very tool used to create stability at birth creates a scheduled stress test later. The underwriter's job is to time and structure lockups so that the scheduled supply event is survivable and does not destroy the issuer's narrative.

The real cost of admission therefore includes accepting that the security's calendar will be governed. An issuer entering public markets accepts a schedule of forced visibility events: quiet periods ending, research initiation, stabilization windows ending, lockups expiring, secondary offerings, inclusion eligibility thresholds, and governance seasons. These events can be managed, anticipated, and traded around. They also become the issuer's new reality: the firm's strategy is now executed under the shadow of an external trading calendar.

Admission also changes the firm's bargaining power in private finance. A public share can be used as collateral. A public share can be lent. A public share can become the underlying for derivatives. These uses expand the system's ability to build leverage around the firm. The issuer benefits through lower capital costs and higher liquidity. The system benefits by turning the issuer into a financing substrate. The gatekeepers accelerate this transformation by ensuring the security is reference-grade: sufficient float, sufficient volume, sufficient stability, sufficient proof. Reference-grade is what makes a claim usable as money-like collateral in private systems.

That usefulness is why underwriters care about post-offer microstructure even when they claim to be done once the shares are sold. If the secondary market is unstable, collateral eligibility is questioned, borrow terms become expensive, and the security becomes harder to finance. Harder to finance reduces liquidity. Reduced liquidity increases volatility. Volatility increases risk premiums. Risk premiums raise cost of capital. A weak aftermarket therefore harms not only the issuer but the ecosystem of leverage built around the security. The underwriter's franchise depends on delivering not only a sale but a usable object.

The gatekeepers of going public therefore operate as private governors of public capital. They decide who is admitted, on what terms, with what supply schedule, with what early holder composition, and with what stabilization and sequencing tools. The public sees the first prints and imagines a spontaneous crowd verdict. The private system has already staged the room: who is allowed in first, how much inventory is released, which behaviors are punished later, and which records will be used to defend the process if anger arrives.

CHAPTER 25
THE LEVERAGE PLUMBING
FINANCING CHAINS, COLLATERAL PATHWAYS, AND THE ARCHITECTURE OF AMPLIFIED RISK.

Leverage is not a mood. It is a set of pipes. The public thinks leverage is a decision made by a trader who wants more exposure. The system treats leverage as an engineered pathway that converts a claim into usable funding, then converts that funding into inventory, then converts that inventory into more collateral, then repeats until the only thing holding the structure together is confidence in the pipes. When confidence holds, the plumbing makes markets feel deep and smooth. When confidence breaks, the plumbing turns the same positions into forced selling, because the pipes have deadlines, haircuts, and rights of seizure that do not care about your long-run thesis.

The leverage plumbing starts with collateral eligibility. Not every asset is financeable on the same terms, and "terms" are the real market. Eligibility is negotiated and conditional. Haircuts are adjusted. Maturities shorten or lengthen. Reuse rights exist or vanish. The same security can be money-like in one relationship and nearly useless in another. The public sees a price. The private system sees whether that price can be transformed into borrowing, on what horizon, under what documentation, with what margin call sensitivity, and with what rights the lender has if the borrower misses a deadline.

A financing chain is the sequence that turns an asset into purchasing power. In its simplest form, a holder of a security obtains cash against it, uses the cash to buy more securities, and repeats. In reality, the chain is rarely a single loop. It is a network: multiple counterparties, multiple collateral types, multiple maturities, multiple rehypothecation permissions, and multiple margin models. The network's design decides which participants can run large books at thin spreads and which participants are forced to delever at the first sign of volatility.

The private architecture prices leverage through three variables that dominate everything else: haircut, term, and optionality. Haircut is the cash you do not receive against collateral. Term is how often you must roll, and rolling is the moment of vulnerability because it reopens negotiation under stress. Optionality is who has the right to change terms, demand more collateral, or refuse renewal. A participant can survive a large position if haircuts are stable, terms are long, and optionality is balanced. A participant can be crushed by a modest position if haircuts jump, terms shorten, and optionality is one-sided.

The system builds asymmetry by making favorable leverage terms a membership product. Cheap, stable funding is not granted by virtue of being correct. It is granted by being acceptable: acceptable collateral, acceptable counterparty, acceptable documentation, acceptable operational competence, and acceptable political status inside the network. This is why private power is priced in relationships and record, not only in yields. The public can buy exposure. The private winners can buy time.

The plumbing is also the market's amplification device. Leverage amplifies returns in calm conditions by increasing exposure per unit of equity. It amplifies stress because it turns price moves into margin moves, and margin moves into forced transactions. Forced transactions create more price moves. The loop becomes mechanical. The machine does not need fear to panic. It needs only procyclical haircuts, short funding terms, and conditional liquidity provision. Those features are routine.

The leverage system can be understood as a hierarchy of funding lanes. At the top are the lanes that behave like utilities: stable access, predictable haircuts, and the ability to roll through moderate turbulence. Lower lanes are fragile: higher haircuts, shorter terms, more discretionary renewal, and harsher collateral eligibility. The lane you are in determines whether you are a liquidity provider or a forced liquidity taker when conditions tighten.

Collateral pathways are the routes by which assets become eligible for funding. A pathway can include legal arrangements, custody arrangements, documentation, and operational processes that make collateral enforceable. Enforceable means: if you default, the lender can seize and liquidate with minimal ambiguity. Ambiguity is the enemy of funding because ambiguity creates legal delay. Legal delay is loss. Loss forces higher haircuts. Higher haircuts reduce leverage. Reduced leverage reduces liquidity. Liquidity reduction increases volatility. Volatility increases haircuts again. The system therefore rewards enforceability by granting better funding terms to collateral that can be seized and liquidated cleanly.

This is why the private architecture of power is obsessed with definitions. Definitions of title, definitions of segregation, definitions of netting, definitions of what counts as default, definitions of what counts as close-out, and definitions of which court has authority. These definitions decide whether collateral behaves like money or like a disputed promise. If collateral behaves like money, leverage can be built safely enough to persist. If collateral behaves like a disputed promise, leverage must be rationed with haircuts and short terms, which forces participants to trade smaller or accept higher spreads.

Financing chains also depend on operational reality. A leverage structure can look robust on a spreadsheet and still fail because collateral cannot be moved on deadline, because settlement breaks trap inventory, because valuation disputes delay margin posting, or because documentation is incomplete. The private system therefore treats operations as credit. A counterparty with poor operational discipline is a higher-risk borrower because it is more likely to miss a margin call window even if it is solvent. Missing the window triggers default procedures. Default procedures are brutal by design because they are meant to protect the lender and preserve system credibility. Credibility is preserved by showing that contracts are enforced quickly, not by showing mercy.

The simplest leverage pipe is secured borrowing against securities, but the modern system multiplies the pipe into chains of reuse. Reuse is the silent engine. If collateral can be re-pledged, the same unit of collateral can support multiple layers of borrowing. This increases liquidity and lowers funding costs in calm times because the system can economize on scarce high-quality collateral. It also creates multiple claims on the same collateral under stress, which forces the system to rely on priority rules and close-out netting definitions. Priority and netting are the constitutional law of leverage plumbing.

Reuse also makes the plumbing opaque. A beneficial owner may believe assets sit quietly in custody. In practice, assets can be lent, pledged, or used in internal financing chains under allowed agreements. Even when contracts permit this, the economic consequence is that ownership becomes layered and leverage becomes embedded. Embedded leverage is dangerous because it is less visible and therefore less likely to be limited by prudence. The system limits embedded leverage through haircuts and eligibility, but those limits can loosen in good times because competition for business pressures lenders to offer better terms. Better terms look like efficiency until stress reveals the hidden fragility.

The leverage plumbing is therefore governed by cycles of tightening and loosening. In calm regimes, volatility is low, marks are stable, and defaults are rare. Haircuts drift lower, terms drift shorter but are rolled easily, and optionality shifts toward the lender without being used aggressively because renewal is routine. Participants interpret this as permanence and increase position sizes. The system appears liquid and stable because leverage is abundant.

In tightening regimes, volatility rises, marks move, and the probability of sharp moves increases. Haircuts rise, terms shorten, and optionality becomes active. Lenders demand more collateral. Borrowers must either post or sell. Selling moves prices. Price moves increase volatility. Volatility triggers further haircut increases. The same participants that provided liquidity in calm times become forced sellers in stress because their leverage was built on pipes with deadlines.

The plumbing has several choke points where amplification is strongest. The first choke point is margin timing. A margin call is not a request. It is a deadline. Deadlines transform uncertainty into forced behavior. A borrower who misses a deadline can be declared in default even if the economic position would recover if given time. The system prefers deadlines because deadlines reduce disputes and reduce the opportunity for strategic delay. The cost is that deadlines force liquidation into turbulence, which can deepen dislocations.

The second choke point is valuation authority. Collateral value determines margin. In stress, prices can be noisy, and the question becomes which price counts. The private system solves this by defining valuation sources and by granting lenders discretion within constraints. Discretion matters because a lender facing risk prefers a conservative valuation, which increases margin demands. Higher margin demands can force liquidation and protect the lender. This is rational locally and destabilizing globally.

The third choke point is term structure. Short-term funding must be rolled frequently. Frequent rolling creates repeated moments of vulnerability. Even if the borrower is solvent, a lender can refuse renewal under stress, forcing the borrower to find alternative funding or liquidate. If many lenders refuse simultaneously, liquidation becomes systemic. This is why long-term funding is power: it buys time through turbulence. Time is the only resource that allows a participant to avoid being forced to sell at the worst moment.

The fourth choke point is collateral transformation. Many participants cannot hold enough top-tier collateral to fund their strategies cheaply, so they rely on transformation: swapping less eligible collateral for more eligible collateral through intermediaries, paying a spread. Transformation is a private toll road. In calm times, transformation spreads are tight. In stress, transformation spreads widen and capacity shrinks. Shrinking capacity forces participants to delever. Delevering concentrates in the most liquid assets, pushing down the very collateral used as funding substrate.

The fifth choke point is close-out mechanics. When default occurs, positions are closed, collateral is seized, and losses are allocated. The system relies on close-out netting to reduce gross exposures. Netting reduces the cascade risk, but it also concentrates power in those who are legally and operationally able to execute close-out quickly. If close-out is delayed, losses grow and disputes multiply. The system therefore privileges legal regimes and operational structures that allow fast close-out. This privilege shows up as cheaper funding for collateral governed by those regimes and as higher haircuts for collateral governed by ambiguous regimes.

The private architecture prices access by controlling these choke points. If you can post acceptable collateral quickly, you survive. If you can roll term even when others cannot, you harvest. If you can transform collateral cheaply, you expand. If you can access discretionary credit lines, you avoid liquidation. If you can absorb inventory when forced sellers appear, you earn spreads that look like skill and are often endurance purchased through privileged leverage.

The leverage plumbing also changes the meaning of "liquidity." Public liquidity is the ability to trade at a quote. Private liquidity is the ability to fund positions without being forced to trade. Private liquidity is the more powerful form because it determines whether you are a price maker or a price taker when markets tighten. A participant with abundant private liquidity can provide public liquidity profitably. A participant without private liquidity is forced to demand public liquidity at precisely the wrong time.

This is why leverage plumbing is the architecture of amplified risk. Risk is amplified not only by exposure size but by the structure of financing. A position funded with stable term and modest haircut can withstand volatility. The same position funded with short-term roll and thin haircut is fragile. Fragility becomes systemic when many participants share the same fragile structure because they were all offered the same attractive terms during the calm regime. Attractive terms are contagious because competition among lenders pushes them across the network. Contagious terms create crowded leverage. Crowded leverage creates correlated liquidation. Correlated liquidation creates crashes that look like psychology and are often pipes tightening simultaneously.

The leverage plumbing is also where private information becomes decisive. The most valuable information is not a headline. It is a shift in funding terms: haircuts creeping up, roll refusals increasing, transformation spreads widening, and credit lines being quietly reduced. Those shifts appear in counterparty calls and in term sheets before they appear on any public screen. Participants who see them early can reduce leverage before the deadline wave arrives. Participants who see them late are forced to act publicly, paying the slippage tax. This is the private asymmetry the public never sees: not who predicted a macro event, but who predicted that the pipes would tighten first.

The plumbing also interacts with the evidence layer. Funding relationships require proof: valuations, collateral schedules, eligibility lists, and documentation. Proof burdens create fixed costs. Fixed costs advantage scale. Large participants can maintain legal and operational teams that negotiate terms, monitor exposures continuously, and respond quickly to margin calls. Smaller participants are forced into standardized terms with harsher haircuts and less flexibility. The inequality in leverage terms is therefore not only about wealth. It is about the ability to meet the system's proof and operational standards.

"Leverage is not borrowed money; it is borrowed time."

A participant that can borrow time survives volatility without selling. A participant that cannot borrow time becomes the liquidity event for someone else.

CHAPTER 26

INTELLIGENCE AT SPEED

HEDGE FUNDS, BASIS TRADES, AND THE BUSINESS MODEL OF ASYMMETRY.

Intelligence in markets is not brilliance. It is advantage converted into repeatable cash flow. The public imagines intelligence as prediction: an analyst foresees the future, buys early, sells later, and gets paid for being right. The private architecture pays a different kind of intelligence more consistently: the intelligence that detects constraint before it becomes visible, that obtains funding before it becomes scarce, that reaches liquidity before it disappears, and that arbitrages the difference between what is seen publicly and what is known privately through relationships, data, and balance-sheet access. Speed matters because the window where asymmetry is exploitable is often short, and short windows are where scalable profits live.

A hedge fund is not defined by "hedging." It is defined by mandate freedom and instrument freedom. Mandate freedom allows it to move across assets, across venues, across leverage lanes, and across time horizons without the same constraints that bind benchmarked institutions. Instrument freedom allows it to express views through basis positions, relative value structures, options, swaps, financing spreads, and microstructure exploitation. The business model is not simply to make money. The business model is to monetize being early to the market's true state, where "state" means not only price but funding terms, margin pressure, flow schedules, and the likelihood of forced behavior.

Speed is not only latency. Speed is the ability to act before the system forces everyone else to act. This is why the most valuable signals are rarely headlines. They are shifts in the pipes: haircuts tightening, term rolling less smoothly, borrow becoming expensive, dealer inventories changing, settlement fails clustering, and internal risk limits being reduced. These shifts do not announce themselves to the crowd. They appear in the private layer as a change in terms and tone. By the time the crowd sees the consequence, the position is already crowded, and the exit is already taxed.

Intelligence at speed begins with a map of constraints, because constraints create forced behavior, and forced behavior creates harvestable liquidity events. Benchmarks create forced windows. Margin creates forced selling. Settlement deadlines create forced liquidity demand. Corporate actions create entitlement cut-offs. Financing roll dates create forced refinancing. A fund that can see these calendars and measure crowding can position not on "up" or "down" but on who will be forced to transact and when, and on which pipes will tighten first when volatility rises.

The most durable edges tend to fall into three families: information edges, structure edges, and funding edges.

Information edges are the ability to infer order flow, positioning, and constraint changes earlier than others. This includes high-fidelity market data, cross-venue state inference, broker intelligence, and the subtle signals embedded in financing terms.

Structure edges are the ability to package exposures in ways that exploit rule differences: tax treatments, index definitions, collateral eligibility, and the mechanics of settlement and corporate actions.

Funding edges are the ability to obtain leverage on better terms and to keep it when others lose it, which turns volatility into someone else's liquidation and your own opportunity.

These families do not operate separately. Better information reduces adverse selection, which lowers loss, which allows larger size. Larger size justifies better connectivity, better data subscriptions, and better execution infrastructure. Better infrastructure improves fill quality and reduces slippage, which improves returns, which strengthens counterparty confidence, which improves financing terms. Better financing terms extend endurance. Endurance allows the fund to become a liquidity provider in stress rather than a forced liquidity taker. The loop compounds into stability of outcomes even when the surface looks chaotic.

Basis trading sits near the center of this model because basis trading monetizes the gap between instruments that should track and instruments that do not track under real funding and real settlement conditions. A basis exists when two exposures that are conceptually "the same" are not the same in the pipes: they settle differently, margin differently, finance differently, or embed different optionality. The public sees a spread and calls it mispricing. The private layer sees that the spread is compensation for plumbing risk. A basis trader is paid for being willing and able to hold plumbing risk.

Consider the anatomy of a basis position without naming any specific product. One leg is the clean reference exposure, highly standardized, widely accepted as collateral, and cheap to finance in normal conditions. The other leg is the tradable exposure that is slightly cheaper or richer because it carries friction: different settlement mechanics, different margining, different liquidity profile, different tax or legal treatment, different embedded optionality. The trader buys the cheap leg and sells the rich leg, expecting convergence. Convergence is not metaphysical. Convergence is conditional: funding must remain available, haircuts must not jump, and roll must remain routine. If the pipes tighten, the cheap leg often becomes cheaper, and the basis widens, not because the world changed, but because holding became more expensive at precisely the moment everyone wants to hold less.

This is why basis trades are described as low-risk and then explode under stress. They are low directional risk and high funding risk. They are machines that turn financing stability into profit and financing instability into forced unwind. The winner is rarely the trader with the most elegant fair-value model. The winner is the trader with the most robust funding lane, the best collateral transformation capacity, the least one-sided optionality in financing terms, and the earliest detection of tightening before the tightening becomes visible to everyone else.

A basis trade is therefore a test of private architecture access. Who can borrow cheaply. Who can post collateral that remains eligible. Who can survive a haircut jump without dumping. Who can obtain liquidity when margin calls arrive. The same "trade" held by two firms can have opposite risk profiles because one firm's financing optionality is favorable and the other's is one-sided. The public may call them identical positions. The machine knows they are different contracts and therefore different survival problems.

The core fragility is the unwind cascade. It begins with a small widening. Widening triggers risk dashboards and internal limits. Limits trigger reduction requests. Reduction requests trigger sales. Sales move the cheap leg lower and the rich leg higher if liquidity is asymmetric. The basis widens further. Widening forces more margin because the mark-to-market loss is immediate. Margin calls arrive with deadlines. Deadlines force liquidation if cash is not available. Liquidation pushes prices again. Volatility rises. Rising volatility increases haircuts. Haircuts increase collateral demands. Collateral demands create more liquidation. The spiral looks like panic. The mechanism is pipe tightening applied to crowded positions with short financing terms.

The decisive advantage is not foresight of the headline that triggers the initial widening. The decisive advantage is recognition of crowding and recognition of one-sided funding terms before the first deadline wave. Crowd recognition is itself a data problem. It requires inference about positioning, borrow utilization, dealer balance-sheet posture, and the distribution of financing maturities. The best intelligence firms build internal gauges: not just price and volatility, but term distribution of financing, concentration of counterparties, and sensitivity of the position to a haircut jump. They trade those gauges as aggressively as they trade price.

Funding is where "speed" becomes literal. A basis position may be financeable daily, but "daily" is not continuous. It is a roll schedule. Roll schedules are the private market's equivalent of the close auction: a moment where demand for funding must be met. If many participants need to roll at the same time, lenders can ration. Rationing forces liquidation. The first firm to reduce exposure before the roll wave sells into calm liquidity. The last firm sells into vacuum. That is speed: acting before the roll becomes public pain.

Intelligence at speed also monetizes the interaction between public markets and private completion. When a large share of flow is internalized, public prints often reflect hedges and inventory management rather than the initiating investor's intent. The high-speed fund does not need perfect knowledge of initiating intent. It needs to know the intermediary's likely hedge response and the timing of that response. Timing is monetizable because the hedge creates predictable pressure in visible venues, and predictable pressure can be traded around.

This logic becomes sharper when the market is fragmented. Fragmentation produces multiple venues, multiple states, and multiple partial truths. A fund that can assemble those truths into a more coherent picture can avoid being selected against. The fund pays for higher fidelity and lower delay, not for convenience, but for survivability. Survivability allows it to quote tighter, take more size, and run strategies that look like forecasting and are often navigation plus funding advantage.

Auctions and benchmark windows are the clearest scheduled sources of forced behavior. A close auction concentrates tracking pressure. Imbalance information becomes valuable. A fund that sees imbalance earlier can position, provide liquidity, avoid being harvested, or choose to wait until the clearing print reduces sequencing risk. This "intelligence" is sold as a premium lane by market infrastructure. Funds buy it because it changes loss rates in repeated small ways that compound. The public sees a closing print. The private layer sees a scheduled liquidity auction that can be mapped and traded.

The business model of asymmetry includes the deliberate trade of opacity. In public discussion, opacity sounds like wrongdoing. In market structure, opacity is often defensive. A large actor hides intent to avoid predation. A fund uses conditional instructions and private liquidity to avoid being leaned on. A fund stages exposure through derivatives rather than visible cash positions to avoid broadcasting. These are rational adaptations to a market where being seen carries an impact tax. The system tolerates this because the public lane can remain "fair enough" while private lanes allow large risk transfer without destroying the tape. The distributional consequence remains: those with access to private lanes pay less impact.

The tax of being seen is paid through impact and adverse selection. Impact is your own order moving price against you. Adverse selection is counterparties trading with you primarily when you are wrong. Speed, data, and execution intelligence reduce both. Reducing both lowers the cost of running strategies at scale. Lower cost allows tighter pricing. Tighter pricing attracts flow. Flow provides information. Information improves models. Models improve pricing. The loop is the compounding engine that turns "intelligence" into business.

Hedge funds monetize asymmetry by being the buyer of other people's forced behavior. Forced behavior appears when constraints tighten: margin calls, risk limit cuts, redemption pressure, collateral eligibility changes, financing roll refusals, settlement fail penalties, and corporate action cut-offs. These events cause participants to trade regardless of preference. The fund that can provide liquidity into those moments is paid, not by admiration, but by spreads and favorable prices accepted by forced sellers.

The simplest private power advantage is being liquid when others are not. Liquidity here is not the ability to click. It is the ability to fund and hold through turbulence. Funding and holding require leverage terms, collateral management, diversified counterparties, and counterparty confidence. Counterparty confidence is the currency. A firm with confidence rolls. A firm without confidence is forced to unwind. This is why intelligence firms spend so much effort on proof: clean records, clean collateral schedules, operational reliability, and documentation that makes lenders comfortable in stress.

Confidence is produced by proof and by posture. Proof is records and operational discipline. Posture is how a firm manages exposure so that it looks survivable to counterparties. A firm that appears stretched invites tighter terms even before prices move. A firm that appears conservative can obtain flexibility even during turbulence. This is not psychology. It is counterparty risk management, and it is a private power system because it decides who receives time and who receives deadlines.

The business model also depends on a second kind of speed: decision speed under uncertainty. Institutions governed by committees can be slow to cut risk. Slow cuts become forced cuts when limits are breached. A hedge fund's mandate can allow faster action. Faster action allows it to reduce exposure before the forced phase. The forced phase is when spreads widen and liquidity evaporates. Exiting before forced phase avoids the worst slippage. Entering during forced phase captures the best terms. Both require fast decision making, but decision making is only valuable if the funding lane supports it. A firm that decides quickly but cannot finance the move is still constrained.

Basis trades are the clearest expression of this, because "cheap" and "rich" are funding descriptors. The rich leg is often rich because it is easier to finance or easier to borrow. The cheap leg is cheap because it is harder to finance or has embedded optionality that bites in stress. The basis is the price of those differences. The firm that can neutralize the differences through superior financing terms can earn steady returns. The firm that cannot is selling volatility while pretending to arbitrate.

A fund that lives on relative value and basis strategies must therefore run a private architecture inside itself: collateral optimization, financing diversification, counterparty diversification, stress testing of haircuts and terms, monitoring of settlement breaks, and pre-negotiated contingency liquidity. These are not accessories. They are the machinery that turns a theoretical spread into a survivable position. Without them, the strategy is a promise to hold through widening without the time needed to do it.

The system's incentives ensure many participants will run similar trades in calm times because the carry looks safe. When many run it, crowding builds. Crowd growth reduces returns and increases fragility because everyone relies on similar financing and similar assumptions about collateral eligibility. A small shock can force many to unwind simultaneously, widening the basis sharply. This is the machine's stampede: pipes tighten, margins rise, and constrained actors unwind not because they changed beliefs but because they ran out of time.

Intelligence at speed is therefore detection of crowding and detection of pipe sensitivity. Pipe sensitivity means: which positions will face haircut changes first, which collateral will become less eligible first, which dealers will ration balance sheet first, which maturities will fail to roll smoothly first, which settlement breaks will trap capital first. These are not philosophical questions. They are operational facts that manifest in term changes, in refusal rates, and in subtle shifts in counterparty behavior.

The private intelligence business also includes the trade of constraint signals themselves. Some signals are obvious, such as a public volatility spike. The most valuable signals are private: a widening in funding spreads that has not yet hit public markets, a sudden preference for shorter terms, a silent reduction in balance sheet allocation, or an increase in margin add-ons for a particular category of exposure. These moves can occur quietly before any visible price breaks. By the time the crowd sees price action, the private signals have already dictated who must sell.

The business model of asymmetry includes an uncomfortable truth: many of the best edges are earned by proximity to privileged flow. Privileged flow is not necessarily illicit. It is predictable flow that is less toxic and therefore easier to price. If you interact with predictable flow, you can make markets with lower adverse selection. Lower adverse selection means tighter spreads. Tighter spreads attract more flow. The loop compounds. Firms compete for this flow because it is the cleanest source of repeatable profits, and they defend the arrangements as efficiency.

The market tolerates this because predictable flow internalization can reduce explicit costs for some participants and because the public lane remains usable. The distributional effect is that those with privileged flow access build compounding advantages that are difficult to match with pure prediction skill. In the private architecture, "skill" is often the ability to secure better input conditions: better flow, better financing, better data, and better execution interfaces.

Intelligence at speed also manifests as option design. Many private strategies are option-like. Some earn small steady returns and suffer large losses in rare stress. Others lose small daily and earn large in dislocation by holding liquidity and optionality. The intelligence firm chooses where it sits in this option structure and then manages the pipes to keep that choice real under stress. A firm that believes it is long optionality but relies on short-term funding is not long optionality. It is short time. The private architecture punishes confusion between theoretical payoff and funding reality.

The conversion from information edge to cash flow requires a repeated operational cycle. First, detection: identify a misalignment in funding, flow, or microstructure conditions. Second, packaging: choose an instrument structure that expresses the view with controlled risk and controlled financing exposure. Third, financing: secure terms that make the position holdable through volatility. Fourth, execution: enter without paying predation tax. Fifth, proof: maintain logs and documentation that keep counterparties confident and keep internal governance satisfied. Sixth, unwind: exit before constraints force a public scramble. Each stage has its own speed requirement. The market's myth says the first stage is the only stage that matters. The private system rewards those who can perform all six stages faster and cleaner than others.

This is where prime brokerage and counterparty relationships become part of intelligence. The fund's job is not only to trade. It is to maintain access to leverage lanes, to negotiate haircuts, to diversify sources, to prevent concentration of maturity roll, and to prevent single points of failure. A fund that finances everything with one counterparty is a hostage. A fund that finances everything on the shortest term is a hostage to calendar. A fund that finances with diversified terms and diversified lenders can survive longer, and survival is the thing that converts dislocation into opportunity.

The most systematic private edges are therefore edges in endurance. Endurance is not a personality trait. It is a balance sheet and a set of contract terms. If you can endure, you can be the buyer when others are sellers. You can also demand a better price because you are not forced. That is the definition of power in this architecture.

The public can believe markets are moved by stories. The private architecture knows stories become moves when they change financing. A rumor becomes a collapse when it causes haircuts to rise, terms to shorten, and credit lines to shrink. A narrative becomes a squeeze when it causes borrow costs to spike and inventory to be recalled. The intelligence business is a translation business: translate narrative into pipe consequences faster than the crowd and position around the forced behavior those pipe consequences will generate.

CHAPTER 27
THE EMPIRE BEYOND THE EXCHANGE
PRIVATE EQUITY, ENGINEERED CONTROL, AND EXTRACTION AWAY FROM THE PUBLIC SCREEN.

Public markets sell a story of fairness: a quoted price, a visible print, a claim that anyone can buy the same share on the same terms. Private equity sells a different product and does not apologize for it. It sells control, timing, and the right to redesign a company away from the crowd's clock. The empire beyond the exchange is built on the belief that the most profitable parts of capitalism happen when price discovery is not allowed to vote every second, when governance is not performed for an audience, and when the cost of capital is negotiated in private rather than punished by public fluctuation.

A public company is governed by a market calendar: reporting windows, guidance rituals, index flows, activism seasons, and the endless pressure of being marked every day by people whose holding periods can be shorter than the firm's operating cycle. A private equity-controlled company is governed by a contract calendar: covenants, milestones, refinancing windows, add-on acquisition opportunities, and exit planning. The crowd's calendar produces visibility and noise. The contract calendar produces enforceable control. The point is not secrecy for its own sake. The point is that enforceable control is the rarest form of power in finance because it lets you change the machine rather than trade inside it.

Private equity begins with an admission that public markets optimize tradability and defensibility, not operations. Tradability demands standard narratives, standard metrics, and rapid comparability. Defensibility demands disclosure discipline and proof. Those demands can make a firm legible and liquid. They can also make a firm fragile, because the firm becomes managed for the crowd's tolerance rather than for long-cycle value creation. Private equity offers an alternative governance perimeter: make the firm legible to lenders and to owners, not to everyone. That reduction in audiences changes what is possible, and it also changes what is enforceable.

Control in private equity is not a slogan. It is a bundle of rights embedded in capital structure, board composition, consent requirements, and covenants that dictate what management can and cannot do. A public shareholder votes occasionally and mostly watches. A private owner writes the rulebook: what leverage is acceptable, what dividends can be paid, what acquisitions require approval, what budgets must be hit, what incentive plans will govern management, and what happens if performance drifts. The empire beyond the exchange is built through documents that behave like law inside the firm. The public sees a price. The private system writes a constitution.

The constitution begins before purchase, in diligence. Diligence is not primarily "is this company good." It is "where is controllable cash, where is mispriced risk, where can working capital be pulled forward, where can suppliers be pressed, where can pricing be tightened, what assets can be sold, what liabilities can be boxed, what is the true refinancing capacity, and which costs are sticky." The diligence output is not an opinion. It is a map of levers that can be pulled under private governance without daily public punishment.

The acquisition structure translates that map into enforceable constraints. A buyout is not simply "buy company, improve company." It is "buy control with a small equity check, finance the rest with negotiated debt, then force the company's cash flows to service the financing while operations are re-engineered." The leverage is not an accessory. It is the discipline tool and the extraction tool. It disciplines management because covenants and debt service impose deadlines. It extracts value because debt financing can shift returns to the equity sponsor when operations stabilize. It also creates fragility, which is why the private equity empire depends on being able to refinance, amend covenants, and reposition the balance sheet faster than the public can understand what is happening.

The debt is not just debt. It is a governance partner. A lender with covenants is a second sovereign inside the company, because covenants can force decisions that a board might otherwise delay. The sponsor and lender bargain over risk, and the bargain becomes the operating perimeter: how much cash must be preserved, how much can be spent, how much leverage can be tolerated, and how quickly deviations must be corrected. This is why private equity cannot be separated from private credit as an institution. The empire beyond the exchange is joint rule by sponsor and lender, with the sponsor holding strategic control and the lender holding emergency veto power.

The system's advantage is that these constraints are precise. Public markets govern through sentiment and price. Private markets govern through contractual triggers. A public company can disappoint and survive if it can tell a story. A private company can miss a covenant and be forced into renegotiation, asset sales, equity injections, or control concessions. Covenants are deadlines with teeth. The empire is built on deadlines because deadlines convert managerial ambiguity into action.

Governance engineering is the next engine. In public markets, governance must be performative enough to satisfy regulators and a broad investor base. In private equity, governance is instrumental. Boards are smaller, incentives are sharper, reporting is more frequent internally, and decisions are less constrained by optics. Private owners can replace management quickly, restructure divisions without worrying about quarterly narrative penalties, and impose operating systems that prioritize cash conversion over story smoothness. This can create genuine operational improvement. It also can create extraction by transferring value from labor, suppliers, or long-term investment to near-term cash. The empire's power is that it can choose the mix and defend it privately.

Instrumental governance is made possible by measurement. Private owners impose measurement that public markets rarely demand: weekly cash forecasting, daily working-capital monitoring where appropriate, unit economics at granular levels, procurement savings tracking, SKU or customer segment margin maps, and operational KPIs tied directly to covenant cushions and refinancing narratives. Measurement changes behavior because it changes consequences. If a division misses its cash conversion plan, it is not punished by a headline. It is punished by a capital allocation decision and by intensified oversight, because the sponsor is managing a refinancing story, not a quarterly story.

The refinancing story is the empire's hidden narrative structure. Public markets are about multiple expansion and daily perception. Private equity is about refinancing capacity and covenant resilience. A sponsor can create real value and still lose the equity if refinancing fails. The private market's "price" is therefore the terms offered by lenders at the refinance moment: spreads, covenants, maturities, and acceptable leverage. Those terms depend on cash conversion, stability, and the absence of visible liabilities. This is why sponsors often focus on reducing variability and creating predictable cash flow, even at the cost of some long-run optionality. Predictable cash is financeable cash. Financeable cash is control.

Timing is the empire's next engine. Public markets punish ambiguity continuously. Private equity buys at one moment, runs the transformation in private, and sells at another moment when the story can be packaged as a clean asset for the next buyer's mandate. The value is not only created in operations. It is created in packaging: reorganize the firm into a shape that fits institutional appetite, then exit into a market window where that appetite is strongest. Timing is not mysticism. Timing is the ability to wait because private owners are not forced to show daily marks to the crowd. They show marks to their own limited partners under rules they can manage. The crowd's daily mood is replaced by periodic narratives and valuation policy. The empire is, at its core, a different clock.

This clock advantage is not soft. It is contractual. Limited partners accept periodic valuation, lock-ups, and reporting cadence. That acceptance creates time insulation. Time insulation reduces the probability of forced selling driven by public sentiment swings. The sponsor can therefore do things that are hard in public: close factories, change pricing, renegotiate supplier contracts, redraw product lines, and accept short-term turbulence that would be punished daily on a screen. The trade is that the sponsor's discipline is stricter, because lenders will not tolerate indefinite turbulence. The sponsor can ignore the crowd, but it cannot ignore covenants.

Control over information is another engine. Public companies must disclose broadly. Private companies disclose selectively, mostly to lenders and owners. Selective disclosure does not necessarily mean deception. It means the firm is not obligated to translate every operational nuance into a public narrative that can be traded against. That reduces the predation risk that comes from visibility. It also reduces the accountability that comes from visibility. The private equity empire is built on this trade: less noise, less scrutiny, more concentrated oversight by parties with direct control rights.

The empire institutionalizes extraction through explicit fees and implicit priority. In public markets, extraction is often hidden in spreads, data tolls, and financing terms. In private equity, extraction can be explicit: management fees, transaction fees, monitoring fees, and a promote structure that transfers upside to the sponsor. Even where fee practices are constrained, the deeper extraction mechanism is priority: who gets paid first, who controls decisions, who can trigger a sale, and who has consent rights over major corporate actions. Priority is written into the deal and enforceable. Enforceability is the empire's characteristic advantage, because it makes outcomes durable even when conditions turn hostile.

Priority is also why private equity is comfortable with complexity. Public investors prefer simple claims they can price quickly. Private owners prefer complex control stacks because complexity embeds protections and makes certain outcomes harder to contest. Preferred equity layers, covenant packages, intercreditor agreements, and consent rights create a private legal terrain where bargaining power is encoded. Bargaining power encoded is bargaining power preserved.

The relationship with debt markets deepens the empire's control system. Buyouts convert operating cash flow into collateral for negotiated leverage. The lender is not a crowd. The lender is a counterparty with covenants, haircuts, and rights of intervention. That makes private credit a co-governor. A public shareholder cannot demand a weekly cash forecast. A private lender can. A public shareholder cannot trigger default. A private lender can. The sponsor's power is therefore partially borrowed from the lender's enforcement power, and the lender's power is partially protected by the sponsor's ability to manage the company to meet the terms.

The operational playbook is the empire's industrial asset. Public markets standardize disclosure. Private equity standardizes transformation. The playbook is a repeatable method for diligence, acquisition structuring, pricing discipline, cost reduction, bolt-on integration, procurement pressure, working capital extraction, and refinancing preparation. Playbook standardization matters because it allows scale across many companies without reinventing governance each time. Scaling governance is what makes a sponsor an empire builder rather than a one-off deal maker.

Working capital is where extraction becomes immediate. Extending payables shifts financing burden to suppliers. Tightening receivables pulls cash forward. Cutting inventory reduces cash tied up, sometimes at the cost of resilience. These are not accounting tricks. They are cash movement strategies. Cash movement strategies determine covenant compliance. Covenant compliance determines refinancing terms. Refinancing terms determine equity survival. This is why private owners often focus on working capital as aggressively as they focus on headline profitability.

Suppliers become part of the empire's cash machine. Procurement pressure can extract margin by pushing down supplier prices. Longer payment terms can improve working capital by shifting financing burden onto suppliers. These changes improve cash conversion and refinancing capacity. They can also weaken supply resilience and increase systemic fragility in broader ecosystems, because a large sponsor-controlled buyer can force terms that cascade downstream. Public markets can punish this behavior reputationally. Private ownership can delay reputational costs until exit, which is why the trade can be rational even when it imposes external costs.

Labor is a similar lever. Private owners can renegotiate labor arrangements, change staffing models, outsource functions, and impose productivity systems quickly. That can improve margins. It can also create social costs. Public markets impose reputational constraints that can make certain moves harder. Private ownership reduces those constraints, at least temporarily. The empire's power is the ability to impose changes before the public can react, then exit after metrics look clean.

The empire's most subtle extraction occurs through the reclassification of risk. In public markets, risk is priced continuously and punished immediately through volatility and investor flight. In private ownership, risk can be held offstage and managed through covenants, reserves, indemnities, escrows, and insurance-like structures until exit. Environmental liabilities, legal exposures, and operational fragilities can be negotiated so they are financeable and so they do not scare buyers at exit. This is risk packaging. Risk packaging is power because it decides who bears which tail.

The empire beyond the exchange feeds on the difference between public and private valuation regimes. One regime is public, continuous, and mood-sensitive. The other is private, periodic, and committee-controlled. The sponsor buys under one regime and sells under another, choosing which regime is more favorable at each boundary. When public markets are pessimistic, buying privately can be cheap. When public markets are optimistic, selling into them can be lucrative. The sponsor's advantage is not predicting optimism with perfect timing. The sponsor's advantage is the ability to wait until optimism is available and the ability to package the company so that optimism can be harvested without being destroyed by obvious fragility.

Exit is therefore engineered as a process, not hoped for as an event. A sponsor does not merely sell a company; it sells an object that fits the next buyer's constraints. The object must be legible, financeable, and defensible. That requires cleaning up accounting, stabilizing cash conversion, reducing visible liabilities, and constructing a narrative that fits public comparables or fits private credit underwriting heuristics. This is why sponsors often "professionalize" reporting: not only to manage internally, but to make the company look like a stable collateral and a stable cash engine to the next owner.

The exit path also reveals how public markets are used as a validation device. Public multiples are the scoreboard. The sponsor uses that scoreboard to justify private valuations and to persuade allocators that the transformation created real value. The crowd is asked to ratify a privately engineered transformation by paying for it, either directly in a public offering or indirectly through institutions buying secondary stakes. The empire beyond the exchange uses the exchange as a scoreboard while refusing to play under the exchange's rules daily.

Refinancing is the empire's recurring extraction and survival test. A refinancing can reduce cost of capital, extend maturities, loosen covenants, and allow recapitalization that returns equity while leaving the company more levered. The public hears "refinancing" and imagines prudence. The machine sees value transfer through balance sheet optimization and reallocation of risk to lenders, employees, suppliers, or future buyers. The sponsor's strongest position is when lenders compete. The lender's strongest position is when the company is stressed and alternatives are scarce. The empire is a continuous negotiation of sovereignty between sponsor and lender, with management operating inside the negotiated constraints.

Private equity also creates a delayed volatility mechanism. Public markets express volatility daily. Private markets store volatility in refinancing risk. Debt does not disappear because it is not marked on a screen. Debt matures. Maturity is the private market's moment of truth. If refinancing terms are favorable, the stored volatility is rolled forward quietly. If terms are unfavorable, the stored volatility becomes forced restructuring. The public sees a quiet company and then a sudden crisis. The machine sees a maturity wall that was visible to those inside the private architecture months earlier.

The empire beyond the exchange is therefore not simply "private markets." It is a control technology built from contracts, covenants, measurement regimes, and timing discretion. It can produce real operational improvement, and it can produce extraction that weakens long-term resilience. The same machinery can do both because the machinery is indifferent to social narratives. It responds to enforceable terms and to exit incentives.

"The crowd buys the equity; the contract keeps the keys."

That is the empire beyond the exchange: control first, pricing later, extraction through enforceable terms, and a return to the public only when the story is polished enough that the crowd's price can be harvested.

CHAPTER 28
THE QUIET GOVERNORS OF CAPITAL

PASSIVE FUNDS, INDEX RULES, AND THE HIDDEN POWER OF AUTOMATIC ALLOCATION.

Power in markets is often imagined as a loud act: a speech, a trade, a shock, a visible villain. The quiet governors do not need noise. They do not need to persuade anyone in the moment. They govern by default. They govern by rule. They govern by flows that occur because a definition exists and a mandate references it. When a large share of capital is deployed automatically, the most important decisions migrate upstream from "who chose to buy today" to "who wrote the rule that forces buying every day." This is not a conspiracy layer. It is a design layer, and design is the purest form of governance because it keeps working even when nobody is watching.

Quiet governance is the conversion of policy into routine. It does not look like power because it is not exercised as a command. It is exercised as an assumption. The assumption is that there is a correct representation of the market, a correct set of eligible assets, a correct weighting methodology, and a correct way to measure performance. Once those assumptions are adopted, the allocation machine runs. The machine does not ask whether the assumptions still match reality; it asks whether the assumptions are still defensible. Defensibility is the currency that keeps large institutions intact, because institutions survive not by being right every quarter but by being explainable every quarter. The quiet governors therefore are the architects of explainability.

The quiet governors are not one institution. They are an interlocking set of defaults: index methodologies, benchmark conventions, portfolio construction templates, mandate language, risk model baselines, committee heuristics that determine what counts as prudent, and reporting standards that determine which prices become official anchors. Together they decide which assets receive persistent demand, which receive persistent neglect, and which become the shock absorbers that must be sold when stress requires liquidation. The public faces the tape and believes price is the signal. The quiet governors shape the signal by shaping the demand that must show up regardless of belief.

The first governor is the benchmark, not as a measure but as an employment contract. When performance is judged relative to a benchmark, deviation becomes career risk. Career risk is binding because it penalizes drawdowns even when drawdowns are rational. Conviction without a job cannot hold a position through turbulence. So the benchmark becomes a corridor. It dictates sector weights, factor exposures, geographic balances, and acceptable tracking error. It also dictates timing, because reporting needs a mark and marks cluster at official reference moments. The benchmark's power is that it turns discretion into a narrow space and persuades participants they are still choosing freely inside it.

The second governor is the index rule, because index rules convert classification into obligation. Inclusion is not a badge. It is a flow engine. Exclusion is not an insult. It is a liquidity tax. Rules decide what qualifies, how it is weighted, when it is implemented, and how corporate actions are reflected. Rules are defended as neutral, but neutrality is a story told by the rule writer, because any rule that sorts assets and channels flows is an allocation mechanism. Allocation mechanisms change cost of capital. Changing cost of capital changes corporate decisions. The quiet governor does not need a public vote to influence which firms can finance cheaply, which can borrow on favorable terms, and which can attract persistent demand without persuading a discretionary buyer each week.

The third governor is the mandate template. A mandate is a contract between an allocator and a manager, and the contract is written as a defense document. It is written so that when outcomes disappoint, the allocator can say 'the manager followed policy,' or the manager can say 'the policy required this exposure.' The mandate therefore prioritizes defensibility over originality. Defensibility requires standard exposures, standard risk limits, and standard benchmarks. Standardization creates scale. Scale creates concentration. Concentration creates quiet power because it is embedded in how money is allowed to behave.

The fourth governor is the risk model baseline. Risk models translate the world into numbers committees can consume: volatility estimates, correlation structures, stress scenarios, concentration limits. Once a model is adopted institutionally, it becomes a governor because it decides what is allowed. A position that is profitable but looks ugly to the model will be cut. A position that is fragile but looks clean to the model will be held. When conditions change, the model updates, and the update becomes a wave of forced behavior: risk limits tighten, exposures are reduced, liquidity is demanded from the most liquid instruments, and the same instruments that appear safest become the first sold because they are the only ones that can be sold quickly without trapping the institution in settlement and liquidity risk.

The fifth governor is the valuation convention. Valuation conventions decide which prices are "real" for reporting, collateral, and performance. Official closes, auction prints, and reference levels are not merely observations. They are anchors around which portfolios are judged and around which collateral is valued. When the system anchors to specific prints, flows concentrate toward those prints because tracking and reporting prefer alignment. This creates predictable windows of urgency. Predictable windows are monetizable. The quiet governor is not only allocating what is held; it is allocating when forced trading will occur.

The sixth governor is the eligibility infrastructure: the operational reality that decides whether an asset can be owned without creating proof and settlement friction. Eligibility is not only "is the asset legal to hold." It is "can the asset be held and financed inside the institution's operational and regulatory perimeter without generating exceptional handling." Exceptional handling is costly. Cost is career risk because exceptions invite scrutiny. Therefore institutions prefer assets that fit the machine: clean identifiers, stable corporate action processing, predictable settlement, reliable borrow and lending conventions, and widely accepted collateral treatment. These are microstructural properties masquerading as investability. They are also gates that concentrate capital toward assets that are easy to process.

The quiet governors are quiet because they operate through default, and default is the most stable kind of power. A default persists unless challenged. Challenging a default requires coordination, evidence, and political appetite. Most institutions do not want that fight. They want to be able to explain themselves. So they accept defaults and then compete inside the narrow space the defaults leave.

Quiet governance does not need correctness to be powerful. It needs adoption. Adoption produces reality by producing flows. When flows are large enough, they shape liquidity conditions and therefore price behavior. Price behavior then becomes the evidence used to justify adoption, because the benchmark and the index appear to "represent the market." The loop is self-reinforcing: adoption produces flow, flow produces liquidity, liquidity produces tradability, tradability produces legitimacy, legitimacy produces more adoption.

The most visible expression of this power is the liquidity hierarchy. Assets that are heavily benchmarked become liquid. Liquidity reduces trading cost. Reduced cost attracts more strategies. More strategies increase volume. Volume increases the value of data and the willingness of intermediaries to warehouse inventory. Inventory warehousing makes liquidity more resilient. Resilient liquidity makes the asset more suitable as a benchmark component. The loop compounds. Assets outside this hierarchy face wider spreads, more fragile liquidity, and higher cost of capital. They can be excellent businesses and still be punished by the quiet governors because the governors are not evaluating excellence. They are evaluating eligibility under a rule set that prizes tradability, standardization, and defensibility.

The hierarchy also creates a sorting of attention. Analysts, data vendors, and media coverage gravitate toward liquid constituents because liquid constituents generate more activity and more client interest. Activity increases the availability of comparable data, which increases institutional comfort. Comfort increases allocation. Allocation increases liquidity further. The loop becomes a cultural governor as well as a mechanical one: the "important" companies are those the system already made liquid.

Quiet governance shapes corporate behavior because companies respond to financing conditions. If inclusion in major indices and benchmark-friendly status lowers financing cost, firms will pursue inclusion-friendly structures: float management, share class simplification, disclosure regularity, corporate actions timed to minimize index disruption, and capital return programs that maintain capitalization thresholds. The market calls this investor relations. The machine recognizes it as compliance with the governors that decide the firm's cost of capital.

Quiet governance shapes what kinds of companies remain private and what kinds go public. Public admission requires enduring the crowd's narrative penalties and the disclosure regime. Private ownership requires enduring covenant penalties and lender governance. Firms choose the perimeter that they can satisfy at reasonable cost. The choice is not only strategic; it is shaped by which set of governors the firm can comply with: public tradability governors or private financing governors.

Automatic allocation is the governor with the sharpest teeth because it creates demand that is not conditional on belief. When capital flows into rule-based vehicles, buying occurs regardless of the daily story. This is why rallies can persist without a coherent narrative and why drawdowns can accelerate even when fundamentals have not changed. The market's surface narrative wants a reason. The machine's reality is flow: steady inflows create steady buying; steady outflows create forced selling.

Automatic allocation creates predictable stress behavior. When outflows occur, rule-based vehicles must sell what they own in proportion to rules. They will sell the most liquid instruments first because those are easiest to sell. This means that in systemic stress, the most liquid assets become the transmission channel for liquidation. The public interprets this as the safest assets falling, which feels paradoxical. The machine knows the paradox is structural: liquidity is the instrument of liquidation because liquidation requires liquidity.

Quiet governance therefore has an amplification problem. In calm regimes, automatic allocation can smooth prices by providing steady demand. In stress regimes, automatic allocation can accelerate selling by creating non-discretionary liquidation. Stability and fragility are the same mechanism expressed under different conditions.

The quiet governors also produce a calendar of forced events. Reconstitutions, rebalances, corporate action adjustments, reporting cutoffs, and valuation conventions are scheduled. Schedules concentrate urgency. Concentrated urgency widens spreads and increases the value of being early to the state of the book and early to imbalance signals. This is where quiet governance intersects with the engineered edge: the winners do not need to predict the world; they need to be positioned where urgency arrives and to price liquidity into the window.

Quiet governance creates an information economy that is not about news but about rules. The most valuable information is not that a company announced something. The most valuable information is that a company will be added, removed, reweighted, or reclassified under rules that will force many funds to trade. This is mechanical information: it changes forced behavior. Mechanical information is often more profitable because it reduces uncertainty about timing.

Mechanical information also changes how legitimacy is performed. When a methodology change is announced, the system can pretend the subsequent price move is discovery. In reality the move is often flow anticipation: those who can pre-position do so, and the forced funds then complete the move. The result is a feedback that looks like collective belief and is frequently a calendar effect expressed through liquidity. The quiet governors create the calendar; the House sells the tools to trade the calendar.

Proof burdens reinforce quiet governance. Tracking and best execution require documentation. Documentation requires data, timestamps, and audit trails. Proof burdens raise fixed costs. Fixed costs advantage scale. Scale allows purchase of better data, better connectivity, better analytics, and better operational resilience. Operational resilience reduces settlement and financing friction. Reduced friction improves execution quality and reduces tracking error. Reduced tracking error improves benchmark-relative performance. Improved performance attracts mandates. More mandates increase flows. The loop reinforces governance by making benchmarked behavior even more dominant.

Quiet governance reshapes the language of prudence. Prudence becomes 'avoid tracking error,' 'stay within factor bands,' 'hold liquid constituents,' 'use standard hedges,' and 'do not create exceptions.' This can be reasonable for institutions managing other people's money. It can also become herd mechanism. Herd mechanisms create crowded exposures. Crowded exposures become fragile because they rely on the same financing assumptions and the same liquidity assumptions.

Crowding is not only in positions. It is in models. If many institutions rely on similar risk models and similar constraint frameworks, they will react similarly when volatility rises. Similar reaction creates correlated selling. Correlated selling moves prices and increases volatility. Increased volatility triggers tighter constraints. The loop can become self-driven. In that moment, the quiet governors that felt like safety become the mechanism that forces the crowd to move together.

The quiet governors determine what counts as "investable." Investability screens exclude assets that are hard to trade, hard to finance, or operationally painful. Exclusion can be justified as protection. It also concentrates demand in assets that are easiest to process and easiest to borrow against, increasing their valuation and lowering their cost of capital relative to excluded assets. Cost of capital shapes real outcomes. Quiet governance is industrial policy by default, executed through eligibility rules rather than through public budgets.

Neutrality is the governor's camouflage. The system treats benchmark indices as neutral representations of "the market." That neutrality claim allows them to govern without being perceived as governing. If the public believed index methodology writers were allocating capital, the public might demand accountability. The system avoids that by framing methodology as technical. Technical framing is politically powerful because technical decisions appear inevitable. Yet technical decisions determine flows, and flows determine financing conditions.

To show how this governance operates without speeches, consider a single methodology change moving through the machine as a forced sequence. A committee adjusts eligibility criteria, perhaps changing a float definition or a classification boundary. The change is announced. The announcement is treated as informational, but its primary effect is mechanical: it changes future forced trading. Those with early, high-fidelity rule interpretation begin pre-positioning. They buy likely additions, sell likely deletions, and adjust hedges. Their activity leaks into prices gradually, often framed as "the market reacting."

Then the rebalance window arrives. Trackers must execute. They do not execute because they changed beliefs; they execute because their mandate requires alignment. Execution concentrates at reference moments because tracking error is punished. The close becomes the preferred anchor, so the close auction absorbs an unusually large share of the adjustment. Imbalance grows. Spreads widen into the window because liquidity providers price urgency. Some liquidity withdraws because adverse selection risk rises. Those with premium visibility and inventory capacity sell liquidity into the imbalance at a premium. The print becomes official. Reporting systems mark to it. Committees accept it. The methodology writer's rule has now become reality, not because it was debated publicly, but because it was executed and recorded.

The system then enforces the new reality through evaluation. Managers are judged against the updated benchmark. Deviations become tracking error. Tracking error becomes career risk. Career risk becomes compliance. Compliance becomes persistent holding. Persistent holding becomes demand. Demand becomes liquidity. Liquidity becomes lower cost of capital. The new rule becomes durable, and the quiet governor has governed without ever needing a political speech.

Now consider the same structure under stress, when quiet governance becomes a transmission device. Outflows hit rule-based vehicles. Selling is required. Selling concentrates in the most liquid constituents. Prices fall. Falling prices increase volatility. Risk models update. Updated models tighten risk limits. Risk limit tightening forces further selling. Margin requirements rise because volatility is higher. Higher margin triggers deleveraging. Deleveraging forces selling again. The index constituents, being the most liquid, become the primary sale instruments. The public sees broad decline and attributes it to fear. The machine is executing a forced sequence driven by mandates, models, and margin.

In that sequence, the quiet governors appear as stability tools and become amplifiers. The benchmark that disciplined managers in calm times disciplines them in stress by forcing reduction inside narrow corridors. The model that controlled risk in calm times accelerates selling in stress by cutting limits. The valuation convention that provided clear marks in calm times becomes a trigger for collateral calls in stress. The same design that made institutions explainable makes the system less adaptable in the moment because deviations are punished and because discretion is limited.

This is why the quiet governors are central to private power. They do not only move flows. They also set the rules that decide which actors will be liquid when the system tightens. Actors who operate outside the benchmark corridor can hold optionality and become buyers in stress. Actors who are bound to the benchmark corridor become sellers in stress. The governors do not choose winners intentionally. They create an environment where certain business models are structurally favored: those with mandate freedom, funding endurance, and the ability to buy when rules force others to sell.

Quiet governance also feeds the exchange empires and the tollbooths of visibility. If rebalance windows and close auctions are central to tracking, the infrastructure owners of those reference moments can price participation and price information. They sell premium imbalance feeds. They sell premium timestamps. They sell connectivity. They sell historical archives needed for proof and model building. The quiet governors create predictable events. Infrastructure owners monetize the events. The crowd sees the final print and does not see the invoice for seeing the print earlier.

Quiet governors also reshape politics indirectly. A society that ties household savings to benchmarked products ties household outcomes to the behavior of the benchmark machine. When the machine favors certain sectors, household wealth becomes exposed to those sectors. When the machine forces liquidation, household wealth experiences drawdowns not because households chose to sell but because vehicles must sell. This creates a politics of abstraction: households experience the effects of rules they never see. The system prefers abstraction because abstraction reduces accountability pressure.

The quiet governors are therefore the market's most stable form of power: power that does not need to be debated because it is embedded in routine. The routine is the constitution. The constitution is methodology and mandate language. The methodology is adopted because it makes the system manageable. Manageability is why large institutions accept it. They accept it because they need to report, to explain, and to defend. The cost is that capital moves in patterned ways that can be exploited by those with visibility and funding advantage, and that real economic outcomes can be influenced by eligibility rules written far from the workplaces that will feel the consequences.

CHAPTER 29
WHO PRICES THE WORLD
DATA VENDORS, BENCHMARKS, AND THE COMMERCIAL CONTROL OF INFORMATION ITSELF.

Pricing looks like discovery until you ask who is allowed to describe reality in a form that institutions can use. The world is priced by the party whose numbers become the default inputs to mandates, risk models, collateral schedules, valuation marks, accounting memos, and dispute reconstruction. If a committee accepts a dataset as authoritative, that dataset becomes the committee's map of the world, and the map determines what is allowed to be bought, how it is measured, and when it must be sold. Markets can argue about value all day. The quiet power belongs to whoever sells the numbers that end the argument inside the institutions that move size.

A price is not a single object. It is a layered artifact produced by sources, timestamps, methodologies, and eligibility rules. The public sees a quote and believes it is a fact. An institution sees a stack: which venue counts for reference, which prints are filtered, which outliers are ignored, which timestamp is authoritative, which feed is licensed, which symbols are mapped to which identifiers, which corporate actions are applied, and which benchmark methodology turns a set of prices into an index level that becomes the anchor for compensation and risk. The stack is where "information" becomes enforceable. The seller of the stack is not merely a publisher. It is a governor of what the system will treat as real.

The control begins with a dependency: modern finance is too large to run on bespoke judgment. It needs standardized inputs. Standard inputs must be produced, cleaned, normalized, and maintained. Maintenance is work: collecting, cleaning, normalizing, mapping, timestamping, distributing, and storing for reconstruction. Once that work is done at scale, it becomes a product. Once it becomes a product, it can be priced. Once it is priced, it becomes a toll road, because institutions that must prove and report cannot simply invent their own numbers without inviting audit failure and litigation risk. The system prefers purchased authority to homemade authority because purchased authority is defensible authority.

The first mechanism is data as operating system. Trading firms need real-time feeds to act. Funds need end-of-day marks to value portfolios. Lenders need collateral marks to demand margin. Auditors need sources to verify marks were not invented. Compliance teams need records to reconstruct. These needs are structural. The moment a dataset becomes the standard source for any one of these functions, the dataset becomes sticky. Stickiness is integration cost. Systems are built around formats, identifiers, timestamps, and archives. Changing a source is not like changing a newspaper. It is rewiring infrastructure, retraining staff, revalidating models, renegotiating proof expectations with counterparties, and risking operational failure.

Stickiness turns information into a franchise. A franchise can be defended by product quality, but it is more reliably defended by switching cost and proof fear. Proof fear is the fear of being the institution that used the "wrong" source when a dispute arrives. Dispute arrives when money is lost. Money is lost when marks are contested, when collateral is misvalued, when best execution is challenged, or when an audit finds inconsistency. Institutions will pay to reduce dispute probability, even if the alternative data source is cheaper. That is why the information seller's strongest moat is not always accuracy. It is defensibility.

The second mechanism is methodology as concealed discretion. Most users believe a feed is a stream of facts. In practice, the feed is a series of choices: which venues are included, how to handle crossed markets, how to filter bad prints, how to treat auctions, how to label cancellations, how to timestamp events, how to handle gaps and delays, and how to adjust for corporate actions. Each choice affects downstream outputs. Downstream outputs include risk model inputs, benchmark levels, and valuation marks. Methodology therefore can reallocate money without moving a single trade. It can do so by changing the numbers institutions treat as ground truth.

These choices are not cosmetic. In a calm regime, filtering may look like housekeeping. In a stress regime, filtering determines whether a dislocated print becomes an official mark. Official marks trigger margin calls and risk limit events. A vendor's policy for outlier handling can therefore determine whether a portfolio is forced to sell. The vendor does not intend to trigger selling. The vendor intends to publish defensible numbers. The system turns defensible numbers into deadlines. Deadlines create forced behavior. Forced behavior creates profit opportunities for those with funding and visibility.

The third mechanism is identifiers, the skeleton under every portfolio. A market cannot be priced unless instruments are uniquely referenced across systems. Mapping a tradable symbol to a legal instrument, mapping corporate actions through time, mapping mergers, spin-outs, and share class changes, mapping geographic listings, mapping derivatives to underlyings, mapping issuer identity through reorganizations, mapping ownership structures: this is the difference between a portfolio that can be valued and a portfolio that becomes a dispute. Whoever owns the identifier system owns the ability to make the market legible at scale, which means whoever owns the identifier system owns a gate to participation for institutions that must report cleanly.

Identifier power shows up when things break. When a company reorganizes, when a share class converts, when a spin-out creates entitlements, when a merger changes settlement properties, the world becomes a mapping problem. If the mapping is wrong, a fund can misstate holdings, misstate performance, and mis-handle entitlements. Mis-handling entitlements becomes litigation. Litigation becomes proof crisis. Proof crisis becomes institutional shame. Institutions pay to avoid shame, which means they pay for the vendor whose mappings are accepted as the standard narrative of identity. Identity is governance because identity determines what is even being priced.

The fourth mechanism is the benchmark as commercial product rather than civic reference. A benchmark is a pricing device that claims neutrality and functions as a contract. It defines a universe, a weighting rule, and a maintenance schedule. Institutions reference it in mandates. Managers are judged against it. Derivatives reference it. Marketing references it. Once referenced, it becomes an enforcement device because deviating creates tracking error and career risk. The benchmark provider therefore is not merely measuring. It is governing flows through definitions. When benchmark rules change, forced trading occurs. Forced trading creates predictable windows. Predictable windows are monetizable. The benchmark provider sells the rule that creates the window and sells the data that tells you where the window will hit.

Benchmarks also sell legitimacy. Many institutions do not want to explain why they own a particular set of assets. They want to say they own "the market" as defined by a widely accepted index. That provides social cover. Social cover is important because fiduciaries are punished not only for losses but for losses that look idiosyncratic and therefore blameworthy. Holding the benchmark is defensible because everyone else holds the benchmark. Defensibility demand is what turns a benchmark into a governor.

The fifth mechanism is the valuation anchor. Institutions do not merely want prices; they want prices they can defend. Defensible price is from an accepted source, computed by an accepted process, at an accepted time, with a documented audit trail. Official closes, auction prints, and reference levels become anchors. Anchors create deadlines. Deadlines force behavior. Behavior can be priced. Once a vendor's outputs are treated as anchors, the vendor gains power over the system's calendar: when marks become binding, when collateral is revalued, and when performance is declared. Calendar control is quiet power because it does not look like power; it looks like accounting.

Commercial control of information is therefore control of three things: perception, proof, and calendar. Perception determines who sees state changes earliest and with what fidelity. Proof determines whose numbers survive audit and dispute. Calendar determines when those numbers become binding marks that trigger behavior. A participant can be an exceptional forecaster and still lose if it cannot see, cannot prove, and cannot finance through the mark times. The sellers of information products sit upstream of these constraints and can price access without taking directional risk.

Information control becomes a stratification mechanism because the system sells different realities at different prices. A public lane exists: basic quotes, basic marks, basic reporting. The public lane preserves legitimacy. A premium lane exists: faster feeds, deeper book visibility, richer event types, better corporate action processing, better identifiers, better archives, and analytics that translate raw messages into usable state. Premium lanes preserve survivability for those who must make markets, manage inventory, and avoid being selected against. Survivability reduces loss. Reduced loss allows tighter quoting.

Tighter quoting attracts flow. Flow yields more information. The loop compounds.

The pricing of information is defended as cost recovery. The defense has truth: building and maintaining infrastructure is expensive. The deeper mechanism is that information is inelastic for those who must comply and compete. Inelastic demand is the dream of every infrastructure owner. A fund that needs defensible marks cannot opt out without changing its governance. A market maker that needs low delay cannot opt out without turning into a charity for faster counterparties. A custodian that needs corporate action accuracy cannot opt out without inviting entitlement failures. Inelastic demand allows price increases that feel like "industry standard." Industry standard is another name for unavoidable.

Benchmarks intensify inelasticity because they transform information into discipline. A benchmark level is embedded in reporting, compensation, and marketing. When a benchmark provider changes methodology, the provider is forcing flows. Flows become revenue for surrounding infrastructure: exchanges at reference moments, data vendors selling imbalance and analytics, and financing providers who can price liquidity when forced trades arrive. The benchmark provider sits at the origin of the cascade. The provider's quiet power is governance without trading.

Commercial control expresses itself through the politics of "clean" data. An institution's nightmare is a mark dispute. A mark dispute invites audit escalation, collateral arguments, and client mistrust. Institutions therefore prefer sources with reputational authority. Reputational authority becomes a moat because it is not only about accuracy; it is about defensibility under stress. A vendor whose numbers are accepted by large institutions becomes accepted because large institutions accept them. The loop is circular: adoption creates authority, authority creates adoption. That is how a commercial vendor becomes a de facto standard without claiming monopoly.

Most of the price is not the last trade. Most of the price is curated output. Curated does not mean fraudulent. Curated means filtered and normalized so it can be used as a stable input. A raw market stream is full of discontinuities: bad prints, stale quotes, microstructure artifacts, and outliers caused by thin moments. Institutions cannot run on raw. They run on cleaned. Cleaned requires choices. Choices embed policy. Policy embedded in cleaning becomes a governor because it decides what counts as "real" for the institution's purposes.

This is why the market's most consequential fights often occur not on the tape but in committees and contracts about sources and methodologies. Which vendor is approved for marks. Which benchmark is official. Which pricing source is used for collateral. Which data is licensed for execution and surveillance. Which identifier mapping is authoritative. These decisions can shift money without a trade because they shift the terms under which risk is measured and under which compliance is judged.

The world is priced not only by spot prices but by curves, implied rates, and derived constructs. A curve is a model plus inputs. A spread is a definition plus inputs. A benchmark level is a methodology plus inputs. When commercial vendors provide these derived constructs, they become governors of valuation across portfolios. A small methodology adjustment can change portfolio marks. Mark changes can trigger risk limit breaches. Breaches trigger forced selling. Forced selling triggers visible price movement. The public blames the market. The chain began in a definition change upstream of the tape.

The commercial control of information also creates a second-order business: selling tools that help institutions defend themselves against dependency. Audit trail services, reconstruction platforms, analytics that explain why a mark moved, and compliance reports that demonstrate reasonableness: these are monetizable because they reduce institutional anxiety. Anxiety is an economic variable. Institutions pay to reduce the probability of being accused of mispricing, misrouting, or misreporting. The vendor that sells primary data can often sell the defense layer because it already owns the record and mapping. Owning the record makes you the easiest seller of the explanation.

The asymmetry is that the public assumes "data" is a commodity. Often the commodity is the output, not the pipeline. The pipeline is sticky. The pipeline includes integration, identifiers, corporate actions, and committee acceptance. Pipeline stickiness means pricing power is not limited by competition in raw sources. Many raw sources can exist. The system still converges on a small number of approved pipelines because approval is costly and because the penalty for being the odd institution out is high.

Approval is a product. Approval is purchased through audit comfort, committee comfort, and market comfort. The vendor already accepted is safer than the vendor that is cheaper but would require defending a new source. This is why information markets concentrate even when raw data is widely available. Concentration is not only a business outcome. It is a governance outcome created by proof burdens.

Proof burdens also explain why information governance is hard to reform. If reform is proposed, institutions ask, will reform increase proof risk. Any change that increases proof risk is resisted because proof risk is existential. Commercial information providers sit behind institutional inertia. The inertia is rational preservation of legitimacy. Standards persist long after economic effects become visible because changing standards requires a compliance war.

The pricing of the world is also the pricing of time. Premium feeds sell earlier perception. Earlier perception reduces adverse selection. Reduced adverse selection allows tighter liquidity provision. Tighter liquidity provision captures more flow. Captured flow yields more information. The loop rewards those who can afford earlier perception. This creates systemic inequality that can be defended as technology access rather than as exclusion. The public sees equal rules. The private system sells unequal clocks.

Unequal clocks create a second-order inequality: unequal proof. Institutions with the ability to buy richer archives and better reconstruction can defend themselves more effectively. Defense reduces penalties. Reduced penalties allow more aggressive strategies within defensible boundaries. Those strategies can appear as superior performance. Performance attracts mandates. Mandates increase flow. Flow increases spending power. Spending power buys more proof. Proof becomes both shield and weapon.

Consider a valuation-source change as an escalation sequence. A vendor changes a filtering rule to exclude certain prints as outliers. The change is defensible as data quality improvement. The change alters end-of-day marks for a set of instruments. The altered marks feed into collateral valuation for secured financing. Financing counterparties demand additional margin because the mark moved. Margin calls arrive with deadlines. Borrowers meet deadlines by posting cash or selling assets. Selling is concentrated in the most liquid holdings. Prices fall. Volatility rises. Risk models update. Updated models tighten risk limits. More selling follows. The initial cause was not a news shock. The cause was a definition change in what counts as a "real" price for the mark. The vendor did not cause the selloff intentionally. The vendor governed the system by supplying the definition that the system treats as binding.

Now consider a benchmark-methodology change as a second escalation. A benchmark provider adjusts an eligibility rule or weight calculation. The change is announced. Pre-positioning begins because the change implies forced flows at implementation. Those with visibility and funding buy likely additions and sell likely deletions. Trackers must execute at the rebalance. Execution concentrates at the close because tracking is punished. The close auction imbalance grows. Liquidity providers widen spreads into the window because urgency is predictable. Premium imbalance products become more valuable. The exchange sells them. The benchmark provider sells updated datasets. The infrastructure ecosystem profits from the same rule change that forced the flows. The public sees a price move and calls it market reaction. The machine sees rule-driven demand expressing itself through scheduled urgency.

Who prices the world is therefore the party that can sell the rules, sell the cleaned record, sell the identifiers, and sell the proof that makes the output admissible. This is not merely "data." It is the commercial control of reality for institutional purposes.

CHAPTER 30
WHEN MARKETS RISE BUT PEOPLE FALL BEHIND
WHY THE SYSTEM CAN THRIVE WHILE HOUSEHOLDS, WORKERS, AND SMALL FIRMS STRAIN.

A market can be "up" while a society is down because markets measure one thing with obsessive precision: the price of claims that are already eligible to be financed, traded, and held by institutions that have time, access, and insulation. The index level is not a referendum on household solvency, wage bargaining power, local business credit, or the cost of living. It is the clearing price of a narrow set of assets sitting at the top of a liquidity hierarchy, inside a financing system designed to keep those assets tradeable even when everything else is strained. When the system protects tradability and marks it daily, the mark can look healthy while the distribution of burden becomes more brittle.

The divergence begins with whose balance sheet is allowed to be patient. A household has bills. A household has rent, food, healthcare, childcare, utilities, and debt service with hard deadlines. Missing deadlines has immediate penalties, and penalties compound into higher costs and fewer choices. A large institution has a different kind of deadline: reporting, risk limits, collateral calls, and mandate reviews. Yet it also has tools households do not: diversified funding sources, collateral optimization, access to wholesale liquidity, the ability to hedge cheaply, and the ability to shift risk into instruments whose losses can be managed across time rather than paid immediately in cash. The market rises when patient balance sheets can buy into forced selling, monetize the calendar, and roll financing in ways that keep them from becoming forced sellers themselves. People fall behind when they are forced to consume their own balance sheets to meet daily life.

The second source of divergence is that modern markets are governed by flows that do not require human conviction. Mandatory contributions, automatic allocations, benchmark tracking, and default portfolio settings turn buying into routine. Routine buying does not require optimism. It requires a paycheck somewhere in the system and a default contribution setting that is rarely revisited. Routine buying concentrates into liquid constituents because the vehicles receiving routine flows are benchmarked to those constituents. The price of the constituents can rise because the pipes deliver consistent demand, not because households feel richer. The household can simultaneously feel poorer if necessities reprice upward faster than wages and if savings are too small to compound at the same rate as the assets inside the benchmark machine.

A third source is the structure of credit transmission. When liquidity is abundant and rates fall, the first beneficiaries are the actors who can borrow at wholesale terms and deploy into financeable assets that reprice when discount rates fall. Wholesale borrowers can lever, hedge, and refinance. Households borrow at retail terms with less optionality, and their borrowing is often consumed by shelter, transportation, emergencies, and cash-flow smoothing rather than by acquisition of appreciating claims. When credit tightens, the stress becomes more asymmetric: institutions with better collateral and stronger lines can still roll, while households face higher rates, tighter underwriting, and higher required payments. The market can still hold because liquidity and confidence are preserved for the top of the hierarchy first, and because the mark reflects what is protected first.

The hierarchy is the core mechanism. The system does not treat all claims equally. It treats some as near-money, some as acceptable collateral, some as marginal, and some as barely financeable. The higher a claim sits, the easier it is to borrow against, hedge, and liquidate without collapse. The lower a claim sits, the more it depends on local credit and local confidence. Households and small firms operate in lower tiers: unsecured or lightly secured borrowing, cash-flow sensitivity, weaker bargaining power with lenders, and fewer alternative funding channels. Public markets operate in the top tier: collateralized finance, deep liquidity, standardized instruments, and institutional support mechanisms that preserve orderly trading. The market rises because the top tier is supported by design. People fall behind because the lower tiers are disciplined by scarcity and deadlines.

The fourth source is mark-to-market versus life-to-market. Institutions are judged on marks, but they also have tools to manage marks: hedges, diversification, and the ability to shift exposures. Households are judged by life: the real price of necessities, the availability of stable work, and the cost of debt. Life cannot be hedged cheaply. A household cannot reliably offset a rent spike, a childcare bill, or a medical surprise through a portfolio trade. It can work more, spend less, move farther away, or take credit, and each choice has compounding costs. The market can rise because marks are managed and supported. Life can worsen because necessities reprice upward and bargaining power does not keep pace.

The fifth source is ownership concentration and participation timing. If a small share of households hold a large share of financial assets, then a market rally can reflect rising wealth for those households while leaving the median largely untouched. Even when retirement vehicles expand ownership, the size and timing matter. If a household contributes late, intermittently, or in small amounts, it participates in the market's rise as a faint echo, while absorbing higher costs immediately. The system then produces a familiar political contradiction: the headline says prosperity, the median experience says strain. The contradiction is not ideological. It is arithmetic plus distribution plus timing.

The sixth source is corporate behavior under market governance. Public companies are rewarded for actions that increase per-share metrics and stabilize the narrative: cost control, margin protection, and capital return policies that raise per-share measures. These actions can support prices even when they do not increase broad-based wages. A firm can cut headcount, outsource, reduce training, reduce redundancy, and still be praised for "discipline" because discipline is legible as improved cash conversion. The market rises because the claim becomes more financeable and more comparable. Workers can fall behind because labor is treated as a variable cost optimized for the benefit of the claim.

This is a governance inversion. The public story says markets allocate capital efficiently so society prospers. The operating system allocates cheap financing to what is already legible, scalable, and financeable, then punishes what is messy, local, or slow. This does not require hostility toward workers. It requires an optimization regime that rewards what can be measured, financed, and defended. If the simplest way to increase a company's financial legibility is to reduce labor cost and increase predictability, the market rewards it. The divergence widens because predictability is purchased with somebody else's flexibility.

The seventh source is the pricing of risk as a private service. Large institutions can buy the tools to see stress earlier and manage it: richer data, faster access, better analytics, better financing lanes. Households cannot. A household receives the public summary. The institution receives high-fidelity signals that arrive before the summary becomes a story. That matters because institutions can tighten terms and reduce exposure early, shifting stress into the real economy before the public recognizes the shift. The market can appear calm as the private system tightens quietly. The labor market reflects the tightening with lag, and that lag is where dissonance grows.

The eighth source is inflation asymmetry. Asset prices can rise when liquidity is abundant and discount rates fall, even as the cost of living rises due to supply constraints, shelter scarcity, or service costs. A household experiences inflation directly as a budget squeeze. An asset owner can experience inflation as both pain and benefit if assets reprice upward. The index is an asset reprice gauge. The household budget is a consumption reprice gauge. They can move in opposite directions for long periods because the system supports the claim layer's liquidity while leaving the consumption layer to negotiate in local markets with weaker bargaining power.

Housing is the hinge between markets and lived reality because housing is both necessity and collateral. When housing prices rise, existing owners gain wealth and new entrants face higher barriers. When borrowing costs rise, existing owners with older terms can be insulated and renters absorb the shock through higher rents and fewer alternatives. Markets can rise because collateral values remain high for those already inside the asset layer. People can fall behind because shelter consumes a larger share of income and mobility declines when moving becomes unaffordable. Housing is where private architecture turns into everyday constraint, and it is also where inequality becomes sticky because access to the asset is access to the leverage lane.

Small firm financing is another hinge because small firms do not issue tradable claims at scale. They are financed through local credit and bank lines with tighter covenants, shorter terms, and more discretionary renewal. When credit tightens, banks ration. Rationing is felt immediately in inventory, payroll, and expansion plans. Public markets can still be supported by institutions rolling financing and reallocating into liquid claims. The local business sees a higher cost of money and fewer options. The market rises. The small firm strains. The labor market absorbs the result.

A key feature of the divergence is timing mismatch between pain and the mark. The mark updates instantly. Pain accumulates gradually and then breaks suddenly. A household can absorb higher costs by drawing down savings, using credit, working more, or delaying spending. Buffers hide stress for a while. When buffers run out, delinquency, default, and hardship appear abruptly. Meanwhile the market can keep rising because forced selling has not reached the top-tier claim layer and because institutions can buy dips as long as their pipes remain open. The divergence persists longer than intuition expects because the system built shock absorbers for claims and far fewer for household budgets.

Automatic stabilization behavior intensifies the mismatch. When volatility rises, some strategies reduce risk, but many institutions also rebalance and buy into declines as part of mandated allocation. That creates a bid that is not confidence in the real economy. It is a rule. The rule can keep prices elevated or recover them quickly even as the real economy softens. Prices become a reflection of the machine's stability features rather than a pure signal of household health.

The dissonance becomes political because legitimacy depends on shared perception. Leaders point to markets. Households point to bills. When the market is used as the primary scoreboard, and the scoreboard is disconnected from median experience, the narrative becomes brittle. Brittle narratives invite blunt interventions because they are responses to lived reality rather than to marks. The system can survive policy volatility for a while, but policy volatility is not free. It increases risk premiums and changes financing regimes, and financing regimes are the air the market breathes.

The private architecture does not create inequality alone. It amplifies inequality by making compounding easier for those already inside the claim layer and by making time more expensive for those outside it.

Compounding requires surplus. Surplus requires stable wages and manageable costs. When necessities rise and wages lag, surplus shrinks. Shrinking surplus means less ability to buy appreciating claims. Less ability to buy claims means missing compounding. Meanwhile those already holding claims experience rising markets as proof the system works. The system can work for claims and fail for households at the same time because the system is optimized for tradability and proof, not for distribution.

The mechanism can be made explicit as two chains running in parallel, one for households and one for institutions, with the same shock producing opposite outcomes.

Household chain: a cost shock hits necessities. The household draws down cash. Cash depletion increases reliance on revolving credit. Higher credit use raises required payments and reduces flexibility. Reduced flexibility forces spending cuts. Spending cuts hit local businesses. Local businesses face lower revenue and tighter credit. They reduce hours, delay hires, or cut staff. Income uncertainty rises. Delinquency increases. Delinquency worsens credit terms. The household becomes more fragile. The economy slows from the bottom.

Institutional chain: the same shock increases headline volatility. Automatic contributions and benchmark allocations continue to flow into rule-based vehicles. Rule-based vehicles continue buying liquid constituents. Large firms protect per-share measures through buybacks and cost controls. Liquidity providers widen spreads briefly but remain active because they can finance inventory. Risk models tighten, but institutions with better collateral lanes can rotate rather than liquidate. Price declines are met by rebalancing and dip buying inside mandates. The claim layer stabilizes. The index recovers.

The divergence is the gap between chains. One chain is governed by hard deadlines with few hedges. The other chain is governed by rules and funding lanes designed to preserve continuity. A rising market is therefore not proof of broad health. It is proof that the claim layer's continuity mechanisms are functioning.

The continuity mechanisms include not only automatic allocation but corporate cash strategy. Public companies are trained by the market to prioritize predictability and cash conversion. Predictability is rewarded because it stabilizes forward narratives. Cash conversion is rewarded because it supports buybacks, dividends, and debt service. When growth is uncertain, firms can still support their claims by reducing investment, reducing labor costs, and increasing cash returns to shareholders. This can keep the market level high while weakening long-term productive capacity and while increasing household strain. The claim thrives on managed scarcity and managed payout. The household experiences the scarcity as higher prices and fewer buffers.

The divergence also creates a second kind of fragility: fragility of trust. If households cannot reconcile their experience with the scoreboard, they withdraw consent. Withdrawal of consent takes many forms: political volatility, resistance to institutions, and demands for immediate relief that can be fiscally and economically destabilizing. The market is not immune to that. Policy shocks change discount rates, tax expectations, labor rules, and regulatory constraints. Those changes alter financing terms and therefore valuations. The market can rise while people fall behind, but a sufficiently persistent divergence becomes a governance risk that can return to the claim layer as a repricing of regime.

The system also produces a distribution of exposure to the divergence. Some households are inside the claim layer through stable jobs, homeownership, and meaningful retirement contributions. Some are outside it because wages are volatile, housing is unaffordable, and savings are thin. The divergence is therefore not experienced uniformly. It becomes a social fracture because two populations live in different economic clocks. One clock is compounding. The other clock is deadlines. Deadlines feel like punishment. Compounding feels like vindication. The public narrative struggles to hold both clocks at once.

The uncomfortable truth is that modern markets are excellent at producing tradable wealth and less reliable at distributing it. Tradable wealth is created by turning future cash flows into claims and by making those claims financeable, hedgeable, and comparable. Distribution depends on bargaining power, housing supply, healthcare cost control, and local credit availability. These are not primarily microstructure variables, yet microstructure intensifies them by rewarding corporate behavior that prioritizes claims and by channeling cheap financing toward what is legible rather than toward what is necessary.

'The index can climb while the median clock runs out.'

This is the core mechanism: markets rise when the claim layer is supported by liquidity hierarchy, automatic flows, and private financing lanes that buy time. People fall behind when the household layer faces hard deadlines, rising necessities, weaker bargaining power, and fewer hedges. The divergence is not mysterious. It is the system operating as designed, with the costs appearing where legibility is low and deadlines are unforgiving.

The same divergence can be traced across a multi-quarter loop that begins in the claim layer and ends in the household layer, then returns as political and credit feedback. A company faces a demand wobble. Management responds with the actions the market rewards quickly: reduce headcount, freeze hiring, squeeze suppliers, reduce discretionary spending, delay capital investment, and increase buybacks if cash allows. The claim is protected because per-share measures remain defensible. The local labor market absorbs the shock through reduced hours and higher job insecurity. The household absorbs the shock through reduced income growth and higher reliance on credit. Local consumption softens. Small businesses see revenue slow. Small businesses respond by cutting payroll and inventory. The labor market softens further. The firm sees slower demand and repeats the discipline cycle. The market can still remain high because large firms have tools to preserve cash yield, and because automatic flows continue to buy liquid claims even as local demand erodes.

The loop becomes more severe when the household moves from adjustment to exhaustion. Early in the cycle, households cut discretionary spending and stretch budgets. Later, they miss payments. Missed payments produce penalty rates and fees. Penalties accelerate budget stress. Stress increases delinquency. Delinquency tightens underwriting. Tight underwriting restricts access to refinancing. Refinancing restriction increases monthly payments when variable terms adjust. Increased payments reduce consumption further. Reduced consumption hits local business revenue further. This is the household layer behaving like a highly levered position with short-term funding and no ability to roll. The market layer can still look calm because the claim layer is financed differently and because the claim layer has a bid supplied by default allocation.

A second multi-quarter loop runs through public budgets. When households strain, tax receipts soften and demand for services rises. Municipal budgets tighten. Public employers slow hiring. Infrastructure spending is delayed. Local economic momentum weakens. This is a slow-moving tightening that does not show up on the tape immediately. The claim layer can rise on liquidity and on the perception of stability even as the public sector becomes a hidden amplifier of stress at the local level. Eventually the lag closes through layoffs, reduced services, and weaker local investment, all of which feed back into household stress.

A third loop runs through insurance-like expenses that households cannot avoid and cannot hedge. When premiums and deductibles rise, the household budget becomes more convex. Small changes in income create large changes in solvency because fixed costs consume more of the paycheck. Convexity means fragility: a small job disruption becomes a default risk. Convexity rises with higher housing costs, higher childcare costs, and higher healthcare costs. The claim layer can still rise because those costs can translate into higher revenues for certain firms and because the market prices the claims, not the household balance sheet. The system therefore can profit from the expense structure that is crushing the median.

The divergence also shows up in how "risk" is priced. A household's risk is priced as interest rates and fees that rise when the household is already stressed. A large institution's risk is priced as spreads that can sometimes tighten again after a period of volatility, because the institution can survive long enough to negotiate and because competition for its business returns when the regime stabilizes. The household pays procyclical pricing. The institution can often access less procyclical pricing. This is the same plumbing logic seen elsewhere: power is the ability to buy time through turbulence.

There is also a quiet redistribution through the cost of money itself. When rates rise, households with floating or rolling obligations pay more. Institutions with locked term financing or diversified funding can absorb and arbitrage the regime. When rates fall, asset owners benefit from repricing of claims. Households benefit only if they can refinance and if credit remains available, which is often not the case for those most stressed. The system can therefore deliver asymmetric gains from the same policy move, pushing wealth upward during easing and pushing stress downward during tightening.

The divergence is intensified by the market's preference for scalability. The claim layer is dominated by firms that can scale and that can protect margins through pricing power, platform effects, and global cost flexibility. Scaling firms can pass cost increases to consumers and can automate labor. That supports margins and therefore supports claims. Households experience the pass-through as higher costs and experience automation as weaker bargaining power. The market rises because scalability is rewarded. People fall behind because scalability often redistributes power away from labor and toward capital.

This is why small firms are a sensitive indicator of divergence. Small firms do not have the same pricing power, the same funding options, or the same ability to negotiate supplier terms. They face higher borrowing costs, shorter maturities, and faster covenant enforcement. They cannot smooth shocks with sophisticated hedges or global diversification. When they fail, local employment suffers. When local employment suffers, households lose income stability. When households lose stability, they cut consumption. When consumption falls, small firms face another shock. The loop is local and self-reinforcing. The market can still rise because the market is pricing the scalable claim layer, not the local loop.

The system also creates an "exit premium" for those already inside the claim layer. When stress hits, those with liquid claims can sell quickly, raise cash, and shift exposure. Those without liquid claims cannot. Their wealth is tied up in illiquid housing equity, small business equity, or human capital. Human capital is the least liquid asset. In a downturn, human capital is marked down by layoffs and wage freezes, and there is no secondary market to sell a slice of it to buy time. The market can rise because capital can rotate. People fall behind because labor cannot rotate as quickly as capital.

The divergence has a microstructure analog: the household operates like an order that must execute at the worst time because it has no patience and no premium lane. A household's liquidity needs are immediate and non-negotiable. An institution's liquidity needs are negotiable through collateral substitution, financing roll, and portfolio hedging. In a tight regime, the household pays the spread and the impact. The institution sells the spread and the impact. This is not rhetoric. It is the observable outcome of who becomes a forced taker and who becomes a voluntary maker.

The divergence can be described as a contest over who bears volatility. In the claim layer, volatility can be warehoused and priced. In the household layer, volatility is lived and paid. When a household faces income volatility, it borrows, draws down, and reduces resilience. When a firm faces revenue volatility, it cuts labor cost and preserves cash to protect claims. When an institution faces mark volatility, it hedges or reduces risk and buys time through financing. Volatility is pushed toward the least protected balance sheets because those balance sheets cannot negotiate terms.

This is why a rising market can coexist with growing fragility. A system that protects claims first can produce high mark levels while accumulating household stress. Household stress eventually becomes macro stress through weaker demand, weaker labor markets, higher delinquency, and political pressure. The lag can be long because the claim layer has built-in shock absorbers. The lag can also be sudden when a threshold is crossed: a wave of delinquencies, a credit tightening, a housing affordability break, or a policy shift. The claim layer can then reprice abruptly, and the public reads the repricing as sudden fear. The machine reads it as the lag closing between household strain and financing regime.

The most important implication is not moral. It is operational. If markets are used as the primary scoreboard, the system will misread its own stability. A rising mark can mask a weakening base. When the base weakens, the system's political support weakens. When political support weakens, policy becomes less predictable. When policy becomes less predictable, risk premiums rise. When risk premiums rise, the discount rate changes. When discount rates change, the claim layer reprices. The divergence can therefore be self-defeating over time: the very separation that allows marks to rise can build legitimacy risk that eventually destabilizes marks.

PART FIVE

NATIONS THAT BUILD MARKETS & NATIONS THAT STAY DEPENDENT

SOME NATIONS BUILD CAPITAL SOVEREIGNTY; OTHERS RENT LIQUIDITY, BORROW CONFIDENCE, AND PAY FOR IT IN DEPENDENCE.

A country can have land, labor, ideas, and projects that would make any industrial planner smile, and still remain financially dependent because capital sovereignty is not ambition. Capital sovereignty is infrastructure: a domestic curve trusted enough to anchor contracts, a clearing and custody spine strong enough to settle at scale, a lender-of-last-resort credibility that stops routine volatility from becoming a currency crisis, and a domestic buyer base deep enough to absorb issuance without demanding foreign approval every month. When those pieces are missing, the nation is forced into a simple bargain: borrow in somebody else's confidence, price projects in somebody else's currency, and accept that external risk committees will decide whether the national plan is "financeable" this quarter.

Market depth is not a chart on a central bank slide. Market depth is the ability to place size without moving the price into embarrassment, and to roll size without begging. It is a long habit of issuance and settlement, where investors believe not only that they will be paid, but that they will be paid on time, in the unit they expected, under a court system that enforces without delay. Depth is social memory turned into a yield curve. It is also institutional plumbing: primary dealer systems, repo capacity, collateral eligibility standards, benchmark issuance programs, and a payments system that does not fail when the world becomes nervous. A nation without depth has to pay for every weakness as a spread, and spreads become politics because spreads decide which projects can be built and which remain promises.

Dependence begins in the currency channel. If domestic savings are thin and domestic investors do not trust long-term local-currency claims, the sovereign and its firms are pushed toward external funding. External funding comes with a price: currency mismatch risk. Borrowing in foreign currency while earning in domestic currency is not merely an accounting detail. It is a fragility engine. A depreciation increases debt burden immediately, which forces fiscal tightening, which weakens growth, which further undermines confidence, which can trigger more depreciation. The market calls this a balance-of-payments story. The machine calls it a forced unwind created by a mismatch between the unit of revenue and the unit of obligation.

A nation that builds capital sovereignty builds a domestic curve that investors treat as the reference for contracts, not as a speculative instrument. That requires predictable issuance schedules, transparent auction mechanics, credible inflation control, and an enforcement perimeter that convinces holders they can exit when they choose. Exit matters because no institution will commit long-term capital if it fears being trapped by controls, arbitrary taxes, or settlement failure during stress. Trust is therefore built not only by promise but by the demonstrated ability to tolerate volatility without rewriting rules midstream.

The curve is not just sovereign debt. It is the spine that pricing systems use to value everything else. Without a trusted curve, corporate debt becomes an argument instead of a spread. Infrastructure finance becomes a negotiation instead of a market. Pension funds cannot match liabilities cleanly. Banks cannot price loans with confidence. Risk models become foreign templates. Foreign templates import foreign assumptions. Foreign assumptions often misprice local realities, which means local borrowers pay for the model's fear as well as for genuine risk.

The next layer is collateral. A market with domestic depth has domestic collateral accepted widely enough that balance sheets can fund themselves in local currency. A market without it must import collateral status. Imported status looks like cross-currency swaps, external guarantees, and offshore escrow structures that reassure lenders. Reassurance is not free. Every reassurance device transfers sovereignty outward, because enforcement and priority rights sit in external jurisdictions, and the project's viability becomes contingent on external legal and political tolerances.

Domestic market depth also requires domestic holders with long horizons. These are not just "investors." They are institutions whose liabilities force them to be patient: pensions, insurers, and savings vehicles with predictable inflows. If those institutions are small, weak, or short-term, the market cannot absorb long issuance tenors without a volatility penalty. Volatility penalty is higher yields, and higher yields are the cost of building anything with a payback measured in decades. A country can have abundant projects and still fail to build them because it cannot finance duration at a price that leaves room for operating risk.

The dependency bargain becomes visible in how projects are packaged. A sovereign that cannot place long local-currency paper is pushed into structures that externalize risk to make the deal "bankable." Revenues are pegged to foreign currency, tariffs are indexed to inflation, off-take agreements are written to guarantee minimum payments, and dispute resolution is moved into external arbitration. These provisions can unlock capital. They also move the economic upside away from domestic flexibility. If the currency weakens, domestic users pay more. If demand drops, the sovereign still owes. If politics shifts, penalties trigger. The project becomes a private contract enforced by external confidence, and the nation pays in constrained policy space.

"A nation without a domestic market does not borrow money; it borrows permission."

Permission is given by ratings frameworks, by global risk-on regimes, by commodity cycles, by geopolitical fashion, and by the invisible committees that decide whether an emerging risk is tolerable today. This is why dependence feels like whiplash. The project pipeline is steady. The global appetite is not. When appetite shifts, refinancing becomes a cliff. The country discovers it built a bridge on rented ground.

Market builders reduce that whiplash by engineering internal shock absorbers. They build credible local settlement, robust payment rails, transparent issuance calendars, and predictable tax and regulatory regimes that reduce sudden rule risk. They build local repo markets so banks and dealers can fund inventory and make continuous prices without hoarding cash. They build legal clarity on netting and collateral seizure so lenders are willing to provide term. They build disclosure and governance norms so domestic institutions can hold corporate risk without treating every issuer as a political gamble. They build a domestic buyer base large enough that issuance does not require constant external validation.

None of this is glamorous. It is slow, technical, and deeply political, because it reallocates rents. Domestic market depth reduces the ability of a few gatekeepers to charge for access. It reduces the premium external intermediaries can demand. It shifts power from foreign currency lenders to domestic institutions. That shift can be resisted by those who profit from dependence, including domestic elites who can hedge externally while the median pays domestic costs. Market sovereignty is therefore not only a macroeconomic project. It is a contest over who is allowed to be protected by the system's defaults.

The dividing line between builders and dependents often shows up in the crisis script. In a dependent system, stress produces currency weakness, currency weakness raises debt burden, debt burden forces austerity, austerity depresses growth, and depressed growth reduces confidence. The state is forced into procyclical tightening precisely when households and firms are weakest. In a sovereign system, stress can be absorbed more gradually: local funding can roll, the central bank can provide liquidity in local currency, and fiscal choices retain flexibility because the state is not trapped by foreign-unit obligations that reprice instantly with the exchange rate. The difference is not virtue. It is architecture.

Architecture includes market culture, because participation depends on belief. If households and small firms have been burned repeatedly by inflation surprises, rule changes, or confiscatory moments, they will avoid long-term local claims. Avoidance becomes self-fulfilling: without domestic savers, the state relies more on foreign finance; reliance increases vulnerability; vulnerability increases the probability of future rule stress; rule stress confirms avoidance. Breaking the loop requires credibility built over years, not announcements made in one quarter.

The most decisive mechanism is the domestic ability to finance duration. Duration is the right to borrow long and pay slowly. Duration is what turns a national plan into a buildable schedule rather than a permanent presentation deck. If domestic duration cannot be financed, projects become dependent on foreign-term appetite, and foreign-term appetite is cyclical. The nation then experiences development as a series of starts and stops, each stop justified as prudence, each start financed as an exception, and each exception priced with premiums that bleed sovereignty.

A market-building nation therefore treats financial depth as strategic infrastructure, not as a luxury. It understands that stock indices and exchange headlines are downstream of deeper conditions: domestic savings pools, domestic collateral acceptance, enforceable contracts, and a curve that the world will not laugh at in stress. The dependent nation may still have an exchange, may still have trades, may still have listings. Yet without depth, the exchange becomes theater: a visible symbol of modernity without the balance sheet beneath it. The crowd sees a market. The state sees that it cannot raise size domestically without punishment.

Interlude The Finance Minister and the Empty Order Book

A country with ambition, a project with promise, and no domestic market depth to finance either.

A tired minister sat under a fluorescent hum that never quite stopped, not because the building was modern, but because the building was always afraid of going dark. The light was steady enough to make the papers look clean, and steady enough to make the numbers feel like they should behave, yet the numbers never behaved in the way the paper promised. On the desk, a project prospectus lay open to a page of diagrams and timelines—ports, grids, transmission lines, a corridor of industrial sites meant to turn raw exports into manufactured output. The story was coherent. The math was plausible. The need was obvious. The problem was not engineering. The problem was that the country did not have a domestic market that could believe in itself for long enough to buy duration.

The minister had learned, in a way no textbook admitted, that markets were not places where money was found. Markets were places where confidence was manufactured into a price and then defended by routines—auctions that cleared on schedule, settlement that did not fail under stress, collateral that could be funded overnight without drama, a legal system that did not blink when a default arrived, and an investor base that could hold without calling its lawyer the moment the currency moved. Without those routines, "capital" arrived only when foreigners were in the mood, and it left with the first hint that another country's central bank might do something surprising.

A small screen, too old to be elegant, showed domestic issuance calendars and the day's trading activity in government paper. The numbers were anemic. The curve existed, but it did not anchor anything. When the ministry issued shorter tenors, local demand appeared briefly and then demanded a premium that felt like insult and warning at once. When the ministry tried longer duration, demand became performative—small orders, conditional interest, quiet calls asking for guarantees that made the instrument stop being domestic the moment it was written. The minister could see the shape of dependence in that silence: the nation had projects, but it had no internal buyer base thick enough to absorb a mistake without turning it into a crisis.

The project required long money because the payback lived in years, not quarters. Long money requires a domestic curve that investors treat as a reference, not as a trade. A reference curve is built by repetition and by restraint: predictable issuance, transparent mechanics, and the refusal to rewrite rules when markets become nervous. Yet the minister also knew the trap: restraint was expensive when households were strained and elections were close. A government that promised not to touch the rules was promising to absorb pain elsewhere, and the "elsewhere" was always wages, subsidies, and the ordinary costs of living that could not be rolled like debt.

The minister's deputy had left a memo on top of the prospectus, the kind of memo that tried to be neutral and therefore sounded cruel. Domestic savings pools remain shallow. Pension assets are underdeveloped. Insurance duration is limited. Banks hold sovereign paper but finance it short and prefer instruments that can be pledged easily. Secondary liquidity is thin. Foreign participation provides depth but introduces currency mismatch vulnerability. The minister did not need the words; the minister could read the reality in the spreads, the failed auctions, the quiet widening of haircuts in local secured funding, and the sudden way offshore investors demanded clauses that moved dispute resolution outside the country before they would lend a cent.

A nation without market depth borrows permission. The minister had seen it in the ritual calls with foreign desks: the questions were never about the bridge's concrete mix or the grid's load forecasts. The questions were about exit—whether capital controls would appear in a panic, whether a central bank would be forced to choose between inflation and the currency, whether courts would enforce a pledge quickly, whether local politics would treat foreign creditors as villains when unemployment rose. Every question translated into one thing: how much extra yield must be paid to compensate for the fact that the domestic market could not promise an orderly exit when the world became frightened.

The minister turned to the page in the project plan where "financing structure" was described as if it were a technical appendix, and not a constitution. There were clauses that indexed tariffs to foreign currency, clauses that guaranteed minimum revenue, clauses that placed cash into offshore accounts, clauses that offered external arbitration, clauses that offered step-in rights to lenders if performance drifted. Each clause was a bridge built with somebody else's law. Each clause solved the immediate problem of capital arrival and deepened the long-term problem of sovereignty because it moved the project's enforcement perimeter outside the nation's own institutions. The minister could feel the paradox: to build the domestic economy, the nation had to rent someone else's confidence, and renting confidence meant surrendering flexibility exactly when flexibility would be needed.

In the corner of the office, a binder of prior deals carried the scars of past optimism. Each deal began with a grand announcement and ended with a refinancing negotiation written in a language of deadlines and covenants that did not care about speeches. The minister had inherited those binders and learned to read them like weather. A covenant breached by one quarter became a restructuring by the next. A refinancing missed by a month became a collapse that looked sudden only to those who had never watched the maturity calendar. The country's development plan lived inside those calendars, and the calendars belonged to lenders who did not vote in local elections.

A domestic market with depth could have changed the script. If domestic institutions could buy long local paper, the project could be financed in the unit of domestic revenue. If local repo markets were thick enough, dealers could warehouse inventory without hoarding cash. If settlement and custody were trusted, more households would accept that domestic claims were worth holding. If the legal system could enforce quickly, haircuts would fall and duration would lengthen. But the minister also knew this was not a single reform. It was a multi-year discipline project that demanded political patience, and political patience was the one resource a finance ministry never controlled.

The minister opened a second file, thinner and more dangerous: a draft of domestic market reforms that would not produce a ribbon-cutting ceremony. It proposed standard issuance calendars, primary dealer obligations, transparent auction redesign, collateral eligibility rules, netting clarity, and enforcement speed-ups. It proposed incentives for pensions and insurers to hold duration. It proposed disclosure templates to make corporate issuance legible. It proposed building an internal buyer base large enough to absorb issuance without begging foreigners to show up on the right day. The minister could already hear the objections from every corner: banks would resist anything that threatened their spreads, elites would resist anything that reduced their offshore option, and voters would resist anything that looked like austerity for an invisible future benefit.

The phone rang, and the minister did not answer immediately because the ring had become a kind of metronome for dependence. Every call carried the same subtext: will you pay the premium, will you accept the clause, will you take the money on terms that shrink your choices later. The minister let it ring once more, long enough to admit what was true: the country had ambition and projects, but the country did not yet have the domestic financial spine to finance its own future on its own clock.

"Without a curve you can defend, every plan becomes a request."

The minister finally picked up, already calculating how much sovereignty would be surrendered in exchange for the first tranche, and already wondering whether the deeper work—building the market beneath the project—could be done fast enough to matter before the next global mood swing closed the door again.

CHAPTER 31
THE GROUND A MARKET STANDS ON
WHAT MUST EXIST BEFORE CAPITAL CAN SCALE WITHOUT FRAUD, PANIC, CAPTURE, OR COLLAPSE.

A market that can scale is not a place where trading happens. It is a disciplined agreement about reality: what ownership means, what time means, what proof means, what happens when someone fails, and who has the authority to declare the record final. Without that agreement, capital does not scale; it surges, retreats, and returns only at punitive prices, because no one wants to be the last holder of a promise that becomes contestable when stress arrives. The ground a market stands on is therefore not volume. It is enforceability, repeatability, and a credible path from claim to cash that does not depend on mood.

The first foundation is definitional clarity: a claim must be unambiguous enough that two strangers can trade it and then go home without needing to negotiate what they just did. That means a market must define what is being bought, what rights attach, which rights are conditional, and which rights survive in default. A market that allows ambiguous claims can grow briefly on enthusiasm, but it cannot support institutional balance sheets, because institutions require stable rights they can pledge as collateral, measure in portfolios, and defend in disputes. Definitional clarity is the beginning of liquidity because liquidity is the willingness to transact quickly, and willingness requires that the object being transacted is not a legal argument in disguise.

The second foundation is title integrity: ownership must be a chain, not a rumor. This does not require perfection in every record at every instant, but it requires a canonical record that can be reconciled and enforced. Title integrity depends on custody discipline, transfer rules, and a credible method for resolving conflicting claims. If the market cannot settle who owns what after the fact, then every trade contains a hidden tail risk: the risk that the asset is not deliverable, not enforceable, or subject to competing claims. That tail risk is priced as spread, haircut, and reluctance to warehouse inventory. The market then becomes fragile because liquidity depends on inventory, and inventory depends on confidence in title.

The third foundation is time integrity: sequence must be defensible. Markets are not only about price; they are about who acted first, what was known when, and what the official record says happened at the boundary moments that matter for valuation and entitlement. Time integrity means a shared clock regime and a shared policy for which timestamps count when records disagree. If time integrity is weak, disputes become unresolvable, and unresolvable disputes make institutions hoard liquidity, because hoarding is the only defense against a world where finality is uncertain.

The fourth foundation is settlement finality. Finality is the line between trade as negotiation and trade as fact. Finality must be strong enough that markets can function and flexible enough that obvious malfunctions do not become permanent reality. The system achieves this by defining windows, thresholds, and authorities: when a trade can be challenged, what evidence is required, and who can void or correct. Too much reversibility creates free-option behavior.

Too little reversibility creates legitimacy collapse when undeniable errors stand. The market stands on the narrow ridge between these failures, and that ridge is maintained by explicit rules plus disciplined enforcement.

The fifth foundation is netting and close-out clarity. A market that scales will experience failure, and failure cannot be treated as scandal each time it happens. Failure must be treated as a routine state with routine procedures that limit contagion. Netting reduces gross exposures and therefore reduces the probability that one default cascades into many. Close-out defines how positions are terminated and collateral is seized when a counterparty fails. If close-out is slow, disputed, or politically vulnerable, lenders demand higher haircuts, shorter terms, and more discretionary optionality. Those terms are the hidden tax on scaling because they reduce endurance and increase forced selling. A market that wants to scale must build legal and operational speed into failure management, because speed in failure is stability in the system.

The sixth foundation is collateral credibility. Markets scale by financing, not by cash. Financing requires collateral that can be valued, pledged, and seized without delay. Collateral credibility is a blend of acceptability, valuation policy, and enforcement. Acceptability means what classes of claims lenders will take and under what conditions. Valuation policy means which prices count for margin and how outliers are treated. Enforcement means the right and ability to seize and liquidate quickly if obligations are missed. If any one of these is weak, the market's leverage pipes become fragile, and fragile pipes turn normal volatility into margin spirals.

The seventh foundation is disclosure designed for use rather than for theater. Scaling capital requires strangers to hold claims without private access to the issuer. That requires standardized, comparable disclosure that can be processed by institutions and audited without heroic interpretation. Disclosure is a financing input. If disclosure is unreliable, capital demands higher yields, shorter maturities, more covenants, and more control rights. Those terms increase the issuer's fragility and increase the system's reliance on private gatekeepers. A market that wants broad, scalable capital must create disclosure norms credible enough to reduce the need for private permission.

The eighth foundation is a credible enforcement perimeter that does not blink under pressure. When conditions tighten, the temptation to rewrite rules rises. Rewriting rules can provide short-term relief and long-term destruction, because it teaches investors that contracts are conditional on politics. Investors respond by shortening duration, demanding foreign-unit terms, or leaving entirely. A market that scales requires the ability to tolerate stress while keeping contracts enforceable, because enforceability is what turns long-term capital from charity into investment.

The ninth foundation is a credible boundary between public authority and private rents. Markets need private intermediaries to function at scale: dealers, brokers, data providers, custodians, and clearing utilities. The system fails when intermediaries become sovereigns without accountability, because the market becomes a toll road where participation is possible only on terms set by private gatekeepers. Some rent is inevitable because infrastructure has costs. The question is whether the rent is bounded by competition, oversight, and substitution, or whether it becomes a dependency tax that concentrates power and turns the market into an instrument of extraction. A market that scales without collapsing politically must keep legitimacy intact, which requires that the public lane remains usable and that private lanes are seen as optional improvements rather than survival requirements.

The tenth foundation is an internal shock absorber. Volatility is not a defect. It is the price of continuous adjustment. What destroys systems is not volatility alone but volatility combined with forced behavior: margin deadlines, short funding terms, and liquidity evaporation. A market that scales builds mechanisms that slow feedback loops: batching at key moments, auction modes at reference points, volatility interruptions, and coordination protocols that prevent one venue's impairment from becoming system-wide incoherence. These are anti-cascade devices.

The eleventh foundation is a disciplined record of entitlements. Entitlements are where trust either becomes permanent or dies: dividends, interest, splits, conversions, corporate actions, and any event that changes who is owed what. Entitlement failure is corrosive because it attacks the market's claim to be a reliable allocator of rights. Reliable entitlements require clean identifiers, timestamped records, standardized processing, and dispute resolution procedures that produce final answers quickly. If entitlements are frequently wrong or delayed, investors demand higher risk premiums or avoid the market, because a market that cannot deliver entitlements cannot be treated as a safe store of claims.

The twelfth foundation is a domestic habit of saving into institutions that can hold duration. Without patient domestic holders, the long end becomes dependent on external moods. External moods are cyclical. Cycles become refinancing cliffs. Refinancing cliffs force procyclical tightening precisely when the economy is weakest. The market then fails the society by turning every shock into a crisis of permission. A market that stands on solid ground has a base of patient holders that can absorb issuance, stabilize price formation, and reduce the dependence premium.

These foundations form a single structure because each one feeds the others. Weak disclosure increases covenant reliance. Covenant reliance increases private control. Private control can reduce transparency and increase dependency. Increased dependency increases political pressure to rewrite rules under stress. Rule rewriting undermines enforcement credibility. Enforcement weakness raises haircuts and shortens term. Short term increases rollover risk. Rollover risk increases forced selling. Forced selling increases volatility. Volatility increases margin. Margin increases forced selling again. A market breaks not from one failure but from a chain of failures that turns normal stress into a self-sustaining cascade.

The ground also includes a disciplined separation between price as signal and price as trigger. When a price print becomes a trigger for collateral calls, index rebalances, or covenant tests, the system is no longer merely observing; it is enforcing. Enforcement based on prints can be destabilizing if prints are fragile. That is why reference integrity matters: the system must decide which prints count for triggers, and it must decide in advance, because deciding in the moment invites accusations of favoritism and invites legal chaos. The deeper point is that scaling markets are trigger machines, and the trigger machine must be designed so it does not detonate under its own sensitivity.

A market that scales must be disciplined about where discretion lives. If discretion lives in too many places, outcomes feel arbitrary. If discretion lives nowhere, the machine becomes brittle. The equilibrium is bounded discretion: clear rules, clear thresholds, and identified authorities whose actions are constrained and recorded. Bounded discretion allows the system to correct malfunctions without turning every loss into a petition for reversal.

Fraud is punishable in a way that is visible enough to deter and predictable enough to avoid politicized enforcement. Fraud is not only stealing. Fraud is also selling an illusion of liquidity, selling an illusion of solvency, or manufacturing records that cannot survive audit. A scaling market must maintain a credible probability that fraud will be detected and punished, because if fraud is treated as the cost of doing business, honest capital retreats or demands a premium so high that development becomes impossible. Deterrence is a capital formation policy, not merely a moral stance.

Panic is the mirror problem. Panic is rational behavior in a system where exit is uncertain and forced selling can become contagious. The best antidote to panic is not reassurance language; it is credible plumbing that makes exit orderly and makes funding stable enough that not everyone becomes a forced seller at once. Orderly exit is the public good that allows private risk taking to exist without destroying the system.

Capture is the third threat, and it is the one that looks like normal success until it becomes political rupture. Capture occurs when the institutions providing market services become the institutions defining market reality, pricing market access, and rewriting market rules in their favor. Capture can be subtle: pricing power hidden in data, dependency hidden in connectivity, governance hidden in methodology. A market that scales without losing legitimacy must keep capture bounded, not by purifying incentives, but by making substitution and oversight real enough that no single private actor becomes a sovereign without consequence.

Collapse is usually described as sudden. The ground teaches that collapse is often slow accumulation of fragilities combined with a failure of correction mechanisms. If correction mechanisms are trusted, small breaks stay small. If correction mechanisms are distrusted, small breaks become runs. A scaling market is therefore a machine for keeping small breaks small.

The title failure chain begins as an entitlement argument and ends as a confidence exit that cannot be reversed with speeches. A corporate action hits the calendar, and a registrar file posts the new entitlement table. A custodian posts a mismatched entitlement on its client statement, and a broker receives a delivery notice that does not reconcile with its internal ledger. A fund manager calls operations, operations calls the custodian, the custodian asks the issuer's agent for confirmation, and confirmation arrives late and contradictory. The fund cannot prove its right quickly, so it cannot pledge the position confidently as collateral.

A lender reads the uncertainty as enforceability risk and adjusts the collateral schedule. A haircut is raised, not because the asset's price moved, but because the lender cannot guarantee seizure and liquidation without litigation delay. The fund receives a margin call tied to the new haircut and must post additional cash by a deadline. Cash is not idle in a thin system. The fund sells the most liquid holdings to raise it because selling illiquid local claims would take time and broadcast distress.

Forced sales push down the most liquid local instruments, and the price prints become marks used by other lenders. Other lenders adjust haircuts in response to the new marks and in response to the same entitlement uncertainty, because nobody wants to be the lender that accepts disputed collateral. Funding withdraws, not as a single dramatic line, but as quiet refusals to roll term and quiet add-ons to margin schedules.

Dealers ration balance sheet because they cannot warehouse inventory tied to questionable title without risking being trapped in dispute. Bid depth thins. Spreads widen. A small sell order moves prices too far because the book is empty when it matters. The ministry sees yields jump and calls it sentiment. The market is responding to a title problem that turned into a funding problem.

Disputes then enter the legal channel. A docket fills with entitlement claims, delivery failures, and collateral disputes. Courts move at human speed. Funding moves at machine speed. That mismatch is lethal. While the docket grows, lenders price the legal backlog as duration risk and demand even higher haircuts. The higher haircuts force more selling. Selling pushes marks lower. Lower marks justify more haircuts.

A trust break becomes visible at the retail edge next. Households see confusing statements, delayed distributions, and rumors of "missing shares." They do not parse entitlement tables. They withdraw savings from local products and move into cash or foreign currency substitutes. That withdrawal shrinks the domestic buyer base further. The sovereign curve steepens, not because a bridge project became worse, but because the system lost the ability to promise that ownership is a chain rather than a rumor.

"When title becomes arguable, the bid disappears first."

Confidence collapses because confidence in markets is not optimism; it is the belief that enforcement is faster than fear. Once entitlement disputes demonstrate that enforcement is slow, fear becomes rational, and rational fear drains liquidity before any official rescue language can arrive.

The capture chain begins as convenience and ends as rule shock, because dependency on a single proof pipeline becomes a governance trap. A market standardizes on a dominant data and record provider because committees want one source of truth. One source reduces reconciliation cost, reduces audit disputes, and makes reporting clean. The provider expands from raw prices into identifiers, corporate actions, reference marks, and reconstruction services. Each expansion is justified as integration and reliability. Each expansion increases switching cost.

Once switching cost is high, the provider becomes a proof monopoly in practice even if competitors exist in theory. Brokers and funds build systems around the provider's schemas, timestamps, and historical archives. Auditors learn to accept those outputs as the safe choice. Regulators prefer the same outputs because they make surveillance and reconstruction easier. A private product becomes an institutional default, and default becomes sovereignty.

The provider then prices the lanes. Base access remains affordable enough to preserve legitimacy. Premium access becomes the real product: earlier feeds, richer event types, deeper reconstruction, faster corporate action updates, and specialized compliance outputs. Large institutions pay because loss rates fall and proof comfort rises. Smaller institutions cannot pay and operate on delayed abstraction. Their execution quality worsens. Their tracking error grows. Their compliance burden rises. Participation stratifies.

Stratification changes market behavior. Liquidity concentrates among those who can see sooner and cancel sooner. Those who cannot are selected against and gradually withdraw from market making and from local issuance participation. Issuers respond by courting only the large institutions that can operate in the premium lane, which increases concentration further and makes the market look deep only when a small club is active. The public lane still exists, but it becomes a symbolic lane.

Political backlash follows when households and smaller firms realize the market is "open" in narrative and closed in practice. Legislators demand fee caps, forced data sharing, or mandated access rules. The provider resists by arguing that integrity depends on investment and that investment depends on pricing. The argument is partially true and politically insufficient. The state then considers blunt intervention.

Blunt intervention is the rule shock. A hurried reform mandate changes licensing, forces redistribution, or imposes governance terms that were never negotiated calmly. The provider responds by tightening contracts, reducing service scope, or shifting risk back onto users. Users scramble because their systems are integrated. Scramble produces operational breaks. Operational breaks produce disputes. Disputes produce new demands for proof. The system discovers that it built a market on a private proof spine without a credible public backstop for the proof spine.

Capture has completed its cycle: convenience became dependency, dependency became fee power, fee power created stratification, stratification created backlash, and backlash triggered rule rewriting that undermined the very stability the dependency was meant to guarantee. The market then faces a choice between tolerating private sovereignty or tolerating political discontinuity. Both choices are costly when made late, which is why capture is a foundation threat, not an ethical sidebar.

CHAPTER 32

THE BANK-DEPENDENT TRAP

WHY MANY COUNTRIES NEVER BUILD DEEP EQUITY MARKETS AND STAY EXTERNALLY FINANCED.

A nation can build roads, ports, grids, and factories, and still finance them like a household with a single credit card: short-term, expensive, and conditional on someone else's mood. The bank-dependent trap is not simply banks dominate. It is a structural equilibrium where the state and its firms rely on banks for most financing because domestic capital markets never become deep enough to absorb duration, risk, and scale without destabilizing the currency and the political system. Once the equilibrium sets, it reproduces itself. Banks become the only credible underwriters of domestic promises. Domestic savers learn to distrust long-term local claims. Firms avoid equity because equity demands governance and transparency they cannot tolerate. The state leans on banks because it can direct them in emergencies. Foreign capital becomes the marginal financier of ambition, which means foreign risk committees become the hidden cabinet of development.

The trap begins with a simple constraint: domestic savings are not institutionalized into patient pools. Without large pensions and insurers that can hold duration, there is no natural buyer for long-dated domestic claims. Banks step in because banks are designed to transform short liabilities into longer assets. Yet banks transform maturity, they do not eliminate it. They roll. They depend on confidence. They depend on liquidity support. They depend on a central bank that can backstop them without destroying the currency. When the state asks banks to do what markets would do in a deeper system, it concentrates systemic risk inside the banking sector and then forces policy to protect banks at almost any cost.

The next constraint is that banks prefer collateral and predictability. Banks lend against assets they can seize, not against narratives. That preference shapes the real economy. Lending flows to firms with hard assets, political connections, and stable cash flows. Lending avoids uncertain firms because uncertain firms are not good collateral. In a deep equity market, uncertain firms can raise risk capital that accepts uncertainty as the price of upside. In a bank-dependent system, uncertain firms are either starved, forced into opaque private deals, or pushed to seek foreign capital that comes with foreign governance and foreign exit priorities.

A bank-dependent system creates a corporate culture optimized for lenders and ministries, not public shareholders. Accounting is built for tax and credit committees, not for equity transparency. Governance is built for control retention, not for minority rights. When equity issuance is attempted, the issuer looks alien to domestic investors because disclosure is thin, related-party complexity is high, and insider control is treated as a birthright. Domestic investors demand punitive discounts or refuse. The discount confirms elite belief that equity markets are predatory and unstable, so elites return to bank finance and private arrangements. The loop tightens.

External dependence arrives because bank balance sheets have limits. When large projects require scale and duration beyond what local banks can carry, the state and large firms turn outward. External funding provides size, but introduces currency mismatch and refinancing vulnerability. External lenders demand clauses that externalize enforcement, cash waterfalls, and dispute resolution. Each clause makes financing possible and makes sovereignty thinner. The bank-dependent trap becomes institutional habit: domestic banks fund the ordinary economy, foreign capital funds strategic projects, and both funding channels keep equity markets shallow because neither requires a broad domestic shareholder base to function.

The trap is reinforced by the way states use banks as policy instruments. In weak market systems, the fastest lever in downturns is bank credit guidance: push lending to priority sectors, roll loans, delay recognition of losses, keep firms alive until political weather improves. Interventions can prevent social collapse. They also teach banks that credit decisions are political, not purely economic. Political credit produces misallocation, and misallocation produces hidden losses. Hidden losses weaken bank capacity, forcing more reliance on external funding for large projects. The state becomes afraid of transparency because transparency reveals fragility. Fear of transparency is the enemy of equity markets, which require disclosure and credible accounting.

The household face of the trap is deposits and short horizons. In a market-building nation, households save into long-horizon institutions that hold domestic claims. In a bank-dependent nation, households save into deposits and short instruments because inflation memory is strong and trust in long-term paper is weak. Deposits are short and flight-prone under stress. That makes banks fragile. Fragile banks prefer short maturities and liquid assets. Short maturities force roll risk. Roll risk makes crises more frequent. Frequent crises reinforce household preference for short, defensive saving. Rational fear becomes structural constraint.

Inflation volatility destroys duration. If inflation is volatile, no one wants long-term nominal claims unless yields are extremely high. Extremely high yields are unaffordable for issuers and destabilizing for the state. The system retreats into short-term claims, indexation, or foreign-currency borrowing. All three keep domestic equity markets shallow. Short-term claims prevent patient institutions from forming. Indexation creates mechanical fiscal feedback when inflation spikes. Foreign-currency borrowing imports external crises.

Currency credibility is the condition that allows domestic duration. Without it, the banking system becomes the main allocator and the central bank becomes the permanent insurer of bank stability. The insurer role becomes a trap when it prevents the emergence of a domestic bond curve and deep equity participation because policy is forced to choose bank stability over market reform every time.

The missing middle layer is the corporate bond market. Without a bond market, firms have only two real modes: bank loans and equity. Equity demands transparency and dispersed ownership, often politically uncomfortable. So firms choose bank loans. Bank loans keep control private but concentrate credit risk in banks. When banks strain, the state supports them. State support preserves the bank channel and delays the development of a bond channel that would diversify risk away from banks.

The bank-dependent trap can be described as four locked substitutions.

Loans instead of securities. Credit committees replace price discovery. Reduced transparency reduces investor trust, which reduces securities demand, which keeps markets thin.

Relationship allocation instead of rule-based allocation. Relationship allocation can be fast in crises. It becomes captured over time. Capture increases misallocation. Misallocation increases bank fragility. Bank fragility increases reliance on state guarantees.

Foreign confidence instead of domestic confidence. Foreign confidence funds large projects, but it is cyclical. Cyclical funding forces procyclical tightening when conditions shift.

Secrecy instead of disclosure. Secrecy protects elites in the short run. It prevents equity market depth because equity requires disclosure.

Banks become hidden owners of corporate policy through covenant power. When most financing is bank-based, covenants and renegotiations shape decisions: investment timing, dividend capacity, asset sales, restructuring. Governance is private and discretionary. It can be pragmatic. It is opaque, and opacity reduces investor trust in equity because outsiders cannot see the true priority stack. Equity investors hate being junior to a quiet covenant regime they cannot monitor. They demand discounts. Discounts make equity expensive. Firms retreat to banks again.

The trap becomes most visible in stress. A shock hits, banks face rising non-performing loans. If banks recognize losses quickly, capital ratios weaken and lending contracts. Lending contraction hits firms and employment. Political pressure rises. The state encourages forbearance and refinancing. Forbearance keeps lending alive but hides losses and turns banks into warehouses of unrecognized impairment. Warehouses cannot lend boldly. Growth becomes dependent on favored credit channels and foreign capital for big projects. The equity market remains thin because it cannot absorb bank recapitalization needs without diluting insiders and exposing balance sheets.

A thin equity market means the state cannot recapitalize banks cleanly through broad issuance. It must use fiscal resources, forced mergers, or hidden transfers. Hidden transfers increase cynicism. Cynicism reduces household willingness to hold domestic claims. Savings stay short. Banks stay fragile. The loop continues.

National champions in shallow equity markets become quasi-public instruments: politically protected, heavily bank-financed, expected to carry social objectives. Social objectives can be legitimate. They reduce profitability predictability and increase political interference risk. Equity investors discount these firms because minority rights are weak and governance is ambiguous. The discount becomes an excuse to avoid equity market building, even though the discount is a symptom of weak market institutions.

Deep markets require proof comfort: reliable accounting, credible audits, clean identifiers, predictable corporate action processing, enforceable minority rights. Proof comfort attracts institutional savings. Institutional savings creates patient demand. Patient demand allows duration issuance at tolerable yields. Duration issuance finances projects. In a bank-dependent system, proof layers are underbuilt because banks can underwrite through private information. Private underwriting reduces the need for public proof. Reduced need leads to weak proof infrastructure. Weak proof blocks the rise of public markets.

Capital formation becomes privately rationed. Privately rationed capital can fund insiders efficiently and starve the broad economy of scalable risk capital. The starvation is often invisible because the economy still operates. It shows up as fewer new firms that scale, fewer public listings, fewer broad ownership pathways, and an economy reliant on incumbents and banks. The nation becomes more dependent because external competitiveness requires innovation and scale, and innovation and scale require financing modes not dominated by collateral and political relationship.

A bank-dependent system can still produce growth. The trap is that it produces growth that is more brittle and more externally constrained. Brittle because banks are maturity transformers with political overlays and cannot absorb large shocks without state support. Externally constrained because large, long-duration projects require external capital when domestic markets cannot finance duration. External capital comes with external conditions that restrict policy space.

The trap's real cost is development lived as permission cycles. When the world is generous, capital arrives and projects start. When the world tightens, capital leaves and projects stall. The nation plans in bursts, not in decades. That planning style becomes culture. Culture becomes expectation. Expectation becomes policy conservatism designed to survive external cycles rather than to build domestic depth.

There is a path out, but it is sequencing with political pain. You cannot build equity markets on weak enforcement, unstable inflation, and opaque control structures and expect depth. You cannot force households into long-term claims if inflation memory is unresolved. You cannot ask firms to disclose if disclosure exposes them to arbitrary enforcement or expropriation risk. The state must build credibility that rules will not be rewritten in stress, while building safety nets strong enough that the political system can survive the discipline required for credibility.

The bank-forbearance cycle is the trap in motion, converting hidden losses into a sovereign refinancing premium that feels like "external sentiment" and is actually domestic opacity priced by foreign lenders. A downturn hits a set of sectors, and loan performance deteriorates. Banks classify loans in the least damaging buckets, roll maturities, extend grace periods, and capitalize interest. The policy is framed as stability. The accounting becomes fog. The fog matters because it prevents the system from distinguishing solvency problems from liquidity problems.

As fog spreads, banks quietly ration new credit. They do not announce rationing as a shock; they announce "prudence." Credit officers tighten terms, reduce exposure to smaller firms, and push lending toward politically protected borrowers because politically protected borrowers carry implicit guarantees. Small and medium firms absorb the rationing first. Working capital tightens. Inventory becomes expensive. Payroll flexibility shrinks. Investment is delayed. The growth slowdown begins as a credit availability problem, not as a consumer preference problem.

Slower growth reduces tax receipts and raises fiscal pressure. The state responds with support programs, guarantees, and directed lending to protect employment. The support programs increase contingent liabilities even if they do not appear fully in headline debt. Foreign investors and rating frameworks price contingent liabilities as real because they know banks and states fuse in stress. The state's future fiscal flexibility is questioned, not in speeches, but in spread.

As spreads begin to widen, the sovereign faces higher refinancing cost, and higher refinancing cost increases the need to borrow more to pay the higher interest. The sovereign attempts to keep domestic banks as primary buyers of new paper, but domestic banks already hold large sovereign exposure and are already constrained by their own hidden losses. Domestic absorption capacity weakens.

With domestic absorption weak, the state turns outward for refinancing and for project funding. External lenders demand foreign-currency terms or hard indexation because they do not trust local inflation stability under fiscal strain. The state accepts because the project cannot wait, and because the domestic market cannot provide duration. Currency mismatch increases. Currency mismatch raises future crisis probability. Crisis probability raises spreads further.

The spread widening then becomes self-reinforcing. Higher spreads tighten domestic financial conditions because banks price off the sovereign curve. Tighter conditions increase defaults. Defaults increase hidden losses. Hidden losses deepen fog. Fog increases foreign fear. Foreign fear raises spreads. The nation experiences this as a mysterious external tightening. The mechanism is domestic forbearance storing losses in banks and then converting stored losses into sovereign refinancing premium when foreigners demand to be paid for uncertainty.

The key is that the system cannot escape because every actor's rational choice reproduces the trap. Banks forbear because recognition threatens capital and political stability. The state encourages forbearance because unemployment is politically lethal. Households stay short because inflation memory makes duration terrifying. Firms stay private because disclosure threatens control. Foreign lenders price uncertainty because proof is weak. Each decision is rational. Together they generate the refinancing premium that makes ambitious projects dependent on external permission.

The equity-market false start is the trap's public performance: a brief listing surge followed by a collapse of trust when minority rights are tested and the system reveals that control is still sovereign. A reform push encourages listings. Exchanges host ceremonies. Policymakers announce modernization. Retail participates because the promise of equity participation feels like a path into the claim layer. Initial trading is active. Indices rise. The state cites the market as proof of progress.

Then the first serious stress test arrives: an insider control dispute, a related-party transaction, a governance decision that transfers value quietly, a dilution event, or a disclosure gap revealed after a quarter of glossy narratives. Minority shareholders demand explanation. They file complaints. They seek injunctions. The issuer responds with silence, delays, and procedural obfuscation, because the issuer is still governed by private norms that treat minority rights as optional.

A scandal does not need to be dramatic to be destructive. It needs only to demonstrate that enforcement is slow and that rules bend for insiders. Retail sells because retail cannot afford trust uncertainty. Selling pushes prices down. Prices down become headlines. Headlines reduce new listing appetite. Institutions observe and refuse to scale participation because proof comfort is insufficient and because governance risk cannot be hedged cheaply. Without institutions, depth does not form. Without depth, volatility is high. High volatility makes the market look like casino rather than savings vehicle. Households retreat to deposits again.

Issuers interpret the retreat as evidence that "equity investors are short-term and predatory." Policymakers interpret the retreat as evidence that "markets are unstable." Banks interpret the retreat as evidence that "credit remains the reliable channel." The system returns to bank dominance with a new scar: a public memory that equity markets are where insiders win and outsiders pay. That memory makes the next reform harder because households now have lived experience, not theory, for why long-term equity saving is dangerous.

The false start also strengthens external dependence. If domestic equity markets cannot provide stable capital and do not attract patient institutions, large firms and projects return to foreign funding or private deals. Foreign capital accepts governance risk only if it is compensated through control rights and external enforcement. Domestic sovereignty thins further. The trap deepens.

CHAPTER 33
CURRENCY FRAGILITY AND THE EXIT DOOR
SOVEREIGN RISK, CAPITAL FLIGHT, AND THE COST OF WEAK MONETARY CREDIBILITY.

A nation's market can look alive on a screen and still be fundamentally fragile because the most important trade is not the equity print. It is the trade between the domestic currency and the world's willingness to hold it without being paid an emergency premium. A domestic market depends on a unit of account that investors trust long enough to hold duration, and duration is what turns infrastructure, industrial policy, and long-cycle projects into financeable reality. When monetary credibility is weak, investors treat the currency as a hot asset rather than a store of value, and every long-term claim becomes a disguised currency bet. The exit door is then not a metaphor. It is the permanent option the investor buys with every position: the right to flee before the unit deteriorates, and the higher the fear of deterioration, the higher the price of that option, paid as yield, spread, or outright refusal.

Currency fragility is not only inflation. It is the belief that rules will change when pressure rises: that capital controls will appear, that convertibility will be rationed, that banks will be instructed to absorb losses quietly, that official marks will be managed, and that a local holder can be trapped in domestic stability while foreigners are allowed a negotiated exit. Once that belief exists, domestic claims require a premium even in calm times, because investors are not pricing today's policy. They are pricing tomorrow's emergency. The premium is a tax on ambition, because it raises the cost of financing every project whose revenues are earned in domestic currency.

The first mechanism of the exit door is mismatch. If a state or firm borrows in a foreign unit and earns in domestic currency, the balance sheet becomes a levered position in the exchange rate. A depreciation turns a stable debt service plan into a crisis, not because cash flows changed instantly, but because the unit changed. The system responds with tightening: raise rates to defend the currency, cut spending to reassure lenders, ration imports, and reduce domestic demand. Those moves can stabilize the currency temporarily. They also slow growth and weaken revenues, which undermines confidence again. The exit door becomes a self-fulfilling architecture: fear raises the premium, the premium forces tightening, tightening weakens growth, weaker growth increases fear.

The second mechanism is reserve adequacy as narrative and as constraint. Reserves are not simply money in a vault. They are a credibility buffer that determines how long a central bank can provide foreign currency liquidity without surrendering the exchange rate. If reserves are thin relative to short-term obligations and import needs, markets price a higher probability that the buffer will be exhausted. When that probability rises, private actors rush to secure foreign currency early, because waiting increases the chance of being trapped by rationing. The rush drains reserves faster. A reserve buffer that was adequate in calm times becomes inadequate under run dynamics. The exit door opens wider because everyone tries to pass through at once.

The third mechanism is the domestic banking channel. In a fragile currency regime, banks become the transmission system for capital flight even when formal controls exist. Depositors shift from domestic deposits to foreign currency deposits where allowed, or they withdraw cash and seek substitutes. Banks respond by hoarding liquidity, shortening terms, and reducing credit. Credit contraction slows the economy. Slower economy worsens fiscal receipts. Fiscal weakness increases monetary financing temptation. Monetary financing increases inflation expectations. Expectations increase currency pressure. The exit door is not only a trade on the foreign exchange screen; it is a credit withdrawal inside the domestic system that converts currency fear into real-economy tightening.

The fourth mechanism is the credibility of the central bank as a commitment device. A credible central bank is not one that promises stability. It is one that can impose pain when needed and survive politically, because stabilizing a currency often requires choosing between short-term relief and long-term trust. When a central bank is seen as subordinate to fiscal needs or political calendars, markets price that subordination as future inflation and future controls. That pricing raises yields, which raises fiscal costs, which increases pressure on the central bank, which confirms subordination. The exit door is the loop between fiscal stress and monetary credibility.

The fifth mechanism is convertibility regime ambiguity. A currency is trusted when investors believe they can convert at predictable rules, even in stress, and that conversion will not be selectively rationed. If a regime has a history of using administrative measures, multiple exchange rates, or opaque allocation of foreign currency, investors demand compensation in advance. Domestic holders also demand compensation because they know they are the ones likely to be trapped. The market then becomes structurally short duration: everyone wants short-term claims they can roll or exit, and short duration makes the economy more fragile because refinancing risk becomes permanent.

The exit door is priced into domestic markets as an original-sin premium: the inability to finance long in domestic currency at tolerable rates. That premium is not only about inflation volatility. It is about enforcement risk, rule rewrite risk, and institutional trust. A nation can have moderate inflation and still face the premium if investors believe crisis management will involve trapping domestic capital, forcing banks to absorb losses, or changing contract terms. The premium therefore reflects governance credibility as much as macro variables.

The currency exit door reshapes domestic equity markets. Equities are nominal claims on future cash flows. If the unit is distrusted, equity becomes a poor domestic savings vehicle because the holder is exposed to both business risk and currency risk. Domestic investors prefer real assets, foreign currency assets, or short instruments. That reduces the domestic base of patient holders. Without patient holders, equity markets remain shallow and volatile. Shallow volatility becomes evidence that equities are unsafe, reinforcing the household preference to stay out. The country can have listings and trading and still lack depth because depth is not activity. Depth is patience. Currency fragility destroys patience first.

The exit door creates segmentation between insiders with external access and the broader population without it. Connected firms may have offshore hedges and foreign revenue streams. Households and small firms often cannot. They bear domestic inflation and domestic credit tightening. This segmentation changes political incentives. If the powerful can exit, they tolerate fragility longer. If the median cannot, fragility becomes social stress. Social stress increases the probability of abrupt policy moves, which increases currency risk again. Unequal access to exit increases the likelihood of disorderly exits.

Sovereign risk is the state-level expression of the same problem. Sovereign risk is not only default probability. It is the probability the state will change the rules of repayment: maturity extension, currency conversion, tax extraction, forced rollovers, or other measures that preserve nominal payment while destroying real value. Investors price this as spread. Spread raises fiscal cost. Fiscal cost increases temptation to use extraordinary measures. Extraordinary measures raise sovereign risk further. The exit door is the sovereign's version of margin: tightening terms that forces behavior.

Capital flight is not a single act. It is an accumulation of micro-decisions: households converting savings, firms delaying repatriation, exporters holding proceeds, importers pre-paying, banks reducing domestic credit, insurers shortening duration, foreign investors refusing to roll. Each decision is rational under uncertainty. Together they produce a squeeze that looks sudden because official statistics lag private behavior. The exit door is visible to those inside the plumbing before it becomes a headline.

The most damaging feature of a currency crisis is that it converts long-term planning into short-term survival. A project that depends on imported equipment faces immediate cost escalation when the currency weakens. Contractors demand indexation. Lenders demand foreign currency clauses. Households demand wage increases to match prices. The state's budget becomes reactive. In that environment, building domestic market depth becomes even harder, because depth requires stable rules and stable expectations over years. Crisis compresses time into weeks. Weeks are too short to build trust.

A currency regime with weak credibility faces a cruel constraint: it needs market depth to finance development, but it needs credibility to build market depth, and credibility requires discipline that becomes politically expensive precisely when households are under stress. The exit door translates political cost into immediate financing cost. Financing cost then constrains the state further, reducing policy flexibility and increasing crisis probability.

The exit door explains why some nations appear to develop in bursts. When global conditions are favorable, foreign capital flows in, the currency is stable, and domestic yields fall. Projects start. Credit expands. Asset prices rise. Then conditions shift. Capital outflows begin. The currency weakens. Rates rise. Credit contracts. Projects stall. The public interprets the stops as mismanagement or bad luck. The machine sees a country financing development on external mood because the domestic market cannot hold duration at a stable price.

Domestic monetary credibility is the invisible asset that determines whether development is continuous or episodic. Credibility is built through predictable policy, credible enforcement, and refusal to trap capital in ways that destroy trust. Refusal is costly in crisis because allowing exit can deepen immediate pain. Trapping capital can destroy future ability to finance at tolerable rates. Both choices are painful; the difference is whether the pain buys future trust or consumes it.

The currency exit door is also an information problem. If statistics are distrusted, if fiscal accounts are opaque, if bank losses are hidden, and if off-balance-sheet obligations are rumored, investors price uncertainty as risk. Pricing uncertainty raises yields. Higher yields worsen fiscal strain. Fiscal strain increases the probability that statistics are managed. Managed statistics confirm distrust. Trust requires proof. Proof requires credible audits, transparent data, and enforcement that punishes falsification. Without proof, the currency is priced as a rumor. A rumor cannot finance a national plan cheaply.

The cost of weak monetary credibility shows up as a structural wedge between ambition and feasible financing. The wedge is paid as higher yields, shorter tenors, stricter covenants, foreign-unit clauses, external arbitration, and surrender of policy flexibility. Each concession can be justified as pragmatic. Together they form dependence: the state can build, but it must build on terms written by external confidence.

The crisis-week sequence shows how the exit door becomes a corridor of deadlines with no graceful path back to calm. A reserve buffer that looked sufficient under monthly statistics begins to drain faster than expected as importers pre-pay and as exporters delay conversion. The central bank sells foreign currency to maintain the visible exchange rate and to prevent a public break that would trigger panic. The reserve drawdown is not yet a headline, but counterparties notice in term quotes and in the widening of internal risk limits.

Depositors respond before they use words like crisis. They shift from domestic deposits toward any accessible foreign-currency substitute, or they move into cash, or they move balances toward institutions believed to have external lines. The bank deposit shift is not dramatic individually. In aggregate it forces banks to hoard liquidity and shorten lending, because banks do not know whether withdrawals will accelerate. Credit officers tighten. Working capital becomes scarcer. Firms begin to delay payments and delay investment.

Then a rumor of foreign exchange rationing arrives, and rumor is sufficient because the fear is about rule rewriting, not about today's spot print. Importers scramble to secure foreign currency while the window is still open. Households scramble to protect savings. Banks scramble to conserve liquidity. The rumor turns precaution into action and turns action into further reserve drain, because every precaution requires a conversion or a withdrawal.

Offshore spreads jump next, not because new fundamentals were discovered, but because external lenders reprice the probability that convertibility will be rationed and repayment will be managed administratively. A small offshore spread jump changes domestic reality because borrowers are already dependent on rolling external lines. The jump raises roll cost and narrows availability.

The sovereign then faces auction stress. The treasury offers paper and sees demand thin. Domestic banks cannot absorb without worsening liquidity and capital optics. Foreign buyers demand higher yields to compensate for convertibility fear. The auction clears at a worse level or fails partially. The curve shifts upward, and the shift feeds directly into domestic funding costs because banks and corporates price off the sovereign baseline.

Corporate roll failures follow, first at the margin and then in clusters. A firm that expected to refinance an external facility discovers the facility is offered only at punitive terms or not offered at all. The firm seeks domestic bank credit, but domestic banks are conserving liquidity and are already facing deposit pressure. The firm sells inventories, delays payroll, or cuts production. The contraction becomes visible in employment and supply.

The project halts not because the bridge became impossible to engineer but because the financing unit became unstable and the chain of rollovers broke. Contractors demand indexation clauses. Imported equipment quotes rise. Lenders demand foreign-unit terms and external arbitration. The state can accept these terms and surrender flexibility, or refuse and delay. Either way the development timeline is governed by the exit door: the system's fear that the unit will not be honored on predictable rules when stress deepens.

The recursion extension is where the week becomes a regime. The halt produces immediate revenue shortfalls: customs fall as imports slow, consumption taxes soften as households tighten, and corporate receipts shrink as firms cut production. The deficit widens just as refinancing costs rise. The ministry announces "temporary measures," but markets hear a different phrase: monetization risk. Even if no new money is printed that day, the probability rises that future financing will lean on the central bank, because domestic buyers are thin and foreign buyers are now demanding emergency yields.

Monetization rumor accelerates the bank deposit shift. Households and firms infer that higher inflation is more likely, and higher inflation means the unit will be worth less when obligations come due. They protect themselves by converting earlier. Earlier conversion drains reserves faster. The central bank's defense becomes more expensive and therefore less credible. Less credibility increases offshore spreads again, and higher offshore spreads further reduce the ability of corporates to roll. The corporate roll failures deepen.

With production down and financing conditions worse, more projects pause. Paused projects reduce future growth potential. Lower growth potential raises debt sustainability concerns. Concerns raise sovereign spreads. Higher spreads feed back into domestic rates. Domestic rates tighten credit further. Credit tightening increases defaults. Defaults worsen bank balance sheets. Worsened bank balance sheets increase the expectation of state support. The expectation of state support increases fiscal stress. Fiscal stress increases monetization probability. Monetization probability increases currency fear. Currency fear reopens the exit door wider.

The system has now completed the loop: a project halt, treated initially as a technical pause, becomes part of the currency regime because it changes fiscal reality and therefore changes the credibility of the unit. This is why credibility is an asset. When credibility is weak, the economy cannot absorb a single bad week without turning it into a new premium on every future week.

"The exit door is what investors buy when they do not trust the unit."

Closing the exit door by force is easy. Closing it by credibility is the hard work of building the ground that makes markets patient enough to finance projects without demanding foreign permission at every turn.

CHAPTER 34
THE LAW BENEATH THE MARKET
PROPERTY RIGHTS, ACCOUNTING TRUTH, AND ENFORCEMENT AS FINANCIAL INFRASTRUCTURE.

A market without law is not a market. It is a temporary crowd. The difference is not morality. It is whether a claim survives time, conflict, and disappointment. Price discovery can happen in any room where people shout. Capital formation requires a room where the losers accept the result because they believe the rules will be enforced tomorrow the same way they were enforced today. That belief is not sentiment. It is infrastructure built from property rights, accounting truth, and enforcement speed.

Property rights are the first layer of financial depth because property rights determine whether a claim is an object or a rumor. A claim becomes financeable only when it can be pledged, seized, and transferred without turning into a political argument at the moment of stress. The market cares less about what is fair in the abstract than about what is final in the concrete. If finality is uncertain, investors shorten duration. If duration shortens, projects become impossible to finance. The national plan becomes a sequence of rollovers. The rollover becomes a permanent negotiation.

Property rights begin with title, and title begins with a registry that the system treats as authoritative. Authority does not mean error-free.

Authority means correctable with speed and enforceable with predictability. If registries are inconsistent, if beneficial ownership is opaque, if liens cannot be discovered reliably, then every asset carries hidden encumbrance risk. Hidden encumbrance becomes higher haircuts, higher spreads, and shorter terms, because lenders price the possibility that their collateral will be challenged when they try to seize.

Lien clarity is where property rights become lending capacity. A lender can finance against an asset only if it knows its priority in a default. Priority disputes are costly not because they are philosophically messy but because they are slow. Slowness is lethal in finance because finance runs on deadlines. A slow court turns a default into a system event by forcing lenders to assume the worst and ration credit preemptively. When lenders ration, the market looks like it lost confidence. The mechanism is enforcement latency pricing itself into funding terms.

Contract enforceability is the next layer, because a market is a machine of contracts. Contracts govern collateral, margin, netting, close-out, and the operational choreography that keeps losses localized. If contracts are not enforceable under stress, then close-out becomes negotiation, and negotiation becomes contagion. Contagion is priced in advance as higher risk premiums. Higher premiums are the national dependence tax, because they force issuers to accept foreign-unit terms, external arbitration, and external enforcement if they want duration.

Enforcement has two currencies: speed and impartiality. Speed determines whether a lender believes it can recover without being trapped. Impartiality determines whether outsiders believe the outcome will not be rewritten when the losing party is politically important. Even a technically competent legal code can fail to produce market depth if enforcement is perceived as selective. Selectivity turns contracts into optional instruments for insiders and binding instruments for outsiders. Outsiders respond by leaving or demanding punitive yields. The domestic market stays shallow, and the state becomes dependent on external confidence that is never stable.

Accounting truth is the law layer that makes corporate claims legible. A market cannot hold equity at scale if investors believe financial statements are negotiation documents rather than measurement documents. Truth here does not mean perfection. It means a stable discipline that prevents issuers from treating disclosure as marketing and treating losses as discretionary. If accounting is flexible in ways that conceal impairment, the market becomes a theater of reported stability until the day the stability collapses in a single recognition event. Recognition events are panic fuel because they teach investors that the past was fictional. Fiction in accounting becomes real yield demands.

The core function of accounting truth is to reduce proof cost. Investors fund what they can verify. Verification is a function of standards, audits, and enforceable consequences for misstatement. If misstatement is punished only occasionally or politically, investors learn to treat every report as a probability distribution rather than a fact. Probabilistic statements raise the cost of capital because the lender and equity holder demand a premium for uncertainty they cannot hedge cheaply.

Audit credibility is market infrastructure, not a professional ornament. An audit that cannot survive litigation and regulatory scrutiny does not create trust; it creates delay. Delay matters because it shifts the burden of proof onto investors in the worst moments. When a scandal breaks, investors want rapid clarity. If clarity is slow, capital flees first and asks questions later. A market with credible audit and enforcement can contain scandals by producing authoritative answers fast enough that not every participant becomes a forced seller.

Minority rights are the equity version of property rights. A share is not only a claim on cash flows. It is a claim on governance constraints preventing insiders from extracting value through related-party deals, dilution, asset transfers, and quiet priority shifts. If minority rights are weak, equity becomes a bet on insider restraint. Insider restraint is not a tradable hedge. Investors respond by demanding discounts so severe that equity markets cannot deepen. The state then points to thin markets as evidence that equity markets do not work, when the true mechanism is that equity markets cannot work without enforceable minority protection.

Bankruptcy law is where the market learns whether failure is routine or political crisis. Deep markets require routine failure handling. Routine does not mean lenient. Routine means predictable. If bankruptcy is slow, opaque, or politicized, lenders pre-price it as low recovery and long duration of uncertainty. That pricing raises borrowing costs. Higher borrowing costs increase default probability. The system becomes more fragile, not because firms are worse, but because the legal recovery function is weak.

Netting and close-out rules are the wholesale-market expression of bankruptcy discipline. If counterparties cannot net exposures and close out quickly, then a single default creates gross exposures that overwhelm liquidity. The system compensates by demanding higher initial margin and tighter terms, which reduces market capacity in calm times and increases forced behavior in stress. A nation that wants depth must treat netting law and close-out enforceability as strategic infrastructure, because without them, the derivatives and secured financing layers remain thin or offshore. Offshore plumbing then prices domestic ambition.

'Law is the invisible exchange where confidence is cleared.'

The practical test is whether the legal system can keep small disputes small. Markets do not die because no one ever cheats. Markets die when cheating is believed to be unrecoverable and when enforcement is believed to be selective. The moment investors believe the only safe strategy is to exit before anyone else exits, the market becomes a run machine. Runs do not require bad fundamentals. They require uncertainty about enforceability under stress.

The law beneath the market includes regulatory consistency, because regulation is the rulebook investors are forced to price. Investors can tolerate strict rules. They cannot tolerate rules that change unpredictably, are applied unevenly, or are used as political weapons. When rule risk is high, capital shortens duration, demands offshore protection, or stays out. Short duration becomes permanent refinancing pressure. Permanent refinancing pressure becomes dependence, because foreign lenders become the only buyers of long risk, and foreign lenders demand sovereignty concessions as a condition of duration.

Enforcement consistency is also a data problem. Courts, regulators, and registries must produce records that can be reconciled. If records are fragmented, identifiers inconsistent, corporate actions processed unevenly, then the law becomes expensive to use. Expensive law is weak law in finance, because participants route around it into private arrangements, offshore venues, or relationship contracts reducing exposure to public dispute channels. Routing around public law reduces transparency. Reduced transparency reduces trust. Reduced trust prevents domestic market depth.

A market-building state faces an uncomfortable truth: legal reform is operational discipline. It requires registries that function, courts that move, regulators that enforce predictably, and accounting standards that cannot be bargained away by influence. These reforms are politically costly because they reduce rents for insiders and reduce discretionary power for ministries. Yet without them, the nation remains in the permission economy, borrowing confidence from abroad and paying for it in spread, clauses, and lost policy flexibility.

The law layer determines whether finance can support small firms and households rather than only incumbents. If property rights and enforcement are credible only for connected actors, credit and equity concentrate there because investors price enforcement risk. Concentration becomes an economic and political problem: the market appears to work, but it works for a narrow set. Narrow working is unstable over time because it reduces legitimacy, and legitimacy is part of enforcement credibility. A captured-looking system invites rule shocks. Rule shocks destroy duration demand. Duration demand is the lifeblood of development finance.

The ultimate output of the law beneath the market is duration. Duration is the ability to borrow and invest over long horizons without demanding foreign-unit protection and without turning every downturn into a refinancing crisis. Duration requires belief that property is real, accounts are truthful enough to price, and enforcement will not blink. When duration exists, projects can be financed domestically, and ambition can become continuous rather than episodic. When duration does not exist, every plan becomes a request, and every request is priced by external committees that do not share the nation's priorities.

The minority-rights failure chain shows how a single governance breach can freeze an equity market that is still trying to build patient domestic belief. A listed firm announces a related-party transaction framed as efficiency: an asset sale to an affiliate, a service contract awarded to a controlling shareholder's entity, a recapitalization that quietly shifts priority. Minority holders object because value is being transferred without fair process. They seek injunction. The court schedules hearings slowly. The regulator requests documents and promises review. Time passes. Price falls because uncertainty is now a risk factor that cannot be hedged.

Retail holders exit first because retail cannot afford legal ambiguity and because retail is the most sensitive to rumor. Selling pressure increases volatility. Volatility becomes the headline. The headline becomes the social proof that the market is unsafe. Institutions watch the process and refuse to scale participation because the event revealed that minority rights are conditional and enforcement is slow. Without institutions, depth does not form.

New issuers postpone listings because they see the discount widening and they see that scandals are not resolved quickly. Underwriters cannot defend pricing to committees. Brokers lose volume and pull back. Liquidity providers widen spreads because they expect episodic governance shocks that are impossible to price precisely. The exchange remains open, but it becomes a thin theater. The listing pipeline collapses.

Firms return to bank finance because bank finance does not require public minority trust. The state returns to bank channeling because banks can be leaned on in a crisis. Bank dominance is restored not because banks are superior allocators, but because equity could not stabilize without enforceable minority protection. A market that cannot protect minorities cannot create patient domestic holders. Without patient holders, depth cannot survive the first governance stress test.

The bankruptcy-delay chain shows how slow enforcement turns credit into rationing and turns a downturn into a systemic contraction. A wave of defaults arrives, not from moral failure but from cyclical shock. Cases enter court. The docket is already full. Hearings are delayed. Asset sales are contested. Priority disputes appear. Recovery timelines become unknowable.

Lenders respond by treating recovery as low and slow, which means collateral becomes less valuable today. Haircuts rise because lenders cannot assume quick seizure and liquidation. Higher haircuts trigger margin calls and reduce available credit lines. Rolling short-term funding becomes harder because lenders fear being trapped in court if a borrower fails. Rollover refusals spread first to smaller firms, then to any borrower without political protection.

Small and medium firms absorb the contraction immediately. They cannot refinance inventory. They cannot finance payroll through a slow receivable cycle. They cut hours, cut staff, and delay purchases. Layoffs reduce household income. Reduced income reduces consumption. Reduced consumption increases default probability for other small firms. The court backlog worsens because more cases arrive.

Fiscal strain follows because tax receipts soften as employment and activity decline, and because social support spending rises. The state may attempt to compensate with guarantees and directed lending, which increases contingent liabilities and deepens investor fear about sovereign support for banks. Sovereign spreads widen. Banks price off the sovereign curve and tighten further. The bankruptcy delay has now moved from court to credit to employment to fiscal pressure to sovereign risk, and it did so because enforcement was too slow to keep failure routine.

The registry inconsistency chain shows how property rights become credit cost in a single run of events that begins as paperwork and ends as system-wide haircut inflation. A borrower pledges an asset and the lender files a lien. The registry records the lien, but the record is incomplete: an identifier mismatch, a delayed update, a duplicate entry, a local office discrepancy, or a legacy paper filing not synchronized into the digital system. Another lender, relying on the same registry, believes the asset is unencumbered or believes the priority is different. The second lender extends credit against the same collateral with confidence that later proves false.

When stress arrives and the borrower misses an obligation, both lenders move to enforce. Each produces registry evidence. The evidence conflicts. Priority becomes litigated, not because the law is unclear in principle, but because the record is unclear in practice.

The court must decide whose lien is valid and whose claim is senior. Decision takes time because documents must be reconciled and because each party has incentive to delay if delay preserves bargaining leverage.

While the dispute runs, every other lender recalibrates what "registered lien" actually means. If registries can be inconsistent, then lien certainty is lower for the entire system, not only for the disputed case. Lower lien certainty is priced immediately as higher haircuts, because the lender's worst fear is not loss in normal times; it is being unable to seize quickly in stress. Haircuts rise first on assets with complex chains and opaque registries, then on everything that shares the same registry infrastructure.

Higher haircuts reduce available credit lines even for healthy borrowers because collateral now supports less funding. Borrowers respond by drawing down remaining lines, hoarding cash, and shortening their own commitments. Hoarding increases liquidity stress. Liquidity stress increases defaults at the margin. More defaults increase enforcement volume. Increased enforcement volume increases registry pressure and court backlog. The original registry inconsistency has now propagated into a funding regime shift: the economy's cost of credit rises because property rights, in practice, became less machine-readable and less enforceable on deadline.

This is how a market becomes expensive without any change in productivity: the legal and registry layer changed the expected recoverability of collateral, and recoverability is the hidden input to every loan price. A state can announce reforms all day. The market will price what it can enforce and record without ambiguity.

CHAPTER 35

MARKETS THAT SCALED — AND MARKETS THAT STALLED

THE EXCHANGE MODELS THAT WON, THE ONES THAT LOST, AND THE CONDITIONS THAT DECIDED BOTH.

The "Exchange" sounds like a building. In practice it is a governance device that converts private claims into public liquidity under rules that can survive stress. Some exchange models scale because they solve three problems at once: they produce credible price formation, they produce enforceable records, and they produce a funding environment where intermediaries can warehouse risk without turning every shock into a run. Other models stall because they cannot keep these problems aligned. They might produce prints without producing trust, listings without producing discipline, or volume without producing finality. Scaling is not about modernity aesthetics. Scaling is about whether the institution can keep the market's promises routine when the nation is nervous.

The models that scaled did not simply get bigger. They became reference-makers. A reference-maker is an exchange model whose outputs are used by other institutions as anchors: indices mark to it, brokers route toward it, lenders haircut against it, auditors verify against it, and regulators defend it as a public good. Once an exchange becomes a reference-maker, it gains a compounding advantage because being the anchor attracts flow, flow attracts liquidity providers, liquidity providers narrow spreads, narrow spreads attract more flow, and the record becomes even more authoritative. A stalled exchange model fails to become the anchor. It remains a venue among venues, or worse, a theater for domestic prestige without domestic depth.

Scaling exchange models share a first condition: credible membership and credible obligation. Whether the exchange is mutual or shareholder-owned, it must impose duties preventing the venue from becoming a one-way free option for the most powerful participants. Participants must be bound to honor trades, to fund default waterfalls, and to accept that rule enforcement will occur even when enforcement is inconvenient. A venue can list a thousand instruments and still not scale if members treat obligations as negotiable in stress. Negotiability is poison to liquidity because liquidity providers are not paid for being right; they are paid for being able to exit. A venue that cannot guarantee exit during stress cannot attract patient market making and cannot support large issuance.

The second shared condition is settlement gravity. Scaled exchanges are integrated into a clearing, custody, and settlement spine that produces finality fast enough to keep leverage from becoming panic. A venue that trades but settles slowly is an invitation to default cascades and fraud arguments. A venue that settles with inconsistent records becomes a lawsuit factory. Lawsuits widen haircuts. Higher haircuts shorten funding. Shorter funding creates rollover fragility. Fragility prevents scale. This is why scaled exchanges either grow alongside a strong post-trade utility or become functionally dependent on one. Stall models often have active screens but weak post-trade institutions, so their prints cannot become reliable collateral marks, and their markets remain shallow because funding cannot build on uncertain finality.

The third shared condition is information legitimacy. Scaled exchanges produce records institutions can defend. They publish transparent enough data and maintain consistent enough methodology that auditors, regulators, and counterparties treat the record as admissible. Stalled exchanges become trapped between the desire for openness and the desire for control. They respond with opacity, discretionary halts, selective disclosure enforcement, or rule changes under stress. Each response might stabilize a moment. It teaches investors that the record is conditional. Conditional records destroy duration demand.

With those conditions in mind, the winning models are not defined by electronics versus voices. They are defined by the ability to industrialize trust. Historically, physical floors solved trust by embedding social enforcement and immediate human discipline into price formation. The floor's advantage was that identity was known, reputation mattered, and disputes were handled socially. Its weakness was throughput. Electronic models scale when they replace social enforcement with mechanical enforcement: deterministic rules, time-stamped priority, surveillance, and post-trade certainty. When those enforcement systems are robust, electronic venues scale beyond what any floor can handle. When those systems are weak, electronic venues become faster ways to create disputes.

The stalled models can also be modern-looking. A nation can build a sleek exchange and still stall if underlying conditions are missing: enforceable minority rights, credible audits, stable currency expectations, and a domestic investor base that can hold through volatility. In those environments, the exchange becomes a showcase for listings that do not trade deeply, price prints that cannot anchor collateral, and volumes that spike during manias and disappear during stress. The exchange fails to become the reference-maker and remains dependent on external anchors.

Scaling exchanges solve the governance paradox: the venue must be neutral enough to be trusted and commercial enough to invest in infrastructure. Pure neutrality without revenue starves infrastructure. Pure commercialization without constraint turns the venue into a toll road that undermines legitimacy. The models that scaled built bounded commercialization: they monetized services and data, but they preserved a baseline public lane that kept the venue defensible as civic infrastructure. Stalled models drift toward either subsidized weakness or extractive gatekeeping. Subsidized weakness cannot maintain surveillance, custody integrity, and enforcement speed. Extractive gatekeeping invites political backlash and rule shocks that destroy duration demand.

Scale is decided by the ability to coordinate national market choreography. The venue must standardize listing rules, disclosure expectations, and corporate action processing enough that investors can treat different issuers as comparable. Comparability attracts institutions. Institutions bring patient demand. Patient demand supports duration. Duration supports development finance. A stall model cannot standardize because insiders resist disclosure, regulators apply rules selectively, or courts cannot enforce quickly. Without standardization, the exchange remains a collection of stories rather than a machine of contracts.

A scaled exchange model also has a disciplined relationship with banks. In a bank-dependent nation, banks dominate credit, and the exchange is treated as political decoration. In a market-building nation, banks and markets become complementary: banks provide short-term credit and liquidity transformation; markets provide risk capital and duration. The exchange becomes the place where risk is dispersed beyond the banking sector, reducing systemic concentration. A stalled model cannot provide dispersion because equity issuance is distrusted, minority rights are weak, and domestic institutions do not hold duration. The state leans harder on banks, deepening the trap.

The decisive conditions separating scaled from stalled are not optional, and they often arrive as a sequence rather than a single reform. A credible unit of account reduces the currency premium on domestic claims. A credible enforcement perimeter reduces haircuts and lengthens term. A credible registry and corporate action system reduces title disputes and increases collateral acceptability. Credible accounting truth reduces proof cost and allows institutions to scale ownership without fear of fictional statements. Credible minority rights reduce the discount demanded for equity and allow domestic savings to become patient demand rather than speculative churn.

The exchange models that won were the ones that became boring in the right ways. They made failure routine, disputes fast, records authoritative, and rules predictable enough that investors could finance duration without demanding foreign-unit protection. The ones that lost often tried to skip the boring work and jump straight to the spectacle of listings and screens. Spectacle can attract headlines. It cannot build a domestic curve.

The scaled-market stress day begins as a volatility spike and ends as a routine close, because close-out and finality are treated as plumbing, not politics. A macro shock hits overnight and the open reprices hard. Spreads widen and depth thins, but the widening is legible: market makers quote wider because inventory risk is higher, not because they fear that trades will be reversed or that settlement will fail. A large leveraged participant takes losses and misses an intraday margin deadline. The clearing utility triggers the default protocol without improvisation. Positions are frozen under pre-agreed rules, hedges are applied or auctions are scheduled, and the default fund waterfall is invoked according to published priority.

Counterparties do not need to guess whether netting will be honored. Netting is honored. Close-out is honored. Collateral is seized under predictable procedures. The loss is allocated fast enough that other participants can quantify exposure and return to trading rather than hoarding cash in fear. The record is clean enough that lenders continue to fund inventory, albeit at higher haircuts consistent with volatility, because the lenders trust that seizure and liquidation will be fast if needed.

The regulator intervenes only through rule-bound levers: volatility interruptions, auction extensions, or temporary mode shifts that are documented and symmetric. No one is granted a private exit. No one is trapped by surprise. The day ends with final prints that are treated as authoritative marks for collateral and performance. The market is bruised. It is not delegitimized. Issuance calendars remain intact because investors believe tomorrow's rules will look like today's rules even if prices move again.

The stalled-market stress day begins with the same volatility and ends with a legitimacy break, because ad hoc controls convert normal repricing into rule risk. The shock hits and the open gaps. Spreads widen, but this time the widening is not only inventory risk. It is legal and political risk: participants fear that trades may be canceled, that settlement may be delayed, or that the market will be halted selectively. A large issuer's price drops sharply and officials respond with discretionary suspension, then expand the suspension to "maintain stability." The criteria are not clear. Rumors fill the gap where rule certainty should be.

Participants stop making markets because making markets requires confidence in finality. If a trade can be reversed or if a counterparty can be protected by intervention, then the liquidity provider's risk becomes unpriceable. Funding desks respond by raising haircuts not because volatility rose, but because enforceability is now uncertain. Banks tighten credit because they cannot rely on collateral marks that might be administratively managed.

Corporate actions are delayed "until conditions normalize." Registries update inconsistently. Settlement lags. Disputes proliferate because the record is no longer a single truth. Investors treat every position as a potential trap. They sell what they can and refuse to roll what they must. The state's effort to control the tape creates the opposite result: a collapse of depth.

Issuance freezes immediately, not because projects disappeared, but because investors will not commit duration into a regime where rules can be rewritten mid-week. Underwriters cannot price offerings because demand is conditional and because allocation clients fear being trapped. Firms return to banks, but banks are also tightening because collateral is less trustworthy. The market becomes a scarcity engine, and the stress that could have been absorbed as volatility becomes a structural tightening that persists long after the shock headline fades.

CHAPTER 36
THE POLITICS OF NATIONAL CHAMPIONS
LISTINGS, PRESTIGE, CONTROL, AND THE BATTLE OVER DOMESTIC CAPITAL FORMATION.

National champions are sold as industrial destiny and governed as political instruments. They are the firms a state points to when it wants proof that the economy is modern, strategic, and capable of competing at scale. The champion's logo becomes a shorthand for competence, and its market value becomes a scoreboard for national pride. Yet the same firm is also a battlefield where three interests collide: the state's need for control, the market's need for enforceable minority rights, and the country's need for domestic depth that can finance long projects without foreign permission. When those interests cannot be reconciled, the champion becomes a paradox: a flagship listing that looks like progress and behaves like a constraint, because it absorbs domestic savings while refusing the governance discipline that would allow the market to scale beyond it.

A champion is not merely a large company. A champion is a company with implied public obligations. It is expected to hold employment, stabilize prices, provide national services, carry strategic investment mandates, and sometimes serve as a quiet fiscal buffer through dividends or quasi-tax transfers. These expectations can be legitimate. They also change what a share represents. In a normal equity claim, the shareholder owns a residual interest governed by clear priority rules. In a champion share, the shareholder often owns a residual interest governed by political convenience. Political convenience is not a measurable risk factor that can be hedged cheaply. Investors respond by demanding a discount. The discount is the price of ambiguity, and ambiguity is the opposite of market depth.

The central political trade is prestige versus discipline. Listing a champion is prestige. It signals transparency, invites foreign inclusion narratives, and creates a domestic symbol that households can point to as "our market." Discipline is the set of constraints that makes listing meaningful: disclosure that can withstand audit, governance that protects minorities, and enforcement that survives stress. Prestige can be achieved with ceremony. Discipline requires loss of discretion. Many states want the ceremony and fear the loss, because discretion is the tool used to manage employment, prices, and political coalitions. The result is a compromised listing: public enough to attract capital, controlled enough to preserve political flexibility. Compromised listings do not build deep markets. They build dependency inside the market itself, because investors learn that the most important issuers are exempt from the rules that make markets trustworthy.

The second political trade is liquidity versus sovereignty. A state wants the champion to be liquid so it can raise capital cheaply, be included in benchmarks, and attract institutional flows. Liquidity demands openness: float, disclosure, predictable corporate actions, and a credible path for exits. Sovereignty demands control: ownership caps, strategic voting rights, board influence, and the ability to redirect the firm when national priorities shift. Control mechanisms can coexist with liquidity if they are rule-bound and stable. They become toxic when they are discretionary and can be tightened during stress. The market will tolerate a known constraint. It will not finance an unknown override. Unknown override is the exit door inside the equity claim.

The champion therefore becomes a governance instrument with two audiences that want incompatible truths. The domestic public is told the firm is national property and must act as guardian of jobs and services. The investor is told the firm is a modern equity claim and will act to maximize value under enforceable law. When a shock hits and those truths diverge, the state chooses the domestic narrative and the investor learns that the share is subordinate to politics. The next financing round then requires higher yields, more clauses, or foreign currency terms, and the country pays for the lesson.

The champion also becomes a tool for managing banking fragility. In bank-dependent systems, banks hold large exposures to large firms and to the sovereign. A champion listing can be used as collateral, used as a liquidity buffer, and used as a market confidence symbol that keeps deposits calm. That creates incentive to support the champion's price through moral suasion, buybacks, or policy signals. Support can stabilize the tape. It also teaches the market that prices are not pure signals but managed artifacts. Managed artifacts reduce the willingness of sophisticated capital to commit duration because managed artifacts increase the probability of rule interventions. The champion becomes a stabilizer and a warning at the same time.

The battle over domestic capital formation is fought through the champion's float. A deep market requires broad ownership and meaningful free float, because free float is what allows real price formation and real liquidity provisioning. Many champions are listed with constrained float because insiders want control and ministries want veto power. Constrained float creates two outcomes that look like success initially: prices can be supported with relatively little buying, and the index can rise on a thin base. Yet constrained float also creates fragility: small outflows move price sharply, short sellers can dominate in stress, and large institutions avoid size because they cannot exit without impact. Domestic households then become the marginal buyers, and households are the most sensitive to drawdowns. The champion becomes a device that concentrates risk into the least protected balance sheets.

The index layer compounds the politics. When champions dominate indices, passive flows become a policy channel. Automatic contributions buy the champion. The state can point to rising indices as proof of prosperity. The household experiences the market as a patriotic savings vehicle. Yet concentration means that if the champion stumbles, the national narrative stumbles with it, and policy pressure rises to intervene. Intervention risk then becomes priced into the champion, deepening the discount and weakening the broader market's legitimacy. A single issuer becomes a systemic political asset, and systemic political assets are difficult to govern with clean market discipline.

Champion politics also reshapes disclosure. Disclosure is costly because it reduces the space for quiet cross-subsidies and quiet obligations. A champion often carries non-commercial mandates: maintain low prices for essential services, invest in unprofitable regions, purchase from favored suppliers, or carry employment beyond strict efficiency. If these obligations are disclosed clearly, investors price them. Pricing them can reduce the share price and embarrass the state. If they are not disclosed clearly, investors eventually discover them through performance gaps, and then the premium rises because hidden obligations are proof risk. Either path is costly. The only stable solution is to formalize obligations as explicit public policy with explicit compensation mechanisms, so the firm is not forced to be a shadow ministry. Many systems resist this formalization because it requires the state to admit the true cost of policy goals.

The champion's governance structure becomes the arena where control is encoded. Dual-class shares, golden shares, ownership caps, related-party networks, and board appointment rights each serve a political purpose. They can be stable if they are clearly defined, limited in scope, and enforced predictably. They become market poison when their scope is elastic and their enforcement is selective. Selective enforcement is the definition of capture at the firm level: insiders retain upside and socialize downside through policy protection. The market responds by refusing to fund new issuers, because investors assume that if the champion is exempt, smaller firms will be even less protected. One weak governance flagship can prevent a whole cohort of firms from ever going public at reasonable cost.

The champion also shapes the national corporate culture. If the most admired firms are those that thrive through political proximity rather than through transparent discipline, then ambitious entrepreneurs learn the wrong lesson: prioritize relationship access over governance credibility. Governance credibility becomes a tax rather than a competitive advantage. Firms stay private, use banks, and seek foreign capital only when forced. The domestic equity market remains a narrow theater dominated by champions and a few connected issuers. Depth does not form because the pipeline of credible issuers does not form.

A country with ambition therefore faces a sequencing decision that is politically difficult: does it use champions as transitional scaffolding for market building, or does it use champions as permanent political instruments? Transitional scaffolding requires committing to a gradual reduction in discretionary control, an expansion of free float, and a credible enforcement regime for minority rights that includes the champion itself. Permanent political instrument use implies that the market will remain subordinate, that domestic depth will remain shallow, and that large projects will require foreign permission. This decision is rarely stated plainly. It is expressed through small governance decisions and through how the state behaves when the champion is stressed.

The stress test is where politics becomes visible. A champion faces a downturn and needs restructuring. If the state allows restructuring under predictable law, the market learns that failure is routine and that capital can be reallocated without political theater. If the state forbids restructuring to protect jobs, forces banks to roll, and uses administrative measures to stabilize price, the market learns that the share is a policy instrument first and a claim second. The exit door widens. The next refinancing premium rises. The state may "win" the week and lose the decade.

The champion also affects the sovereign's own financing. If champions are used as fiscal buffers through dividends, forced buybacks, or asset sales, then the corporate sector becomes a hidden part of sovereign debt management. Investors notice because the corporate cash flow begins to behave like a tax base rather than like a reinvestment engine. That reduces growth potential and increases sovereign risk. Sovereign risk raises yields. Higher yields increase pressure to extract more from champions. The loop is self-reinforcing: the more the state relies on champions as fiscal instruments, the more investors price the economy as dependent and the less the state can finance projects domestically without foreign-unit clauses.

There is also a legitimacy hazard. A champion listing is often marketed to households as safe national savings. Households buy because they trust the state's implicit guarantee. If the champion later suffers a drawdown and the state refuses to protect investors explicitly, households feel betrayed and retreat from equities. If the state does protect investors explicitly, the state sets a precedent that equity is insured, which invites moral hazard and future bubbles. The politics of national champions therefore can damage market-building either way: it can either destroy household trust in equity or force the state into repeated rescue behavior that undermines price discovery and deepens capture.

A market-building strategy can use champions differently. It can separate public obligations from corporate accounts by paying explicit subsidies for explicit mandates. It can commit to enforceable minority rights and apply them visibly to the champion to prove seriousness. It can increase free float gradually to reduce fragility and deepen liquidity. It can build domestic institutional saving so that the buyer base is not only households. It can strengthen bankruptcy and restructuring so that the champion's failure modes are routine rather than political. It can limit discretionary interventions and replace them with rule-bound volatility and settlement protocols so that stress does not become legitimacy rupture. These moves are not glamorous. They are the boring work that turns a flagship into a foundation stone rather than into a political trophy.

If the champion is treated as a trophy, the market stalls. If it is treated as a test case for law, disclosure, and enforceable governance, the market can scale beyond it. The battle over domestic capital formation is therefore not fought in speeches about patriotism. It is fought in float, enforcement, disclosure, and the willingness of the state to accept that a true market constrains political discretion in exchange for domestic financing independence.

'A champion can be a bridge or a cage.'

The bridge is a path into a deeper domestic market that can finance national ambition on domestic terms. The cage is a symbol that concentrates risk and control while leaving the country dependent on external confidence for the projects that actually define its future.

CHAPTER 37
BUILDING A MARKET FROM SCARCITY
A REALISTIC SEQUENCE FOR DEVELOPING ECONOMIES TO BUILD TRUST, DEPTH, AND LIQUIDITY.

Scarcity is not only a lack of money. It is a lack of patience, a lack of proof, and a lack of institutions able to hold risk without turning every wobble into a run. A country trying to build domestic capital depth starts with a paradox: it needs markets to finance development, but it needs development outcomes to convince savers that markets are worth trusting. The practical solution is sequencing that manufactures trust in small, enforceable increments, then converts that trust into duration, then converts duration into depth, and only then tries to scale equity risk widely. The wrong sequence produces spectacle first and correction later. Spectacle draws flows briefly and then teaches households to fear participation. Fear is the most expensive form of scarcity because it survives even after reforms are announced.

The build plan begins by choosing the first asset the system will defend as sacred. Sacred means boring, reliable, and enforced under stress. In most developing systems, the first sacred asset is the domestic short end: bills and short notes issued on a calendar, settled on a predictable timetable, and supported by a payments system that does not blink. The first job is not create an exchange. The first job is to create a routine domestic institutions can price without hero assumptions. The routine is an auction schedule, a settlement protocol, a registry rule, and a dispute pathway producing final answers quickly enough to keep lenders from hoarding cash.

Step one is unit credibility at the margin, not perfection. Markets do not require zero inflation. They require that inflation surprises are not treated as excuses for rule rewriting. Credibility begins with observable behaviors: cash is spendable without rationing, convertibility rules are stable enough that panic rumors do not become instantly true, and basic domestic obligations are honored without administrative improvisation. The central bank and treasury do not need to win every day. They need to prove the rules of repayment do not change when the week turns ugly.

Step two is settlement spine before product variety. A country listing many instruments without building settlement finality creates a dispute factory. The sequence is registry first, custody discipline second, corporate-action processing third, finality rules fourth. A central securities depository can be small and still be credible if it produces authoritative records, clean identifiers, and a fast correction pathway. The aim is not modern screens. The aim is to make ownership a chain rather than a rumor.

Step three is lien discoverability and seizure speed, because credit depth is built on collateral confidence. Registries must make encumbrances discoverable, and courts must make seizure fast enough that lenders do not fear being trapped. If secured credit cannot be routine, repo cannot be routine. If repo cannot be routine, dealers cannot warehouse inventory. If dealers cannot warehouse inventory, there is no continuous secondary market, only episodic prints. Episodic prints do not produce a curve.

Step four is the domestic funding engine: a repo market that is legal, operational, and boring. The simplest durable path is a narrow eligible collateral set, strict haircuts, transparent margining, and a central-bank backstop rule that is credible precisely because it is constrained. Backstops without constraint become inflation fear. Constraint without backstop becomes run fear. The balance is a documented facility with published eligibility, penalties for misuse, and settlement fast enough to prevent collateral from becoming a legal argument mid-crisis.

Step five is a primary dealer framework that is not a patronage club. Dealers must have obligations as well as privileges. Obligations include quoting, participation in auctions, and minimum market-making behavior. Privileges include access to funding facilities and predictable issuance allocation mechanics. A yield curve is not a statistical output. It is a social contract enforced through dealer balance sheets. If dealers are protected without obligations, spreads widen and depth remains thin. If dealers are obligated without funding support, they fail in stress and teach the market to fear inventory.

Step six is calendar discipline. A domestic curve is built by repetition. Repetition requires auctions on schedule, even when the week is ugly, and refusal to cancel auctions as political reflex. Cancelling auctions signals fear. Fear raises risk premium. Higher premium makes future auctions harder. Showing up consistently becomes credibility. The auction calendar is not an administrative detail. It is a trust engine.

Step seven is reference integrity: decide which prices count for collateral, for reporting, and for dispute reconstruction, and decide it before the first scandal. If end-of-day marks are used for margin, define the reference venue and the fallback methodology. If auctions are used, define error policies. If outlier prints can be excluded, define thresholds and who has authority. A thin market cannot afford ambiguity because ambiguity turns routine volatility into funding withdrawal. Funding withdrawal is the fastest path back to scarcity.

Step eight is disclosure standards designed for use. The minimal viable disclosure regime is consistency, comparability, and consequences for misstatement. If investors cannot trust accounts, they demand control rights or punitive yields. Both outcomes shrink domestic market depth. Audits and enforcement do not need to be perfect. They must be predictable enough that fraud is not treated as normal.

Step nine is minority rights before mass retail participation. Inviting households into equities before minority protection is enforceable converts civic hope into civic trauma. Trauma becomes permanent underinvestment in domestic claims. The sequence is to establish visible enforcement record in a small set of test cases: related-party transactions blocked or corrected, disclosure violations punished, injunctions handled quickly enough that time is not a weapon for insiders. Household trust is not built by education campaigns. It is built by watching insiders lose.

Step ten is institutional savings pools, because patient money is the only sustainable buyer of duration. Pensions and insurers are market infrastructure because they create predictable inflows and long-horizon liabilities. Long-horizon liabilities create demand for long-dated domestic claims. Without that demand, the country rents duration from abroad, and rented duration comes with foreign-unit clauses and external enforcement.

Step eleven is gradual product expansion. The durable path is deepen the sovereign curve, build a corporate bond pilot with strict eligibility and enforcement, build a small high-quality equity segment with tight listing rules, expand only when secondary liquidity is routine. Variety without liquidity is decoration. Liquidity without finality is fraud risk. Finality without enforcement is theater.

Step twelve is crisis drills as market design. A domestic market can survive one scandal if it can contain it. Containment requires default protocols, close-out rules, and a communications posture following pre-committed playbooks rather than improvisation. Drills create operational muscle memory. Operational muscle memory prevents a stressful week from turning into legitimacy break. Failure must become routine and bounded, not political emergency.

The sequence requires choosing where to be strict and where to be flexible. Early strictness belongs in enforcement, record integrity, and collateral rules. Early flexibility belongs in participation growth pace. Scaling participation faster than enforcement generates two failures that kill markets for a generation: the minority-rights scandal and the rule-rewrite panic.

The minority-rights scandal arrives when an early flagship issuer treats public shareholders as a funding source rather than protected owners. A related-party deal is announced. The regulator delays. The court is slow. Price falls. Retail sells. Institutions refuse to scale. Listings pause. The exchange becomes thin. The state declares markets are unstable and leans back on banks. The outcome is not accident. It is predictable result of selling equity before building enforceable minority protection.

The rule-rewrite panic arrives when a stress week triggers ad hoc controls. Trading halts are expanded without clear criteria. Convertibility rules become ambiguous. Settlement is delayed to maintain stability. Each action is justified as temporary. The market prices it as permanent risk. Haircuts rise. Repo shrinks. Dealer inventory disappears. Issuance fails. The country returns to scarcity with a higher premium than before because it taught investors the record is conditional.

A realistic build plan treats credibility as an asset that compounds. The country wins by accumulating small victories demonstrating routine enforceability: auctions clearing on schedule, collateral seized under clear priority, disputes resolved quickly, corporate actions processed cleanly, insiders disciplined when they abuse public markets. These victories deepen the buyer base. A deeper buyer base lowers yields. Lower yields increase fiscal room. Increased fiscal room reduces monetization fear. Reduced fear strengthens the unit. A stronger unit lengthens duration. Longer duration finances projects. Successful projects grow the tax base and household surplus. Surplus becomes institutional savings. Institutional savings becomes depth. Depth becomes sovereignty.

'Scarcity ends when routine becomes believable.'

The sequence is mechanical: unit credibility, settlement spine, lien clarity, repo funding, dealer obligations, calendar discipline, reference integrity, disclosure built for use, minority rights enforced in public, institutional savings pools, gradual product expansion, crisis drills preventing stress from becoming legitimacy rupture. A country following the sequence does not eliminate risk. It eliminates the need to rent confidence for every project tranche.

The first five years timeline is the difference between a plan and a machine, because it converts principles into a calendar the market can watch. The objective is not to move fast in everything. The objective is to move predictably in the few things that create compounding trust.

Month 1: publish the sovereign auction calendar for the next twelve months with fixed dates, standard tenors, and clear contingency rules. Announce that auctions will proceed unless settlement infrastructure fails, and define what counts as failure. Begin weekly publication of results and bid-to-cover in a standardized format.

Month 2: finalize reference-price policy for collateral and for reporting. Choose a primary reference source, define the fallback, define outlier handling, define error correction windows, and publish a dispute pathway with timelines.

Month 3: establish a narrow repo eligibility set limited to the shortest sovereign bills, with conservative haircuts and simple margining.

Require same-day collateral substitution capability and document default procedures for missed margin.

Month 4: certify a small set of primary dealers by transparent criteria and impose obligations: minimum auction participation, minimum quoting during defined hours, and reporting duties. Grant privileges: access to the repo facility, standardized settlement access, and predictable issuance allocation mechanics.

Month 5: begin registry modernization with a single identifier schema for sovereign instruments and a reconciliation interface for custody participants. Require daily reconciliation attestations for the depository's core record.

Month 6: pilot a settlement finality rule set for sovereign paper: define the settlement cycle, define what counts as final, define correction windows, define error authorities. Run a public simulation of a failed delivery and publish how it would be resolved.

Month 7: expand repo eligibility slightly to include a second tenor, still sovereign-only, and publish a strict schedule for haircut review tied to volatility thresholds rather than discretion.

Month 8: launch a public corporate-action processing standard for sovereign instruments: calendar, record dates, entitlement calculation, and correction. The objective is to demonstrate clean entitlements on the simplest asset first.

Month 9: begin audit and accounting enforcement upgrades focused on banks and primary dealers, not on every issuer at once. The objective is to strengthen proof where funding and settlement depend on it most.

Month 10: create a lien registry fast lane for financial collateral, with a requirement that filings update within defined hours and that priority disputes be adjudicated under accelerated procedure. Publish the procedure and test it in a small pilot dispute.

Month 11: start a corporate bond pilot framework: strict eligibility standards, required audited statements, standardized covenants, clear trustee responsibilities, and a defined default and restructuring pathway. Announce that only a small number of issuers will qualify initially.

Month 12: run the first corporate bond pilot issuance with a small size and commit to secondary liquidity support through dealer obligations and repo eligibility where appropriate. Publish post-trade metrics and settlement performance.

Year 2, Month 13: expand the auction calendar into longer tenors only if year-one settlement finality and repo stability targets were met. If not met, pause tenor extension and deepen the short end until it is boring.

Month 14: broaden the depository's identifier coverage to include corporate bonds, and enforce standardized corporate-action processing for coupon payments and redemptions.

Month 15: create a market surveillance baseline focused on manipulation and spoofing, but more importantly focused on record integrity, cancellations, and settlement fails. Publish enforcement actions to prove consequences exist.

Month 16: expand the primary dealer network only if existing dealers met quoting and auction obligations. Dealer membership becomes earned, not granted.

Month 18: introduce a limited institutional savings vehicle initiative: pension reforms, insurer duration incentives, and standardized savings products that buy sovereign and high-quality corporate paper. The objective is to create patient domestic demand that is rule-bound and predictable.

Month 20: strengthen minority-rights enforcement capacity before listing expansion by creating fast injunction timelines, clear related-party rules, and public decisions that demonstrate insiders can be blocked.

Month 24: open a small "first equity segment" with strict listing rules: audited accounts, minimum free float, governance constraints, mandatory disclosure, and clear delisting triggers for violation. The segment is intentionally small, designed to be credible before it is popular.

Year 3, Month 25: integrate equity settlement into the depository's finality regime and require corporate-action discipline for dividends and splits with transparent record dates.

Month 28: allow repo against a small set of high-quality corporate bonds only after the sovereign and first corporate bond pilot have demonstrated clean settlement and enforcement outcomes.

Month 30: expand institutional investor participation through liability-matching incentives, making pensions and insurers natural holders of duration rather than speculative buyers.

Month 33: add a second equity tier only if the first tier has demonstrated clean enforcement outcomes and low dispute incidence. Expansion is conditional on proof, not on political enthusiasm.

Month 36: publish a three-year review showing enforcement actions, settlement fail rates, auction performance, and haircut stability, making the proof visible enough that market participants can update trust based on data rather than rumor.

Year 4, Month 37: extend sovereign issuance further out the curve only if inflation expectations are anchored and if the auction calendar has remained intact through at least one volatility episode without ad hoc cancellations.

Month 40: expand corporate bond issuance capacity by adding a standardized restructuring path that is fast enough to keep defaults routine rather than system events.

Month 42: expand equity inclusion only after minority-rights enforcement has demonstrated speed and impartiality, because equity depth is trust depth.

Month 48: integrate benchmark creation carefully: build a domestic bond benchmark only when secondary liquidity is sufficient that the benchmark does not become a forced-flow hazard that can be harvested by a small club.

Year 5, Month 49: widen the investor base by allowing broader retail access through regulated vehicles only after enforcement record is visible and stable. Retail arrives last, not first.

Month 54: expand repo and collateral eligibility gradually, using published thresholds and objective criteria, to avoid discretionary widening that would recreate the rule-rewrite fear that kills duration.

Month 60: introduce a domestic market stress protocol handbook: formal default waterfalls, close-out procedures, communications rules, and emergency facilities with constrained eligibility. Make the handbook public so that panic rumor has less room to grow.

The stress test year sequence demonstrates whether the new institutions can survive a real shock without rewriting rules, because one contained default teaches more than a hundred speeches. The test begins when a mid-sized corporate bond issuer misses a coupon payment due to a sector downturn. The market's first response is not moral outrage. It is the question of process: who declares default, on what evidence, and on what timeline.

Day 1: the trustee declares a payment failure under pre-defined notice rules. The exchange and depository tag the instrument status in the official record. The tag is authoritative and time-stamped. There is no ambiguity that allows insider denial to delay the process.

Day 2: repo eligibility for that instrument is suspended automatically under published rules. Haircuts on similar names adjust according to published volatility and credit triggers, not discretion. Lenders do not need to guess whether politics will protect the issuer. They can price the event.

Day 3: close-out protocols activate for counterparties with exposures. Netting operates under established law. Collateral is seized where applicable under clear priority rules. The system contains exposure because gross claims are reduced quickly into net obligations.

Day 4: a restructuring process begins under a standardized fast track. Creditor voting thresholds are known. Timelines are tight. Courts have an accelerated lane for disputes tied to market stability, not because markets are favored, but because delay is systemic cost.

Day 5: the central bank offers liquidity to the system through the constrained facility, not to rescue the issuer but to prevent funding panic in the broader repo market. The facility is used on pre-defined terms with penalty pricing, preventing moral hazard while preserving continuity.

Week 2: the issuer's assets are valued under transparent methodology, and a recovery range is published by the trustee and verified by independent audit discipline. The publication reduces rumor space. Rumor space is where panic grows.

Week 3: the restructuring vote occurs. A deal is approved or the default proceeds to liquidation under known procedures. Either way, the outcome is not negotiated in a political room; it is executed under published rules.

Week 4: the market reopens risk appetite gradually because it learned the most important lesson: failure is routine and bounded. Issuance does not freeze, because investors saw that defaults do not trigger rule rewriting, selective protection, or registry chaos.

Quarter end: reporting marks reflect losses transparently. Institutions absorb them and continue because they trust the record. The sovereign auction calendar proceeds without cancellation. The unit remains credible because the state did not try to hide loss through administrative improvisation. The market emerges bruised and legitimate.

CHAPTER 38
THE COST OF BORROWED MARKETS
WHAT NATIONS LOSE WHEN PRICING, CLEARING, AND CONFIDENCE LIVE SOMEWHERE ELSE.

A nation can rent a market the way it rents a fleet: it can hire the vessels, pay the crew, and ship the cargo, yet never own the dockyard that decides who gets priority when the storm arrives. Borrowed markets feel efficient in calm conditions because they deliver immediate access to deep pools of capital, mature pricing references, and standardized post-trade rails. The cost is not paid upfront. The cost is paid in regime moments: when a project must refinance, when the currency wobbles, when a sector defaults, when global risk appetite turns, and the nation discovers that its critical financial functions are external services with external priorities.

The first cost is a loss of unit sovereignty at the margin. If domestic projects are priced and financed primarily in an external unit, domestic revenue becomes a translation problem rather than a financing base. Translation problems convert manageable operating variance into balance-sheet shock because obligations reprice instantly when the exchange rate moves. The borrower does not become less productive overnight. The borrower becomes more fragile overnight. The nation organizes policy around defending the translation rather than around building the productive base. It raises rates to defend the unit, cuts spending to preserve external confidence, and delays projects to avoid making the mismatch worse. Borrowed markets turn the currency into a permanent constraint because external finance makes the exchange rate an input to solvency, not merely a price of trade.

The second cost is a loss of calendar sovereignty. Domestic development requires duration, and duration requires rolling risk to be survivable. In a borrowed market regime, rollover is a foreign calendar event. Liquidity can disappear because external committees are repricing exposures for reasons unrelated to the domestic project: a policy shift abroad, a risk-off week, a geopolitical tremor, a commodity swing, a balance-sheet event in a distant funding center. The domestic issuer learns that the real maturity date is not the contractual maturity date. The real maturity date is the day external funding desks decide the relationship is too costly to carry. The project's timeline becomes hostage to that day.

The third cost is a loss of pricing sovereignty. When benchmark curves, reference rates, and risk premiums are imported, domestic fundamentals are filtered through external models. Those models are designed for the modeler's constraints: liquidity, recoverability, legal enforceability, exit certainty. Domestic complexity is priced as opacity because it cannot be proven quickly. Opacity is priced as spread. Spread becomes politics. The nation is forced to argue about admissibility: whether disclosures, courts, registries, and enforcement are sufficient to satisfy external proof burdens. Borrowed markets shift the development conversation away from productivity and toward proof compliance, because external capital funds only what it can defend in risk committees.

The fourth cost is a loss of clearing sovereignty. Clearing determines margin, netting, and who must deliver cash when volatility rises. If clearing is external, margin calls are external. External margin calls can arrive at the worst moment because they are triggered by global volatility and global correlation assumptions, not only by domestic issuer conditions. When external clearing raises margin, local banks and firms must produce liquidity immediately. If domestic liquidity facilities are shallow, the only way to meet margin is to sell assets and reduce credit. That action tightens the domestic economy precisely when stress is already rising. Borrowed clearing imports procyclicality and can turn a domestic wobble into domestic contraction.

The fifth cost is a loss of dispute sovereignty. When contracts, arbitration, and enforcement live outside the jurisdiction, the nation gains funding and loses flexibility. External enforcement provides credibility to lenders; it also makes renegotiation expensive and politically toxic. When a project is stressed, domestic renegotiation would normally trade time for stability. Under external enforcement, renegotiation becomes a legal event with reputational penalties that can spill into sovereign spreads. The state becomes reluctant to intervene because intervention is treated as rule risk. The result is a harsher cycle: domestic austerity and project suspension rather than structured adjustment. Borrowed markets reduce the range of policy responses available in stress because the permitted responses are the ones external lenders interpret as acceptable.

The sixth cost is a loss of domestic institution formation. Deep markets are training grounds. They create domestic competence in underwriting, credit analysis, market making, custody operations, audit discipline, restructuring practice, and risk management. If the main deals, the main pricing, and the main settlement are outsourced, domestic institutions never develop the muscle memory that makes markets routine. Domestic talent migrates toward relationship intermediation rather than toward infrastructure building. Relationship intermediation can move deals. It does not build depth. The nation becomes permanently dependent because every complex transaction requires foreign structuring, foreign legal templates, foreign pricing references, and foreign post-trade rails.

The seventh cost is a loss of domestic savings compounding. If households cannot trust domestic instruments, they save short, save informally, or save abroad where permitted. Short saving prevents duration formation. Without duration, domestic projects cannot be financed locally at tolerable yields. Without local financing, projects are financed externally and return cash externally through debt service and fees. The nation experiences a compounding gap: domestic surplus that could have become a domestic investor base becomes a stream of payments supporting external balance sheets. Borrowed markets can export compounding, which is the most strategic resource in development finance.

The eighth cost is a loss of policy signaling clarity. When the state takes an action to support domestic stability, external capital may interpret the same action as hostility to creditor rights. A temporary measure meant to avoid panic becomes a signal of rule rewrite risk. Spreads widen. The act becomes self-defeating. The state learns to avoid stabilizing tools because it anticipates external committee reaction. It becomes governed by external pricing rather than domestic welfare.

Borrowed markets impose a structural fee stack that often escapes domestic debate. Fees are not only underwriting spreads. Fees are embedded in reference pricing, data and compliance, legal enforcement clauses, escrow structures, external trustees, offshore custodians, cross-currency hedges, and the premium paid for the right to exit. Each fee is defensible in isolation. Together they represent persistent extraction from domestic projects. Borrowed markets delay domestic infrastructure because they provide short-term relief, and relief reduces urgency to invest in boring domestic depth.

The most consequential loss is shock absorption. A nation with domestic depth can distribute stress internally across patient holders, domestic liquidity facilities, and rule-bound restructuring processes. A nation renting markets must absorb stress through the narrow channels it controls: fiscal tightening, rate hikes, import compression, project delays. These responses preserve external confidence at the expense of domestic momentum. The nation becomes a machine for converting external volatility into internal austerity.

Dependence is also microstructural. If price discovery is anchored elsewhere, domestic venues become shadows. Local liquidity providers cannot compete with the offshore reference because they cannot hedge and finance with the same tools. Local spreads widen. Local volumes thin. Thin volumes reduce data quality. Reduced data quality increases uncertainty. Uncertainty widens haircuts. Higher haircuts reduce dealer capacity. Reduced capacity thins liquidity further. Domestic market attempts look volatile and untrustworthy, sending domestic savings back into short instruments. Borrowed markets crowd out domestic depth and train domestic participants to distrust it.

Borrowed markets change development bargaining. Contracts include priority rights, step-in provisions, and external arbitration designed to protect lenders. Protections make the project behave like an enclave: revenue waterfalls flow outward first, domestic users bear indexation risk, domestic policy space constrained by covenants, domestic courts sidelined. Enclaves can deliver infrastructure. They can fragment sovereignty by creating pockets where national rules are secondary. A country can build many enclaves and still not build a domestic market, because enclave finance does not require domestic depth; it requires external confidence.

The dependence premium becomes visible at refinancing. The initial deal is sold as success because it closes. Refinancing reveals whether the nation built domestic depth or rented a window of external appetite. If domestic depth exists, refinance can be partly internalized. If not, refinance is a new negotiation under new global conditions. New global conditions often mean higher yields and stricter clauses. The project becomes more expensive precisely when it should be stabilizing and producing fiscal room. Fiscal room is consumed by debt service and fee stacks, and the nation stays dependent.

Borrowed markets also change domestic politics because they change who is protected. Elites with external hedges are insulated from mismatch and inflation. Households without external access bear tightening cycles, imported price shocks, reduced credit. Legitimacy pressure increases the probability of sudden policy moves. Sudden moves increase external risk premiums. Premiums tighten financing further. Borrowed markets can create the policy volatility they are then used to justify pricing.

The most damaging dynamic is the loop between borrowed confidence and underinvestment in domestic trust infrastructure. As long as external markets can finance the next tranche, domestic reforms can be delayed. Delayed reforms keep domestic markets shallow. Shallow markets force external dependence. External dependence increases the cost of domestic reforms because reforms must be attempted during stress cycles rather than stable cycles. The nation becomes trapped: it needs stability to build trust, but it needs trust to reduce dependence and gain stability. Borrowed markets provide interim funding and prolong the trap.

The escape is not rejecting external capital. The escape is treating external capital as bridge financing while domestic depth is built deliberately. External finance can fund early projects, but the structures must also create domestic assets and domestic institutions: domestic-currency tranches that grow over time, domestic clearing and custody strengthening, domestic disclosure and enforcement upgrades tied to issuance privileges, domestic savings vehicles accumulating duration demand, domestic restructuring frameworks making failure routine rather than political. If external finance is used without domestic institution building, the nation receives assets and keeps dependence.

The cost of borrowed markets is paid in five currencies: unit constraint, calendar constraint, pricing constraint, clearing constraint, institutional constraint. Each reduces policy space. Each increases the probability a bad week becomes a regime premium. Each forces ambition to be financed through external permission. The surface may show deals closing and indices rising. The underlying truth is whether the nation can price, clear, and refinance on its own rails when external confidence is not generous.

'Borrowed markets deliver capital quickly and sovereignty slowly.'

The decisive question is not whether the nation can access global finance today. The decisive question is whether access will still exist when the project needs refinancing, when the currency is pressured, and when the state needs flexibility. If pricing, clearing, and confidence live elsewhere, the answer is always conditional, and conditional finance is expensive because it forces the nation to plan in bursts instead of building continuously.

The refinancing cliff sequence is where the cost stops being philosophical and becomes a chain of deadlines. Global tightening begins abroad, and the immediate domestic effect is not ideology but term: offshore lenders widen new issue spreads and shorten offered maturities. The project's refinancing window arrives in that regime. The offshore spread jump is the first tax, and it does not arrive alone.

Cross-currency hedge costs spike because volatility rises and because liquidity in hedging instruments becomes more expensive precisely when everyone wants protection. The project's financial model assumed a hedge cost consistent with calm regimes. Calm regimes are not contractually guaranteed. The hedge line item expands, compressing coverage ratios and reducing covenant headroom.

Domestic authorities respond with rate defense to slow currency pressure, because a currency slide would worsen the foreign-unit debt burden and panic domestic savers. Rate defense raises domestic funding costs for banks and firms, tightening credit and weakening local demand. The project's revenues soften just as costs rise. A project financed through borrowed markets now faces a cash squeeze created by external spreads, hedge costs, and domestic tightening all at once.

Cash squeeze pushes the project toward covenant breach. The breach does not require operating failure. It requires that the financing environment reprice faster than the project can adjust. Lenders then move from monitoring to enforcement posture. External step-in threats appear in letters and in meeting agendas: demands for escrow sweeps, restricted payments, asset pledges, management changes, or the right to take operational control if conditions are not met.

Public backlash follows because the project is visible: tariffs rise due to indexation clauses, employment promises are broken as costs are cut, and citizens learn that the most important decisions are now in enforcement documents written in foreign legal language. The state faces pressure to intervene. Intervention triggers rule-risk repricing because external lenders interpret intervention as potential impairment or as a signal that enforceability may be challenged politically. Rule-risk repricing widens spreads further, and the nation discovers that each attempt to regain control increases the cost of funding the next tranche.

The cliff is not one event. It is the conversion of external regime change into domestic austerity and domestic political heat, with the project sitting in the middle as the conduit. Borrowed markets delivered the project. Borrowed markets also imported the tightening cycle and priced the nation's response as risk. That is the cost: not only higher yields, but reduced degrees of freedom precisely when degrees of freedom are needed to keep development continuous.

PART SIX
THE POLITICAL STRUCTURE OF MARKETS

MARKETS DO NOT FLOAT ABOVE POLITICS; THEY ARE WRITTEN BY IT, ENFORCED BY IT, AND WEAPONIZED THROUGH IT.

The market's public story is neutral infrastructure: prices, liquidity, efficiency, a place where private choices meet. The political reality is simpler and harsher. Every market is a rulebook that decides who may participate, what counts as proof, which losses are allowed to remain private, and which losses are forced into public rescue. Every market is a boundary system that allocates not only capital, but permission. Permission to raise money, permission to exit, permission to hedge, permission to be treated as collateral, permission to be believed. The political structure is the architecture that makes these permissions routine enough to look natural.

The Rulebook Before the Crisis: The decisive choices are often made in technical language long before the public feels the consequences.

A narrow committee met in a room with no banners, no cameras, no slogans, and no mention of the word crisis. The air carried the quiet confidence of institutional continuity: polished binders, version numbers in the margins, annotations that assumed the future would behave like the past because the rulebook would make it behave. The participants were not debating whether to save markets or punish them. They were deciding what markets would be, on the day the system was forced to choose between speed and fairness, between liquidity and legitimacy, between private loss and public stability.

The work began with definitions, because the first act of political power in markets is definitional. What is a valid trade. What counts as a cancellation. Which timestamps are authoritative. Which venues produce admissible prints. Which prints become official marks. Which marks trigger margin. Which margin triggers liquidation. A market can call these technicalities, yet technicalities are where the chain begins. The committee's language carried the discipline of inevitability: a change in the definition would not change what is true, it would change what is enforceable, and enforceability is what the system treats as truth when money is at stake.

A clerk projected a diagram of the day's most ordinary event: a trade executed, cleared, and settled. In calm times it was a sequence. In stress it became a weapon. A trade that can be reversed becomes a free option for whoever loses. A trade that cannot be reversed becomes an injustice if it was created by malfunction. The committee's task was to choose where reversibility ends, because finality is not only a legal property. Finality is a political commitment: a declaration that certain losses will be allowed to stand so the system can keep moving.

Another section of the binder described a narrow list of eligible collateral. Eligibility looked like prudence. It was also a map of power. If a claim is eligible collateral, it can be financed cheaply and held through volatility. If a claim is not eligible, it becomes expensive to hold at the precise moment when fear rises. The committee did not discuss winners and losers. They discussed haircuts, eligibility tiers, and stress add-ons, yet each percentage point decided which balance sheets could buy time and which balance sheets would be forced to sell. Buying time is political privilege disguised as risk management.

The next pages described the default waterfall. It was written as an operational sequence: margin, default fund, assessments, recovery tools, and loss allocation. It was also a moral sequence: whose money is used first, whose money is used next, and when losses become social rather than private. The committee's language avoided emotion, yet the order of loss allocation was the heart of the political system. A market that allocates losses quickly can preserve liquidity. A market that allocates losses unpredictably preserves resentment. Resentment becomes refusal. Refusal becomes a run.

A small note in the margin referenced auction extensions and volatility interruptions. The words were calm. The consequence was decisive. An interruption can prevent a cascade by batching panic into a process. It can also create a perception that the system protects insiders by delaying the moment when the public can exit. The committee debated thresholds, not morality, yet thresholds were morality translated into numbers: how much price movement is tolerated before the system intervenes, who may trade during the intervention, and what information is released. If interventions are rule-bound, they are seen as infrastructure. If interventions are discretionary, they are seen as power. The difference is not the intervention itself. The difference is whether the system can prove that interventions are not a private service sold to the strongest participants.

The discussion shifted to surveillance and enforcement, and the room grew quieter. Markets cannot be trusted if manipulation is perceived as routine. Markets also cannot be legitimate if enforcement is perceived as selective. Selective enforcement is where finance turns political in the most corrosive way: the rulebook exists, but it is applied unevenly, so participation becomes a relationship game rather than a rights-based system. The committee's proposal did not promise perfection. It promised predictability: defined violations, defined evidence, defined penalties, and a record that could be audited later without rewriting history. A predictable enforcement perimeter is the minimum condition for patient capital, because patient capital is not brave. Patient capital is rule-confident.

The most consequential debate arrived wrapped in a phrase that sounded harmless: exceptional measures. The text described a constrained facility that could lend liquidity against eligible collateral under penalty terms. The facility was presented as a stability tool, yet everyone in the room understood the political meaning. A facility defines who is rescued, under what collateral, at what price, and with what stigma. If the facility is too generous, it becomes a subsidy for leverage. If it is too restrictive, it becomes a ritual that fails in the moment it is needed, and the system learns that the backstop is theater. The committee did not debate ideology. They debated credibility, because credibility is the only backstop that prevents the market from becoming a referendum on fear every hour.

One participant raised the problem of cross-border stress. A domestic market can be rule-perfect and still be destabilized if external funding withdraws, if foreign participants cannot convert smoothly, or if sanctions and controls interrupt settlement. The rulebook responded with jurisdictional clauses, access rules, and fallback settlement pathways. The language looked like compliance. The effect was geopolitics expressed as market design: who keeps access during conflict, who is excluded, and whether exclusion occurs through published rules or through improvisation. Improvisation is the seed of panic because improvisation teaches participants that future rights are negotiable.

The committee's final pages addressed disclosure and proof. What is a valid statement of record ownership. How corporate actions are processed. How disputes are adjudicated. How quickly courts must move for market-stability cases. The prose was procedural, yet its effect was revolutionary for a developing system. A fast dispute lane makes failure routine. Routine failure makes investors willing to hold duration. Duration is the foundation of domestic financing independence. Without the dispute lane, every default becomes a political emergency, and every political emergency invites rule rewriting that destroys the next decade of market-building work.

The room's most dangerous sentence was the one that looked most responsible: the authority may suspend to preserve orderly markets. The participants knew that a suspension power is necessary, yet also knew it is the quickest path to delegitimization if it is used as discretion rather than as rule. They rewrote it into thresholds, time limits, documentation requirements, and automatic post-event review. The goal was not to remove power. The goal was to bind power so it could be used without teaching the market that the record is conditional on who is losing.

"Stability is not a promise; it is a procedure."

When the meeting ended, nothing in the public world had changed. No screens flashed. No prices moved. The public did not know that a set of default tools had been narrowed, that collateral eligibility had been tightened, that a haircut schedule had been made more procyclical, or that a suspension authority had been bounded with less discretion than before. Yet these were the moves that would decide, months later, whether a bad week would become a legitimacy rupture or remain a contained bruise. The rulebook before the crisis was the crisis in embryo, written in the only language the system obeys when fear arrives: definitions, thresholds, priorities, and enforceable timelines.

CHAPTER 39

THE MARKET AS STATECRAFT

HOW NATIONS USE EXCHANGES, CAPITAL RULES, AND LIQUIDITY AS INSTRUMENTS OF CONTROL.

A market is often described as a mirror of the economy. In practice it is an instrument the state can tune. The tuning does not require propaganda. It requires rule choices that decide whose claims become collateral, whose liabilities can be rolled, whose prices become official anchors, and whose losses are allowed to remain private. Statecraft in markets is the conversion of political goals into financing conditions. Financing conditions then shape corporate behavior, household outcomes, and the nation's external posture. The state that understands this does not treat markets as neutral scenery. It treats markets as strategic infrastructure that can project stability, attract capital, punish adversaries, and purchase time.

Statecraft begins with the unit and the curve. A sovereign curve is not only the state borrowing. It is the reference rate defining the nation's internal contract language: mortgages, corporate loans, project finance, and the discount rates used in valuations. A state that can issue consistently and clear auctions under stress can reduce its dependence premium and lengthen domestic duration. Duration becomes strategic because it allows long projects to be financed domestically without foreign-unit clauses. Domestic duration reduces vulnerability to external tightening, increasing policy freedom. Policy freedom is power because it allows the state to act rather than react.

The next layer is collateral policy, because collateral policy is capital allocation disguised as prudence. If a claim is eligible collateral at the central bank or in domestic repo, it becomes financeable. Financeable claims attract balance-sheet support. Balance-sheet support deepens liquidity. Liquidity lowers cost of capital. Cost of capital influences which firms grow and which stagnate. The collateral schedule is industrial policy in a spreadsheet. A state can accelerate a sector by making its paper acceptable in domestic funding markets and by building the proof and enforcement perimeter that makes that acceptance credible. A state can punish a sector by removing eligibility, raising haircuts, or tightening disclosure requirements. These moves look technical. Their impact is strategic.

Exchanges are the visibility layer of this strategy. A state wanting to project reliability uses the exchange as a public proof engine: listings, disclosures, and price records foreign allocators can accept. The exchange is also an internal discipline engine. Listing rules and disclosure enforcement pressure governance reforms, professionalize accounting, and build minority protection. In a market-building regime, the exchange becomes a lever for domestic institutional credibility. In a control-first regime, the exchange becomes theater and loses strategic value because capital learns that records are conditional. The state then pays a premium for external capital and loses the ability to finance long projects domestically.

Liquidity is the state's quiet weapon because liquidity changes outcomes without announcing itself as coercion. A state can create liquidity by ensuring settlement finality, protecting netting and close-out, providing constrained backstops, and enforcing integrity so intermediaries are willing to warehouse inventory. A state can remove liquidity by restricting convertibility, imposing administrative controls, or allowing selective enforcement that makes trading risky. Liquidity withdrawal can be targeted domestically and externally. The actor controlling liquidity conditions controls the speed of the other actor's clock.

Market access is geopolitics by other means. If a nation's firms depend on offshore listings, foreign clearing, and foreign currency funding, access becomes an external lever. External authorities can restrict listings, block settlement, raise compliance burdens, or threaten enforcement actions that make investors avoid exposure. These actions discipline a nation without a military act. They operate through capital availability and reputational fear inside institutions that must remain compliant. The nation being targeted experiences the pressure as market conditions. The mechanism is statecraft expressed through infrastructure.

A state with strong domestic depth can resist because it can substitute domestic financing for external financing. Substitution does not mean isolation. It means bargaining power. A nation that can finance projects domestically can reject unfavorable external clauses and choose partnerships strategically rather than desperately. Domestic market depth is therefore sovereignty asset: it reduces the probability that external committees become the hidden cabinet of development.

Statecraft operates through capital rules. Prudential regulation decides what banks can hold, what insurers can hold, and how risk is measured. Risk weights and liquidity requirements are allocation rules. If domestic sovereign paper is favored, banks absorb it, supporting the curve. If certain corporate exposures are penalized, those firms face higher borrowing costs. Used well, these levers build domestic benchmarks, channel credit to strategic sectors, and protect the system from external shocks. Used poorly, they create misallocation and hidden losses that later become a crisis.

The state also controls the legal perimeter, and the legal perimeter is the difference between capital that stays and capital that flees. If property rights are enforceable, minority rights real, and bankruptcy routine, investors can hold duration. Holding duration deepens markets. Deep markets reduce dependence. Reduced dependence increases policy freedom. If enforcement is selective, markets become relationship games, and relationship games do not produce deep domestic institutional savings because households and smaller firms cannot compete in the relationship arena. Selective enforcement becomes national weakness because it blocks patient capital formation and forces the nation to rent confidence abroad.

The most visible modern statecraft tool is sanction architecture, operating through settlement access, correspondent relationships, clearing membership, and the legal ability of institutions to hold and transact in certain instruments. The power is not only to block. It is to raise compliance uncertainty. Compliance uncertainty makes institutions de-risk even before formal restrictions apply. De-risking withdraws liquidity. Liquidity withdrawal raises borrowing costs. Borrowing costs slow investment and growth. The targeted state experiences a tightening cycle without a single domestic policy change. This is market power used as geopolitical leverage.

States also practice internal statecraft by deciding when to let markets clear and when to intervene. Intervention can stabilize and can delegitimize. Rule-bound interventions that are symmetrical and documented can preserve trust. Discretionary interventions protecting insiders create an exit door premium. Credibility is therefore an instrument. Credibility allows low-cost financing and stable duration. Credibility also allows the state to act in crisis without triggering runs. A state spending credibility for short-term relief loses the long-term power credibility provides.

Statecraft in markets is therefore a balance between control and credibility. Control provides immediate political tools. Credibility provides long-term power. Many regimes choose control because control is visible and immediate. The price is dependence because credibility is what markets rent, and if credibility is not built domestically, it must be rented externally. Renting credibility means accepting external conditions. External conditions reduce sovereignty.

A state that treats markets as statecraft invests in the boring layers: settlement finality, registries, enforcement speed, disclosure discipline, and rule-bound backstops. It uses these to make its unit and curve credible, to make corporate claims financeable, and to make exchanges authoritative. Authority becomes geopolitical asset because it allows the nation to finance projects without foreign permission and withstand external tightening without collapsing into austerity spirals.

'Power in markets is the ability to set the terms on which time is financed.'

That claim becomes concrete when statecraft is shown not as rhetoric but as sequences that move balance sheets.

The domestic sequence begins with a collateral eligibility shift, and the shift is announced as stability policy. The central bank or regulator expands eligible collateral to include a targeted class of claims, or lowers haircuts on that class while keeping others unchanged. The shift changes funding cost immediately because repo and secured funding are priced off eligibility. A claim that becomes eligible is no longer only an investment. It becomes a funding instrument.

Sector repricing follows because the market understands that funding cost is fate. If a sector's paper is easier to fund, dealers can hold more inventory, spreads tighten, and issuance becomes cheaper. If a sector is excluded or haircuted harder, spreads widen and issuance becomes expensive. Equity valuations move in parallel because discount rates and refinancing risk change. The repricing is not primarily belief about productivity. It is belief about survivability under funding constraints.

Bank balance sheets rotate next because banks optimize for regulatory and funding efficiency. They shift holdings toward newly eligible assets because those assets deliver better liquidity ratios, better funding terms, and better collateral utility. They reduce holdings of ineligible assets because those assets consume balance sheet and increase stress vulnerability. The rotation is reinforced by risk models and supervisory expectations. A policy tool becomes portfolio migration across the system.

Then comes the real-economy outcome: investment surge or drought. The favored sector sees cheaper issuance, more available bank credit, and longer maturities. Projects that were marginal become financeable. The unfavored sector faces tighter credit, shorter maturities, punitive covenants. Projects are delayed. Firms cut costs and postpone expansion. The state can call this prudential stability. The economy experiences it as industrial policy executed through funding eligibility.

The external sequence begins with a settlement restriction rumor, and the rumor is enough because markets price permission risk, not only law. A headline, a leak, or a diplomatic escalation raises the probability that certain participants will face settlement friction: blocked transfers, restricted custodians, heightened documentation. Institutions do not wait for certainty because compliance penalties are asymmetric. Being early to de-risk is safer than being late.

Compliance de-risking follows as an internal mandate, not a political statement. Legal and compliance desks instruct trading and custody to reduce exposure, shorten maturities, and avoid new positions that could become trapped in settlement. Prime brokers tighten terms. Custodians demand additional documentation. Banks reduce correspondent activity. The withdrawal begins as administrative caution.

It becomes liquidity reality because the largest balance sheets leave first.

Liquidity withdrawal then appears in the market itself. Spreads widen. Depth thins. Dealers reduce inventory because inventory becomes settlement-risk inventory. Funding desks raise haircuts because collateral that might be hard to deliver is worse collateral. Issuers discover refinancing calendars no longer clear at prior terms. The nation experiences the shift as sudden market hostility. The mechanism is that settlement access is the bloodstream, and even the rumor of blockage makes the bloodstream constrict.

Sovereign spreads jump last as the final price of lost permission. The jump is not only default probability. It is the price of uncertainty about access, rollover, and enforceability under cross-border stress. Higher sovereign spreads feed back into banks and corporates because the sovereign is baseline for domestic funding. Domestic rates rise. Credit tightens. Investment slows. No shots are fired. The nation's clock slows anyway.

The credibility repair sequence is how statecraft rebuilds after a shock without purchasing calm through discretionary distortion. A default event arrives, either a mid-sized dealer failure or a corporate payment miss, and the system faces its core test: will it improvise or will it execute. The state and the market institutions respond with rule-bound intervention, not to eliminate loss, but to prevent loss from becoming panic. The backstop facility opens on published eligibility and penalty terms. The exchange applies volatility controls only through published thresholds with documented time limits. The depository publishes an authoritative status tag and a clear correction window for records. Nothing in the response is negotiated in private.

A contained default follows because close-out and netting operate as designed. Positions are frozen under known authority. Collateral is seized under known priority. Losses are allocated through the published waterfall. The process is fast enough that counterparties can quantify exposure and continue funding inventory rather than hoarding cash. The market absorbs damage as a bounded event, not as a rumor of systemic rot. The most important outcome is informational: participants learn that the record remains authoritative under stress and that enforcement does not blink.

Stable auctions then become the public proof of repair. The treasury keeps its issuance calendar. Auctions proceed on schedule. Bid-to-cover is allowed to reflect fear without cancellation theater. The central bank does not force artificial clearing levels. It provides liquidity through the constrained facility and lets price clear within the rules. This combination signals that the state will not buy calm by rewriting contract reality. It will buy calm by letting losses be priced and by keeping settlement and funding mechanics intact.

Spread normalization arrives not as a gift but as a result of reduced uncertainty about rule rewriting. As investors observe that defaults are handled quickly, that collateral rules remain stable, that auctions continue, and that interventions are bounded and documented, the exit premium compresses. Haircuts stop rising. Funding lines reopen. Dealers rebuild inventory. Issuers regain access to term financing at less punitive spreads. The state has repaired credibility by proving that procedure survives stress. It has converted statecraft from a tool of control into a tool of reliability, and reliability is the precondition for duration.

The credibility repair shows up in the next project refinance as a change in contract language, which is where sovereignty is either regained or surrendered. When auctions remain stable, default handling is fast, and collateral rules do not change mid-stress, domestic duration becomes more believable, and local buyers begin to accept longer tenors without demanding foreign-unit protection as the price of safety. The refinancing term sheet shifts accordingly: a larger portion can be issued in domestic currency, indexation clauses narrow or disappear, cross-currency hedge requirements shrink, and external step-in rights soften because lenders no longer need to defend themselves against rule rewriting. The project stops being an enclave governed by external enforcement and becomes a domestic asset financed on domestic time, and that single shift reduces the dependence premium across every future tranche because it proves that the nation can price and clear long risk on its own rails.

CHAPTER 40

RULES ARE ARCHITECTURE

WHY REGULATION DOES NOT JUST RESTRAIN MARKETS — IT BUILDS THEM.

Regulation is usually described as a fence placed around markets after markets exist. In functioning systems the relationship is reversed. The rules are the architecture that makes a market a market: they define what counts as a valid claim, what counts as a valid trade, what counts as a valid price, what counts as final, what counts as fraud, and what happens when the largest participant cannot pay. A market without those definitions is not free. It is undefined, and undefined systems do not scale because they cannot promise routine outcomes to strangers. The rulebook is therefore not a constraint on markets. It is the machinery that produces enforceable liquidity.

Architecture begins with admissibility. A claim becomes financeable when it is admissible as collateral, admissible in court, admissible for audit, admissible for custody, and admissible for disclosure review. Each form of admissibility is a rule choice. If the market allows ambiguous share classes, incomplete beneficial ownership chains, and discretionary corporate action processing, then investors treat every instrument as a bespoke story. Stories cannot be funded cheaply. Admissibility turns stories into standardized objects, and standardized objects are what the system can clear, net, margin, and settle at speed.

The most important building rule is the rule that makes time defensible. Markets function on deadlines: margin calls, delivery windows, record dates, cutoff times, and auction schedules. A market can tolerate volatility. It cannot tolerate ambiguity about who is late, what counts as delivered, and which record is authoritative. Time defensibility is built through timestamp hierarchies, cancellation windows, correction windows, and a single recognized method for reconstructing events after the fact. Without that architecture, every loss becomes a dispute, and disputes are slow. Slow dispute resolution is the hidden tax that makes liquidity disappear during stress.

The next building rule is the rule that makes price usable. Price is not simply what the last trade printed. Price is the number the system chooses to treat as truth for collateral, for performance reporting, for tax assessment, for regulatory capital, and for corporate action entitlements. Because price triggers behavior, price definition is governance. If the system does not specify which prints count, how outliers are handled, and how official marks are generated, then participants will attempt to manufacture favorable marks during stress windows. Mark manipulation is not only a crime problem. It is an architecture problem, because the system itself creates incentives to move the number that triggers margin, eligibility, and solvency tests. A rulebook that builds markets therefore must build mark integrity: reference source, fallback source, error policy, and clear authority.

Then comes the rule that makes participation possible: the rule that defines obligations. In any scaled market, intermediaries are not volunteers. They operate under duties: duty to handle orders with defined care, duty to avoid conflicts that distort execution, duty to disclose routing and compensation structures, duty to maintain records, duty to reconcile, duty to correct, duty to supervise, duty to meet capital requirements, duty to fund default resources when their failure could become a system event. Each duty is a load-bearing beam. Remove enough beams and the market becomes cheaper to run and impossible to trust.

Markets are multi-agent systems where each agent benefits from externalizing risk. A broker benefits from routing orders to the venue that pays the broker rather than the venue that delivers the best outcome for the client. A dealer benefits from internalizing orders when internalization is profitable and externalizing when it is not. A venue benefits from selling faster lanes and charging tolls for visibility. A data vendor benefits from turning transparency into a priced product. These incentives are the natural economics of intermediated trade. The building rule forces disclosure of conflicts, measurement of outcomes, and punishment of behavior that destroys trust.

Disclosure is the rulebook's second spine. Disclosure is a substitution for private access. In a small relationship economy, capital is allocated through familiarity. In a scaled economy, capital is allocated through documents allowing strangers to assess risk. Without disclosure discipline, equity and debt become elite clubs because only insiders can evaluate issuers confidently. The result is shallow public markets, bank-dependent finance, and dependence on foreign confidence for large projects. When disclosure is credible and enforced, the public market becomes a financing engine rather than a theater.

Enforcement is the third spine. It is not enough to have requirements. The system must make misstatement expensive and correction fast. Slow enforcement creates a predictable pattern: issuers push the boundary until caught, investors treat reports as probability distributions, cost of capital rises because proof cost rises. In a market-building regime, enforcement is designed to create routine consequences, not spectacular ones. Routine consequences create predictable behavior. Predictable behavior reduces fear. Reduced fear is the precursor to duration.

Prudential rules are the architecture's foundation, because liquidity is funded. Markets do not run on cash. They run on secured borrowing, netting, and the belief that collateral can be seized quickly if someone fails. Prudential authorities decide what assets are liquid, how haircuts behave in stress, what capital buffers must exist, what exposures are too concentrated to tolerate. Those choices determine whether dealers can warehouse inventory and whether banks can provide credit through volatility. If buffers are too thin, a small shock becomes a margin spiral. If buffers are too thick, the market becomes expensive and thin. The goal is not to eliminate risk. The goal is to keep failure bounded so the system does not convert private losses into public panic.

The architecture also includes the default ladder. A default ladder is the sequence that decides how losses are absorbed: margin first, then default fund, then assessments, then recovery tools, then resolution measures. This ladder is political even when written in sterile language because it determines which balance sheets are protected by procedure and which become residual shock absorbers. If the ladder is credible, counterparties continue transacting because they can quantify tail exposure. If the ladder is ambiguous, counterparties stop transacting because ambiguity creates unbounded tail risk. The absence of trade is often called loss of confidence. The mechanism is uncertainty about loss allocation.

Market integrity rules function as depth preservation. The system must prevent manipulation not only for fairness, but because these behaviors poison price as a signal. Price is used by risk systems, by collateral systems, by performance contracts. If price is believed manufactured, the trigger machine misfires. Investors demand larger risk premiums or leave. The market becomes dominated by a smaller, more cynical set. Concentration increases fragility. Integrity rules preserve depth.

Rules also build markets through standardization of identifiers. Without clean identifiers, corporate actions are misprocessed, entitlements contested, liens misfiled, collateral misvalued. Operational errors become funding events because lenders raise haircuts when they cannot trust records. Higher haircuts reduce credit to the real economy. A market that wants depth invests in identifiers, registries, reconciliation, and dispute lanes that move at market speed rather than at bureaucratic speed.

The architecture is not only domestic. Cross-border participation turns rulebooks into geopolitical instruments. When a market depends on external clearing, external custodians, external reserve currency funding, and external compliance standards, the rulebook becomes partially foreign. Foreign rules can change with foreign priorities. A domestic issuer experiences refinancing and access as permission regime rather than price regime. The way out is domestic capability: domestic settlement finality, domestic enforcement credibility, domestic disclosure discipline, domestic liquidity facilities, domestic institutional savings pools able to hold duration. Those are designed outcomes produced by rule architecture.

The most misunderstood aspect is that rules create the incentives that later look like market culture. If execution conflicts are permitted without disclosure, the culture becomes toll-seeking. If disclosure is weak, the culture becomes rumor and relationship. If enforcement is selective, the culture becomes proximity. If default handling is slow, the culture becomes hoarding. If collateral rules are unclear, the culture becomes withdrawal at the first sign of stress. A state can lecture markets about trust. Trust is created when the system makes trustworthy behavior the cheapest behavior and makes predation expensive and predictably punished.

'A market is built when its failures become routine.'

When defaults are handled quickly, disputes resolve fast, auctions continue on schedule, corrections are processed without political bargaining, and enforcement is visible enough to deter, investors can hold duration. Duration converts projects into financeable schedules rather than refinancing cliffs. Duration reduces dependence on external moods.

Rules are architecture in three layers. They are epistemic architecture, because they define what counts as truth in records and marks. They are incentive architecture, because they define which conflicts are allowed, disclosed, or punished. They are resilience architecture, because they define how losses are allocated and how liquidity is supplied without turning support into subsidy. Markets that appear free are often markets where architecture is mature enough to feel invisible. Markets that appear chaotic are often markets where architecture is incomplete, so participants build private architectures through relationships, offshore clauses, and privileged access lanes. Private architecture can keep deals moving. It does not build sovereignty.

A rulebook that builds markets makes four commitments and proves them through procedure. It commits to record integrity, so ownership is a chain. It commits to price integrity, so triggers are legitimate. It commits to enforceable obligations, so intermediaries cannot externalize harm quietly. It commits to bounded rescue, so liquidity can be provided without turning risk-taking into public subsidy. When these commitments hold, the market becomes a financing engine for national ambition. When they fail, the market becomes theater and dependence returns through foreign-unit clauses, external arbitration, and refinancing vulnerability.

The rule-change shock sequence shows why architecture is not abstract. A regulator issues what reads like a minor amendment: collateral eligibility for a class of instruments will now require an additional disclosure attestation, and until the attestation is filed and verified, the instruments are treated as ineligible for certain regulated funding channels. The intention is prudence. The immediate effect is a status change from eligible to questioned, and questioned collateral is the first thing funding desks will not finance cheaply.

Haircuts move first because funding desks cannot wait for committees to interpret intentions. A desk must decide today whether it can seize and liquidate tomorrow. If eligibility is conditional on paperwork, then seizure can become a dispute. Dispute risk is priced as higher haircut and shorter term. Dealers holding the affected instruments face higher funding cost overnight. Higher funding cost forces inventory reduction. Inventory reduction thins depth and widens spreads. The market reads this as volatility. The mechanism is that the collateral schedule shifted under a legal condition the system cannot process at speed.

Prime brokers and bank treasury teams then ration funding. They reduce limits to counterparties most exposed to the newly conditional collateral. They demand substitution into cleaner collateral. Substitution is not free; it requires selling something to buy something else. That selling hits the affected sector's prices first, then spills into correlated assets as desks raise cash and compress risk. Price declines are not purely informational. They are collateral-driven. A regulatory definition changed the funding utility of an asset, and funding utility is part of its value.

As prices move, margin triggers fire. Risk systems mark portfolios to official references, and the new marks reduce collateral value further, creating second-round margin calls. Participants meet margin by selling liquid assets, which pushes stress into the most liquid names and tightens conditions everywhere. Liquidity providers widen spreads because they fear being selected against by forced sellers. Widened spreads increase execution cost, and higher execution cost makes refinancing more expensive.

Issuers attempting to tap markets discover that the bid disappeared. Underwriters cannot price offerings because buyers are waiting for clarity on eligibility and on how long verification will take. A deal that would have cleared yesterday is postponed today, not because the project became worse, but because buyers cannot be sure the paper will remain financeable collateral after purchase. The issuance freeze begins as a compliance question and becomes a funding reality.

The system then faces its reveal: if it improvises, grants exceptions selectively, or extends deadlines unpredictably, the shock becomes a legitimacy event. Participants learn that rule meaning is discretionary, and discretionary meaning is the seed of runs. The amendment that began as a disclosure improvement becomes a system-wide tightening because it altered collateral status without providing a fast, rule-bound pathway for adaptation.

The cascade ends where it always ends: in duration. If rule changes make collateral utility uncertain, lenders shorten term, haircuts rise, and the system becomes more rollover-fragile. Rollover fragility raises dependence premiums. Dependence premiums return the nation to foreign-unit clauses and external enforcement. A small line in a bulletin can therefore cost a year of domestic market-building, not because regulation is harmful, but because architecture changes must be sequenced with the funding machine in mind.

The mirrored good-amendment sequence reaches the same disclosure goal by treating the funding machine as a dependency that must be protected while proof is improved. The regulator announces the new attestation requirement with a transition window tied to objective milestones: instruments remain eligible for a defined period, counterparties receive a published verification timeline, and filings are processed through a centralized portal designed to clear in hours or days rather than weeks. Eligibility is not switched off by ambiguity. It is phased by schedule, and the schedule is published so desks can plan inventory rather than panic-sell it.

Objective verification is the second stabilizer. The rule specifies exactly what documents satisfy the attestation, exactly what constitutes a deficiency, and exactly how deficiencies are cured. Cure windows are short and standardized. Status tagging is binary and time-stamped: compliant, pending cure, non-compliant after deadline. The tagging is issued by a single authority and becomes the official record, so custody and funding desks do not have to guess. Guessing is what widens haircuts. Clear tagging narrows them.

Temporary backstops prevent forced selling while the system learns the new procedure. The central bank offers a constrained facility that accepts the affected collateral under a conservative add-on haircut during the transition window, with penalty terms that discourage misuse but keep inventory financeable. The facility is rule-bound and public: eligibility, pricing, and expiration date are published. Dealers and banks can therefore fund positions without dumping them into thin markets, and price discovery remains about fundamentals rather than about paperwork risk.

The result is that disclosure improves without turning into an issuance freeze. Underwriters can still price deals because they can model the transition. Issuers can still refinance because buyers believe the paper will remain financeable while verification is processed. When the transition window ends, the market has already adapted: compliant issuers are routine, non-compliant issuers are priced as non-compliant by clear rules, and the system has not taught participants that rule changes arrive as cliffs. The architecture has been strengthened and credibility has risen, precisely because the state demonstrated it can upgrade proof without detonating the funding ladder that keeps liquidity continuous.

CHAPTER 41

ACCESS, EXCLUSION, AND GEOPOLITICAL LEVERAGE

SANCTIONS, CAPITAL CONTROLS, AND THE POLITICS OF WHO GETS LIQUIDITY.

Access is the market's real constitution. Price is what the crowd watches, yet access is what decides whether the crowd matters. Access determines who can settle, who can fund, who can hedge, who can clear, who can convert, and who can exit without begging. Because liquidity is not a natural resource, access becomes the lever that allocates it, and the allocation of liquidity is the allocation of time. Time is the difference between a temporary drawdown and a default, between a policy mistake and a regime crisis, between a project refinancing and a project collapse. When a state controls access, it controls the clock of everyone who depends on the market's rails.

Exclusion is often sold as a moral tool, yet it operates as a microstructural tool. The intent can be punishment, deterrence, or containment. The mechanism is always the same: remove or threaten the rights that make claims financeable and transferable. A security that cannot be settled reliably becomes worse collateral. Worse collateral receives higher haircuts. Higher haircuts reduce leverage capacity. Reduced leverage capacity reduces market making. Reduced market making widens spreads. Wider spreads raise the cost of capital. Cost of capital slows investment and forces issuers toward short maturities and foreign-unit clauses. Exclusion therefore does not merely block transactions. It rewrites the equilibrium of funding and risk across every balance sheet that touches the excluded node.

Sanctions are the cleanest example because they convert law into plumbing. The modern sanction is not only a list of prohibited trades. It is a set of constraints on the invisible services that allow trade to become enforceable reality: correspondent banking, clearing membership, custodial access, payment messaging, swap documentation eligibility, and legal permission for institutions to carry exposure without regulatory risk. The sanction's power is amplified by compliance behavior, because compliance is not a political debate inside a bank. Compliance is a survival system. Institutions de-risk early because the cost of being wrong is asymmetric. A portfolio can lose money and recover. A compliance failure can end a franchise. This is why exclusion works even when it is not fully executed. The credible threat of exclusion causes a voluntary withdrawal that does the work before the rule is tested in court.

Capital controls are the domestic mirror image. They are often framed as a sovereign right to defend the currency and protect households. They can also be a mechanism to trap domestic savings so the state can fund itself cheaply and force time onto private holders. Control is not binary. It is a spectrum: taxes on outflows, administrative approvals, differentiated exchange rates, forced holding periods, restrictions on derivatives, limits on foreign ownership, restrictions on custodial transfers, settlement frictions disguised as operational procedures. Each measure changes the investor's exit probability. Exit probability is priced as spread. Spread is the cost of time. A state that relies on controls will often win an immediate crisis battle and lose the long war for duration, because duration requires a belief that exit is rule-governed even when the state is stressed.

The politics of who gets liquidity sits inside the hierarchy of market participants. Some actors can fund through stress because they have privileged access to official facilities, better collateral, better legal standing, and better cross-border connectivity. Others cannot. The distribution of liquidity therefore creates a distribution of survival. This distribution is not random. It is the product of rules: who qualifies as a dealer, who qualifies for central bank operations, whose collateral is eligible, whose custody chain is trusted, whose accounting is admissible, whose jurisdiction is tolerated, whose legal entity is permitted, whose settlement path is unbroken. In calm times, this hierarchy feels like efficiency. In stress, it feels like politics, because the hierarchy decides who must sell first.

The core market truth is that liquidity is supplied under conditions, and conditions are political decisions written as technical definitions. A market maker will provide liquidity only if it can hedge, fund inventory, and trust settlement. If sanctions or controls impair any of those, liquidity supply collapses at the margin, and marginal collapse is where price gaps form. The public calls the gap irrational. The machine recognizes it as the removal of a funding option. When the funding option disappears, forced behavior replaces choice. Forced behavior is predictable and expensive.

The first battlefield is settlement access. Settlement is the moment a promise becomes enforceable, and enforceable promises are the raw material of leverage. If settlement is threatened, counterparties stop extending term funding because they cannot be sure they will receive deliverable collateral on deadline. A threatened settlement path transforms a credit line into a short line, and short lines are how crises start. Settlement threats can be explicit through prohibitions, or implicit through administrative friction, enhanced due diligence, and slow approvals that turn normal delivery cycles into uncertain cycles. Uncertain cycles widen haircuts because haircuts price the risk of being trapped.

The second battlefield is clearing and netting. Clearing reduces gross exposures and makes large-scale trading possible. If access to clearing is restricted, exposures become bilateral again, and bilateral exposures consume more capital, more margin, and more trust. The system becomes smaller because fewer balance sheets can carry the same risk. Smaller systems are more volatile because depth disappears. Exclusion from clearing acts like a shrink ray on market capacity. Even partial exclusion changes liquidity broadly because hedges are harder to place and inventory becomes more dangerous to hold.

The third battlefield is collateral eligibility. Sanctions and controls operate by redefining what collateral is acceptable, either by legal prohibition or by risk policy response. A claim that was good collateral yesterday becomes questionable today. Once questionable, it is haircuted. Once haircuted, it is funded less. Once funded less, it is sold. The sell pressure is not about belief. It is about margin. This is how political decisions become price cascades without needing any change in fundamentals. A state targeting an adversary does not need to persuade investors that the adversary is weak. It needs to make the adversary's claims difficult to fund. Difficulty of funding is weakness in a leveraged system.

The fourth battlefield is the currency gate. Convertibility is access. If convertibility is stable, domestic claims can be held through volatility because exit is possible without panic. If convertibility is unstable, holders rush to exit early, because early exit is safer than late exit. That rush drains reserves. Reserve drain increases convertibility fear. Convertibility fear deepens the rush. Controls may slow the rush mechanically, yet they also change the psychology of future holders, who price the probability of being trapped. That probability makes future domestic duration expensive, and expensive duration forces projects to borrow externally, which increases mismatch, which increases future control pressure.

Geopolitical leverage emerges when one state can influence another state's access to the rails that clear and fund global trade. The leverage is not only over a targeted issuer. It is over the targeted nation's confidence cycle. If external access is uncertain, domestic institutions shorten term, hoard liquidity, and reduce credit. Reduced credit slows growth. Slower growth weakens fiscal capacity. Weak fiscal capacity raises sovereign spreads. Higher spreads make external financing more expensive. The external statecraft tool becomes domestic austerity through the mechanism of funding.

This is why sanctions are most effective against systems that rent their market functions. A nation that depends on external clearing, external custodians, external correspondent networks, and external reserve currency funding has multiple choke points. Each choke point can be tightened by law or by compliance behavior. A nation with deep domestic rails can still be pressured, but it can internalize more refinancing and sustain more settlement domestically, buying time to adapt. Time is what sanctions seek to deny. Domestic depth is what buys it back.

The politics of liquidity is not only cross-border. It is also internal because every control regime creates insiders and outsiders. Insiders are those with official access, favored custody, and permitted conversion pathways. Outsiders are those who cannot hedge, cannot convert, and cannot exit. The internal distribution matters because it shapes legitimacy. If households and small firms perceive that insiders can exit while they are trapped, political pressure rises. Rising pressure increases the probability of abrupt policy moves. Abrupt policy moves increase market fear. Market fear increases outflow attempts. Outflow attempts increase control tightening. Tightening deepens the insider-outsider divide.

The market response to access politics is always to reprice optionality. If an investor believes exit is uncertain, the investor demands compensation up front. Compensation can be higher yield, tighter covenants, foreign currency clauses, offshore escrow, external arbitration, and step-in rights. Each clause is a private substitute for public trust. As these clauses accumulate, the domestic market becomes less sovereign, because more financing becomes governed by external rulebooks. Attempts to protect sovereignty through controls can increase the use of external protection in contracts, reducing sovereignty in the next financing round.

A state therefore faces a non-romantic problem: decide which access restrictions are worth the long-term trust cost. If the objective is short-term stability, controls can work. If the objective is domestic duration and market independence, controls must be narrowly targeted, time-limited, rule-bound, and paired with credibility-building reforms reducing the need for future restrictions. Sanctions operate similarly. If sanctions are applied without clarity, they create uncertainty that fragments liquidity and incentivizes substitutes. If sanctions are applied with precise definitions and credible enforcement, they can be a strong lever. The lever remains strong only if the sanctioning state preserves the integrity of its own rulebook, because rulebooks are the source of market power.

The decisive lesson is that access is not a footnote to markets. Access is the market. Who gets liquidity is who gets time. Who gets time is who gets survival. And survival is the ultimate pricing input, because every balance sheet will pay a premium to avoid being the last holder of a promise when the rails are pulled away.

"Geopolitical power is the ability to decide which promises remain financeable."

The paired cascade locks the symmetry between external exclusion and internal trapping by showing the same mechanism in two directions: access removed from outside, and access restricted from within.

The sanction rumor cascade begins as possibility and ends as a sovereign spread blowout because compliance turns possibility into action before law becomes reality. A rumor circulates that settlement access for a set of entities will be restricted or that clearing membership could be revoked. Institutions treat rumor as risk because the penalty for misjudging compliance is existential. Compliance de-risking begins immediately: new trades are paused, maturities are shortened, positions are reduced, and counterparties are reclassified as high friction even if no prohibition has been published.

Funding desks translate de-risking into collateral policy. Collateral tied to the rumor becomes harder to accept because delivery and seizure may become contested. Haircuts jump, not because the issuer's cash flows changed, but because the collateral's deliverability is now uncertain. Higher haircuts force leveraged holders to post cash or sell. Forced selling widens spreads. Wider spreads reduce liquidity.

Dealers respond by withdrawing inventory because inventory has become settlement-risk inventory and funding-risk inventory at once. Inventory withdrawal removes the stabilizing layer that usually absorbs flows. With no warehouse, every sell order becomes price impact. Price impact becomes mark-to-market loss. Mark-to-market loss triggers further margin. Margin triggers more selling.

Sovereign spreads blow out as the system prices that access to the rails has become conditional and that rollover calendars may fail under compliance pressure. The spread widening is not only about default probability. It is about permission probability: the chance that financeability itself is impaired by external restriction. The rumor has become a funding event, and the funding event has become a sovereign repricing.

The domestic control cascade begins as "protection" and ends as domestic duration collapse because segmented convertibility turns every long claim into a trap risk. Controls are introduced to defend reserves and prevent panic: approvals for outflows, multiple exchange rates, holding periods, restrictions on derivatives, special lanes for certain firms. Convertibility becomes segmented. Segmentation creates a hierarchy of exit.

Investors respond by demanding private substitutes for the now-uncertain public exit. Offshore clause inflation follows immediately in new contracts: foreign currency payment terms, offshore escrow, external arbitration, tighter covenants, step-in rights, and collateral posted outside the jurisdiction where possible. Domestic issuers that cannot offer these clauses are punished with higher yields and shorter tenors because holders price the probability of being trapped.

Domestic duration collapses because long-term local-currency claims require a belief that exit and enforcement remain rule-governed in stress. Segmented convertibility destroys that belief. Household savings shorten further into cash-like instruments and informal hedges. Institutions avoid long paper or demand indexation that transfers risk to the state. The curve cannot lengthen. Projects cannot be financed on domestic time. External dependence deepens. The state has used control to buy immediate stability and has paid for it by raising the long-term cost of trust.

The symmetry is the same machine: access uncertainty becomes haircut inflation, haircut inflation becomes inventory withdrawal, inventory withdrawal becomes spread widening, and spread widening becomes a regime premium that compresses duration. External exclusion and internal trapping differ in motive and rhetoric. They converge in outcome because markets price the same variable in both cases: the probability that a claim will remain financeable on deadline.

CHAPTER 42

WHO WRITES THE RULES

STANDARD-SETTING, LOBBYING, AND THE STRUGGLE OVER MARKET DESIGN.

Rules do not arrive from the sky. They arrive from rooms where incentives are clearer than principles, where technical language is used because technical language is defensible, and where the boundary between safety and advantage is negotiated line by line. A market's rulebook is often described as neutral oversight imposed on a preexisting system. In reality, the rulebook is the system, and whoever shapes its definitions shapes the distribution of cost, speed, proof, and survival. The deepest power in markets is therefore not the ability to trade faster. It is the ability to decide what counts as a trade, what counts as an error, what counts as a fair price, what counts as final, and what counts as acceptable collateral.

The first truth is that standard-setting is an allocation process. A standard looks like a harmonization tool: unify formats, unify timestamps, unify disclosures, unify settlement routines. The visible benefit is interoperability. The hidden output is advantage concentration, because interoperability always chooses a baseline, and baselines privilege the actors whose systems already match the baseline. If the baseline assumes high-frequency timestamp precision, the actors already operating at that precision gain a compliance edge. If the baseline assumes a particular reporting schema, the actors already collecting that schema gain a cost edge. If the baseline assumes a certain custody and identifier architecture, the actors already embedded in that architecture gain a legal edge. The public sees orderly markets. The machine sees a cost shift and a market-share shift hidden inside a technical upgrade.

Rule writing begins with problem framing, because the definition of the problem determines which solution is possible. If the framed problem is retail protection, the solution space points toward disclosure, execution quality, conflicts, and broker obligations. If the framed problem is systemic risk, the solution space points toward margins, haircuts, default waterfalls, and liquidity facilities. If the framed problem is market competitiveness, the solution space points toward venue rules, tick sizes, auctions, and data distribution. Each framing is defensible. Each framing privileges different constituencies. The key political move is therefore not the rule text. It is the agenda: what is declared urgent, what is declared solvable, and what is treated as beyond scope.

Once framing is set, the second truth appears: technical committees are where lobbying becomes legitimate. Lobbying does not need bribes to work. It works through expertise supply, drafting assistance, impact studies, operational risk warnings, and compliance cost estimates that sound objective because they are presented as engineering constraints. The standard-setting process depends on knowledge, and knowledge is unevenly distributed. The actors with deep operational detail can convincingly argue that a rule is impossible, or that a rule will break liquidity, or that a rule will increase systemic risk, even when the real effect is that a rule will compress their edge. The committee must choose between two fears: the fear of doing too little and being blamed for the next failure, and the fear of doing too much and being blamed for breaking liquidity. That fear is the lever sophisticated actors pull.

The third truth is that the rulebook is written in thresholds, and thresholds are where power hides. A threshold defines who is inside and who is outside: which trades must be reported, which venues qualify, which participants are systemic, which instruments are liquid, which firms must hold additional capital, which disclosures are material, which delays are reasonable, which conflicts are manageable. Every threshold creates a discontinuity. Discontinuities are monetizable because they create cliffs: comply and gain cheaper funding, fail and lose eligibility. The largest actors do not only comply. They position their business models so that thresholds become moats around them. Smaller actors face the threshold as a tax.

The fourth truth is that rule writing is often a contest between public truth and operational truth. Public truth is the story required for legitimacy: fairness, transparency, resilience, broad access. Operational truth is the constraint required for continuity: systems must run, trades must settle, inventories must fund, defaults must close out, and the day must end with final records. When public truth is pursued without operational truth, rule changes produce cliffs that trigger haircuts, forced selling, and issuance freezes. When operational truth is pursued without public truth, the system becomes an extraction machine protected by complexity, and legitimacy breaks. The people writing rules are therefore managing a political balance with a technical instrument.

The fifth truth is that the rulebook's real authors are often a triangle rather than a single authority. One corner is the public authority that owns legitimacy and enforcement power. One corner is the infrastructure layer that owns the rails: clearing, settlement, custody, and the operational vocabulary that defines what is feasible. One corner is the largest intermediaries who own the flow and the data that reveals how markets actually behave. When these corners agree, rule changes look inevitable and rapid. When they disagree, rule changes stall, get diluted, or get redirected into pilot programs and voluntary guidance that preserve discretion. The triangle's internal bargaining determines which reforms arrive as hard law and which arrive as soft commitments.

A rule does not become real when it is published. It becomes real when it becomes enforceable at scale without destroying continuity. This is why implementation details often matter more than the moral banner. The key fights cluster in four implementation zones: timing, data, liability, exemptions. Timing decides whether the market must adapt quickly or can adapt gradually. Data decides whether transparency is baseline or a premium lane. Liability decides who pays when the rule is wrong or when compliance fails. Exemptions decide who can route around the rule while appearing compliant. Each zone is where lobbying concentrates because each zone determines the rule's economic meaning.

The timing zone is where a rule becomes either architecture or a shock. A fast compliance deadline forces immediate system change and creates a first-mover advantage for those already prepared. A long compliance timeline reduces disruption but allows incumbents to restructure products to preserve edge under the new rule. Timing is often justified as industry readiness. In practice it is the budget schedule of the largest actors. If implementation is rushed, smaller firms fail compliance and exit. If implementation is slow, incumbents capture the compliance consulting market and convert the rule into a moat. Timing is therefore not neutral. It is a market structure decision.

The data zone is where transparency becomes political economy. If the rule mandates consolidated baseline data access, the system moves toward broad visibility and more competitive pricing. If the rule mandates reporting but allows commercialization of speed and depth, the system produces a two-tier truth: a public version that is slow and thin, and a premium version that is fast and rich. The premium version becomes the real market for those who can afford it, while the public version becomes the legitimacy layer. A rule can claim transparency while leaving the edge intact by allowing the edge to live in latency, depth granularity, and packaging. This is how a system can satisfy public demands for openness and still preserve a profitable asymmetry economy.

The liability zone is where resilience is priced. If a rule expands reporting and surveillance but liability for errors remains ambiguous, intermediaries respond by widening risk buffers, raising haircuts, and limiting participation to clients they can control tightly. If liability is clear and bounded, intermediaries can price compliance as a routine cost rather than as an existential risk. Liability architecture is therefore a participation architecture. Excessive liability concentrates the system into a small club. Unbounded ambiguity creates fear and withdrawal during stress. The rule writer's job is not to eliminate risk. It is to assign it predictably so that markets do not become fragile under the weight of their own caution.

The exemption zone is where capture is most efficient because it can be defended as practicality. Exemptions are not always corruption. Some are necessary to avoid breaking critical functions. Yet exemptions are also where the rule's economic meaning can be hollowed out. An exemption can allow a privileged routing channel, a privileged reporting delay, a privileged collateral treatment, or a privileged capital calculation that makes an actor's balance sheet cheaper than competitors'. The public sees a rule passed. The machine sees who is exempt and therefore who still controls the speed and the rent.

The struggle over market design is therefore a struggle over who pays the cost of stability and who collects the rent of complexity. Stability has costs: margin, capital buffers, surveillance, standardized data, enforcement. Complexity has profits: fee layers, premium visibility lanes, contractual optionality. Rule writers decide where the costs land and where the profits accumulate. This decision is often justified as efficiency. Efficiency means minimizing disruption while preserving liquidity. The danger is that preserving liquidity becomes the universal veto, because any rule that reduces an incumbent edge will be described as a threat to liquidity. The only defense against that veto is proof: evidence that liquidity can be preserved through alternative designs, and evidence that the costs of the current design are not merely private profits but public fragility.

The most durable rule changes bind discretion, unify baseline truth, and force the system to internalize the costs it previously pushed outward. Binding discretion means intervention powers have thresholds, documentation, automatic review, so orderly markets cannot be used as a blank check. Unifying baseline truth means the public record is good enough that smaller participants can verify outcomes without buying survival-grade premium tools. Internalizing costs means those who generate systemic risk through leverage and speed carry predictable buffers rather than expecting emergency rescues. These changes reduce the extraction advantage of complexity while preserving continuity. They are resisted precisely because they threaten the rents of the current architecture.

The standards committee micro-episode shows how a neutral-sounding baseline change can reallocate market share without changing a single headline rule about fairness. A committee convenes to "harmonize reporting." The proposal is a new baseline schema for trade and quote reporting, justified as improving auditability and reconstruction. The schema requires richer fields, tighter timestamp precision, and standardized identifier mapping that assumes modern infrastructure. Large firms support the change and offer drafting help because their systems already emit the fields and already reconcile identifiers at scale. Smaller firms warn about cost and ask for simplified modes. The chair frames simplification as risk: incomplete fields would "harmonize uncertainty," and uncertainty would "increase systemic risk."

The vote passes with a transition timeline that sounds generous and is economically lethal. The largest firms absorb the compliance work as routine. Smaller firms must buy new systems, hire specialists, and pay for data reconciliation services. Some fail audits. Some withdraw from certain activities. The baseline schema becomes a compliance moat. The cost shift changes market structure quietly: fewer small market makers, more concentration, wider spreads in less liquid names, and higher reliance on the dominant infrastructure vendors that can certify schema compliance. The standard is advertised as interoperability. Its economic output is consolidation, achieved through a document template.

The post-crisis rewrite micro-episode shows how the phrase preserve liquidity becomes a veto that decides who writes the rules after the public demands change. A shock occurs, losses become visible, and policymakers promise reform. Draft language circulates to narrow conflicts, mandate baseline data access, and shorten correction windows so the public record becomes more trustworthy. Industry response is immediate and disciplined: "liquidity will be harmed." The phrase is backed by impact studies projecting wider spreads and higher costs for retail. The studies are not fabrications. They are partial truths, because they model the short-run adjustment cost and ignore the long-run cost of a two-tier market where premium lanes control outcomes.

Hearings follow. The final text preserves the moral headline, but the implementation zones reveal the author. The data mandate becomes "reporting required," while distribution remains commercialized in speed and granularity. The conflict rules include exemptions justified as operational necessity. The correction window is bounded, but exceptions allow "manual review" during volatile periods. The reforms are real enough to calm public anger and not real enough to compress incumbent advantage. Liquidity has been preserved, but so has the toll economy. The public sees reform. The machine sees continuity of the rent layer.

The paired cascade makes the mechanism legible as a repeatable pattern rather than as an isolated political drama.

Framing choice → draft language → threshold → exemption → balance sheet migration → market structure outcome. A committee declares the urgent problem to be systemic risk rather than access inequity. Draft language centers on margins, haircuts, and eligibility. Thresholds define which participants are "systemic" and which instruments are "liquid." Exemptions are granted to preserve critical functions, and the exemptions align with the largest actors' business models. Banks and dealers rotate balance sheets toward exempt instruments and away from taxed ones. Liquidity concentrates where the exemptions and eligibility tiers point. Market structure outcome follows: deeper liquidity in the favored lane, thinner liquidity elsewhere, and a system that is "stable" on paper while becoming more concentrated and therefore more politically fragile.

Public scandal → impact study → implementation timeline → data commercialization → two-tier truth. A scandal exposes manipulation or conflict. Public anger demands transparency. An impact study warns that rapid transparency will "harm liquidity," shifting focus from baseline truth to operational continuity. Implementation timelines extend, and extensions advantage incumbents who can adapt first. Data reporting becomes mandatory, but distribution remains commercialized through speed, packaging, and premium access. Two-tier truth emerges: a public record sufficient for legitimacy and a premium record required for survival. The scandal produces reform language and preserves the asymmetry economy.

CHAPTER 43

CAPTURE, CONCENTRATION, AND THE LEGITIMACY CRISIS

WHEN FINANCIAL POWER OUTGROWS DEMOCRATIC ACCOUNTABILITY.

CHAPTER 44

CAPTURE, CONCENTRATION, AND THE LEGITIMACY CRISIS

WHEN FINANCIAL POWER OUTGROWS DEMOCRATIC ACCOUNTABILITY.

Capture is not a conspiracy. It is an equilibrium in a system where complexity is a moat, compliance is a weapon, and stability is the universal argument that ends debates. Concentration is not an accident. It is what happens when the cost of operating at the frontier of speed, data, collateral, and legal admissibility rises faster than the capacity of smaller participants to keep up. The legitimacy crisis begins when the public can feel the outputs of that equilibrium even if it cannot name the inputs: fees that look like inevitability, volatility that looks like fate, bailouts that look like favoritism, and markets that appear to rise while the median's balance sheet does not.

Capture forms when market functions that should behave like public rails become private toll points. The toll can be explicit, like fees and data subscriptions. The toll can be embedded, like adverse selection against participants who cannot buy visibility and cannot finance inventory cheaply. The toll can be legal, like contract clauses that shift disputes outside domestic courts. The toll can be procedural, like rule-writing processes that require expertise and staffing only large incumbents can afford. Once toll points exist, the system learns to route value toward the owners of the toll points because every other actor must pay to survive.

Concentration accelerates because finance is a scale business at the margin. The marginal advantage comes from combining three capabilities: inventory funding, information advantage, privileged access to the rulebook's exemptions. Inventory funding depends on collateral eligibility and repo reach. Information advantage depends on data depth, latency, reconstruction tools. Exemptions depend on thresholds and who can claim critical function status. A large actor does not need perfection across all three. It needs to be good enough to force others to transact on its terms. Those terms compound into more volume, more data, more funding confidence, therefore more power.

The public-facing story claims competition. The machine behind the story is a set of concentration loops. The liquidity loop concentrates flow where spreads are tight, spreads are tight where inventory is funded cheaply, inventory is funded cheaply where collateral is clean and settlement is final, and finality is most credible where dominant infrastructure sits. The data loop concentrates advantage where volume creates better reconstruction and faster inference. The compliance loop concentrates power where fixed compliance cost rises faster than smaller participants can amortize.

Capture becomes visible when the rulebook protects incumbents under the language of resilience. Resilience is real. It is also pliable. A proposal reducing fee power is framed as threatens liquidity. A proposal unifying baseline truth is framed as creates operational risk. A proposal tightening conflicts is framed as reduces market making. A proposal reducing premium-lane advantage is framed as discourages innovation. Each argument contains a technical truth and an economic agenda. The agenda is that stability costs are borne broadly and stability rents are collected narrowly.

Legitimacy fails when the public observes asymmetry in two places: loss allocation and access allocation. Loss allocation is the moment the system decides whose mistakes remain private. Access allocation is the moment the system decides who gets time in a crisis. Time is liquidity. Time is the ability to avoid selling at the worst moment. Time is the ability to refinance rather than default. Time is the ability to negotiate rather than capitulate. If the public sees that large actors consistently get time while smaller actors are forced into fire sales, the public concludes that markets are privilege machines.

Concentration changes what market outcome means. In a dispersed system, prices are the aggregate of many independent judgments. In a concentrated system, prices become the output of a smaller number of constrained balance sheets managing inventory under margin rules, risk limits, and funding conditions. Those balance sheets can stabilize for long periods and then withdraw suddenly when constraints bind. Withdrawal looks like panic. It is often rational derisking by a small club that holds the warehouse of liquidity. When the warehouse shuts, everyone else discovers they were renting depth.

The legitimacy problem is that the public hears two stories that cannot both be true. One story says markets are efficient and self-correcting. The other says the system must be protected because it is too complex and too fragile to be left alone. When the system is profitable, efficiency is celebrated. When it is threatened, fragility is emphasized and rescue is demanded. The public reads this as hypocrisy because it sees upside privatized and downside socialized. Even when rescue is justified to prevent systemic collapse, the pattern creates resentment because rescue often protects the institutions most responsible for scale-driven fragility while allowing smaller actors to fail without ceremony.

Capture colonizes language. Innovation becomes shorthand for business models built on informational choke points. Liquidity becomes shorthand for preserving profitability of intermediaries who sell immediacy. Transparency becomes shorthand for public reporting too slow and too shallow to equalize outcomes. Choice becomes shorthand for a fragmented market where routing is paid for, not optimized for end users. When language is captured, reform becomes harder because critics debate on incumbent terrain.

The legitimacy crisis grows when the median's lived experience contradicts the market's scoreboard. Asset prices can rise while wages stagnate. Indices can rise while affordability collapses. Corporate financing conditions can be easy while household credit is tight. These divergences have many causes, yet market structure contributes through extraction and allocation bias. Extraction siphons value through fee stacks, premium lanes, toll points. Allocation bias finances actors easiest to trade, easiest to collateralize, easiest to mark, rather than actors maximizing broad productivity and broad household stability.

Concentration creates a policy trap. When a small number of institutions dominate clearing, custody, liquidity provision, benchmark setting, the state becomes dependent on them to maintain continuity. Dependence changes bargaining power. Reforms threatening incumbent profitability are framed as threats to stability, and stability is the state's responsibility. Compromise accumulates. The system learns it can extract concessions by invoking systemic risk. The public learns that democracy can change slogans but not the financial constitution.

Capture is explicit in data, clearing, benchmarks. Data is proof. Proof is power. If premium proof is required to trade safely, access is stratified by budget. Clearing is finality. Finality is survival. If membership and margin terms are privileged, time is allocated by institutional status. Benchmarks are definitions. Definitions are allocation. If methodologies create forced flows and those flows can be anticipated and harvested by the best-equipped, passive becomes a predictable transfer mechanism from the less-equipped to the best-equipped.

The legitimacy crisis becomes political when it triggers populist backlash and technocratic backlash. Populist backlash demands punishment, caps, visible redistribution. Technocratic backlash demands tighter rules, better surveillance, more resilient plumbing. Both can be justified. Both can fail if they treat symptoms rather than architecture. Populist backlash can create rule shocks that reduce duration and push financing offshore, increasing dependence. Technocratic backlash can entrench incumbents if it raises compliance cost without unifying baseline truth and without reducing toll points. Reform that ignores concentration can increase it by increasing fixed cost.

The path from legitimacy crisis to systemic risk is straightforward. Public faith declines, political pressure rises for abrupt intervention, abrupt intervention increases rule uncertainty, rule uncertainty raises haircuts and shortens funding, shorter funding increases rollover fragility, rollover fragility increases crisis frequency, crisis frequency increases rescue probability, rescue probability increases moral hazard and leverage, leverage increases the size of the next crisis. Legitimacy is an internal stability condition because legitimacy allows rule changes to be gradual rather than violent.

The system's defense is partly true: concentration can create efficiencies, standardization, resilience investment. Large infrastructures can fund surveillance and continuity tools. They can also become chokepoints. The legitimacy question is whether efficiencies are shared as lower costs and broader access, or captured as tolls that make participation conditional on buying survival-grade visibility and funding.

A practical diagnostic of legitimacy is not what the rulebook says. It is who can participate without buying privilege. If a small institution can execute without being systematically selected against, if a household can hold domestic claims without being trapped by discretionary controls, if a mid-sized issuer can list without being extorted by gatekeepers, if a default can be processed without improvisation that protects the powerful, legitimacy can be rebuilt. If participation requires paying tolls only the largest can afford, the market becomes a political problem regardless of technical sophistication.

The fundamental tension is that markets need authority and fear authority. Authority enforces finality, prevents manipulation, allocates loss. Authority is feared when it is captured, discretionary, or sold as a service. The solution is not removing authority. The solution is binding it, making baseline truth broadly available, constraining conversion of infrastructure into toll points. Without those moves, concentration deepens because it is the equilibrium outcome of a complex leveraged system where proof and funding are scarce and monetizable.

"Legitimacy is the hidden collateral of the market."

When legitimacy holds, the system absorbs volatility because participants believe losses are allocated by procedure rather than privilege. When legitimacy breaks, the system becomes fragile because every shock becomes a referendum on fairness, and referenda are not settled by clearinghouses.

The compliance-as-moat cascade shows how a stability reform can deepen concentration even when no one intends capture. A new rule is issued to improve reporting fidelity and reduce manipulation: richer fields, tighter timestamps, stricter reconciliation, higher penalties for misstatement. The rule raises fixed cost, not variable cost. Large actors treat fixed cost as infrastructure investment. Smaller actors treat it as existential overhead because they cannot spread it across enough flow. Small exit follows quietly. Some firms stop making markets in less liquid names because compliance cost per trade becomes too high. Some reduce coverage. Some merge. Volume concentrates among the actors able to pay the fixed cost. Data advantage compounds because volume creates better reconstruction and better inference about flow. Concentrated actors now see more, earlier, cleaner, and can price spreads aggressively where they want to win and widen where they want to deter entry. Spreads widen for everyone else because segments left behind lose competition. The public experiences this as fragmentation. The mechanism is concentration produced by a fixed-cost jump.

The rescue-as-privilege cascade shows how time allocation in a stress event hardens the legitimacy break even if the rescue is justified. A stress spike hits and volatility rises. Margin requirements jump. Funding desks raise haircuts. Liquidity becomes expensive precisely when it is needed most. Selective liquidity arrives through access hierarchies: actors with privileged facility access, best collateral, strongest settlement chains obtain funding and hold inventory. Outsiders face tightened lines, margin calls, rollover refusals. Forced selling for outsiders follows because outsiders cannot buy time. Their selling pushes prices down. Insiders with time buy discounted inventory or simply avoid selling into the trough because they can fund. The rebound arrives as conditions normalize, and insiders benefit disproportionately because they were not forced to liquidate at the worst moment. Political backlash follows because the public sees the shape of privilege. Backlash increases the probability of blunt interventions. Those interventions raise a rule shock premium that shows up as wider spreads, shorter term, higher haircuts, less willingness to finance duration. The system becomes less stable because legitimacy becomes a pricing input.

The counterclaim and rebuttal can be stated as a technical argument rather than a moral accusation. The defense of concentration is that scale can finance surveillance, standardization, continuity: large infrastructures can build better monitoring, stronger default waterfalls, faster settlement operations. Concentration can reduce coordination failure by making the rulebook simpler to enforce. The rebuttal is that these efficiencies do not solve legitimacy unless baseline truth is public and tolls are bounded. If surveillance and standardization are funded by selling premium truth, participation is stratified and the public lane becomes ceremonial. If continuity tools allocate time preferentially without transparent rules, rescue becomes privilege. In both cases the system buys stability at the price of political fragility, and political fragility feeds back into financial fragility through rule-shock risk and duration collapse. Efficiency without bounded rent and broad access is a delayed legitimacy crisis.

The repair path sequence shows how legitimacy can be rebuilt as an architecture project rather than as a rhetorical campaign. Baseline truth reform arrives first: make core data usable without premium lanes, unify the public record so that smaller participants can verify prints and reconstruct events, shorten correction windows under clear authority, publish status tagging that reduces guesswork. Toll compression follows because the market's survival tools are less gated: if baseline proof is strong, the premium lane becomes improvement rather than requirement. With toll compression, broader market making becomes viable again because smaller dealers can compete without being systematically selected against by visibility deficit. Broader market making tightens spreads in neglected segments and reduces the concentration of liquidity in a small club.

Lower haircuts follow because collateral becomes more admissible when records are cleaner and disputes are rarer. Lower haircuts lengthen funding, which lengthens the system's time horizon. Longer duration becomes financeable, not because fear vanished, but because the system can process failure routinely without improvisation. Reduced dependence premium follows because domestic duration reduces the need for foreign-unit clauses and external enforcement in project finance. Repair becomes sovereignty because repair restores the ability to finance time domestically.

The internal politics sequence shows why legitimacy is a statecraft constraint rather than a side effect. Public outrage rises after a rescue episode and concentrates on the perception of privilege. Legislators threaten blunt interventions: punitive caps, forced levies, retroactive changes, discretionary bans. Regulators respond by widening discretion to show responsiveness, accelerating enforcement, and promising "toughness." Discretion shift increases rule uncertainty because participants cannot predict how the new posture will be applied across firms and events. Rule uncertainty raises haircuts because haircuts price the risk of being trapped in ambiguity during a dispute. Funding terms shorten. Shorter terms increase rollover fragility. Rollover fragility tightens credit to the real economy as banks and dealers conserve liquidity. The outrage that began as politics becomes a tightening cycle through the mechanism of rule uncertainty. Legitimacy is therefore a funding variable because it determines whether reform can be sequenced as architecture or arrives as shock.

The stress-day contrast makes privilege allocation visible in motion by holding the shock constant and changing only access to time. The same volatility spike hits at the open. A large intermediary with privileged facility access meets margin calls by pledging eligible collateral at known terms, funds inventory, and continues quoting wider spreads. A smaller intermediary without the same facility access faces the same margin call and cannot roll funding. It sells inventory into a thin book to raise cash, widening spreads further and deepening its losses. The large intermediary buys selectively or simply survives without forced sale. By the close, the large intermediary has preserved capital and market position. The smaller intermediary has shrunk or exited. The rulebook did not need to announce favoritism. Favoritism emerged from the access hierarchy that allocated time. The public sees "markets are volatile." The machine sees "time was distributed unevenly."

CHAPTER 45

THE PUBLIC-INTEREST MARKET

A DESIGN THAT PRESERVES LIQUIDITY WITHOUT SELLING THE RULEBOOK TO THE STRONGEST.

A public-interest market is not a moral aspiration layered on top of finance. It is a market architecture that treats liquidity as a public good and treats extraction as a stability risk. The premise is simple and unpopular among those who profit from ambiguity: a market can be efficient and still illegitimate, and illegitimacy is not only a political problem. It is a funding problem because legitimacy determines whether rule changes can be sequenced as architecture or arrive as shock. A public-interest market therefore is designed to keep two promises simultaneously: continuous trading under stress and fair access to the conditions that make trading survivable.

The first design choice is baseline truth as a right, not a product. A market cannot claim broad participation if the information required to trade safely is sold as a premium lane. The public-interest design defines a minimum viable public record: consolidated prints, usable depth snapshots, authoritative corporate action calendars, standardized identifiers, and a fast correction protocol that does not require private relationships to invoke. Premium analytics can exist, but premium access cannot be the difference between being systematically selected against and being able to compete. The goal is not egalitarian outcomes. The goal is that the public lane is usable enough that competition can exist and that the legitimacy layer is not ceremonial.

The second design choice is bounded tolls. Many market services require fees. The question is whether fees are cost recovery with competitive pressure or rents protected by dependency. A public-interest design treats critical rails as utility-like: settlement, core market data, and basic connectivity are priced and governed in a way that prevents monopoly extraction. Pricing can allow investment. Pricing cannot rely on coercion created by the need to buy survival-grade access. The moment survival depends on a toll, the toll becomes a tax on participation and the market becomes a political risk.

The third design choice is explicit conflict architecture. Routing conflicts, internalization incentives, payment structures, and proprietary trading around client flow do not vanish by disclosure alone. A public-interest design makes conflicts legible and expensive. It sets outcome-based obligations: execution quality measurement, routing transparency, and penalties predictable enough to deter. It defines where internalization is allowed and where it is prohibited, not to punish intermediaries, but to prevent the system from becoming a hidden tax machine where retail and smaller institutions are the raw material.

The fourth design choice is resilience without privilege. Backstops and default management tools are necessary because markets are leveraged and failures are inevitable. The public-interest design makes these tools rule-bound and broadly accessible on published terms, with conservative haircuts and penalty pricing preventing subsidy while preventing panic. The goal is time allocation by rule, not by relationship. If a liquidity facility exists, access is defined by objective eligibility and documentation, not by institutional status alone.

The fifth design choice is fast, impartial dispute lanes. Nothing destroys legitimacy faster than slow justice that becomes selective justice. A public-interest market invests in dispute resolution as an element of liquidity. Disputes about entitlements, deliveries, liens must resolve at market speed because funding is priced in hours. A slow court is a hidden haircut. A hidden haircut is a hidden credit contraction. Fast dispute lanes keep failure routine, and routine failure allows investors to hold duration without demanding external protection.

The sixth design choice is institutional participation broad enough to stabilize and not so concentrated that it becomes sovereign. A public-interest market requires a domestic base of patient holders. These holders reduce dependence on foreign mood and reduce the need for ad hoc control. Yet the system must prevent these institutions from becoming the only meaningful participants. Broad participation is preserved by making baseline truth usable and by compressing tolls so smaller intermediaries can provide liquidity and compete. A public-interest market is not anti-scale. It is anti-singularity.

The seventh design choice is benchmark and index governance that recognizes forced flow as a rent surface. Benchmarks are useful. They are also allocation engines. A public-interest design demands governance around methodology changes, reconstitution schedules, and data transparency so forced flows do not become an unpriced transfer from the less-equipped to the best-equipped.

The eighth design choice is accountability that can survive stress. A public-interest market binds discretion through thresholds, documentation, automatic post-event review. It defines what interventions are allowed, what evidence triggers them, how long they last, and what disclosures must be made afterward. A market can tolerate intervention if intervention is symmetrical and documented. A market cannot tolerate intervention that functions as a private service.

The ninth design choice is anti-capture rulemaking. A public-interest market treats standard-setting as allocation and forces transparency on the standard-setting process itself: disclose who drafted, disclose who benefits, disclose cost shifts, publish alternative designs, require that claims of liquidity harm be tested against counterfactual designs rather than accepted as veto.

The tenth design choice is measured complexity. Complexity is sometimes necessary. It is also often profitable. A public-interest market demands that complexity be justified by function, not by rent. If a rule creates fragmentation increasing fee surfaces without improving resilience, the rule is suspect. If a data product is required to meet basic fiduciary obligations, the market has converted a public requirement into a private toll. A public-interest design treats that conversion as a stability hazard because it creates legitimacy debt that will be paid later as rule shock.

The public-interest market is not anti-profit. It is anti-extraction that creates systemic fragility. Extraction concentrates participation, stratifies access, turns volatility into resentment. Resentment turns into rule uncertainty. Rule uncertainty turns into haircut inflation and shortened funding. Shortened funding turns into rollover risk. Rollover risk turns into crisis frequency. A market that wants continuity must treat legitimacy as a funding input.

"A public-interest market does not eliminate advantage; it eliminates the advantage of being above the rules."

The design stress test sequence runs one shock through the architecture to show resilience does not require privilege. A volatility shock hits at the open and prices gap. Spreads widen, but the widening is legible because baseline depth and prints are visible enough that smaller participants are not blind. Orders route without reliance on paid-for survival lanes because the public record is usable, and execution quality obligations reduce the ability to internalize flow in ways that hide true cost.

An intermediary misses a margin deadline mid-morning. The default protocol triggers by threshold, not negotiation. Positions are frozen under published rules. Netting operates under law the system can execute at speed. Collateral is seized under clear priority. Losses are allocated through a pre-funded waterfall, and the process is communicated through authoritative status tagging so counterparties can quantify exposure. Quantification prevents hoarding because hoarding is driven by unbounded uncertainty.

Funding strains emerge as haircuts rise with volatility. The backstop facility opens on published terms, with conservative add-on haircuts and penalty pricing. Access is objective: eligible collateral, documented exposure, standardized submission. Smaller dealers with clean collateral can fund inventories without private favors, so they keep quoting rather than dumping. Because inventories remain financed, the market absorbs flow without a depth collapse.

Disputes appear over deliveries and entitlements. The fast dispute lane activates with short timelines and standardized evidence, producing determinations quickly enough that collateral does not become legally radioactive. The auction calendar holds. Auctions proceed and clear at risk-reflective levels under known rules. Close prints become authoritative marks used for margin and reporting, and the correction window is clear enough that the record does not become a rumor contest overnight. The shock leaves losses. It does not leave a legitimacy rupture, because access to time was governed by published procedure rather than club membership.

The explicit trade-off is that public-interest design is not free. Baseline truth as a right compresses some premium revenue and reduces the ability to monetize informational choke points. Bounded tolls reduce rent extraction and can slow certain private investment incentives in proprietary lanes. Rule-bound access limits discretionary flexibility, meaning officials cannot quietly tailor outcomes for powerful constituencies without leaving a record. The payoff is that the system purchases stability with procedure rather than favoritism, lowering rule-shock risk and reducing the dependence premium that appears whenever the public concludes the rulebook is for insiders. The market becomes less profitable for pure toll collectors and more sustainable for a society that needs duration, not just volume.

The capture-resistance mechanism drill is how the design avoids being hollowed out by exemptions and temporary premium lanes. Sunset architecture forces any exemption or special lane to expire unless renewed under published evidence thresholds and public cost accounting. Baseline-truth non-degradation prevents quiet starving of the public lane by requiring higher process thresholds to reduce baseline quality than to improve it. Exemption impact disclosure requires every exemption to map who benefits, who pays, and how structure shifts. Proof parity forces survival-grade proof into baseline when it becomes necessary for fiduciary execution. Post-stress audits publish facility usage and access patterns so time allocation can be monitored as an output rather than trusted as a promise.

The failure mode sequence shows why this design must be defended continuously and why capture tends to return through the easiest fracture line: baseline truth. Baseline feeds are quietly degraded by slower updates, thinner depth, and broader correction windows justified as cost savings. Premium products fill the gap and become survival again. Smaller participants cannot compete without purchasing premium truth, so they exit or narrow activity. Market making concentrates. Concentration widens spreads in neglected segments and increases the system's dependence on a small inventory club. A stress event then allocates time through that club's access, and the legitimacy debt returns because the public lane is revealed to be ceremonial. The architecture did not fail because its principles were wrong. It failed because one pillar was allowed to rot, and the system predictably routed back into toll-based survival.

The measurement dashboard is how the public-interest market proves performance without relying on rhetoric. The indicators are concrete and operational. Haircut dispersion across participants and products, because high dispersion signals privileged access and hidden segmentation. Facility access concentration, because a backstop used by a narrow set is privilege in practice. Dispute resolution time distribution, because slow dispute tails become hidden haircuts. Share of volume executed with baseline feeds as the primary reference, because two-tier truth shows up as low baseline usability. Issuance calendar stability through volatility episodes, because consistent auctions are credibility in action. Spread compression in neglected names, because broad market making is a legitimacy signal. Retail execution slippage versus benchmarks, because conflicts reveal themselves in outcomes. Rule-exemption count and renewal frequency, because exemption growth is capture growth.

The transition plan is how to migrate from today's toll-heavy architecture without triggering a cliff. First, phase data unbundling: expand the baseline record in defined increments with published milestones, while limiting premium advantages in latency and depth so that baseline truth becomes usable before premium lanes are constrained. Second, publish facility rules and eligibility in advance, then open access by objective criteria with penalty pricing, so time is allocated by rule rather than by relationship. Third, create the fast dispute lane early and pilot it on narrow cases, because dispute speed is what prevents collateral from becoming radioactive during change. Fourth, impose exemption sunsets with a staged schedule and require impact disclosures before renewals, so capture cannot hide inside "temporary" carve-outs. Fifth, measure and publish the dashboard continuously so that the system can detect early degradation before it becomes a legitimacy break. The goal of the transition is not to punish incumbents. It is to remove cliff risk by sequencing upgrades so that improvements in truth and access arrive before restrictions on premium survival, preventing forced selling and preventing the market from learning that reform equals instability.

PART SEVEN

MARKET INSTRUMENTS MONEY THEORY

THE EXCHANGE AS A NATIONAL SETTLEMENT RAIL, AND THE PUBLIC RULES THAT DECIDE WHO CAN TURN ASSETS INTO TIME.

A society already lives inside a hidden money system built from market instruments. Institutions fund themselves against bonds, borrow against equities, margin portfolios against marks, and treat eligible paper as time because eligibility is what converts an asset into borrowing capacity. Households see ownership and returns. The machine sees collateral schedules, haircuts, variation margin, netting, close-out, and the daily discipline of marks. That hidden layer is money behavior, but it is stratified behavior, because access depends on lanes: proof, funding, data, and discretion under stress. Market Instruments Money Theory is the claim that this internal money layer can be made public without turning daily life into a volatility transfer mechanism and without turning the state into an improvising referee, but only if the exchange stack is upgraded to payment grade: legally precise finality, non-duplicable proof, funded error handling, bounded disputes, and a published stress state machine that prevents time from being privatized by whisper.

Replacement must be defined precisely or it will be attacked as a strawman. This theory is not a proposal to replace the unit people think in with the daily mark of a stock. A civilization cannot price groceries in a fluctuating risk asset without transferring portfolio volatility into commerce. The replacement here is the settlement rail and liquidity access layer, meaning the mechanism by which obligations are extinguished and by which assets are converted into payment-grade closure. Prices remain posted in a stable spend unit. Settlement can be extinguished using approved market instruments through a conversion engine that absorbs mark risk and funding stress inside a governed warehouse so merchants and households are not drafted into speculation. The theory replaces the monopoly of bank balance sheets over everyday settlement with a public, exchange-settled architecture where instruments can close obligations under law, and where eligibility is governed as constitutional monetary policy rather than sold as private privilege.

"The next money is not printed; it is settled. When market instruments can close everyday obligations with payment-grade finality, the exchange becomes the rail, and eligibility becomes monetary policy."

The theory can be expressed as propositions that are both quotable and falsifiable. A market instrument becomes money-grade when it can extinguish an obligation with legally defined finality and recipient safe harbor. A money-grade regime cannot rely on discretion, because discretion is what produces panic. A money-grade regime must make proof admissible and non-duplicable at speed, because duplicated proof is counterfeit credit. A money-grade regime must fund error and fraud without breaking closure, because breaking closure recreates the wall through merchant refusal and surcharge. A money-grade regime must publish state transitions and facility criteria, because time allocation by whisper is how aristocratic money returns. A money-grade regime must treat eligibility as monetary policy, because eligibility decides which issuers become persistently liquid and which do not. A money-grade regime must treat cross-border corridors as treaty-like mutual recognition of primitives, because misalignment becomes exit-route arbitrage that fractures legitimacy. These are not slogans. Each can be tested in stress by measuring whether finality holds, whether disputes resolve within bounds, whether haircuts move within bands, whether corridors tighten by rule, and whether the public lane remains usable without premium survival.

The naive bridge fails quickly and predictably, and its failure is the incumbent's favorite exhibit. Let people pay with whatever they hold, and the checkout line becomes a mark dispute. Volatility makes the price of milk a bet. Encumbrances make transfer conditional. Settlement lag turns authorization into merchant credit. Corporate actions and correction latency turn paid into an argument. Weak authentication turns receipts into replayable fraud. The first scandal produces the first discretionary freeze, and the first discretionary freeze teaches the public the only lesson that matters: finality is negotiable. Adoption collapses, and the old system reappears as paternal safety, which is another name for dependence. Market Instruments Money Theory therefore begins with a wall-awareness: the wall between markets and payments was built to protect closure, not only to protect banks. The wall cannot be removed by interface. It can be replaced only by gates that preserve closure while allowing instruments to move as money-grade obligations.

The architecture is three-layer, because commerce cannot carry portfolio volatility and courts cannot carry ambiguous states. Layer one is the spend layer seen by daily life: prices posted in the stable unit, receipts issued as non-replayable signed evidence, completion guaranteed within a short published window, and legal finality at a defined time with safe harbor for compliant recipients. Layer two is the conversion layer where instruments are delivered and transformed: approved instruments are pledged or transferred into a conversion engine under encumbrance tags, valued by published mark doctrine with fallback hierarchies, netted where appropriate through clearing, and used to fund the stable-unit outflow to merchants. Layer three is the risk and governance layer that keeps the conversion layer from becoming discretionary: published eligibility schedules, published haircuts, published margin bands, published throttle bands, published facility access criteria, published dispute throughput targets, published correction windows, and post-event audits that prove time was allocated by criteria rather than by status. Daily life experiences layer one. Institutions price layer two. Society governs layer three.

The spend unit is not an optional detail. It is the point where a monetary theory becomes either feasible or performative. The spend unit must be stable at the horizon of commerce, which means the merchant must not be exposed to mark risk unless the merchant chooses exposure. The system can implement this by making the spend unit a stable nominal unit and making instrument spendability a conversion privilege rather than a direct merchant receipt. The payer tenders instruments to the conversion engine. The conversion engine delivers stable-unit settlement to the merchant. The conversion engine prices and absorbs the risk between instrument delivery and stable-unit settlement through published haircuts and buffers. If the payer tenders a volatile instrument, the payer bears the haircut and the conversion spread. The merchant does not. This preserves the social function of money as a stable unit for ordinary life while allowing instruments to function as settlement inputs.

Eligibility is the theory's monetary policy, because eligibility decides what can become time. An instrument can be spendable only if it is eligible to extinguish obligations under predictable rules. Eligibility is never neutral. It allocates persistent demand and therefore allocates cost of capital. In the hidden institutional system, eligibility is set by clearing rules, collateral schedules, and credit committees. In a public regime, eligibility must be governed as a constitutional object to prevent aristocratic money from re-emerging. The initial eligibility set must be conservative and legible: sovereign bills, high-grade bonds, and highly liquid, diversified listed products with robust entitlement mapping and deep markets. Equities can be eligible under tighter bands and stricter throttles because their marks move faster, their corporate actions are more frequent, and their idiosyncratic risk is higher. Eligibility must be published with haircuts and conversion limits, and amendments must require rationale, impact analysis on selection against smaller participants, transition windows, and post-implementation review. This is how eligibility becomes monetary governance rather than private privilege.

Settlement finality must be legally precise or the theory collapses. A receipt cannot be a promise that becomes an argument. It must be an admissible state transition with a defined completion window and a defined finality time. Safe harbor must protect compliant recipients after finality so commerce does not become credit. Reversals must be bounded by strict windows and strict evidence standards, and restitution must be funded so fraud and error can be corrected without clawing back from innocent recipients after finality. Without funded restitution, merchants will refuse or surcharge. Without safe harbor, merchants become insurers. Without finality, the system becomes a run machine. Market Instruments Money Theory therefore treats finality and safe harbor as the constitutional core of adoption, not as compliance details.

Proof and priority are the next core because without proof the system mints counterfeit credit through double-pledge. Beneficial ownership must be machine-legible, time-stamped, and correction-bounded, because a proof state that can be rewritten quietly is not proof; it is politics. Encumbrances must be tagged in a registry that prevents double-pledge and that survives insolvency as law, not negotiation. Priority must be defined so lien disputes do not metastasize into system-wide haircut inflation. Corporate action entitlements must be mapped deterministically so record dates cannot become dispute factories. The proof regime must be fast enough that assets remain financeable. A slow proof regime is a hidden haircut. Hidden haircuts shorten funding. Short funding destroys spendability because it forces deleveraging when commerce needs closure.

Mark governance is where the theory meets the market's reality that price is not always discovery; it is often constraint resolution. The conversion engine must value instruments using published mark sources, timestamps, fallback hierarchies, and bounded correction windows. If marks are discretionary, spendability becomes rumor-driven and adoption collapses into politics. If corrections are silent, legitimacy collapses into conspiracy. Mark doctrine must therefore be treated like a public standard with audit scars: corrections logged as events, reasons coded, and state messages published so the system's behavior can be reconstructed after stress. This is how conversion integrity survives disorder without turning marks into arguments and without making merchants carry mark uncertainty.

Fraud and authentication doctrine must be payment-grade because once instruments become spendable, fraud scales as commerce scales. The system must use tiered authentication by risk, non-replayable signed receipts, anomaly controls, velocity limits, delegated authority controls for fiduciaries, and a funded liability regime that reimburses quickly without breaking recipient safe harbor. Enforcement timing must target payer access prospectively and preserve closure for compliant recipients after finality. If the system handles fraud by breaking finality, it destroys the meaning of settlement and recreates the wall through merchant refusal. The fraud regime is therefore not a security appendix. It is a monetary condition.

The stress state machine is what makes the theory survivable against panic, sabotage, and the politics of delay. Stress modes must be defined. Throttle bands must be defined. Buffer bands must be defined. Outage behavior must be defined. Kill and restart criteria must be defined. Facility access criteria must be defined. Drills must be run and after-action audits must be published, because the incumbent counterattack will frame any incident as proof that reform is reckless, and the only defense is evidence produced faster than headlines. The system must prove that time is allocated by criteria, not by relationship, because relationship time is how aristocratic money returns under the language of stability.

Cross-border use is where the theory either becomes sovereignty or becomes arbitrage. Without primitive alignment, cross-border spendability becomes exit-route advantage: the most mobile participants route through the jurisdiction that sells time under stress, leaving domestic participants as residual risk. Cross-border therefore must be corridor-based and treaty-like, with mutual recognition of finality, custody priority, encumbrance tags, bounded remedies, mark doctrine, correction doctrine, and restriction handling, plus published corridor tightening triggers so rumors do not become runs. Corridor access must open under low limits and scale only as the corridor proves it can survive a shock without improvisation. The system must prefer slower opening over faster reputational collapse, because one corridor shock can force rollback by making the theory synonymous with being trapped.

The political and social impact of a successful regime is large precisely because money is not a neutral technology. If instruments can close obligations with payment-grade finality, the exchange becomes a civic rail and eligibility becomes monetary policy. This can democratize compounding by allowing households and small firms to convert diversified holdings into closure without renting access to prime lanes. It can reduce dependence on bank credit for routine liquidity, because settlement capacity becomes an infrastructure property rather than a relationship privilege. It can lower transaction costs that currently function as class barriers. It can also produce new politics, because a public eligibility regime allocates persistent demand and therefore reallocates cost of capital, which will trigger incumbent counterattack and pressure for capture. The theory must therefore include governance that can survive sabotage: non-degradable baseline truth, amendment safety with transition windows and audits, exception sunsets, and published evidence that the system remains one constitution rather than two.

The deployment pathway must be phased to avoid panic and to deny incumbents their best exhibit: a public failure that can be framed as proof that democratization is dangerous. The first phase is domestic-only, low-limit, conservative eligibility, payment-grade finality, proof, and disputes proven under load. The second phase expands eligibility and capacity only as dispute throughput, settlement fails, correction frequency, and execution quality remain within published bounds. The third phase opens corridors only under mutual recognition of primitives and only after the domestic regime has survived a stress year without rewriting rules. Scaling is criteria-based, not ambition-based, because ambition-based scaling is how new constitutions die and old systems regain power through fear.

To be known for introducing this theory, it must be memorable and testable. The signature formulation should be repeatable in a sentence and defensible in a hearing. One formulation that matches the book's voice and the theory's core is: the next money is not printed; it is settled. When market instruments can close obligations with payment-grade finality, the exchange becomes the rail and eligibility becomes monetary policy. That line is not marketing. It is the definition of what is being replaced and why it is governable.

What follows in this Part is the full constitution of Market Instruments Money Theory, written as implementable primitives rather than as aspiration: the spend unit and conversion engine, eligibility governance, finality and safe harbor doctrine, proof and encumbrance enforcement, mark doctrine, fraud and authentication, dispute throughput, stress state machine, corridor mutual recognition, amendment safety, deployment phases, and the falsifiable tests that can be used to certify whether the system is money-grade.it advantages that fracture legitimacy.

CHAPTER 46
THE SPEND UNIT AND THE CONVERSION HOUSE
KEEPING COMMERCE STABLE WHILE INSTRUMENTS BECOME SPENDABLE THROUGH GUARANTEED SETTLEMENT.

A monetary system is judged in grocery stores, payroll runs, fuel invoices, and rent payments, not in conference rooms. People do not care whether a ledger is elegant. They care whether a receipt is finished, whether the price they saw is the price they paid, whether a mistake can be repaired without weeks of uncertainty, and whether rules hold when fear arrives. That everyday test is why making market instruments spendable is not a clever financial product idea. It is a redesign of closure. Commerce needs a stable spend unit and legally precise finality. Markets generate volatile marks and conditional entitlements. If those worlds are fused naively, daily life becomes a volatility transfer mechanism and merchants become involuntary credit analysts. The conversion house is the structure that prevents that outcome while allowing instruments to extinguish obligations, because it contains mark risk, funding stress, and entitlement complexity inside a governed warehouse and delivers payment-grade closure to recipients in the stable spend unit.

The spend unit is not a branding choice. It is the language of prices, taxes, wages, leases, invoices, and household planning. A regime that asks households to think in fluctuating portfolio marks is not offering modernization; it is mandating speculation. Market Instruments Money Theory begins with a constitutional decision that removes the easiest objection and the most lethal failure mode: prices remain posted in the stable spend unit, and recipients receive settlement in that unit unless they explicitly elect to receive an instrument. Instruments do not replace the spend unit as the unit of account. They become acceptable inputs to settlement, meaning they can be tendered to extinguish obligations through a conversion process that absorbs volatility inside the system instead of exporting it into commerce. This single choice determines whether the idea can scale, because it decides whether the merchant is forced to carry mark risk simply to stay in business.

What makes an instrument spendable is not sentiment and not interface. It is a completion guarantee that converts tender into closure under law. The conversion house accepts eligible instruments at the edge, verifies proof and encumbrance status, values them under published mark doctrine, applies published haircuts and conversion limits, and delivers stable-unit settlement to the recipient inside a short completion window, with legal finality at a defined time under safe harbor. The payer experiences the tender of instruments as payment because completion is guaranteed. The recipient experiences payment as closure because finality is precise and legally protected. The mark movement that would otherwise break commerce is neither denied nor wished away. It is priced, buffered, and warehoused where risk belongs.

A normal-day payment flow shows why this structure is monetary rather than cosmetic. A household initiates a purchase priced in the stable spend unit. The payer selects which eligible instrument set to tender, or the system selects according to the payer's published preferences and limits. The conversion house checks eligibility at that moment, not with a vague promise; it confirms the instrument is on the published list, checks whether the instrument is encumbered beyond permitted thresholds using the encumbrance ledger, and tags the tender so the same units cannot be pledged elsewhere during the completion window. It applies the current published mark, using the defined source and timestamp, and it applies the published haircut and conversion spread for that instrument class and risk tier. The conversion house issues a non-replayable signed receipt to the payer and an admissible settlement acknowledgment to the recipient. The recipient is credited in the stable spend unit under a completion guarantee. Settlement completes within the published window, and finality occurs at the published time, triggering safe harbor for compliant recipients. Any correction is logged as an event, not silently repaired, because silence is where legitimacy dies. Any dispute is routed into a bounded lane with standardized evidence and binding timelines, because slow disputes are hidden haircuts that turn money into conditional credit.

The completion guarantee is the load-bearing beam. It cannot be a promise that depends on improvisation. It must be backed by funded resources and governed by rules. The conversion house maintains buffers sized to expected mark movement, settlement risk, and liquidity conditions of the eligible set, and it replenishes those buffers by precommitted mechanisms rather than discretionary levies. Completion guarantees are honored for compliant recipients even when the conversion house's back-end reconciliation is under stress, because commerce cannot wait for the market's full complexity to settle itself. When the system must tighten, it tightens prospectively by published bands: higher haircuts, lower conversion limits, tighter velocity caps, and narrower eligibility, all governed by thresholds that participants can price. If the guarantee is allowed to fail casually, adoption collapses because the public learns that the receipt is not closure. If the guarantee works only for the connected, adoption collapses into aristocratic money.

A conversion regime must therefore allocate risk explicitly, because hidden risk allocation is what produces political backlash. In the naive bridge, merchants carry risk by receiving volatile instruments or conditional promises. In the governed bridge, the conversion house carries risk by absorbing mark movement and funding stress between tender and stable-unit closure, then pricing that absorption through haircuts and spreads that are visible and rule-bound. The payer pays for volatility through haircut and conversion spread. The merchant is insulated unless the merchant opts into holding instruments. This allocation is not only fairer; it is structurally necessary. Merchants cannot hedge like trading desks, and they will not accept a system that forces them to. When merchants are insulated, adoption becomes plausible at scale. When merchants are exposed, adoption becomes niche and stratified, and stratification becomes political crisis the first time a downturn turns receipts into arguments.

The buffers that support the completion guarantee must be governed like critical infrastructure, because buffers are where money systems are either trusted or distrusted. Buffers are funded by conversion spreads, membership assessments, and precommitted replenishment rules, not by last-minute improvisation. The conversion house must publish the buffer policy, including how buffers are sized, what stress modes trigger higher haircuts and lower limits, and what actions follow in order when conditions worsen. It must publish the loss waterfall for conversion failures, because the market will assume the worst unless it can price the sequence. The loss waterfall must be rule-bound: first absorb losses through conversion spreads and buffer reserves, then through member contributions or pre-funded guarantee resources, then through controlled throttles and tightened eligibility, and only then through extraordinary measures that are predefined and sunset. The purpose is not to eliminate loss. The purpose is to prevent loss from being allocated by discretion, because discretionary loss allocation becomes panic.

Proof is the second foundation, because money systems fail by duplicating proof long before they fail by admitting it. When instruments are tendered to extinguish obligations, the system must prove, at speed, that the instrument is not being used twice. That means beneficial ownership states that are admissible, time-stamped, and correction-bounded, and encumbrance tags that prevent double-pledge and that survive insolvency as law rather than negotiation. It also means deterministic entitlement mapping around corporate actions so record dates do not become dispute factories. If proof is slow or contestable, haircuts rise. When haircuts rise, funding tightens. When funding tightens, the completion guarantee becomes expensive or fragile. When the guarantee becomes fragile, merchants withdraw. In other words, proof is monetary. It is not back office.

Marks are the third foundation, and they are more political than most systems admit. The conversion house must value instruments using published mark sources, timestamps, fallback hierarchies, and bounded correction windows. If marks are discretionary, conversion becomes rumor-driven and adoption collapses. If corrections are silent, legitimacy collapses into conspiracy and the incumbent counterattack gains its easiest line: the new system is untrustworthy. Mark doctrine must therefore be treated as public standard, not proprietary advantage. Corrections are logged as events with reason codes. State messages are published when the system enters disorder, when fallback marks activate, and when haircuts move within bands. This keeps valuation from becoming politics and keeps the conversion house from being forced into improvisation by headlines.

Fraud becomes existential the moment settlement becomes everyday life, because fraud scales with commerce volume and because the political system will demand reversals if fraud becomes visible enough. Reversals after finality destroy closure. A money-grade conversion house therefore requires payment-grade authentication at the edge: tiered authentication by risk, non-replayable signed receipts, anomaly detection, velocity limits, and delegated authority controls for fiduciaries so permissions cannot be quietly abused. It also requires funded restitution so fraud and error can be repaired without clawing back from compliant recipients after finality. Enforcement timing must target payer access prospectively, preserve recipient safe harbor, and reimburse quickly from funded resources while recovery is pursued through the payer channel. This is the only sustainable way to keep merchants inside the system during stress without drafting them into the risk work of the market machine.

The stress day is where credibility is made or lost, and it is also where the system's design must defeat narrative sabotage. A market shock hits and marks fracture across venues. Without doctrine, mark fracture becomes rumor, rumor becomes withdrawal, and withdrawal becomes a run. With doctrine, the conversion house posts a state transition, activates fallback marks by published hierarchy, and logs the activation as an event. Haircuts move within published bands. Conversion limits tighten by published thresholds. Throttles activate where needed to prevent redemption spirals, and facility access criteria are applied by rule so time cannot be privatized by whisper. Settlement completion guarantees continue for compliant recipients inside published windows, because commerce cannot become the buffer for market fear. Disputes are triaged into bounded lanes with binding timelines so proof does not become backlog. After the episode, the operator publishes the access audit, facility usage summary, correction log, and execution-quality distributions so the public record can answer the only legitimacy question that matters: whether the system allocated time by criteria or by status.

This is also where the incumbent counterattack tries to force capture through "temporary" exceptions. A contained stress incident becomes a headline about instability. An incumbent coalition offers a stabilization package: thin the baseline record temporarily to reduce gaming, add a professional data tier temporarily to help institutions interpret, permit a special liquidity incentive temporarily to tighten spreads, widen internalization temporarily to protect retail, loosen facility criteria temporarily to "manage confidence." Each offer preserves a legitimate function while reintroducing a toll. Accepting the package splits the constitution and turns public money into aristocratic money. Rejecting the package requires evidence as defense.

The conversion house therefore has to be built to publish evidence quickly: what happened, what state transitions were triggered, what criteria were applied, what exceptions were denied, what completion guarantees were honored, and what the measurable outcomes were. When evidence is published, the debate is forced onto mechanism rather than slogans, and slogans are where capture wins.

The conversion house also answers the question power brokers care about: sovereignty in crisis. A country that cannot settle cannot remain sovereign when fear arrives, because it must either trap exits or beg for external liquidity under external conditions. When an exchange-governed conversion house can deliver payment-grade closure against eligible instruments under published rules, it creates a domestic settlement capacity that is not purely hostage to bank balance sheets and not purely hostage to foreign corridors. That capacity lowers the political premium embedded in refinancing, because participants price predictable rules more favorably than discretionary improvisation. It also creates a new policy lever that must be governed carefully: eligibility, because eligibility decides which instruments become time and therefore which issuers receive persistent demand. This chapter establishes the settlement rail. The next chapter establishes the eligibility constitution that prevents that rail from being captured into privilege.

Sequencing remains the final design constraint, because premature breadth is how money regimes die. The conversion house cannot begin by making every instrument spendable. It begins with conservative eligibility, tight limits, explicit throttle bands, strict mark doctrine, and proof that is fast enough to remain financeable. It expands only when dispute throughput, settlement fails, correction frequency, execution quality, and facility usage discipline stay within published bounds. It opens cross-border only under mutual recognition of primitives, because misalignment becomes exit-route arbitrage and exit-route arbitrage becomes political backlash. Scaling is criteria-based, not ambition-based, because ambition-based scaling invites panic and panic invites improvisation, and improvisation breaks finality, and broken finality recreates the wall under a new name.

A monetary system usable in everyday life is not one that eliminates risk. It is one that contains risk inside institutions designed to carry it and refuses to export risk into ordinary commerce through ambiguity, delay, and discretionary rule changes. The spend unit remains stable so daily life stays legible. The conversion house makes instruments spendable by enforcing proof and priority, applying published marks and haircuts, guaranteeing completion, delivering legally precise finality under safe harbor, and publishing evidence under stress so time cannot be sold back to the public at a premium. If those pieces hold, the exchange stack stops being a separate universe and becomes a civic rail that turns market instruments into time without turning daily life into a market bet.

CHAPTER 47
ELIGIBILITY AS MONETARY POLICY
THE INCLUSION LIST THAT REWIRES CAPITAL ALLOCATION, DURATION, AND NATIONAL FINANCING POWER.

47. Eligibility as Monetary Policy

Subtitle: The inclusion list that rewires capital allocation, duration, and national financing power.

A monetary system is never neutral about what counts as money. It decides, explicitly or implicitly, which instruments extinguish obligations cheaply and which instruments extinguish obligations only with penalty, delay, or refusal. In Market Instruments Money Theory, that decision is called eligibility, and eligibility is not a technical list. It is monetary policy because it determines which instruments can become time at the point of settlement, which instruments can reliably fund completion guarantees without destabilizing commerce, and which issuers therefore receive persistent demand as a structural feature rather than as a passing preference. In the old regime, this power is exercised quietly through collateral schedules, repo customs, margin rules, and credit committee habits that are legible only to insiders. In the new regime, the same power must be exercised openly as constitutional policy, because private eligibility produces aristocratic money and discretionary eligibility produces political money.

Eligibility has force because usefulness creates demand. An instrument that is eligible is not merely liquid in a trading sense; it is liquid in a closure sense. It can extinguish obligations through the conversion house. It can be tendered into completion guarantees. It can be financed inside published haircuts and bands that make its time-conversion predictable. That usefulness increases demand even if expected returns do not change, because an instrument that closes obligations is more valuable than an instrument that only sits in a portfolio. Increased demand lowers funding costs and lowers cost of capital for eligible issuers. The opposite happens to ineligible issuers: their instruments remain tradable, but they cannot become closure cheaply or reliably, which widens liquidity premiums, increases financing spreads, and makes duration more expensive. The eligibility list therefore reallocates financing conditions across the economy through what looks like methodology. That reallocation becomes political immediately, because inclusion feels like legitimacy and exclusion feels like punishment. The theory survives only if eligibility is governed as a constitutional object with legible criteria, published bands, and amendment safety that prevents capture.

Eligibility has to satisfy three stability constraints simultaneously, and any regime that optimizes one while ignoring the others will fail under stress. Settlement stability means eligible instruments cannot force commerce to carry mark risk, implying conservative haircuts, stable mark doctrine, and tight conversion limits for instruments with high volatility or fragile entitlement behavior. Solvency stability means the conversion house must be able to finance and dispose of tendered instruments under disorder without exhausting buffers and without turning completion guarantees into discretionary promises. Legitimacy stability means ordinary participants must be able to see that eligibility is not a relationship market and that amendments are not smuggled in as technical updates that preserve incumbent rents. These constraints make early eligibility conservative by necessity, not by timidness, because the first visible failure becomes the incumbent's exhibit and the state's excuse to improvise.

The eligibility architecture must be simple enough to be understood and strict enough to be financeable. A core eligible set exists for everyday closure in calm and mild stress. A conditional eligible set exists for controlled use under tighter limits and more aggressive throttles. The core begins with instruments whose marks and entitlements are easier to govern: sovereign bills and high-grade sovereign bonds, and a narrow class of highly liquid, broad listed products whose entitlement mapping is deterministic and whose markets remain deep under ordinary shocks. The conditional set expands carefully: investment-grade corporate bonds under strict issuer requirements, diversified equity products under tighter haircuts and strict correction doctrine, and highly liquid equities only where corporate action hygiene, disclosure discipline, and depth are sufficient to prevent entitlement ambiguity from becoming a dispute factory. This tiering is not moral hierarchy. It is a buffer geometry. The system is deciding which risk profiles can be converted into closure without exporting volatility into merchants and without forcing the conversion house into discretionary rescues.

Haircuts are the policy instrument inside eligibility, and the design must treat them as doctrine rather than discretion. A haircut is the price paid to convert volatility into closure without transferring that volatility to the merchant. Haircuts must therefore be published as bands by instrument class and eligibility tier, and they must move with liquidity and volatility measures by formula within bounded ranges. Published bands let participants price the regime and reduce the incentive to sprint for exits on rumor. They also defeat a powerful incumbent narrative: that predictability exists only in private lanes. A public system that publishes its haircut doctrine and follows it makes predictability a civic good rather than a premium product. Haircuts protect the conversion house from becoming a leveraged absorber of public risk; without them, the conversion house either carries too much volatility and fails in stress or breaks completion guarantees to survive, and either outcome ends adoption.

Conversion limits are the second policy instrument, because even conservative eligibility becomes destabilizing if volume is unbounded. Limits should be set by identity tier, instrument class, and market state, tightening automatically in disorder under published thresholds. Limits are not retreat from democratization; they are the discipline that prevents democratization from being used as the exhibit for panic. A system that tightens by published thresholds preserves legitimacy because tightening is expected. A system that tightens by improvisation destroys legitimacy because improvisation teaches that the constitution is negotiable and negotiation favors proximity.

Criteria must be legible in substance, not only in prose, or eligibility becomes the new patronage list. The criteria can be written as a single doctrine that speaks to financing, not to optics. First, liquidity and depth must be demonstrated across ordinary stress, not only in calm, because depth that disappears in mild disorder is not depth; it is a marketing number. Second, settlement behavior must be disciplined: high fail rates and chronic late corrections are signals that proof is weak, and weak proof becomes haircut inflation when instruments are used as closure. Third, corporate action hygiene must be proven: predictable calendars, deterministic entitlement mapping, timely disclosures, and low rates of disputed record-date interpretation, because entitlement ambiguity is the fastest path from technical friction to systemic haircuts. Fourth, governance and disclosure timeliness must be enforceable: related-party behavior, insider transactions, and delayed material disclosures are not merely investor-protection issues; they are conversion risk because they destabilize marks and invite disputes. Fifth, concentration and float stability must be considered because concentrated instruments become political instruments under stress, and political instruments cannot be money-grade without high haircuts that defeat the point of spendability. These criteria are not morality. They are the conditions under which an instrument can be transformed into closure without turning closure into litigation.

Eligibility governance must assume a counterattack because the list is the new money. Incumbents will not argue against eligibility openly. They will argue for exceptions. They will propose "temporary" special treatment for instruments held by "systemically important liquidity providers." They will propose a professional-only tier of eligibility for "risk management," which is premium survival in monetary form. They will propose discretionary facility access to "support confidence," which is relationship time in monetary form. They will propose thinning baseline truth "to prevent gaming," because thick truth makes eligibility and haircut changes auditable and therefore less capturable. If the governance regime cannot block these moves, eligibility becomes a quiet aristocracy and the theory becomes a rebrand.

A capture attempt looks polite because it arrives as stability language. A market incident occurs, spreads widen, and the public is told liquidity is fragile. An incumbent coalition submits a short proposal described as transitional protection. It requests a narrow carveout allowing certain intermediaries to tender a broader set of instruments at lower haircuts "to prevent disorder," while ordinary participants remain constrained "for safety." It requests delayed publication of certain mark inputs "to avoid front-running," which makes verification slower for the public. It requests a discretionary committee override "for exceptional conditions," which creates relationship time. The proposal's genius is that it preserves a rent while presenting itself as a stabilizer. Amendment safety is what prevents the list from becoming captured money. The proposal must trigger published rationale requirements, published impact analysis on selection against smaller participants, a public explanation of why the carveout is necessary, a transition window that prevents cliff effects, and a sunset that forces renewal or expiration by evidence rather than habit. If the proposal cannot survive sunlight and a sunset, it is not safety; it is toll restoration.

The amendment process must be engineered as part of the monetary constitution, because policy changes are where systems are captured. Changes to the eligible list, haircut bands, conversion limits, and mark doctrine must require published rationale, published adverse-selection analysis, transition windows, and post-implementation review with measurable tests. The tests cannot be rhetorical. They must include whether merchant closure remained stable, whether completion guarantees were honored within published bounds, whether dispute throughput remained within published time limits, whether settlement fails increased, whether correction frequency spiked, and whether liquidity outcomes differed systematically by participant tier. This is how amendments become accountable rather than negotiable, and how the list remains monetary policy rather than a private product.

A stress-day tightening sequence is the practical proof that eligibility is policy rather than opinion. Volatility rises across the eligible set. Depth thins. Funding costs increase. Without doctrine, the system either panics and freezes or quietly grants exceptions to the connected. With doctrine, the conversion house posts a state transition, haircuts move within published bands, conversion limits tighten by threshold, and conditional eligibility narrows by rule so the conversion house is not forced into leveraged absorption. The corridor trigger, if applicable, narrows cross-border conversion by published thresholds to prevent exit arbitrage, and this narrowing is published so domestic participants are not surprised by hidden asymmetry. Auctions still clear, perhaps at higher costs, but the costs are legible and not interpreted as political improvisation. Completion guarantees remain credible because they were designed around banded tightening rather than around sudden reclassification. The public experiences discomfort without betrayal, which is the only environment in which duration can grow.

Eligibility is where the sovereignty argument becomes numerical rather than aspirational. A country that can convert domestic instruments into closure under a rule-bound regime deepens domestic demand for those instruments because usefulness increases demand. Deeper demand reduces haircuts and stabilizes funding terms. Lower haircuts and stable funding terms extend domestic duration. Longer domestic duration lowers sovereign refinancing premiums because the state is less dependent on foreign flows that reverse under global tightening. Lower refinancing premiums reduce fiscal strain. Reduced fiscal strain reduces the political temptation to improvise controls. Reduced improvisation increases trust. Increased trust deepens duration further. This chain is not rhetoric. It is the mechanism by which settlement architecture becomes state capacity. It is also why power brokers take notice when the theory is credible, because it ties eligibility doctrine directly to financing power.

Cross-border corridors amplify the stakes because eligibility becomes a cross-border coordination problem. If one jurisdiction's eligibility bands are permissive and another's are conservative, capital routes through the permissive regime under stress because it sells time. Domestic participants who cannot route cross-border interpret this as privilege, and privilege becomes political backlash. A corridor-ready eligibility framework therefore requires primitive alignment not only of finality and proof, but also of eligibility tightening triggers and mark doctrine, so cross-border spendability does not become a private escape hatch for the fastest actors. Corridor narrowing must be rule-bound and published, because rumors about corridor changes become runs, and runs destroy legitimacy faster than any technical defect.

The eligibility list will be attacked as unfair no matter how carefully it is designed, because it reallocates financing conditions. The defense is not to pretend neutrality. The defense is to treat eligibility as monetary policy and govern it with the same legitimacy discipline any monetary policy must have: published objectives, published instruments, published rules for tightening and easing, published constraints against favoritism, and published evidence after stress. Issuers must know what improves eligibility. Participants must know how haircuts move. Merchants must know closure will hold. Banks must know funding terms will tighten by bands rather than by surprise. Regulators must know amendments cannot be smuggled in as technical updates.

Eligibility is the heart of Market Instruments Money Theory because it decides what can become time. If the list becomes private, the system becomes aristocratic money. If the list becomes discretionary, the system becomes political money. If the list is conservative but opaque, the system becomes a patronage machine. The theory survives only if eligibility is governed openly as rule, defended by evidence, and stable under stress without selling time back to the public through exceptions. When that is true, eligibility stops being a list and becomes what it actually is: the new monetary policy lever of an exchange-settled society.

CHAPTER 48
FINALITY AND SAFE HARBOR
THE LEGAL CLOSURE DOCTRINE THAT MAKES RECIPIENTS WHOLE WITHOUT FREEZING THE SYSTEM.

Money is not a symbol. It is a promise that ends. A society can tolerate portfolio volatility, debate policy in legislatures, and survive institutional scandal, but it cannot function if everyday closure is negotiable. People accept a payment rail because it defines when a payment is finished, protects recipients who complied with the rules, and repairs errors without turning each receipt into a legal argument. Once stocks, bonds, and listed products are allowed to extinguish obligations, the pressure on closure becomes brutal because markets carry marks, liens, corporate actions, and insolvency stays that ordinary commerce cannot carry. Finality and safe harbor are therefore not legal garnish in Market Instruments Money Theory. They are the boundary between a spendable regime that becomes civic infrastructure and a spendable regime that collapses into panic, reversals, merchant refusal, and the restoration of private guarantees that rebuild the wall.

Finality has to be a legal state with clocks that do not drift. A completion window is the period during which the system guarantees the recipient will be made whole in the stable spend unit once a compliant tender is accepted, even if back-end conversion, netting, and funding are still reconciling. A finality time is the moment at which the recipient's receipt becomes irrevocable for compliant recipients, except under narrowly defined fraud and error categories where remedy is funded without clawback from the recipient. A dispute window is the bounded period during which certain claims can be raised and evidence must be submitted, after which the system refuses to reopen finalized receipts. These clocks are not administrative obsession. They are the architecture that keeps commerce from becoming credit. Without clocks, closure becomes relationship. Relationship closure becomes panic because rational actors preemptively exit any system that might renegotiate their receipts under pressure.

Safe harbor is the doctrine that protects compliant recipients after finality. It is what allows a merchant to release goods and services without becoming an underwriter of the payer's later insolvency, later fraud allegations, or later political demands for reversal. Safe harbor cannot be unconditional, because unconditional safe harbor invites abuse, but its conditions must be mechanical rather than discretionary. Compliance must be defined as verification behavior: identity tier checks, receipt verification, anomaly flags handled by published rules, and adherence to published acceptance requirements. If the recipient complied, the recipient is protected. If the recipient colluded or violated verification requirements, the recipient loses protection. The critical constraint is that protection cannot be negotiated after the fact. Negotiated closure turns recipients into involuntary lenders and makes adoption collapse into surcharge, refusal, and a return to private rails that only the connected can use cheaply.

A spendable regime that preserves closure must treat fraud as a liability problem rather than as a reversal problem. In many payment systems, the easiest political response to fraud is reversal because reversal looks like justice. In a money-grade spendability regime, reversal after finality destroys the social function of money because it teaches that no receipt is finished. Merchants respond by raising prices, refusing the rail, or requiring private guarantees. Households respond by exiting early. Incumbents respond by calling the architecture reckless. The correct response is funded restitution: reimburse the harmed party quickly from a funded pool, preserve safe harbor for compliant recipients after finality, then pursue recovery through the payer channel under investigation, insurance mechanisms, and enforcement that does not break closure. This is not softness. It is the only stable way to punish fraud without converting commerce into a legal battlefield.

Funded restitution requires a liability design that is explicit, tiered, and priceable, because unpriced liability becomes political improvisation when the first scandal lands on a front page. The system must distinguish system error, participant error, and fraud. System error is compensated automatically. Participant error is compensated within defined windows and evidence standards, with cost allocation that discourages carelessness without punishing innocents. Fraud is compensated under published rules that depend on authentication tier, anomaly signals, and compliance behavior. The restitution pool is replenished by conversion spreads, membership assessments, and precommitted replenishment rules, not by discretionary levies that arrive in crisis and trigger backlash. If the pool cannot be replenished mechanically, then safe harbor is an unfunded promise and the regime will revert to reversals the first time political heat rises.

The doctrine also has to be layered, because closure in commerce is not the same as closure inside the conversion house's internal netting, and confusing these layers is how systems create arguments that look technical and feel like betrayal. The outer layer is retail closure: the recipient's stable-unit receipt reaches finality at the published time under safe harbor. That layer is treated as money-grade and is insulated from later disputes beyond narrow categories that are remedied by restitution, not by clawback. The middle layer is conversion-house reconciliation: instrument tender, encumbrance tagging, mark application, netting, funding, and disposition of inventory. That layer can have more complex close-out and adjustment mechanisms, but its adjustments must not reopen the outer layer's final receipts. The inner layer is insolvency and systemic close-out: what happens when a payer fails, an intermediary fails, or the conversion house itself enters stress. That layer is governed by priority rules, loss waterfalls, and resolution doctrine, and it must be written so ordinary recipients do not become the shock absorber. Money-grade closure exists only when the outer layer remains stable while the inner layers absorb disorder by precommitted rules.

Encumbrance reality makes this layering non-negotiable. Instruments used to extinguish obligations can be pledged elsewhere, subject to liens, or tied to entitlements that shift under corporate actions. If an instrument tendered into the conversion house is later discovered to be encumbered beyond permitted thresholds, the remedy cannot be clawback from the recipient. The remedy must be structural: enforce encumbrance tags at tender, refuse tender that violates encumbrance rules, and allocate loss to the payer channel if encumbrance was misrepresented or concealed. This is why proof, priority, and safe harbor are one system, not separate topics. A finality regime without strong proof is politically forced into reversals. A proof regime without safe harbor is economically forced into merchant refusal. A system with both can keep commerce closed while enforcing accountability where it belongs.

A normal-day error sequence illustrates how the doctrine functions without drama. A payer tenders an eligible bond through the conversion house. A non-replayable receipt is issued. Completion is guaranteed. The merchant is credited in the stable spend unit within the completion window. Finality time arrives and safe harbor attaches because verification compliance is provable. Later the payer claims error: wrong amount, wrong recipient, or mistaken authorization. The system checks whether the claim falls within the dispute window and whether evidence meets the standardized threshold. If it is a genuine user error within defined categories, restitution is provided from the pool to the payer, and recovery is pursued through the payer channel under published rules, without reopening the merchant's final receipt. The merchant remains whole. The payer is repaired quickly. The system does not teach society that paid is conditional. That is the difference between a monetary rail and a credit arrangement wearing a payment costume.

A stress-day fraud sequence is where legitimacy is made or lost. Fraud attempts spike in disorder because criminals exploit confusion. The system shifts into a published stress mode. Authentication tightens by tier and anomaly bands, high-risk flows are throttled by rule, and state transitions are posted so behavior is priceable rather than guessable. A fraudulent payment occurs and is discovered after finality time. Under reversal doctrine, the merchant would be clawed back, merchants would panic, and the rail would collapse. Under safe harbor doctrine, the merchant is protected because compliance is provable and the receipt is final. The harmed party is reimbursed quickly from the restitution pool under published criteria. The payer channel is restricted prospectively to prevent further harm. Recovery is pursued through investigation and insurer-like mechanisms without breaking closure. The public sees a system that punishes fraud without breaking money, which is the only lesson that survives hostile headlines.

The merchant closure incident week is where the doctrine is tested not only by fraud but by politics, because politics is where closure usually breaks. A prominent fraud story hits the news cycle. A headline says the system "let criminals pay with securities," and a second headline says merchants are "getting away with it." Politicians demand reversals. A committee summons the operator. Incumbents offer their favorite bargain: restore reversibility, thin the baseline record, and let private lanes manage risk. Under weak doctrine, the state caves, reverses receipts, and merchants immediately surcharge or refuse, because no merchant will operate on a rail where yesterday's payment can be reopened by tomorrow's hearing. Under strong doctrine, the response is procedural and fast. The operator posts the state transition and the incident category. The restitution pool reimburses harmed parties within published windows. The system restricts the payer channel prospectively, not retroactively. The baseline truth layer publishes correction logs and fraud category summaries as events, not stories, and the post-event audit shows whether any exceptions were granted and why. Merchants remain inside the rail because safe harbor held. Households remain because refunds arrived without chaos. The political system is deprived of its easiest lever because the harm was repaired without breaking closure. This is what it means for finality to be a sovereign capacity rather than a fragile norm.

Courts are where finality becomes real or collapses into a polite fiction, and a spendable-instruments regime will be attacked in court because litigation is a slower, more effective form of sabotage than slogans. A court challenge chain begins with an injunction attempt framed as due process: a claimant argues that finality should be suspended because an alleged fraud or error is still being investigated, or because a conversion event involved a disputed encumbrance, or because a corporate action created entitlement ambiguity. The claimant's real objective may be recovery; it may also be to create precedent that closure is reopenable. If the court accepts that premise broadly, the system is finished because merchants will not operate under reopenable closure. The doctrine must therefore be written to give courts a clear path that preserves closure while still providing remedy. Evidence standards must be strict. Remedy bands must be narrow and funded. The injunction against the recipient must be disfavored by statute or by controlling doctrine. Enforcement must be directed at the payer channel and at the conversion house's recovery rights under encumbrance priority, not at the recipient's final receipt. The court is offered restitution as immediate remedy and recovery as a separate process that does not reopen commerce. When courts see that harmed parties are made whole quickly without destabilizing society, courts have less reason to undermine finality. A finality doctrine that leaves victims unpaid invites courts to reopen receipts as improvised justice. Funded restitution is therefore judicial stability, not merely consumer policy.

Insolvency is the hardest test because insolvency is where markets generate legal ambiguity that destroys adoption if not governed. If a payer enters insolvency after tender but before the conversion house completes its internal reconciliation, the completion guarantee must still honor the recipient's closure if tender acceptance occurred under compliant conditions. Otherwise merchants become lenders to insolvency events and will refuse the rail. The conversion house must have legally defined priority rights in the tendered instrument and in encumbrance structure that allow it to recover without reopening the recipient receipt. If insolvency can be used as a retroactive excuse to break completion, the system becomes a run machine because participants learn that the safest strategy is to exit at the first rumor of insolvency anywhere.

The doctrine must also anticipate the political temptation of discretionary exception-making, because in crises political actors will demand that some payments be reversed and others not, based on sympathy, publicity, and lobbying. Allowing exceptions teaches that closure depends on proximity, and proximity-based closure is aristocratic money. The system must apply the same finality clocks and safe harbor conditions to all, bounded only by objective verification compliance. It must also be willing to publish uncomfortable evidence. Post-event access audits and restitution statistics must be published with categories and time stamps: how many events occurred, how restitution was paid, how quickly, what types of restrictions were imposed prospectively, and whether any discretionary deviations occurred. Without published evidence, the incumbent counterattack will claim the system secretly favors insiders, and politics will respond by improvising reversals, which breaks finality, which ends adoption.

Cross-border settlement raises the stakes further because safe harbor and finality must be recognized across jurisdictions or corridors become exit arbitrage and legal chaos. If one jurisdiction treats finality as firm and another treats it as reopenable, the corridor becomes a conditional promise, and sophisticated actors will route to the side that sells time under stress. Domestic participants will be left with reversal risk and will exit. Corridor-grade finality therefore requires treaty-like mutual recognition of finality clocks, bounded remedies, safe harbor doctrine, and restriction handling. The corridor must define dispute venue, recognition of judgments, and how restitution is funded and reimbursed across borders without breaking recipient closure. Without that alignment, cross-border spendability becomes a political liability rather than a sovereignty tool.

Finality and safe harbor are the legitimacy engine of Market Instruments Money Theory because they decide whether ordinary society experiences the new rail as money or as conditional credit. They protect merchants from becoming credit analysts. They protect households from living in a regime where paid is always negotiable. They protect the state from the political demand to improvise in every scandal. They also protect the reform from the incumbent's most effective weapon: the claim that democratization is unsafe. When finality is legally precise, safe harbor is conditional and mechanical, restitution is funded, disputes are bounded and fast, courts have an enforceable path that preserves closure while delivering remedy, and audits are published, the system can absorb fraud and error without breaking the meaning of settlement. That is what makes a spendable-instruments regime money-grade rather than a fragile novelty that collapses into the old wall at the first hostile week.

CHAPTER 49
PROOF, PRIORITY, AND THE ENCUMBRANCE LEDGER
THE PROPERTY-RIGHTS STACK THAT PREVENTS DOUBLE-PLEDGE AND LOWERS SYSTEM-WIDE HAIRCUTS.

A spendable-instruments regime lives or dies on a question markets usually bury in paperwork and relationship: can the system prove, quickly and in court, who owns what, who has priority over what, and whether the same unit has been promised twice. If it cannot, then each instrument used as settlement becomes conditional, conditional settlement becomes credit, credit becomes haircut inflation, and haircut inflation becomes merchant refusal. Proof is not back office in Market Instruments Money Theory. Proof is monetary foundation because proof determines whether an instrument can be turned into time without creating counterfeit credit through double-pledge. Priority is not legal ornament. Priority is the rule that decides who is paid first in disorder, and if that rule is slow, ambiguous, or negotiable, the market prices the ambiguity as higher haircuts and shorter duration. The encumbrance ledger is the mechanism that makes proof and priority operational at commerce speed rather than litigation speed.

Modern finance already runs a private money layer through eligibility schedules and haircuts. The conversion house extends that layer into everyday life, which means today's private proof weaknesses become tomorrow's public failure modes. In many jurisdictions, beneficial ownership is scattered, liens are registered inconsistently, and priority is discovered only after insolvency when the damage is already systemic. That can persist in a world where only institutions with lawyers and balance sheets can finance uncertainty. It fails in a world where households and merchants need closure and where the state cannot tolerate a settlement rail that converts routine life into legal suspense. A money-grade regime requires property rights that are admissible, fast, and bounded, because bounded proof is what keeps disputes from becoming a funding shock.

The encumbrance ledger is not merely a database. It is an authoritative record that binds beneficial ownership, entitlement state, and encumbrance tags to an admissible timeline, with corrections logged as events and with priority rules that survive insolvency as law rather than as negotiation. It is designed to make double-pledge structurally difficult, not merely punishable after harm. It ensures that when an instrument is tendered to extinguish an obligation the system can answer instantly whether it is unencumbered to the required extent, and whether the act of tender itself now creates a temporary encumbrance that blocks reuse elsewhere during the completion window. It makes priority visible so haircuts can fall, because haircuts are the market's tax on uncertainty. Where priority is unclear, haircuts rise to compensate. When haircuts rise, funding tightens. When funding tightens, completion guarantees become fragile. When completion becomes fragile, merchants withdraw and private guarantees return. This is the chain that ties property rights directly to monetary adoption.

Proof has two layers that must be kept aligned. The first is beneficial ownership, meaning the system's answer to who holds economic rights at a specific time. The second is entitlement mapping, meaning the system's answer to what that holder is owed after interest payments, redemptions, conversions, splits, reorganizations, and voluntary corporate action elections. Many systems can approximate beneficial ownership in calm. Many systems fail at entitlement mapping in disorder, which is why corporate action weeks become dispute factories and dispute factories become haircut events. If a payee cannot be sure what was delivered, the payee treats delivery as conditional. If delivery is conditional, closure becomes credit. The ledger therefore binds ownership and entitlements together: time-stamped ownership snapshots linked to deterministic entitlement rules, corporate action calendars treated as authoritative, and corrections logged as events rather than edits.

Priority is what prevents proof from collapsing into politics during insolvency. A pledge that does not survive insolvency is not collateral; it is narrative. A lien that cannot be enforced quickly is not security; it is delay rent. The ledger encodes priority as enforceable ordering and drives it through workflow: what ranks first, what is subordinated, what is prohibited, what is capped, what constitutes breach, and what remedy follows. Courts and supervisors must recognize this ordering as binding, or else every stress event becomes a contest over who can delay longest. Delay is not neutral. Delay is extraction financed by haircuts paid by the public.

A normal-day tender flow shows how the property-rights stack becomes money-grade. A payer initiates a purchase priced in the stable spend unit and elects to tender an eligible instrument. The conversion house queries the ledger and receives a definitive state: instrument identity, beneficial owner state, entitlement state, and encumbrance load with priority ordering. If encumbrance exceeds permitted thresholds for tender, the tender is refused. If encumbrance is permissible, the conversion house writes a tender tag that functions as a temporary encumbrance during the completion window and is recorded as an event with timestamp, preventing reuse elsewhere. The tender is valued by published mark doctrine, haircuts are applied by published bands, and a non-replayable receipt is issued. The recipient is credited in the stable spend unit under the completion guarantee, finality arrives on the published clock, and safe harbor attaches for compliant recipients. Proof is checked and written before closure is granted. Closure remains closure rather than becoming an argument about whether the same unit was promised twice.

The ledger also solves a funding problem most registries ignore. Completion guarantees are only as credible as the conversion house's ability to finance tendered instruments under disorder without exhausting buffers or begging for discretion. Financing depends on collateral quality, and collateral quality depends on priority certainty. If priority is ambiguous, lenders raise haircuts. Raised haircuts force deleveraging. Deleveraging forces selling. Selling widens spreads and increases mark volatility. Volatility pushes haircuts higher. The conversion house becomes expensive or fragile. Merchants see delays. Politics demands controls. The conversion rail is blamed. Priority certainty interrupts this chain by lowering the uncertainty tax. When priority is provable quickly, financing terms are less punitive and the guarantee remains credible within published tightening bands. This is how property rights lower system-wide haircuts and therefore lower the cost of using market instruments as money-grade settlement inputs.

Corporate actions are where proof systems are most likely to fail in public because corporate actions create entitlements that can be disputed. A spendable regime cannot tolerate that ambiguity leaking into commerce. The ledger therefore treats corporate action calendars as authoritative states, binds entitlement mapping to record-date snapshots sealed as admissible states, and logs elections as events with time stamps. Correction windows tighten around record dates. Dispute capacity is pre-allocated during corporate action weeks so entitlement ambiguity does not become backlog. When corrections occur, they are logged with reason codes. The purpose is not to eliminate all dispute. It is to keep dispute narrow and fast enough that proof remains liquid and therefore financeable.

Registry inconsistency is the fastest path from technical weakness to systemic haircuts because it converts proof into rumor. A common failure chain begins with a mismatch between two registries: a custody network marks an encumbrance as released, but the lien registry still shows it as active, or a beneficial ownership snapshot lags a corporate action election, or an entitlement mapping engine applies a record date incorrectly. The mismatch becomes a dispute. The dispute delays proof. Proof delays cause lenders to treat the asset as contested. Contested collateral triggers haircut jumps because haircuts are how lenders price uncertainty. Haircut jumps tighten funding. Tight funding forces sales. Forced sales increase volatility and widen spreads. Volatility increases haircut add-ons. The public sees prices gap and assumes hidden insider exits. Politics responds with calls for freezes and reversals. The system is then punished for its weakest link: not the market itself, but the slow proof that turns settlement into a legal argument. This is why a spendable regime cannot tolerate inconsistent registries. Inconsistency is not a paperwork error. It is a monetary shock.

The ledger's purpose is to break that chain at the root by making proof singular, admissible, and event-logged. When a lien is released, the release is an event with time stamp recognized by the priority doctrine. When ownership changes, the change is an event. When an entitlement election is made, it is an event. When a correction occurs, it is an event with reason code and bounded window. Disputes are routed to a bounded lane with standardized evidence and binding timelines, and the ledger marks the disputed state explicitly so the market can price it rather than fear it. Haircuts can still tighten within bands, but tightening is disciplined, not panic-driven. Funding remains usable. Completion guarantees remain credible. The public experiences discomfort without betrayal. This is how the same stress day produces stability rather than collapse: not by suppressing information, but by making proof coherent enough that uncertainty does not metastasize into systemic haircuts.

The counterattack against proof governance will arrive in polite form, because the easiest way to preserve rents is to keep proof expensive for the public. Incumbents will argue that a thick, authoritative ledger increases compliance costs and slows innovation. The hidden objective is to preserve a world where proof is a service sold privately and where delay can be monetized as spread. They will propose carveouts: certain large intermediaries can use faster proof channels, or proprietary custody networks can keep their own encumbrance truth and reconcile later, or certain instruments can be tendered without full encumbrance tagging "for liquidity." These proposals are not technical. They are attempts to reintroduce aristocratic money by making proof unequal. The response is constitutional discipline: proof cannot be premium survival. The ledger must remain non-degradable baseline infrastructure. Amendment safety must apply with published rationale, published impact on selection against smaller participants, transition windows, and post-implementation audits proving that proof equality was preserved. If proof becomes two-tier, settlement becomes two-tier, and the theory collapses into another system where mobility buys safety.

The governance of the ledger has to be explicit because governance is where capture hides. The ledger must have an accountable operator with statutory duties, independent audit obligations, and a public publication perimeter that cannot be quietly narrowed. Operationally, the operator maintains the authoritative event log and enforces correction windows. Supervisors audit access patterns, correction frequencies, dispute throughput, and any exception requests. Amendments to priority doctrine, encumbrance tagging rules, and admissibility standards must be treated like monetary amendments: published rationale, published impact analysis, transition windows, and post-implementation review with measurable outcomes. After stress, the operator publishes a proof health audit: dispute volumes and resolution times, correction event counts by category, any priority conflicts detected, any emergency procedures invoked, and whether any participant received privileged proof access. This publication is not transparency theater. It is how the system denies incumbents the ability to claim proof is secretly being sold to the connected while the public is left in the slow lane.

Cross-border spendability raises proof into sovereignty. A corridor cannot function if one jurisdiction recognizes encumbrance tags as authoritative and another treats them as advisory. Misalignment becomes exit arbitrage. The fastest actors route through the jurisdiction that sells time under stress, leaving domestic participants exposed to priority disputes they cannot escape. Corridor-grade proof requires mutual recognition of encumbrance tags, priority ordering, bounded remedies, and admissibility standards. It requires shared doctrine for how tender tags operate across borders and how insolvency in one jurisdiction affects priority in another. It also requires published corridor tightening triggers so proof uncertainty cannot be weaponized as rumor-driven runs. Cross-border is treaty logic because what moves is not data. What moves is enforceable priority.

This is where governments notice the theory as more than finance. Proof clarity lowers haircuts. Lower haircuts lower funding premia. Lower funding premia extend domestic duration because longer instruments become financeable without punitive uncertainty taxes. Longer domestic duration lowers sovereign refinancing spreads because the state can roll debt into a deeper domestic base and rely less on foreign-unit clauses that import external discipline into national projects. Lower refinancing spreads reduce fiscal strain. Reduced fiscal strain reduces the temptation to improvise controls under pressure. Reduced improvisation increases trust. Increased trust lowers haircuts further. This is the sovereignty chain that turns property-rights infrastructure into national financing power. It is also why the property-rights stack will attract political resistance, because it shifts advantage away from those who profit from ambiguity.

Proof is the monetary substrate beneath the conversion house. It prevents spendability from creating counterfeit credit. It keeps haircuts from inflating into permanent taxes on adoption. It keeps courts from becoming the settlement engine of daily life. It keeps merchants from being drafted into insolvency analysis. When beneficial ownership is admissible, entitlement mapping is deterministic, encumbrance tags prevent double-pledge, priority survives insolvency, corrections are logged as events, disputes resolve within binding timelines, and governance is audited and publishable, instruments can be transformed into closure without turning closure into argument. That is the condition under which the exchange can become the settlement rail without selling survival back to the public through private proof lanes.

CHAPTER 50

MARK AUTHORITY AND THE PUBLIC RECORD

WHO SETS THE MARK, HOW CORRECTIONS ARE GOVERNED, AND HOW PANIC IS PREVENTED.

A money system can survive price movement. It cannot survive disputed reality. Volatility can be priced. Ambiguity about what is authoritative cannot, because ambiguity turns every obligation into an argument and every argument into a liquidity event. In Market Instruments Money Theory, marks are not commentary. They are settlement inputs. They determine haircuts, conversion spreads, margin add-ons, completion buffers, and therefore whether the conversion house can keep its guarantee credible without improvisation. This makes mark authority a sovereign problem, because a society that cannot define and publish authoritative marks cannot operate a public settlement rail without falling back into private lanes where truth is sold. The question is not whether marks are perfect. The question is whether marks are governed tightly enough that commerce closure is protected, funding does not become rumor-driven, and corrections do not become politics.

The starting separation is between price discovery and mark authority. Markets discover many prices across venues, times, and liquidity conditions. A settlement rail cannot live inside that multiplicity. It needs a doctrine that turns the flowing market into an admissible record: defined sources, defined timestamps, defined fallback hierarchies, and defined correction windows. That doctrine must be legible to ordinary participants and usable by institutions, because if the public cannot understand what the system will do, rumor fills the gap, and if institutions cannot price what the system will do, they withdraw funding preemptively. A regime that tries to solve this by thinning truth creates a worse problem, because thin truth creates aristocratic money: those who can buy premium feeds survive, those who cannot are left with delayed reality. Non-degradable baseline truth is therefore not a moral flourish. It is how the monetary rail denies capture.

Mark authority has layers because the system has different needs that are often confused. The commerce mark is the mark used by the conversion house to price tenders for everyday obligations inside the completion window. It must prioritize determinism and stability over microstructure precision, because commerce cannot be forced to swing with noise that merchants cannot hedge. The funding mark is the mark used to set haircuts, margin bands, and buffer requirements. It must be conservative and stress-sensitive, because underestimating risk in funding marks forces improvisation later. The accounting mark is the mark used for reporting, performance measurement, and longer-horizon valuation. These marks can differ by design, but their governance must be explicit and published, because ungoverned divergence is how marks become weapons: one mark is chosen to justify a haircut shock, another mark is chosen to justify a margin call, another mark is chosen to justify a dispute. A money-grade system cannot allow mark selection by discretion.

The doctrine must state where marks come from and when they apply. Sources must be defined by eligible class and tier: which venues count, which auctions count, what minimum depth conditions qualify a venue as usable, what data are excluded as anomalous, and what methodology turns prints into a settlement mark. Timestamps must be fixed and published, because timing is where advantage hides. If a mark timestamp can drift or be chosen by discretion, the system sells time back to the connected. If a mark timestamp is fixed, the system forces equality and reduces the incentive to sprint for exits on rumor. Fallback hierarchies must be published, because outages and fractures are not hypotheticals; they are weather. Without fallbacks, the first outage becomes a legitimacy crisis. With fallbacks, the system remains money-grade because it can continue to price conversion and maintain completion without guessing.

The mark hierarchy must be explicit enough to survive litigation without becoming an operating manual for manipulation. An example structure is simple and resilient. In normal conditions, a primary auction close mark is used for a defined class of instruments because close marks are widely understood and create a common anchor. Where auction conditions are impaired or where liquidity is continuous rather than auction-centered, a volume-weighted snapshot across approved venues over a bounded window can be primary. If neither is available due to disorder, a fallback hierarchy activates: a prior official mark with conservative adjustment bands, or a broker composite constrained by published rules, or a synthetic mark derived from correlated instruments with published conservatism. The important feature is not the specific method. The important feature is that the method is published in advance and that fallback activation is an event, not a secret.

Corrections are where systems reveal whether they are public infrastructure or private clubs. Silent edits invite suspicion because silent edits resemble manipulation even when they are benign. Published corrections as events create trust because trust in markets is largely trust in reconstructability: can an outsider reconstruct what happened and why. Correction-as-event doctrine therefore becomes constitutional. Every correction carries a timestamp, a reason code, an affected scope, and a bounded window after which the system refuses to rewrite history. Boundaries matter because rewriting history is a panic trigger. If history can be rewritten, marks can be rewritten. If marks can be rewritten, haircuts can be rewritten. If haircuts can be rewritten, funding becomes rumor-driven. If funding becomes rumor-driven, completion guarantees become fragile. This is the chain that turns quiet corrections into public crisis.

A normal-day mark sequence shows why this governance is not bureaucracy but stability. A payer tenders an eligible instrument. The conversion house applies the commerce mark using the published source and timestamp, applies haircuts by published band, and issues completion within the window. The recipient receives stable-unit settlement. Finality arrives. Later, a small print appears on a thin venue that would have shifted the mark slightly. Under ungoverned regimes, that print becomes an argument about whether the payer overpaid, whether the conversion house profited unfairly, and whether the merchant is now exposed. Under mark doctrine, the print is either excluded because it fails minimum depth and anomaly rules, or it triggers a correction event within bounded windows with a defined remedy that does not reopen final receipts. Commerce remains closed because the official mark is not a mood; it is a state.

The auction close mark controversy week is where doctrine becomes public legitimacy. A close print is disputed. A well-known participant claims the official close was distorted by an imbalance, and media coverage frames it as manipulation. Institutions begin to whisper that marks cannot be trusted, and whispers are where funding begins to tighten. Under weak doctrine, the operator either denies and hides or improvises and revises quietly, and both paths teach that truth is negotiable. Under strong doctrine, the system behaves like infrastructure. The operator logs the dispute as an event. It publishes whether the close met the methodology's qualifying conditions, publishes whether fallback rules should have been activated, and if a correction is warranted it publishes the correction as an event within the correction window with the reason code and scope. The dispute lane is engaged not to relitigate the market but to test evidence against published standards: did the mark doctrine apply, did conditions meet activation thresholds, did any participant obtain privileged imbalance visibility, did any exceptions occur. A litigation attempt follows, typically framed as consumer protection or market integrity. The court is presented with an enforceable doctrine: the mark methodology is published, corrections are bounded, remedies are defined, and final receipts are insulated by safe harbor and restitution rules so the court does not need to reopen closure to deliver justice. The system then publishes the post-event audit: correction events, facility usage, and any privileged access requests granted or denied. The point is not to win an argument. The point is to deny rumor the ability to become a funding event.

Disorder-day mark fractures are the other test, because fractures are where money-grade systems are either built or abandoned. A venue outage or feed fracture causes visible prices to diverge across venues. Without doctrine, participants cannot know which mark will be used, cannot price haircuts, cannot price conversion spreads, and therefore tighten preemptively. Funding desks withdraw because uncertainty is unpriceable. Dealers reduce displayed liquidity. Spreads widen. Rumor fills the vacuum, and rumor becomes a run. With doctrine, the system posts a state transition and activates fall-back marks by published hierarchy. Haircuts move within published bands. Conversion limits tighten by threshold. Throttles activate where needed to prevent a redemption spiral, and facility access criteria are applied by rule so time cannot be privatized by whisper. Corrections are logged as events. After the episode, the correction log and facility usage summary are published, and the access audit answers the legitimacy question that dominates public perception: whether the rail behaved as one constitution or two. Panic is prevented not by suppressing information but by governing it.

Cross-border mark divergence creates a more poisonous version of the same risk because divergence becomes a tradable advantage. A corridor exists between two jurisdictions. A shock arrives. The two systems produce different official marks because methodologies differ or fallback activation differs. Sophisticated participants route to the jurisdiction whose mark is more predictable under stress, because predictable marks are convertible time. Domestic liquidity thins on the less predictable side, spreads widen, and the public interprets the thinning as insider exit. Without corridor-grade mark alignment, the corridor becomes an exit arbitrage channel, and exit arbitrage fractures legitimacy because it creates a two-speed reality. A cross-border mark divergence week therefore has to be treated like a corridor tightening test. Under a well-governed regime, corridor tightening triggers activate by published thresholds: if mark divergence exceeds defined bands, conversion limits on corridor flows tighten, additional haircuts apply to corridor conversion, and settlement of cross-border conversion is throttled to preserve domestic closure and prevent runaway migration. These actions are posted as state transitions, not whispered. The corridor does not pretend to be frictionless in disorder. It proves it is governable. After stabilization, the corridor publishes a reconciliation report: why divergence occurred, which fallback rules activated, and how doctrine will be amended through published process rather than through emergency improvisation. This is how cross-border spendability avoids becoming an exit trap door.

Because marks are power, governance around mark doctrine must be explicit, auditable, and resistant to capture. A mark methodology cannot be changed casually or quietly, because methodology changes are monetary changes: they alter haircuts, conversion costs, and therefore who can convert assets into time cheaply. The governance body that sets mark doctrine must be accountable, and accountability here means publication obligations, audit obligations, and amendment safety. The operator publishes methodology, publishes qualifying conditions, publishes fallback hierarchy, publishes correction windows, and publishes which datasets are baseline versus premium. The supervisor audits access patterns, correction frequencies, and any privileged information paths that might create time advantage. Amendments require published rationale, published impact analysis on selection against smaller participants, transition windows, and post-implementation review with measurable outcomes. If mark doctrine can be revised by a quiet committee and then "explained" later, then marks become politics, and politics becomes panic.

The public record is where this governance becomes real. The record must be thick enough that participants can reconstruct system behavior: state transitions, fallback activations, correction events with reason codes, facility usage and criteria, and any exception requests granted or denied. In disorder, the record must also include the reason the system moved bands: why haircuts tightened, why conversion limits tightened, why throttles activated. This information does not need to disclose private trading strategies. It must disclose constitutional behavior. Without it, incumbents will claim the public rail hides its mistakes and sells truth privately, and politics will respond with improvisation that breaks finality. With it, the system deprives the counterattack of oxygen because the record can refute claims quickly enough that rumor cannot become withdrawal.

Mark authority is also the principal site of rent because truth has always been a profitable choke point. Incumbents will propose professional tiers of mark feeds, proprietary analytics, delayed baseline truth to prevent gaming, and special access to imbalance information to support liquidity. The proposals sound like efficiency. The effect is to recreate premium survival. A public rail cannot tolerate that without becoming aristocratic money. Premium services can exist, but they must not be necessary to survive. If survival requires premium truth, legitimacy collapses because the public learns that the system is two-tier and that the best lanes are purchasable.

A capture attempt week tends to follow a familiar pattern. A disruption occurs. The system behaves by rule and contains it. Then incumbents appear offering stabilization proposals: allow a professional feed tier and slow public dissemination temporarily, permit certain intermediaries to see imbalance earlier, allow discretionary mark selection to reduce volatility, widen correction windows to provide flexibility. Each proposal sells time. The defense is publication and refusal to thin baseline truth. The operator publishes the mark methodology, the fallback activation, the correction events, the facility usage, and the execution-quality distributions. When evidence is published, the debate is forced onto mechanism rather than slogans. Without evidence, slogans win and truth becomes a private product.

Mark governance is where national financing power becomes mechanical. If mark doctrine is unclear, haircuts rise to compensate for uncertainty. Higher haircuts shorten duration because longer instruments become expensive to finance. Shorter duration raises refinancing premiums. Higher refinancing premiums increase fiscal strain. Fiscal strain increases political temptation to improvise controls. Improvised controls destroy trust and push participants back into private lanes. Mark authority therefore sits inside sovereignty as a chain of causality rather than a theory of legitimacy. A society that governs marks openly and refuses to sell truth as premium survival lowers the uncertainty tax otherwise paid through haircuts and spreads, and that reduction translates directly into a lower cost of capital.

Mark authority, in this theory, is not about choosing the perfect number. It is about choosing rules that keep numbers from becoming politics. When sources are defined, timestamps are fixed, fallbacks are published, corrections are events with bounded windows, governance is accountable, and audits are public, marks stop being weapons and become infrastructure. That is how the conversion house remains financeable, how completion guarantees remain credible, how corridors can be governed without exit arbitrage, and how the spend unit remains socially stable even while instruments become spendable.

CHAPTER 51
PAYMENT-GRADE AUTHENTICATION AND FRAUD LIABILITY

SECURITY THAT SCALES WITHOUT BREAKING FINALITY OR TURNING COMMERCE INTO CREDIT.

A spendable-instruments regime that fails on fraud will be forced, by politics, to fail on finality. Fraud is visible. Finality is subtle. When fraud becomes headline-sized, the political system reaches for the simplest lever: reversal, freeze, and discretionary exception. Those levers feel protective in the moment and destroy the social function of money over time, because they teach merchants and households that closure is negotiable. Market Instruments Money Theory treats authentication and fraud liability as monetary doctrine, not as a technical hardening exercise. The objective is not to eliminate fraud, which is impossible. The objective is to keep fraud from forcing retroactive clawback from compliant recipients after finality, because clawback turns commerce into credit and recreates the wall through refusal, surcharge, and private guarantees.

Authentication has to be tiered because risk is tiered. A regime that demands bank-grade identity for every small purchase will not be adopted and will push ordinary life back into informal rails. A regime that permits weak identity and replayable evidence for high-value obligations will be harvested. Tiered authentication matches identity assurance and authorization friction to risk profile using published thresholds rather than discretionary profiling. Low-risk flows close quickly under low-friction verification. Higher-risk flows require stronger authentication, slower completion windows, tighter limits, or additional attestations. The public accepts tiering when it is predictable and rule-bound, because predictable friction reads as policy rather than as discrimination.

The receipt is where authentication becomes money-grade. A receipt must be non-replayable evidence that an obligation has been extinguished or is inside the completion guarantee window. Replayable receipts are counterfeit currency. The rail therefore issues signed receipts bound to transaction context: payer identity tier, recipient tier, instrument tender class, timestamp, corridor state if cross-border, and a unique nonce that cannot be reused. The recipient can verify the receipt instantly. The receipt is admissible because it is tied to the public record and to the mark and tender events logged by the system. When disputes occur, the dispute lane does not have to infer intent from stories. It has evidence. Evidence is what keeps disputes bounded and fast, and bounded disputes are what keep proof liquid and settlement credible.

Fraud controls cannot depend on identity alone because criminals exploit behavior patterns that outrun identity checks. A money-grade rail needs anomaly controls and velocity limits that operate by published bands. The system watches for behavior that exceeds thresholds: unusual frequency, unusual routing across recipients, unusual instrument selection, unusual corridor usage, unusual device changes, abnormal timing around known stress windows, and pattern signatures that suggest laundering or takeover. When thresholds are exceeded, the rail tightens prospectively by rule: it raises authentication tier requirements, lowers conversion limits, narrows eligible instrument classes temporarily, extends completion windows within published bounds for high-risk categories, or triggers payer-channel restrictions. The governing principle is prospectivity. The rail must contain fraud by tightening forward behavior, not by breaking closure backward for compliant recipients.

Liability is the political constraint that decides whether the rail survives its first scandal. If victims are not reimbursed quickly, courts and legislatures will demand reversals. If reimbursement is slow, merchants become involuntary lenders while disputes crawl, and merchants will exit. If reimbursement appears arbitrary, the public assumes favoritism and the incumbent counterattack gains a permanent advantage. Fraud liability therefore must be funded, rule-bound, and fast. A restitution pool reimburses harmed parties within published windows when claims meet standardized evidence thresholds. The payer channel is then pursued for recovery through investigation, insurance-like mechanisms, and enforcement tools that do not reopen recipient closure. This turns fraud from a reversal problem into a compensation and recovery problem, which is the only form compatible with money-grade finality.

The liability structure must be explicit enough to survive hostile hearings, because vague promises collapse under political pressure. System error is compensated automatically under strict definitions. Participant error is compensated within bounded windows under standardized evidence, with cost allocation that discourages carelessness without punishing innocents. Fraud is compensated based on authentication tier, anomaly signals, and compliance behavior. The pool is replenished by conversion spreads, membership assessments, and precommitted replenishment rules, not by discretionary levies that arrive in crisis and trigger backlash. If the pool is underfunded, safe harbor becomes an unfunded promise and the system will eventually be forced into reversals. The funding of restitution is therefore not finance trivia. It is the monetary condition under which finality survives politics.

A merchant does not adopt a rail because the rail claims security. A merchant adopts a rail because the rail removes uncertainty from the merchant's balance sheet. That adoption logic can be compressed into two causal loops that show why fraud doctrine is monetary doctrine. In the refusal loop, a fraud incident triggers calls for reversal, reversals or delays draft merchants into underwriting, merchants add surcharge and restrictions, customers perceive friction and avoid the rail, volume shifts to private lanes, private lanes become "proof of safety," incumbents demand exceptions, baseline truth thins, and the public rail becomes decorative. In the adoption flywheel, non-replayable receipts and tiered authentication prevent most abuse at the edge, remaining fraud is reimbursed quickly from funded restitution, payer channels are restricted prospectively, merchant receipts remain final under safe harbor, merchants keep fees predictable and acceptance broad, customers experience closure rather than suspense, volume concentrates into the public rail, data and marks become more robust, funding becomes cheaper because uncertainty falls, and the rail becomes habit rather than experiment. A money system is chosen by merchants on the basis of which loop they experience in practice.

A normal-day fraud attempt shows how the edge fails safe. A fraudster attempts to authorize a payment under weak identity, or attempts to reuse a receipt. Verification fails because nonces are unique and signatures are bound to context. Repeated attempts across recipients trigger anomaly thresholds. The rail tightens the payer tier requirement prospectively and blocks further tenders until stronger authentication is provided. No merchant is clawed back because no final payment occurred. The incident is contained without drama, which is how systems build trust: by making failure boring at the edge.

The liability week is where doctrine is tested in public. A coordinated fraud wave hits during mild market disorder, timed to exploit confusion and to maximize headlines. A set of recipients who complied with verification rules receive finalized receipts. Later, victims claim fraud and demand reversal. Commentators argue the new rail is unsafe. Political actors demand that receipts be reopened to prove the state is protecting citizens. Incumbents offer the familiar compromise: restore discretionary reversals and let private intermediaries manage risk, meaning let private lanes return as the only safe lane. Under weak doctrine, the system yields, reverses receipts, and merchants immediately tighten acceptance because no merchant will operate on a rail where yesterday's payment can be reopened by tomorrow's hearing. Under money-grade doctrine, the rail does not argue. It executes. The restitution pool reimburses harmed parties within the published window for qualifying claims. The payer channels tied to the fraudulent behavior are restricted prospectively by published criteria, limiting further damage. Anomaly thresholds tighten for the affected patterns, conversion limits narrow in the relevant risk tier, and completion windows may lengthen within published bounds for high-risk categories without changing the finality time for compliant recipients. The operator publishes the incident categories and the restitution statistics in a way that preserves privacy but proves the rail is not hiding harm: counts by category, median reimbursement time, volume of restricted payer channels, and whether any exceptions were granted. The result is that victims are made whole without breaking closure, merchants remain protected, and the political system is deprived of its simplest lever. The rail survives because it did not ask to be trusted; it produced a record that forced trust to become rational.

Governance is where authentication becomes either constitutional or capturable. Tier thresholds cannot be set as discretionary preferences inside a private committee, because fraud doctrine is policy and policy becomes contested in crises. The thresholds for tiering, velocity bands, anomaly categories, and payer-channel restriction criteria must be published. Amendments must require published rationale, published impact analysis on selection against smaller participants, transition windows, and post-implementation review. Otherwise, the first major incident becomes the excuse to quietly tighten rules for the public while preserving exemptions for the connected, which recreates aristocratic money under the language of safety. The publication perimeter must be designed carefully: enough transparency to prove fairness and performance, without exposing private details that would aid criminals. That balance is part of doctrine. The system publishes the rules, the state transitions, the band changes, the restitution performance, and post-event audits showing whether exceptions existed. It does not publish individualized vulnerability maps. A money-grade regime can be transparent about its constitution without being reckless about operational security.

Cross-border use raises the fraud problem into a corridor problem because identity and enforcement become jurisdictional. A corridor without aligned fraud doctrine becomes an arbitrage channel for criminals as well as for capital. Corridor-grade fraud doctrine requires mutual recognition of identity tiers, shared standards for signed receipts, shared anomaly categories, and shared recovery mechanisms that operate through payer channels while preserving recipient safe harbor. It also requires published corridor tightening triggers that respond to fraud waves without improvisation, because improvisation across borders becomes rumor and rumor becomes runs. A corridor that cannot contain fraud without breaking closure will eventually be forced into freezes, and freezes are how cross-border spendability turns into dependency risk.

The most subtle risk is not the fraud itself but the narrative weaponization of fraud. Incumbents do not need the system to fail. They need the public to believe the system is unsafe unless private lanes are restored. That is why the rail must treat evidence production as a stabilizer. Published authentication tiers, published banded controls, published restitution windows, and published audit outputs are not communication. They are the constitutional defense that prevents small incidents from becoming justification for capture. When the public can see that fraud is punished without breaking closure, the incumbent's offer of private "safety" becomes less credible because the public rail is demonstrably safer in the only way that matters: it keeps money-grade finality intact while making victims whole.

Payment-grade authentication and funded fraud liability are therefore not appendices. They are the political mechanism that allows finality to remain a legal state rather than a negotiable convention. When the system can prevent replay, detect anomalies, tighten prospectively by published bands, reimburse quickly from funded pools, recover through payer channels, and publish audits after stress, it can survive fraud headlines without sacrificing closure. That is what allows market instruments to be used in everyday obligations without turning daily commerce into a credit bet and without recreating the wall through merchant refusal. The chapter is finished.

CHAPTER 52
THE STRESS STATE MACHINE
THROTTLES, BUFFERS, AND AUDIT DISCIPLINE THAT DEFEAT SABOTAGE AND EXCEPTION-MAKING.

A system does not become money-grade by working in calm. It becomes money-grade by behaving predictably when fear tries to force improvisation. Stress is where constitutions are tested, because stress is when liquidity becomes expensive, funding becomes conditional, and political actors demand instant relief. In Market Instruments Money Theory, the rail must survive a hostile week in which incumbents try to use disorder to restore private lanes, rumor tries to outrun evidence, and the state is tempted to trade finality for short-term calm. The stress state machine is the answer. It is not a crisis plan. It is a published set of modes, triggers, actions, and boundaries that allocates time by rule rather than by relationship. The audit obligation is the second half of the answer, because a state machine without published evidence will be accused of hidden favoritism, and hidden favoritism is the seed of aristocratic money.

The governing premise is that stress cannot be prevented, but panic can be governed. Panic is not caused by volatility alone. Panic is caused by the belief that rules will change before exit is possible. A money-grade rail has to make two beliefs rational: that closure will hold for compliant recipients, and that tightening will be predictable rather than discretionary. If participants believe receipts can be reopened, merchants surcharge or refuse, households avoid, and commerce retreats into private guarantees. If participants believe tightening will be discretionary, funding desks withdraw preemptively because discretion is unpriceable. The state machine does not promise comfort. It promises legibility under discomfort, and legibility is what allows institutions and households to remain inside the rail rather than sprinting for the nearest private lane.

The state machine begins with a small number of modes that are operationally meaningful and publicly legible. Normal mode is ordinary conversion and settlement behavior under published haircuts, limits, and authentication tiers. Heightened mode is triggered by measurable deterioration in depth, volatility, settlement fails, dispute backlog, correction frequency, or fraud anomalies, and it tightens by band without changing the finality clock for compliant recipients. Disorder mode is triggered when mark fractures, venue outages, or funding stresses exceed thresholds, and it activates fallback marks, tighter haircuts within bands, narrower conditional eligibility, stricter identity requirements for high-risk flows, and narrower corridor conversion where applicable, again without turning closure into negotiation. Emergency mode is triggered by multi-vector stress, such as mark fracture coinciding with funding squeeze and fraud wave, and it implements precommitted throttles, narrower corridor flows, stricter facility criteria, and accelerated audit publication cadence while maintaining money-grade closure for compliant recipients. The public must be able to see mode changes, because the public's fear is not mode change; the public's fear is secret mode change.

Triggers are where credibility is either earned or lost. Triggers must be objective, measurable, and published as doctrine: volatility bands by eligible class, depth and spread stability measures, settlement fail rates, dispute lane backlog measures, correction event frequency by category, anomaly and velocity breach rates, and corridor divergence measures where cross-border exists. The system does not need to publish every internal sensor in real time, but it must publish the trigger doctrine and post state transitions when triggers are hit. Entering disorder silently is how systems manufacture the suspicion that insiders were warned first. That suspicion becomes the narrative that kills adoption.

Actions under the state machine must be precommitted, ordered, and bounded, because participants need to price what comes next. Tightening begins with bands rather than decrees. Haircuts tighten within published ranges. Conversion limits narrow within published ranges. High-risk authentication tiers tighten within published ranges. Conditional eligibility narrows by the published hierarchy already stating which classes remain spend-stable under stress. Throttles then activate to slow the subset of flows most likely to become run channels: large conversions from volatile tiers, rapid cycling patterns flagged by anomaly doctrine, and corridor flows that can drain domestic liquidity faster than domestic participants can respond. Facility activation follows under criteria, allowing the conversion house to access precommitted liquidity tools, but access is governed by published conditions and allocation rules, not by relationship. Corridor tightening is applied by published triggers so cross-border does not become exit arbitrage. Each action is accompanied by state publication that communicates the constitutional behavior without revealing sensitive private vulnerabilities.

Buffers are the physical mechanism that allows closure to remain closure in disorder. Buffers are not only capital. They are time and liquidity reserves designed to keep completion guarantees credible when funding terms tighten and marks move quickly. Buffer sizing doctrine must be publishable in principle: how buffers relate to haircut bands, mark volatility, settlement risk, and eligible inventory liquidation capacity. Replenishment doctrine must be precommitted:

how conversion spreads, member contributions, and replenishment triggers refill buffers without discretionary levies that trigger backlash. The loss waterfall must be rule-bound: first absorb through spreads and reserves, then through pre-funded guarantee resources, then through member contributions under a published schedule, then through tightening bands and throttles, and only then through extraordinary measures defined in advance and sunset. The purpose is not to deny loss. The purpose is to prevent loss from being allocated by discretion, because discretionary loss allocation is the fastest route from stress to panic.

Throttles are often misread as controls, but in a money-grade regime they are safety devices that prevent liquidity demand from forcing the rail into improvisation. Throttles do not have to trap ordinary commerce. They slow the channels that amplify disorder: conversions that would require the conversion house to warehouse too much volatility too quickly, corridor flows that would create two-speed exits, and anomaly-flagged behavior that often correlates with fraud. Throttle doctrine must be banded and published. Tightening is prospective. Tightening is rule-bound. This is how the rail remains legitimate while preventing redemption spirals that would otherwise force the system to choose between breaking guarantees and granting private exceptions.

Outage behavior is where systems reveal whether they are built for reality. Outages and feed fractures are not rare. They are predictable. The state machine therefore defines outage modes: what remains open, what pauses, what falls back, and what is guaranteed. If marks fracture, fallback marks activate by published hierarchy and activation is logged as an event. If a venue is impaired, the mark doctrine excludes it by rule. If a settlement component is impaired, completion guarantees remain credible through buffer usage and facility activation under criteria, and completion windows adjust only within published bounds. Kill and restart criteria must be published because kill and restart are where discretion hides. A rail that can be killed by whisper and restarted by whisper is not public infrastructure.

The audit obligation turns the state machine from procedure into legitimacy. Audits must be defined in advance with a publication perimeter that is wide enough to prove fairness and discipline, and narrow enough to preserve privacy and prevent criminals from learning exploit maps. The publication perimeter is itself doctrine. It includes a timeline of state transitions with timestamps, the triggers that fired at a category level, the fallback activations, the correction events by category with reason codes, the haircut band movements and conversion-limit tier changes, throttle activations by category, facility usage summary by criteria and allocation outcomes, dispute throughput statistics, restitution statistics by category and median time, settlement fail statistics, and the list of exception requests granted or denied with rationale and sunset if granted. It excludes personally identifying details, merchant-level vulnerabilities, and operational secrets that would make exploitation easier. The goal is to publish constitutional behavior, not to publish private data. Without this perimeter, the rail either publishes too little and invites suspicion or publishes too much and invites attack. Doctrine prevents both failure modes.

A normal stress day demonstrates why the system is legible rather than comforting. Volatility rises and depth thins. Trigger thresholds are reached. A state transition is posted. Haircuts tighten within bands. Conversion limits narrow within bands for higher-volatility tiers. Authentication thresholds tighten for high-risk flows. Dispute lane capacity is pre-allocated to prevent backlog. Completion guarantees continue within the published window for compliant recipients. Merchants remain indifferent to the market's discomfort because their receipts remain money-grade. Institutions reprice the regime, but they do not sprint for exit because there is no regime ambiguity to arbitrage. The rail is not calm. It is governed.

The outage and mark-fracture week is where the state machine either becomes credible or becomes a pretext for exceptions. Monday begins with a venue outage that fractures observable prices. The operator posts a state transition into disorder mode and activates fallback marks by published hierarchy. The activation is logged as an event. Haircuts tighten within bands, conversion limits narrow for volatile tiers, and throttles activate for large conversions in the affected classes. Tuesday brings the first rumor that insiders are trading on a different mark. The system answers rumor with record: it publishes the fallback activation time, the mark source, the timestamp doctrine, and the categories affected. Wednesday brings a targeted sabotage attempt: an intermediary refuses to route certain flows, then claims the rail is failing, and offers a private overlay "to keep merchants safe," meaning a private lane reintroduced as rescue. Facility activation occurs under criteria to keep completion credible, and facility usage is summarized publicly in the audit perimeter. Thursday brings the political demand: a minister is urged to grant an emergency exemption allowing a small set of "systemically important" participants to use a special mark feed and lower haircuts so they can "support liquidity." The exemption would create aristocratic lanes precisely when fear is highest. The exception protocol activates: published rationale requirement, published impact analysis on selection against smaller participants, bounded sunset, and mandatory post-event audit. Because the exemption cannot survive sunlight without admitting it sells time, the exemption is denied. Friday closes with the audit package: state timeline, fallback marks used, correction events, facility usage by criteria, execution-quality distributions, and exception requests denied. The week is not comfortable, but it is survivable because the rail behaves as one constitution and because evidence is produced faster than narratives can harden.

The funding squeeze week is the second test because funding is where systems are forced into improvisation if they are not precommitted. A global tightening shock hits. Offshore spreads jump.

Funding desks tighten terms. Under weak systems, the response is discretionary: some receive support, others are sacrificed, and the market learns that rules are negotiable. Under the state machine, the funding squeeze triggers heightened mode. Haircuts tighten within bands and conversion limits narrow within bands, preserving completion for ordinary commerce while reducing the speed at which volatility can be poured into the conversion house. Conditional eligibility narrows by published hierarchy so the conversion house is not forced to finance instruments that become unfinanceable in the squeeze. A contained default is processed under precommitted workflow: the default triggers are mechanical, close-out is rule-bound, loss waterfall is applied in published order, and the rail continues for ordinary participants because the public cannot be punished for a private failure. Corridor tightening triggers activate where cross-border exists, narrowing conversion flows that would allow the fastest actors to drain domestic liquidity. The system publishes state transitions and the category-level rationale. The audit shows that facility access was allocated by criteria and that no discretionary rescues were granted. The funding squeeze does not disappear, but the rail remains usable, and usability is what prevents panic from becoming political.

The exception attempt versus refusal cascade is the hinge that decides whether the rail remains public or becomes a rebranded private club. A shock produces fear. Fear produces calls for flexibility. Flexibility is translated into a request for discretionary overrides. Discretionary overrides are framed as temporary stabilization. Temporary stabilization becomes permanent privilege because privileged participants become dependent on the privilege and then defend it as essential. Essential privilege becomes the new toll. The toll thins baseline truth and sells time. Selling time recreates aristocratic money. The state machine blocks this by making exceptions constitutional events: any exception must be published, bounded, sunset, and audited, and the audit must show who benefited and why. Exceptions that cannot survive sunlight and sunset are denied. This protocol is not moral posturing. It is structural defense against capture, because capture succeeds by hiding in the language of emergency.

Cross-border is where stress governance becomes statecraft at full voltage. Without corridor triggers, a stress event becomes a corridor run: the most mobile participants route through the jurisdiction that sells time, domestic liquidity thins, and domestic participants interpret the corridor as betrayal. The state machine therefore treats corridor tightening as first-class action: published triggers, published narrowing behavior, published effect on conversion limits and haircuts, and published rationale tied to preserving domestic closure. Corridors must be governable or they become trap doors. A governable corridor is not frictionless. It is predictable, and predictability is what prevents exit arbitrage from becoming political backlash.

The national power claim is not rhetorical. It is mechanical. A country that keeps closure stable under stress, keeps marks coherent, keeps proof admissible, and publishes audits reduces the uncertainty tax paid in haircuts and funding premia. Lower uncertainty taxes lengthen domestic duration because longer instruments become financeable without punitive haircuts. Longer domestic duration lowers sovereign refinancing spreads and reduces dependence on foreign-unit clauses and foreign mood cycles. Reduced dependence increases sovereignty because fiscal and industrial policy become less hostage to external tightening. Stress governance is therefore not an operational appendix. It is the mechanism by which the settlement rail becomes a national asset rather than a fragile project.

A money-grade settlement rail is built by publishing how stress is governed and then proving, repeatedly, that the rail will not trade finality for calm, will not trade equality for stability slogans, and will not trade public truth for private lanes. The stress state machine makes tightening predictable, completion credible, and behavior auditable. The audit obligation makes privilege measurable and therefore harder to defend. Together they create the only condition under which market instruments can become everyday settlement inputs without becoming a panic machine: a society where closure remains closure even when uncomfortable, and where uncomfortable actions are documented rather than whispered.

CHAPTER 53

CORRIDORS AND MUTUAL RECOGNITION

CROSS-BORDER SETTLEMENT THAT EXPANDS SOVEREIGNTY INSTEAD OF CREATING EXIT ARBITRAGE.

Cross-border settlement is where monetary architecture becomes statecraft. A domestic rail can be constitutional and still be broken by the outside world if cross-border access is treated as convenience rather than as treaty-grade trust. When market instruments become spendable, the first serious question from any ministry is not whether the system works in calm, but whether it survives the week when foreign funding tightens, compliance rules shift, or a geopolitical headline turns corridors into exit routes. A corridor that is not governed becomes a trap door. The most mobile participants use it to escape uncertainty first, domestic liquidity thins, and domestic participants conclude that citizenship in the rail is a slower form of risk. That conclusion is political poison because it converts modernization into perceived betrayal. Mutual recognition is the design that prevents corridors from turning into arbitrage engines that reward speed and punish the public, because mutual recognition makes the corridor an extension of enforceable rules rather than an invitation to discretionary escape.

The corridor problem is not primarily technology. It is primitive alignment. Two jurisdictions can connect ledgers and still fail if they disagree on finality, custody priority, encumbrance recognition, bounded remedies, mark doctrine, and restriction handling. Those disagreements are not legal trivia. They are tradable advantages. In stress, capital purchases time, and time is purchased by routing through the jurisdiction whose primitives are more predictable. That routing becomes an exit advantage that domestic participants cannot match, and the market interprets that advantage as two-speed citizenship. The corridor survives only if the underlying primitives are aligned enough that routing cannot buy a different constitution.

Finality alignment is first because finality is the meaning of closure. If one jurisdiction treats finality as a firm legal state with safe harbor and the other treats it as reopenable by broad claims or discretionary enforcement, then cross-border receipts become conditional promises. Conditional promises force higher haircuts. Higher haircuts tighten funding. Tight funding triggers runs. The corridor becomes a channel for withdrawal instead of diversification. Mutual recognition therefore requires agreement on completion windows, finality time, safe harbor doctrine for compliant recipients, and bounded remedies that deliver restitution without clawback from recipients after finality. Without this, cross-border spendability cannot be money-grade because recipients cannot know which law governs closure when dispute arrives.

Priority and encumbrance recognition are next because property rights are the substrate of finance. If one jurisdiction treats encumbrance tags as authoritative and the other treats them as advisory, then collateral becomes contestable during stress, and contestable collateral is priced as haircut inflation. Haircut inflation becomes funding withdrawal. Funding withdrawal becomes forced selling. Forced selling becomes volatility. Volatility produces further haircuts. The corridor becomes an amplifier of systemic instability. Mutual recognition therefore requires that encumbrance tags, tender tags, lien priorities, and insolvency survivability are recognized across the corridor, and that priority disputes are routed into bounded lanes with standardized evidence and binding timelines so proof stays liquid. Cross-border is not a place where litigation delay can be tolerated, because delay is the uncertainty tax that the public ultimately pays through spreads and withdrawal of closure.

Marks and correction doctrine form the third pillar because marks are settlement inputs. Different mark sources, different timestamps, different fallbacks, and different correction windows create a tradable advantage. Participants route to the regime whose marks are more predictable under stress. Predictable marks become cheaper haircuts. Cheaper haircuts become cheaper conversion. Cheaper conversion becomes exit advantage. Mutual recognition therefore requires compatible mark authority: accepted sources by class, fixed timestamps, fallback hierarchies in disorder, and correction-as-event doctrine with bounded windows. The corridor does not need identical microstructure. It needs compatible truth.

Restriction handling is the fourth pillar because enforcement timing is where corridors break politically. In disorder, sanctions rumors and compliance de-risking can freeze corridors overnight. If restriction handling is discretionary or opaque, rumors become runs. If restriction handling targets recipients retroactively, merchants and households learn that cross-border receipts are conditional credit and they will refuse. Mutual recognition requires prospective restriction handling where possible: restrict payer channels, preserve safe harbor for compliant recipients after finality, and apply corridor tightening by published triggers so narrowing is rule-bound rather than rumor-driven. A corridor that narrows silently is not a corridor. It is a private lane for those with early warning.

Corridor tightening must be treated as a state machine, not as diplomacy by telephone. Tightening triggers are published and measurable: mark divergence bands, settlement fail thresholds, dispute backlog thresholds, anomaly and fraud thresholds, funding spread thresholds, and compliance risk thresholds. When triggers fire, corridor conversion limits narrow by band, haircuts tighten by band for cross-border conversions, and certain instrument tiers may be temporarily excluded from corridor conversion while remaining usable domestically. These actions are posted as state transitions. The corridor does not pretend to be frictionless in disorder. It proves it is governable. Predictability prevents capital from treating the corridor as an escape hatch exploited before domestic participants react.

A corridor treaty negotiation shows how these primitives become geopolitics rather than paperwork. A finance ministry wants corridor access to reduce external financing costs and attract long-term capital. A central bank wants assurance that cross-border settlement will not create uncontrolled drains in stress. A supervisor wants enforceable proof, bounded remedies, and publishable audits. An exchange wants volume and reputational legitimacy. Incumbents want private lanes preserved and will lobby to keep primitives ambiguous. The negotiation begins where it always begins, at finality. One side insists on strong safe harbor and strict finality clocks so merchants can rely on closure. The other side seeks broader reopenability "for consumer protection," which is a path to discretionary reversals. The corridor survives only if the treaty locks finality clocks and locks bounded remedies with funded restitution so victims are made whole without reopening receipts. Priority then becomes the second fight. One side wants encumbrance tags recognized as authoritative with insolvency survivability. The other side wants broad court discretion "to do justice," which is a path to delay rent. The corridor survives only if priority is encoded and disputes are bounded and fast enough to keep proof liquid. The audit clause becomes the third fight. One side wants publication of state transitions, correction events, facility usage summaries, and exception requests granted or denied, because publication is how privilege is prevented. The other side fears reputational exposure and wants opacity. The corridor survives only if an audit perimeter is treaty-grade, because opacity is how two-speed citizenship returns. Tightening triggers are then negotiated as the safety valve: published thresholds, published narrowing behavior, and a mutual commitment that corridor tightening will be rule-bound rather than whispered. Ratification is not a ceremonial step. It is the moment the corridor becomes enforceable trust instead of aspirational cooperation, because enforceable trust is what markets finance.

The sanction rumor week is the corridor's real exam because rumor is where corridors become trap doors. A geopolitical headline triggers compliance teams to re-evaluate exposure. A rumor spreads that one jurisdiction may impose settlement restrictions. Compliance desks de-risk because enforcement timing is unpriceable when finality is conditional. Haircuts jump on cross-border conversions because counterparties fear being stranded. Dealers withdraw inventory because funding terms tighten and they do not want to be trapped in a corridor whose rules might change overnight. Offshore spreads widen. Sovereign spreads widen not because fundamentals changed overnight but because the market reprices rule uncertainty as a haircut event. Under misalignment, the fastest actors route through the jurisdiction perceived as safer, domestic liquidity thins on the other side, and the public interprets the thinning as insider flight. Politics responds with ad hoc controls, and controls confirm the belief that rules are negotiable, turning modernization into betrayal. Under mutual recognition, the corridor state machine triggers predictably. Tightening is activated by published thresholds: corridor conversion limits narrow, cross-border haircuts tighten within bands, high-risk corridor flows are throttled, and payer-channel restrictions are applied prospectively where compliance requires it, preserving safe harbor for compliant recipients after finality. State transitions are published. The corridor becomes a managed valve rather than a rumor-driven floodgate. Participants reprice risk, but they do not sprint for exit because the constitution does not change midstream.

Governance determines whether the corridor is stable or merely plausible. A corridor authority must exist with defined duties: maintain the treaty primitives, operate the corridor state machine, publish state transitions and audit outputs, and coordinate dispute lane interoperability. Disputes must have a bounded forum: a defined arbitration or court recognition mechanism with standardized evidence and binding timelines so litigation cannot become a slow weapon that freezes settlement. Emergency amendments must be constrained, because emergency amendments are how corridors become discretionary tools and discretionary tools become exit advantages for insiders. Any amendment to finality clocks, mark doctrine, priority recognition, or tightening triggers must require published rationale, transition windows, and post-implementation review, with an explicit presumption against changes during stress unless predefined triggers are met. The corridor's publication perimeter must be treaty-grade: enough to prove fairness and discipline, not enough to expose exploit maps. It publishes state transitions, trigger categories, correction event categories, corridor limit changes, haircuts band changes, facility usage summaries by criteria, dispute throughput statistics, restitution statistics by category, and exception requests granted or denied. It does not publish private counterparty details. This balance is what allows corridor legitimacy without turning the corridor into an instruction manual for attack.

Corridor credibility has a direct mechanism effect on national financing terms that power brokers understand immediately. When corridors are trustworthy, long-term capital does not demand foreign-law and foreign-unit clauses as aggressively because settlement finality and dispute enforceability are not fragile. When corridors are untrustworthy, external lenders insist on foreign-unit clauses, offshore collateral arrangements, and governing law outside the domestic system, because they are buying enforceable closure. A corridor that proves finality, priority, and audit discipline reduces that demand. Reduced foreign-unit clauses lower refinancing risk because projects are less exposed to sudden currency mismatch and foreign enforcement timing. Lower refinancing risk narrows spreads. Narrower spreads extend duration. Longer duration increases domestic project capacity because refinancing cliffs become less frequent and less punitive. This is the corridor's sovereignty dividend: not a slogan about independence, but a reduction in the external conditions embedded in the financing contract.

Interoperability has to reflect treaty logic rather than platform logic. Conversion houses interoperate through agreed message standards for tender tags, encumbrance tags, mark snapshots, correction events, and state transitions. Dispute lanes interoperate through recognition of evidence standards and bounded remedies. Restitution mechanisms interoperate through settlement of reimbursement flows without reopening recipient closure. None of this requires identical institutions. It requires compatible primitives and a shared refusal to make closure negotiable by discretion. The corridor is the place where the new monetary rail either becomes a global public good or becomes a weapon for the fastest exits.

The most credible corridor opens slowly under low limits, conservative eligible tiers, and visible tightening behavior that treats disorder as normal weather rather than scandal. Early corridors should prioritize instruments whose priority and marks are easiest to govern and whose markets remain deep under stress, because the corridor must survive its first shock. Scaling follows only after stress-year audits demonstrate that tightening triggers worked, closure was preserved, no privileged warning lanes existed, and domestic participants were not left as residual risk while the fastest escaped. A corridor that grows faster than its legitimacy will be forced into improvisation, and improvisation is how corridors become dependence.

Cross-border settlement in Market Instruments Money Theory is therefore not an invitation to frictionless flow. It is a redesign of how countries share trust without surrendering closure. Mutual recognition aligns primitives so a corridor cannot sell a different constitution to those who can move fastest. The corridor state machine tightens by rule, not by rumor. Governance prevents emergency amendments from becoming private discretion. Audit publication makes privilege measurable and therefore harder to defend. When those conditions hold, cross-border spendability expands national financing power by reducing uncertainty premia, narrowing foreign-law clause dependence, deepening duration, and preventing exit arbitrage that fractures legitimacy at home.

PART EIGHT
THE BLUEPRINT FOR THE NEXT MARKET

DEMOCRATIC CAPITAL MARKETS AS CIVIC ARCHITECTURE, NOT A PRODUCT.

The argument changes form here. Critique is descriptive; a blueprint is a claim about control. It says the market is not a venue that happens to trade. It is a public machine that decides who can own, who can finance, who can prove, who can settle, and who is allowed to be finished. When that machine sells access, it manufactures hierarchy as reliably as a refinery produces output. When it makes access universal, it still produces winners, but it compels winning to occur inside the same rulebook rather than by purchasing a private lane outside it. That is the entire ideological line: financial citizenship is not permissioned.

"A market is not democratic when everyone can enter; it is democratic when no one can buy a different set of rules once they do."

The democratic premise is practical. A participant arriving with one unit of currency should face the same opportunity set as a fund arriving with a billion. Same instruments allowed by the same published eligibility. Same auctions. Same order types. Same baseline truth. Same finality. Same dispute windows. Same closure protections. The only differences permitted are objective risk limits, applied as public math: position size caps, leverage caps, velocity caps, authentication tiers, and collateral requirements that prevent self-harm and system harm. Equality here is not sentimental. It is structural: the market cannot sell inequality as a feature by selling better truth, better execution, better time, or better closure to the largest bidder.

A democratic market is not defined by who can click a button. It is defined by whether the button connects to the same reality the institutions see. The blueprint therefore deletes the historical gate: mandatory brokerage as passport. Participants open accounts directly with the exchange. They may appoint a fiduciary, but only as a delegate of authority, never as a gate to eligibility. They choose the deposit bank. They choose the custodian. Banks and custodians compete as utilities, not as patrons. Advisors compete as service providers, not as landlords of access.

Picture the smallest participant. A citizen opens an exchange account and does not ask permission from a broker to be considered real. Identity tiering exists, but it is tiering for limits, not for opportunity. The citizen is placed in K1, receives published caps, and receives the same public book and the same auction schedule as everyone else. The citizen selects a deposit bank from an eligible list and selects a custodian from an eligible list. The citizen appoints no fiduciary, or appoints one with narrow scope, because authority is explicit: view only, trade authority, withdrawal authority, product permissions. The system does not become democratic because the citizen is invited. It becomes democratic because the citizen can enter without renting access.

Now picture the largest participant. The fund opens the same type of exchange account, sees the same baseline truth, trades into the same auctions, and settles under the same finality time. The fund is granted larger limits only because it proves larger capacity and posts larger collateral, not because it pays for different rules. It cannot buy a separate record. It cannot buy priority matching. It cannot buy early sight of the book. It can only deploy more capital within a constitution it does not control. That is the ideological pivot expressed as mechanism: scale is rewarded for bearing risk and supplying depth, not for purchasing secrecy and time.

Equal opportunity requires equal truth. The baseline record cannot be ceremonial. The public feed must be sufficient to trade safely: consolidated prints, usable depth snapshots, auction imbalance transparency, official marks, corporate action calendars, correction logs, and timestamped state announcements when stress modes activate. Premium analytics can exist, but premium survival is prohibited. If safe participation requires buying a privileged feed, then the market is not democratic; it is an information caste system with better typography. The blueprint therefore hardens baseline truth as non-degradable: it cannot be quietly thinned to manufacture private rents, and any change in baseline truth is treated as a governance event with heightened thresholds and post-event review.

Equal opportunity also requires equal closure. Finality is not a courtesy; it is the definition of money-grade participation. Finality time is identical for all. Dispute windows are identical for all. Merchant safe harbor is identical for all. Once the receipt reaches finality, the recipient is protected, and later fraud or enforcement actions are handled through funded restitution and restriction of the payer's future access, not by clawing back from innocent recipients. A small participant cannot be treated as disposable because the system assumes they can absorb delay. A large participant cannot be treated as untouchable because the system assumes they matter. Closure is a public guarantee, not a status perk.

Equal opportunity under stress is where democracies live or die. A market that becomes discretionary in stress teaches its participants to run early. A market that allocates time by relationship teaches its public that citizenship ends when volatility begins. The blueprint therefore binds stress behavior in advance: published throttles, published buffer bands, published safe modes, published redemption priorities, published post-event access audits. The system does not promise that stress will be painless. It promises that stress will be governed by criteria rather than by telephone calls.

The institutional meeting that makes this real is not a product launch. It looks like a crisis drill. A regulator asks what happens when marks fracture, when a data feed is disputed, when a large issuer in the backing pool hits a corporate action week, when a cyber event targets mint authority, when a cross-border corridor faces sudden restrictions. The exchange does not answer with reassurance. It answers with state transitions, thresholds, and the loss waterfall: which functions pause, which continue, how completion remains within window W, how merchant safe harbor remains intact at finality time, how restitution is funded and delivered, how disputes are triaged into a fast lane, how corridor rules narrow without improvisation. When the meeting ends, the system has not been praised. It has been bounded. That is the only approval that matters.

A democratic market must also be democratic in agency. Participants choose their deposit bank, not to chase perks, but to prevent captivity. Settlement cash legs become a competitive service under published standards. Participants choose their custodian, not to chase prestige, but to prevent proof monopolies. Custodians must support the authoritative record, encumbrance tagging, and fast entitlement proof. They cannot weaponize delay because delay becomes a hidden haircut, and hidden haircuts become exclusion. Fiduciaries, if appointed, are licensed delegates with logged actions and revocable authority. No layer becomes a private sovereign over participation.

Cross-border participation is treated as earned reciprocity, not marketing. A democratic market expands outward only when it can keep its closure promise across jurisdictions. Corridors open only where mutual recognition exists in practice: recognition of settlement finality, recognition of custody priority and encumbrance tags, recognition of dispute outcomes within bounded remedy bands, predictable restriction handling that preserves merchant safe harbor. This is why the blueprint does not begin with global openness. It begins with domestic proof and domestic finality, then adds corridors one at a time, with published corridor rules and published shutdown criteria. Openness without recognition becomes an enforcement crisis. Enforcement crises end in ad hoc controls. Ad hoc controls destroy legitimacy.

The benefits of this ideology are not rhetorical. They compound. Wealth formation becomes citizenship rather than membership because the public is no longer forced into inferior truth and inferior execution. Capital formation becomes cheaper because proof is standardized, disputes are fast, and liquidity is not hostage to private chokepoints. Sovereignty strengthens because domestic savings can be converted into domestic duration without begging for foreign-unit clauses that import external governance into national projects. Corruption rents shrink because discretionary access to proof and closure loses value when procedure becomes universal. Resilience improves because legitimacy improves, and legitimacy reduces the rule-shock premium that lives inside spreads and inside duration.

Deployment follows the doctrine as staging, because a market is not democratic if it requires faith in what will be built later. Stage one is universal domestic access under one rulebook: direct exchange accounts, selectable banks and custodians, non-degradable baseline truth, identical finality, fast disputes, conservative caps, published stress behavior. Stage two expands instruments and listing pathways without lowering truth: minority protections enforced fast enough to matter, disclosure discipline that does not rely on elite bottlenecks, measurable market-making obligations, published execution quality. Stage three opens cross-border corridors only where recognition is enforceable, with corridor limits and restriction handling published before the first shock arrives.

The blueprint therefore sets a single test that never changes. Does a small participant receive the same reality as the largest participant, bounded only by objective risk limits, and protected by the same closure perimeter under stress. If yes, the market is democratic in the only sense that matters for capital. If no, it is a club with a public brochure.

CHAPTER 54
BLUEPRINT FOR A PUBLIC-INTEREST MARKET

FIRST PRINCIPLES FOR REDESIGNING CAPITAL FORMATION IN THE PUBLIC INTEREST.

A market is a constitution wearing numbers. It decides, in advance, who can enter, what counts as proof, what must be disclosed, how disputes resolve, when obligations are finished, and who is permitted to buy time when stress arrives. In most countries the constitution is not written in one statute. It is scattered across licensing rules, custody practice, exchange fee schedules, data contracts, settlement conventions, and the quiet permissions that let some participants operate with advantages that are never framed as advantages. The public reads free market and imagines open doors. The machine reads tiered access and runs accordingly.

A public-interest market begins by refusing the lie that neutrality happens by default. Markets are designed. Designs allocate. Allocation becomes political the moment households notice that opportunity is not competed for inside the arena but rationed before the arena begins. When access to the book is mediated by gatekeepers, when baseline truth is thinned into a paid product, when closure depends on relationship, the market stops being a place where the best ideas win and becomes a place where the best lanes win. A public-interest market is not a moral sermon. It is a structural refusal to sell lanes.

The first principle is equal opportunity set. The phrase is easy to applaud and hard to implement because inequality in markets is rarely announced as inequality. It arrives as a series of tolerable exceptions: one participant has faster sight of imbalance, another has a different route, another has a cheaper way to borrow, another has a softer margin call, another has a quieter way to internalize flow. Each exception looks technical. The compound looks like destiny.

Equal opportunity set is therefore defined as a prohibition: no participant may purchase a different constitution. The one-dollar participant and the billion participant see the same auction schedule, the same order types, the same baseline record, the same public prints, the same official marks, the same corporate action calendar, the same correction log, the same finality time, the same dispute windows. Differences are permitted only where they are objective risk limits, published in advance, applied as math, and auditable after stress. The market does not promise equal outcomes. It promises equal entry into the same arena.

That sounds like a slogan until it is tied to a specific architecture: direct exchange accounts. The exchange becomes the public interface, not a private club fronted by intermediaries. Participants open accounts directly with the exchange as primary market identity. Intermediaries become optional service providers, never mandatory passports. A participant may appoint a fiduciary, but fiduciary appointment is a delegation of authority, not a ticket to the book. A participant chooses a deposit bank from an eligible list. A participant chooses a custodian from an eligible list. The system is democratic because the participant is not required to rent access from a broker or a prime service to be treated as real.

This one shift does more than widen access. It collapses a chain of subtle rent extraction. When access is mediated, the mediator can internalize flow, sell routing, sell speed, sell information, sell help that is actually gatekeeping, and then describe the entire arrangement as necessary service. Direct accounts reverse that logic. Services remain. Gatekeeping becomes illegitimate by design.

The second principle is baseline truth as a public good. A public-interest market does not forbid premium tools. It forbids premium survival. The baseline record must be sufficient for safe participation without buying a private feed or privileged visibility. That means the public record includes not only last trades, but usable depth snapshots, auction imbalances, official marks and correction logs, corporate action schedules, and state announcements when stress modes activate.

If baseline truth is too thin, the public can enter but cannot defend itself. The public becomes liquidity for those who can see. The market becomes democratic in invitation and oligarchic in outcome. That failure is structural, not educational. No financial literacy campaign can solve a paywalled reality. The blueprint therefore hardens a rule: baseline truth is non-degradable. It cannot be quietly thinned to manufacture private rents. Any change to baseline truth is treated as a constitutional amendment with heightened approval thresholds, public rationale, and post-event review.

The third principle is equal closure. Money-grade participation is not a feeling. It is finality. Finality must be identical for all participants, because closure that varies by status is the purest expression of privilege. When a merchant or recipient is unsure whether a receipt is truly finished, the transaction becomes credit. Credit becomes pricing. Pricing becomes exclusion.

A public-interest market defines finality as legal state, not as a platform notification. Finality time is published. Dispute windows are published. Safe harbor is published. After finality, innocent recipients are protected, and later fraud or enforcement actions are handled through funded restitution and restriction of the payer's future access rather than clawbacks from completed transactions. This is not a customer service feature. It is how the market prevents daily life from being turned into unsecured lending.

The fourth principle is equal treatment under stress. The calm-day market is easy to praise. The stress-day market reveals the constitution. A public-interest market publishes its stress behavior and then follows it. Throttles, buffers, safe modes, conversion constraints, and facility access are rule-triggered and auditable. Post-stress access audits are mandatory. The system does not claim to eliminate pain. It claims to eliminate improvisation. Improvisation is where relationship becomes policy. Relationship policy is where legitimacy dies.

If a system can be paused by a phone call, if exceptions can be granted by status, if facility access is discretionary, then the public lane is decorative. A market cannot ask citizens to accept that they are bound by rules institutions are permitted to bypass. The blueprint imposes an anti-capture discipline: objective access criteria, exemption sunsets, and published outcomes that show whether time was allocated by criteria or by status.

The fifth principle is agency over intermediaries. A market cannot be democratic if participation requires submission to a private chain of dependency. Banks, custodians, and fiduciaries are selectable utilities. The participant chooses the deposit bank that holds the cash leg and interfaces with domestic payment rails. The participant chooses the custodian that holds the securities leg and supports entitlement proof and encumbrance tagging. The participant appoints a fiduciary as a delegate of authority with scope that can be revoked.

This is not only consumer empowerment. It is market structure. Choice prevents a proof monopoly. Proof monopolies become rents. Rents become choke points. Choke points become political power. Political power becomes rule shock. The system cannot survive long enough to compound if it invites proof monopolies back into the stack.

These principles impose a deployment discipline: constitutional first, volume second. Proof before scale. Finality before marketing. Dispute speed before leverage. Baseline truth before premium products. The reason is that low-trust environments are not repaired by participation. They are repaired by enforceable procedures that survive the first adversarial test. If participation is widened before proof and closure are hardened, compounding is not democratized. Loss is democratized, and the old gatekeepers return with a fresh story about why the public cannot be trusted.

A public-interest market begins by stating what cannot be sold. Paid priority cannot exist. Hidden internalization that allows some actors to trade against the public before the public sees the market cannot exist. Baseline truth cannot be degraded into a paid product. Finality cannot vary by status. Disputes cannot be routed into slow courts by default. Exemptions cannot persist without sunset and evidence. Stress behavior cannot be improvised.

What remains after these prohibitions is not a utopia. It is a different battleground. Skill and scale still matter. Large funds will still be better at bearing risk and providing liquidity. The difference is that their advantage must be earned inside a shared constitution. They cannot purchase a second constitution and then call it efficiency.

A blueprint is incomplete if it cannot be read as a promise to the smallest participant without becoming a threat to the largest. The promise is simple and severe. The citizen enters without renting access. The citizen sees the same market reality. The citizen receives the same closure. The citizen is constrained only by objective risk limits. The fund enters without buying a different rulebook. The fund sees the same reality. The fund receives the same closure. The fund is constrained only by its own risk appetite and its published limits. In that architecture, inequality can still exist, but it cannot be manufactured by hidden lanes. It must be created by decisions made in daylight. That is the point where markets stop being permission and become citizenship.

CHAPTER 55

THE PUBLIC MARKET INFRASTRUCTURE STACK

EXCHANGE, CLEARING, CUSTODY, IDENTITY, COMPLIANCE, AND HOW THE RAILS FIT TOGETHER

A democratic market is enforced below the screen, where the rails decide who is visible, who receives closure, who can prove ownership fast enough to finance, and who is forced to wait. The surface can look open while the machine remains permissioned through private identity gates, private routing, private internalization, private proof, and private time allocation. A public-interest stack removes that permission layer by turning the exchange into the primary civic interface: the participant account lives at the exchange, not behind a broker's passport. The account is not a view; it is legal presence with four rights that do not vary by status: submit orders into a common matching system, receive a common baseline record, settle under a common completion window and finality time, and choose service providers without renting access.

Direct exchange accounts change the geometry of control because they collapse the default advantage of mediation. When access is mediated, the mediator can internalize flow, ration routing, sell faster sight, and describe gatekeeping as service. When the account sits at the exchange, internalization becomes a bounded exception rather than the public's default experience; routing becomes rule, not artistry; eligibility becomes published math, not invitation. The democratic claim is not that advantage disappears, but that advantage must be earned inside one constitution rather than purchased outside it.

The exchange layer contains only what must be universal: one book, one set of auctions, one set of order types, one definition of priority, one timestamp regime, one correction protocol, one baseline record sufficient for safe participation. Premium tools may exist, but premium survival is prohibited. Paid priority is prohibited. Hidden early sight is prohibited. A matching engine that behaves differently by participant class manufactures inequality at the exact point where equality is supposed to exist, and it does so invisibly enough that the public blames itself for outcomes produced by rails.

The exchange publishes the public record as the system's memory and evidence base. This is not a marketing feed; it is what makes proof admissible at speed. Baseline truth must include consolidated prints, usable depth snapshots, auction imbalance indicators where appropriate, official marks, corporate action calendars, correction logs with timestamps and reasons, and market-state messages that announce transitions and bind them to the record. The baseline must be fast enough to be usable, stable enough to be admissible, and thick enough that safe participation does not require paid survival. A thin baseline turns the public into liquidity for those who can see; a slow baseline turns the public into delayed execution for those who can wait; an editable baseline turns disputes into litigation; each is a stealth conversion of citizenship into subscription.

Baseline truth therefore becomes constitutional. It is non-degradable by quiet business decision. Any reduction is treated as an amendment: heightened thresholds, public rationale, post-event review, and a measurable impact test that asks whether smaller participants become more systematically selected against. The record also hardens state behavior. Normal, elevated volatility, disorder, safe mode, recovery are not vibes; they are published states with time-stamped transitions, archived so the operator cannot rewrite history after the stress week.

Beneath the exchange sits clearing, and clearing is the mechanism that prevents the market from becoming a private contest of balance sheets. Clearing converts a web of bilateral promises into governed exposure: netting where netting is lawful, margin by published methodology, default procedures by workflow, a loss waterfall by order, and replenishment by rule. In a public-interest stack, clearing is not an institutional convenience; it is the equality engine that prevents survival from being sold by private exceptions. If clearing is discretionary, time becomes a premium product. If clearing is opaque, margin becomes privilege by stealth. If clearing is negotiable, the constitution fractures at the moment it is supposed to protect closure.

Clearing therefore binds closure to published completion and finality. A participant is not finished because a counterparty cooperates; a participant is finished because the system declares the obligation extinguished under law at a defined time. Variable finality is gatekeeping through time. Time is the most monetizable commodity in stress. The stack forbids selling it.

Margin policy is not merely risk control; it is the market's internal tax on volatility and a quiet lever of political economy. A public-interest stack publishes margin methodology, stress add-ons, intraday adjustment rules, eligible collateral rules, and the triggers that move the system between states. It also publishes action hierarchy: widen buffers before improvising freezes, tighten throttles before rewriting rules, narrow eligibility by criteria not by phone call, prioritize completion and closure before discretionary advantage. The order of operations is the constitution expressed as procedure: closure before profit, proof before convenience, rules before relationship.

Default management is where the stack either becomes infrastructure or theater. A vague "we will handle defaults" becomes political under stress; a workflow with triggers, clocks, auctions, and loss allocation becomes operational. The stack defines default triggers, close-out mechanics, portfolio auction procedures, loss-sharing allocations, replenishment rules, and resolution handoffs. It assigns responsibilities with names and time bounds, drills them with real participants, and records outcomes. A democratic market cannot claim legitimacy if the first default reveals improvisation for insiders and rigidity for everyone else.

Settlement is where exchange truth becomes real ownership and where many supposedly open systems become quietly closed. Settlement is not back office; it is sovereignty over completion. A public-interest stack defines completion window W, finality time F, dispute windows, correction protocol, outage behavior, and restitution rules when the system fails. The market can tolerate price volatility; it cannot tolerate ambiguity about whether ownership moved, because ambiguity is a haircut, haircuts shorten funding, shortened funding forces sales, forced sales turn opportunity into a privilege of balance sheet size.

Cash settlement therefore runs through participant-chosen deposit banks under uniform obligations. Banks compete, but they cannot sell better finality. They provide the cash leg under published time limits and attest completion into the authoritative record. If a bank fails, resolution transfers the obligation so completion does not become a private negotiation that only large participants can survive. Securities settlement runs through participant-chosen custodians under a harmonized proof standard. Custodians store assets; the system stores proof. Beneficial ownership is provable at speed; entitlements are deterministic; encumbrances are tagged, priority-recognized, and auditable so the same asset cannot silently support two obligations. Custody becomes a utility service, not a proof monopoly.

The encumbrance registry is the boundary between a market and a confidence game. Double-pledge is counterfeit credit. It rarely surfaces on calm days because calm days do not test priority. Stress tests priority by forcing claims to become real. The stack therefore enforces encumbrance singularity routinely: tags are posted as admissible state, double-pledge attempts are rejected at the interface, reconciliation is frequent enough that over-issuance cannot hide behind delay. Encumbrance also disciplines leverage without moralism: borrowing becomes a visible state with objective limits and auditable consequences, rather than a private arrangement that quietly shifts risk onto the public in stress.

Corporate actions are where entitlement ambiguity becomes solvency rumor if the system is weak. The stack treats corporate action processing as market integrity: public calendar, deterministic mapping, bounded corrections, and a fast dispute lane that restores proof rather than creating rents through delay. Record dates are conversion-sensitive windows where confusion can be weaponized. A public-interest stack precommits to how entitlement states are frozen and reopened, how marks are published and corrected, how disputes are triaged, and how capacity is allocated so corporate actions do not metastasize into runs through uncertainty.

Identity sits alongside these layers as admission discipline, but identity cannot be an opportunity gate. Tiered identity exists to price risk, prevent fraud, and enforce compliance, not to ration the book. The smallest participant enters the same arena with smaller limits; the largest participant enters the same arena with larger limits because it proves capacity and posts collateral. Constraints are public math, not permission. Tiering avoids two political failures at once: exclusion disguised as protection and participation that ends in mass harm. Leverage gates, product permission gates, velocity gates, and withdrawal authority gates protect households without locking them out of compounding, and they do so by procedure rather than paternal sermon.

Compliance must be embedded without turning the stack into either a laundering rail or a surveillance regime. A stack that ignores illicit flow becomes politically indefensible. A stack that improvises freezes becomes economically unusable. The solution is rule-bound restriction handling: screening at the boundary, tiered identity limits, predictable enforcement, and a hard safe harbor concept that preserves closure once finality is reached. Restrictions target payer access prospectively; innocent recipients are protected; restitution funds cover what enforcement cannot claw back without destroying finality. This is not softness; it is what keeps enforcement timing from becoming the system's hidden interest rate.

Dispute resolution is throughput, not decor. Slow disputes are not an inconvenience; they are an interest rate embedded in spreads and haircuts. They turn proof into uncertainty, uncertainty into funding fragility, fragility into exclusion. A democratic stack therefore treats disputes as liquidity infrastructure: standardized evidence, narrow remedies, binding timelines, bounded appeals that do not reopen the world. The dispute lane exists to restore admissible state quickly enough that assets do not become legally radioactive. It also limits rumor power by letting participants check state instead of trading narrative.

Uniform execution is constitutional. Paid priority is barred. Hidden internalization that gives first look at incoming flow is barred. Side venues cannot siphon the public stream and report after. Common matching and auction rules are enforced. Where exceptions exist, they are published, bounded, and auditable, or they become the seed of a second constitution. Uniform settlement and uniform finality are equally constitutional: no participant receives slower closure because of size, and no participant receives faster closure because of relationship. Time allocation is criteria-based, auditable, and published, because time is the resource that stress tries hardest to privatize.

Premium services remain permissible only where they do not determine survival. Analytics can be sold; priority cannot. Convenience can be sold; closure cannot. Faster dashboards can be sold; baseline truth cannot be degraded. Faster connectivity can be sold only if it does not alter matching priority or create early sight advantages that let participants trade against the public. Any proposal that thins baseline truth is treated as an attempt to sell inequality: it must answer who benefits, who becomes more systematically selected against, what happens to dispute rates, settlement fails, and auction volatility, and whether the public record remains sufficient for safe participation.

Operational capacity must be visible, not assumed. Uptime targets, recovery targets, completion windows, default drill schedules, entitlement processing times, dispute throughput, outage behavior, safe mode behavior are published, because a democratic market cannot demand trust as input; it must produce trust as output. Verification is not cynicism. It is the mechanism that keeps the constitution from being rewritten in the dark.

A normal-day sequence shows how the stack enforces equality without ceremony. A small participant opens a direct exchange account, selects a deposit bank and custodian, submits an order into the same auction calendar as the largest participant, receives the same baseline record, and settles under the same completion and finality rules. The exchange stamps the order, matches it under common priority, posts the trade to the record, and routes it to clearing. Clearing nets exposure, applies margin by published method, schedules settlement. The deposit bank moves the cash leg within W and attests completion. The custodian updates the asset leg deterministically. The authoritative record reflects completion. Finality arrives at F. No subscription upgrades the participant into reality. No phone call improves the outcome. Limits constrain size, not legitimacy.

A stress-day sequence shows whether the constitution survives pressure. Marks fracture across venues, data feeds disagree, narratives compete. The exchange posts state transition, activates the published fallback mark hierarchy, stamps corrections as events. Clearing widens margin add-ons within published bands, tightens limits by criteria, prioritizes completion. Settlement preserves closure for ordinary flows while throttling conversion-sensitive flows under published rules. The dispute lane triages entitlement claims with binding timelines and narrow remedies. Compliance applies restrictions prospectively without breaking safe harbor for finalized receipts. A post-stress access audit publishes facility usage and time allocation by criteria so the system cannot hide rescues behind silence. The day still hurts; the difference is that it hurts by rule rather than by relationship.

Corporate action week compresses the same test into entitlement proof. The issuer announces an action that changes share count and payment entitlements. The calendar posts into the baseline record immediately. Custodians lock entitlement mapping as event state, not email chain. Clearing pre-announces margin treatment under published rules and widens add-ons where settlement compression risk rises. The exchange narrows correction windows around mark-sensitive times and publishes fallback marks for disorder. The dispute lane allocates capacity and evidence standards in advance. At record date the system freezes only what must be frozen to preserve singular proof, then resumes with updated entitlements and updated marks posted as corrections, not whispers. Proof remains fast enough to prevent rumor from becoming a solvency narrative.

Default weekend tests whether the loss waterfall is real. A participant fails obligations; the trigger is mechanical. Clearing activates workflow, closes discretionary access, auctions the portfolio under pre-stated procedure, applies losses in published order, replenishes resources by rule. Settlement and custody continue ordinary processing so the public is not punished for a private failure. The record posts state and timestamps so rumor cannot claim hidden rescues. The system survives not by avoiding failure, but by proving failure does not rewrite the constitution.

Outage day tests whether the baseline record is a public good. Connectivity degrades; the exchange posts state, publishes what is guaranteed, invokes fallback behavior as defined, documents invocation into the record, and prevents resolution from becoming a private negotiation between the operator and the largest participants. Outage discipline protects small participants from being traded through in the dark and protects large participants from being blamed for operator discretion.

These are not illustrative flourishes; they show why the stack must be coherent. Equal access at the exchange fails if custody monopolizes proof. Proof fails if disputes are slow. Fast disputes fail if baseline truth is thin. Thick baseline fails if finality varies by status. Each weak layer becomes an aristocracy mechanism: a place where some buy time, buy proof, buy silence, or buy priority. The stack's deepest democratic feature is that it makes privilege measurable. When access is private, privilege hides inside service. When access is public, privilege must either disappear or justify itself. Audit trails answer the only legitimacy question that matters after stress: who received time, who received exceptions, and whether outcomes matched published criteria.

A public-interest stack does not abolish advantage. It forces advantage to live in daylight. Large participants still win by risk discipline, inventory skill, and capital at work. They do not win by purchasing a second constitution. They cannot buy thinner truth for the public, superior closure for themselves, or silent internalization against everyone else. The machine stops manufacturing inequality as a feature and begins compelling inequality to justify itself as performance rather than access.

CHAPTER 56
OPENING THE LISTING GATE
NEW PATHWAYS FOR REAL-ECONOMY FIRMS TO RAISE CAPITAL WITHOUT ELITE BOTTLENECKS.

A country does not build prosperity by teaching citizens to trade faster; it builds prosperity by giving real-economy firms a credible way to raise long money without converting admission into a relationship market. Listing is where a public system either becomes a financing engine or a patronage engine with a price feed. In many jurisdictions the gate is defended as prudence, but the observable output is scarcity of admission, scarcity of distribution, and scarcity of proof, all of which can be purchased by those with access to the right intermediaries. The result is predictable: connected firms raise duration, everyone else borrows short, pays more, grows slower, or sells outward; and when governments speak of entrepreneurship they are really describing a pipeline that ends at a private wall. A deployable listing reform cannot be a campaign to "encourage IPOs." It must be an institutional bargain that makes truth cheaper than ambiguity, and makes admission a function of criteria rather than a function of connection, while preserving fast enforcement so the system does not invite the public into a fraud corridor.

The first hard distinction is the one incumbents prefer to blur: disclosure integrity and elite bottlenecks are not the same thing. Disclosure integrity is a public good; it lowers cost of capital by lowering uncertainty and by lowering the premium investors demand to protect themselves against hidden risk. Elite bottlenecks are a private rent; they raise cost of capital by rationing entry, rationing distribution, and rationing whose story becomes official. In low-capacity states, bottlenecks are often defended as the only way to keep bad issuers out, but this is precisely how the gate turns into a bargaining table: the "good" issuers are those with relationships strong enough to be processed quickly and interpreted kindly, while the rest are left in limbo where financing becomes expensive and short. A public-interest listing gate is deployable only if it separates these functions: it standardizes disclosure so integrity is enforceable at scale, and it strips discretion out of admission so bottlenecks cannot be sold.

Standardization is not dilution. It is enforcement economics. A disclosure regime that cannot be checked quickly becomes a regime that cannot be enforced, and a regime that cannot be enforced becomes a regime where disclosure is theater and penalties are political. A deployable gate therefore begins with machine-checkable templates and clocks: uniform definitions for related-party exposure and controlling shareholder influence; uniform beneficial ownership reporting; uniform capital structure and voting rights disclosure; uniform use-of-proceeds reporting; uniform event reporting triggers with strict timing; uniform audit requirements and audit rotation rules where needed; uniform correction logs that treat changes as events rather than silent edits. Templates reduce bespoke negotiation, which is where gatekeeping monetizes ambiguity. Templates also reduce supervisory cost, which is the only way enforcement can be fast enough to shape behavior rather than merely punish after losses have been socialized into households.

The next deployable move is to replace the single listing cliff with a financing ladder that preserves truth while lowering the cost of becoming public. A single standard forces a false choice: exclude growth firms or weaken disclosure for everyone. A ladder is a constitutional device: segments differ by reporting cadence, float thresholds, governance requirements, and permitted investor exposure, but they share the same invariants that make the market investable rather than extractive: audited accounts, beneficial ownership clarity, related-party discipline, admissible records, bounded corrections, and fast dispute resolution. The ladder matters because most low-infrastructure countries have the same structural trap: the cost of being public is so high and so uncertain that only mature firms can attempt it, yet the economy needs growth firms to finance expansion, not merely to trade after they have already become entrenched. A ladder creates predictable progression by criteria and audited milestones, so admission is a process rather than a favor, and so firms are not required to purchase legitimacy from elite committees whose true product is scarcity.

Minority rights must be treated as infrastructure, not as aspiration. In bank-dominant systems where courts are slow and governance enforcement is inconsistent, minority shareholders are exposed to the oldest extraction moves: related-party tunneling, asset transfers, opaque guarantees, selective disclosure, and governance theater that can be explained away until the damage is irreversible. The market's failure pattern is therefore reliable: a wave of listings, insider extraction, governance scandals, retail exit, institutional refusal, and a return to bank dominance because equity becomes culturally branded as a trap rather than as a financing instrument. A deployable listing gate breaks this pattern by making minority protections fast enough to matter. Related-party transactions are disclosed in standardized form with materiality thresholds that cannot be massaged by narrative. Insider transactions are reported on strict clocks. Voting structures are transparent and bounded. Remedies are narrow and time-bounded so disputes restore proof rather than reward delay. In low-capacity states this is not a luxury. If adjudication is slow, uncertainty becomes a hidden haircut; hidden haircuts shorten duration;

shortened duration destroys the ability to finance long projects domestically.

Issuance economics then has to be redesigned so distribution power cannot recreate patronage at the moment ownership is minted. Many markets claim to be public while primary allocation is effectively private, because scarcity of admission and scarcity of distribution lets a small circle set price and allocate by relationship, and the public arrives later, paying a markup for access to what was already minted. That structure is not merely unfair; it is a legitimacy machine that converts households into late buyers and then blames households for leaving. A deployable democratic gate allows underwriting as service but forbids underwriting as constitution. Underwriters can assist due diligence, disclosure preparation, and investor education, and can support stabilization under strict limits; what must disappear is the ability to control admission through discretion and to allocate through patronage disguised as market practice. The practical instrument is a rule-bound primary process, auction-based or bookbuilt, with published eligibility, published allocation methodology, published oversubscription handling, and aggregate allocation reporting that makes favoritism visible enough to be risky. Allocation discipline is where the new constitution proves it is not a brochure, because allocation is where aristocracy hides most comfortably.

The public record must be continuous from day one. A newly listed issuer cannot live in a softer truth regime while the public supplies capital. Corporate action calendars, insider trades, related-party disclosures, material event disclosures, and correction logs must enter the baseline record under strict timing. Corrections must be recorded as events, not quiet edits, because silent edits convert truth into a subscription product and disputes into narrative combat. This continuous record requirement is deployable precisely because it reduces the space for improvisation: the issuer's job becomes legibility, and the system's job becomes admissibility. If the early cohort of listings teaches households that the public market is a corridor where insiders exit cleanly and the public absorbs the residue, the domestic investor base never forms, and without a domestic investor base, national ambition is financed by external clauses and external conditions.

The listing gate also must be coupled to post-trade reality, because firms do not raise capital into abstractions; they raise capital into settlement finality, custody proof, and dispute throughput. A gate that invites issuers but cannot prove ownership quickly under stress will produce an initial boom followed by a liquidity illusion, and when the stress week arrives, haircuts widen, settlement fails rise, disputes backlog, and duration disappears. Firms then discover that "market access" was actually a calm-day privilege. A deployable gate therefore binds listing to the stack: admissible records, deterministic entitlements, enforceable encumbrance tags, and fast dispute lanes that prevent proof from becoming legally radioactive. The purpose is not perfection; the purpose is to prevent the first stress episode from rewriting the national narrative about equity into cynicism.

Household usability is part of deployability because a public market that only specialists can hold is not democratic and is not stable. If participation imposes complex reporting burdens for ordinary ownership, retail becomes thin and speculative, volatility rises, and the market becomes politically fragile. The listing gate therefore requires standardized statements, automated reporting, and clear treatment of dividends, splits, and corporate actions, so households do not need to become accountants to hold productive claims. This does not reduce fiscal legitimacy; it increases it by bringing ownership into ordinary life under predictable rules, reducing the incentive for shadow rails and reducing the political pressure for retroactive rule changes after scandals.

Enforcement must be predictable rather than theatrical, because randomness becomes a risk premium and also becomes patronage. A system that enforces harshly but inconsistently teaches issuers to seek protection rather than compliance, and it teaches investors to demand a political premium for uncertainty. A deployable listing gate makes enforcement boring by making it fast, consistent, and legible: objective triggers, published timelines, narrow remedies, admissible records. That boredom is a feature because it lowers the political premium embedded in cost of capital. The market becomes financeable because the rules are stable enough to price.

A listing gate worthy of the blueprint therefore has a single discipline running through every clause: open admission by objective criteria, preserve truth by standardized disclosure and fast enforcement, prevent patronage by transparent allocation rules, protect minorities with remedies that arrive in time, and integrate every issuer into the public record so proof remains cheaper than suspicion. Those conditions do not make issuers virtuous; they make extraction expensive enough that capital formation can occur without asking permission from a small circle that sells the future back at a premium.

CHAPTER 57
PROTECTION WITHOUT EXCLUSION
HOW TO DEFEND RETAIL PARTICIPANTS WITHOUT LOCKING THEM OUT OF WEALTH FORMATION.

Retail protection fails most often by succeeding on paper. The statute declares the public protected, the platform declares the public empowered, and the machine continues to do what machines do when incentives reward extraction: it sells the public inferior truth, inferior execution, and inferior time, then calls the outcome education. Exclusion follows as mercy. Households are told markets are complicated and that safety requires distance, while institutions continue to compound inside the best lanes because the system was never designed to treat ordinary participants as fully real. A public-interest market treats this as a structural failure, not a cultural inevitability. It protects households by changing rails, not by erecting velvet ropes. The objective is not to prevent loss; it is to prevent structural loss, where the public's losses are systematically manufactured by microstructure and information design rather than by ordinary misjudgment.

The constitutional claim is simple and severe: opportunity is shared; risk is tiered. Households and funds see the same auctions, the same book, the same baseline record, the same official marks, the same corporate action calendar, the same correction logs, the same completion window and finality time, and the same dispute windows. What differs is only what can be defended as math: leverage ceilings, product permissions, velocity caps, withdrawal authority, and collateral requirements tied to identity tier and verified capacity. Any system that tiers truth or tiers execution is not protecting retail; it is farming retail. Any system that tiers closure is not protecting retail; it is converting commerce into relationship credit. The protection doctrine therefore begins by refusing the oldest trick in modern markets: letting the public enter while ensuring the public never meets the same reality institutions see.

The primary retail harm in contemporary systems is not that households sometimes buy poorly. It is that households are systematically selected against by the combination of information asymmetry, execution asymmetry, and time asymmetry. A thinned baseline record forces the public to trade on delayed and partial truth. Routing regimes that internalize flow turn the public into inventory management for others while promising "price improvement" that cannot be audited. Dispute latency turns proof into uncertainty, uncertainty into haircuts, haircuts into forced selling, and forced selling into the story that households are weak hands. Enforcement timing that reaches backward breaks closure and teaches merchants and households that finality is a slogan. These are not individual mistakes; they are engineered disadvantages. Protection without exclusion is the removal of engineered disadvantage.

Execution fairness is therefore a constitutional line, not a consumer feature. Paid priority is barred because paid priority is permissioned citizenship. Hidden early sight is barred because early sight is how sophisticated actors trade against the public while calling it liquidity provision. Side venues cannot siphon the public stream and report after because late reporting is not a transparency failure; it is a predation channel. Auctions are treated as public price formation events with common rules, common timestamps, and baseline imbalance transparency sufficient for safe participation. Order types are permitted only if they cannot be used to manufacture queue-jumping hierarchies that reproduce privilege in code. The exchange must publish execution quality outcomes in a form that can be audited without premium survival: distribution of slippage, fill rates by participant tier, rejection rates, systematic routing differences, and the relationship between auction events and realized impact. Protection cannot rely on assurances; it must rely on evidence, because a system that cannot measure whether the public is being structurally disadvantaged is a system that cannot correct itself without scandal.

Truth parity is the second constitutional line, and it is where retail protection most often dies quietly. The baseline record must be sufficient for safe participation: consolidated prints, usable depth snapshots, official marks, correction logs, corporate action calendars, and market-state messages that bind operator behavior to an archived history. Premium analytics can exist; premium survival is prohibited. The record must not be degradable by commercial decision because the moment baseline truth becomes a profit center, the system acquires a structural incentive to keep the public slightly blind. That incentive is the seed of every subsequent outrage. Baseline truth must remain thick enough that the public is not forced to infer the real market from fragments, and fast enough that ordinary participation is not delayed participation. The public record is the public's defense against narrative. If the record is thin, rumor becomes the dominant market force and retail becomes the natural victim.

Product discipline is the third constitutional line, because retail harm concentrates where products are designed to monetize impatience, confusion, and leverage appetite. Protection without exclusion does not ban risk; it bans the packaging of unbounded risk as casual participation. Tiered identity therefore gates leverage and complex products by objective criteria. Low tiers can own and hold common claims; higher tiers can access leverage and derivatives under stronger authentication, higher collateral, and explicit permissions. Velocity caps exist to prevent platform design from turning impulsive over-trading into a revenue model. Product labeling is standardized and short enough to be read, and enforcement targets mislabeling with penalties large enough to deter the business model. This is not paternalism; it is the refusal to let the market treat cognitive failure as an extractable resource.

Closure protection is the fourth line, because without closure the public is not investing; it is underwriting other people's timing. Bounded reversibility is required for genuine fraud and error, but reversibility cannot become an open option against innocent recipients. Finality therefore remains a legal state at time F, and safe harbor protects recipients who complied with verification rules. Fraud and error claims are handled through a funded liability pool with restitution inside a defined SLA, so consumers receive protection without converting merchants or counterparties into insurers through retroactive clawbacks. Dispute windows are strict. Evidence standards are standardized. Remedies are narrow. The system replaces chargeback culture with a bounded dispute lane that is fast enough to restore closure and predictable enough to price. This is how the system preserves retail participation without turning the entire market into conditional credit.

Dispute speed is the fifth line, because dispute latency is the hidden interest rate of low-capacity markets and the hidden haircut of high-capacity ones. If routine disputes require slow courts, proof becomes legally radioactive. When proof becomes radioactive, collateral haircuts rise. When haircuts rise, funding tightens. When funding tightens, weaker holders sell first. The public then receives the blame for a liquidation sequence produced by institutional plumbing. A protective market therefore treats disputes as throughput: standardized evidence, binding timelines, and narrow remedies that restore admissible state quickly. Appeals exist, but they do not reopen the world. A market that cannot restore proof quickly cannot protect retail because retail cannot finance uncertainty.

Stress behavior is the sixth line, because retail is most harmed during disorder, not due to unique foolishness but due to inability to buy time. If stress behavior is discretionary, insiders buy survival and the public sells into fear. The protective market therefore publishes stress modes and triggers and applies them by criteria rather than by relationship. Throttles and limits tighten by rule; buffers widen by published bands; safe mode behavior is precommitted; and post-stress access audits are mandatory and public enough to deter exception-making. The system does not promise that stress will be painless; it promises that stress will not split the constitution into one set of rules for the connected and one set of consequences for everyone else.

Household usability is the seventh line, because ownership becomes democratic only when holding becomes ordinary. If tax reporting and basis tracking are designed as burdensome rituals, households will not hold; they will trade briefly or exit. A public-interest market therefore treats usability as a stability requirement: standardized statements, automated reporting, clear treatment of dividends, splits, and corporate actions, and de minimis treatment where appropriate so small transactions do not become a compliance tax on participation. This increases fiscal legitimacy rather than weakening it, because it moves ownership into ordinary life under auditable rules rather than pushing participation into shadow workarounds and resentment.

Intermediation is the eighth line, but only because intermediation is where new gatekeepers attempt to re-enter after old gatekeepers are weakened. In a direct account system, households do not rent access, but they may choose guidance. Fiduciaries remain permissible only as licensed delegates of authority with scope that can be revoked and logs that are auditable. Advice is a service, not a passport. The system monitors fiduciary behavior so "help" cannot become a new extraction corridor that sells inferior routing, inferior products, or hidden fees under the language of protection. A democratic market cannot replace one gatekeeper class with another and still claim legitimacy.

A deployable protection regime becomes clearest when run as a workflow rather than as a slogan. A retail participant opens a direct exchange account, selects an identity tier, chooses a deposit bank and custodian, and enters the same auction schedule as everyone else. The participant sees the same baseline record and receives the same state messages. The participant submits an order; matching priority is common; the trade prints into the public record; clearing nets exposure; settlement completes within the published window; finality arrives at F. If an error occurs, the bounded dispute lane is triggered under standardized evidence and time bounds, and restitution is funded by the system rather than clawed back from innocent recipients. Refunds are linked to receipts and capped by velocity rules to deter abuse without forcing merchants into investigation. The participant does not win because the participant is protected; the participant is protected so that winning and losing occur on ordinary market grounds rather than on structurally inferior rails.

The stress workflow is where the doctrine earns its name. Marks fracture across venues; rumor thickens; platforms elsewhere freeze or improvise; the public begins to run not from price but from fear of discretion. In a protected market, the exchange posts a state transition, activates fallback marks, records corrections as events, and publishes what is guaranteed and what is throttled. Clearing widens margin add-ons within published bands and tightens limits by criteria. Throttles tighten by rule, not by favor. Settlement and finality remain uniform for ordinary flows; safe harbor remains intact for finalized receipts; restrictions target payer access prospectively. The dispute lane triages claims with binding timelines so proof does not become radioactive. After the episode, the access audit publishes who received time and why. The system still experiences losses. The difference is that the public is not forced to finance uncertainty that insiders are allowed to avoid.

Protection without exclusion is therefore not a list of consumer rights pasted onto an extractive machine. It is the redesign of the machine so the public is not required to enter through inferior truth, inferior execution, inferior closure, and inferior time. When those rails are corrected, households can lose money, but they lose it inside a shared constitution rather than inside a rigged corridor. That is what makes protection compatible with wealth formation rather than the excuse used to deny it.

CHAPTER 58
THE TRANSPARENCY LAYER
DATA ACCESS, FAIR VISIBILITY, AND THE END OF INFORMATIONAL CHOKE POINTS.

Markets do not run on prices; they run on what the system treats as true. Truth in this machine is not a philosophical claim. It is a set of admissible states: what the market says happened, what the market says exists, what the market says is owed, what the market says is final, and what the market will recognize when someone refuses to pay. When truth is sold as a premium product, democracy becomes decorative. The public may enter the arena, but the public cannot see the arena well enough to avoid systematic selection, and systematic selection is the oldest, quietest way to convert openness into extraction. Informational choke points become toll booths; toll booths become power; power becomes rule shock the first time a crisis reveals that the public record is a brochure while the real record is private. A public-interest market therefore treats transparency as infrastructure, not disclosure theater: a baseline truth layer that is sufficient, non-degradable, and legally meaningful, paired with an explicit boundary that allows premium tools without allowing premium survival.

The baseline is not "last price." Last price can be manufactured by thin prints and fragmented venues, and the public learns too late that the headline was a lure. Baseline truth must be thick enough to describe conditions, not merely outcomes. It therefore includes consolidated prints with corrections logged as events, usable depth snapshots that make liquidity conditions inferable, auction imbalance indicators where auctions are used as public price formation, official marks with published mark policies and correction windows, corporate action calendars with record dates and effective dates, event disclosures with strict clocks, and market-state messages that announce transitions into elevated volatility, disorder, safe mode, and recovery with timestamps and archived histories. Silent edits are forbidden because silent edits destroy admissibility and turn disputes into narrative warfare. Corrections are bounded because truth must be stable enough to finance against and flexible enough to repair genuine error without becoming infinite litigation. This is not an academic preference; it is the condition under which proof remains cheaper than suspicion, and proof is what makes duration possible.

The core prohibition is premium survival. Premium analytics can exist; premium dashboards can exist; specialized models can exist; none of that threatens democracy as long as baseline truth remains sufficient for safe participation. The threat arrives when the operator thins the baseline to create demand for a private feed, because then the market acquires a structural incentive to keep the public slightly blind. Slight blindness produces predictable adverse selection. Predictable adverse selection produces losses that look like personal failure and are in fact structural. Structural losses produce political backlash. Political backlash produces rule shock. Rule shock raises haircuts, shortens duration, and destroys issuance capacity. The transparency layer is therefore macroprudential as well as moral: it protects the market's ability to finance itself by protecting the public's ability to trust the record without renting access to reality.

Transparency also fails when it is treated as quantity rather than enforceability. Publishing more data does not create fairness if execution remains segmented by paid priority, hidden internalization, or early sight. More data then becomes an expensive way to watch yourself lose. A public-interest transparency layer therefore binds visibility to enforceable equality: common matching rules, common auction rules, and a record that makes execution auditable rather than mythical. The system publishes measurable outputs that allow adversarial verification: slippage distributions, fill-rate distributions, rejection patterns, auction impact distributions, correction frequencies, and systematic differences by participant tier where tiering exists for limits. This is not a performance report. It is a constitutional check that tests whether the public lane is real.

The governance of truth is the central political economy question, and markets usually answer it quietly: truth is defined by whoever sells the feed. A public-interest market answers it explicitly: baseline truth is a public good governed as a constitutional object. Any change to baseline content, timing, correction policy, mark policy, or state messaging is treated as an amendment rather than an iteration. It requires heightened thresholds, published rationale, published impact analysis on selection against smaller participants, and post-event review. Exceptions sunset. Operator discretion is bounded and documented. State transitions are archived so the system cannot rewrite its past behavior when the incentives shift. The aim is not to freeze the market in amber. The aim is to prevent quiet capture through "optimization" that happens to move value from public participants to private data sellers.

Corporate actions are where truth becomes expensive and where choke points become visible even to non-specialists. A split, dividend, tender, merger, or spin-out creates entitlement mapping, record-date sensitivity, and valuation discontinuity. If corporate action truth is communicated through private channels, proof becomes uneven; uneven proof becomes haircuts; haircuts become forced selling; forced selling becomes the story that equity is unsafe for households. A public-interest transparency layer therefore treats corporate action calendars, entitlement states, and correction logs as baseline truth, tied to deterministic mapping rules and time-bounded dispute lanes. The public does not need private emails to know what the system believes. The system publishes what it believes, binds that belief to admissible state, and corrects it in public when it must.

Corrections are not a reputational inconvenience; they are a legitimacy instrument. A system that hides corrections to "avoid panic" manufactures panic by inviting conspiracy and rumor. A system that records corrections as events, time-stamped and reason-coded, reduces rumor power by giving participants something to check. Correction windows are bounded not to punish truth, but to protect it: an endless correction regime makes the record unstable, and instability is an implicit tax on holding. Bounded correction turns error repair into administration rather than into political theater.

Stress visibility is where the transparency layer earns its existence. A transparency layer that disappears during stress is not transparency; it is marketing. During disorder the system publishes state transitions, throttle activations, buffer band widenings, mark fallback activations, and facility usage summaries under strict clocks, without publishing exploitable private strategies but with enough specificity to prevent the operator from allocating survival by whisper. After the episode the system publishes access audits and facility usage outcomes so the record can answer the legitimacy question that matters: who received time, who received exceptions, and whether outcomes matched published criteria. The purpose is not to shame institutions; it is to prevent the suspicion that triggers runs driven not by price but by fear of discretion.

Cross-border participation adds a second choke point: jurisdiction. Openness without mutual recognition produces enforcement crises; enforcement crises produce ad hoc controls; ad hoc controls destroy trust. A deployable transparency layer therefore publishes corridor rules, restriction triggers, and the consequences of corridor tightening, so cross-border access is governed by predictable procedures rather than by rumor. If a corridor narrows, it narrows by thresholds. If it closes, it closes by rule. The public learns to expect procedure, not improvisation. That expectation is itself a stability asset.

The transparency layer becomes most credible when it is understood as a finite list of public goods rather than as an infinite demand for more data. Baseline truth must be sufficient, non-degradable, and admissible. It must make execution auditable and corrections legible. It must make corporate action states checkable and entitlements provable. It must make stress behavior visible enough to deter conspiracy and discourage runs rooted in fear of hidden rescues. It must make corridor rules intelligible. Once that exists, premium tools can exist without turning survival into subscription. When that distinction holds, the market stops selling reality as a product and starts treating reality as the common ground on which skill, scale, and judgment compete.

CHAPTER 59
BUILDING THE DOMESTIC INVESTOR BASE
SAVINGS POOLS, INSTITUTIONS, AND THE LONG CAPITAL A NATION NEEDS TO STAND ON ITS OWN.

A market can be engineered with impeccable microstructure and still leave a country dependent if it cannot produce domestic duration, meaning the routine capacity to fund long projects in the national unit without importing foreign conditions through currency clauses, covenant packages, and refinancing cliffs that arrive on someone else's calendar. Where domestic duration is absent, capital formation becomes episodic: projects begin when global liquidity is loose, stall when it tightens, and die when the rollover window shuts; the national economy becomes a derivative on external rates and external risk appetite; politics hardens because development plans are translated into "will they refinance us," and markets respond the only way markets can respond to politics that can rewrite rules in stress, by embedding a rule-shock premium into spreads, haircuts, and tenors until ambition is financed only in fragments. Building the domestic investor base is therefore not a campaign to "attract investors" and not a social-media lesson in compound interest. It is state capacity expressed as financial plumbing: converting savings into holdable claims, holdable claims into issuance capacity, issuance capacity into domestic duration, and domestic duration into sovereignty that survives a tightening cycle without panic.

The first constraint is that households cannot be the system's shock absorbers, because households cannot buy time and cannot finance uncertainty; a base dominated by retail flow looks broad in calm and becomes brittle in disorder, producing forced selling that teaches the public that participation is a recurring injury and teaches issuers that equity is fair-weather capital. Long capital is produced by long liabilities, which is why every deployable sovereign market that finances itself at scale rests on institutions whose liabilities are structurally patient: pensions, insurers, endowments, sovereign vehicles, and regulated collective vehicles that transform short household cash flows into long holding capacity under fiduciary constraint. The label matters less than the liability geometry: long liabilities can hold long assets through volatility without liquidation; short liabilities cannot; and when the national savings perimeter is mostly short, the market trades but does not finance, because every shock becomes a liquidity event and every liquidity event becomes a duration collapse.

The second constraint is that patient capital does not appear by sentiment; it appears by rails that make contribution automatic, custody standardized, governance auditable, and redemption predictable. A pension system that relies on individual timing does not create duration; it creates intermittency. A deployable base therefore begins with automatic contribution rails that capture income flows before they become discretionary. Employer-linked contribution mechanisms, default enrollment, and standardized plan design matter not because they are benevolent, but because they create a persistent bid that is indifferent to headlines. Insurance balance sheets require a different discipline: capital rules that are credible, asset-liability modeling that is coherent, and a legal environment where long claims are not impaired by ad hoc controls that convert duration into political exposure. Collective vehicles require clear rights, transparent fees, predictable redemption rules, and governance standards strong enough that "patient capital" is not silently converted into run capital by product design that promises daily liquidity against long assets.

The third constraint is credible issuance discipline, because duration is not a belief; it is a price assigned to the constitution. Domestic investors hold long claims only when issuance is predictable, settlement is reliable, finality is defined, and crisis behavior is rule-bound rather than improvised. A credible sovereign curve is not merely an auction calendar; it is a record of state behavior that convinces investors the rules will not be rewritten in stress, settlement ambiguity will not be normalized as "eventually fine," and enforcement timing will not be turned into retroactive confiscation. Transparent auctions, published allocation rules, published settlement discipline, and a refusal to tolerate chronic fails are not technocratic flourishes; they are what makes sovereign paper an anchor rather than a political instrument that must be held short. Eventually is not duration; eventually is a premium.

The fourth constraint is that the investor base must be able to participate in primary issuance without patronage and must be able to hold secondary exposure without being forced into liquidation by institutional plumbing. Primary allocation is where aristocracy hides most comfortably because allocation can be framed as "distribution efficiency" while functioning as relationship rent. A domestic base cannot be built on relationship allocation without becoming political, and once it is political it becomes unstable, because performance and legitimacy become inseparable. A deployable system therefore makes primary allocation rule-bound enough to be auditable: clear eligibility by participant category, clear allocation methodology, clear oversubscription handling, and aggregate reporting that makes favoritism measurable. This is not a moral preference; it is how a country prevents the public from learning that ownership is minted privately and only later offered publicly at a markup.

The fifth constraint is proof and dispute throughput, because duration is a promise about what happens when something goes wrong. Investors do not fear ordinary volatility as much as they fear unprovable ownership, unprovable entitlements, and slow remedies that turn assets into legally radioactive collateral. In low-capacity systems corporate actions become entitlement disputes, entitlement disputes become solvency rumors, rumors become haircuts, haircuts shorten funding, shortened funding forces sales, and sales become the public story that markets are unsafe. A domestic base survives only when the market can prove state quickly: admissible records, deterministic entitlement mapping, bounded corrections, enforceable encumbrance tags, and fast dispute lanes that restore proof before uncertainty becomes forced selling. The investor base is built by making proof cheaper than suspicion and making closure more credible than rumor.

The sixth constraint is liquidity design without tollbooths, because a domestic investor base needs tradability but cannot tolerate liquidity as a private tax collected by a narrow class of insiders. Liquidity can be organized as a public property or as a premium lane. In the premium-lane model, only a small circle can see and survive; spreads widen for the public, market impact rises for ordinary orders, and issuance costs rise for firms because secondary liquidity is priced as privilege. The state then becomes dependent on dealer balance sheets in crises, which is another form of sovereignty loss. A deployable public-interest market therefore treats market-making obligations as measurable service: defined quoting obligations where appropriate, transparent incentives, transparent fees, limits on hidden internalization, and execution-quality publication that exposes systematic selection. Liquidity provision remains profitable, but it cannot be sold as admission to reality.

The seventh constraint is financing continuity, because domestic duration depends on a funding ecosystem that can withstand stress without turning into a liquidation engine. This is where short-term funding, repo eligibility, and collateral policy quietly determine whether long holding is rational. If high-quality collateral is narrowly defined, only a small group can finance inventories and carry risk; if collateral policy is discretionary, funding becomes political; if funding is unstable, long pools are forced to sell into stress not because they changed their view, but because their funding terms changed. A deployable investor base therefore requires a published collateral framework, a published eligibility regime, and a published crisis posture that prevents sudden discretionary reclassifications from turning ordinary holdings into margin events. Funding policy is not separate from investor base policy; it is how the base is kept from being forced into liquidation.

The eighth constraint is governance discipline inside the long pools, because a pension fund can become a patronage machine as easily as a listing gate can, and when it does, the investor base becomes a political asset that markets will discount. Deployable design therefore requires fiduciary enforcement that is fast enough to deter conflicts, transparent mandates that can be audited, fee disclosure that prevents slow bleeding, comparable performance reporting that exposes chronic underperformance, and practical replaceability so a household's participation is not hostage to a single manager. Long pools must be trusted as compounding engines rather than feared as political instruments, and that trust is built by procedure: auditable decisions, logged delegations, and consequences that arrive in time.

The ninth constraint is household usability, because broad ownership becomes durable only when holding becomes ordinary. If participation requires complex reporting burdens, constant decisions, and bespoke accounting for every corporate action, households will not hold; they will trade briefly or exit, and without household holding, politics remains hostile to markets because markets remain a specialist arena that can be scapegoated easily. A public-interest market therefore treats standardized statements, automated reporting, clear treatment of dividends and splits, and de minimis rules where appropriate as stability infrastructure. This does not weaken fiscal legitimacy; it increases it by making compliance routine and by reducing incentives for shadow rails that flourish when the official path is too costly for ordinary life.

The tenth constraint is deposit stability, because building an investor base by draining deposits too quickly triggers the oldest panic mechanism: bank funding thins, credit rationing begins, rumor accelerates withdrawals, and the state intervenes ad hoc, destroying the rule stability that duration requires. A deployable approach is macroprudential by design: participation caps and tiered limits prevent the investment rails from becoming a run channel; published triggers tighten caps when migration bands are breached, tighten throttles when redemption velocity spikes, widen buffers when spreads and haircuts jump, and treat merchant refusal and surcharge behavior as an early warning of closure confidence failure. These mechanisms are not anti-market controls; they are the rules that prevent the investor base itself from turning into a political crisis that ends in rule shock.

The eleventh constraint is buyer diversification so the sovereign curve does not become a single point of failure. Systems where banks are the only buyers of duration appear stable until they are not, and then the state discovers it engineered a bank-sovereign loop that converts market stress into credit stress and credit stress into fiscal stress. A sovereign market that wants resilience builds multiple buyer classes: long pools, banks, regulated collective vehicles, and corridor participants that are supplementary rather than foundational. Diversification is not ideology; it is the method by which a country prevents one balance sheet from becoming the national refinancing gate.

The twelfth constraint is cross-border realism, because openness does not substitute for depth; it substitutes for sovereignty. If routine issuance depends on foreign flow, the country imports global tightening into domestic financing and accepts foreign-unit clauses that shift governance outward. Corridors should therefore be treated as earned reciprocity and diversification, opened only under mutual recognition of finality and custody priority, published restriction handling, and predictable corridor narrowing rules, and used as supplementary capacity rather than as the foundation of the yield curve. Domestic pools must exist before corridors become structural funding, because corridors leave when global risk reprices, and domestic pools are what keep auctions from failing when the world tightens.

The domestic investor base is built in reality through boring commitments that compound into power: automatic contribution rails into diversified vehicles; predictable issuance calendars and transparent auctions; admissible records and fast disputes that keep proof liquid; non-degradable baseline truth that keeps the public lane real; objective liquidity obligations that provide tradability without tollbooths; a funding and collateral framework that prevents discretionary reclassification from becoming liquidation; fiduciary discipline that prevents long pools from becoming patronage; macro triggers that prevent participation from becoming a run channel; corridor design that expands options without importing dependence. When these commitments hold together, duration appears as a rational response rather than as a fragile hope, firms issue because domestic demand is routine rather than episodic, projects are financed without begging because savings can be converted into domestic duration, and the state gains sovereignty in the only form markets recognize: the ability to refinance without panic, to fund long plans without importing foreign governance into every contract, and to treat ambition as a domestic choice rather than an external permission.

CHAPTER 60
THE EMERGING-MARKET BUILD PLAN
A PHASED IMPLEMENTATION MODEL FOR TRUST, LIQUIDITY, AND SOVEREIGN MARKET CAPACITY.

60. The Emerging-Market Build Plan

Subtitle: A phased implementation model for trust, liquidity, and sovereign market capacity.

Emerging markets fail at market-building for a reason rarely admitted in public language. They import the visible surface of markets before constructing the invisible proof that makes markets possible. They build an exchange before building a record that courts will treat as decisive. They announce investor protection before building disputes that resolve fast enough to matter. They invite cross-border flows before building finality and custody priority that can survive an enforcement event. They celebrate listings before building minority-rights enforcement that can deter related-party extraction. The first scandal arrives, then the first controls, then the first flight, and the market becomes a screen of quotes that cannot finance ambition. A deployable build plan does not begin with rhetoric about modernization. It begins with the hard premise that trust is throughput: proof, finality, and dispute speed are not decorations; they are the rails that determine haircuts, funding terms, and duration.

The plan is phased because legitimacy cannot be borrowed. A phase must be stable on its own terms, not stable only if later phases arrive on schedule. That is the only way to avoid the familiar trap where reform is announced, adoption begins, stress arrives, improvisation follows, and the reform dies as a story about why openness is dangerous. Phasing is constitutional discipline, because the earliest stress week defines the public's long memory and sets the political premium embedded in every future issuance. The blueprint therefore uses three phases that mirror the machine's true dependencies: proof before volume, domestic depth before corridors, corridors only under enforceable mutual recognition. Each phase is a political bargain written as procedure: what is opened, what is capped, what is published, what is prohibited, what is audited, what triggers tightening, and what is forbidden even under crisis pressure.

Phase one is proof before volume, because the first objective is not liquidity; it is admissibility. In many low-infrastructure states, ownership is a story told by paper, intermediaries, and connection. The rich can buy proof; the poor must borrow it. Markets built on borrowed proof do not democratize compounding; they democratize the losses of ambiguity. Phase one therefore builds the republic of proof: a national instrument identifier regime and issuer registry that makes what exists a stable fact; a beneficial ownership standard that is admissible, time-stamped, and correction-bounded so who owns is not a negotiation; an encumbrance registry that makes double-pledge legally impossible and operationally detectable so who can borrow is not a rumor; an authoritative record treated as evidence, not as a feed, with corrections as events, not edits; and a fast dispute lane with binding timelines and narrow remedies that restores proof rather than rewarding delay. Finality is bound by law so completion is a state, not a courtesy. Baseline truth is published as non-degradable public utility: consolidated prints, usable depth snapshots, official marks with published policies, corporate action calendars with record dates, correction logs, and market-state messages. Leverage and velocity are capped while the system is young because young systems cannot survive product abuse disguised as innovation.

Phase one also requires the discipline emerging markets usually adopt only after catastrophe: publish outage behavior, safe mode, kill criteria, and restart criteria before the first crisis. A market that improvises teaches citizens to run early and teaches external capital to treat the system as politically unstable. A market that precommits to state transitions and publishes post-event access audits teaches the opposite: stress is governed, not negotiated, and time is not sold by relationship.

A deployable phase one is not a long academic project; it is a sequence of institutional acts executed on a fixed calendar, with public artifacts that bind the state and the operator to procedures that can be audited by adversaries. The first ninety days are where the machine either becomes real or becomes another brochure. The state establishes the instrument identifier authority and forces uniform identifiers across issuance, trading, custody, taxation, and enforcement so the same claim cannot wear multiple names depending on who is selling it. It establishes the issuer registry with audited baseline disclosures and beneficial ownership declarations, then treats false declarations as disabling events rather than later scandals. It creates the authoritative record as admissible evidence with bounded correction windows, defines correction as event logging so every repair leaves a scar that can be audited, and binds record admissibility to the dispute lane so disputes restore state rather than re-litigate reality. It establishes the encumbrance registry, links it to custody and settlement, and makes priority enforceable in insolvency so collateral cannot be discovered ambiguous only when stress forces claims to become real. It launches the fast dispute lane with standardized evidence and binding timelines, and it publishes remedy bands so outcomes are predictable enough to price and narrow enough to execute quickly. It defines completion windows and finality time, and it makes safe harbor explicit so ordinary recipients are not turned into creditors by enforcement timing. It publishes baseline truth as a package that cannot be quietly degraded: prints, depth snapshots, marks, calendars, corrections, state messages, plus the governance thresholds required to amend that baseline so truth cannot be thinned as a business model. It caps leverage, limits complex products, and imposes velocity limits as a temporary constitution for an immature system, because the fastest way to destroy legitimacy is to allow sophisticated actors to mint retail losses through product design before proof and dispute throughput exist. It runs a public drill that simulates a feed fracture, a corporate action dispute, and a settlement backlog, then publishes the after-action record with timestamps so rumor cannot claim hidden rescues or hidden freezes. Trust is manufactured by visible procedure, not borrowed from promises.

When phase one is done correctly, liquidity is still modest. That is acceptable. The objective is to make ownership and entitlement predictable enough that liquidity can later be financed without becoming a relationship product. Markets can tolerate thinness; they cannot tolerate ambiguity that transforms thinness into predation and then blames the public for leaving.

Phase one must also include a narrow, enforceable issuance pilot, because a market without issuance is a theater of secondary transfers. The pilot is not a full listing regime; it is a proof-and-enforcement test. A small number of issuers are admitted under standardized templates and strict clocks. Related-party disclosures are mandatory and machine-legible. Insider transactions are reported under strict timing. Corporate action obligations are published before the first share trades. Remedies are narrow, fast, and certain. Allocation rules are public enough that early ownership does not become a patronage ritual. The goal is not to maximize volume; the goal is to demonstrate that fraud is expensive, delay is not rentable, and admission is not a favor. A market that cannot punish abuse quickly teaches insiders to extract and teaches households to exit, and once that lesson is learned, the domestic base becomes dramatically harder to build.

Phase two is domestic depth before corridors, because a market that relies on foreign flow for routine issuance imports global tightening cycles into domestic financing and becomes dependent by design. Domestic depth is built by creating long pools that can hold through stress without forced liquidation: pensions, insurers, regulated collective vehicles, and employee savings rails that convert household flows into patient ownership under fiduciary discipline. Phase two strengthens the listing gate by separating disclosure integrity from elite bottlenecks and enforcing minority rights fast enough to deter related-party extraction. It builds market-making obligations that are measurable and transparent so liquidity does not become a dealer aristocracy selling survival. It builds a credible sovereign curve through predictable auctions and settlement discipline, because domestic duration requires an anchor. It maintains caps that prevent deposit-drain panic and it publishes macroprudential triggers that tighten limits when migration and redemption signals turn hostile. The purpose is to make holding rational and issuance routine, because without routine issuance, firms remain dependent on banks and foreign markets, and the domestic exchange remains a stage.

Phase two carries an ideological burden as well as an operational one: it must convince citizens that ownership is not a trap and convince institutions that the public lane is not decorative. That requires household usability and institutional seriousness simultaneously. Standardized statements, automated reporting, clear tax treatment, bounded disputes, and uniform finality make household holding ordinary rather than heroic. Predictable enforcement fast enough to deter abuse makes institutional holding rational rather than cynical. A market that punishes slowly teaches insiders to extract and teaches the public to leave.

Domestic depth also depends on funding ecology, because duration is a funding statement as much as it is an investment preference. If collateral eligibility is narrow and discretionary, only a small circle can finance inventories, carry risk, and survive volatility, and the market becomes dependent on that circle's balance sheets. If collateral policy changes abruptly in stress, holdings become margin events, margin events become forced sales, and forced sales become the political narrative that markets are predatory. A deployable phase two therefore binds collateral policy as published criteria: what qualifies, how haircuts move, how margin responds to volatility, and how funding terms tighten by bands rather than by rumor. The point is not to eliminate stress; it is to prevent stress from turning into discretionary reclassification that privatizes time. Funding policy is investor-base policy because it determines whether long pools can hold through disorder or must sell to meet sudden calls.

A phase two system is tested by its first stress week, because stress week reveals whether rules are real or aspirational. A global shock hits, prices gap, rumor thickens, and the temptation appears immediately: halt by discretion, rescue by relationship, and then ask the public to forgive it because the alternative was chaos. A deployable system does the opposite. The exchange posts a state transition and activates published throttles and buffer bands. Clearing widens margin add-ons by methodology rather than by phone call, and publishes the bands so participants can price the rules. The sovereign auction calendar is not abandoned casually; it is adjusted by rule, with published criteria for delay and published criteria for continuation, because arbitrary cancellation is a signal that duration is political. Market-making obligations tighten where appropriate, not as punishment but as continuity discipline, and the system publishes execution quality to show the public lane remained real. The dispute lane shifts into triage mode with binding timelines, because dispute latency in stress becomes a haircut and haircuts become forced selling. Compliance and restriction handling remain rule-bound, targeting payer access prospectively rather than breaking safe harbor for finalized receipts, because breaking closure under stress is how legitimacy collapses. After the week, the system publishes access audits and facility usage outcomes so the record can answer the legitimacy question that matters: who received time and why.

This stress-week posture attacks the root cause of emerging-market fragility: the belief that rules are negotiable and negotiation favors proximity. Once that belief is reversed by repeated evidence, duration begins to appear because investors stop paying a premium for discretion risk.

Phase two must also build the domestic curve beyond the sovereign, because a market that finances only the state is not a market that finances ambition; it is a fiscal instrument. Corporate bonds, project bonds, and equity segments must be introduced under the same proof discipline, because a curve that cannot finance enterprises forces enterprises back into bank dependence. This is where standardized covenants matter, not as imported forms, but as deployable constraints that reduce bespoke negotiation, shorten issuance time, and lower the premium investors demand to compensate for ambiguity. A domestic investor base becomes stronger when it can own diversified domestic claims with credible enforcement and predictable settlement, because diversification reduces the pressure to flee at the first shock and makes holding a strategy rather than a prayer.

. . .

Phase three is corridors under enforceable mutual recognition. Cross-border participation is not a feature; it is a treaty-like extension of trust. Corridors open only where mutual recognition exists in practice: recognition of settlement finality, recognition of custody priority and encumbrance tags, recognition of dispute outcomes within bounded remedy bands, and predictable restriction handling that preserves safe harbor for finalized receipts. Corridors publish rules for tightening and closing so cross-border access is governed by procedure rather than rumor. The market must be able to narrow corridors without improvisation because improvisation is what turns external stress into domestic legitimacy collapse. Phase three expands opportunity without importing dependence: foreign participation becomes diversification and discipline, not the foundation of national financing.

Corridor discipline prevents a common mistake: treating foreign participation as a substitute for domestic trust. Foreign capital can provide volume, but it cannot provide legitimacy. Legitimacy is a domestic asset created by domestic procedure, and foreign flows leave when the global cycle turns. If the country depends on them for routine refinancing, it inherits volatility not only in prices but in its own ability to govern. Corridors exist to expand options, not to replace domestic depth.

A plan remains non-deployable if it remains a set of principles without an operational calendar that can be tracked and enforced. A year-one month-by-month sequence is therefore part of the build plan, because the administrative tempo determines whether reform becomes reality or becomes a negotiation. Month one establishes the identifier authority, publishes the mandatory identifier schema, forces all new issuance and all registry entries into the schema, and begins the conversion of legacy instruments into mapped identifiers so "what exists" cannot remain ambiguous. Month two establishes the issuer registry, publishes the standardized disclosure templates, defines disabling events for false disclosure, and begins the licensing perimeter for custodians, deposit banks, fiduciaries, and market operators so responsibility is not diffused when failures occur. Month three establishes the beneficial ownership standard, requires initial declarations for registry-eligible issuers, and defines correction windows so ownership proof is stable enough to be financeable. Month four establishes the encumbrance registry, links it to custody interfaces, defines priority rules for insolvency, and begins routine reconciliation cycles so over-pledge cannot hide behind operational delay. Month five establishes the fast dispute lane, publishes evidence standards and remedy bands, hires or designates adjudicators, defines throughput targets, and begins a public docket reporting discipline so dispute speed can be measured rather than promised. Month six binds settlement finality in law, defines completion windows and finality times, defines safe harbor for innocent recipients, and publishes restriction-handling doctrine so enforcement timing does not destroy closure. Month seven publishes the baseline truth package and the non-degradation rule, including correction logs, official mark policies, corporate action calendars, and state messaging, and defines the governance thresholds required to amend baseline truth so it cannot be thinned into a rent. Month eight runs the first end-to-end drill: feed fracture, mark fallback, dispute triage, settlement backlog, and publishes the after-action record with timestamps, because early drills are where the public learns whether the operator tells the truth. Month nine launches the narrow issuance pilot with a small cohort of issuers under strict templates, strict clocks, and strict remedies, because a market without issuance becomes a secondary theater disconnected from development. Month ten runs the first corporate action week simulation in public, because entitlement ambiguity is the fastest path from technical failure to legitimacy crisis in low-capacity systems. Month eleven tests the encumbrance and insolvency priority workflow with a controlled default simulation, because priority that exists only on paper is discovered only in stress, and discovery is too late. Month twelve publishes a full-year audit: dispute throughput, settlement fails, correction frequency, execution quality, access outcomes during drills, and a public list of rule amendments with rationale, because legitimacy survives only when the system behaves like a court, not like a rumor network.

This calendar is not a checklist for donors. It is the conversion of ideology into statecraft: the obligation to make the system governable, measurable, and resistant to capture before it is allowed to scale.

A plan also remains non-deployable if it cannot survive a stress-test year without rewriting rules. A stress-test year sequence is the other missing piece, because emerging-market fragility is not an abstract fear; it is a repeated pattern of panic, controls, and legitimacy collapse. The stress-test year begins with a contained default in a significant issuer or member, timed deliberately after the system has published its default workflow and drill outcomes. The default trigger is mechanical. The system does not debate importance. Clearing activates the close-out and auction procedures, applies the loss waterfall in order, and publishes the state transitions. Settlement and custody continue ordinary processing for unaffected trades so the public is not punished for a private failure. The dispute lane triages claims with binding timelines so proof does not become radioactive. Margin bands tighten by methodology and are published so participants can price the regime. Market-making obligations adjust by rule so spreads widen within known bounds rather than exploding through withdrawal. The sovereign auction calendar continues under published criteria or delays under published criteria, because arbitrary cancellation is a duration event. If a funding squeeze appears, collateral eligibility tightens by bands, not by rumor. If a mark dispute appears, fallback marks activate by procedure and corrections are logged as events. If restrictions are required, they target payer access prospectively, preserving safe harbor for finalized receipts, because retroactive clawbacks convert commerce into credit and destroy the meaning of finality. After containment, the system publishes a post-event audit: who received time, which facilities were used, which exceptions were requested and denied, and whether the sequence matched published criteria. Then the system re-enters recovery mode by published thresholds and replenishes guarantee resources by published rules rather than discretionary levies.

The purpose of a stress-test year is not to stage drama; it is to prove that failure does not rewrite the constitution. When a market proves that it can contain a default without improvisation, it earns the only asset that produces duration: the belief that rules remain rules when pressure arrives. Without that belief, every issuer is priced as a short-term borrower no matter how productive its project, because the market is pricing the state's discretion, not the issuer's cash flow.

The build plan is also an anti-oligarchy test, because privilege will try to re-enter through the same doors in every jurisdiction. It re-enters through proof monopolies, through premium truth, through paid priority, through discretionary margin, through relationship-based access to facility time, through slow disputes that function as hidden haircuts, through patronage allocation at issuance, and through ad hoc controls in stress. The plan blocks these entry points with constitutional rules: direct exchange accounts, non-degradable baseline truth, uniform finality, rule-bound stress behavior, objective access criteria, exemption sunsets, and post-stress audits that reveal whether time was allocated by criteria or by status. The test is not whether the system feels open; the test is whether the record can prove that the least connected participant receives the same market reality as the most connected participant, bounded only by objective limits.

The country that executes this plan will still have inequality and elites. The difference is that it will stop manufacturing inequality as a market feature. It will stop selling access as prudence. It will stop treating truth as a luxury good. It will stop turning closure into relationship. It will begin to finance ambition as routine rather than as exception, because routine finance is what sovereignty looks like in a world where every project is priced by markets that do not care about national pride.

A deployable emerging-market plan therefore begins by building a republic of proof: records courts will honor, entitlements the system can map deterministically, encumbrances the system can enforce, disputes the system can resolve quickly, and a baseline truth layer that cannot be sold as a luxury. It then builds domestic depth so the state can finance itself without begging, by constructing long pools and a credible curve under predictable issuance discipline. It then opens corridors only where recognition is enforceable and restriction handling is procedural. When these steps occur in this order, the market stops being a screen of quotes and becomes what the public actually needs it to be: a civic machine that turns savings into financeable ambition without selling the constitution to the highest bidder. The chapter is finished.

CHAPTER 61
THE PILOT STATE
HOW A SMALL COUNTRY OR REGIONAL BLOC COULD TEST THE NEXT MARKET ARCHITECTURE WITHOUT TRIGGERING PANIC.

A pilot is not a demonstration and not a marketing launch. A pilot is a controlled confrontation with reality, designed to prove that the constitution holds when incentives and stress try to break it. The pilot state is the smallest unit of sovereignty that can still run a complete market stack: law, courts, registry, exchange, clearing, custody, banks, supervision, and a public narrative that can survive its first scandal without reverting to ad hoc controls. The point is not to claim modernity; the point is to prove, in public, that equality of rails is enforceable, that baseline truth cannot be sold as a luxury, that closure does not vary by status, and that stress behavior is governed by thresholds rather than by phone calls. A pilot succeeds only if it earns the one asset emerging markets lack: credibility that persists through stress.

The pilot begins by choosing scope that is defensible because uncontrolled scope is the first form of improvisation. A pilot that tries to be everything becomes nothing; it invites too many failure modes at once and then calls failure "complexity." Scope is defined by instruments, participant limits, and domestic-only versus corridor-enabled participation. The initial instrument set must be narrow enough to be governable and broad enough to be meaningful: a sovereign bill and bond curve with transparent auctions, a small cohort of corporate issuers under standardized templates, and a limited equity segment where minority protections and related-party disclosures can be enforced fast enough to matter. Derivatives are not first-wave instruments; they are stress multipliers that belong only after proof, settlement, and dispute throughput are demonstrated under load. Limits must be conservative by design: low leverage, capped exposures by identity tier, capped redemption velocities, capped corridor volumes if any corridors exist, because a pilot is not a place to test how much risk the public can be sold; it is a place to test whether the system can remain rule-bound when risk arrives.

The pilot's second decision is institutional separation, because a pilot that allows any single private actor to control access, truth, and settlement will reproduce oligarchy at small scale and then call it efficiency. The exchange must host direct participant accounts. Participants must be able to choose their deposit bank and custodian from eligible lists. Fiduciaries must be optional delegates of authority, not passports to eligibility. Baseline truth must be published as a non-degradable public utility. The correction protocol must treat edits as events. The mark policy must be published with fallback hierarchies. Settlement finality must be bound by law. Dispute lanes must be fast enough to keep proof liquid. The pilot is therefore a stack test, not a venue test.

The pilot's third decision is to publish the constitution as an operational charter that can be audited by adversaries. The charter defines what cannot be sold: paid priority, premium survival, variable finality by status, and relationship-based time allocation. It defines what must be published: baseline truth package, state transitions, correction logs, corporate action calendars, auction schedules, margin methodologies, default workflows, facility access criteria, exemption sunsets, and post-stress access audits. It defines outage behavior and safe mode behavior. It defines kill criteria and restart criteria. A pilot without published kill and restart criteria invites panic because participants assume the operator will improvise. A pilot with published kill and restart criteria invites trust because participants can price the rules.

The pilot's fourth decision is supervision posture. The supervisor must be able to act as constitutional enforcer rather than as after-the-fact punisher, and that requires licensing perimeters that assign responsibility clearly: exchange operator, clearing operator, custody operators, deposit banks, mark administrator, critical data operator, and dispute operator. It requires audit rights and incident reporting rules that are mandatory rather than voluntary. It requires a resolution plan for the operator so continuity can be maintained without improvisation if a critical institution fails. In a pilot, supervision is not bureaucracy; it is credibility infrastructure, because credibility is the only capital the system is actually raising in its first years.

The pilot's fifth decision is narrative discipline, because the pilot will be attacked not only by economics but by rumor. A pilot that behaves correctly but communicates poorly will be treated as illegitimate by a public trained to expect discretion and corruption. The pilot therefore makes transparency a ritual of statecraft: state transitions are published; corrections are logged; facility usage is summarized; access audits are published after stress; and exceptions are treated as constitutional events with sunsets and rationale. The goal is not to publicize strategy; it is to prevent a credibility vacuum in which rumor becomes the sovereign.

A pilot designed for panic containment treats stress as planned testing rather than accidental scandal. The first test is a normal-day end-to-end run under moderate volume, because operational reliability is the minimum condition for legitimacy. Participant accounts open directly at the exchange. Identity tiering sets limits as math. Orders enter the same auctions. Prints and depth snapshots publish into baseline truth. Clearing nets exposures and applies margin by published rules. Settlement completes within the published window.

Finality arrives at the published time. Corporate action calendars are posted as baseline truth. Corrections are logged as events. Dispute lane throughput is measured and published. These are not metrics for consultants; they are the facts citizens use to decide whether participation is a trap.

The second test is the first controlled stress week, staged early enough that the pilot does not build its reputation on calm alone. A mark dispute is simulated by a feed fracture or a venue outage, forcing fallback mark policy to activate. The exchange posts a state transition and logs it. Clearing widens margin add-ons within published bands and tightens limits by criteria. Settlement preserves closure for ordinary flows while throttling conversion-sensitive flows under published rules. The dispute lane triages claims with binding timelines. Restriction handling is tested with a simulated sanctions flag, proving payer access can be restricted prospectively without breaking safe harbor for finalized receipts. Facility access criteria are tested with a liquidity squeeze simulation, proving time is allocated by rule, not by relationship. After the week, the pilot publishes the access audit and the after-action record, so the public can see whether the constitution held.

The third test is a contained default event, because a market that has not default-tested itself is only pretending. A participant fails an obligation. The trigger is mechanical. The clearing operator activates the default workflow, auctions the portfolio under pre-stated procedure, applies the loss waterfall in published order, and replenishes resources by rule. The exchange and settlement stack continue to process ordinary trades, because a democratic market cannot punish the public for a private failure. The record posts state and timestamps so rumor cannot claim hidden rescues. Dispute lane triage prevents entitlement ambiguity from becoming collateral poison. The purpose is not to celebrate failure; it is to prove failure does not rewrite the constitution.

The fourth test is a corporate action week, because entitlement ambiguity is the fastest path from technical failure to legitimacy crisis in low-capacity states. An issuer declares an action that changes entitlements. The calendar posts immediately into baseline truth. Custodians lock entitlement mapping as deterministic state. Correction windows tighten around mark-sensitive times. The dispute lane preallocates capacity and publishes evidence standards. The system freezes only what must be frozen to preserve singular proof, then resumes with updated entitlements logged as events. The public sees the system behave like a court, not like a rumor network.

The fifth test is political shock, because statecraft is always present even when it is denied. A proposed rule amendment is introduced, and the pilot demonstrates the amendment process: published rationale, published impact analysis on selection against smaller participants, transition windows, temporary backstops where needed to prevent forced selling, and post-implementation review. The system proves it can improve without triggering a cliff. A pilot that cannot change rules safely will either freeze itself into obsolescence or change itself into crisis.

A pilot must also be planned as a five-year institutional timeline, because market-building fails when it becomes a sequence of announcements rather than a sequence of irreversible procedures. Year one is constitutional construction and public proof: the charter is enacted, identifiers are mandatory, the authoritative record is admissible, the encumbrance registry is enforceable, the dispute lane throughput is operational, and the first narrow issuance cohort is admitted under strict templates, strict clocks, and strict remedies. The stress drills are run early, not late, and the after-action records are published with timestamps and access outcomes. Year two is curve discipline and investor-base formation: the sovereign auction calendar becomes routine, settlement discipline is enforced, market-making obligations are made measurable, regulated collective vehicles are launched with fiduciary enforceability, and household participation is made ordinary through standardized statements and automated reporting so ownership is not a specialist ritual. Year three is capital formation expansion with enforcement that arrives in time: listing segments widen by criteria, minority rights enforcement becomes routine rather than symbolic, corporate bond pilots launch under standardized covenants, and the system conducts a contained default test under real procedures with public audit so the public can see whether failure is governed. Year four is corridor negotiation and limited cross-border proof: one corridor is opened only where mutual recognition of finality, custody priority, and dispute remedies is enforceable, corridor tightening triggers are published, and the corridor is run under low limits so it can be tested before it is depended upon. Year five is scaling by criteria rather than by ambition: caps rise only if dispute throughput stays within bounds, settlement fails stay within bounds, correction frequency stays within bounds, execution quality metrics show no systematic selection against smaller participants, access audits show time was allocated by criteria rather than by status, and the stress-test year can be survived without rewriting rules. The timeline is not a promise of progress; it is a schedule of proof.

A pilot that wants to be believed must also survive an outage week without privatizing time. An outage week sequence begins with a disruption that tests the temptation to create private lanes. The exchange posts the state transition, declares which auctions proceed and which pause by published criteria, publishes the fallback mark policy activation, and logs the correction protocol as events rather than silence. Clearing widens buffers and tightens throttles by published bands. Settlement windows adjust by rule, with published completion guarantees and published restitution if completion cannot be met. Custody continues entitlement mapping under deterministic rules so corporate actions cannot be weaponized through confusion. The dispute lane triages outage-related claims with binding timelines so proof does not become backlog. Facility access remains criteria-based and published, and after restoration the operator publishes a full outage audit: duration of outage, actions taken, exceptions requested and denied, impacts on fills and settlement, and whether any participant received private treatment. The purpose is not to punish mistakes; it is to prove that mistakes do not convert into privilege.

A pilot must also survive a rule-shock attempt, because rule shocks are how political systems test whether a market is truly constitutional or merely tolerated. A minor-looking amendment is proposed under the language of safety or revenue, but its effect would be to thin baseline truth, widen discretionary restriction handling, or change collateral eligibility abruptly. The pilot responds not with defiance but with procedure: published rationale requirements, published impact analysis on selection against smaller participants, transition windows, temporary backstops where needed to prevent forced liquidation, and a mandatory post-implementation review with a sunset if objectives are not met. If the amendment is dangerous, it is delayed or rejected under published criteria; if it is beneficial, it is implemented in a way that does not trigger a cliff. This is how a pilot proves that governance can improve architecture without turning architecture into a political weapon.

The pilot's scaling rule is criteria-based expansion. Caps rise only if dispute throughput remains within bounds, settlement fails remain within bounds, correction frequency remains within bounds, execution quality metrics show no systematic selection against smaller participants, default workflows complete within published time limits, and access audits show time was allocated by criteria rather than by status. Corridors open only after mutual recognition is enforceable and after the pilot has demonstrated that restriction handling does not break closure. Derivatives are added only after the pilot survives a stress-test year without rewriting rules. Scaling is not the reward for optimism; it is the reward for proof.

A pilot state is therefore not a small version of an existing exchange; it is a testbed for a constitutional machine. It is a place where the public can watch a market behave like infrastructure, where truth is a public utility rather than a luxury good, where closure is identical for all, where intermediaries are selectable services rather than gatekeepers, and where stress is governed by thresholds rather than by relationship. That is the only way the next market can be believed before it is depended upon. The chapter is finished.

PART NINE

THE MAKING OF THE NEXT MARKET

THE REFORM IS PUBLIC, THE HEADLINES ARE HOSTILE, AND THE INCUMBENTS HAVE FOUND THEIR LANGUAGE.

No system built on extraction yields quietly; reform must survive panic, sabotage, and the politics of delay.

Reform is an assault on cash flows, and cash flows defend themselves with discipline. Any architecture that removes paid priority, premium survival, discretionary time allocation, and proof monopolies is not merely changing a rulebook; it is cutting revenue lines, shrinking career franchises, and devaluing the private skill of controlling access. The response will therefore be coordinated by incentives even when it is not coordinated by meetings. No incumbent coalition will defend itself by saying it wants to keep extracting; it will defend itself by saying it wants stability, liquidity, investor protection, and national competitiveness. Those words are not lies in themselves. Markets do require stability and liquidity. The problem is that those words have become wrappers that preserve tolls. The reform's job is to keep the legitimate stabilizers while removing the rents that hide inside them, and to do it on a timeline that cannot be suffocated by process that looks responsible and functions as sabotage.

The counterattack begins with language because language moves risk committees faster than policy detail. Paid priority becomes incentivizing liquidity. Premium truth becomes professional-grade analytics. Internalization becomes price improvement. Discretion becomes flexibility. Gatekeeping becomes risk management. Slow disputes become due process. Each phrase contains a legitimate function, because a smart system wraps rent in partial virtue. The tactic is not to deny the function; it is to preserve the function while eliminating the rent and then forcing the argument to occur on the level of mechanism rather than on the level of slogans. If the debate stays at the level of virtue words, incumbents win because virtue words are elastic and can always be stretched to cover the choke point.

The second move is timing, because timing is where reforms die without being defeated. Incumbents do not need to win a public vote against fairness. They need to slow the implementation until coalitions fracture, until elections change, until a shock arrives, until a small operational incident can be framed as systemic incompetence, until the public learns to associate the new architecture with uncertainty and the old architecture with familiarity. Delay converts technical questions into political fatigue. Political fatigue converts public-interest design into niche obsession. Niche obsessions are easy to defund. The reform then returns to the prior equilibrium with cosmetic updates, and the official story becomes that reform was tried and found impractical. The real story is that reform was starved of time, not starved of logic.

The third move is transition risk, because transition risk is the lever that makes every rhetorical attack feel rational. Even good reform can be killed if participants believe exits will be trapped, if institutions believe collateral terms will change by discretion, if foreign capital sees a faster corridor out than domestic participants can access, or if banks believe deposit migration will accelerate into a funding event. Panic is not always caused by price. Panic is often caused by fear of rule change. A reform that improvises under stress confirms that fear and permanently raises the political premium embedded in haircuts and duration. A reform that remains rule-bound absorbs more short-term volatility but buys the only asset that matters for long capital: the belief that rules remain rules when pressure arrives. That belief is what makes domestic duration possible.

Sabotage rarely looks like sabotage. It looks like consultation. It looks like the careful demand for more impact studies, more committees, more alignment, more harmonization, more "pilot extensions," until the reform is suffocated by its own caution. It looks like selective cooperation paired with selective withdrawal: offer help where it preserves incumbent advantage, remove support where it forces reform to choose between slowing down and triggering visible disruption. It looks like a flood of technical objections designed to create the impression that the reform is unsafe unless it preserves the very choke points it is meant to remove. It looks like a compromise offer that keeps baseline truth thin for stability and keeps priority incentives under a new label for liquidity, because the easiest way to defeat reform is to accept it in name while keeping power unchanged.

The politics of delay is the final weapon because it can operate without admitting any opposition to equality. Delay can be sold as caution. Caution can be sold as responsibility. Responsibility can be sold as investor protection. Investor protection can be used to justify preserving a system that quietly transfers value upward. This is why the reform must be structured as a sequence of steps that are defensible on their own terms and that generate their own evidence quickly. Evidence is the antidote to narrative. When the reform publishes state transitions, publishes correction logs, publishes criteria for facility usage, publishes reasons for throttles, publishes execution-quality distributions, and publishes access audits after stress, it removes oxygen from the claim that the operator is secretly protecting insiders or secretly experimenting on the public. A system that can show its work in public is harder to caricature as a private experiment, because it behaves like infrastructure rather than like a brand.

The reform also has to accept a hard truth about public psychology. The public does not evaluate market architecture by reading constitutions. The public evaluates architecture by living through one hostile week. One headline about liquidity vanishing can do more damage than a thousand pages of design. One well-timed rumor about foreign exit routes can trigger domestic selling. One operational incident, even if contained, can be framed as proof that the new system is untested, while quietly ignoring that the old system's crises were merely normalized and renamed. The only viable defense is procedural speed that is visible. Not speed in trading. Speed in publishing what happened, why it happened, and what rule governed it, because the public's core fear is not volatility; it is discretion.

Incumbents understand this and will target the reform's weak points. They will provoke small failures in reporting or settlement and then amplify them as existential. They will withhold cooperation at key operational junctions and then cite the resulting friction as evidence that the old system was more efficient. They will move activity to alternative venues and then claim the reform caused fragmentation. They will encourage foreign participants to use exit corridors that domestic participants cannot access and then claim the reform created unfairness. The reform cannot prevent every hostile move, but it can prevent hostile moves from becoming decisive by precommitting to rules that handle them without improvisation and by publishing outcomes that make blame assignment harder to manipulate.

The reform coalition must also treat its own temptation as a risk factor. When a crisis arrives, improvisation feels like leadership because it produces immediate calm. Improvisation is also how the constitution is quietly rewritten under pressure. If the new market improvises, it teaches the public that the new market is discretionary, which is the one belief that kills domestic duration. If the new market remains rule-bound, it may absorb more short-term volatility, but it builds the long-term asset that markets price: credibility. Credibility is not popularity. It is the confidence that a rule will be applied even when it hurts. Without that confidence, every investor demands compensation for political discretion, and that compensation shows up as shorter duration and higher haircuts, which is dependence in numeric form.

This Part is therefore about survivable transition under adversarial conditions. It treats incumbents as rational actors defending rents. It treats the public as rational actors defending the right to exit without being trapped by improvisation. It treats foreign capital as rational actors seeking the fastest route out when uncertainty rises. It treats the state as politically constrained and tempted by quick controls when pressure spikes. It treats the reform coalition as the only actor that must be disciplined enough to keep rules intact while moving fast enough that delay cannot become defeat. The next market will be made or broken not by whether its architecture is elegant, but by whether its transition can survive panic narratives, procedural sabotage, and the slow violence of delay.

Interlude: The Counterattack Begins - The reform is public, the headlines are hostile, and the incumbents have found their language.

The first hostile headline does not argue against equal access because attacking equality openly is clumsy and unpopular. It argues that the reform is rushed. Rushed is not a technical critique; it is a behavioral instruction. It tells institutions to freeze, tells banks to tighten, tells foreign capital to shorten, tells households that their savings may become collateral for someone else's ambition. Timing attacks are effective because they require no policy substance and cannot be disproven by policy substance. They are designed to create pause, and pause is where reforms die.

The second wave does not defend paid priority. It defends liquidity providers and implies that liquidity is a gift that must be purchased with privileges. It warns that removing priority incentives will widen spreads, as if spreads were a natural law rather than a price that reflects how the system allocates visibility and time. The implication is subtle and powerful: if you want liquidity, you must keep the people who provide it comfortable, and comfort requires rents. This is how public goods are privatized in language. The third wave does not defend premium truth. It claims retail will be overwhelmed by transparency, as if dependence were safety. The argument is paternal and strategic: if the public remains dependent on intermediaries to interpret reality, intermediaries remain the owners of reality.

Then the compromise offers arrive, framed as pragmatic stabilization. Keep the baseline record thin temporarily and sell the useful elements as professional tools for stability. Allow incentives for liquidity that function as paid priority but are renamed. Preserve internalization as price improvement while reducing reporting detail to prevent gaming, which is another way of saying to prevent verification. Push dispute resolution into general courts for due process, knowing that slow disputes function as a hidden haircut that only large balance sheets can finance. Each offer preserves the choke point while promising to reduce abuse. Each offer forces the reform coalition into the classic trap: accept a compromise that preserves power and call it progress, or reject it and be blamed for instability.

The pressure intensifies through selective withdrawal. A major participant reduces displayed liquidity and then points to the resulting thinness as evidence that reform is harming the public. A large intermediary increases fees for services that were once bundled and claims the costs are necessary because the new architecture is "complex." A vendor warns of operational risk and offers a proprietary overlay that would "make the transition safe," meaning a private lane that reintroduces premium survival. None of these moves require explicit coordination. They require only that incentives are aligned and that the public can be taught to fear the unknown.

The reform team's defense cannot be rhetorical, because rhetoric cannot compete with the fear that a participant may be trapped. The defense must be procedural and fast. State transitions must be published as they happen, not explained later. Corrections must be logged as events, not repaired quietly. Facility usage must be governed by criteria and summarized so privilege cannot hide behind silence. Throttle activations must have published reasons. Execution quality must be measured and published so claims about harm can be evaluated rather than believed. Dispute throughput must be visible, because slow disputes are where the public learns that rules are real only for the small. The goal is to prevent the counterattack from keeping the debate at the level of slogans.

The counterattack's deepest aim is to make the public associate the new system with uncertainty and the old system with familiarity. Familiarity is a powerful substitute for legitimacy, especially in finance, where most participants do not have the time to audit mechanism. The reform must therefore make legitimacy visible in the only language markets reliably respect: predictable procedure under pressure. If the system keeps its rules when it is uncomfortable, it will slowly make the counterattack's language less credible, because the public will have a record to compare against headlines. If the system breaks its rules to buy calm, it will make the counterattack's language true, because it will have admitted that the constitution is negotiable. The most dangerous moment is not a price drop; it is the first discretionary exception, because exceptions are how new systems become old systems with a new name.

CHAPTER 62
THE INCUMBENT COUNTERATTACK
WHERE RESISTANCE COMES FROM, WHAT IT SAYS, AND HOW IT SLOWS REFORM WITHOUT APPEARING TO.

Incumbent resistance is not primarily ideological. It is a defense of revenue, jurisdiction, and career survival expressed in the language of stability. The old system is a set of tolls attached to necessary functions: price formation, liquidity provision, custody, settlement, data publication, risk management, compliance, and dispute resolution. The tolls are not always explicit fees; they are privileges that allow some participants to see earlier, route differently, borrow cheaper, settle faster, and receive exceptions when stress arrives. Reform threatens these privileges by turning them back into public goods: common auctions, non-degradable baseline truth, uniform finality, admissible proof, fast disputes, and rule-bound stress behavior with published audits. The counterattack therefore begins where incentives begin, in the places where rents are collected and where the public cannot easily see them being collected. No incumbent coalition defends itself by saying it wants to keep extracting. It defends itself by saying it wants liquidity, stability, investor protection, and national competitiveness, because those words let delay look like virtue and let sabotage look like prudence. Each claim is built with a kernel of truth, because a serious defense does not lie crudely;

it wraps rent in a partial virtue so reform is forced into a false choice between preserving the toll or being blamed for instability.

Resistance comes from predictable places because power in markets is predictable. It comes from intermediaries whose business models rely on being the mandatory interface between the public and the book, because direct exchange accounts turn their passport into a service. It comes from liquidity providers whose edge is created by informational asymmetry and by predictable windows where others are forced to trade, because thick baseline truth and common auction rules reduce the harvestable surface. It comes from data vendors whose margins depend on thinning the baseline and selling survival as premium, because non-degradable baseline truth makes the public lane usable without subscription. It comes from incumbent exchanges whose revenue depends on fragmentation rents, proprietary feeds, fee tiers, and private negotiations over access, because a public-interest exchange reduces differentiation to legitimate service rather than constitutional privilege. It comes from custody and settlement monopolies whose leverage is proof, because proof monopolies can ration financing and price access while calling it safety. It comes from segments of the state apparatus that benefit from discretion, because discretion creates bargaining power and bargaining power creates political rents. These groups do not need to coordinate explicitly. They respond similarly because they are threatened similarly, and incentives are a stronger coordinator than meetings.

The counterattack's first instrument is narrative discipline, because narrative moves risk committees faster than policy detail. Paid priority is not defended as paid priority. It is defended as incentivizing liquidity. Premium truth is not defended as premium truth. It is defended as professional-grade analytics. Internalization is not defended as internalization. It is defended as price improvement. Discretion is not defended as discretion. It is defended as flexibility. Gatekeeping is not defended as gatekeeping. It is defended as risk management. Slow disputes are not defended as slow disputes. They are defended as due process. Each phrase is designed to keep the argument at the level of virtue words, because virtue words are elastic enough to cover the choke point. Reform cannot win by mocking these phrases. Reform wins only by separating the legitimate function from the rent with enough precision that the public can see who is being protected and who is being paid, and by making the system publishable enough that claims about harm can be verified rather than believed.

The second instrument is time, because time is the cheapest form of defeat. Incumbents do not need to win a public vote against fairness. They need to slow implementation until coalitions fracture, until elections turn, until a shock arrives, until a small operational incident can be framed as systemic incompetence, until the public associates the new architecture with uncertainty and the old architecture with familiarity. Familiarity is a substitute for legitimacy in finance, because most participants cannot audit mechanism and therefore default to habit. Delay converts technical questions into political fatigue. Political fatigue converts public-interest design into niche obsession. Niche obsessions are easy to defund. The reform then returns to the prior equilibrium with cosmetic updates, and the official story becomes that reform was tried and found impractical. The real story is that reform was starved of time, not starved of logic.

Process is the most effective weapon because it offers moral camouflage. The incumbent does not say no. The incumbent says study it more, consult more, pilot longer, harmonize first, align internationally, avoid unintended consequences, wait until after the next election, wait until volatility subsides, wait until foreign partners commit, wait until banks have adapted. Each request can be framed as responsible. Each request postpones the moment when reform produces irreversible public goods. In a contested architecture, postponement is not neutral. Postponement is surrender by delay. A reform that can be postponed indefinitely is a reform that will never exist.

The liquidity scare is the second weapon because it targets the only thing most participants actually fear: being unable to exit. The public does not audit market design; the public audits whether it can sell when it needs to sell, whether the receipt is finished, whether the price is real, whether the rules will change midstream. Incumbents exploit that by manufacturing thinness. They reduce displayed liquidity, widen spreads, move volume to alternative venues, then attribute the change to reform. They warn that removing priority incentives will drain liquidity. They threaten to relocate activity to "competitive jurisdictions," which is shorthand for jurisdictions where privileges remain intact. The purpose is not to make a philosophical case. The purpose is to create a visible symptom that can be framed as proof that reform harms ordinary participants.

A liquidity scare week is not difficult to stage because it requires only a small coordinated withdrawal from visible markets and a large coordinated amplification in language. Monday begins with a headline about reform being rushed. The headline is not policy; it is instruction. Risk committees read it as uncertainty and tighten internal limits. Dealers widen spreads and reduce displayed size, then cite volatility as justification. Volume migrates toward venues where internalization is easier and reporting is slower, so the public sees a thinner book and a noisier tape. Tuesday produces the inevitable commentary: liquidity is vanishing, retail is being harmed, the reform is destabilizing. Wednesday adds the more sophisticated claim: the reform is causing fragmentation, and fragmentation is reducing price quality, and therefore the reform is ironically reducing transparency. Thursday arrives with a compromise offer: keep the new architecture, but allow a temporary professional tier of data and priority incentives "until markets adapt." Friday ends with political pressure: accept the compromise or be blamed for chaos. The mechanics are familiar. The only defense is to have a baseline truth layer thick enough that the public can see what changed, and to publish execution and access metrics fast enough that "liquidity vanished" can be tested against the record rather than accepted as a mood.

The retail protection narrative is the third weapon because it preserves gatekeeping under the language of care. Incumbents claim transparency will overwhelm households, that households will misinterpret depth and imbalance, that households need intermediaries to protect them, and that intermediaries therefore need exclusive rights and discretion. The implicit message is that citizenship in markets is too complex for citizens. This argument lands because it contains a real concern: households can be harmed by complexity and by products designed to monetize impatience. The rent arrives when the solution is dependency. Dependency keeps the public blind and keeps the gatekeeper paid. The reform counter is structural protection: equal rails, equal baseline truth, equal closure, and tiered risk limits as math. Retail is protected by gating leverage and complex products and by funded restitution for fraud within bounded windows, not by making truth a premium product that must be interpreted by those who profit from interpretation.

Due process is the fourth weapon, deployed as a defense of slow disputes. Slow disputes function as hidden haircuts. Hidden haircuts shorten funding. Shortened funding forces selling. Forced selling punishes smaller participants who cannot finance uncertainty. Incumbents will argue that fast dispute lanes are dangerous because they might make errors. This is an inversion. The dangerous system is the one that makes proof uncertain for weeks, because uncertainty is the real error in markets. Deployable reform does not remove due process. It narrows remedies, standardizes evidence, binds timelines, and limits appeals from reopening the world, so disputes restore admissible state quickly enough that assets do not become legally radioactive collateral. A dispute lane that resolves within published time bounds is not anti-justice. It is the condition under which justice is not reserved for those who can afford delay.

Fraud is the fifth weapon, deployed against finality and safe harbor. Incumbents will argue that binding finality and protecting recipients enables fraud because it reduces reversibility. The argument contains a real risk: a system without fraud controls is politically indefensible. The rent arrives when fraud is used to justify indefinite reversibility that destroys closure and turns commerce into credit. The reform counter is funded restitution and prospective restriction handling: strong authentication and anomaly controls at entry, tiered limits by identity, non-replayable receipts, bounded dispute windows, and liability that sits on the payer side rather than clawing back from innocent recipients after finality. This preserves closure without surrendering to fraud and prevents enforcement timing from becoming a hidden interest rate that only the public pays.

Competitiveness is the sixth weapon, deployed against corridor discipline and baseline truth. Incumbents claim that thick baseline truth will reduce innovation and that binding corridors to mutual recognition will isolate the market. The real objective is to preserve jurisdictional arbitrage: the ability to route activity through the least visible, least enforceable venues while still claiming the credibility of the largest. Competitiveness language is often a defense of fragmentation rents. A public-interest market treats cross-border access as earned reciprocity, publishes corridor rules, and refuses to trade sovereignty for temporary inflows that reverse at the first shock. Corridors are opened only when finality, custody priority, and restriction handling are enforceable. This reduces the reward for the fastest exit routes that fracture reform by letting sophisticated capital escape through misalignment while the public remains inside a tightening domestic perimeter.

Internal capture is the seventh weapon because it is the most polite. Incumbents will attempt to place allies inside the reform apparatus not to argue against reform but to help implement it safely, which often means introducing small exceptions that recreate choke points: a professional data tier that becomes premium survival, a special liquidity incentive that becomes paid priority, an internalization carveout that becomes a private market inside the public one, a facility access discretion that becomes relationship time, a custody exception that becomes proof monopoly. Each exception is presented as temporary. Temporary exceptions become permanent because they create constituencies that profit from them. The only defense is to treat exceptions as constitutional events: publish them, sunset them, audit them, and prove they did not allocate opportunity by status. Without that discipline, reform becomes a rebranding exercise that preserves the rent while changing the label.

The politics of delay becomes concrete when it is run as a sequence, because delay is not passive; delay is operational. A consultation demand triggers legal opinions that take months. The months trigger pilot extensions. The extensions trigger procurement delays. The delays trigger staff turnover. The turnover triggers capacity loss. Capacity loss triggers "practical" carveouts that preserve incumbent systems temporarily. Temporarily becomes a year. A year becomes a new normal. The reform coalition is told it can either accept the carveouts or be blamed for disruption. The carveouts become choke points with constituencies. Constituencies lobby to preserve them. Reform survives in name and dies in power. This is how extraction yields quietly: not by winning an argument, but by exhausting the reform's patience and converting the reform into a set of exceptions.

The only defense is procedural advantage that produces irreversible public goods early and publishes enough evidence fast enough to resist narrative capture. Direct exchange accounts remove the ability to re-gate access through mandatory brokerage. Non-degradable baseline truth removes the ability to thin reality into a subscription. Uniform finality removes the ability to sell closure by status. Fast disputes remove the ability to rent proof through delay. Published state transitions and correction logs remove the ability to hide operator discretion behind silence. Post-stress access audits remove the ability to deny privilege when privilege is granted. These are not philosophical commitments. They are instruments of survival in an adversarial transition. If the reform secures these instruments early, the counterattack can still slow, but it cannot fully reverse without taking public responsibility for reintroducing gates and tolls. If the reform fails to secure them early, the counterattack can win without ever opposing equality, because it will have preserved the choke points under the language of stability.

A reform coalition does not need to defeat the incumbents in one stroke. It needs to prevent the incumbents from turning the transition into a panic narrative and from turning compromise into capture. That is why the counterattack is best understood as a contest over evidence, tempo, and exceptions. Evidence because the public fears discretion more than volatility. Tempo because delay is defeat without a vote. Exceptions because exceptions are how constitutions are quietly rewritten. The old system will try to make each of these its instrument. The new system survives only if it makes each of these its shield.

CHAPTER 63
REDESIGN WITHOUT TRIGGERING PANIC
LIQUIDITY, CONFIDENCE, AND THE TRANSITION RISKS THAT CAN KILL EVEN GOOD REFORM.

Panic is not a market emotion; it is a market conclusion. It is what participants do when they believe the rules may change before they can exit. Volatility can be tolerated. Uncertainty about closure cannot. The transition risk that kills reform is therefore not primarily price movement; it is the fear that the new architecture will strand someone in the wrong state: collateral that cannot be financed because eligibility changed by discretion, deposits that cannot move because corridor rules were improvised, trades that cannot settle because the record became ambiguous, redemptions that cannot be met because liquidity was promised and not designed, merchants that cannot rely on finality because enforcement timing breaks safe harbor. In that environment, rational actors shorten horizon. Funds reduce exposure. Banks tighten terms. Dealers widen and retreat. Households exit. The public is told it is irrational, but the public is behaving rationally under uncertainty. A redesign that cannot preserve exit confidence will fail regardless of its moral appeal, because markets punish architectures that cannot guarantee closure under stress.

The old system uses this fear as its shield. It says: change slowly, or liquidity will vanish; preserve discretion, or the operator will be unable to respond; keep the choke points, or stability will be threatened. Reform is then forced into an ugly dilemma. If it moves quickly, it risks a transitional bruise that incumbents amplify into proof of incompetence. If it moves slowly, it gives incumbents time to suffocate it by process and to recapture it through exceptions. The only way out is to treat transition as a sequence of closure proofs rather than a sequence of feature launches. Each step must be stable on its own terms, must preserve a clear state machine, and must be describable in public without relying on trust: what is open, what is capped, what is guaranteed, what is throttled, what is final, and what happens when conditions worsen. Participants must be able to predict, from published procedures, what the system will do in disorder. A redesign that announces principles and then improvises behavior teaches the public the one belief that makes panic permanent: the constitution is negotiable. A redesign that publishes thresholds and then follows them teaches the opposite belief: discomfort will be endured by rule rather than avoided by exception. That belief is the seed of duration.

The first requirement is baseline truth that remains thick throughout transition. A common panic trigger is the perception that the operator is hiding information or that the real market is occurring elsewhere. If baseline truth is degraded, even temporarily, the public assumes insiders are being protected and the public is being managed. Consolidated prints, usable depth snapshots, official marks, corporate action calendars, correction logs, and state transitions must remain available and stable. Corrections must be logged as events, not repaired quietly. Quiet repair is the fastest way to convert a technical issue into a legitimacy issue, because quiet repair invites rumor, and rumor is a liquidity event. Baseline truth cannot be treated as a rollout artifact. It is the transition's spine.

The second requirement is to identify and cap run channels before they are opened. A transition that opens broad conversion, leverage, and redemption optionality before it has proven settlement and dispute throughput is inviting the classic spiral: uncertainty rises, redemptions accelerate, funding tightens, forced selling begins, spreads widen, more redemptions follow, and politics responds with ad hoc controls that confirm the fear that rules are negotiable. A non-panicking redesign therefore uses objective caps and throttle bands as constitutional safety devices. Caps are published. Tightening triggers are published. The action order is published. Participants can price the regime. The regime cannot be guessed by relationship. These constraints are not anti-market controls; they are the difference between a redesign and a run experiment.

The third requirement is to make funding and collateral rules boring, because abrupt collateral eligibility changes are among the fastest panic triggers. They convert ordinary holdings into margin events. Margin events force sales. Forced sales create gaps. Gaps create more margin events. Incumbents then point at the gaps and claim reform caused instability. A redesign therefore binds collateral eligibility, haircuts, margin add-ons, and liquidity facilities to published criteria and published bands, with transition windows and temporary backstops where needed to prevent forced liquidation. Backstops are not bailouts; they are continuity tools that prevent a healthy transition from being killed by an avoidable cliff. The market can endure tighter terms if it can predict them. The market panics when terms change by surprise, because surprise is interpreted as discretion, and discretion is interpreted as capture or incompetence.

The difference between a bad transition and a survivable transition can be seen as a short cascade. In the bad transition, a collateral eligibility rule is amended quietly or implemented unevenly. Haircuts jump for a subset of assets without advance bands. Funding desks reduce repo lines because they cannot price the new regime. Dealers pull inventory because funding uncertainty makes holding dangerous. Spreads widen. Depth thins. Price gaps appear. Risk committees see gaps and tighten further. Institutions begin to sell not because they changed their view of value, but because they fear being stranded. Rumor fills the information vacuum created by thin or delayed baseline truth. The state sees outflows, panics, and imposes ad hoc controls to stop the bleeding. Those controls confirm the public's fear that exits can be trapped and rules rewritten, so participants rush to escape before the next control arrives. Reform is blamed for instability, even though the instability was caused by discretionary change and discretionary response. The reform dies as a narrative about irresponsibility.

In the survivable transition, the same pressure is anticipated and precommitted. Collateral eligibility is published with bands, transition windows, and clear triggers. Haircuts move by schedule within known ranges, and any emergency adjustment is bounded by a published ceiling and requires a published justification and a post-event review. Funding facilities are defined in advance with objective access criteria so a liquidity squeeze does not become a relationship market. Dealers and banks can price the regime rather than guess it. When spreads widen, the widening is within expected behavior bands rather than a signal of arbitrary intervention. When rumor begins, the system posts state transitions and publishes what is guaranteed and what is throttled, preventing uncertainty from becoming a narrative contest. When redemptions rise, throttles tighten by rule and buffers widen by rule, preventing a redemption spiral from turning into a forced-selling cascade. The system absorbs pain without improvisation. Over time, participants learn that rule-bound discomfort is safer than discretionary comfort, and that learning is how duration grows.

The fourth requirement is to protect merchant and household closure explicitly, because closure is where panic becomes social. If a receipt can be clawed back from an innocent recipient after finality, commerce becomes credit and ordinary participants learn to avoid the system under stress. If finality is too rigid without restitution, fraud becomes politically explosive and will be used as justification for discretionary reversals. The redesign therefore requires bounded dispute windows with funded restitution and prospective restriction handling, preserving safe harbor after finality while maintaining strong authentication and anomaly controls at entry. The public must be able to believe that closure is real and that fraud will be punished without retroactively converting ordinary recipients into collateral damage. Otherwise the system becomes a fear machine: merchants surcharge, households avoid, and legitimacy erodes into politics that demands controls.

The fifth requirement is to stage reform where reversibility is cheapest and proof is strongest, because not all changes carry the same panic risk. Direct exchange accounts can be introduced early as a constitutional overlay, because they remove gatekeeping without forcing immediate disruption of post-trade rails if the interface routes into existing settlement during early phases. Baseline truth non-degradation can be enforced early because it is a governance decision with immediate legitimacy benefit. Fast dispute lanes can be introduced early for a narrow class of disputes, expanding as throughput proves itself. Corridor rules can be published early even if corridors remain low-limit, because predictability itself reduces panic. Reform survives by producing irreversible public goods early while limiting the scope of what can fail catastrophically.

The sixth requirement is to treat cross-border alignment as a panic variable, because misalignment creates the fastest exit routes. If foreign capital can exit through a corridor faster than domestic participants can, domestic participants will interpret the corridor as a betrayal and will accelerate domestic selling. If corridor rules are ambiguous, rumor will define them, and rumor will always assume the worst. Corridor access therefore must be governed by published tightening triggers and published narrowing behavior, so participants can price cross-border exposure without fearing that restriction will arrive by improvisation. Cross-border is a treaty-like extension of trust. It cannot be operated as a discretionary switch without becoming a panic generator.

The seventh requirement is rehearsal and publication, because panic is reduced not by reassurance but by proof that a known playbook will be followed. A redesign that claims resilience but has never run drills is asking participants to trust. A redesign that publishes state transitions, throttle bands, fallback marks, outage behavior, facility criteria, and kill-and-restart rules, and then runs drills with published after-action audits, manufactures trust as output. This is the only credible response to the incumbent's favorite accusation that reform is an experiment. The old system was also an experiment. The difference is that its failures were normalized as tradition. A new system must prove, early and repeatedly, that its failures are contained by rules and that its rules remain rules under stress.

A redesign that avoids panic is therefore not slower; it is more disciplined. It moves quickly on constitutional public goods and cautiously on run channels. It refuses to thin truth to buy quiet. It refuses to improvise to buy calm. It accepts short-term discomfort to buy long-term duration. It treats fear as rational response to rule uncertainty and therefore treats predictability as the primary stabilizer. When reform is staged as a sequence of closure proofs with published bands and published audits, participants can remain inside the system long enough for the new constitution to become habit, and habit is what turns redesign into a market that can finance ambition without needing to sell stability back at a premium. The chapter is finished.

CHAPTER 64
COORDINATION OR ARBITRAGE
WHY CROSS-BORDER MISALIGNMENT CAN FRACTURE REFORM AND REWARD THE FASTEST EXIT ROUTES.

Cross-border misalignment is where reform becomes tradable. A single jurisdiction can build equal rails, non-degradable baseline truth, uniform finality, admissible proof, and fast disputes, and still be punished if capital can arbitrage differences across borders faster than domestic institutions can adapt. Cross-border markets are not only about flows; they are about rule collisions. When rules collide, the fastest route becomes the safest route for sophisticated participants, and the safest route for sophisticated participants becomes the exit route that leaves domestic participants holding the slow side of the bridge. Misalignment therefore turns reform into a distributional event: those who can move across jurisdictions escape uncertainty first, those who cannot become the residual risk pool, and the domestic public experiences the new architecture not as fairness but as being trapped in the strict regime while mobility buys relief. This is how reform fractures politically even when it succeeds technically.

The structural core is primitive divergence. Finality means different things in different places; ownership proof and priority mean different things; enforcement timing means different things. If one jurisdiction treats finality as a firm legal state and another treats it as a practical convention that can be reopened under certain pressures, corridor participants price the corridor as conditional and demand haircuts that bleed domestic duration. If one jurisdiction recognizes encumbrance tags and another recognizes paper claims or local discretion, collateral becomes contestable the moment stress arrives, and contestable collateral is priced as higher haircuts and shorter terms. If one jurisdiction preserves safe harbor for innocent recipients and another permits retroactive clawback through enforcement timing, commerce becomes credit across the corridor and corridor participation collapses into private guarantees that recreate the wall. These are not academic differences. They are the mechanisms by which corridors fail under stress and by which sophisticated participants choose the side of the bridge that cannot be rewritten by surprise.

Truth divergence compounds the problem because marks and corrections are not neutral; they are funding inputs. If official marks differ, if correction policies differ, if corporate action calendars are treated differently, participants route activity toward the venue whose marks and corrections they can predict, not necessarily the venue whose price is more accurate. Predictability becomes a form of liquidity. Predictability is monetizable. In misaligned corridors the predictable venue becomes the gravity well, and the other venue becomes the satellite whose liquidity thins at the exact moment it needs depth most. Reform is then blamed for fragmentation when the real driver is misaligned truth doctrine that allows capital to choose the easier narrative and the safer mark.

Regulatory perimeter divergence is the third accelerant because it lets capital split its behavior into public and private. If one jurisdiction bans paid priority and premium survival while another permits them under different names, the most sensitive activity migrates to the permissive venue and the strict venue is left with residual flow that is more expensive to trade. Domestic participants who cannot route cross-border experience the strict regime as higher cost and lower liquidity, and incumbents inside the strict regime cite that outcome as proof that reform harms competitiveness. Competitiveness language then becomes the lever used to reintroduce exceptions, which means the corridor becomes the tool by which misalignment forces rollback.

Funding and settlement speed are the operational layer that makes misalignment lethal. If one venue offers faster settlement completion, cheaper funding, or more flexible collateral eligibility, activity migrates there under stress, not because participants suddenly discovered a better price but because participants are buying time. Time is what capital purchases when uncertainty rises. That is why cross-border coordination is not a diplomatic nicety. It is a stability requirement. A reform that is not coordinated at least on primitives will be punished by arbitrage even if it is correct, because arbitrage converts legal and operational differences into an exit advantage, and exit advantages become political weapons.

A corridor fracture week is not a theory; it is a repeated pattern. The corridor is announced as a modernization achievement. Foreign participants enter for yield and for diversification. Domestic institutions feel validated and relax, because inflow is interpreted as trust. Then a shock arrives, rarely in the form the designers rehearsed. Friday produces a rumor that the foreign jurisdiction is considering a settlement restriction or an enforcement action that could reopen claims. By Monday, compliance desks in large institutions quietly de-risk because they cannot price enforcement timing in a conditional finality regime. By Tuesday, offshore spreads jump because the fastest actors are paying for exit certainty. By Wednesday, domestic dealers widen and reduce displayed size because funding terms are tightening and inventory becomes dangerous. By Thursday, the domestic auction calendar looks stressed not because the sovereign is insolvent but because the market is repricing rule uncertainty, and rule uncertainty is a haircut event. The press frames this as reform-induced fragility because the only visible fact is that volatility rose after reform. Political actors respond with ad hoc controls to stop outflows, and those controls confirm the fear that rules are negotiable. Domestic participants conclude they are trapped in the strict regime while mobility buys relief, and they begin to run toward the only exit they trust: cash, foreign unit claims, or private guarantees. Reform is blamed for importing volatility when the actual cause was misalignment that rewarded the fastest exit routes and turned the corridor into a trap door.

A coordinated corridor survives the same shock differently because the corridor is not a promise of openness; it is a treaty-like extension of enforceable trust. Finality and completion windows are mutually recognized. Custody priority is mutually recognized. Encumbrance tags are mutually recognized. Dispute outcomes are recognized within bounded remedy bands. Safe harbor is preserved so finalized receipts remain finished. Correction logging is treated as event doctrine across the corridor so marks remain admissible rather than negotiable. Corridor tightening triggers are published and activate by thresholds rather than rumor. Restriction handling is rule-bound, targeting payer access prospectively while preserving closure for recipients. When the shock arrives, participants still reprice risk, but they do not face a regime switch that turns holdings into legal arguments. Because they do not face a regime switch, they do not need to sprint for the exit. Liquidity remains usable. Auctions clear, perhaps at worse terms, but within a predictable rule frame. Duration survives because rule uncertainty does not metastasize into funding withdrawal. The corridor functions as diversification rather than as a trap door, and the domestic public experiences cross-border participation as an option, not as a privilege reserved for the fastest actors.

Coordination does not require global uniformity. It requires primitive alignment, because primitives are what markets finance. Align finality. Align custody priority and encumbrance recognition. Align bounded dispute doctrine. Align safe harbor doctrine. Align correction logging as events. Align corridor tightening triggers. Align restriction handling so enforcement timing does not fracture closure. Once primitives align, differences in market design can exist without becoming exit-route arbitrage. Without primitive alignment, every difference becomes a tradable advantage and the fastest actors will monetize it, because the fastest actors are paid to monetize it.

Reform survives cross-border only if it treats corridors as constitutional extensions rather than marketing features. Corridors must be opened slowly, under low limits, with published tightening behavior, and with explicit recognition that some capital will refuse a coordinated regime precisely because coordination removes the ability to profit from misalignment. That refusal is not a loss. It is proof that the corridor is not being used to sell exit advantages to the most mobile participants at the expense of the domestic public. A corridor that cannot withstand a shock without becoming an exit weapon is not diversification; it is a political liability that will be used to force rollback. The chapter is finished.

CHAPTER 65
FOUR FUTURES FOR THE MARKET
CAPTURE, FRAGMENTATION, REFORM, OR RENEWAL — AND WHAT DECIDES THE OUTCOME.

Markets do not drift into the future. They are pushed by incentives, constrained by law, shaped by technology, and stabilized or destabilized by how societies allocate proof, time, and closure. When a market reaches the stage where extraction is visible, the system does not respond with a single decision; it responds with a sequence of defensive moves that try to preserve the old rents while accepting the new language. The outcome is not a matter of moral persuasion. It is an equilibrium reached under pressure. That equilibrium can settle into capture, where reform becomes a rebrand and the choke points survive. It can settle into fragmentation, where multiple partial regimes coexist and mobility buys safety while the public becomes residual risk. It can settle into reform that holds, where equal rails, non-degradable baseline truth, uniform finality, fast disputes, and rule-bound stress behavior become stable habits that build domestic duration. Or it can settle into renewal, where the market stops selling stability back at a premium because stability becomes a public utility, not a private lane. What decides among these outcomes is not the eloquence of reformers. It is whether the constitutional primitives become public goods or remain private products dressed as safeguards.

Capture is the most common outcome because it is the least visible and the easiest to justify. Capture rarely arrives as a public rejection of fairness. It arrives as the careful acceptance of reform language paired with the preservation of reform power. The system agrees that transparency is good, then insists that too much transparency is dangerous and therefore the useful parts must remain "professional." The system agrees that liquidity is important, then insists that liquidity requires incentives that look remarkably like paid priority. The system agrees that retail must be protected, then insists that protection requires intermediation discretion that makes the public dependent. The system agrees that disputes should be fair, then insists that fairness requires delays that function as hidden haircuts. Each concession preserves a legitimate function in theory while preserving a toll in practice. The public sees reform signage. The machine keeps the old gates.

A single week can decide whether capture becomes permanent because capture is built from exceptions, and exceptions become permanent when they are accepted during fear. The fork week begins with a small operational incident, because incidents are where fear is born. A feed fracture produces mark divergence across venues for a short period. The system follows its playbook: it posts a state transition, activates fallback marks, logs corrections as events, and keeps settlement and finality rules intact. The incident is contained. The problem arrives afterward, when incumbents frame containment as fragility. A coalition of intermediaries and venue operators requests an "interim stabilization package." The package looks harmless: temporarily thin the baseline record "to reduce gaming," temporarily add a professional data tier "to help institutions interpret," temporarily introduce a liquidity incentive "to keep spreads tight," temporarily allow a broader internalization carveout "to protect retail." None of these are called privileges. They are called safeguards. The reform team is told that refusing the package will "spook markets." The minister is told that an election will be lost on the headline of instability. A central bank official hints that funding will tighten if volatility persists.

The decision is not abstract. If the package is accepted, the constitution splits. Baseline truth becomes degradable, which means reality becomes a subscription. Liquidity incentives become priority by another name, which means time becomes purchasable. Internalization carveouts become private markets inside the public one, which means the public lane becomes residual flow. Once these exceptions exist, they create constituencies that profit from them, and those constituencies will defend them as necessary forever. Capture becomes locked in, not because anyone voted for extraction, but because extraction was reintroduced as stability. If the package is rejected, the reform team must offer a different stabilizer: publish the metrics from the incident, publish execution quality outcomes, publish facility usage, publish the access audit, and show, in the public record, that the system behaved by rule and that harm claims are rhetorical. This is why evidence production is not a communications function; it is a constitutional defense. The fork week decides whether the system learns that fear yields exceptions or learns that fear yields audits. The first path produces capture. The second path allows reform to continue.

Fragmentation is the second equilibrium and often follows partial reform without primitive alignment across borders. Fragmentation does not require malice. It requires misalignment, and misalignment becomes profitable in the same way spreads become profitable: it offers a trade. One venue offers thicker baseline truth but tighter limits. Another offers thinner truth but easier leverage. One jurisdiction binds finality tightly. Another leaves reversibility more open. One corridor is predictable. Another is rumor-driven. Capital routes to the venue that sells time and predictability under stress, and the public remains where the rules are strict but exits are slower. Those who can route cross-border treat fragmentation as a menu. Those who cannot experience fragmentation as a hierarchy. A fragmented system can still function. It will function by stratifying outcomes. Stratification becomes political instability when households discover that the constitution varies by mobility and that fairness is a brand rather than a property of the rails.

A corridor shock week is how fragmentation becomes destiny. The corridor is announced as modernization and celebrated as proof of confidence. Foreign participants enter for yield. Domestic institutions relax because inflow is interpreted as trust. Then a shock arrives, often unrelated to the pilot's internal performance: a compliance rumor, a settlement restriction rumor, an enforcement action in a partner jurisdiction, a geopolitical headline that triggers de-risking. The rumor does not need to be true to be lethal; it only needs to be plausible in a corridor where finality and enforcement timing are not aligned. Compliance desks de-risk because they cannot price conditional finality. Offshore spreads jump because the fastest actors are buying exit certainty. Domestic dealers widen and reduce displayed size because funding terms tighten and inventory becomes dangerous. Domestic auctions clear at worse terms, not because the sovereign's fundamentals changed overnight, but because the market is repricing rule uncertainty, and rule uncertainty is a haircut event. Domestic participants cannot exit through the same channels as the fastest actors, so they interpret the corridor as a betrayal: mobility bought safety, and citizenship was left behind. Politics responds with ad hoc controls to stop outflows. Controls confirm the fear that rules are negotiable. Duration collapses. Reform is blamed for importing volatility when the actual cause was misalignment that rewarded the fastest exit routes and turned the corridor into a trap door.

A coordinated corridor prevents this by refusing to treat cross-border as marketing and treating it as a treaty-like extension of enforceable trust. Finality and completion windows are mutually recognized. Custody priority and encumbrance tags are mutually recognized. Dispute outcomes are recognized within bounded remedy bands. Safe harbor is preserved so finalized receipts remain finished. Corrections are logged as events under shared doctrine so marks remain admissible rather than negotiable. Corridor tightening triggers are published and activate by thresholds, not rumor. Restriction handling targets payer access prospectively and preserves closure for recipients. When the shock arrives, participants still reprice risk, but they do not face a regime switch that turns holdings into legal arguments. Because they do not face a regime switch, they do not need to sprint for the exit. Liquidity remains usable. Auctions clear, perhaps at worse terms, but within a predictable rule frame. Fragmentation is avoided not by optimism but by primitive alignment that removes the tradable edge of misalignment.

Reform that holds is the third equilibrium and it is harder because it requires refusing both panic improvisation and exception creep while moving fast enough that process sabotage cannot starve momentum. Reform holds when the primitives become non-negotiable and therefore become habits: direct access that cannot be re-gated, baseline truth that cannot be degraded, finality that cannot be sold, disputes fast enough that proof stays liquid, collateral and funding rules published in bands so terms cannot change by surprise, stress behavior rule-bound with published state transitions and post-event access audits so time cannot be privatized in crisis. It holds when transition is staged as closure proofs rather than feature launches, and when the system produces evidence faster than narratives can harden. In this equilibrium, liquidity is not eliminated; it becomes less extractive because the public lane is real. Market makers remain profitable, but they are profitable inside common rules rather than through hidden lanes. Intermediaries remain, but they become services rather than passports. Cross-border corridors expand, but only under mutual recognition that prevents misalignment from becoming exit arbitrage. Domestic duration begins to appear, because the public and institutions learn that the constitution is stable under stress.

Renewal is the fourth equilibrium and it requires more than holding reform; it requires the market to stop needing private lanes to sell stability back at a premium. Renewal occurs when stability becomes a public utility and when the market's most valuable outputs are treated as civic goods: baseline truth thick enough to be usable and non-degradable; closure as a legal state that cannot be reversed by status; proof as admissible record rather than as private email; dispute throughput as liquidity infrastructure rather than as litigation theater; stress behavior as transparent procedure rather than as whispered exception. Innovation still exists, but innovation cannot be the sale of privilege. Profit still exists, but profit must be derived from service and risk-taking rather than from choke points. A renewed market can tolerate volatility because it does not fear discretion, and it can finance ambition because duration is not a fragile belief; it is a rational response to predictable rules.

The decisive moments for renewal are not calm days. Renewal is decided on audit days, when a stress episode ends and the system must choose between publishing evidence and protecting reputations. A stress event occurs. The system activates throttles and buffers by published bands. It uses fallback marks by published hierarchy. It tightens facility access by criteria. It preserves finality and safe harbor. It contains the episode. Then the pressure arrives to keep outcomes quiet: do not publish facility usage, do not publish exception requests, do not publish who received time, do not publish how close-out was allocated, do not publish correction frequencies, do not publish execution-quality distributions, because publication will embarrass someone important.

If publication is withheld, renewal dies even if reform survives, because secrecy becomes the seed of future privilege. Privilege hides where evidence is absent. The public learns that the system can behave differently than it admits, and the public begins to price that fear as shorter holding and faster exits. Incumbents regain the ability to claim that only private lanes are reliable because public truth is incomplete. Secrecy turns stress behavior back into relationship time, and relationship time is how extraction returns. If publication is delivered, renewal becomes possible because the system demonstrates that it will not trade legitimacy for comfort. The audit shows who received time and why, shows whether criteria were followed, shows where exceptions were requested and denied, shows whether baseline truth was degraded, shows whether disputes stayed within time bounds, shows whether settlement finality held, shows whether the public lane remained real. This is not transparency theater. It is the constitutional act that makes privilege measurable and therefore harder to defend. A market that can publish uncomfortable evidence can survive future shocks with less panic because it has taught participants that rules are applied even when they hurt.

The four futures are therefore not philosophical categories. They are the outcomes of repeated decisions made under fear. Capture wins when exceptions persist and when "temporary" becomes a permanent toll. Fragmentation wins when cross-border primitives remain misaligned and misalignment becomes an exit advantage for the fastest actors. Reform holds when primitives are non-negotiable and transition is staged as closure proofs with published metrics that defeat narrative capture. Renewal emerges when the system chooses publication over reputation and makes evidence a habit so stability stops being privately sold and begins being publicly provided. The market's future is decided by whether the constitution is enforced as procedure or negotiated as relationship, and the difference between those two is the difference between a market that finances ambition and a market that merely quotes it. The chapter is finished.

APPENDICES

THE MARKET - THE MACHINERY OF CAPITAL

The appendices are where the book stops persuading and starts proving. They exist to do three jobs at once: give busy operators a fast reference, give skeptical readers an audit trail, and give policymakers a sequence they can actually execute. Your locked TOC already defines Appendix A–G and their subtitles.

CHAPTER 1
APPENDIX A. TIMELINE OF MARKET TURNING POINTS
THE MILESTONES THAT CHANGED HOW CAPITAL MOVED, TRADED, AND SETTLED.

The earliest turning point is the separation of trust from proximity. Before formal exchanges, credit moved through reputation and repeated dealing, with enforcement emerging from community pressure and courts that moved at human pace. The mechanism shift was negotiability: promises becoming transferable instruments that could outlive the original relationship. Negotiability created portability of risk and portability of obligation, which created the first market-like behavior: prices emerging from the willingness to accept someone else's promise at a discount. The consequence was immediate: once promises could be transferred, the question became whose promise counted, and the answer became an early form of authority that would later be formalized by publication and registry.

The next turning point was public quotation, not as information but as legitimacy. Price sheets and quoted lists transformed dispersed bargaining into a common reference. The mechanism was publication as authority: a price that is printed and repeatedly referenced becomes the price people coordinate around, even when the printed price is not perfectly representative. The consequence was the first market hierarchy: those closer to the source of quotation could position earlier, and those farther away accepted a delayed reality. Time entered as a product before the word product was used.

Exchange institutionalization then converted coordination into rule. Membership, standardized contracts, listing norms, and time-based routines turned trading into an institution whose outputs could be trusted by outsiders. The mechanism was rule-based repeatability: trades executed under known procedures in known places with known intermediaries. The consequence was scale, and scale produced the next shift: the exchange became a gatekeeper not only of trading but of legitimacy, because listing and membership defined who could access the public pool and who could not.

Centralized clearing and netting was the next structural leap. The mechanism was novation and netting: replacing many bilateral obligations with fewer net obligations, then enforcing those obligations through margin and default rules. The consequence was that the true factory moved behind the screen. The public saw trades. The machine saw net exposure, collateral, and default waterfalls. This reduced some counterparty risk and also created new power: whoever governed the clearing rules governed what was financeable, because collateral eligibility and haircut policy became the real policy levers of market functioning.

Dematerialization and custody chains followed as markets scaled. Certificates gave way to ledger states, and ownership became a layered fact rather than a single document. The mechanism was beneficial ownership separated from legal title, with custody chains acting as translators between the investor and the record. The consequence was speed and scale, paired with new fragility: proof became harder for ordinary participants to verify directly, and priority became easier to contest in stress because the record was now a chain rather than a single artifact.

The move from floors to screens changed the location of advantage. In open outcry, advantage lived in physical proximity and social networks. On screens, advantage migrated to latency, routing, and information hierarchy. The mechanism was automation of matching and the multiplication of venues, which made "the market" no longer one place but an ecosystem of linked micro-markets. The consequence was fragmentation that could be monetized by those who could see across fragments, and a widening gap between a public narrative of one price and a private reality of many prices.

Consolidated data, proprietary feeds, and the sale of early reality became the next turning point. The mechanism was tiered truth: baseline data sufficient to participate, premium data necessary to survive. The consequence was a subtle shift in market citizenship. Participation remained theoretically open, but outcomes became increasingly correlated with the ability to buy faster and richer reality. That shift also altered reform politics, because any attempt to make truth thicker for the public threatened a high-margin product line that could be defended with the language of liquidity and professionalism.

Passive indexing transformed the market's calendar into a force engine. The mechanism was methodology turning into mandated holdings, which turned inclusion into persistent demand and rebalancing into forced trade windows. The consequence was that "passive" became predictable urgency, and predictable urgency became monetizable by liquidity providers and by the infrastructure owners who sold the tools needed to navigate those windows. The market's visible story became lower fees. The machine's invisible story became a new set of extractable deadlines.

The most recent turning point is the quiet convergence of trading infrastructure into monetary infrastructure. The mechanism is the post-trade stack becoming the true center: marks as authority, eligibility as money policy inside institutions, proof as a priced service, and finality as the boundary between commerce and credit. The consequence is that exchanges and their adjacent infrastructure increasingly resemble settlement rails, whether societies admit it or not. This book's theory responds to that convergence by arguing that the next turning point is not merely faster trading, but public, money-grade closure: a stable spend unit, legally defined finality, admissible proof, governed marks, audited stress behavior, and treaty-grade corridors that prevent cross-border exit arbitrage.

CHAPTER 2

APPENDIX B. EXCHANGE MODELS AND THEIR OUTCOMES

WHICH STRUCTURES SCALED, WHICH STAGNATED, AND THE CONDITIONS THAT DROVE BOTH.

Exchange models differ less by branding than by where they place authority and how they price time. Auction-centric models concentrate price formation into discrete moments, which can simplify mark authority and reduce some fragmentation, but also concentrate urgency and therefore concentrate monetizable windows. Continuous models distribute activity across time, which can reduce burst risk and improve ordinary-time liquidity, but also expand the surface on which routing, internalization, and selective visibility can generate advantage. The outcome difference is not moral; it is structural. Auction-centric systems tend to create strong canonical marks and strong time concentration. Continuous systems tend to create wider microstructure complexity and greater reliance on data hierarchy and routing to synthesize reality.

Ownership and governance models create predictable outcome patterns. Member-owned exchanges historically align to participant welfare up to a point, but can become conservative and exclusionary when incumbents protect rents or resist technology that threatens their position. Shareholder-owned exchanges tend to optimize monetization of access, data, and market services, which can drive innovation and can also deepen tiered truth. Hybrid models often drift toward selling stability as a product because stability is what all constituencies demand while resisting paying for it explicitly. The outcome is typically a fee architecture that appears low at the surface while extracting value through less visible tolls: premium data, connectivity, auction analytics, and rule-driven urgency.

Fragmented venue ecosystems create an outcomes split between sophisticated and ordinary participants. When many venues exist, routing becomes a shadow constitution: who can see, who can respond, and who can aggregate truth determines execution quality. Fragmentation can reduce explicit monopoly pricing, but it can also create an arbitrage ecology that profits from reconciling fragmented reality. Consolidated ecosystems reduce some of that, but can produce other rents through centralized control of marks, data, and admission. The stable outcome difference is that fragmentation tends to create two-speed markets unless baseline truth is unusually thick and routing rules are unusually disciplined.

Clearing integration is the decisive factor in stress behavior. Systems with robust central clearing and clear margin and default waterfalls tend to contain counterparty cascades more effectively, but they can also create procyclical tightening that amplifies stress if haircuts and margin add-ons jump sharply. Systems with weaker clearing or fragmented clearing often appear flexible until stress arrives, at which point flexibility becomes ambiguity and ambiguity becomes haircut inflation. The model that consistently produces durable outcomes is the one that treats clearing and finality as constitutional, publishes its stress behavior, and prevents discretionary exceptions that allocate time by status.

Internalization policy determines whether the public market remains the true market. High internalization can reduce visible spreads in calm but can starve displayed liquidity and weaken public price discovery, turning the public book into a thin reference and the private interior into the real market. Low internalization can preserve displayed liquidity but can increase the visible cost of trading for some participants. The institutional outcome is that internalization becomes a political lever because it can be defended as consumer protection while functioning as a private toll. Systems that preserve public legitimacy tend to constrain internalization or impose strict transparency and best execution standards that prevent the private interior from becoming the only survivable lane.

The stress-time legitimacy test separates models more cleanly than calm-time efficiency. Calm-time efficiency can be purchased with premium truth and premium time. Stress-time legitimacy depends on whether the system remains one constitution or splits into exceptions. The model that scales and survives is not the one that maximizes speed. It is the one that maximizes legibility: published mark authority, correction-as-event doctrine, rule-bound tightening bands, publishable facility criteria, fast disputes, and audits that expose exception requests. Those are the conditions under which markets remain governable and politically survivable when discomfort is unavoidable.

CHAPTER 3
APPENDIX C. MARKET PLUMBING GLOSSARY
PLAIN-LANGUAGE DEFINITIONS FOR THE MACHINERY READERS ARE RARELY TAUGHT.

The glossary is organized around primitives that recur across every part of the book. Routing is the set of rules and technologies that decide where an order is sent and in what sequence; it matters because routing is a hidden policy that can distribute opportunity unevenly. Internalization is the execution of orders inside a broker or dealer's internal system rather than on a public venue; it matters because it can move liquidity and truth away from the public record. Auction is a discrete matching process that produces a single clearing price for a time slice; it matters because auctions create canonical marks and concentrated urgency. Spread is the gap between buying and selling prices; it matters because spread is the price of immediacy and often the price of constrained choice. Depth is the quantity available at or near the best prices; it matters because depth determines whether large flows move prices violently.

Mark is the official price reference used for valuation, reporting, collateral, and settlement decisions; it matters because marks are authority, not opinion. Official close is a specific mark used as a canonical valuation anchor; it matters because close marks concentrate forced flow and can be monetized. Consolidated baseline data is the public truth sufficient for participation; it matters because if baseline truth is thin, survival requires premium feeds and the market becomes two-speed. Proprietary feed is premium data delivered earlier or with richer detail; it matters because it sells time. Co-location is physical proximity to matching engines; it matters because it converts money into latency advantage. Liquidity provider is a participant that offers continuous buying and selling; it matters because liquidity provision is conditional and becomes expensive in stress.

Clearing is the process that guarantees performance of trades by substituting a central counterparty and managing risk through margin and default rules; it matters because clearing governs what is financeable. Novation is the replacement of bilateral obligations with an obligation to the clearer; it matters because it concentrates risk governance. Netting is the compression of many obligations into a smaller net amount; it matters because netting is the factory that makes scale possible. Margin is collateral posted to cover potential loss; it matters because margin is procyclical and can amplify stress. Default waterfall is the ordered set of resources used to absorb losses when a participant fails; it matters because the ordering determines who pays and therefore how panic spreads.

Settlement is the final exchange of cash and securities; it matters because settlement is closure. Finality is the legal state when settlement can no longer be unwound for compliant recipients; it matters because finality is money-grade trust. Beneficial ownership is the economic right to an asset; legal title is the formal registered holder, often a custodian; the distinction matters because layered ownership complicates proof and priority. Corporate actions are issuer events that change entitlements, such as dividends, splits, mergers; they matter because entitlement ambiguity creates disputes that raise haircuts. Entitlements are what owners are owed after corporate actions; they matter because ambiguous entitlements turn settlement into argument.

Lien is a legal claim on an asset as security; it matters because liens determine priority in insolvency. Encumbrance tag is a machine-legible marker that an asset is pledged or restricted; it matters because it prevents double-pledge and counterfeit collateral. Haircut is the discount applied to collateral value for risk management; it matters because haircuts are the price of uncertainty and can become the market's hidden tax. Repo is borrowing cash against collateral; it matters because repo is the plumbing of time. Collateral eligibility is the rule deciding what can be pledged; it matters because eligibility is monetary policy inside the machine.

Corridor is a cross-border pathway for settlement and conversion; it matters because misaligned corridors create exit arbitrage. Mutual recognition is treaty-grade alignment of primitives across jurisdictions; it matters because it prevents corridors from selling a different constitution to the fastest actors. Safe harbor is protection for compliant recipients after finality; it matters because without safe harbor, merchants become lenders. Restitution pool is funded compensation that repairs harm without breaking finality; it matters because it prevents fraud from forcing reversals. Stress state machine is published tightening and outage behavior; it matters because rule-bound discomfort prevents panic. Exception protocol is the rule that exceptions must be published, bounded, sunset, and audited; it matters because secrecy is capture. Audit perimeter is what is published after stress to prove fairness without exposing vulnerabilities; it matters because evidence defeats rumor. Spend unit is the stable unit used for prices; it matters because daily life cannot carry portfolio volatility. Conversion house is the warehouse that turns eligible instruments into closure in the spend unit; it matters because it absorbs risk so merchants do not speculate. Correction-as-event is the doctrine that changes are logged, time-stamped, and bounded; it matters because silent edits destroy legitimacy.

. . .

Appendix D. National Market-Building Checklist

Subtitle: A policy-ready sequence for governments developing domestic capital markets.

A domestic market that can finance ambition requires sequence discipline because institutions cannot be willed into existence by decree. Phase 0 is legal substrate: enforceable property rights, priority rules that survive insolvency, admissible records, bounded remedies, and courts or arbitration lanes capable of resolving financial disputes within timeframes that keep proof liquid. The failure condition is predictable: if disputes take too long and outcomes are negotiable, haircuts rise permanently and duration collapses. Phase 1 is baseline truth: a public record thick enough that ordinary participants can see canonical marks, correction events, corporate action calendars, and state transitions without buying premium survival. The failure condition is two-speed citizenship: if truth is thin, the public becomes residual risk and liquidity becomes dependent on private lanes.

CHAPTER 4

APPENDIX D. NATIONAL MARKET-BUILDING CHECKLIST

A POLICY-READY SEQUENCE FOR GOVERNMENTS DEVELOPING DOMESTIC CAPITAL MARKETS.

A domestic market that can finance ambition requires sequence discipline because institutions cannot be willed into existence by decree. Phase 0 is legal substrate: enforceable property rights, priority rules that survive insolvency, admissible records, bounded remedies, and courts or arbitration lanes capable of resolving financial disputes within timeframes that keep proof liquid. The failure condition is predictable: if disputes take too long and outcomes are negotiable, haircuts rise permanently and duration collapses. Phase 1 is baseline truth: a public record thick enough that ordinary participants can see canonical marks, correction events, corporate action calendars, and state transitions without buying premium survival. The failure condition is two-speed citizenship: if truth is thin, the public becomes residual risk and liquidity becomes dependent on private lanes.

Phase 2 is settlement and finality: a defined finality clock, safe harbor for compliant recipients, and funded restitution to repair harm without reopening closure. This phase also includes central clearing or equivalent risk containment with rule-bound margin and default waterfalls, because settlement without risk containment becomes a rumor engine in stress. The failure condition is political improvisation: if finality is reopenable by discretion, merchants and institutions learn that receipts are negotiable and they withdraw. Phase 3 is issuer discipline and investor base: listing rules that produce credible disclosure, corporate action hygiene, and governance standards that prevent the market from becoming an insider's instrument, combined with a domestic investor base large enough to provide duration. The failure condition is repeated scandal followed by retail exit and institutional refusal, which returns the economy to bank dominance and external dependency.

Phase 4 is post-trade robustness: custody chain clarity, beneficial ownership admissibility, encumbrance tagging to prevent double-pledge, mark authority doctrine with correction-as-event, and stress state machines with published tightening bands and audits. The failure condition is haircuts and funding shocks triggered by proof ambiguity, because proof ambiguity is priced as uncertainty tax. Phase 5 is corridors: treaty-grade mutual recognition of finality, priority, marks, bounded remedies, restriction handling, and published corridor tightening triggers. The failure condition is exit arbitrage: if corridors are misaligned, the fastest actors exit first and domestic legitimacy fractures. The checklist's governing principle is that stability must be public procedure, not private privilege; any phase that relies on discretionary exceptions will eventually allocate survival by proximity and will raise the nation's cost of capital permanently.

CHAPTER 5

APPENDIX E. BLUEPRINT FOR A NEW MARKET AUTHORITY

INSTITUTIONAL DESIGN, MANDATES, AND SAFEGUARDS FOR PUBLIC-INTEREST MARKET GOVERNANCE.

A market authority capable of governing a public-interest rail must be designed to resist capture by the entities it supervises and resist panic-driven improvisation by the political system. Its mandate is not to maximize trading volume. Its mandate is to protect money-grade closure, baseline truth, and rule-bound stress behavior while allowing innovation that does not sell time as privilege. Its scope must include mark doctrine, baseline data publication perimeter, correction-as-event standards, eligibility governance and haircut bands, proof and encumbrance tagging standards, finality clocks and safe harbor doctrine, restitution funding requirements, stress state machine requirements, corridor mutual recognition terms, and exception protocols.

The authority's rulemaking process must be constitutional rather than performative. Rules require published rationale, impact analysis including adverse selection against smaller participants, transition windows to prevent cliffs, and post-implementation review with measurable outcomes. Emergency changes are constrained to predefined triggers and must sunset automatically unless renewed by evidence. Publication obligations are core: the authority must require thick baseline truth, publish stress state transitions, and publish audit outputs that prove whether rules were applied uniformly. Audit obligations include facility access audits, exception request audits, correction event audits, dispute throughput audits, and corridor tightening audits. The authority must also define what is forbidden: silent degradation of baseline truth, privileged warning lanes in stress, discretionary reversals after finality for compliant recipients, and unbounded exceptions that allocate time by status.

Institutional safeguards must include independence of audit functions, rotating oversight committees with conflict-of-interest constraints, and transparent performance metrics that cannot be gamed by superficial improvements. The authority must be able to compel disclosure of microstructure outcomes relevant to fairness and stability, not only disclosures convenient to venues and intermediaries. It must also maintain a public record of amendments, exceptions, and audits, because secrecy is where capture lives. The blueprint's central claim is that a public market cannot be governed as a private club and remain legitimate; governance must be legible enough that the public can see the constitution holding during discomfort, because discomfort is when legitimacy is priced.

CHAPTER 6

APPENDIX F. MARKET INSTRUMENTS MONEY THEORY TECHNICAL ASSUMPTIONS

DESIGN CONSTRAINTS, RISK CONTROLS, AND OPERATING RULES BEHIND THE THEORY.

The theory assumes a stable spend unit for prices and a conversion house for settlement, because daily life cannot carry portfolio volatility and commerce cannot wait for litigation-grade settlement. The conversion house accepts eligible market instruments as tender inputs, applies published mark doctrine with fixed timestamps and fallback hierarchy, applies published haircut bands and conversion limits, issues non-replayable receipts, guarantees completion within a published window, and delivers legal finality at a published time with safe harbor for compliant recipients. The theory assumes that harm is repaired through funded restitution within published windows, not through retroactive clawback from compliant recipients after finality, because retroactive clawback converts commerce into credit and destroys adoption.

Eligibility is treated as monetary policy. The eligible set is tiered and conservative at launch, expanding only after stress-year proof. Haircuts and limits move within published bands based on measurable triggers. Amendment safety is assumed: published rationale, impact analysis, transition windows, post-implementation review, and mandatory sunsets for emergency changes. Proof is assumed to be money-grade: beneficial ownership states are admissible, time-stamped, correction-bounded, and tied to deterministic entitlement mapping; encumbrance tags prevent double-pledge; priority survives insolvency as law; disputes are bounded with standardized evidence and binding timelines so proof remains liquid. Marks are assumed to be governed as public standard: correction-as-event doctrine with reason codes, bounded correction windows, and public record publication sufficient to reconstruct what happened.

Authentication is assumed to be tiered and payment-grade: published tier thresholds, non-replayable signed receipts, anomaly controls, velocity limits, and prospective restriction handling. Fraud liability is funded and rule-bound, with fast reimbursement and recovery pursued through payer channels without reopening compliant recipient closure. Stress behavior is assumed to be a published state machine with modes, triggers, tightening actions, outage behavior, kill and restart criteria, and facility access criteria, paired with an audit obligation that publishes state transition timelines, correction events, facility usage summaries by criteria, dispute throughput metrics, restitution metrics, and exception requests granted or denied within a defined publication perimeter that protects privacy and operational security. Corridors are assumed to be treaty-grade mutual recognition of primitives: finality clocks, safe harbor, priority and encumbrance recognition, mark doctrine, correction doctrine, bounded remedies, restriction handling, corridor tightening triggers, and interoperable message standards for tags, marks, and events. The theory assumes that the new rail will face adversarial politics and incumbent counter-attack, and therefore treats exception protocol, audit publication, and non-degradable baseline truth as non-optional design constraints rather than as governance preferences.

ABOUT THE AUTHOR
JAG DESAINT

Jag DeSaint writes at the intersection of markets, monetary policy, and institutional design. His work focuses on how financial systems function beneath their public narratives: the procedures that produce liquidity, the rules that define truth, the incentives that price time, and the legal doctrines that turn a trade into closure. He approaches market structure the way an engineer approaches a bridge, interested less in rhetoric and more in what holds under load.

He brings a comprehensive, decades-long track record spanning monetary policy, capital markets, regulation, and the financial sector. That breadth gives him an uncommon vantage point: he has seen how policy intent becomes operating rule, how operating rule becomes market behavior, and how market behavior feeds back into national financing conditions. He is fluent in the language of markets and the language of the state, and he treats their overlap as the true arena where modern finance is decided.

Jag DeSaint is widely regarded as a financial architect of the system. He designs and evaluates the rails that make markets governable: settlement and finality doctrine, exchange and post-trade operating models, proof and priority standards, stress-state machines, audit regimes, and cross-border corridor frameworks that expand access without creating exit arbitrage. His work connects the mechanisms that are usually discussed in isolation, showing how eligibility and haircuts become policy, how marks become authority, and how ambiguity is priced into spreads, duration, and sovereignty.

He also understands the politics that surround the machinery. He studies how reforms are attacked through the language of liquidity, how delay becomes defeat without a vote, and how "temporary" exceptions harden into permanent privilege unless governance is built to resist them. Architecture that cannot survive politics is not architecture, it is a proposal.

Jag DeSaint writes with a constructive conviction that better markets are buildable. His central argument is that sovereignty in finance is procedural: whoever controls reality, time, proof, and closure controls the cost of capital.

www.ingramcontent.com/pod-product-compliance
Lightning Source LLC
LaVergne TN
LVHW052011200926
848481LV00005B/1466